UNITED STATES BUSINESS HISTORY, 1602–1988

UNITED STATES BUSINESS HISTORY, 1602–1988

A Chronology

Compiled by
Richard Robinson

GREENWOOD PRESS
New York • Westport, Connecticut • London

Library of Congress Cataloging-in-Publication Data

Robinson, Richard.
  United States business history, 1602-1988 : a chronology /
compiled by Richard Robinson.
    p.   cm.
  Includes bibliographical references.
  ISBN 0-313-26095-8 (lib. bdg. : alk. paper)
    1. United States—Industries—History. 2. Business enterprises—
United States—History. 3. Businessmen—United States—History.
4. Women in business—United States—History. I. Title.
HC103.R595 1990
338.0973—dc20   90-34102

British Library Cataloguing in Publication Data is available.

Library of Congress Catalog Card Number: 90-34102
ISBN: 0-313-26095-8

First published in 1990

Greenwood Press, 88 Post Road West, Westport, CT 06881
An imprint of Greenwood Publishing Group, Inc.

Printed in the United States of America

The paper used in this book complies with the
Permanent Paper Standard issued by the National
Information Standards Organization (Z39.48-1984).

10 9 8 7 6 5 4 3 2 1

To
Marjory and Raymond Robinson

Contents

Preface

The business chronology is designed to provide a basic calendar of representative events taking place in the evolution of U.S. business. Business events have been cited, to the extent they can be dated, as they occurred for better or worse from 1600 through 1989.

The descriptive historical data has been presented so readers might ask questions or make interpretations about why such happenings took place when they did. Readers can also draw their own conclusions as to what changes and trends are evolving as U.S. business impacts on and/or reacts to its historical setting in time. Such determinations are necessary for a better understanding of what is taking place in the business system today and what might happen tomorrow. Perhaps the chronology might also arouse a browser's curiosity about the surprises and oddities appearing at times in business history and be encouraged to pursue their study in more depth elsewhere.

The calendar is first of its kind in the field of business history to arrange its data by a specific time framework instead of using the customary coverage to present categories of subject matter in general time periods. The two approaches complement each other. The traditional books paint an overall picture of business evolution, while the chronology presents what historical minutiae it can here and there in timely fashion to provide some of the details missed by the broad strokes depicting the panorama of U.S. business. In essence, the pointillist method was deliberately used so readers can visualize for themselves how the U.S. business system travels through time.

In so doing, attention is paid to a diverse sampling of the many worshippers, good and bad, continually seeking the wonderous favors of the Roman goddess Fortuna. These enterprising individuals, regardless of age, sex, race, nationality, religion or ability, appear higgledy-piggledy on the historical stage in an ever-changing kaleidoscope of business activities ranging from spectacular conglomerates to prosaic undertakings of individuals. In reviewing their adventures and misadventures, one may gain some insight about, or at least an appreciation for what it takes to win the rewards Fortuna offers to the victorious.

The historical data has been classified into two categories: General Events and Business Events. General Events attempts to give an overall background of business, by showing changes in living conditions and lifestyles for possible impacts on the marketplace. Demographics provide statistical data on who the buyers and sellers are. Economic conditions

mirror the rise and fall of the business system. Governmental actions,
laws, and court decisions help define the marketplace and rules of
competition. Social indicators, such as changes in fashions, assist in
revealing underlying trends in social values. Educational developments
are identified for their contributions to the evolution of business
activities. Events in architecture and housing show physical changes
where people live and work. Guild and/or union activities give reactions
of workers to commercialization and industrialization. Agriculture is
covered as it contributes to social welfare and provides wealth for
business activity. Inventions, including those of everyday items
necessary for a desired standard of living, are identified as instruments
of change and well-being. Advancements in science herald the use of
technology for productivity. Significant political happenings, such as,
major wars, appear as known markers for the passage of time.

In addition, certain articles and books are included in General Events to
note the concerns of a particular time. Activities of non-business
organizations, such as religious, government, military and educational,
are included at times to show their use of business methods and their
influence on the organizational and managerial practice of business. For
example, military innovations in planning and organizing, such as, staff
units, precede such developments in business.

Business Events identifies occurrences in the rise and fall of those
enterprises engaged in producing goods and/or providing services. These
activities cover the following fields of endeavor: finance and
accounting, transportation, communications, insurance, retailing,
manufacturing, construction, extractive industries, wholesaling,
entertainment and sports, real estate, marketing, and personal services
of one kind or another. When possible, brief accounts are given as to
what happens to the business activity in question.

With this chronological material, perhaps readers will see how much
business is interwoven in the fabric of society. Another realization is
that business encompasses so much more than the usual large manufacturing
firms in textiles, metals, automobiles, chemicals and electronics,
transportation giants in railroads, shipping and airlines, media powers
in publishing and broadcasting, national and international retail chains,
and conglomerates in diverse activities. Such noteworthy enterprises are
of concern for the magnitude of their size and energy as trendsetters and
change-makers in U.S. business history. Nevertheless, small and medium-
sized firms, a necessary foundation for big business, are presented
whenever possible to show the eclectic vitality, diversity and complexity
of the business system serving the American public.

Business Events also identifies at times the managerial practices of
enterprises as they appear and disappear in history. The data shows, to
the degree specific methods exist for citation, what techniques managers
use to plan, direct, organize, staff and control their organizations.
The formal techniques used by managers at particular times can reveal the
complexity of operational problems requiring resolution just as
inventions show what individual and social needs are of concern.

As the business system is composed of people working with people for people, the chronology focuses whenever possible on the colorful array of enterprising Americans engaged in capitalizing on whatever opportunities are available in business activity. The coverage includes entrepreneurs, i.e., Sarah B. Walker, Colonel John Stevens, Commodore Vanderbilt, Helena Rubinstein, George Halas, Ray Kroc, and Walt Disney; promoters, P.T. Barnum, William Durant, and C.C. Pyle; managers, Rose Knox, Alfred P. Sloan, Jr., and Julius Rosenwald; builders, Henry J. Kaiser and James Ling; retailers, Eugene Ferkauf, Clarence Saunders and Sam Walton; frauds, Charles Ponzi and Anthony De Angelis; raiders, Daniel Drew, Louis E. Wolfson and T. Boone Pickens; merchants, Marshall Field and Leslie Wexner; losers, Jim Fisk, Barry Minkow and Joe Hunt; eccentrics, Isaac Singer, Hetty Green and Howard Hughes; organizers, J.D. Rockefeller, Charles Frohman, Mort Tennes and Royal Little; financiers, Jacob Schiff and J.P. Morgan; inventors, Oliver Evans, Thomas A. Edison, Edwin Land and the McDonald brothers; idealists, Henry Noble Day and J.C. Penney; gurus, Frederick W. Taylor, Peter F. Drucker and Kenneth Blanchard; manufacturers, Patrick Tracy Jackson and Henry Ford; heroes, Olive Beech, Colonel Sanders, Victor Kiam, Lee Iacocca and Peter Uberroth; forgotten, Caspar Wistar, Frederic Tudor, Henry Hackenfeld, Gustave Whitehead and Robert Young; and then those flavoring history, such as, Jay Gold and Al Capone. At times, brief accounts are given on the historical personages in one place for a quick review of their destiny, unfinished in some cases, as time isn't finished with them.

Of course, a complete accounting of business activity through time is impossible, unfortunately, as it would no doubt be a fascinating saga. With this reality in mind, the chronology focuses on presenting those events that pioneered trends and those that represented what was generally happening at a particular time. A problem with pioneering events is that such occurrences aren't always known, then or even now when precedents are ever being discovered. Then too, to compound this problem, different sources did not always agree as to the specific date when a particular event took place. The best that could be done in handling this issue, other than dropping the item from history as if it had never occurred, was to identify it as being in a general period of several years, a decade, etc.

Representative events raised the subjective issue as to what is representative. In many cases, references also differed as to what activity would show the common practice of a time period. To resolve such conflicts, the chronology includes different events so that readers can make their own judgments.

Another problem in compiling the chronology is that there must be an end at some date for publication. In this instance, the work finishes with the year 1988. However, as time is seamless and ever evolving, the reality is that accounts of many events cannot be completed as their stories are still unfolding. Thus, this chronology can only finish with "to be continued."

CAVEAT LECTOR

Of course, no project of this magnitude is a singular effort. My thanks go to Kathy Grove for her assistance in the beginning struggle to assemble the raw data in a logical order. Patty Taylor deserves a medal for her efforts to transcribe my rambling thoughts and translate my illegible notes into readable material. Students and others are to be thanked for contributing items to the cause, a quest lasting over ten years, and using the material to seek clues for understanding the U.S. business system of today and tomorrow.

1602

General Events

English pilot Bartholomew Gosnold discovers Cape Cod... Spanish vessels explore Pacific Coast to San Francisco.

1604

General Events

France starts settlement in Maine (moves to Nova Scotia later).

1606

Business Events

Merchants from Plymouth, Bristol, Exeter form joint stock Plymouth Company to colonize North Virginia, area of NYC (sends 2 expedtions, 1st captured by Spanish and 2nd surveys Atlantic Coast, is followed by 11 other colonizing companies, such as New Scotland for Nova Scotia, Adventurers to Canada, Massachusetts Bay, and Providence Islands for Carolinas, by 1630)... 715 merchant adventures charters joint stock London Company to settle South Virginia (send 105 colonists in 1606, settle Jamestown in 1607, losing 73 to disease).

1607

General Events

Plymouth Company's 3rd expedition, led by Sir George Popham and sponsored by Sir Fernando Gorges, tries to start first New England colony on Sagadahoc River, ME (-1608 when abandoned after dissension, unwillingness to work, failure to find quick wealth, and death of Popham).

1608

General Events

Jamestown ships cargo of "gold," really mica, to England... Jamestown exports first shipment of glass, pitch, soap, tar, lumber, iron ore to England... Polish, German glassmakers land in Jamestown.

1609

General Events

Captain John Smith cultivates Indian corn at Jamestown to ward off starvation... Spain founds Santa Fe in New Mexico (-1610)... Henry Hudson, Dutch East India Company, sights Newfoundland, explores New England Coast and Hudson River in searching for Northwest passage.

Business Events

London Company is chartered as Virginia Company with Sir Thomas Smythe,

Governor of East India Company, as Treasurer (is granted 7 years of imports without taxes and duties, is required to give 20% of all gold, silver to England).

1610

Business Events

By law, Virginia Colony uses daily drum-rolls to muster laborers for work.

1612

General Events

James I sponsors lottery to raise funds for Virginia Colony.

Business Events

Virginians colonize Bermudas... John Rolfe plants first tobacco in Virginia with seeds from West Indies (exports Colony's first shipment in 1614, shipping some 50,000 pounds in 1615 and by end of 1600's 40 million pounds to England and 25 million pounds to Europe)... Dutch merchants start fur trading on Manhattan Island (start post in 1613 and Fort Nassau, later Fort Orange, near Albany in 1614).

1614

Business Events

Captain John Smith explores, charts coast of New England for London merchants (returns with cod fish)... Dutch merchants, ship owners form United New Netherland Company, becomes Dutch West India Company in 1621, to trade with Hudson River Valley Indians with 3-year monopoly (with colony at mouth of Hudson, New Amsterdam in 1624, build first large ship of 16 tons in North America).

1615

General Events

Captain John Smith, Admiral of New England for Plymouth Colony, attempts to start colony in new land.

Business Events

Sir Fernando Gorges undertakes fishing, trading voyage to New England for Plymouth Company.

1616

Business Events

All investors in Virginia Company receive dividend of 100 acres per share, pooled by investors to form plantations.

1619

General Events

First representative assembly in North America meets (July 30) in Jamestown with delegates from 11 plantations (bans all forms of amusement on Sunday)... To encourage immigration, investors in Virginia Company receive 50 acres for paying sea passage of each new colonist... Polish glassblowers in Jamestown win first strike in North America to protest denial of voting rights... Virginia Company ships marriageable women, planters pay 120 pounds of tobacco for each passage, and slum children as apprentices to Jamestown.

Business Events

Virginia starts first iron works in North America... Dutch ship sells 20 African blacks as indentured servants in Jamestown.

1620

General Events

London ironmonger Thomas Weston and London clothmaker John Peirce receive patent from Virginia Company (form joint-stock company with Leyden separatists, land on Cape Cod as result of storm, sign Mayflower Compact, form Council for New England with reorganization of Plymouth Company)... Council of London Company, governor of Virginia Colony set first fixed wage rates for different occupations.

1621

Business Events

Plymouth Colony starts salt works... Dutch merchants charter Dutch West India Company with trading monopoly and rights to colonize North America, (-1791).

1622

General Events

Privy Council bans lottery to raise funds for Virginia Colony (forces enterprise into receivership)... By law all craftsmen in Virginia must work their trade, banned from farming... Council for New England receives trading, fishing monopoly.

1623

General Events

Council for New England grants 20 patents for settlements from Maine to Rhode Island... Holland creates New Netherlands as province in North America (starts settlements in 1624)... Immigrant fishermen, farmers from Dorchester found Gloucester, MA (ship first salted cod to Spain in 1623).

1624

General Events

England revokes (May 24) charter of bankrupt Virginia Colony   (creates royal colony)... First cattle are shipped to New England... Virginia levies fines in tobacco on those not attending Sunday church.

1626

General Events

Seaport of Salem is founded, MA,... Peter Minuit becomes Director General of Dutch Colony on Manhattan Island (-1631, buys island from Canarsie Indians for $24 in goods, builds first colonial flour mill to run on horse power)... Plymouth Colony prohibits cutting of timber on public lands without permission.

Business Events

Plymouth pilgrims buy out London stockholders in Council for New England with loan guaranteed by 8 colonists in return for trade monopoly, tax on shareholders until debt repaid.

1627

General Events

Cardinal Richelieu creates Company of New France with fur trading monopoly... Charles I charters New England Company as commercial enterprise to develop resources of area (settles Charlestown in 1630)... London managers send some 1,500 kidnapped children to Virginia Colony.

Business Events

New Amsterdam, Plymouth colonies start trading... Plymouth Colony starts trading post on Maine's Kennebec River.

1629

General Events

Dutch West India Company issues land grants with freedom from taxation for 8 years and grants feudal rights to patroons, Amsterdam pearl merchant Kiliaen Van Rensselaer most successful with some 700,000 acres on Upper Hudson... Massachusetts Bay Company, formerly New England Company, is chartered by Puritans as joint-stock enterprise to start religious community.

Business Events

Brick kiln is started at Salem and leather tannery at Lynn, MA.

1630

General Events

Massachusetts Bay colonists taste (February 22) first "popped corn" at first Thanksgiving dinner... Massachusetts Bay Colony sets wage ceiling for workers in building trades, abolished 1631 and revived 1633.

1631

General Events

Sir Fernando Gorges obtains land grant to settle area in Maine, New Hampshire... Virginia prohibits export of hides (MA in 1646, MD in 1685, PA in 1700).

Business Events

John Winthrop, Jr., MA, launches first large colonial-made vessel, fishing boat of 30 tons (pioneers American fleet as 3rd largest in world by 1776).

1632

General Events

Roman Catholic Lord Baltimore obtains charter for 10-20 million acres in Maryland... Land along Connecticut River is granted to Puritans by Council for New England (build Fort Saybrook in 1635).

Business Events

New Amsterdam builds first colonial public brewery, Philadelphia's first by William Penn in 1685.

1633

General Events

Massachusetts prohibits sales of certain commodities at prices over one-third of those in England.

1635

General Events

Plymouth Colony hires James Morton to teach children to "read, write, and cast accounts."

Business Events

Dutch trading post is started on Delaware River... To eliminate battles of customers buying goods on arriving English ships, 9 Massachusetts towns buy cargoes for resale to public at 5% above cost.

1636

General Events

College to train Puritan ministers is started in Massachusetts (becomes Harvard in 1638)... Massachusetts allows freemen of each town to set rates of pay... Maine fishermen strike to protest withholding of wages.

1637

General Events

New Sweden Company of Dutch and Swedish investors settles Fort Christina on Delaware River, Peter Minuit leader (introduces log cabin).

Business Events

Massachusetts grants Captain Sedgwick exclusive rights to start brewery.

1638

General Events

Plymouth Colony creates a pension plan, first in colonies, for disabled soldiers.

Business Events

Stephen Daye starts first colonial printing press, MA... Indentured servants of Captain Sibsey mutiny to protest intolerable living conditions.

1639

Business Events

Boston builds wharf, crane to unload ships, site for 15 private wharves by 1645... Boston merchant Robert Keayne is admonished by church, fined by civil court for making too much money... Edward Rauson builds first known gunpowder mill at Pecoit, MA.

1640

General Events

Dutch Colony is started on Delaware River near Sweden's Fort Christina (is captured by Swedish in 1654, is recaptured by Dutch in 1655 to end Sweden's colonization)... Massachusetts fines anyone fasting, feasting, or refusing to work on Christmas Day... Massachusetts offers bounties to increase production of woolen cloth (DE in 1662, MD in 1682)... Maryland authorizes county courts to regulate wages .(-1642)... Massachusetts Bay Colony, first colonial study of child labor, calls for town magistrates to determine possibility of teaching children spinning of yarn.

1641

General Events

Plymouth Colony adopts English system for inspection, regulation of shipwrights... General Court, Massachusetts Bay Colony, establishes Code of Liberties (grants towns authority to regulate wages and prices, specifies no man should take money for representing another in court).

Business Events

Massachusetts merchant Samuel Maverick starts exporting whale oil to Bristol for clapboards, selling clapboards to Spain for fruit shipped to Bristol (credits returns to Bristol account)... John Winthrop, Jr., Massachusetts promoter and manager, submits plans for iron works at Lynn to London investors (with 11 English gentlemen charters Company of Undertakers for Iron Works in New England with 21-year monopoly, free 3-square miles of land for each furnace, an exemption of workers from military service and of taxes for 20 years, starts production 1648, is fired in 1650 for financial losses, is purchased by Boston merchant William Paine in late 1650's and abandoned in 1676).

1642

General Events

Richard Graves, Yankee peddler first cited, is sentenced to whipping post, stocks for kissing Goodie Gent twice... Massachusetts regulates saltpeter works, leather tanneries.

1643

General Events

New Plymouth taxes individuals on estates, facilities (taxes tradesmen, craftsmen in 1646 on returns, gains)... Massachusetts, Plymouth, New Hampshire, Connecticut colonies form United Colonies of New England to cooperate in returning run-away servants, slaves (-1698 when dissolved).

Business Events

Massachusetts offers exclusive rights to mill corn to anyone building tide mill.

1644

General Events

Guilds of shipbuilders, shoemakers are formed, MA, followed by NYC coopers in 1644 and weavers in 1702, Philadelphia cordwainers and tailors in 1718... Massachusetts charters company to build ships... New Haven Colony grants impressed labor to three businessmen for approved undertaking.

1645

General Events

New Haven colony requires all men to do public work as needed.

1646

General Events

Virginia Colony starts training program to teach children carding, knitting and spinning at public cost.

1647

General Events

Rhode Island regulates working conditions, setting penalties for those in building trades leaving their work and prohibiting masters to fire a servant without sufficient cause.

Business Events

Boston takes business census: 6 enterprises in wood-working, 7 in metal-working, 3 in leather (shows existence of weavers, ropemakers, feltmakers, furriers, brickmakers, tilemakers).

1648

General Events

Massachusetts charters Boston coopers with self-government (grants coopers power to supress craftsmen not approved by society).

1649

General Events

Iroquois Confederation attacks Hurons to establish fur monopoly.

1650

General Events

Parliament bans (October 30) foreign shipping not having special license for trading with colonies.

1651

General Events

Parliament passes (October 9) first Navigation Act to require colonial trade with England must be in English ships (instigates Anglo-Dutch War of 1652 - 1654)... Connecticut grants John Winthrop, Jr., monopolies in lead, copper and tin.

1652

General Events

Boston starts (June 7) first colonial mint, issues Pine Tree Silver Shilling... Rhode Island passes first colonial law to abolish slavery.

1656

General Events

Massachusetts decrees all women, girls and boys, unless otherwise occupied, must do spinning (sets penalties for families not meeting production quotas).

1657

General Events

Porters in New Amsterdam refuse to carry salt as they never had to do it in the past.

Business Events

Anthony Langsten proposes to build ironworks, employing 144 workers, in Virginia.

1658

General Events

New Amsterdam forms first colonial police force... Plymouth establishes work house for vagrants, idlers, rebellious children, and stubborn servants, seen in Boston, NYC, Philadelphia, Charleston in 1700's... New Amsterdam sets detailed hours for working day.

1659

General Events

Massachusetts passes law to punish anyone observing holidays, repealed 1681... Bakers of New Amsterdam hold two strikes to protest low prices set for wares... White servants in York County, VA, strike to settle grievances, again 1661.

1660

General Events

Parliament requires (October 10) all goods to and from England to be shipped in English-manned, English-built ships in 2nd Navigation Act (requires all colonial sugar, tobacco, cotton, wool, indigo to be shipped to England).

1661

General Events

Massachusetts bans "wampum" as legal tender, NY in 1701... Virginia requires counties to start tanneries and train shoemakers, tanners.

1662

Business Events

Porters in New Amsterdam create common fund to protect members when ill.

1663

General Events

King Charles II charters Carolina Colony (allows proprietors to establish feudal society based on English estate system, settles Charleston in 1670).

Business Events

Boston merchant John Hall acquires small trading vessel (operates 8 ships with partners in 1665-70, 14 in 1670-83).

1664

General Events

Duke of York's forces seize New Amsterdam, renamed New York (is recaptured by Dutch in 1673 and returned to England in 1674)... Connecticut is formed by independent colonies.

1666

General Events

Virginia counties are required to provide public loom... Due to overproduction, Maryland forbids commercial cultivation of tobacco for one year.

1670

Business Events

Merchants Exchange, first in colonies, appears in NYC... Newark, NJ, offers anyone starting corn mill 3 days of work by every man, woman with town allotment.

1671

General Events

French explorers reach Sault Saint Marie to claim interior land for France.

Business Events

Dr. H. Woodward grows first true colonial rice, VA.

1672

General Events

Massachusetts bans giving wine or strong liquor to workmen.

1673

General Events

Regular overland mail service is started between NYC, Boston...
Massachusetts passes first colonial copyright law (grants protection for
7 years)... Father Jacques Marquette, trader Louis Joliet explore
Mississippi River to Arkansas River.

Business Events

Benjamin Harris prints first colonial paper, <u>Public</u> <u>Occurrences</u>, in
Boston, suppressed after first issue.

1674

General Events

Father Jacques Marquette starts mission on Lake Michigan, becomes site of
Chicago.

1675

General Events

NYC passes law to protect coopers from competition by outsiders from
Boston... War with Indians starts in New England (-1676)... Boston ship
carpenters force apprentice to leave for failing to serve full
apprenticeship of 7 years.

Business Events

Over 600 vessels, some 4,000 men in New England fish for cod.

1676

General Events

Nathaniel Bacon leads insurrection of servants, workers, sharecroppers,
and poor in Virginia to demand frontier security, tax reforms, and
settlement of grievances, granted reforms.

1677

General Events

Massachusetts appoints postmasters... Licensed cartmen strike, NYC.

Business Events

Salem Captain Phillip English signs contract with English agent to ship goods from France to Boston, Boston to Spain, Spain to French and English ports (gives agent 30% for his investment, operates with 12 vessels, wharf, 14 buildings by 1692).

1678

General Events

Joseph Moxon: The Doctrine of Handy-Works (-1680 with illustrations of basic production machines, i.e., lathes and blacksmith forge).

1679

General Events

Boston forms first paid colonial fire department.

1680

General Events

Massachusetts bans business activities on Sunday.

1681

General Events

Charles II grants William Penn Royal Charter for Pennsylvania (requires 1 acre in trees to be left for every 5 acres cleared).

1682

General Events

French explorer La Salle reaches mouth of the Mississippi to claim territory for France (founds St. Louis)... Royal agent Edward Randolph reports Massachusetts as refusing to enforce the navigation acts.

1683

General Events

William Penn opens first Pennsylvania post office.

1684

General Events

France charters Mississippi Company.

1686

General Events

Porters petition NYC for redress on work done by Negro, Indian slaves.

Business Events

Cornelius Steenwych, NY's "richest" merchant, dies, leaves estate of $25,000... Some 6 booksellers do business in Boston (evolves with first known in Williamsburg in 1736, 5 in Philadelphia in 1742).

1687

Business Events

Francis Perot's Son's Malting Co., perhaps U.S.' oldest continuing business, is started in Philadelphia.

1689

General Events

Jacob Leister, former trader for Dutch West India Company, captures NYC (-1691, bans trading monopolies in 1690).

1690

General Events

Massachusetts issues bills of credits, first colonial paper money, to pay soldiers in expedition against Port Royal, Quebec.

Business Events

Samuel Carpenter, partners build first colonial paper mill.

1691

General Events

Thomas Neale obtains 21-year monopoly to operate colonial postal system (-1706, is replaced by English postal service in 1707-75).

1692

Business Events

Boston Almanac advertises patent medicine, guaranteed to cure "Gripping of the Guts," "The Dry Belly Ache".

1695

General Events

Rice is cultivated in Carolina... For first time, English law prohibits exports of textile machinery, blueprints.

1696

General Events

Board of Trade and Plantations is formed in London to regulate North American commerce (-1768)... Parliament passes (April 10) Navigation Act to limit all colonial trade to English-built and colonial-built ships (voids laws of colonial assemblies counteracting navigation acts, gives colonial customs commissioners powers of forceable entry, of requiring bonds, and of collecting plantation duties)... Royal African Trade Company, formed 1660, loses monopoly for transporting slaves (results in rise of New England slave trade).

1698

Business Events

First colonial tannery is built, NJ.

1699

General Events

Parliament passes Wool Act to limit wool production in Ireland, ban export of wool from American colonies... Board of Trade urges Parliament to prohibit woolen workers leaving country... French trading post is started at Biloxi (moves to Mobile Bay in 1702)... New Orleans holds first North American Mardi Gras festival.

1700s

Business Events

Taos fairs of Pueblo Indians are visited by Comanches to exchange dry meat, skins, tallow, and suet for maize, squash, melons, blankets, poultry, and turquoise jewelry, other Indian trading centers at villages of Mandans, Hidatsas, Arikaras.

1700

General Events

Rhode Island taxes peddlers.

1701

General Events

Cotton Mather: A Christian and His Calling (advocates diligent Christian follow occupation with industry to reap just rewards)... France starts settlement at Detroit to control Illinois trade.

1702

General Events

New Jersey is created (April 17) as Royal Colony.

Business Events

England charters Asiento Guinea Company to ship slaves to American Colonies (starts colonial slave trade with Spanish patent from Asiento Treaty of 1713).

1703

Business Events

South Carolina issues paper money to pay soldiers for attack on St. Augustine.

1704

Business Events

Weekly Boston Newsletter is first regularly published colonial paper (-1776, prints advertisements).

1705

General Events

New England passes trade act (-1713, expands number of colonial products for export to only English ports, sets bounties to encourage manufacture of rice, molasses, and naval stores)... Virginia requires all masters to teach apprentices reading, writing... Virginia allows the formation of merchant guilds to develop ports, towns (prohibits monopoly combinations)... England limits (June 18) currency value of shillings in American colonies... Virginia formulates "slave code," defines slaves as property.

1706

Business Events

First important colonial custom house is built at Yorktown, VA.

1707

General Events

Philadelphia mechanics join together to oppose competition of hired black slaves.

1708

General Events

England passes currency act to fine those guilty in offering illegal exchange rates for foreign coins.

1709

General Events

Connecticut Assembly charters first colonial mining venture to export copper to England... First mass of Germans emigrate to Pennsylvania from Palatinate... Some private schools teach bookkeeping... Coke replaces wood in colonial iron production.

1710

General Events

London's Postmaster General becomes Postmaster General of American Colonies.

1711

Business Events

English politicians create South Sea Company as trading enterprise, granted monopoly on trade to eastern coast of South America with power to issue stock for funding public credit (obtains 30-year Spanish Asiento in 1713 to ship slaves to North American and Spanish colonies, ruins investors in 1720 with collapse of speculative "South Sea Bubble," dissolves in 1854 after retiring all debts).

1712

General Events

NYC condemns 18 slaves to death for rebellion.

Business Events

Nantucket ship blunders on pod of sperm whales in open North Atlantic, efficient deep-sea whaling replaces dangerous shoreline catches (becomes port for 15 whalers by 1715)... French trader Antoine Crozat is granted monopoly on trade from Mississippi to Pacific Coast (-1717 when acquired by John Law's Company of the West, is acquired by French Crown in 1731).

1713

General Events

England continues bounties of 1705 Act for 11 years and extends subsidy for hemp for 16 years... Captain Andrew Robinson builds first colonial schooner in Gloucester, MA.

1714

General Events

Massachusetts Land Bank is created to lend money on security of land... Tea is first exported to American colonies.

Business Events

Iron works is started, VA (imports Germans to operate blast furnaces).

1715

General Events

Maryland prohibits imports of Pennsylvania bread, flour, and beer.

Business Events

Sybilla Masters, Philadelphia, gets British patent for pulverized maize (sells "Tuscarora Rice" as cure for consumption).

1716

General Events

French establish Natchez on Mississippi.

1717

General Events

Connecticut requires peddlers entering State to pay fees... American vessels are allowed to carry expensive rum from French West Indies to

colonies... France's Louis XIV grants John Law trading monopoly for
Louisiana Territory (forms Mississippi Company to issue shares in 1718,
obtains tobacco monopoly in 1718, ruins speculating investors with
collapse of "Mississippi Bubble" in 1720).

Business Events

Presbyterian Synod of Philadelphia creates corporation to provide funds
to needy ministers and families (becomes insurance company later as
Presbyterian Ministers' Fund).

1718

General Events

San Antonio is founded by Spanish in Texas as presido-mission
(establishes 10 missions, 4 presidios by 1722)... New Orleans is settled
by French colonists... Philadelphia cordwainers, tailors are granted
corporate privileges to regulate their crafts... Vermont is first
settled... Parliament authorizes 7 years at bound labor in colonies for
lesser crimes, 14 years for offenses punishable by death (results in some
10,000 convicts being shipped 1717-1775).

1720

General Events

Colonial population is estimated as 474,000, Boston with 12,000,
Philadelphia with 10,000, New York with 7,000.

Business Events

Alexander Spotswood starts iron furnace in Virginia, William Bird
operates four in 1732 with some 100 slaves... Relatives of England's
Darby Family of ironmongers start first colonial blast furnace to make
iron at Coalbrookdale, PA... Principio Company of England starts furnace,
forge near head of Chesapeake Bay (-1781, uses coal from mines of partner
Augustus Washington, father of George, to evolve with 30,000 acres, four
furnaces, two forges by 1767)... Phillip Renault works lead mines in
Missouri... In period, group of Scottish merchants of Glasgow organize
Chesapeake tobacco trade with chain of permanent stores and buy tobacco
direct from planters, previously handled by independent planters and
merchant houses in London, Bristol, and Liverpool (by 1750s supplies 40%
of French monopoly, ships 12% of England's imports)... With land grant
from Penn family British investors form Free Society of Traders to
develop industrial enterprise near Philadelphia (-1729, after recruiting
settlers, build tannery, sawmill, gristmill, glass factory and brick
kiln, go broke from under-financing, absentee ownership).

1721

Business Events

John Copson opens first colonial office in Philadelphia to underwrite
marine and fire insurance, first Boston insurance office in 1724.

1722

General Events

Parliament adds copper, beaver, other furs to items only for export to England (removes hemp, lumber, naval stores from export duties, permits colonies to mint copper coins).

1723

General Events

Benjamin Franklin travels 100 miles from NYC to Philadelphia in 4 days.

Business Events

Connecticut charters trading corporation, wharf company by MA in 1772 and Philadelphia Contributorship, fire insurance business, by PA in 1776.

1724

General Events

France builds Fort Vincennes on Lower Wabash River... Irrigation of rice in southern colonies increases crop production... Philadelphia house carpenters, workers, and owners organize, Carpenters' Company of the City and County of Philadelphia in 1792, to provide training, assistance to injured members and widows (sets standard prices for work later)... 32 Boston barbers join to set uniform prices for shaves, wigs... Philadelphia carpenters are able to buy ready-made sash windows for houses.

Business Events

After finishing 7-year apprenticeship in book trade, Thomas Hancock opens Boston shop to publish and bind books (-1763, starts importing other goods from London about 1728 with exports of whale oil, sells goods wholesale, accepting commodities in exchange, to country traders and peddlers, supplies British troops in 1940-48 War of Austrian Succession and 1755-63 French and Indian War to become wealthy).

1725

General Events

Virginia forbids shipment of seed tobacco, overruled by English Board of Trade.

Business Events

The New York Gazette is City's first regular newspaper (-1745).

1727

General Events

Benjamin Franklin and others, mostly artisans, form "Junto" discussion club as secret brotherhood for mutual improvement in business of getting ahead (-1750).

1729

General Events

Parliament renews bounties on naval stores (-1774).

Business Events

Benjamin, James Franklin buy 1728 newspaper to start Pennsylvania Gazette (becomes Saturday Evening Post in 1821).

1730

General Events

Virginia passes tobacco inspection law to set product quality standards for export... Nicholas Bayard builds NYC's first large sugar refinery... First commercial kiln in NYC for making stoneware is started (develops City as colonial pottery center)... Newport, RI, is visited by wealthy vacationers from as far away as Carolinas, West Indies.

Business Events

Central Market opens at Lancaster, PA, for farmers, operates continuously from 1742.

1731

General Events

Parliament prohibits immigration of factory workers to American colonies... Benjamin Franklin, Junto Club form the Library Company of Philadelphia (uses suggestion box to select books for acquisition).

Business Events

Dr. Charles Carroll, others found Baltimore Iron Works.

1732

General Events

Parliament passes Hat Act to ban shipments of hats between colonies (sets limit of two apprentices per colonial manufacturer, forbids use of black apprentices and requires craftsmen to serve 7-year apprenticeships)... James Oglethorpe founds colony of Georgia... Alexander Malcolm's grammer school, NYC, teaches bookkeeping, also at David Dore's school in 1759.

Business Events

Benjamin Franklin starts (December 19) <u>Poor Richard's Almanack</u> to encourage temperance, prudence, integrity, economy, punctuality, courage, and perseverance (-1757, views lotteries, gambling, swindling, striking, betting, stock market as vices)... <u>The South Carolina Gazette</u> prints advertisement on availability of skilled negro artisans for work... First regularly scheduled colonial public stage coach line is operated between Burlington, Amboy, NJ.

1733

General Events

Parliament passes (May 17) Molasses Act to set heavy duties on all molasses, rum, sugar imported to American colonies from West Indies... James Oglethorpe, followers settle planned Savannah, GA... Bounty is established to encourage colonial construction of whalers over 200 tons.

Business Events

Colonist obtains patent from King George to make, sell Dr. Bateman's Pectoral Drops to cure consumption.

1734

General Events

First colonial women's labor organization is formed by NYC maids to protest abuses from mistresses' husbands.

Business Events

Colonel Pepperell, New England trader, owning 35 vessels with interests in 20 others, dies.

1735

General Events

Massachusetts passes general incorporation law for wharves, water power mills, community service enterprises... Benjamin Franklin, others start Philadelphia's City Watch (-1752)... Benjamin Franklin, friends start Philadelphia's Union Fire Company, first colonial volunteer unit... Massachusetts lends Joseph Plaistel funds to operate potash business... Parliament allows Georgia to export rice to other countries besides England.

Business Events

Friendly Society for the Mutual Insurance of Houses Against Fire, first colonial fire insurance company, is chartered in Charleston (-1741), (declares bankruptcy after disastrous fire)... First colonial commercial grower of grapes, Pennsylvania Vine Co., is established near Philadelphia.

1736

General Events

South Carolina passes act to encourage production of silk... Jonathan Hulls obtains British patent for Newcomen-driven steamboat, used in boats of Marquis de Jouffroy in 1776, 1783.

1737

General Events

Annual Hanover County Fair is first held in Virginia (provides entertainment with feasts, music contests, wrestling bouts, beauty contests)... Richmond, VA, is founded... Connecticut mints first colonial copper coins.

Business Events

Paper currency is issued by land bank, NY (charters its first state bank in 1784).

1738

Business Events

Huguenot potter Andrew Duche discovers clay near Savannah, GA, for making Chinese-style porcelain (exports clay to England in 1743).

1739

General Events

French explorers sight Rocky Mountains... Georgia sets maximum wages for servants, laborers... Parliament permits colonies to export sugar to ports south of Spain's Cape Finisterre... Some 100 slaves revolt on Stone plantation near Charleston.

Business Events

Caspar Wistar starts large glass factory, NJ, with German glassblowers (-1780, starts second in 1740 to make window, bottle glass with Belgian glassblowers, becomes one of first successful worker cooperatives in colonies).

1740

General Events

Massachusetts establishes land bank to issue notes on land mortgages, dissolved by Parliament in 1741... Boston voters approve building Faneuil Hall as public market (holds first colonial town meeting in 1743).

Business Events

Boston News-letter prints ads to sell property.

1741

General Events

Danish Vitus Bering explores Alaska, Aleutian Islands for Russia... N.Y. Bakers strike to protest City's price regulations... Boston ship caulkers protest payment of salary by notes instead of money... To develop new export for South Carolina, Elizabeth Lucas, age 16, experiments with West Indies indigo on father's farm she manages (-1744, shares seeds with other planters to enable colony to export 135,000 pounds of dye stuff in 1747).

Business Events

Marblehead, MA, fishing fleet numbers 60 boats, Gloucester with 70... Andrew Bradford, Philadelphia, publishes <u>American Magazine</u>, first in colonies.

1742

Business Events

Marine Society of Boston is created to provide assistance to distressed shipmasters and families... Ringwood Iron Company is started by Ogden family of Newark, NJ (-1763, is acquired in 1764 by Peter Hasenclever to start industrial complex).

1743

General Events

Benjamin Franklin, Junto Club form American Philosophical Society, first colonial science organization.

1744

Business Events

Benjamin Franklin issues mail-order catalog.

1745

Business Events

Russian fur traders start settlement at Attu Island, reach end of Aleutians by 1759.

1746

General Events

Savannah carpenters strike for better working conditions.

Business Events

Philadephia bankers, merchants form financial market to exchange information, instruments.

1747

General Events

Maryland passes tobacco inspection law to maintain quality standards...
Virginians, Englishmen form Virginia-based Ohio Company with grant for
500,000 acres along Ohio River (start first settlement 1748, obtain
700,000 acres from England in 1749)... Building trades workers petition
New York governor to stop competition of NJ workers in NYC construction
projects, rejected... New York Gazette uses lottery to raise funds for
King's College, Columbia University in 1784.

1748

Business Events

Benjamin Franklin: "Advice to a Young Tradesman" (suggests Industry and
Frugality as Way to Wealth).

1749

General Events

Virginia grants Loyal Company 800,000 acres for development in Ohio.

1750

General Events

Maryland requires overseers of iron works to send one employee of every
ten to work on highways... Jacob Yoder of Pennsylvania develops flat
boat... U.S.' share of world manufacturing output is 0.1%, 0.8% in 1800,
2.4% in 1830, 7.2% in 1860, 14.7% in 1880 and 23.6% in 1900 to top
Britain's 18.5%... Conestoga wagon is built, PA, to carry household goods
of westward families.

Business Events

To escape persecution of Jews in Portugal, merchant Aaron Lopez starts
shop in Newport, RI (with funds borrowed from Jewish families sells soap
to New York merchants and candles to Philadelphia retailers, operates
some 30 ships and whaling fleet by mid-1770s, dies 1782 as town's
wealthiest merchant)... Some 200 merchant traders or shipping wholesalers
do business in Philadelphia, 450 by 1790.

1751

General Events

Currency Act forbids New England colonies to print money (covers all
colonies in 1764).

Business Events

Boston businessmen form Society for Encouraging Industry and Employing the Poor (operates with elected trustees to appoint management).

1752

Business Events

Benjamin Franklin, others form Philadelphia Contributorship for Insurance of Houses from Loss by Fire (operates only chartered business in colonial time, underwrites some $2 million of insurance by 1781).

1753

General Events

Benjamin Franklin, William Hunter are appointed joint postmasters for colonies (-1774, extend post roads from Maine to Florida)... Benjamin Franklin publishes data on experiments with electricity in <u>Poor Richard's Almanac</u> (invents lightning rod - first installed in England in 1760)... Phillip Schuyler, owner of copper mine, NJ, imports Newcomen engine, about 5 horsepower, to pump water from deep levels, first in colonies (leads to 72,000 horsepower steam engine of Interurban Transit Co., NY, in 1900).

1754

General Events

Benjamin Banneker, black mathematician, astronomer, and surveyor, builds first Colonial clock (issues almanac in 1891).

Business Events

Board of Brokers is formed as guild to operate financial market at Philadelphia's London Coffee House.

1755

General Events

Virginia pays Anglician clergy in currency instead of tobacco, used as payment in 1662, with failure of crop from drought.

1757

General Events

Parliament forbids American colonies to export outside empire... Benjamin Franklin: <u>Poor Richard Improved</u> (suggests prosperity result of industry and diligence, using time wisely, and not trusting others too much)... Parliament allows unrestricted duty-free import of American iron into England.

1759

General Events

Virginia forms public corporation to encourage growth of manufacturing (awards premiums for new enterprises).

1760

General Events

Benjamin Franklin introduces gypsum for fertilizer... Boston, Providence, NYC, Philadelphia, Baltimore, and Charleston are connected by rough road... 39 masters form Cordwainers Fire Company in Philadelphia to recover runaway apprentices.

1761

General Events

63 Boston merchants submit case to Massachusetts court to oppose use of general warrants by English custom officials to search anywhere, anytime for smuggled goods.

Business Events

To eliminate bitter competition Nicholas Brown and competitors in Boston, Philadelphia form United Company of Spermaceti Candle Manufacturers of Providence and Newport to fix prices, ban new plants, and limit dealers (-1775 as first American monopoly)... Some 83% of colonial exports shipped to England by 1765 are from Virginia, Maryland, Carolina, Georgia.

1762

General Events

Boston Gazette reports attempted counterfeiting.

1763

General Events

Parliament reduces bounties on indigo... Boston forms Society for Encouraging Trade and Commerce... Philadelphia is first colonial town with population over 20,000... George Washington, associates form Mississippi Company with grant (September 9) by English Crown for 2.5 million acres at junction of Ohio, Mississippi Rivers... Charleston grand jury protests combination of black apprentice chimney sweeps to fix prices... Proclamation Line bans settlements west of Appalachians, redrawn 1768 for land companies.

Business Events

Indiana Company is formed for land development (-1767)... John Hancock becomes partner in uncle's general business (-1775, is arrested, fined in

1768 for illicit trading).

1764

General Events

France settles St. Louis... Parliament bans immigration of skilled workers to colonies (bans export of textile machinery, plans, models in acts of 1774, 1781, 1782)... Parliament passes (April 5) Sugar Act to raise revenues from duties... England forbids (April 19) colonies, particularly Virginia, to issue paper money with Currency Act.

Business Events

Boston merchants boycott English luxury goods, supported by mechanics... Society for the Promotion of Arts, Agriculture and Economy is formed, NYC, as employer combination... German-born ironmonger Heinrich "Baron" Stiegel starts glass factory in Pennsylvania with foreign glassmakers (starts 2nd in 1769 as American Flint Glass Manufacturing, declares bankruptcy in 1774 and goes to debtors' prison)... Peter Hasenclever, German agent for group of London merchants organized as American Company, starts two industrial complexes in Northern NJ (operates 6 blast furnaces, 7 forges, one stamping mill, 3 steel mills, and one grist mill as possibly largest colonial employer by Revolution).

1765

General Events

Indian trader Alexander Henry discovers copper on Michigan Penninsula... Parliament passes (March 22) Stamp Act to tax all printed material... Maryland county is first to repudiate Stamp Act... Some 200 New York merchants join in opposing Stamp Act and 1764 trade act, supported by over 400 Philadelphia merchants.

Business Events

Chocolate is first manufactured in U.S., world's leading producer in 1980s (leads to Hershey chocolate candy bar in 1894).

1766

General Events

Parliament repeals (March 18) Stamp Act... Illinois Company is formed for land development... Parliament revises 1764 Trade Act to lower import duties on molasses... Oldest colonial medical society forms at Duff's Tavern in New Brunswick, NJ (fails to establish uniform fees, licensing system)... Printers in Philadelphia strike.

Business Events

Thurber family opens woman's apparel store in Providence, RI, (is acquired in 1805 by George W. Gladding, partner to operate oldest U.S. specialty store, remains family-owned until 1968)... Samuel Bowen, former British seaman, is first in colonies to cultivate soybeans (exports soy sauce, noodles to England - Henry Ford processes crop in 1920s-30s to produce enamel and plastics).

1767

General Events

Moravian missionary visits oil springs near Titusville, PA, used by Indians for ointment... Parliament passes (June 29) Townshend Act to tax colonial imports, partially repealed in 1770... Committee is formed, NYC, to develop industry in reducing City's reliance on English goods... Friendly Society of Tradesmen House Carpenters is formed, NYC (as mutual-aid and group-benefit society provides loans, funeral expenses, support to widows).

Business Events

Boston Post Boy advertises services of Elizabeth Shaw, London-born shoemaker... New York Gazette and Weekly Post Boy reports French Huguenot refugees cultivate silkworms, SC... Dr. Turnbull plants mulberry trees, grape vines in Florida (recruits workers from Greece, Italy).

1768

General Events

In first strike 20 journeymen tailors, NYC, "turn out" for higher wages.

Business Events

Boston merchants boycott (August 1) English goods, supported by NYC... In Boston, Mr. Michaelson starts first foundry in colonies to cast printer's type... New York City Chamber of Commerce is formed in Fraunces' Tavern... John Hancock's Liberty is seized by English Customs for carrying illicit wine, released by mob.

1769

General Events

Philadelphia (March 10), Baltimore merchants (March 30) join non-importation movement... Grand Ohio Company is formed in England to buy 20 million acres for settlement... St. Charles is first white settlement on Missouri River... Vandalia Company, Benjamin Franklin member of Anglo-American syndicate, seeks permission from England's Board of Trade to buy 2.4 million acres in Eastern Kentucky, approved 1775... Franciscan friar Father Junipero Sera founds San Diego de Alcala Mission as first settlement on West Coast, 8 more by 1784 to San Francisco... New Jersey rewards Hibernia Ironworks for plant construction with exemptions from taxes for 7 years... Guild of building trades' workers is started, NYC.

Business Events

Boston Society for Encouraging Industry and Employing the Poor builds "manufacturing house" as spinning school.

1770

General Events

Parliament drops (April 12) duties on all American imports except tea.

Business Events

Philadelphia china factory advertises for workers with apprenticeships from England, France, Germany.

1771

General Events

Over 40 tailors, Philadelphia, form company to fix prices and limit wages of journeymen.

1772

General Events

English banking system undergoes crisis (July), forces reduction of credit (requires colonial merchants to liquidate inventories)... English customs schooner Gaspee is burned by colonials after running aground near Rhode Island.

Business Events

Over 250,000 barrels of flour and 38,000 casks of bread are exported annually by mills on Delaware River.

1773

General Events

Parliament passes Tea Act (May 10) to grant near-bankrupt English East India Company right to sell tea to colonies without having to use middlemen... "Mohawk braves" dump 342 chests of tea into Boston harbor... First public museum in colonies opens in Charleston, SC.

Business Events

Phillip Mazzei of Virginia imports workers, materials from Italy to start silk industry.

1774

General Events

Transylvania Company is formed by land speculators in Kentucky... First Continental Congress is held (September 5) in Philadelphia's Carpenter Hall... Illinois, Wabash Land Companies are formed to buy tracts of Western territory... Mother Ann Lee, former English Quaker, starts first Shaker village, NY, as socialistic Christian society practicing celibacy, shuffling holy dances (evolves by 1860s with over 6,000 members of United

Society of Believers in Christ's Second Appearing in 19 communal farms from Indiana to Maine with inventions of flat broom, circular saw, wrinkle-resistant cotton, one-horse farm wagon, Poland China pigs, clothespin and iced tea and improvements in screw propeller, hand-powered and steam-powered washing machines, silk culture, turbine waterwheel, and horse collars, fades away in 1980s).

1775

General Events

Parliament declares (February 9) Massachusetts in state of rebellion... Revolution is started (April 18-19) with attack of English troops on Concord, MA (-1781)... Second Continental Congress convenes (May 10) in Philadelphia (establishes postal system with Benjamin Franklin as Postmaster, authorizes army with Colonel Washington as Commander, creating staff sections of adjutant general, commissary, quartermaster and paymaster with each supervising similar staff units in three line division.

Business Events

Some 80 apprentices, 175 forges are used to make some 30,000 tons of iron per year in colonies, more than all other countries except Russia, Sweden... United Company of Philadelphia for Promoting American Manufacture is first colonial joint stock company to make cotton goods (employs some 400 women spinners - most in own homes, ends with British occupation)... New Jersey storekeeper starts wampum factory... Samuel Wetherill, pioneer dyer, starts cloth factory with spinning jennies in Philadelphia... Lawyer John Lowell moves to Boston (amasses fortune in handling confiscated Tory property and selling prize vessels captured by American privateers, leaves estate of $80,000 in 1802 to merchant son, Frances Cabot Lowell).

1776

General Events

Jeremiah Wilkinson, RI, devises method for making a dozen nails at one time (invents "first" cold-cut nail in 1777)... Spanish mission is started at Yerba Buena, known as San Francisco in 1849... Congress declares (April 6) colonial ports open to all marine traffic except that of England... New York with population of 22,000 is second largest city after Philadelphia with 26,000... Congress authorizes loan of $5 million to finance war.

Business Events

Paul Revere starts gunpowder factory at Canton, MA... John Sears builds salt works on Cape Cod to evaporate salt from sea water.

1777

General Events

Oliver Evans devises machine to improve productivity of wool manufacturing.

1778

General Events

Congress establishes works to cast cannon at Springfield, MA, U.S. armory in 1794... Baron Friedrich Wilhem von Steuben, former staff officer in Prussian Army, becomes Inspector General for Continental Army with responsibility for military training... South Carolina adopts general incorporation law for religious societies, followed by NY in 1784, NJ in 1786 and DE in 1787.

Business Events

Merchant peddler Thomas Danforth opens store in Rocky Hill, CT (sends peddlers throughout area to sell hardware to retail dealers and outfit local peddlers, establishes sons in branches along East Coast to Savannah).

1779

General Events

Spain starts settlement at Nacogdoches, TX... Pelatiah Wester: Essay On Free Trade and Finance (opposes regulations on prices, wages)... Baron von Steuben: Steuben's Regulations for the Order and Discipline of the Troops of the United States, official training manual for 33 years (covers drilling, regulations, tactics, military routine).

Business Events

St. Louis' Solard Market for farmers is oldest west of Mississippi.

1780

General Events

Congress passes Forty to One Act as deflationary move to redeem Continental paper money at 1/40 of face value... William Coxe: Account of the Russian Discoveries Between Asia and America (reveals wealth in Northwest fur trade).

Business Events

Andrew Cabot starts Boston's trade with Sweden, Russia by 1784... Pennsylvania Packet prints ad to offer employment to master workman (offers share of ownership as inducement).

1781

General Events

Congress appoints (February 20) Robert Morris as Superintendent of

Finance to resolve financial crisis (accepts providing he can continue with private business interests)... Faced with problem of worthless money, Bank of North America is chartered, December 31... Netherlands extends large loan to U.S.

Business Events

First U.S. pharmaceutical firm is started... Robert Morris, associates form North American Land Company, first American trust, to sell Western lands from holdings of nearly 6 million acres in six states... When Philadelphia Contributorship refuses to insure houses surrounded by trees (fears lightening), Mutual Assurance forms (provides one-payment fire insurance).

1782

General Events

U.S., Netherlands sign commerce treaty... Bank of North America, first commercial bank, opens in Philadelphia.

1783

General Events

Revolutionary War is ended (September 3)... British West Indies' trade is closed to U.S... U.S. is permitted to export manufactured goods to England.

Business Events

Over 300 business corporations are chartered by 1801... Empress of China, financed by Robert Morris and partners, is first U.S. vessel to visit Canton (-1785, earns profit of $37,000 on investment of $120,000 in cargo of ginseng, brandy, wine, tar, and turpentine, returns with imports of tea, silks, nankeens, chinaware)... Pennsylvania Evening Post is Philadelphia's first daily.

1784

General Events

Tennessee Companyis formed to make land grants to settlers... At request of Robert Morris, Congress creates (May 28) Treasury Board to replace Superintendent of Finance... Russians establish permanent colony on Kodiak Island... Benjamin Franklin suggests daylight savings time as way to cut down on use of candles... James Rumsey of Virginia tests small steam-powered boat (uses mechanically-driven poles for propulsion)... Benjamin Franklin, annoyed by having to switch glasses, invents bifocals... Ship carpenters form guild in NYC... James Rumsey petitions Virginia for patent on model steamboat, rejected (is given large land grant from Congress on urging of George Washington for successful demonstration, fails to make practical boat, invents watertube boiler and steam pump in 1785, steamboat powered by backward jet of water in 1786 and piston-driven hydraulic sawmill in 1787 - workhorse of U.S. industry in 1850s).

Business Events

United States sails to India from Philadelphia... Bank of Boston is
founded (still extant)... Financier William Duer, Alexander Hamilton
start Bank of New York (still extant)... Salem merchant Elias Hasket
Derby sponsors trading voyage to Russia... Privileges for mining
bituminous   coal   in   Pittsburgh's   Coal   Hill   are   sold...
The Pennsylvania Packet and Daily Advertiser is first U.S. daily
(provides more advertising than news)... George Hogg, British-born
pioneer chain store merchant (operates 15 wholesale groceries in Ohio and
61 stores in Pennsylvania, New York), is born (-1849).

1785

General Events

Congress fails to persuade individual states to grant more power to
Federal Government to regulate foreign commerce... Congress passes (May
8) land ordinance of 1785 to survey northwestern territories...
Massachusetts forbids export of U.S. goods in English vessels...
Pennsylvania passes bankruptcy law for "merchants, scriveners, bankers,
brokers, or factors"... U.S., Prussia sign commerce treaty to support
free trade, ban privateering... Virginia builds first U.S. turnpike...
James River Company opens waterway to navigation to West (operates first
U.S. canal-and-lock system in 1789)... Patowmack Company, George
Washington as president, is formed to develop Potomac River for traffic
inland (opens 1808, operates at loss, establishes bank in 1828, is
operated by Chesapeake and Ohio Canal Company 1828-30)... New York City
shoemakers form union, Philadelphia printers in 1786 - permanent by 1802,
Philadelphia cordwainers in 1789 - Federal Society in 1794...

University of Georgia is first state university... U.S., Russia sign
commercial treaty... Thomas Jefferson: "Cultivators of the earth are the
most valuable citizens. I consider the class of artificers as the
panders of vice and the instruments by which liberties of a country are
generally overturned"... Congress appoints James Madison to persuade
states to grant more power to U.S. to regulate foreign commerce,
rejected.

Business Events

Carey and Lea book publishing business is started in Philadelphia
(sponsors five book fairs 1802-06)... New York grants first stagecoach
franchise... Salem merchant Elias Hasket Derby sends Grand Turk to Canton
(-1786, returns $200,000 on investment of $40,000)... Oliver Evans builds
automated flour mill, uses belt, screw and bucket conveyors, on
Brandywine River, DE (gets Maryland patent in 1787 and U.S. patent in
1790, licenses over 100 by 1792).

1786

General Events

Congress adopts coinage system based on Spanish milled dollar...
Interstate commercial conference is held (September 11-14) at Annapolis,
MD... Rhode Island State Court rules (September 25) in Trevett v. Weeden

that a creditor need not have to accept paper money in payment of a debt... Congress mandates (October 16) a U.S. mint... New Ohio Company of Associates is formed by Boston investors to develop over 1.5 million acres at junction of Ohio, Muskingum Rivers (founds Marietta in 1788)... Pennsylvania makes interest-free loan to individual making steel... New Jersey grants John Fitch 14-year monopoly to build, operate steamboat on Delaware River (builds and demonstrates practical vessel in 1787, by 1790 becomes discouraged with low-pressure steam engine in lacking power to carry passengers upstream)... Oliver Evans seeks monopoly from Pennsylvania on propelling vehicles with steam on state roads (after rejection, is approved by Maryland)... Philadelphia journeyman printers strike to protest wage cuts to minimum of $6 per week.

Business Events

NYC's Chamber of Commerce forms tribunal to hear disputes on seamen's wages... Mr. Hall advertises commercially made ice cream in New York Gazette, followed by ice cream parlors, NYC, in 1790s.

1787

General Events

Fugio Cent, first U.S. coin, is minted with "Mind Your Business" as motto... Congress passes (July 13) Northwest Ordinance to create 3-5 states... Oliver Evans designs non-condensing, high-pressure steam engine, opposed by James Watt as too dangerous... James Rumsey demonstrates (December 3) steamboat for George Washington on Potomac.

Business Events

Pennsylvania Society for the Encouragement of Manufacture and the Useful Parts is founded with Benjamin Franklin as Patron and William Duer as Governor (-1790 when textile business is burned - perhaps arson by hand-loom weavers opposing powered machinery)... "First" U.S. cotton factory is built at Beverly, MA... Tench Coxe, Alexander Hamilton create The New Jersey Society for Establishing Useful Manufacturers, U.S.' first large industrial enterprise, at falls of Passaic River (fails during panic of 1792, sells real estate holdings to City of Paterson in 1940)... Boston merchants send Captain Gray in Columbia to Vancouver Island to trade cheap iron chisels for furs (continues to Hawaii and Canton for tea, loses money on damaged goods).

1788

General Events

Constitution is ratified (in pioneering formal plan provides for sharing of authority between central government and states)... Losantiville is established (August 17) on Ohio by land speculator John Cleve Symmes, NJ settlers (becomes Cincinnati in 1790)... Virginia passes general incorporation law for fire companies, KY 1798... North Carolina offers 5,000 acres to anyone starting successful iron works.

Business Events

Woolen factory is started at Hartford, CT... Fur trader Julian DuBuque operates lead mining, smelting enterprise with Indian labor in upper Mississippi Valley... Thomas Handasyd Perkins starts Boston merchant house (ships opium to China in 1807).

1789

General Events

Congress passes (July 4) first U.S. tariff legislation to protect some 30 items (taxes imports on U.S. ships 10% less than those on foreign vessels)... Congress creates (September 2) Treasury Department (names Alexander Hamilton first Secretary of Treasury)... Tennessee laws require elected officials to be paid in deer, raccoon, otter, muskrat, beaver, or mink skins... Samuel Osgood becomes Postmaster General, supervises 75 post offices, 13,468 by 1840, and some 2,000 miles of post roads... Alexander Hamilton, Secretary of Treasury: Report on the Public Credit (favors federal government's responsibility to assume debts of states fighting Revolution and use of tariff system to pay interest to landholders, advocates federal fiscal power to establish flexible monetary system)... Baltimore tradesmen petition Congress for tariff protection.

Business Events

Philadelphia and Lancaster Turnpike Company is formed (starts construction 1790, reaches Philadelphia in 1794)... Over 1/3 of 46 foreign vessels sailing into Canton are U.S. ships... Jonathan Lucas builds revolutionary South Carolina rice mill with water-powered system of cogwheels, pulleys, conveyors, mortars, and pestles, (builds first U.S. tidal-powered mill in 1792)... Samuel Slater, former apprentice to Jedediah Strutt, secretly leaves England with spinning technology for employment in NYC with New York Manufacturing Society (forms partnership in 1790 with William Almy, Moses Brown to build textile mill with Arkwright's machinery in Pawtucket, RI - others in 1800, 1812, 1815)... Reverend Elijah Craig, KY, is pioneering distiller of bourbon whiskey in state, followed by Old Grand-Dad of Basil Hayden, Sr., in 1796, Dr. James Crow in 1835, and Jack Daniels in 1857.

1790

General Events

Some 7,500 water mills operate in U.S., some 55,000 by 1840 with more in manufacturing than steam engines in 1870... Congress creates (April 4) Revenue Marine Service to police contraband trade, smuggling... President Washington signs (May 31) first copyright act (protects plays, books, maps for 14 years, allows renewal for 14 more years)... New York legislature grants loan to manufacturer for importing European labor to start earthenware factory... First U.S. census is taken, reports Philadelphia with 42,000 people, NYC with 33,100, Boston with 18,300, Charleston with 16,400 (shows 700,000 as slaves - 2 million 1820 and over 4 million 1860)... Congress requires written contracts between ship's master and seamen to specify voyage, wages... Congress passes (April 10)

U.S.' first patent law to make process easier, cheaper than in Britain, first to Samuel Hopkins for improvements in making potash (leads to 3 patents in 1790, 41 in 1800, 223 in 1810, 155 in 1820, 544 in 1830, 477 in 1840, 986 in 1850, and 4,588 in 1860, is amended 1793 to award patents without tests of originality and usefulness, remedies cost of challenging infringements in 1836 law).

Business Events

Sand, Taylor & Wood Co. is started in Brighton, MA, oldest U.S. flour company in continuous operation... Cabinet-maker Duncan Phyfe opens shop in NYC... Some 3,000 bales of cotton are produced, 333,000 in 1820, 1,438,000 in 1840, and almost 4 million by 1860... Alexander Barnov becomes manager of Russian fur post at Kodiak (-1817, becomes Alaska's first governor)... After dissolving partnership with brother in wine and shipping, Stephen Girard invests profits of $30,000 in numerous voyages (invests some $500,000 by 1810 in First Bank of the United States)... John Fitch starts regular steam-powered boat service on Delaware River... Insurance Co. of North America is formed in Philadelphia, 33 by 1800 with Massachusetts Fire and Marine in 1795 and Insurance Co. of New York in 1796.

1791

General Events

After seeing John Fitch's steamboat on Delaware River, Colonel John Stevens patents engine improvements... Over objections of Thomas Jefferson, First Bank of the United States is chartered (February 25) with branches in 8 major cities (-1811)... Construction is started to build Knoxville Road (-1795)... Pennsylvania charters company to build canal to link Schuylkill, Susquehanna Rivers... Alexander Hamilton: Report on Manufacturers (advocates tariff system for protection, agricultural bounties, federal aid for public works)... Philadelphia carpenters fail in strike to win a 10-hour day, overtime pay... Massachusetts Secretary of State grants Boston sail-cloth maker exclusive use of mark for goods.

Business Events

Although not chartered, Tontine Association of Boston sells 100,000 shares to investors... Moses Brown, others start Providence Bank, U.S.' 5th largest.

1792

General Events

Congress passes (April 2) Coinage Act (creates Philadelphia mint)... Law firm of Caldwalader, Wickerstrom & Taft is formed, 300 attorneys in 1987... New York charters Western Island Lock Navigation Company (opens canal on Mohawk River in 1796)... Construction is started in South Carolina to build Santee Canal (-1800)... Proprietors of the Locks and Canals on the Merrimack River is formed to build canal around Pawtucket Falls (-1823)... Philadelphia shoemakers form first U.S. local craft union for collective bargaining... Captain Gray in Columbia discovers

Columbia River, claims all land for U.S.

Business Events

Thomas, James Perkins start Boston merchant house with profits from trading with China, West Indies (operate 7 ships by 1793, control 50% of U.S. trade with Canton by 1830)... Subscribers of Universal Tontine Association form Insurance Company of North America to issue marine, fire insurance (receives first U.S. general insurance charter in 1794, provides model for 3 New York corporations in 1798)... New Hampshire grants all breweries a tax exemption to encourage production so as to reduce public's consumption of hard liquor... Guild of stock brokers is formed, NYC, at Merchant's Coffee House, forerunner New York Stock Exchange in 1817... Robert B. Thomas publishes The Farmer's Almanac (gains fame with prediction, printer's error, for July cold snap with blizzards in 1816).

1793

General Events

Middlesex Canal of Massachusetts is chartered to build 27-mile waterway from Boston to Merrimack River... Congress replaces U.S. Patent Board with registration system... Steampowered boat, designed by James Rumsey, is successfully tested on London's Thames River after his death... Federal lottery is used to raise funds for Union Public Hotel, Washington (opens 1810 to house Post Office and Patent Office with rooms).

Business Events

Mercantile exchange is started in Baltimore as meeting place for buyers, sellers... John Harrison of Philadelphia produces U.S.' first sulfuric acid... Jabez Ricker starts inn, stagecoach house at Maine's Poland Spring (evolves by 1840's as resort for those seeking cures of water's healing properties, starts bottling water in 1845)... Noah Webster publishes American Minerva as first NYC daily paper... Eli Whitney, backer Phineas Miller receive patent for cotton gin (lose 1797 infringement suit, regain rights after 60 cases a year before patent's expiration, legal debacle results in Patent Law of 1800)... Lehigh Coal Mine Co. is created to mine anthracite coal at Mauch Creek, PA... British-born Arthur, John Scholfield starts making wooden textile machinery, MA (although a failure leads to diffusion of technical knowledge)... After clockmaking apprenticeship Eli Terry, one of first to protect inventions with patents, starts clock business at Plymouth, CT, in this time (takes over old mill around 1800 to design water-powered machinery to mass produce wooden clock movements - 200 clocks in 1802, sells clocks with free trial, guarantee of satisfaction, and installment purchase plan, signs contract with two Waterbury merchants in 1807 to make 4,000 wooden clock movements in 3 years with interchangeable parts, sells factory to 2 employees in 1810 to retire, designs new clock in 1814 for manufacture by unskilled workers - 1822 model industry standard for 15 years).

1794

General Events

Congress bans (March 22) slave trade with foreign nations... Whiskey Rebellion breaks out in western Pennsylvania by farmers opposing federal excise tax on liquor, stills... Federal Society of Journeyman Cordwainers is organized in Philadelphia (-1806)... NYC printers form Typographical Society.

Business Events

73-room Corre's Hotel, first U.S. hostelry so named, is opened, NYC... Parson Weems, peddler and fiddler, hawks books over New Jersey roads.

1795

General Events

Connecticut Land Company buys large track of land along Lake Erie, agent Moses Cleaveland lays out City of Cleaveland in 1796 (becomes Cleveland about 1830)... Crude wooden-rail tramway is built on Boston's Beacon Hill... Congress funds trading posts in Northwest Territory (in 12 years puts posts at Detroit, Fort Wayne, Sandusky, Chicago, etc.)... North Carolina adopts general incorporation law for businesses... U.S. exports 2,000 tons of cotton to Britain, 96,000 tons 1830 and over 550,000 in 1860... Congress creates U.S. Corps of Artillerists and Engineers (commissions Louis de Tousard of France as major to instruct officers on skills of artillery and engineering - stresses interchangeability of parts, proposes school for artillerists and engineers - model for West Point)... Jacob Perkins invents nail-making machine, called "greatest technological advance at the turn of the century" (produces some 200,000 nails/day).

Business Events

New York lends funds to manufacturer making scythes, nails, tobacco products... Jonathan Carnes of Salem nets over some 700% on voyage to Sumatra... John Fitch builds practical model of locomotive (-1798)... Irish-born Robert Oliver, Baltimore agent for Belfast House, records profits of $111,898 on working capital of $11,000 (retires later to invest some $1-2 million in land, urban real estate and securities to become City's wealthiest merchant)... Jacob Beam starts making Bourbon whiskey, KY (becomes distinctive U.S. product by Congress in 1964).

1796

General Events

Mohawk Canal is built in New York to link Albany, Troy... Hamilton Manufacturing Society, chartered 1797 to make glass, is exempted from New York taxes for five years, employees excused from jury duty, highway work and militia service... Congress passes (May 18) Land Act to survey public lands in Northwest Territory (permits public auctions of lands for minimum of $2 per acre in minimum lots of 640 acres with one year to pay, results in rise of land speculators)... Boston's _Otter_ is first U.S.

vessel to visit Monterey, Spanish California... New York passes general incorporation law for public libraries.

Business Events

William Mitchell of Philadelphia writes first U.S. text on accounting... New Haven's <u>Neptune</u> sells some 80,000 sealskins in Canton for $3.50 each (returns to U.S. in 1799 with cargo of tea, silks, jades, teakwood, etc., to pay duties of $75,000)... Dutch bankers form Holland Land Company to settle Western NY, PA... English-born Thomas W. Dyott, former London apothecary's apprentice, starts livelihood in Philadelphia by cleaning, polishing shoes (with savings starts drug store to sell line of 13 family remedies by 1815, pioneers U.S. patent medicine industry)... Robert Morris, former U.S. Superintendent of Finance, and others form syndicate to speculate in real estate (is jailed later in debtor's prison for 3 years).

1797

General Events

Charles Newbold, NJ, patents cast-iron plow (although better than rivals, is rejected by farmers on suspicion it would poison land and stimulate growth of weeds)... First New York turnpike corporation is chartered, some 500 in 1797-1847... New York passes general licensing law for chartering ferry operations... First U.S. vessel visits Japan (starts almost annual trips in 1809 to represent Dutch interests)... Nathaniel Briggs, NH, patents washing machine... Amos Whittemore, New England, invents card-making machine, first c.1780 by Oliver Evans, so efficient as to make 60 men, 2,000 children in Boston factory redundant.

Business Events

Foundry owner Nicholas Roosevelt, NY politician and financier Robert R. Livingston, and steamboat designer Colonel John Stevens form informal partnership to develop workable steamboat (sign 20-year contract in 1800)... Albert Gallatin adopts first U.S. profit-sharing plan at New Geneva, PA, glassworks.

1798

General Events

After receiving marine patent in 1792, Colonel John Stevens builds first steamboat... Congress creates (April 7) Mississippi territory... Congress orders (May 28) U.S. Naval vessels to sieze any French ships interfering with U.S. commercial shipping... Congress abolishes (June 6) imprisonment of debtors.

Business Events

Eli Whitney signs cash-advance contract with Secretary of Treasury to make 10,000 muskets for delivery in 1799, 1800 (receives 2nd contract in 1800, demonstrates use of interchangeable parts in 1801 with idea possibly from French gunsmith Honore Le Blanc to Thomas Jefferson, U.S. Minister to France, and then to Secretary of War Jeffers, produces first muskets from New Haven armory in 1801, completes first contract in 1809)... Gunsmith Simeon North signs cash-advance contract with War Department to make 500 horse pistols (uses mechanical operations, precision standards, interchangeable parts at Middletown plant, CT)... After working as sail loft foreman, James Forten, black sailmaker, takes over when owner retires (runs successful business with up to 40 white and black workers).

1799

General Events

Massachusetts passes general incorporation act for operators of aqueducts... Federal marshals arrest John Fries, leader of tax payer's rebellion, PA... Russian Czar grants Russian-American Co. virtual monopoly for trade in Northern Pacific (establishes headquarters at New Archangel, called Sitka in 1804)... Massachusetts, New Hampshire ban private issue of bank notes, NY in 1804... Federal Society of Cordwainers holds 9-day strike in Philadelphia against employer's association (after lockout wins higher wages from association)... English-born engineer Benjamin H. Latrobe starts building Philadelphia Waterworks with steam engine to pump water from Schuylkill River via underground tunnel for almost a mile to City (-1801 as U.S.' first major construction project, performs critical role by training U.S. engineers).

Business Events

Aaron Burr, others form Manhattan Company to deliver pure water to NYC, completed 1842.

1800

General Events

Congress passes (April 4) first Federal bankruptcy act (applies only to merchants and traders, is repealed 1803)... Congress passes (May 10) Public Land Act of 1800 (causes rise of real estate speculation with liberal credit terms)... U.S. census cites population of 5.3 million with .3 urban and 5.0 rural (shows 1 million Blacks and Virginia as most populace state with 900,000).

Business Events

Paul Revere builds first U.S. copper rolling mill (still extant)... Tontine Association builds City Hotel, NYC (operates as major hostelry to 1830's)... Irish-born auctioneer Alexander Brown starts Brown Brothers & Co. trading house, Baltimore (starts Charleston branch in 1806, starts international clearing house for British, U.S. merchants with son's Liverpool agency in 1809, starts agencies at Savannah in 1810, Philadelphia in 1818, NYC in 1825, Boston in 1844)... Robert R. Livingston, Nicholas Roosevelt and Colonel John Stevens form 20-year partnership to build steamboats... In this time Holland Land Co. is formed to settle western New York (-1836 donates 100,000 acres for Erie Canal)... In this time John Meeker operates chain of at least 15 stores in upstate New York.

1801

General Events

Philadelphia establishes U.S.' first major municipal waterworks.

Business Events

Alexander Hamilton publishes New York <u>Post</u> (flirts with closure in 1988)... William Jackson: <u>Bookkeeping in the True Italian Form for Debtor and Creditor by Way of Double Entry or Practical Bookkeeping</u>... Eli Whitney demonstrates use of interchangeable parts in making muskets to governmental officials (uses mechanization, patterns for uniformity, detailed cost analysis, span of management, and work specialization for unskilled labor at Connecticut plant, pioneers U.S. housing for workers, records one of highest rates of labor turnover in U.S. arms industry)... York, PA, hosts annual "publick fare" market... Crane & Co. starts cotton pulp business in Dalton, MA (stressing quality supplies stationery to Tiffany & Co. and currency paper to U.S. Mint, realizes sales over $100 million in 1987).

1802

General Events

Congress abolishes (April 6) all excise duties... Colonel John Stevens invents screw propeller... Henry Morgan, master armorer, becomes superintendent of Springfield Armory, MA (-1805, organizes workers as barrelmakers and forge men, filers, stockers and assemblers, grinders and polishers)... Kentucky charters Lexington Insurance Co., first

institution west of Appalachians to issue notes as currency... Oliver
Evans, DE, and Richard Trevithick, Britain, independently patent high-
pressure steam engines... Colonel John Stevens tests screw-propelled
model steamboat, mechanical failure... Oliver Evans fails in attempt to
build Mississippi steamboat... President Jefferson appoints Swiss-born
tea merchant Albert Gallatin as Secretary of Treasury (-1809, reduces
U.S. debt from $83 million to $57 million)... New York City uses militia,
first U.S. use of armed intervention in strikes, to crush strike of
sailors demanding wages of $14/month... Peale's Museum of Natural
History, Objects and Portraits, named Philadelphia Museum later, is
opened by painter Charles Wilson Peale (pioneers form of public
entertainment in U.S.)... U.S. Military Academy is established at West
Point, NY, first national center for engineering and science (is followed
by Rensselaer Polytechnic in 1824, science courses at Harvard in 1847,
Dartmouth in 1851, Cooper Union in 1859, Yale in 1861).

Business Events

After rejection by Colonel Stevens, brother-in-law of Livingston, to
join them, Robert R. Livingston and his son-in-law Robert Fulton form
partnership to build steamboats... French-born Eleuthere Irenee du Pont,
former apprentice of Antoine Lavoisier, starts powder mill on Brandywine
River, DE (with President Jefferson's support wins government contracts
to become largest U.S. industrial enterprise by 1812, drops powder
business in 1987).

1803

General Events

U.S. buys (May 2) Louisiana Territory from France for about $15
million... New York grants John Fitch's steamboat rights to operate on
Hudson River to Robert R. Livingston, Robert Fulton... Pennsylvania court
rules in Thurston v. Koch that business losses should be distributed
among many creditors rather than ruin a few entrepreneurs... Maryland
farmer, Thomas Moore, devises double-walled box to deliver fresh butter
to market, followed by ice box in 1830's.

Business Events

New York sawmill is first U.S. operation to use steam power.

1804

General Events

Meriwether Lewis, William Clark explore to determine feasibility of water
route to West Coast (-1806)... Congress passes (March 26) Land Act of
1804, reduces price of public lands to $1.64/acre... Oliver Evans builds
steam dredge to operate on land, water... Master craftsmen form
Plasterers Co. of Philadelphia (still extant)... Colonel John Stevens
tests Little Juliana, steam-propelled boat with twin-screw propellers.

Business Events

Illinois merchant William Morrison sends pioneering trading expedition to

Santa Fe... Boston's Perkins & Co. appoints John Cushing as Canton agent (-1831, amasses fortune over $600,000 as most influencial of all foreigners trading with Chinese, particularly hong merchant Houqua)... John Marshall, Philadelphia, produces nitric, hydrocholoric acids.

1805

General Events

Benjamin Prescott becomes superintendent of Springfield Armory, MA (-1813, institutes piece-rate system)... Oliver Evans exhibits prototype for compressed ether refrigerating machine, Philadelphia... Boston and Worcester Turnpike is chartered (opens 1809)... Strike of Philadelphia's Federal Society of Journeymen Cordwainers for higher wages is suppressed (results with arrest of leaders under English Common Law for criminal conspiracy)... New York starts fund with money from land sales to lend long-term working capital to manufacturers... U.S., Tripoli end Barbary wars with treaty, allows U.S. ships to sail Mediterranean... Cattle are driven from Ohio to Baltimore, pioneers supply of beef to East Coast.

Business Events

On whim, Frederic Tudor, MA, starts shipping ice to Caribbean (expands from 130 tons in 1806 to 146,000 tons throughout world in 1856)... Spruce tree gum is first sold commercially for chewing, idea from Indians, replaced by chicle around 1872.

1806

General Events

Noah Webster: Compendius Dictionary of the English Language (gives first U.S. listing of advertisement)... Congress authorizes building of federally-financed Cumberland Road from Maryland to Wheeling, VA, on Ohio River (starts building in 1811, reaches Wheeling 1817, is extended as National Road to Columbus, OH, in 1833, ends in Vandalia, IL, around 1850)... Non-importation Act bans (April 18) certain English goods (is suspended by President Jefferson December 19 and reinstated 1808)... President Jefferson orders U.S. Mint to stop coining silver dollars (-1836).

Business Events

First U.S. operation to bottle carbonated water is started in New Haven, CT... Exchange Coffee House opens in Boston, provides hotel arrangements on upper floors... Wheaton & Dickson store in Dedham, MA, advertises goods for cash only... Samuel Slater forms new partnership to start spinning mill in upstate Rhode Island (plans new community of Slaterville, employs over 100 children, ages 4-10, at Pawtucket Mill)...Mountain man John Colter traps beavers in Yellowstone Valley... English-born William Colgate starts tallow chandlery, silk business (places first ad in 1817, merges with Palmolive-Peet in 1928).

1807

General Events

Congress prohibits (March 2) importation of slaves... Embargo Act bans (December 22) all trade with foreign countries and forbids U.S. ships to sail to foreign ports, reinforced by two acts of 1808 (results in 1808-09 depression)... Montreal-based North West Co. builds Kootenae House, first trading post on Upper Columbia River (builds second in 1810 near Spokane)... New York abolishes mercantile arbitration tribunals.

Business Events

Quaker Henry Shreve captains keelboat from Pittsburgh to New Orleans in 40 days... Silas Whitney builds horse-powered railroad in Boston... New Orleans lists over 1,800 boats or rafts arriving downstream, only 11 departing... Boston merchant Thomas Perkins starts Monkton Iron Co. (expands by vertical integration, provides workers with housing, company store)... Robert Fulton, Robert R. Livingston demonstrate steam-powered _Clermont_, "Fulton's Folly" (use Boulton & Watt engine to power paddlewheel, by 1810 receive returns of $50,000/year on investment of $60,000)... Pelican Life Insurance of England opens agency in Philadelphia... Manuel Lisa, St. Louis, sends party of fur trappers to Rockies (builds fort at mouth of Bighorn River in 1808)... John Wiley starts printing business in NYC, publishing firm in 1980s... To keep up with U.S. literature and periodicals, merchants start Boston Athenaeum as reading room... Oliver Evans starts Mars Iron Works, PA (builds 50 steam engines by 1819).

1808

General Events

Napoleon orders seizure of any U.S. vessels entering ports of France, Italy, Hanseatic League (-1810)... Albert Gallatin, Secretary of Treasury: _Report on Roads, Canals, Harbors, and Rivers_ (describes U.S.' transportation needs, recommends "a great turnpike road" and canals at a total cost of $20 million from surplus tariff revenues)... Simeon North, Connecticut gun-maker, recommends use of interchangeable parts to make pistols in letter to Secretary of Navy.

Business Events

First regular bank in Northwest Territory opens at Marietta, OH... Manuel Lisa forms Missouri Fur Co... Anthracite coal is first tested as fuel at Wilkes-Barre, PA... John Jacob Astor creates American Fur Co. (-1834, evolves with virtual monopoly on western furs by 1817).

1809

General Events

Enforcement Act halts (January 9) smuggling used to avoid Embargo Acts... Non-Intercourse Act repeals (March 1) Embargo Acts to open overseas commerce, except to France and England, to U.S. shipping... President Madison reinstitutes (April 19) trade with England (reinstates ban

March 1)... On request of George Washington, Major Lewis de Tousard: <u>American</u> <u>Artillerist's</u> <u>Companion</u> (promotes French ideas on standardization, uniformity)... Robert Fulton with associates Robert R. Livingston, De Witt Clinton and others send Nicholas Roosevelt to survey Ohio, Mississippi rivers (form Ohio Steamboat Co. in 1810, launch first river steamboat in Pittsburgh in 1811 after securing exclusive rights from Louisiana Territory for 14 years)... Massachusetts passes first general incorporation act for business enterprise, New York in 1811... Robert Fulton receives first steamboat patent, 2nd in 1811... Printers, NY, establish price list, sent to other typographical groups... United Society of Believers in Christ's Second Appearing, the Shakers, starts colony at Pleasant Hill, KY (pioneers scientific farming in State, invents flat broom, and opens market in Midwest, South).

Business Events

Thomas Leiper builds horse-powered railroad in Delaware County, PA... 1792 Boston Crown Glass Co., first successful U.S. works making window glass, incorporates... Pennsylvania Company for Insurance on Lives and Granting Annuities issues first U.S. whole life insurance... Colonel Stevens operates steamboat <u>Phoenix</u> between Manhattan and Brunswick, NJ (moves vessel to Delaware River in world's first ocean voyage by steamboat to avoid seizure by New York on urging of Fulton, Livingston).

1810

General Events

U.S. Supreme Court (March 16): <u>Fletcher</u> <u>v.</u> <u>Peck</u> (nullifies Georgia law rescinding 1795 sale of Western Georgia lands in Yazoo land fraud)... Macon Bill reopens (May 1) trade with Britain, France... Maryland authorizes lotteries to raise funds for Potowmack Company, chartered 1784-85, to improve river transportation to West... New York charters 10 banks... Striking members of NYC's Journeyman Cordwainers are convicted as illegal conspiracy by using strike to demand higher wages, conspiracy doctrine overturned by Massachusetts' Supreme Court in 1842... U.S. census records population of 7.2 million, 0.5 urban and 6.7 rural with some one million slaves (cites New Orleans with 24,000, Cincinnati 2,540)... New York City grants Colonel Stevens right to operate ferry service to Hoboken, NJ, for 24 years (despite opposition of Fulton and Livingston, starts world's first steam ferry operation in 1811, uses first steam-powered, double-ended ferries in 1823 to develop Hoboken as pleasure resort)... Census shows 390 watermills: 29 fulling mills, 11 paper mills, 1 gunpowder mill, 12 clover mills, 148 gristmills, and 189 sawmills, 66,000 in 1840 with 23,700 gristmills, 31,650 sawmills, 2,600 fulling mills, and 8,200 tanneries... Census shows leather goods, iron and steel, flour milling and food products as leading industries (lists 88 banks with capital of $23 million - 1,562 in 1860 with nearly $500 million).

Business Events

Lukens Steel is started, PA (-1847, is inherited in 1825 by widow Rebecca Lukens to develop business internationally by marketing quality products)... In survey Tench Coxe, Albert Gallatin find every other New Hampshire farm house operating looms to weave cloth for Boston merchants... Cornelius Vanderbilt starts regular ferry service between Staten Island, Manhattan (-1818)... William Sturgis forms partnership in Boston to trade with China, Pacific Coast (handles over 50% of U.S. trade by 1840, invests profits in railroads, other ventures)... John Jacob Astor founds Pacific Fur Co. (-1813, locates headquarters at Fort Astoria on Columbia River).

1811

General Events

New York passes limited incorporation act for manufacturers (incorporates 362 firms by 1848, is followed by Connecticut in 1817 and all states by 1860) and law to regulate bankruptcies... Thomas Cooper produces first U.S. potassium at Joseph Priestley's laboratory, PA... Congress fails (February 20) to renew charter of First Bank of the United States, attacked as being unconstitutional, having majority ownership by British citizens and stifling formation of state banks... Elkanah Watson holds pioneering Pittsfield Fair, MA, to introduce new agriculture techniques (spawns county, state fairs).

Business Events

Robert Fulton, associates launch steam-powered New Orleans, first paddlewheeler on Ohio and Mississippi rivers, at Pittsburgh, 20 by 1818, 60 by 1820, 200 by 1830, 450 by 1842 and 1,200 by 1848 (takes 4 months to reach New Orleans)... John Jacob Astor, Montreal merchants form South West Fur Co... Samuel Slater forms new partnership to start spinning mill at Oxford, MA... Oliver Evans sends son to Pittsburgh to build high-pressure steam engines for boats on western rivers.

1812

General Events

Fort Ross is built (February 2) north of San Francisco by Russian-American Fur Co. as agricultural colony, base for hunting sea otters (-1841 when acquired by John Augustus Sutter)... Louisiana is 18th state... President Madison proclaims (June 19) U.S. at war with Great Britain (-1814)... Congress raises tariffs on imports and issues $5 million in bonds to raise funds for war effort... Charles D. Wadsworth becomes U.S. Army's first Chief of Ordinance (receives authority in 1815 to operate federal armories, institutes French system of uniform manufacturing)... Colonel Stephens: Documents Tending to Prove the Superior Advantages of Rail-Ways and Steam Carriages over Canal Navigation... North Carolina grants 20-year monopoly for steamboating to Colonel Stephens, opposed by Robert Fulton and Oliver Evans.

Business Events

Fur trader Robert Stuart leads expedition from Astoria to St. Louis for John Jacob Astor (discovers Oregon Trail)... National City Bank of New York is created to replace City's branch of defunct First Bank of the United States... Seth Thomas starts clock factory, CT (forms Seth Thomas Clock Co. in 1853 which merges in 1931 with Western Clock of La Salle, IL, to form General Time Corp.)... Trading expedition of Robert McKnight

reaches Santa Fe, goods confiscated and imprisoned to 1821... New York
Manufacturing Co. is chartered with banking powers to make iron and brass
wire... Stephen Girard acquires First Bank of the United States, becomes
Girard Bank.

1813

General Events

Steamboat lines carry mail.

Business Events

First governmental contract to require interchangeable parts is granted
to Simeon North by U.S. Navy to make 20,000 pistols... Boston
Manufacturing Co. is chartered by Francis Cabot Lowell, Boston associates
with Patrick Tracy Jackson as President and Paul Moody as Master Mechanic
(builds first U.S. plant with all textile operations under one roof in
1814)... New York charters Commission Co. to lend money to manufacturers
for marketing products... John Jacob Astor's Pacific Fur Co. sells
trading post of Fort Astoria to Montreal's North West Co., renamed Fort
George... Nathaniel Stephens starts woolen mill in North Andover, MA
(evolves to include 10 New England woolen mills in becoming parent
company of today's J.P. Stevens & Co. of South Carolina, U.S.' 2nd
largest with 1982 sales of some $2 billion, is acquired 1988 in hostile
takeover by West Point-Pepperell for $1.2 billion).

1814

General Events

Cleveland is incorporated in Ohio as village, city in 1836... Pittsburgh
Cordwainers resolve not to accept members of other societies until proof
is given of previous membership... Congress repeals (April 14) Embargo,
Non-Importation Acts (establishes duties for 2 years to protect new U.S.
manufacturing industries)... Pennsylvania charters 14 banks.

Business Events

Henry Shreve, barge captain between Pittsburgh-New Orleans in 1811,
pilots steamboat _Enterprise_ to challenge monopoly of Fulton, Livingston
on Ohio, Mississippi rivers... Massachusetts Bank employs president, vice
president and 9 employees from cashier to clerks.

1815

General Events

Van Ness Mansion, Washington, installs pioneering indoor bathroom...
Territorial act of Indiana permits individuals to issue bank notes so
long as the banker's name is on the note... W.T. James, New York, patents
cook stove... 36-hour coach trip from Boston to New York City is
advertised... President Madison vetoes (January 20) proposed Second
National Bank as being undercapitalized, lacking power... Congress
authorizes (March 3) policy of trade reciprocity with all nations...

"National Panorama and American Museum of Wax Figures" tours Northwest Territory... Congress creates Ordinance Department "to draw up a system of regulations... for the uniformity of manufactures of small arms."

Business Events

Troth & Co., wholesale jobber of drugs and other goods, is started, Philadelphia (serves some 300 customers by 1840's)... Amos, Abbot Lawrence start Boston cotton trading business with $50,000 (start Lawrence Corp. in 1830 with $1.35 million to finance textile mills and export fabrics, start Essex Co. in 1845 to build textile mill and community of Lawrence on Merrimack River)... Eli Whitney, Seth Thomas assemble some 500 wooden clocks with replaceable parts... Schuylkill Navigation Company is created to build canal to transport anthracite coal to Philadelphia (-1825)... The New York General Shipping and Commercial List is pioneering business publication, first specialized business paper in 1827... Colonel Stephens obtains first U.S. railroad charter for line from Trenton to New Brunswick, NJ (fails for lack of funds)... Samuel Drake's theatrical company tours western communities, first called barnstorming... Colonel Roswell Lee becomes superintendent of Springfield Armory, MA (-1833, transforms craftwork to industrial system in using standard guages for parts, increases specialization of tasks from 36 to 100 by 1825, uses lathes and special purpose machines of Thomas Blanchard in 1826 to eliminate most hand labor in making gun stocks, establishes formal lines of authority, bookkeeping controls and inspections for quality control).

1816

General Events

Connecticut gunmaker Simeon North builds earliest known milling machine... In response to widespread unemployment caused by dumping of English goods on market, Congress passes first protective tariff... Congress authorizes (March 14) Second Bank of the United States (-1836, opens 1817 with Stephen Girard as primary underwriter)... Gaslight Company of Baltimore is formed, U.S.' first city utility for streetlighting... Indiana is 19th state... John Jacob Astor persuades Congress to limit role of foreigners in U.S. fur trade (assumes control of Canadian fur operations in U.S. with passage of Act).

Business Events

Fort Howard is built at Green Bay, WI (becomes center for area's fur trade)... Philadelphia Savings Fund Society is formed as first U.S. savings association, followed by Boston Provident Institution for Savings in 1816 to pay interest on savings and Oxford-Provident Building Association in 1831 to finance home building... Hotel is built on Washington's Pennsylvania Avenue (becomes site for elegant Willard Hotel, City's finest, in 1850)... New York City's American Society is U.S.' "first" protective tariff association... Employers successfully prosecute striking Journeymen Cordwainers of Philadelphia as being common-law conspiracy in restraint of trade... Ex-keelboater Henry Shreve launches steamboat Washington, first practical paddlewheeler with shallow draft for western rivers, in Wheeling (wins suit against Fulton, Livingston after boat's seizure in New Orleans for violating monopoly).

1817

General Events

New York authorizes (March 15) building of Erie Canal (opens 1825)...
Seth Hunt patents automatic pin-making machine... New York sets $25 as
minimum debt for imprisonment... Connecticut passes limited liability law
for corporations, Massachusetts in 1820... Construction of 130-mile
Cumberland Road to Ohio River at Wheeling is finished, used by such stage
lines as June Bug, Pioneer, National, Good Intent, Oyster and Shake-
Gut... Congress mandates resumption of payments and hard currency...
Mississippi is 20th state... Richard Roberts devises first effective
planning machine, first published description by Joseph Clement in early
1830s.

Business Events

Four Harper brothers start NYC printing business, publishing firm in
1980s... John H. Hall, ME, completes contract to make 100 rifles,
experiment in mass volume, for U.S. Army (obtains 1819 contract to make
1,000 breechloaders with interchangeable parts at Harpers Ferry Armory
by 1821 - completed 1824)... New York Stock and Exchange Board is
created... S. & M. Allen & Co. holds lottery to finance Union Canal,
PA... Jethro Wood, NYC, makes cast iron plows with replaceable parts...
Oliver Evans' Mars Works builds steam-powered pump, U.S.' first, for
Philadelphia Municipal Water System... Competing salt producers of
Kanawha Valley, OH, form Kanawha Salt Co. to set quotas, prices...
Quakers Jeremiah Thompson, Thomas T. Cope start Black Ball Line as
scheduled packet service between NYC, Liverpool (-1877).

1818

General Events

Congress grants (March 18) veterans of Revolutionary War lifetime
pensions... Congress postpones reductions in textile duties and increases
levies on iron imports... Walk-in-the-Water is first steamboat on Great
Lakes (-1829)... Eli Whitney devises milling machine, first universal
milling machine in 1862 by J. Brown of Providence, RI... David Beatty
finds oil drilling for water, KY (abandons well)... New York
Typographical Society forms (omits articles in charter on wages, working
conditions)... Thomas Blanchard devises machine at Harpers Ferry Armory
to turn musket barrels (develops lathe in 1819 to turn gun stocks,
receives contract in 1822 by Springfield Armory to make gun stocks with
battery of machines, uses 14 by 1826 to mechanize production)... Illinois
is 21st state.

Business Events

Steamboat operators on upper Ohio River join to regulate rates,
schedules... First steamboat trip from New Orleans to Louisville takes 35
days, 90 days usual for flat boats (drops to 10 days by 1824, 5 by
1850)... Stage line operates between Louisville, KY, and Vincennes, IN,
first Michigan stage line in 1827... James A. Bennet starts bookkeeping
school in NYC (publishes bookkeeping book in 1820)... Siam is visited by
first U.S. merchant vessel, 3 in 1819 and 4 in 1821... Brooks Brothers

clothing business for men is started, NYC, as a "gentlemen's store run by gentlemen" (by 1859 advertises large assortment of ready-made clothes, develops reputation with such customers as Abraham Lincoln and J.P. Morgan, opens first store for ready-made apparel in 1894 - 35 more in 28 cities by 1980 and 21 in Japan, introduces English button-down collars in 1900 on classic shirts, is acquired from Federated Dept. Stores in 1988 by Britain's Marks & Spencer for $750 million)... Massachusetts Hospital Life Insurance Co. is chartered (is reorganized as investment trust in 1823 - format used to organize Standard Oil Trust in 1882)... Quaker Josiah White leases land in Leigh Valley to mine anthracite coal (substitutes coal for coke in 1838 to produce iron in hot-blast furnace, achieves success in 1840)... Southern planter Thomas Gibbons starts steamboat service between NYC and Elizabeth, NJ (employs Cornelius Vanderbilt as ferry captain to fight monopoly of Fulton and Livingston, wins battle in 1824 with case of <u>Gibbons v. Ogden</u>)... Nicholas Longworth starts vineyard near Cincinnati, one in Indiana by Swiss settlers in early 1800s... First U.S. professional horse racing meet is held, regular meets by 1830s.

<h2 style="text-align:center">1819</h2>

General Events

Triggered by revival of Europe's agriculture, financial panic, first major economic disaster, arises from curtailment of credit and 1817 congressional mandate for resumption of payments in hard currency (-1822, results in collapse of many state banks and foreclosures on western real estate by Second Bank of the United States)... U.S. Supreme Court (February 2): <u>Trustees of Dartmouth College v. Woodward</u> (rules private corporate charter a contract that cannot be revised or broken by state)... U.S. Supreme Court (March 6): <u>McCulloch v. Maryland</u> (rules states may not tax U.S. agencies)... Steam-powered <u>Savannah</u> travels to Liverpool (uses sails after 80 hours when coal supply exhausted)... Harpers Ferry Armory contracts with gunsmith John H. Hall to make rifles (-1824, develops process to make patented breechloading rifle with interchangeable parts)... Apprentices Library opens, Philadelphia, as reading room for mechanics... Alabama is 22nd state... Chillicothe, OH, holds fair, first state fair in area by Michigan in 1849... First U.S. lodge of Independent Order of Odd-Fellows, genesis in England in 1700s as secret society of mechanics, forms in Baltimore... Jordon Mott, NYC, invents stove to burn anthracite coal (leads to mining of coal, PA, to supply demand for home heating - 210,000 tons in 1830 to 1,164,000 in 1837 with delivery by network of canals, railroads).

Business Events

Thomas Lloyd publishes first U.S. shorthand system... First Missouri River steamboat is launched... New York cannery of Ezra Daggett, Thomas Kensett preserves oysters, lobsters, salmon... Bank for Savings opens, NYC... Aetna of Hartford, CT, does business as reinsurance agency... Boston's Suffolk Bank becomes central bank for New England (-1860s)... John Stuart Skinner publishes first U.S. journal on sports.

1820

General Events

Maine is 23rd State... Public Land Act reduces (April 24) price and size of land purchase (abolishes credit in purchasing western land)... Tenure of Office Act limits (May 15) political appointments to 4-year terms... Fort is built near head of navigation on Mississippi River at St. Anthony Falls (evolves as Minneapolis by 1856)... Blanchard Lathe for turning axe-handles, shoe lasts is patented... U.S. Census records population of 9.6 million with 0.7 urban and 8.9 rural (counts over 7,000 in Pittsburgh, 9,000 in Cincinnati, and 1,400 in Detroit, identifies some 6.5 million farms - 5.6 million in 1950 and 2.4 million in 1980, for first time tries to count labor force)... Robert Eastman, ME, invents first U.S. circular saw... Missouri taxes bachelors, 21-50, $1/year.

Business Events

Josiah White, Erskine Hazard ship anthracite coal to Philadelphia to compete with bituminous coal from fields of James River, Nova Scotia, Britain... Daniel Lambert opens (-1829) Boston Museum with curiosities to entertain paying customers... Philadelphia hotel installs bathroom.

1821

General Events

Missouri merchant Moses Austin, after losing bank, lead mine and real estate in Panic of 1819, obtains permission from New Spain to settle 300 American families in Texas, colonizes 1825... Missouri is 24th state... Czar Alexander I of Russia claims all of American Pacific Coast north of 51st parallel (closes waters to commercial shipping of other nations)... John Jacob Astor persuades Congress to abolish U.S.' trading posts... War Department: The General Regulations for the Army of the United States (provides officers with guidelines for administration and organization in 1st U.S. management manual)... Kentucky abolishes imprisonment for debt, OH in 1828, VT and NJ in 1830, NY in 1832, CT in 1837, LA in 1840 and MO, AL in 1848... First strike of women factory workers occurs at Boston Mfg. Co. to protest cut in wages.

Business Events

Some 20% of imports to U.S. are sold by auction (-1830, peaks in 1827 when $24 million of U.S. total of $79.4 million is auctioned)... Reverend Dr. Nott, combustion expert, is asked by Lehigh Valley Coal Mine Co. to design efficient stove to burn anthracite coal... First U.S. gas well is drilled at a "burning spring" near Fredonia, NY... Trader Captain William Becknell takes (September 1) wagon-train of goods from Independence, MO, over 780-mile Santa Fe Trail to New Mexico... With insufficient power at Waltham, MA, Patrick Tracy Jackson, Boston Associates (evolves as informal group of partners by 1850s to control 20% of State's cotton spindles, 30% of railroads, 40% of insurance, 40% of Boston's banking) start new textile operation, named Merrimack Manufacturing in 1822, at fork of Merrimack, Concord rivers (builds Lowell as planned industrial community, starts operations in 1823, starts Appleton Manufacturing in 1828)... Richard Borden starts Fall River Iron Works, MA (starts steamship line in 1827, builds American Print Works in 1834, runs City's first steam-powered textile mill in 1843, starts railroad in 1846).

1822

General Events

Boston streets are lit by gas lamps... Congress passes (April 29) Cumberland Road Tolls Bill to finance repairs of Cumberland Road, vetoed by President Monroe as Federal Government lacks jurisdiction... Some 4,000 miles of turnpike are used in New York, over half abandoned by 1836... First U.S. Mechanical and Scientific Institute opens in NYC... Fur traders are forbidden by law to take liquor in Indian territory.

Business Events

William Underwood starts pioneering U.S. food business in Boston to preserve fruit, pickles, seafoods and condiments in glass or ceramic jars (prepares famed deviled ham in 1868)... Public market is started in Lower Manhattan by butchers, fishmongers, produce dealers (becomes Fulton Fish Market as world's largest wholesale mart for fish, is controlled by mobsters from early 1920's-1980's is sued 1987 by U.S. in Federal takeover)... Merchant Thomas Handasyd Perkins builds 54-room hotel in Boston... Scottish-born fur trader Kenneth Mackenzie starts Columbia Fur Co. in St. Louis, acquired by John Jacob Astor in 1827 after competitive battle... Fur trader William H. Ashley advertises in St. Louis to recruit young men for Missouri fur trade (evolves as Rocky Mountain Fur Company)... Red Star, Blue Swallowtail packet lines are started to compete with Black Ball line on transatlantic service to Britain, times of eastbound trips average 24 days, fastest in 17 days, and westbound ships average 38 days, fastest in 24 days)... John Jacob Astor reorganizes American Fur Co. with Western, Northern departments... Thomas P. Cope, Philadelphia merchant, starts monthly packet service to Liverpool.

1823

General Events

Philadelphian Nicholas Biddle becomes head of Second Bank of the United States (-1836, develops bank with sound financial policies)... Champlain Canal is opened to link Hudson River and Lake Champlain for commercial traffic... St. Paul, MN, is visited by first Mississippi steamboat... Hay rake is invented (allows man, boy and horse to do work of six men, one-two oxen)... Pennsylvania charters Pennsylvania Railroad of Colonel John Stevens, father of Pennsylvania system, to operate between Philadelphia, Susquehana River (fails for lack of funds)... Hagerstrum-Boonsboro Road, MD, is macadamized.

Business Events

Samuel Slater purchases 3 cotton mills (introduces first U.S. power loom, erects first U.S. steam mill at Providence in 1827)... Boston's Russell & Co. sends John Green to Canton as super cargo (builds merchant house as market leader in China trade with opium, tea, textiles before retiring in 1829)... Irish-born Alexander Stewart opens small shop, NYC, to sell

Irish lace (moves to larger quarters to open dry goods store in 1826, opens Marble Palace in 1848)... Merrimack Mfg. starts textile production at Lowell, MA (uses production system of departmentation and specialization, hires farm girls of good character to earn money for dowries, and provides pleasant working conditions, supervised housing, hospital, school, Improvement Circles for personal development, savings bank, library and lecture series, requires employees to support Episcopal Church with wage deductions)... Bijou Theater opens, NYC (becomes music hall in late 1800s).

1824

General Events

U.S. Supreme Court (March 2): <u>Gibbons v. Ogden</u> (rules monopoly granted by New York for steamboat navigation between NYC and New Jersey is unconstitutional as Federal Government regulates interstate commerce)... Congress passes (May 22) Tariff Act (raises rates on wool, cotton and iron imports and sets duties on linen, silk, glass and lead to protect home industries)... Pioneering Rensselaer School of Theoretical and Practical Science is founded, NY, for study of science, engineering... Fort Vancouver is built on Columbia River by Hudson's Bay Co. to replace Astoria as western headquarters... Work is started in New Jersey to build Morris County Canal to link NYC with Delaware River (-1832)... Franklin Institute is opened, Philadelphia, by business leaders and University of Pennsylvania professors to promote scientific study of mechanical arts, others in Baltimore in 1826 and Boston 1827 (stages annual exhibition to encourage, publicize inventions, continues to present)... Pennsylvania Society for the Promotion of Internal Improvements is created (sends civil engineer William Strickland to England with secret instructions to study building of canals, railroads)... Women textile workers strike at Pawtucket, RI... Work is started in building Chesapeake and Delaware Canal (-1829)... General Survey Bill authorizes surveys for national roads, canals... English High School, U.S.' first public school, opens in Boston, instruction may have covered bookkeeping and accounting.

Business Events

James Gordon Bennett starts Permanent Commercial School, NYC (-1835, provides instruction in elocution, history and geography, penmanship, arithmetic, algebra, astronomy, moral philosophy, commercial law, political economy, English, French, German)... Some 10 lottery dealers in NYC operate as underwriting syndicates, about 150 by 1833 to underwrite at first colleges and church... Missouri wagon train reaches Santa Fe (sells goods of some $35,000 for about $190,000)... Joseph Chapman plants first commercial grapevines, CA, near Los Angeles, followed by planting of first French cuttings by Bordeaux immigrant Jean-Louis Bignes in 1831.

1825

General Events

Delaware and Hudson Co. is capitalized with $1 million to build canal for shipping coal (opens 1828)... Maryland charters (January 31) Chesapeake and Ohio Canal Co. (finishes building 1829)... Congress authorizes survey of Santa Fe Trail to New Mexico... Congress authorizes extending

Cumberland Road from Wheeling through Ohio as National Road... Dr. Joseph Buchanan successfully tests steam-road carriage in Louisville, KY (abandons project to do other things)... Work is started to build Miami Canal from Cincinnati to Toledo (-1845, is followed by Ohio Canal in 1825-32 to link Ohio River and Cleveland, Louisville and Portland Canal in 1826-31, Wabash and Erie Canal, longest at 452 miles to Evansville, in 1832-56 - a failure, Illinois and Michigan Canal in 1836-48)...

First phase of canal connecting Lehigh Valley, Schuylkill River is completed to Philadelphia (delivers some 9,500 tons of anthracite coal first year - 210,000 tons in 1830)... Work is finished in building 363-mile Erie Canal to link NYC with Great Lakes (recovers cost of some $8.5 million in less than 10 years)... Colonel John Stevens tests model locomotive, U.S.' first, at Hoboken, NJ... United Tailoresses of New York is formed as first U.S. labor organization for women only... Ezra Daggett, nephew Thomas Kensett patent process to store food in tin cans... Boston house carpenters win 10-hour day after striking employer-contractors... Rapp religious community of Harmonie in Indiana, founded 1814, is purchased by Robert Owen, Scottish industrialist and social reformer, to establish utopian community of New Harmony (-1827, establishes first U.S. kindergarten, trade school, and free public school system, fails due to lack of competent farmers and businessmen, loses most of fortune)... Codorus is U.S.' first iron ship - Britain's first 1829.

Business Events

Hamilton Mfg. starts plant at Lowell, MA, to join Jackson's Merrimack Mfg., area evolves as world's largest textile center with some 12,000 looms... Barnam's City Hotel is built in Baltimore (-1826, is followed by Manhattan's Astor House in 1832-36 with over 200 rooms, St. Charles with 309 rooms and 17 bathrooms in New Orleans in 1837, 600-room Continental Hotel in Philadelphia in 1858-60)... Modern Sebastiani Vineyards is started in Sonoma Valley, CA... Edmund Dwight starts Boston and Springfield Manufactory (operates in 1841 with 4 mills, some 3,000 workers)... First annual rendezvous of fur traders and Indians, organized by William H. Ashley, is held on Green River in Rockies, last meeting in 1840... Merrimack Mfg. starts independent machine shop, master mechanic Paul Moody in charge, at Waltham, MA (launches local machine tool industry)... Some 30 Louisville boat operators form combination to set rates for barrel goods.

1826

General Events

U.S., Denmark sign treaty of amity, commerce and navigation... Mountain man Jedediah Strong Smith leads first overland expedition from Great Salt Lake to California... Boston merchant Thomas Handasyd Perkins builds first U.S. railroad, Granite Railway Co., as 3-mile track for horse-drawn wagons to carry granite from Quincy quarry to Neponset River... New York charters Mohawk and Hudson Railroad... Work is started to build 359-mile Pennsylvania Main Line Canal between Philadelphia, Pittsburgh (-1834, links with Ohio canals in 1836-40)... Day's New York Bank Note List and Counterfeit Detector is published... British-born T.P. Jones becomes editor of Journal of the Franklin Institute (-1848, prints practical information on mechanical arts, manufacturing, general science, inventions)... Colonel John Stevens builds steam locomotive, U.S.' first to pull train, for Philadelphia and Columbia Railroad, 1828-34.

Business Events

First U.S. calico printing is produced at New Hampshire, MA... Samuel Lord, George Washington Taylor open dry goods store in NYC (still extant)... Former associates of William H. Ashley start Rocky Mountain Fur Co. (joins Astor's American Fur Co. in 1834).

1827

General Events

Maryland charters Baltimore and Ohio Railroad to local merchants to compete with canals for inland business (starts construction in 1828, completes first section for horse-drawn train in 1829, tests Peter Cooper's Tom Thumb locomotive in 1829, operates steam train in 1830, replaces horses with steam engines by 1831, reaches Wheeling on Ohio River in 1853 and St. Louis in 1858)... Ohio passes safety law to protect passengers on stagecoaches... Pennsylvania Assembly considers bill to prohibit minors from working in textile mills... When strike of journeymen carpenters fails to win 10-hour day, unions of painters, carpenters, bricklayers, glaziers, cordwainers, and hatters in Philadelphia form Mechanics' Union of Trade Associations as first U.S. City-wide labor organization (results in formation of Working Men's Party in 1828-32)... Philadelphia building trades win 10-hour day after strike.

Business Events

Dr. John McLoughlin, factor at Hudson's Bay Co.'s Fort Vancouver, starts first commercial sawmill on Columbia River (-1846, employs indentured Hawaiians, ships cargo of lumber to Hawaiian Islands in 1828 and China in 1833)... Carl Fisher starts music publishing business (still extant)... After competitive battle John Jacob Astor's American Fur Co. absorbs Columbia Fur Co... 9-mile Mauch Chunk gravity railroad is built, PA, to haul coal from Carbondale to Lehigh River...

General merchants' exchange is started, NYC, used as model by other cities... Matthew Baldwin builds stationary steam engine at iron works (builds first locomotive of Baldwin Locomotive Works in 1831)... Consolidated Association of the Planters of Louisiana is formed as first bank for planters... Foster's Commercial School, first successful business school, opens in Boston (provides studies in penmanship, arithmetic, bookkeeping, and countinghouse procedures, moves to NYC in 1837 as Foster's Commercial Academy)... South Carolina Canal and Railroad is built from Charleston to Hamburg (-1833)... Samuel Slater builds U.S.' first large steam-powered mills operated in MA... The New York Journal of Commerce is published (still extant)... First Hudson Valley vineyard, U.S.' oldest wine district, is estalished, followed by area's Brotherhood Winery, oldest continuously operated vineyard, in 1839... Gadsby's National Hotel opens in Washington, City's first first-class hotel.

1828

General Events

Pennsylvania provides funding, first such recorded case, for proposed railroad between Philadelphia and Columbia... "Tariff of Abominations" is signed (May 19) into law by President Adams... Reciprocity Act nullifies (May 28) all discriminatory import duties on trade with reciprocating nations... Delaware and Hudson Canal opens for commerce, used to ship Pennsylvania anthracite coal to New York, New England... Working Mens' Party forms in Philadelphia to work for social reforms: universal education, abolition of the militia, cheaper law system, lien laws for workers, no laws on religion (-1832)... The Mechanics Free Press of Philadelphia is first U.S. labor paper... New York passes limited liability law for all corporate stockholders... Factory workers in Paterson, NJ, strike to protest changing of dinner hour and to demand 10-hour day (results in first U.S. use of militia to quell strikers who win dinner hour issue).

Business Events

Peter Cooper, after operating retail grocery store and factory making glue and isinglass - U.S. monopoly, starts Baltimore iron works (builds Tom Thumb locomotive to save Baltimore & Ohio Railroad from bankruptcy)... Gunsmith Eliphalet Remington starts plant on Erie Canal (purchases Springfield factory in 1844 for his first U.S. arms contract, starts making agricultural implements in 1856)... Tremont Hotel, U.S.' first modern hotel, opens in Boston with water closets and bathrooms (is followed by NYC's St. Nicholas Hotel and The Hoffman House, later by Grand Union and United States hotels in Saratoga Springs, St. Charles in New Orleans, Willard in Washington, DC, Palace in San Francisco, and Palmer House in Chicago)... 1785 Patowmack Co. declares bankruptcy after failing to build water route along Potomac River to Appalachians, acquired by Chesapeake and Ohio Canal Co... Samuel, David Collins mass produce axes at Connecticut plant (as one of largest U.S. firms, employ some 300 workers in 1830's)... New American Institute holds U.S. trade fair, NYC, to encourage industrial development... Abbot-Downing partnership forms in New Hampshire to make quality Concord coaches (-1847, 1865-1900's)... Delaware & Hudson Canal Co. of Pennsylvania sends engineer Horacio Allen to England to buy locomotives for proposed railroad (tests Stourbridge Lion successfully in 1828, is used as stationary power engine as too heavy for flimsy railroad tracks)... Illiterate farmer James White, LA, starts ranch, TX (handles some 3,000 cattle by 1831, 30,000 longhorn on 40,000 acres by 1842).

1829

General Events

American Society for Encouraging Settlement of Oregon Territory forms in Boston... Rev. Sylvester Graham, temperance lecturer seeking to save souls through the stomach, devises Graham Cracker... U.S.' first gold rush occurs in northeast Georgia... William Burt, Detroit, patents Family Letter Press, impractical typewriter as 6 others by 1857... John Henry builds pioneering electro-magnetic motor... New York sets up Safety Fund System to protect depositors, investors of participating banks... New

York Working Mens' political party forms to fight for 10-hour day... The Mechanics Free Press reports use of child labor (cites 1/3 to 1/2 of New England factory workers as children under 16 and use of boys in Philadelphia to work from dawn to 8 p.m.)... Chicago issues first tavern license, sells night's lodging for 12.5 cents and 3 meals for 25 cents... Jacob Bigelow: Elements of Technology (coins word "technology")... Franklin Institute begins study, first U.S. scientific research of technology, of water wheels... New Jersey legislature charters Delaware and Raritan Canal, Camden and Amboy Railroad with right to buy either after 30 years
(-1830).

Business Events

Memphis and Charleston Railroad starts construction (-1857)... Thomas Ward of Boston is commissioned by London banking house of Baring Brothers to gather credit information on U.S. businessmen (develops credit rating system)... Cornelius Vanderbilt starts steamboat business on Hudson River with $30,000 (operates new, improved boats to earn average profits of some $30,000/year for 1830-35 - line worth $500,000 by 1836, acquires Daniel Drew's competing line when Drew slashes rates and proclaims Vanderbilt robs passengers with excessive charges, is acquired in 1839 by Hudson River Association to eliminate his competition)... First U.S. cooperative stores are seen in Philadelphia, NYC... The American Turf Register, first U.S. sports magazine, is published in Baltimore... Red Rover, U.S.' first opium ship, is launched... Case Co. starts making steam-powered tractors (is followed by France's steam locotractor in 1856 and Hussey's steam plow in 1885).

1830s

General Events

Penitentiary inmates are leased to private contractors (are restricted in use by state laws in 1840s).

Business Events

Chemist Luther Dana, Merrimack Manufacturing Co., tests organic chemicals for dyeing... Daily sugar auctions are held in New Orleans... Chemistry professor at Medical College of Ohio removes impurities from copper, saves Cincinnati bell foundry from ruin... Dr. J. Gorrie devises air cooling system, FL, to purify bedrooms of patients with malaria, yellow fever (gives public demonstration in 1850)... James Neilson develops "hot blast" process to use anthracite coal in iron furnaces... Dr. Mile's Compound Extract of Tomato is sold as popular patent medicine (becomes catsup with commercial production by H.J. Heinz in 1876)... Daniel Craig uses carrier pigeons to carry news from incoming vessels to participating newspapers, U.S.' first recorded commercial news service... Brass rolling appears, allows for first time cheap, good-quality clocks to compete with those of wood.

1830

General Events

Isaiah Jennings patents Camphrene, U.S.' first synthetic oil lamp illuminant (results in use of distillation techniques for coal, petroleum)... U.S. Supreme Court (March 12): <u>Craig v. Missouri</u> (rules circulation of state loan certificates as bills of credit are unconstitutional)... Congress lowers (May 20-29) duties on tea, coffee, salt, molasses... Town of Chicago is located at site of Fort Dearborn... Jedediah Strong Smith, William Sublette of Rocky Mountain Fur Co. guide first wagon train of settlers to Rockies... Project is started, IL, to link Lake Michigan with Mississippi, work in 1836-48... New Jersey re-charters Camden-Amboy Railroad to sons of Colonel John Stevens (grows as one of U.S.' largest corporations by 1834 in carrying 105,000 passengers, 8,400 tons of freight with receipts of nearly $500,000 and expenditures of $257,000, pays locomotive engineers $40/mo. and firemen $32/mo. for 6-day week - yearly bonus of 2 or 3 months' pay)... 178-mile Miami Canal between Lake Erie and Wabash River is finished... U.S. records 530 inventions, 77 yearly average for 1790-1811, 6,460 for 1841-50, and 25,250 for 1851-60...

Robert Stephens designs T-rail for railroads... U.S. Census records population of 12.9 million with 1.1 urban and 11.8 rural... During long voyage to Singapore, Samuel Colt whittles wooden model for repeating revolver (obtains patent in 1832)... Jurisdiction of mercantile arbitration tribunals, abolished by NY in 1807, are limited to preliminary hearings... Pre-emption Act gives squatters option to buy 160 acres after making improvements... Society for preventing theft forms in Detroit... Ohio grants first railroad charter... Massachusetts passes limited liability legislation for manufacturing firms... Only 26,000 people, some 0.5% of labor force, are union members, around 5,000, 0.1% , in 1860... Samuel F.B. Morse visits Italy, amazed by inefficiency of standard European axe in balance, heft of American axe for felling trees.

Business Events

Louis A. Godey publishes <u>Godey's Ladies Book</u>, U.S.' first successful women's magazine (provides color plates of fashions, articles on morality and taste)... Boston merchant and former sea captain John Mackay and Jonas Chickering, piano-maker since 1819, form partnership to make pianos (produce 177 pianos in 1831 with 20 employees - 350 per year in mid-1830's for dealers in 9 cities from Providence to New Orleans, employ work force of some 200, working in 20 separate departments in veneer factory, to produce with uniformity 1,000 quality pianos of industry's 9,000 in 1850)... South Carolina Railroad starts first U.S. scheduled railroad service between Charleston and Hamburg, operates world's longest line of 136 miles in 1833... Work is started in building Boston and Worcester Railroad (-1835)... Construction of Lexington and Ohio Railroad is started (-1832)... Boston & Lowell Railroad is chartered, financed in 1835 by informal group of Boston investors... B&O Railroad issues first railway timetable.

1831

General Events

Instead of trying to improve father's reaper, Cyrus McCormick builds new practical reaper, VA (spurred by 1833 demonstration of Obed Hussey's reaper at Cincinnati fair, patents machine in 1834)... New Copyright Act provides protection for 28 years, renewal for 14... New York abolishes (April 26) prison terms for debtors... Protective tariff convention is held in New York... William Manning, NJ, receives first patent for mowing machine... Truck Act prohibits payment of wages in goods instead of money... Thaddeus Fairbanks, in foundry business since 1823, invents platform scale... New England Association of Farmers, Mechanics, and Other Working Men forms, RI, as labor organization, political party (-1834)... New York Typographical Association forms to maintain just, uniform scale of prices... Mechanics at 3 NYC boat yards win 10-hour day.

Business Events

First horse-drawn buses in NYC are seen, built by Irish-born John Stephenson (builds horse-cars for City's street railway in 1832 - bankruptcy in 1837 Panic)... Yellowstone, operated by American Fur Co., is first steamboat to travel upper Missouri River... First U.S. bank robbery occurs with theft of $245,000 from NYC's City Bank... Oxford Provident Building Association, early savings and loan association, is created in Philadelphia, followed by 5 others by 1840... First river showboat, Floating Theatre, is built at Pittsburg by British-born actor William Chapman... The Spirit of the Times, pioneering sporting sheet, is issued in NYC... John Cox Stevens, brother open Elysian Fields in Hoboken as large amusement park... South Carolina Railroad is first to carry mail... Boston Society for the Diffusion of Knowledge launches paperback line of books (fails)... Edward Collins takes over New Orleans shipping line (starts packet line between NYC, Britain in 1836 to acquire fortune)... John Cushing, agent for Perkins & Co. in Canton, returns to Boston (recommends textile exports to Boston Associates who acquire control over 56% of U.S. cotton trade with China by 1859)... Daniel Whitney's sawmill is first to operate in Wisconsin... Boston & Providence Railroad is chartered... Joseph Henry shows 1st industrial use of electromagnet at iron works, NY... Philadelphia and Columbia Railroad uses horse-drawn vehicles to compete with Erie Canal, locomotives and cars in 1834.

1832

General Events

Wagon Train, guided by Nathaniel Wyeth, former manager of Frederic Tudor's ice business and inventor of ice-harvesting machine, leaves Missouri for Columbia River to open up Oregon Trail, settlers to develop businesses in salmon, furs, timber and tobacco... Tariff Act requires (July 14) high duties for textiles and iron... Thomas Larkin opens first store in Monterey, CA... Horse-drawn streetcar carries first passengers in NYC... Lewis McLane, Secretary of Treasury, issues report on U.S. industry (lists 106 manufacturers with assets of $100,000 or more - 88 in textiles and 12 in iron, lists 36 firms with 250 or more workers - 31 in textiles and 12 in iron, lists only 15 with assets of $50,000 or more with steam-power)... President Jackson vetoes bill to recharter Second Bank of the United States... Franklin Institute is hired by Secretary of Treasury to find reasons for boiler explosions on steam engines (results in 1838, 1852 laws)... Michigan grants first railroad charter... On returning from Europe Samuel Morse, professor of painting at New York University, sees device of Charles T. Jackson for conducting electricity over long distances (develops working model for electric telegraph in 1835, devises code in 1838, shows invention to Congress in 1843).

Business Events

Baltimore merchant launches <u>Ann McKim</u> (starts evolution of clipper ship with narrower hull, sharper bow)... New York and Harlem Railroad is built (-1852)... John Matthews, NYC, starts business to make carbonating equipment, to sell charged water to retail stores... British-born Dr. W. Gerrard starts making first U.S. crucible steel in Cincinnati... Most tailors carry large stock of ready-made clothing.

1833

General Events

U.S. signs (March 20) commercial treaty with Siam... Roger Taney, U.S. Secretary of Treasury, transfers (September 26) funds from Second Bank of the United States to Philadelphia's Girard Bank (transfers funds to 23 other state banks)... Obed Hussey patents first successful horse-drawn grain reaper (moves plant to Baltimore)... Lutheran Minister Dr. Fedrick Geissenhainer patents process to burn anthracite coal with blasts of hot air... U.S. whaling fleet is composed of 392 ships and some 10,000 seamen, almost doubled by 1843... Thaddeus Lowe makes steel-blade plowshare...

Chicago carpenter Augustine Taylor builds St. Mary's Church, first use of balloon frame (changes nature of home-building)... John T. Howe patents pinmaking machine (operates Connecticut plant 1838-76)... Journeymen shoemakers in Geneva, NY, strike successfully for wage increase... General Trades Union is formed, NYC, by journeymen of trade unions to seek higher wages and better working conditions, 12 federations in major cities by 1838 (leads to National Trades Union of all crafts in 1834)... Philadelphia Typographical Association forms to seek just, uniform prices... Samuel Preston invents machine to peg shoes... Soda fountain is patented.

Business Events

After failed attempt in Philadelphia in 1830, <u>New York Sun</u> is first successful penny newspaper... Brentano's bookstore opens, NYC (files for bankruptcy in 1982)... 486-mile Erie Railroad is chartered to link Hudson River, Lake Erie (-1851)... Western Railroad is chartered to link Worcester, MA, with Albany, NY, as first transectional road (-1841)...

Bent's Fort is built on Arkansas River in Southwestern Colorado (-1849, develops trading monopoly with Cheyennes, Plains Indians, mountain men, explorers, and military, operates stage depot in 1861 for service between Kansas City, Santa Fe)... Some 200 lottery offices operate in

Philadelphia, used to raise money for new businesses...   Shipowner John Randall starts Sailors Snug Harbor, Staten Island, for elderly sailors...

Holt's Hotel, NYC, uses steam-powered lift for baggage, Fifth Avenue Hotel with first practical passenger elevator in 1852... William Dodge, father-in-law Anson Phelps form Phelps, Dodge & Co. to develop Lake Superior copper, Pennsylvania ore (starts mining Arizona copper in 1880's - by 1910 one of largest U.S. copper producers)... Charles, Elias Cooper start Mt. Vernon Iron Works, OH, to make plows, maple syrup kettles, wagon boxes, etc. (expands to make internal combustion engines by 1900 and pipeline compression engines in 1920's, start diversification in 1929 to develop Cooper Industries with diesel locomotives and marine engines in 1930, builds first industrial jet-powered gas turbine in 1960)...

Erastus Corning, Albany merchant, incorporates Utica and Schenectady Railroad (-1836, evolves by 1843 as one of interconnecting roads between Albany and Buffalo, consolidates 1853 with other lines as New York Central)... Three Boston merchants start trading house in Honolulu (start first sugar plantation in 1835 with 1,000-acre lease to partner William Hooper from King Kamehameha III)... After discovering use of sawdust as insulation material, Frederick Tudor, MA, ships ice to East Indies, Calcutta (exports 12,000 tons in 1836, 65,000 in 1846, and 146,000 in 1856 with 363 cargoes to 53 destinations throughout world)... Grand rendezvous of some 300 trappers, 600-700 Indians meets on upper Green River... Thomas W. Dyott: Exposition of the System of Moral and Mental Labor Established at the Glass Factory of Dyottsville (describes use of homeless boys as workers with new methods, technology at 5 glassworks near Philadelphia).

1834

General Events

Henry Blair, inventor of corn planter, is "first" black to obtain U.S. patent... Walter Hunt devises sewing machine with vibrating arm to hold a curved needle... Workers on Chesapeake and Ohio Canal riot during strike for closed shop (requires for first time use of Federal troops to quell violence)... Some 1,200 women workers at Merrimack Mfg. mills strike to protest cuts in wages and raises in boarding charges (fail, fail again in 1836)... Boston craft union forms to achieve labor, political goals (-1835).

Business Events

Jacob Perkins, MA, devises first ice-making machine (uses 1823 compression principle of Michael Faraday)... John March opens shop, NYC (provides customers with pioneering soda fountain)... Board of Trade forms in Philadelphia... John Jacob Astor sells fur business (concentrates on interests in Manhattan real estate, banking)... Bowery Savings Bank is chartered, NYC, to handle savings of individuals rather than corporate funds (evolves by 1890 as City's largest bank in assets, declines in 1920's with competition from commercial banks, is forced to reorganize in 1985)... Regular steamboat service is started between Chicago, Buffalo... Boston Stock and Exchange Board is officially organized... R. Montgomery Bartlett starts private business school in Philadelphia (starts Cincinnati commercial college 1838-1909)... Jerome

Case starts business making threshing machines...

Nathan P., James T. Ames start pioneering machine tool shop, followed by Robbins & Lawrence, Brown & Sharpe, and Pratt & Whitney... F. & W.M. Faber Co. is formed in Pittsburgh to use steam power to produce $60,000 worth of steam engines and other machinery by 1860 with 35 workers as City becomes industrial center for steam power... Nathaniel Currier opens printing business, joined by James Ives, artist and businessman, in 1852 (-1880, uses kind of production line to produce thousands of prints by lithography, appears in U.S. in 1820, for mass market).

1835

General Events

National Trades Union forms as federation of city centrals unions (goes from some 26,000 members to over 100,000)... Congress authorizes (March 3) U.S. mints in New Orleans, Charlotte, NC, and Daholohega, GA... Franklin Institute offers award for first successful anthracite smelting process (declares British-born Benjamin Perry winner in 1839)... Philadelphia grants City employees 10-hour day, Federal workers with 10-hour work day in 1840... 10-hour day is won by Union of Trade Organizations, society of 15 labor groups, after strikes in Boston, Philadelphia, Baltimore... New York courts uphold "conspiracy doctrine" in Geneva Cordwainers' case (makes collective action to raise wages illegal)... U.S. finishes paying off national debt... Alexis de Tocqueville: _Democracy_ _in_ _America_ (notes Americans, addicted to practical science, wanted to make money by "every new method that leads by a shorter road to wealth, every machine that spares labor, every instrument that diminishes the cost of production").

Business Events

Samuel Colt obtains French and English patents, U.S. in 1836, for revolving pistol (starts Patent Arms Manufacturing Co. in Paterson, NJ, loses U.S. Army contract in 1837 as pistols are complicated, sells revolvers to Sam Houston around 1839 for use by Texas Navy and Rangers, closes plant in 1842 with lack of business)... Construction is started to build Louisville, Cincinnati and Charleston Railroad (-1839)... New York Stock Exchange lists three railroads, 10 in 1840 and 38 in 1850... James Gordon Bennett publishes _New_ _York_ _Herald_ (-1867, innovates with editorials, special sections, scandal, European correspondents)...

Zachariah Allen incorporates Manufacturers Mutual to underwrite fire insurance for cotton mills... Boston, New York capitalists form American Land Co. (invest $400,000 in Mississippi cotton land, $250,000 in Arkansas land, $350,000 in rural lands and town sites in 6 western states)... Old Crow Distillery is started, KY, State's first in 1793 by Evan Williams... John Cox Stevens promotes "Great Race" spectacle, offering $1,000 to anyone running 10 miles in less than one hour (is watched by some 20,000 bettors, fans)... P.T. Barnum promotes exhibition of George Washington's "nurse" over "160 years of age"... Textile industrialist Samuel Slater, interests in 10 mills, two machine shops, and wholesale and commission firm, dies (1768-)... Hawaii's first successful sugar mill is operated on Kauai.

1836

General Events

Thomas Haliburton: The Clockmaker; or The Sayings and Doings of Samuel Slick of Slicksville (satirizes Yankee peddler)... Closed Second Bank of the United States is rechartered (March 1) as Bank of the United States of Pennsylvania... Congress forms (April 30) Wisconsin Territory... Arkansas is 25th State... Deposit Act places surplus revenues in one or more banks in each state to curb inflation and land speculation (divides $28 million government surplus among 26 states)... President Jackson issues (July 11) Specie Circular to mandate only gold and silver be used to buy government lands to halt wild use of credit in buying western land, $2.6 million in 1832 to $24.9 million in 1836 (triggers Panic of 1837)... Sam Houston is (October 22) first President of Republic of Texas... Swedish-born inventor John Ericcson patents pioneering screw propeller... Philadelphia Navy Yards adopts 10-hour day... Massachusetts passes first state law to regulate child labor (restricts employment of those under 15 in manufacturing work unless provided 3 months of school per year)... Hiram Moore, J. Hascal patent grain combine... National Cooperative Association of Journeymen Cordwainers is formed as first national craft union...

Thomas P. Hunt: The Book of Wealth: In Which It Is Proved From the Bible That It Is the Duty of Every Man to Become Rich... Work in building Monongahela Canal, PA, and Morris Canal, NJ, to link Hudson, Delaware Rivers is finished... Henry Taylor: The Statesman (discusses business of government)... 58 different trade unions are listed in Philadelphia, 51 in NYC, 24 in Baltimore and 14 in Cincinnati... Alonzo Phillips patents phosphorus match.

Business Events

Work is started to build Erie and Kalamazoo Railroad, Richmond and Petersburg Railroad... Maine lumberman Charles Merrill buys Michigan timberland, pioneers westward movement of forest operations... First steamboats are seen on Columbia River... Nashville printer publishes Davey Crockett's Almanack, forerunner of dime novels first issued in 1860... Cyrus H. McCormick, father and others start iron business, VA (start making reapers in 1843, after bankruptcy in Panic of 1837 start new plant in Chicago in 1847)... John Deere, VT, starts blacksmith forge in Grand Detour, IL (makes first steel and wrought-iron plow in 1837 - 25/week by 1842 before moving factory to Moline on Mississippi River to produce 1,000 plows for prairie farming in 1846 - 10,000/year in 1850's, forms Deere & Co. in 1868 with son, son-in-law)... Merchant George Peabody starts business in Boston to specialize in foreign exchange (moves to London in 1837 to compete with Barings, Rothschilds)...

After experimenting by trial and error with India rubber fabrics since 1834 to make waterproof shoes, Nathan Hayward purchases Eagle Rubber to manufacture products (sells factory to Charles Goodyear and starts successful Hayward Rubber in 1847)... Former operator of New Orleans shipping line, Edward Collins starts "Dramatic Line," names ships after famous actors, to provide service to Britain (after becoming millionaire with success starts United States Mail Steamship Co., "Collins Line," in 1847 with government financing to build 4 ships larger, faster, and more

elegant than competitors - failure 1857-58)... Connecticut factories
produce over 80,000 wooden clocks, a record.

1837

General Events

Michigan is 26th state... U.S. Supreme Court: <u>Briscoe</u> <u>v.</u> <u>Bank</u> <u>of</u>
<u>Commonwealth</u> <u>of</u> <u>Kentucky</u> (rules state banks may issue bills of credit)...
U.S. Supreme Court: <u>Charles</u> <u>River</u> <u>v.</u> <u>Warren</u> <u>Bridge</u> (rules against bridge
monopoly over transportation route)... Connecticut is first state to pass
(June 10) general incorporation law... Artist and inventor Samuel Morris
demonstrates electric telegraph at College of the City of New York...

Michigan is first state to pass free-bank law, New York in 1838... First
U.S. plank road is built in Syracuse, NY... Hiram, John Pitts, ME, invent
U.S.' first successful threshing, winnowing machine... Dr. B.W. McCready:
<u>On</u> <u>the</u> <u>Influence</u> <u>of</u> <u>Trades,</u> <u>Professions</u> <u>and</u> <u>Occupations</u> <u>in</u> <u>the</u> <u>United</u>
<u>States</u> <u>in</u> <u>the</u> <u>Production</u> <u>of</u> <u>Diseases</u> (is first U.S. publication on
occupational health hazards)... Pennsylvania Senate forms committee to
study child labor (passes first law in 1847 to prohibit minors working in
textile mills)... After bankruptcy in hardware business, Charles Goodyear
patents process to make rubber articles (discovers vulcanizing process
for rubber by accident in 1839 - patent in 1844, sells license for
discovery to pay debts)... Unemployed workers, NYC, demonstrate against
high rents and high prices of food and fuel.

Business Events

Herman Briggs & Co., major New Orleans cotton house, fails as price of
cotton drops nearly 50%... New York banks stop payments in specie,
followed by banks in Baltimore, Philadelphia, Boston - 618 during year
(starts Panic of 1837)... Work is started to build Michigan Central
Railroad, reaches Chicago in 1852, and Michigan Southern Railroad,
reaches Chicago in 1852... Charles Tiffany, friend start business in NYC
selling stationery, fancy goods (start importing quality jewelry,
including Esterhazy diamonds and French crown jewels, and novelties from
Europe in 1841, rename business Tiffany & Co. in 1853, open London branch
and Switzerland watch factory in 1860's, win first prize for silverware
by 1867 Paris Exposition)... First U.S. process to make sugar from beets
is started at Northhampton, MA...

Some 38,000 wooden clocks are made in Bristol, CT (results in use of more
credit, style changes with intense competition)... A.A. Lowell, started
as Canton clerk in 1833, becomes partner of New York's Russell & Co.,
largest U.S. business in China trade (starts own trading house in
1840)... Austrian-born Francis Drexel, after working as portrait artist
in Philadelphia and making money from currency transactions while
painting portraits in South America, opens brokerage house in Louisville,
KY (moves to Philadelphia in 1838 to pioneer City's investment banking
business)... August Belmont is U.S. agent for London's N.M. Rothschild &
Sons... A day coach is rebuilt as crude sleeping car, world's first, for
railroad between Harrisburg and Chambersburg, PA... After operating
Boston shop, Charles F. Hathaway starts shirt-making business in
Waterville, ME... William Procter, James Gamble start soap and candle
business in Cincinnati (use first trademark in 1851 which evolves as

moon-and-stars by 1870's)... Lehigh Crane is formed to develop "hot-blast" method in using anthracite coal to make iron, successful in 1840, (is used by 28 Pennsylvania furnaces by 1845 - over 60 by 1853)...

Chauncy Jerome, pupil of Eli Terry, starts clock business in Bristol, CT (mass-produces brass clocks)... Lewis Tappan, former credit manager for silk jobber, starts Mercantile Agency, NYC (reorganizes as R.G. Dun & Co. in 1859)... Artist George Catlin opens Indian Gallery business, NYC, to exhibit Indian paintings, some 600 of 48 tribes after 7 years of travel, to paying public... After food business was destroyed by New York's Great Fire of 1835, Swiss-born Delmonico brothers, one started wine shop in 1825 and other operated catering business, open new restaurant to feature European cuisine, show hamburger steak on menu (-1922 with end of family, continues to closing in 1977, is revived in 1983)... Silas Richard sails from Canton to NYC in 91 days... British-born James B. Francis becomes chief engineer for The Proprietor of Locks and Canals of Lowell, corporate developer of city (uses science in developing innovative, practical hydraulic turbine with mathematician-engineer U.A. Boyden).

1838

General Events

Congress designates (July 7) use of railroads for postal service... Congress establishes federal inspection system for steamboats on inland waters, 2nd safety law in 1852... New York passes banking law (permits qualified individuals to issue money)... Treasury Secretary Woodbury reports on U.S.' use of stationary steam engines (cites over 1,600 in use with over 930 in 10 northeastern states and over 600 in 19 states for processing crops - 274 used by Louisiana sugar mills, shows steamboat engines generating about 60% of U.S.' total steam power)... T. Davenport, VT, develops practical electric motor... Master armorer Thomas Warriner reorganizes Springfield Armory, MA, to operate manufacturing system with interchangeable parts... Major S. Ringgold transforms U.S. Army's light artillery unit into mobile force with carriages, horses (develops standardized loading, firing procedures for precision firing)... Transatlantic steam service starts when Britain's Sirius docks, NYC, after 17-day trip... U.S. reports 337 locomotives in use, only 82 foreign-built... 133 steam engines are used in Pittsburgh, almost 50% in glass industry with others in sawmills, machine shops and iron rolling mills.

Business Events

New York banks make payments in specie... Steamship Great Western starts service between NYC and Bristol, England... Boston-born merchant George Peabody starts Peabody, Riggs & Co. in London (becomes J.S. Morgan & Co. with retirement in 1864 and Morgan Grenfell in 1910)... Tredegar Iron Works is started in Richmond, VA (operates locomotive plant in 1850, trains slaves as skilled labor, serves Confederacy as major armory during Civil War)... Lehigh Coal & Navigation Co. completes canal for transporting anthracite coal to East... Work is started in building Raritan Canal, NJ.

1839

General Events

D.S. Rockwell invents horse-drawn corn planter, seeds 2 rows at one time... American Statistical Association is formed... U.S. Supreme Court: Bank of Augusta v. Earle (rules corporation can do business in other states)... Steam shovel is invented, used for strip-mining in 1881.

Business Events

Pennsylvania banks suspend specie payments, resume 1842... William F. Harnden uses railroads to pioneer package delivery service between NYC, Boston (extends service to Philadelphia in 1840, to Britain with Cunard line in 1841 to operate offices in Liverpool, London, Paris, Scotland, Germany, Ireland)... Commuter passenger railroad is started in Boston... Dodd, Mead publishing business is started (still extant)... Freeman Hunt publishes Merchant's Magazine and Commercial Review... First successful smelting of iron with anthracite coal is performed at Mauch Chunk, PA... Puff's Business College, H.J. Heinz a graduate, opens in Pittsburgh (still extant)... Lake House opens as Chicago's first hotel of note... Samuel Cunard uses Boston as U.S. port of entry for British steamship line (shifts to NYC in 1868)... William Underwood uses tin cans to preserve food products... Slater textile business uses elementary cost accounting.

1840s

General Events

Some 300 miles of canals, 6,000 miles of railroad are built by 1850... Shawnee Trail opens for cattle drives from Texas to Kansas City, Sedalia, St. Louis... Skilled workers, artisans, tradesmen and some white-collar workers form Native American Clubs.

1840

General Events

President Van Buren mandates 10-hour work day for federal employees in public work jobs... President Van Buren signs (July 4) Independent Treasury Act (allows Government to handle own funds, provides for depositories to hold Government funds)... U.S. Gross National Product is estimated 40-60% more than France and near that of Britain... Blacksmith Thomas Davenport builds world's first press powered by small electric motor... U.S. Census records population of 17.1 million with 1.8 urban and 15.3 rural, Britain with 18.5 (registers immigration of 599,000 from 1831)... John Griffiths builds test tank, NYC, to evaluate hull-resistance studies of Englishman Mark Bautry (proposes ship design with sharp bow, narrow beam - scorned by other designers, captains)... Isaac Winslow, ME, invents process for canning corn... Regular apprenticeships for shoemakers ends, MA.

Business Events

Last rendezvous of fur trappers, Indians is held... Welsh-born Davis

David Thomas successfully burns anthracite coal with hot air for Lehigh
Crane Co... Henry Disston starts company, Philadelphia, to make saws,
first U.S. saw manufacturer to standardize products and use   trade
name... Lowell Offering is published by women workers in Lowell textile
mills... J.L. Hooper starts business to represent advertisers...
Antoines, U.S.' oldest restaurant with single-family ownership, opens,
New Orleans, as French-Creole boarding hotel... Alvin Adams, Ephraim
Farnsworth start Adams & Co. as express service between NYC, Boston for
merchants (extends service later to Philadelphia, Baltimore, Washington,
Pittsburgh, Cincinnati, Louisville, and St. Louis, enters California
market in 1849 only to lose competitive battle with Wells Fargo by
1855).

1841

General Events

Independent Treasury Act is repealed (August 13)... Uniform Bankruptcy
Law permits voluntary declarations (-1843, is used by 33,737
individuals)... George Ripley, Brook Farm Association start Brook Farm
Institute of Agriculture and Education near Boston as cooperative
community... U.S.' first Fourierist community, economic unit of some
1,620 people sharing communal dwellings and dividing work by ability, is
started, OH... Congress authorizes U.S. Navy to operate first training
ship, supplements training on fleet vessels... New York licenses 302
peddlers, including 22 by foot, 71 by horse, 1 by canal boat and 3 by
two-horse team (licenses 10,669 in 1850 and 16,594 in 1860)... U.S.S.
Princeton is first propeller-driven man-of-war... President Tyler vetos
revival of Second Bank of the United States.

Business Events

Horace Greeley publishes New York Tribune (-1872)... To augment sales of
laundry soap, Colgate makes quality soap after discovering secret
saponification process of English and French soap makers (evolves as
largest U.S. operation until Procter & Gamble's Ivory Soap in 1879)...
Two passenger trains of Western Railroad operating between Albany,
Worcester collide, kills two persons (results in new organizational
structure with 3 adjoining operating divisions under assistant master of
transportation to coordinate train movements)... Volney B. Palmer starts
pioneering advertising business in Philadelphia to broker newspaper space
to advertisers as side-line for real estate, coal enterprise (forms
American Newspaper Advertising Agency in 1850)... Dr. James Cook buys
drugstore (promotes "Ayer's Cherry Pectoral" as patent medicine with
extensive advertising, introduces sugar-coated pills in 1854,
sarsaparilla extract in 1855 and ague cure in 1857, sells "Ayer's Hair
Vigor" in 1869, prints first formulas on labels before 1906 Pure Food and
Drug Act)...

Thomas Jones: Principles of Accounting, first U.S. text on accounting
theory... Comptroller of Erie Canal, previously political position,
becomes regular administrative office in The Canal Department... Eben
Jordan, Benjamin Marsh open retail business, Boston (becomes City's
largest, oldest department store to pioneer enlightened personnel
relations)... Ann T. Lohman, NYC entrepreneur in quack medicine, is
arrested for performing abortions (starts branches during mid-1840's in

Boston and Philadelphia, uses traveling salesmen to peddle various compounds and abortion pills, spends some $60,000/year on advertising)... After serving as ship's captain out of New Orleans, William Leidesdorff, black merchant, moves to San Francisco (builds City's first hotel, opens importing-exporting business, ship chandlery, lumberyard and shipyard, obtains Mexican citizenship in 1844 to acquire 350,000-acre land grant, serves as U.S. Vice Counsel to Mexico in 1845, provisions U.S. Army during Mexican War, serves as San Francisco's first City Treasurer before death in 1848, leaves estate of some $1.5 million as U.S.' first black millionaire).

1842

General Events

Springfield Armory mass-produces first regular issue muskets with interchangeable parts (ends assembly of flint-locks)... Congress passes (March 30) Protective Tariff Act... Massachusetts' Chief Justice Lemuel Shaw rules in Commonwealth v. Hunt that a union is a lawful organization, that a union is not responsible for illegal acts of its members, and that a closed shop strike is legal (negates conspiracy doctrinal)... Work on canal from Toledo to Cincinnati is finished... First adhesive postage stamps are used by NYC private mail service... John Howe, CT, invents automated pin-making machine... Massachusetts, Connecticut are first States to limit children in factories under age of 12 to 10-hour work day... George Washington Eastman starts Rochester Mercantile College, NY... Louisiana passes banking law to set standards for insuring deposits, maintaining reserves... J. Fowler, Baltimore, patents balanced self-rising flour, perhaps first baking mix... Henry L. Ellsworth, Patent Commissioner: "The advancement of the arts, from year to year, taxes our credulity and seems to presage the arrival of that period when human improvement must end."

Business Events

Joseph Dart builds first U.S. grain elevator in Buffalo, NY (bases design on principles used by Oliver Evans in 1785 automated flour mill)... Adam Gimbel, Bavarian-born pack peddler, starts trading post at Vincennes, IN (starts branch stores at Dannville, IL, and Washington, IN, in 1882, opens Milwaukee store as Gimbel Brothers in 1887, buys Philadelphia store in 1894, opens Manhattan store in 1910 - by 1930 world's largest department store business)... Civil Engineer Edward Anthony opens photo shop, NYC (evolves through mergers, acquisitions to become Ansco Photo Products in 1929 as part of German holding company - General Aniline & Film in 1939 before U.S. seizure in World War II to become G.A.F. Corp.)... Stephen F. Whitman starts candy business in Philadelphia (introduces Whitman's Sampler in 1912)... Mutual Life of New York is first mutual insurance company, New England Mutual first chartered...

Franklin is advertised as first variety theatre in NYC... P.T. Barnum opens American Museum, NYC, to exhibit curiosities, oddities, and hoaxes... F. & M. Schaefer Brewing Co. is started, NYC (is acquired by Detroit's Stroh Brewery in 1980)... Cheney & Co. Express business is started to serve Boston, Montreal (merges with American Express in 1879)... Jerome I. Case starts selling threshers in Racine, WI (invents combined thresher and separator in 1844, forms J.I. Case Co., largest west of Buffalo, in 1863).

<h2>1843</h2>

General Events

North American Phalanx is formed in Red Bank, NJ, as Fourierist community with agrarian-handicraft economy (-1854)... U.S. obtains trading privileges as most-favored nation from China... Congress contracts with Samuel Morris to build telegraph line between Baltimore, Washington... Board game, The Mansion of Happiness, is devised by clergyman's daughter as courtship game (provides moves through vices, virtues to obtain happiness)... Samuel Morris devises first workable teleprinter.

Business Events

Smith and Dimon shipbuilding firm builds "first" clipper Rainbow, designed by John Griffiths (-1844, earns profits on one voyage twice cost of construction)... Henry Wells, partner start express line between Buffalo, Albany (start new line to Detroit in 1844)... After operating small machine shop since 1834, Benjamin Babbitt starts business, NYC, to make yeast, baking powder, and soap powder (advertises "Babbit's Best Soap" with free samples)... Boston capitalist John Murray Forbes, partner in Russell & Co. mercantile house since 1834, starts investing in railroads (joins with Boston investors in 1845 to rescue Michigan Central and extend line to Chicago in 1852, finances development of Burlington system in 1850's)... Stanley Bolt Manufactory is started in New England (evolves to make tools)... Fur trapper, scout Jim Bridger and trader Louis Vasque build Fort Bridger on Oregon Trail, joins some 150 trading posts in West (trades 1 ordinary horse for 8 buffalo robes or 1 gun and 100 loads of ammunition, racing horse might equal 10 guns, 3 lbs. of tobacco, 15 eagle feathers or 5 tepee poles)...

Pierre Lorillard, maker of snuff and tobacco, dies, first use of French term millionnaire in obit... Watchmaker Aaron L. Dennison starts family stationery firm when unable to get boxes for watches, joined by brother Eliphalet in 1849 - sole owner of stationery business in 1855 (as "father of American watchmaking" for use of machinery, interchangeable parts in mass assembly starts American Watch, becomes Waltham Watch after bankruptcy, in 1859).

<h2>1844</h2>

General Events

First U.S.-China Treaty is signed (opens 5 ports for trading)... W.F. Ketchum patents mower... Walker Tariff sets duties for categories of goods instead of individual commodities... Houqua clipper is launched with flat bottom, sharp bow and narrow beam (sails to Canton in 95 days, returns in 90)... Oriental trader, New York merchant Asa Whitney petitions Congress for railroad land grant from Michigan to Columbia River to prevent Oregon forming separate nation and monopolizing Asia trade... Russian-American Fur Co. abandons all settlements in Northern California... William Gregg complains to Charleston, SC, on ordinance banning use of steam power.

Business Events

Best Brewing is started, Milwaukee (becomes Pabst in 1889)... Rowland Hussey Macy opens thread and needle store in Boston (opens fancy dry goods store in Manhattan in 1858)... Former cattle drover Daniel Drew starts Wall Street office (invests in Erie Railroad in 1853 - director in 1857)... William P. Clyde starts steamship line to serve Atlantic ports... Savage Iron Work, MD, makes iron rails, all previous rails from Britain.

1845

General Events

Florida is 27th state, Texas 28th... Postal Act reduces postage rates to 5 cents/one-half ounce for 300 miles (grants subsidies to steamship lines carrying mail)... Potato famine develops in Ireland (starts Irish immigration to U.S. - some 1.5 million by 1850)... Lawrence is founded on Merrimack River, MA, as manufacturing center for woolens... Dr. Henry Day patents pressure-sensitive adhesive... Louisiana Constitution forbids private corporate charters in requiring incorporation with general laws, copied by Iowa in 1846... National Reform Association meets, NYC, as industrial congress to lobby for 10-hour day... Sarah Bagley of Lowell starts Female Labor Reform Association... New York Knickerbockers is first organized baseball club... Miners form Green Club Claim, WI, to protect property rights from claim jumpers (pioneers trend of associations or unions by 1866: 500 in CA, 200 in NY, and 100 in AZ, ID and OR).

Business Events

Boston's Eastern Exchange Hotel is first U.S. steam-heated building... New England Protection Union is created as central purchasing agency by retail stores... Erastus Bigelow builds power loom for weaving carpets... Abram Hewitt, son-in-law of Peter Cooper, starts South Trenton Iron Co. (incorporates later with new funds as Trenton Iron Works, one of first in industry to start verticle integration)... Baltimore & Ohio railroad adopts new organizational structure: general superintendent of operations supervising departments of transportation, construction, machine maintenance, treasury... Luxurious Ocean House opens in Newport, RI, for wealthy vacationers... After intensive lobbying campaign, William Gregg incorporates, legal form not in general use in South until after Civil War, cotton mill, SC... Henry Wells, former employee Willam Fargo form partnership to start new express service from NYC to Cincinnati, Chicago (after helping to form American Express in 1850 start Wells, Fargo & Co. in 1852 to deliver lightweight valuables throughout California - within 15 years every major rival in State either absorbed, bankrupted, or retired, acquire Butterfield Overland in 1866)... New York's Tiffany Store issues "A Catalogue of Useful and Fancy Articles"...

Swiss-born John Brunswick starts business to make billiard tables... Samuel Kier, former canal boat operator, and father drill well for salt near Pennsylvania Canal (discover petroleum, sell "Kier's Rock Oil" as patent medicine with medicine shows, start promoting oil as illuminant in late 1850's)... Cornelius Vanderbilt enters railroad business when named director of Long Island Railroad (invests in Providence & Stonington

Railroad on advice of Daniel Drew)... After working for John Sutter, John Bidwell starts Rancho Chico with Mexican land grant of 22,000 acres, CA (starts area's first important farm and nursery to develop almonds, casaba melons, olive trees, Chinese sugar cane, grapevines for wine)...

National Police Gazette publishes lurid stories with explicit pictures of sex, sports and crime (-1977, prospers to 1932 only to falter with Depression and ladies invading barbershops)... Peter Cooper, operator of glue and iron works, starts rolling mill in Trenton, NJ, first to provide structural iron for fireproof buildings in 1854 and first to use Bessemer converter in 1856 (invents process for rolling iron, washing machine, and compressed air propulsion for ferry boats, starts Cooper Union in 1857-59 to educate poor)... Mark Cross starts business to make fine leather goods...

1846

General Events

Congress declares (May 13) state of war with Mexico (-1848 with U.S. receiving areas of California, Nevada, Utah, most of New Mexico and Arizona, and parts of Wyoming, Colorado)... New Yorks beat Knickerbockers in first match baseball game, over 200 clubs in 1866... Congress readopts Independent Treasury Act... Iowa is 29th state... Commodore James Biddle visits Japan to establish trade relations... Maine bans sale of liquor... J.M. Shively prepares guide book for travelers to Oregon, California... For Mexican War U.S. Army forms first field army staff for its expeditionary force.

Business Events

Pennsylvania Railroad is chartered (hires J. Edgar Thomson as Chief Engineer in 1847)... Nancy Johnson invents first hand-crank device to make home-made ice cream, not patented (leads to Jacob Fussell, Baltimore, with first commercial ice cream plant in 1851)... A.T. Cross starts business, RI, to make elegant writing instruments (is acquired in 1916 by Boss family, acquires leather-goods stores of Mark Cross in 1983)... Sea Witch, first true clipper ship, is launched (sails from Hong Kong to NYC in 74 days, 14 hours - record never broken)... Some 1,000 head of Texas cattle are driven to Ohio, Texas herds to New Orleans in 1842 and Missouri in 1846... Although viewed as mad, William Kelly, Eddyville, KY, kettle-maker, tries blowing cold air through molten iron to oxidize carbon impurities with advice of 4 experts from China, made steel from cast iron in 100s B.C. (after hearing of Bessemer's work, gets U.S. patent in 1852 with evidence of prior rights, shows process to Daniel J. Morrell, general manager of Cambria Iron Works - no action due to Panic of 1857, licenses rights to Kelly Process Co. in 1861, approves merger of Kelly with U.S. holders of Bessemer rights in 1866)... Resort hotel is built on Boston's North Shore...

John Murray Forbes, Boston associates refinance Michigan Railroad (extend line to Chicago in 1852)... Elias Howe patents a sewing machine, as inefficient as those designed in England in 1776, Austria in 1814, U.S. in 1826, and France in 1830 (after improvements by I.M. Singer in 1851 wins patent war in 1854)... After mortgaging holdings in Kansas to buy 14 wagons and 16 mules, Ben Holladay starts Holladay Overland Mail &

Express to operate on Santa Fe Trail, later to Salt Lake City (eliminates competition by cutting prices, expands business to operate with some 15,000 employees, 20,000 vehicles, 150,000 animals, and 16 steamers, acquires Central Overland stage coach business in 1862, declares bankruptcy in Panic of 1873)... Charles Scribner's Sons publishing is started (opens famed bookstore in 1913)... Over 700 whalers are commissioned by U.S., only 41 by 1906... T.T. Pond, Utica druggist, starts business to make Extract herbal medicine with curative powers from witch hazel (introduces Cold Cream products in 1907, uses endorsements of American heiresses and British beauties in 1920s to become world's largest producer of face creams by W.W. II, merges with Chesebrough vaseline products in 1955).

1847

General Events

Congress approves (March 3) use of adhesive postage stamps, first mail carriers in 1863... New Hampshire sets 10-hour day for workers, Pennsylvania for certain workers in 1848... Amos Lawrence, Boston merchant and textile industrialist, endows Lawrence Scientific School at Harvard, charity donations of $700,000 during lifetime inspires J.D. Rockefeller... S. Page patents disc harrow... New York passes General Incorporation Act for villages, rural cemeteries, plant roads, turnpikes... Ship's Captain Hanson Crockett supposedly discovers doughnut after poking fork through a "fried cake".

Business Events

Mike Simmons, George Bush start first Puget Sound sawmill... After devising lozenge cutter, first U.S. candy machine, Oliver Chase starts business to make lozenges... Chicago Tribune is published... Small side-wheel steamer is used to carry vacationers from Manhattan to Coney Island, operates early roller coaster ride in 1844... Steam is used to power textile mills in Salem and New Bedford, MA... Edward K. Collins starts United States Mail Steamship Co. with U.S. subsidy to compete with Britain's Cunard line (loses mail subsidy in 1856 to Vanderbilt with loss of Arctic and Pacific vessels, auctions 3 remaining vessels in 1858 to satisfy creditors)... Benjamin H. Latrobe, Chief Engineer for B & O Railroad, prepares operations manual (creates two administrative departments: general superintendent over operations, treasurer over collection and disbursement of revenues)... Ezra Cornell starts Erie and Michigan Telegraph Co. (co-forms Western Union in 1856 to consolidate several major, minor lines)... German-born Emanuel Lehman starts cotton brokerage business in Alabama with brothers, opens offices in New Orleans in 1850s and NYC during Civil War (moves to NYC after Civil War to underwrite ventures in railroads, iron enterprises, textile mills, land and timber companies, banks and trust companies - Sears in 1906, Underwood in 1910, Studebaker in 1911, F.W. Woolworth in 1912, Continental Can in 1913, is sold to Shearson American Express in 1984)...

Cyrus McCormick starts Chicago plant to make reapers (loses patent in 1848 after fighting infringement suits, out-performs machine of Obed Hussey in field competition at London's 1851 Crystal Palace Exhibition, uses some 1,000 carpenters and machinists, using patterns for standardization, to produce some 5,000 reapers/year by 1858, uses advertising, guarantee of satisfaction or money back, easy credit terms, and competitive field trials in competing with over 100 rivals in 1860's market)... After closing arms business in 1842, Samuel Colt obtains government contract to make 1,000 revolvers for Mexican War, subcontracts to New Haven Armory of Eli Whitney, Jr. (employs Elisha K. Root, mechanic and inventor with Collins axe business, in 1848 as production superintendent at twice former salary, to design special-purpose machines for making interchangeable parts, builds new modern plant in 1853-55 at Hartford, CT, to make arms, machine tools with trained Yankee mechanics - fails to achieve precision required for true interchangeability of parts, employs Indian painter George Catlin to do series of paintings to promote hunting, builds London plant in 1855 to introduce "American system" of manufacturing)...

French-born 3 Lazard brothers open clothing store in New Orleans, expand with banks in Paris, London, and NYC (with no male heirs pass control to David-Weill family in Paris, is last family investment bank in NYC in 1988 when Salomon Bros. and Lehman Bros. become corporate entities)... With mail subsidy for $199,000/year for 10 years William H. Aspinwall, others form Pacific Mail Steamship Co., builds 1st of 3 ships for Pacific service (makes 1st sailing in 1848 for West Coast to become profitable in Gold Rush with transportation across Isthmus of Panama, starts first trans-Pacific trade to Yokohama, Hong Kong in 1867).

1848

General Events

Cincinnati iron molders form cooperative society, one of over 800 organized 1845-60... Wisconsin is 30th State... Gerrit Smith, NY, is nominated for Presidency by representatives of labor organizations meeting in Philadelphia... U.S., Great Britain sign postal treaty... Pennsylvania is first State to set 12 as minimum age for employment in factories... British-born Robert Hoe perfects rotary press for printing newspapers... New York passes general incorporation law for societies, toll bridges and businesses... Linus Yale devises pin-tumbler lock (forms Yale Lock Mfg. in 1868)... Federick W. Howe, VT, designs milling machine to make Sharp's breech-loading rifle, first universal milling and grinding machine developed later by partner Joseph Brown.

Business Events

James Marshall, NJ mechanic, discovers (January 24) gold in building sawmill for John A. Sutter on American River, CA (is reported by New York Herald on August 19 and confirmed by President Polk on December 5)... Six NYC daily newspapers form New York News Agency, becomes Associated Press in 1856 (is followed by number of regional subsidiaries)... J. Curtis sells spruce resin for chewing, William Semple with patent for chewing gum in 1869... In Manhattan William Tollner opens hardware store with wares displayed in velvet-lined cases and salesmen wearing morning coats (becomes Hammacher Schlemmer in 1867, is acquired from Schlemmer family in 1950's to become known as super-specialty store with fancy gadgets)...

American President Line is formed... New Jersey Zinc Co. is created... Cyrus McCormick forms partnership in Chicago to make reapers (acquires full ownership by 1851)... Warren, Wheeler and Woodruff is formed to make small metal articles (accepts sewing machine inventor Allen Wilson as partner in 1851, reorganizes in 1855 to employ William Perry, former inside contractor at Samuel Colt's armory, as production superintendent, uses Colt system of manufacture in 1857 to become leading producer until 1867)... Alexander Majors starts Missouri freight service business to Santa Fe... Bavarian-born Joseph Seligman, brothers start clothing business in Manhattan (transforms mercantile operation into international banking house by 1862 with branches in Frankfort, London, Paris, San Francisco and New Orleans, enters railroad securities field in 1869)...

Alexander T. Stewart opens Marble Palace in Manhattan as retail, wholesale business (evolves as department store in 1850's, pioneers with fashion shows, single-price policy, handsome floor-walkers, and foreign merchandise, moves to Cast-Iron Palace in 1862 to employ some 2,000 people and gross some $50 million in 1870 as world's largest retail business with foreign offices and warehouses before death in 1876)... Chicago Board of Trade is founded to systematize buying, selling of grains (incorporates 1859)... J.C. Lee, G. Higginson start Boston-brokerage firm (lose reputation for soundness and trust with 1932 financial collapse of Ivar Kreugar's International Match)... Ester Howland of Worcester, MA, starts commercial Valentine business in home... William Sellers starts manufacturing concern in Philadelphia to make machine tools (invents bolt machine in 1857, basis for commercially interchangeable nuts and bolts, and gear cutting machine, one of first to be automatically operated)... American Factors starts business, HI (becomes Amfac, state's largest employer with 1986 sales of $1.96 billion, with interests in agriculture, food, wholesaling, retailing and land, 56,700 acres and leases 94,000, sheds all mainland operations in 1987 to restructure after losses)... Curtis Paper Co., U.S.' oldest continuously operating paper mill in 1980s, is started, ME.

1849

General Events

Walter Hunt, NY, invents safety pin to pay creditor $15... Gail Borden devises food concentrate (wins award for meat biscuit at 1851 Crystal Palace Exhibition in London)... New York passes general incorporation law for insurance companies... George H. Corliss patents steam engine with rotary valves and governor (starts Providence plant in 1856, builds Corliss steam press, largest and most powerful of time, for 1876 Centennial Exhibition in Philadelphia)... After initial efforts in 1846, Oneida is founded in New York by John Humphrey Noyes, medium of God's will, and followers as harmonious community of men and women living, working together in open love relationships (after division in 1879, evolves as Oneida silversmith business in late 1890's - international corporation in 1970's worth close to $100 million)... Chicago Gas Light and Coke Co. is chartered... California's Chinese population numbers 325, 25,000 by 1851 and over 300,000 by 1882 as they flee Southern China from war, corruption, natural disasters and poverty despite laws to execute anyone leaving or returning.

Business Events

California lands (February 28) at San Francisco with first boat load of gold miners... Pacific Railroad, named Missouri Pacific later, is chartered to link St. Louis, Kansas City... Mail is carried by stagecoach between Independence, MO, and Santa Fe... Poor's Publishing is started to provide financial data, advice (is rescued from bankruptcy in 1933 by Paul Babson of Standard Statistics to form Standard & Poor's in 1941)...

Henry Varnum Poor becomes Editor of <u>American Railroad Journal</u> (-1862, advocates use of organization, communication and information to improve management of railroads)... Clipper <u>Memmon</u> sails from NYC to San Francisco in 122 days, usually 200 days good time for voyage... Chemical business of Charles Pfizer & Co. is started, NY... Hiram Sibley co-founds New York State Printing Telegraph (organizes New York and Mississippi Valley Printing Telegraph in 1850 - lines to Detroit and Chicago in 1854, reorganizes lines as Western Union in 1856)... Yankee peddler Collis P. Huntington goes to California with trade goods (forms partnership in 1854 with Mark Hopkins to operate Sacramento hardware business)...

Alexander Todd starts first major express business in California to deliver mail between San Francisco, mine fields... German-born Jew Isaac Friedlander joins California gold rush (obtains first fortune in 1852 by cornering local flour market as "Grain King of California," declares bankruptcy in 1878 after over-chartering vessels)... Some 40,000 gold miners, settlers are seen on Oregon, California trails (form quasi-military, joint-companies in New England, foreign nations for transportation to gold fields, sell trade goods in San Francisco to pay for travel costs, dissolve companies after distribution of profits)...

John Bradstreet starts credit agency in Cincinnati (merges with Dun & Co. in 1933 to form Dun & Bradstreet)... James Lanier starts pioneering investment bank, NYC, to underwrite railroad securities... Adams & Co. is started, CA, as branch of Eastern Express Co. (collapses in Panic of 1855)... Partnership of Pope & Talbot is formed, CA, with $500 to start lumber business (moves to Puget Sound in 1853, by 1863 produce some 18 million feet of lumber yearly with 35,000 acres of timberland)... German-born Captain Henry Hackfeld sails from Germany to Honolulu with cargo of merchandise for missionaries, settlers (opens store, becomes part of Amfac after seizure by U.S. in 1918 as alien property, grows as 29-store Liberty House chain, expands to mainland in buying 17 Rhodes Western department stores, WA, OR and CA, in 1969, acquires I. Magnin's 51 stores, started 1890, in 1969)... Challenging monopoly of Pacific Mail and U.S. Mail transporting California-bound passengers across Panama, Cornelius Vanderbilt, operating 8 steamers to Nicaragua, forms Accessory Transit Co. (gets Nicaragua train charter 1850-1853 to earn over $1 million yearly).

1850s

General Events

Chinese craftsmen, merchants form guilds, based on those in China, in San Francisco to stabilize prices (combine later with secret societies as tongs).

Business Events

E. & T. Fairbanks start regional agencies to sell mass-produced scales... Some 280,000 brass clocks are made at 2 plants of Chauncey Jerome, CT (uses mechanization in mass-manufacturing but not interchangeable parts)... Sharps rifle factory is built in Hartford, CT, used later by Weed sewing-machine business and Alfred Pope to make bicycles.

1850

General Events

Congress abolishes (September 28) flogging in U.S. Navy... Governmental mail contract for Independence to Salt Lake City is let to Samuel Woodson, linked with Sacramento by operation of Absalom Woodward, George Chorpenning... U.S. Census shows population of 23.2 million, 3.5 urban and 19.7 rural (indicates 45% west of Alleghenies, some 1,713,000 immigrants since 1841, and 1,479 southern plantations with over 100 slaves - 56 over 300, 9 over 500, and two over 1000)... National Road from Columbus, OH, reaches Central Illinois... First significant U.S. railroad land grant is awarded to line from Illinois to Mobile, AL (results in construction of Illinois Central in 1851-1856)... U.S., Britain sign Clayton-Bulwer Treaty (agree projected canal across Central America would be neutral operation)... California is 31st state... Herman Melville: White-Jacket (reveals poor working conditions, inhumane treatment of U.S. sailors)... Dry good clerks, NYC, form association to seek shorter hours... John F. Heath invents grain binder...

Act for the Government of Masters and Servants is established, HI (compels immigrant laborers under contract, passage paid by planter to work one-five years for wage of $4/month with food, lodging, and medical care, to work or go to prison, punishes planters for "any cruelty, misusage, or violation of the contract")... Massachusetts is first state to study occupational safety (passes first laws requiring factory safeguards in 1877 and factory inspections in 1879).

Business Events

Henry Willard acquires site for elegant hotel two blocks from White House... P.T. Barnum promotes U.S. tour of Jenny Lind, Swedish Nightingale... Clipper Sea Witch sails from NYC to San Francisco in 97 days (sells cargo of $84,624 for $275,000)... U.S. clipper Oriental sails from Canton, China, to London in record 97 days (amazes British with daring design)... Edward Collins launches steamship Atlantic to compete with Britain's Cunard Line on Atlantic service (operates as United States Mail Steamship Co. with annual government subsidy)...

Aaron Dennison, others start venture, MA, to make watches by machines (evolves after 1859 as American Watch Co. with men trained at Springfield Armory to produce some 70,000 timepieces in 1865, becomes Waltham Watch Co. later to compete with Elgin in 1864, Waterbury in 1879, Hamilton in 1892)... Aetna Life Insurance issues its first life insurance policy... Stroh Brewery is started in Detroit, State's oldest... Henry Varnum Poor, editor of American Railroad Journal, advocates use of railroad mortgage bonds to raise funds for construction (warns public in 1852 on dangers on investing in railroads, issues studies on railroads seeking investment capital)...

Lewis Luckenbach starts tugboat business in NYC's harbor   (expands business with salvage operations, moves to Philadelphia to evolve as worldwide business by death in 1906)... Merchants Abraham Kuhn, Solomon Loeb open general merchandise store in Lafayette, IN (move to Cincinnati later, dissolve partnership in 1865, open NYC investment house in 1867 to sell government, railroad bonds)... Butterfield & Wasson, Livingston & Fargo Co. express agencies merge to create American Express with Henry Wells as President... Henry Hopkins starts grocery business in Sacramento (forms partnership in 1854 with Collis P. Huntington to run iron, hardware business)... Richard King starts Rio Grande riverboat business, operates 22 vessels by 1865...

The Mercantile Agency credit service hires Robert G. Dun (becomes partner in 1854, acquires ownership in 1859, starts publishing credit reference books in 1859)... Modern Gibson greeting card business is started... Group of mechanics start rolling mill on flat boat at Pittsburgh (acquire funds for expansion in 1853 from Jones, iron merchant, and Laughlin, pork packer, to operate blast furnace, five rolling mills and 25 nail-machines as Jones & Laughlin steel business). German-born Henry Miller sails to California with $6 (starts career as butcher, with savings purchases water rights to control of some one million acres, CA, by 1900's with holdings, NV and OR, and interests in packing houses, retail stores, lumber yards, hotels, banks)... Illiterate machinist Isaac M. Singer redesigns Blodgett & Lerow sewing machine with $40 from partner George Zieber and shop facilities from partner Orson C. Phelps (acquires Zieber's interest for $6,000 and buys out Phelps to form new partnership with lawyer Edward Clark in 1851, assembles machines in 1852 by hand with finishing, assembling of components by Boston job shop, starts French factory in 1855 - aborted, produces first home sewing machine in 1856)...

Work is started in building Louisville & Nashville Railroad (-1859)... Scottish-born Allan Pinkerton starts detective agency, Chicago (becomes only investigating agency for interstate crime for some 50 years)...

Nova-Scotian Donald McKay, "Father of Shipbuilders," launches <u>Stag</u> <u>Hound</u>, his first clipper, in Boston (builds last in 1869)... Empire City Steamship, NYC, enters Pacific market with 3 vessels, 2 purchased by rival Pacific Mail to cut competition... U.S. Mail Steamship, formed for Atlantic trade in 1847, invades Pacific Mail's market with 4 ships, Pacific retaliates with Atlantic service (leads to each buying other's ships to monopolize original markets and to cooperate on Panamian traffic).

1851

General Events

Congress authorizes (March 3) minting of three-cent silver coins... Maine prohibits (June 2) sale, manufacture of intoxicating beverages, followed by MA, VT, and LA in 1852, NH, NY, IA and NE Territory in 1855... California requires high schools to provide instruction in bookkeeping... When ice shipments from Boston are halted by labor dispute, Dr. John Gorrie, director of U.S. Marine hospital, FL, patents first ice-making machine to keep malaria, yellow fever patients cool... J. Brown, Providence, invents first vernier caliper... James Bogardus erects cast-iron frame building... Johnathan Baldwin Turner advocates "State University for the Industrial Classes" to teach agriculture, manufacturing, bookkeeping, etc., passage of Morrill Land Grant act in

1862... Horace Greeley's _Tribune_ publishes weekly budget of $10.37 for skilled-worker's family of five (gives $12 budget in 1853)... Massachusetts permits forming of industrial firms under $200,000 with specific state charters, extends limits to $500,000 in 1870.

Business Events

New York Daily Times is first published, becomes _New York Times_ in 1857... Hudson Railroad provides service between Albany, NYC... Donald McKay's clipper _Flying Cloud_ sets record of 89 days, 8 hours sailing from NYC to San Francisco, beaten in 1989... Two local associations, called Huigan (6 by 1870's), are formed, San Francisco, in this time by Chinese to recruit workers from certain areas in China (provide protection and social services for new immigrants who arrive on funds borrowed from middlemen)... Erie Railroad, formed 1833, is completed by Erastus Corning from Hudson River to Lake Erie, world's longest line with 483 miles of track (employs Daniel McCallum as General Superintendent, 1854-57, who establishes job descriptions, merit promotions, formal organizational chart and internal communications with hourly, daily, monthly records for evaluating performance)... Present Almaden vineyard is started, CA...

Blatz brewing business is established in Milwaukee... Hiriam Sibley forms New York and Mississippi Valley Printing and Telegraph (reorganizes as Western Union Telegraph in 1856, forms pool with 5 competitors in 1859 to divide U.S. telegraph market as North American Telegraph Association with Peter Cooper as President)... Independent Ohio salt manufacturers form joint-stock company to regulate productivity... Western and Atlantic Railroad completes line across southern Appalachians... Asa Simpson, ME, starts sawmill at Astoria, OR (moves operations to Grays Harbor, WA, in 1880's, operates 7 mills, 2 shipyards and 15 ships in 1882)...

Prussian-born Simon Lazarus opens retail business in Columbus, OH (becomes F. & L. Lazarus Department Store)... Richard Bonner buys NYC's _Merchant's Ledger_, just _Ledger_ in 1855 (uses creative printing to advertise publication in other publications)... Georgia plantation of Farish Carter records profit of 1.25% on investment of $150,000... British-born Amory Houghton starts small glass factory, MA (operates Brooklyn Flint Glass in 1864, starts Corning Flint Glass, NY, in 1868 - fails, restarts Corning Glass Works in 1875)... Construction on Missouri Pacific Railroad, chartered 1849, is started (reaches Kansas City in 1860's, fails to extend line to Pacific when blocked by Jay Gould's Texas & Pacific line, Collis P. Huntington's Southern Pacific)... For defending Isaac Singer in patent suits, lawyer Edward Clark becomes equal partner in sewing machine business to handle finances and sales (starts branch stores in 1856 to compete with rival Grover & Baker - 14 competitors by 1859, introduces installment buying in 1856, innovates with sewing demonstrations and trade-in allowances, becomes president in 1875 on death of Singer)...

Gail Borden receives medal from London's Great Exhibition for meat biscuit (loses fortune in making food concentrate for U.S. Army)... Nathaniel Heywood, Southern planter with some 2,000 slaves working 4,500 acres of rice land on 14 plantations to earn annual income of nearly $90,000 on investment of some $1 million, dies... Benjamin, Robert Knight start cloth firm at Providence, RI (adopt red apple label in 1856 for Fruit of the Loom fabrics - first trademark label for cloth).

1852

General Events

Congress establishes (July 3) branch of U.S. Mint in San Francisco...
National Typographical Union is formed in Cincinnati by journeymen
printers, first national union to last to present (is followed by unions
of hat finishers in 1854, journeyman stonecutters in 1855, cigar-makers
in 1856, and iron molders, machinists and blacksmiths in 1859)... Samuel
Johnston devises mechanical rake... American Society of Civil Engineers
is formed, followed by Institute of Mining Engineers in 1871, Society of
Mechanical Engineers in 1880, Institute of Electrical Engineers in
1884... Massachusetts passes first State safety law in setting standards
for steam engines... Congress requires river pilots to be licensed...
Congress provides land grant to build Sault St. Marie Canal, built 1853-
54 by Erastus Corning's St. Mary's Falls Ship Canal Co... U.S. presents
599 exhibits, covering all facets of U.S. industry from artificial leg,
dentifrice and false teeth to machinery for woodworking, agricultural and
firearms production, at London's Crystal Palace Exhibition (wins 159
awards of 5,084 total prizes with McCormick's reaper most celebrated,
Borden's meat biscuit and Colt's revolver, although no prizes gets
publicity for pianos, Hobb's "unpickable locks," and America yacht).

Business Events

Representatives from 11 southern states convene, New Orleans, to discuss
economic development... Michigan Southern Railway of Henry Farnum reaches
Chicago... Pittsburgh, Philadelphia are linked by Pennsylvania Railroad
(uses different guage of track to prevent use by New York's Erie
Railroad)... Potter Palmer, age 26 with $5,000 and 8 years' experience,
starts distinctive dry goods store in Chicago (employs Marshall Field,
age 21, in 1855, starts wholesale business in 1860, forms partnership in
1865 with Field and Levi Leiter)... James Smith & Sons, restaurant
operators in Poughkeepsie, NY, advertise cough drops, operated by sons
after death in 1866... Modern St. Louis Globe-Democrat newspaper is
published (-1986)... Platt Roger Spencer opens Spencerian Commercial
Academy, Pittsburgh (starts series of copy books on penmanship in
1859)... Adams & Co. express business opens bank in San Francisco's
Chinatown (declares bankruptcy for bank after failing to exorcise demons
from building, is reopened successfully by Wells, Fargo with appropriate
ritual to Chinese god of wealth, collapses in Panic of 1855)...

Mountain Man Richard Wootton drives some 9,000 sheep from Taos to
Sacramento (clears $45,000 on investment of $5,000, Scout Kit Carson
makes $30,000 on sheep drive in 1853)... Wisconsin Marine and Fire
Insurance circulates some $1,500,000 in notes as money in IL, IA and
other bankless states... J.L. Robinson's Wisconsin tent show advertises
as U.S.' oldest vaudeville company... Bavarian Brewery, one of some 430
in U.S. - 1,269 by 1859, is started in St. Louis (becomes Hammer & Urban
in 1857, is acquired by Eberhard Anheuser in 1860, employs son-in-law
Adolphus Busch in 1864 - Anheuser-Busch Brewery in 1879)... Advised by
Robert E. Lee, Captain Richard King, partner acquire 75,000 acres of
ranch land, TX (build Santa Gertrudis Ranch to operate over 100,000 head
of cattle on some 600,000 acres with some 1,000 Mexicans, diversify into
paper business, stagecoach line, ice plant, railroad)... Boston Board of
Trade is formed by James Converse, others... Henry, Clem Studebaker start

blacksmith business, South Bend, IN, with $68, two sets of tools (after making wagons on order and for Government contracts during Civil War, form Studebaker Brothers Mfg. in 1868)... Edmund Richardson starts cotton factorage in New Orleans (leases convicts in 1868 to work Mississippi plantations, evolves to operate some 50 plantations with 25,000 acres - world's largest cotton planter)... M.A. Hanna starts wholesale grocery business, OH (acquires fleet of ships to deliver goods throughout Great Lakes, starts acquiring Lake Superior iron and copper mines and coal mines, OH and PA, in 1857, expands into steel-making, shipping, ship-building, and railroads, operates with assets over $120 million by 1953)...

Elisha Otis builds first hand-powered hoist with automatic safety device for Yonkers bedstead manufacturer (patents safety elevator 1853, shows elevator at New York World's Fair in 1854, starts elevator business in 1854, installs first safety elevator for passengers in 1857, first U.S. commercial use, at E.V. Haughwout Department Store, obtains patent for steampowered elevator in 1861, devises U.S.' first high-speed hydraulic elevator for commercial buildings in 1878, introduces first electric elevator, invented 1880 by Germany's Werner Von Siemens, in 1889 - automated in 1894, introduces escalator in 1900)... John E. Thomson becomes president of 246-mile Pennsylvania Railroad, operates 1,538 miles of track by death in 1874 (organizes railroad with financial, treasury and accounting, and operating departments, creates central headquarters with secretary's office, legal and purchasing departments)...

Wells, Fargo & Co. express service is started, CA (becomes virtual monopoly with 108 stations by 1860)... John Stephenson, after bankruptcy in 1837 Depression, starts building streetcars, NYC (evolves as world's largest builder)... With backing of John Murray Forbes and his Boston associates, James F. Joy, former president of Michigan Southern Railroad, acquires Chicago & Aurora Railroad (acquires Central Military Track Railroad in 1856 to form Chicago, Burlington & Quincy Railroad, acquires Burlington & Missouri Railroad in 1857, adds two more roads to develop "Joy System" by 1870 as first combine west of Mississippi)...

Charles Crocker opens dry goods store in Sacramento, soon one of town's wealthiest (co-founds Central Pacific Railroad in 1861 with Mark Hopkins, Collis P. Huntington, Leland Stanford)... Leland Stanford joins brothers in Sacramento mercantile business... Henry J. Heinz peddles food, by 1860 with 3 employees making deliveries to Pittsburgh grocers (starts partnership in 1869 to make, sell horseradish, declares bankruptcy in 1875)... Thomas A. Scott becomes assistant superintendent of Pennsylvania Railroad, superintendent of western division in 1858 and president in 1874... Boston, Concord & Montreal Railroad stages first annual Harvard-Yale rowing event on Thames River, CT, to promote interest in area as summer resort... French-born Paul Masson starts vineyard near Santa Clara, CA.

1853

General Events

Congress passes (February 21) Coinage Act (establishes subsidiary silver system to reduce amount of silver in coins, permits minting of $3 gold pieces)... Army Appropriation Act provides (March 4) funds for surveying transcontinental railroad routes... Commodore Matthew Perry's black fleet sails into Yedo Bay, opens Japan to Western trade... Inspired by plight of mothers, children immigrating to U.S. in steerage, Gail Borden invents condensed milk at New York Shaker colony (obtains patent in 1856 rejections, starts first plant in 1861 to achieve success during Civil War, becomes $6.5 billion food business by 1988)... George Scheutz builds "difference machine" calculator...

Elizur Wright compiles actuarial tables for mortality rates... New York Crystal Exhibition shows technology of all nations (is attended by England's Joseph Whitworth, leading toolmaker, and George Wallis, headmaster of design school, who tour U.S. manufacturers in 15 cities, report to Britain on extensive U.S. use of special-purpose machinery in place of manual labor and interchangeable parts)... Modern thin, crisp potato chip is created from thick-fried potatoes in Saratoga Springs, NY, by either G. Crum or Indian Kate Moon... U.S. signs treaty with Mexico, acquires strip of land, Gadsden Purchase, along southern border, AZ and NM (provides railroad route to California)... Commission of British mechanics, entrepreneurs tour U.S. to study technology, manufacturing methods (are amazed by working of wood: 7,000-10,000 shingles/day, 4,500 matches/minute)... Herman Melville: "Bartleby the Scrivener," _Putnam's Monthly Magazine_ (describes typical office with staff of 2 or 3 copiers, bookkeeper, cash keeper, and confidential clerk to take charge when partners are away).

Business Events

Baltimore & Ohio Railroad reaches Wheeling... 120 clipper ships are launched, 3 in 1859... Union Railway Station is built in Indianapolis, first U.S. central depot for city's lines (becomes complex of restaurants, shops, and hotel in mid-1980's)... Andrew Carnegie is hired as telegraph operator, personal clerk by Thomas A. Scott, assistant superintendent of Pennsylvania Railroad (with funds from mother's home mortgage invests in Adams Express on advice of Scott in 1856, earns $45,000/year from such investments by 1863)... With fortune of $11 million yielding 25% yearly Cornelius Vanderbilt turns over management of 1849 Accessory Transit Co. to Charles Morgan and Cornelius K. Garrison while sailing on yacht, U.S.' first, to Europe (loses control to duo by 1855 through stock manipulations)...

Erastus Corning creates New York Central Railroad by combining 10 Upstate lines to link Buffalo, Albany (retires as president in 1866, is followed by control of William G. Fargo, associates and then Cornelius Vanderbilt in 1867)... Samuel Colt builds Hartford Armory to make machine-made small arms (trains machinists on "American system of manufacture," opens London plant 1853-57 to introduce manufacturing techniques to Britain)... H.B. Bryant, H.D. Stratton open private business college, Cleveland (operate 10 schools by 1863 - chain of 48 such colleges in 18 south and southwest states operated by J.F. Draughon and chain of 30 schools operated in Illinois by G.W. Brown)... German-born Henry Steinway, sons start piano manufacturing business, NYC (perfects modern iron-frame piano for rich tones in few years)... Mount Vernon Hotel, running water and bath in every room, is built at Cape May, NJ... New York Clearing House is created to settle accounts between banks... Menomonee Valley Brewery is started, WI (becomes Frederick Miller Brewing in 1888)... Aetna Life & Casualty Co. is started in Hartford, CT (evolves as largest U.S.

investor-owned)... German-born Gottlieb Heileman starts brewery in La Crosse, WI (still extant)... Dr. Brewer, associates lease land near Titusville, PA, to develop oil, deed land in 1854 to Jonathan, George Bissell... Baltimore millwright Henry Yesler starts steam sawmill on Puget Sound's Elliott Bay (leads to development of Seattle as City's largest enterprise by 1860's)... American Brass Assn. is formed by producers to regulate prices... Sailing packets make some 1,000 Atlantic crossings, trips average 30-40 days... Philadelphia Board of Presidents is formed, first permanent association of bankers... German-born John Jacob Bausch starts optical shop in Rochester, NY (joins Henry Lomb in 1866 to form Vulcanite Optical Instruments as base for modern Bausch & Lomb business)...

Bavarian-born peddler Levi Strauss sails to San Francisco with stock of heavy canvas (sells to prospectors for use as tents and wagon covers, makes canvas "pantaloons" when miners want sturdy work pants - later uses serge de Nimes from France to make blue-dyed denim work trousers for miners, cowhands, lumberjacks, gandy-dancers)... Oregon ships first apples, $1/pound, to San Francisco.

1854

General Events

Commodore Perry, Japan sign treaty of Kanagawa (opens 2 ports to trade for U.S. vessels)... Congress forms Kansas, Nebraska Territories... Emigrant Aid Co. is formed in New England to settle Kansas... David Halladay, Connecticut tinkerer, devises self-governing windmill to withstand high winds on western plains... Ketchum mower is patented for cutting hay... Robbins & Laurence, VT, build turret lathe.

Business Events

John Murray Forbes, Boston associates invest in Burlington & Missouri River Railroad, IA (in 1856 finance Canadian Great Western Line to link Chicago with East Coast)... George Fitz takes over rundown 1851 Cambria ironworks at Johnstown, PA (operates industry's most technically advanced plant with some 2,000 workers by Civil War, develops Bethlehem Iron in 1860's)... After pleas of Daniel Drew, Cornelius Vanderbilt advances Erie Railroad $400,000 (serves as Director 1859-66)... Boston's National Shawmut Bank uses Indian as trademark on bank notes... In this time, Peacedale Manufacturing starts pioneering employee library (by 1909 is adopted as common facility by other employers)... Cornelius Vanderbilt acquires bonds, stock in Harlem Railroad, connecting with Western Railroad to reach Albany (serves as Director in 1857, President in 1863)... Junius Spencer Morgan, dry goods merchant, becomes partner in London investment house of George Peabody & Co. (changes name of international banking house in 1864 to J.S. Morgan & Co., handles $50 million loan in 1870 for France during its war with Prussia to become premier financial institution)... Hampton County Cotton Spinners' Assn. is formed, MA, to regulate competition (evolves as New England Cotton Spinners' Assn. in 1865)... Boston Five Cents Savings Bank is created...

Daniel Drew lends Erie Railroad $1,500,000 for chattel mortgages on rolling stock (becomes Treasurer of Railroad in 1857, declares first bankruptcy in 1859)... A railroad is built to Atlantic City (changes

fishing village into fashionable resort, builds Boardwalk in 1870)...
R.H. Macy, former Nantucket Whaler, adopts one-price policy for dry goods
store in Haverhill, MA (needs standardization for large number of
clerks)... Civic promoter Henry Noble Day's business "empire" in Hudson,
OH, collapses during Depression, used funds from family, local Western
Reserve College to start housing development, bank to finance houses and
building supply business... Irish-born Samuel Carson, John D. Pirie open
retail business in Amboy, IL (open 4 branch stores in nearby towns by
1858 before starting Chicago store in 1864)... George H. Bissell, partner
form Pennsylvania Rock Oil Co. to lease land at oil spring near
Titusville, PA (hire pharmaceutical manufacturer Luther Atwood and Yale
Professor Benjamin Silliman to determine possible uses of oil other than
as patent medicine, receive 1855 report to suggest valuable products
possible with refining, re-incorporate, CT, in 1855 and commission
"Colonel" E.L. Drake, former railroad conductor, to drill for oil)...

John S. Chisum, partner start Texas cattle business, by 1870's with herds
of 60-100,000 (start operation, NM, in 1866)... Alvin Adams, William B.
Dinsmore incorporate express agency business, CA (-1855, after losing
competitive battle with Wells, Fargo, reorganize to operate on smaller
scale)... First commercial flour mill in Minneapolis is operated...
Russell, Majors & Waddell freight business is started at Leavenworth to
haul materials for U.S. Army (nets some $300,000 on first contract,
starts bank in 1857, receives 2nd contract from U.S. Army in 1858,
operates on prairies as largest freight hauler with 500 wagons, 7,500
oxen, and 700 men, declares bankruptcy after loss of some $500,000 when
U.S. Army refuses to pay for wagons destroyed during 1857 Mormon War,
refinances in 1859)... Most coach lines in Northern California are
combined as California Stage Co., operates 110 coaches over 1400 miles of
road...Nova Scotian Dr. Abraham Gesner starts New York Kerosene Oil Works
(coins term "kerosene")...

Daniel McCallum becomes General Superintendent of Erie Railroad (-1857,
submits stockholder report with principles of railroad operation:
establish division of responsibility, provide sufficient power, provide
means to measure performance and require promptness in correcting
problems and reports to detect errors, in first known U.S. organizational
chart shows board of directors, president and five operating divisions:
engine repairs, cars, bridges, telegraph and printing, and service,
resigns when Daniel Drew assumes control to start bridge construction
company)... While serving as Troy alderman Russell Sage starts career as
financier and speculator by buying City's railroad for $200,000, sells to
New York Central for over $800,000 (joins Jay Gould in 1870's).

1855

General Events

Chicago police subdue mob of 21,000 protesting trial of people accused of
violating Sunday closing laws... Southern corn crop of $209 million
exceeds combined value of area's cotton, tobacco, sugar, and rice
crops... Railroad is built across Isthmus of Panama with U.S.
financing... Joshua C. Stoddard of Worcester, MA, patents steam
calliope... Stone cutters form national union... James B. Francis:
Lowell Hydraulic Experiments (from research provides guidelines for
building turbines)... Amana religious colony is established, IA, as self-

sufficient community (separates religious activities from governmental, business interests during "Big Change" of 1932 in forming Amana Society as corporation)... "First" U.S. household bathroom is installed in George Vanderbilt's NYC residence... Alexander Parkes discovers composition of celluloid, developed commercially as first synthetic plastic by John W. Hyatt in 1872... Olympic Club is founded, oldest U.S. athletic club... Atlanta is among first with streets lighted by gas.

Business Events

Eliphalet W. Dennison, brother to watchmaker Aaron, assumes control of family business making cardboard boxes (invents new kind of shipping tag in 1863 to enter stationery business)... Parker House of Boston is first U.S. hotel to adopt "European Plan"... After operating inn, brewery near Stuttgart, S. Liebmann's Sons Brewing is started, Brooklyn (operates 5 plants by 1957, is acquired in 1964 by Pepsi-Cola and renamed Rheingold)... American Iron Assn. is formed to pool interests of members... Bradstreet's Improved Commercial Agency, originated St. Louis, is started, NYC, as mercantile credit business... After taking over Vanderbilt's 1849 Accessory Transit Co., Charles Morgan and Cornelius K. Garrison finance adventurer William Walker's takeover of Nicaragua with 58 followers (cancel Vanderbilt's 1850 charter to acquire monopoly, by 1857, after series of maneuvers by Vanderbilt, are ruined when Walker surrenders to Vanderbilt's force, with $1.2 million from U.S. Mail, Pacific Mail to stay out of Panama market resumes business to earn some $10 million before dissolving Accessory in 1863).

1856

General Events

Congress adopts (January 1) adhesive postage stamp... Railroader Henry Farnum builds first railroad bridge accross Mississippi between Rock Island, IL, and Davenport, IA... Townsend Harris opens U.S. Counsul Office in Japan... Henry Bessemer of Britain applies for U.S. patent on steel-making process (is challenged successully by William Kelly for having prior rights with discovery of process in 1846 - support by Charles Cargill who claims "discovery" of method in 1842)... David Christy: <u>Cotton is King</u>... Herman Melville: <u>The Confidence-Man: His Masquerade</u>... Obed Hussey develops steam-powered tractor for farming... "Snowshoe" Thompson uses skis to deliver mail to Placerville, CA... Boston is first U.S. city with streetcar line (electrifies 97% by 1902)... English-born David Hughes, Kentucky school teacher, devises telegraphic printer.

Business Events

Illinois Central Railroad, first U.S. land grant line (sells land for $15.3 million to pay for most of construction costs), is opened between Chicago and Cairo... After 4-1/2 years, whaler <u>E L B Jenney</u> returns to New Bedford, MA, with 2500 barrels of sperm oil... Some 4,000 reapers are made at Cyrus McCormick's Chicago plant (uses advertising, guarantee of satisfaction or money back, competitive field trials and credit terms to sell machines)... President of Michigan Central Railroad sends letter to President of Michigan Southern line to suggest joint cooperation on rates (provides first evidence in industry on mutual regulation of rates)...

Jay Gould starts tannery in Lehigh, PA, with backing of Zadoc Pratt, wealthy tanner (sells out to Gould after discovering mismanagement of funds in speculation, who then consumes funds of new patron, Charles Leuppi, within a year in an attempt to corner hide market)... Construction of Pittsburgh, Fort Wayne and Chicago railroad is finished (provides link with East via Pennsylvania Railroad)... Joseph Schlitz acquires 1849 brewery of August Krug in Milwaukee... Eagle Pencil Co. is started, NYC, as importer, manufacturer of pencils by Bavarian-born Berol family (introduces first U.S. pencil with inserted eraser in 1872, first mechanical pencil in 1879, and first successful pocket pencil-sharpener in 1893, opens London branch in 1906)... James Birch, developer of California's largest stage system in 1849-54, acquires mail contract for Texas to California route... Edward Clark, I.M. Singer & Co., adopts "first" installment-purchase plan for customers buying sewing machines (requires $50 down-payment and $100/month for 6 months)...

Great Sewing Machine Combination, first important U.S. patent pool, is formed by Orlando Potter of Grover & Baker Sewing Machine Co., Isaac Singer, Elias Howe, Allen B. Wilson to eliminate expensive legal suits on patent infringements (-1877)... After losing _Arctic_ and _Pacific_ in disasters, United States Mail Steamship Co., "Collins Line," loses Government mail subsidy (is forced to auction assets to satisfy creditors in 1858)... Rancher Charles Goodnight starts cattle business, TX... J.P. Morgan starts working for father's London banking house, employed by New York agent in 1857 (forms J.P. Morgan & Co. in 1861)... Hiram Sibley, Ezra Cornell form Western Union to consolidate several major, minor lines (provides telegraph service from New York to Mississippi River)...

Cadwallader C. Washburn, partner form Minneapolis Mill Co. (develop new milling process for purer flour in 1866 - called Gold Medal in 1880)... German-born Ferdinand Schumacher starts German Mills American Oatmeal Factory in Akron, OH (with success in selling oatmeal, makes rolled oats in 1878 as City's largest employer)...

After brother opens famous Equinox House in 1853 for tourists visiting Green Mountains, Charles F. Orvis starts business in Manchester, VT, to make bamboo fishing rods - 6 competitors, including Thomas Chubb, VT, as volume producer, in 1870-1900 (opens Orvis Hotel in 1861, relies on catalog, claims to be oldest U.S. mail-order firm, for advertising in 1872 - casting demonstrations and tournaments at county fairs in 1860s, pioneers modern fly reels with patent in 1874, with only 2 employees left from Great Depression sells to Dudley C. Cockran in 1939, makes ski poles for U.S. Army 1941-44, uses national advertising in late 1940s, starts Christmas catalog in 1954, introduces fiberglass rods in 1960 - graphite in 1974, sells business in 1965 to Leigh Perkins - expands mail-order business with over 2.5 million catalogs in 1979, opens U.S.' first fly fishing school in 1966 - over 10,000 graduates by 1980, sponsors American Museum of Fly Fishing in 1968, opens shooting school in 1973, after operating outlets in retail stores opens first retail store, San Francisco, in 1980 - 8 by 1988 to sell up-scale apparel and general merchandise)... George W. Brown Co. is first U.S. clockwork toy maker, followed by Ives, U.S.' largest, of Plymouth, MA, in 1868... Dr. C.H. Phillips moves little beeswax and camphor factory from NYC to Glenbrook, CT (patents Milk of Magnesia in 1873 as antacid and laxative).

1857

General Events

Congress negates (February 21) foreign coins as legal tender... Tariff act lowers (March 3) average duties on imports by 20%... U.S. ships are allowed by treaty with Japan to trade in port of Nagasaki... Businessman Peter Cooper founds Cooper Union to provide working class with free education in engineering and arts (offers evening courses)... Hinton Rowan Helper: The Impending Crisis of the South (suggests slavery has impoverished many Southern whites)... Thomas Hill patents multiple-order, key-driven calculating machine... Lammont Du Pont develops nitrate-based formula for making explosives, used to mine anthracite coal...

Massachusetts enacts law to grant all manufacturing, mining companies right to engage in interstate commerce... Leon Scott suggests idea for phonograph... Robert Mushet, Britain, acquires U.S. patent for Spiegelesen, composed of carbon, manganese, iron... "Arithmometer" is patented, impractical... University of Michigan installs first U.S. college chemistry laboratory... International Typographical Union and molders union survive Depression (-1862) while unions of stone-cutters, hat-finishers, machinists, blacksmiths fail... With rampant speculation in U.S. railroads and land and exports of Russian wheat first worldwide financial crisis occurs.

Business Events

New York branch of Ohio Life Insurance & Trust Co. fails (triggers commercial and financial panic with 4,932 business failures, including those of Erie, Illinois Central, Michigan Central and Reading Railroads)... St. Louis, NYC are linked by rail... Pennsylvania Railroad acquires State's main canal system to eliminate competition... Employee Oliver Winchester acquires Connecticut plant becomes New Haven Repeating Arms Co. (starts producing carbine repeating rifle in 1860)... First brewery on West Coast opens at Vancouver on Columbia River (-1985)...

Bavarian-born Aaron Meier, partner open dry goods store in Portland, OR Territory (-1864, starts new store in 1864)... Baltimore & Ohio Railroad reaches St. Louis... Augustus Wolle starts Saucona Iron Co., named Bethlehem Iron in 1861 and Bethlehem Steel in 1899... Cornelius Vanderbilt lends funds to New York and Hudson Railroad (acquires control in 1863-64)... Spalding & Rogers' European Circus is first to tour along Missouri River (features clowns, minstrels, equestrians from France, Germany and Britain, and museum of wonders exhibiting boa-constricter, assorted oddities)... Retired merchant Cyrus Field forms Atlantic Telegraph Co. to lay Atlantic cable (achieves success in 1866 after several failures)...

Butterfield Stage Line provides mail service between St. Louis, San Francisco (evolves with Eastern, Western divisions, each with 18 subdivisions, to supervise some 2,000 employees, 250 coaches, 1,000 horses, 500 mules, and 141 way stations, charges $200 for each trip - meals not included)... J. Edgar Thomson, President of Pennsylvania Railroad, reorganizes central headquarters by creating secretary's office and two departments, one for legal, controller and auditing activities (uses ratios to analyze performance) and one for purchasing to adopt

military line-and-staff and divisional organizational structure...
Hungarian-born A. Haraszthy starts first successful winery in
California's Sonoma Valley... Scottish-born James Oliver purchases South
Bend foundry (patents innovative Oliver Chilled Iron Plow in 1869 to
operate business with some 2,000 workers producing 200,000 plows/year)...
Norvin Green combines six large telegraph systems to create North
American Telegraph Co. (merges with Western Union in 1866).

1858

General Events

Minnesota is 32nd State... U.S. and China sign (June 18) treaty of peace,
friendship and commerce... Treaty is signed by U.S., Japan to open more
ports for trade... Gold is discovered some 90 miles from Pikes Peak...
Lewis Mill patents mowing machine... Charles Wesley March patents
harvester which bundles grain (becomes strong competitor of McCormick)...
Lyman R. Blake devises machine to stitch soles of shoes to uppers ... By
this time, due to high cost in printing catalogs to list books available
for reading, libraries in Boston, Philadelphia have established card
files for patrons... Harvey Brown, NY, receives first chainsaw patent...
"Sons of Vulcan" is formed as first U.S. union of iron, steel workers...
National Association of Baseball Players is formed... J. Mason patents
food preservation jar.

Business Events

Overland Mail Stage Co. completes first run from San Francisco to St.
Louis in 23 days and 4 hours, westbound stage reaches San Francisco in 24
days, 20 hours... Mathew B. Brady opens photography studios in NYC,
Washington... Dr. Edward Robinson Squibb, former director of first
laboratory at Brooklyn Naval Hospital in early 1850's, starts business to
supply reliable drugs to military... Pennsylvania Railroad acquires
interest in Pittsburgh, Ft. Wayne and Chicago line (acquires road in 1869
for linkage with Chicago)... After starting dairy in 1830's with earnings
as laundress, Margaret Haughery starts bakery business, New Orleans
(-1882, operates South's first steam-powered bakery, pioneers packaged
crackers)... Henry Varnum Poor proposes uniform annual reporting system
for U.S. railroads in American Railroad Journal (in 1860's provides
methodology to study productivity of various railroads and reports on
administration of British railroad system in comparison with military,
governmental bureaucracies)...

As a result of stockholder conflict in Pennsylvania Rock Oil Co.,
"Colonel" Irwin Drake is hired by Seneca Oil, CT, to drill for oil at
Titusville, PA (succeeds 1859)... Butterfield Overland receives
governmental contract to deliver mail from St. Louis and Memphis to Ft.
Smith, AR, to El Paso, Los Angeles, and San Francisco (travels 2,795
miles in 24 days, 18 hours, 26 minutes)... John D. Rockefeller, Maurice
Clark start commission house, Cleveland, to trade in grains, hay, meats,
and other goods (-1865 when Rockefeller sells interests to focus on oil
refinery business)... Prussian-born Joseph Getz starts general store
(starts overseas trading with trip to China in 1885, is acquired and
revived by wealthy Pritzker Family of Chicago in 1981 - by 1985 largest
non-commodity U.S. international trader with sales of some $500
million)... Cornelius Vanderbilt starts Atlantic shipping line to take

over government contract of "Collins Line" (sells fleet in 1864 for $3 million)... Thomas A. Scott becomes General Superintendent of Pennsylvania Railroad's western division (with protege Andrew Carnegie, mentor J. Edgar Thomson and Theodore Woodruff starts Woodruff Sleeping Car Co. in 1858, succeeds Thomson as President in 1874)... Brown & Sharpe machine business of Providence, RI, is contracted by Willcox & Gibbs Sewing Machine Co. to make sewing machines (uses manufacturing system of small arms factories to produce machines with American System instead of traditional job shop process)... R.H. Macy opens fancy dry goods store, NYC (succeeds with cash only, low prices and advertising, operates with 8 departments and some 400 employees by 1877)...

Benjamin P. Hutchinson opens small meat packing plant, Chicago (-1885, pioneers conversion of waste parts into profitable products)... First commercial wine in Napa, CA, is produced... Singer introduces light-weight "family" sewing machine.

1859

General Events

Oregon is 33rd State... John F. Appleby devises self-knotting mechanical grain binder... Prospector files claim in six-mile canyon of Nevada (becomes first U.S. major discovery of silver with mining of Comstock Lode, produces over $300 million in high-grade ore before depletion in 1940's)... At Philadelphia convention union of machinists and blacksmiths is first to demand 8-hour day... Virginia City is founded, NV, as Comstock Lode mining center (flourishes to 1870's, declines in 1880 when richest mine ceases operation)... New York creates insurance department...

George Jackson accidentally discovers gold at Pikes Peak, CO, when searching for food... National Molders' Union is formed (is reorganized in 1863 by William Sylvis as Iron Molders' International Union to become first stable factory labor organization).

Business Events

Annual Southern Commercial Convention meets in Vicksburgh, MS, to promote economic development of area (supports slavery)... Merchants Grain Forwarding Assn. is formed, Chicago, to improve distribution of crops... J.P. Morgan, employee for New York agent of father's investment business in London, makes first financial coup by selling coffee shipment in New Orleans without approval of superiors (although enraged, approve profitable transaction)... First horse street railway in Chicago appears...

First Pullman sleeping car is tested on railroad line between Bloomington, IL, and Chicago... Atchison, Topeka & Santa Fe Railroad is created by Cyrus K. Holliday (opens first section for traffic in 1869, expands from Kansas to Colorado, New Mexico, Arizona, and California by 1885 to operate 7,373 miles of track, declares bankruptcy in 1893)... Mormon millionaire Sam Brannan develops Calistoga, "Hot Springs of the West," Nappa Valley, CA, as health spa modeled on New York's Saratoga Springs... Machine-made blotting paper is made by nephew of John Slade, inventor of Slade's Original Hand-Made Blotting... Commercial school opens in Poughkeepsie, NY (registers some 4800 students in 1865)...

Henry Varnum Poor publishes comparative statistical studies of railroads in <u>American Railroad Journal</u>... German-born master brewer Henry Weinhard opens brewery at Ft. Vancouver (moves to Portland in 1860, merges with local Blitz Brewery in 1928, sells to Pabst in 1979)... Furniture manufacturing is started in Grand Rapids, MI... After being forced out of Mutual Life Insurance Co., Henry B. Hyde starts Equitable Life Insurance Society, world's largest in 30 years (-1899, innovates with training of salesmen, sales conventions, national sales organization and advertising, issues its first tontine policy in 1868)...

William Russell, partners start Leavenworth & Pikes Peak Express Co... Randolph B. Marcy: <u>Prairie Traveler, A Hand-Book for Overland Expeditions</u> (provides guidelines for organizing wagon trains)... Central Virginia Railroad reaches Mississippi River... Former farmer, frustrated miner George Hearst discovers gold, NV (evolves as multimillionaire by 1870's with interests in Comstock Lode, Utah mines, Homestake Mine in South Dakota)... Tailor Ebenezer Butterick uses patterns to reproduce garments in unlimited quantities (starts commercial production in 1863, publishes magazine to promote sales, sells some 6 million patterns in 1871, opens branches in London, Paris, Berlin, Vienna by 1876)...

Russell, Majors & Waddell freight business is re-financed as Central Overland, California & Pike's Peak Express, known as "Clean Out of Cash and Poor Pay" (starts Pony Express in 1860, declares bankruptcy in 1861)... George Huntington Hartford, age 26, buys shipload of tea from China, sells it at dockside for third of usual price (with success opens store, The Great Atlantic Tea Co., in lower Manhattan with George Gilman to sell imported tea at discount prices in bypassing wholesaler, opens 5 stores by 1865 and 11 by 1869 as The Great Atlantic & Pacific Tea Co. to sell coffee, spices, and groceries, operates 100 A & P stores by 1880 and almost 500 by 1912 from East Coast to Chicago, operates over 15,000 stores by 1930)... For first time baseball fans are charged admission, 50 cents each, to see Brooklyn play New York... NYC's Fifth Avenue is first hotel with elevator... Banking house of Ladd & Tilton, Portland, OR, is first north of San Francisco.

1860s

General Events

Molly Maguires, secret Irish-American society, is formed by Pennsylvania miners (-1875 when violence is exposed by Pinkerton agents and 10 leaders executed 1876)... Working Woman's Protective Association is formed... Irish-born Patrick Gilmore forms U.S.' first concert band, popular entertainment in Europe during 1700s with touring bands from Turkey.

Business Events

After opening Volney Palmer's Boston advertising office, Samuel Pettengill opens advertising agency, NY (becomes City's largest)... Master Car-Builder's Assn. is formed (sets standards for exchange of railroad equipment)... Chicago serves as hub for 11 different railroads... Some 2,000 oil wells, PA, pump 1,165 barrels of crude oil daily... Only 6 industries report employing more than average of 100

employees/plant, cotton textile industry averages 120 employees/plant...
U.S. vessels carry about two-thirds of U.S. ocean shipping, some 10% by
1914... Railroads hire press agents to place favorable stories in
newspapers.

1860

General Events

Massachusetts Institute of Technology obtains State Charter (opens
1865)... Population census records population of 31.4 million with 6.2
urban and 25.2 rural, NYC at 814,000 and Chicago at 109,000 (counts
immigration of 2,589,000 since 1851, shows 58% of labor force in farming
- around 50% in 1880 and 38% in 1900)... Gold is found near Leadville, CO
(-1862 with silver in 1875-80, copper and zinc in 1880's)... With men
earning $3/week and women $1/week with 16-hour days, largest strike prior
to Civil War is held in Lynn, MA, by some 6,000 - 10,000 shoemakers,
joined by others in MA, NH and ME (although failing to win union
recognition get higher wages)... War Department creates position of
Chief Signal Officer (forms Signal Corp in 1863 to use portable
telegraph, flag signaling in campaigns)... U.S. produces some one million
tons of pig-iron (makes 36 million tons in 1900 as world's No. 1 in
manufacturing iron and steel products)... San Francisco is first city in
West with rail-transit system, shifts to steam engines after horse-drawn
carts.

Business Events

Irwin P. Beadle & Co. publishes first dime novel... Pony Express mail
service is started between St. Joseph, MO, and Sacramento (-1861, covers
route in some 8 days)... Arm & Hammer mustard, spice business is acquired
by Church & Dwight (introduces popular baking soda in 1867, forms joint
venture with Armand Hammer's Occidental Petroleum in 1968)... Some 2,000
commercial banks, 149 savings banks, and 81 general insurance companies
operate in U.S. (expands to nearly 25,000 commercial banks by 1910, 2500
savings banks and 500 insurance firms by 1900)... Francis A. Pratt, Amos
Whitney start business to make precision machinery (incorporates 1869,
survives to 1980's)... J.P. Morgan resigns from New York office of
father's investment business in London (becomes new agent for London
house, reforms business in 1861 and 1863 with partners, participates in
dubious 1861 loan to enterprise with government contract to rifle
carbines - defective, buys $4 million in gold on margin with Edward
Ketchum in 1863 when Union military reverses push price up -possibly
attempts to corner market, ships 50% to England to make $160,000, forms
Dabney, Morgan & Co. in 1864-71)...

Hiram Sibley obtains government subsidies to build transcontinental
telegraph line (-1861, acquires American Telegraph Co. and its Atlantic
cable in 1867)... Charles H. Morgan devises first commercial paper-bag
machine, follows one operated in Bethlehem, PA, in 1852 (is patented by
Luther C. Crowell in 1867)... Ellen C. Demorest, former owner of
successful millinery business in Saratoga Springs, starts fashion
magazine, NYC (provides readers with dress patterns, mail-order
"purchasing bureau")... Henrietta Green receives $20,000 from aunt
(obtains $8,000 from mother's will and $1 million from father's estate in
1865, after 1874 invests in government bonds, railroad stock, real

estate, and speculations to amass some $100 million at death in 1916 by sensing when to enter, leave the market)...

In drugstore at Dutch Flat, CA, Theodore Judah learns of feasible route over Sierras (creates Central Pacific Railroad in 1861 with funds from Collis P. Huntington and Mark Hopkins, partners in Sacramento hardware store, Leland Stanford, wholesale grocer, and Charles Crocker, dry goods merchant, is ousted by partners in 1863 who continue   with Huntington to lobby Congress, Mark Hopkins as financier, Leland Stanford in California politics, and Crocker to supervise construction of transcontinental line).

1861

General Events

Kansas is 34th State... Jefferson Davis is elected (Feruary 9) President by Confederate Provisional Congress...   President Lincoln declares (April 15) state of insurrection (-1865, introduces first railway war, use of logistics, electric telegraph, canned rations, rifle, mass forces with small arms, and trench warfare)... Congress passes (August 5) first income tax to finance war, 3% tax on all income over $800 (-1870, 1894-1902)... Pioneering camp, Gunnery School for Boys, opens in Washington, DC, followed in 1881 by first camp for girls, CT... Samuel Goodale, Cincinnati patents motion picture peep-show machine... U.S. adopts world's first passport system... California Governor sends Colonel Haraszthy to Europe to gather cuttings for improving state's vineyards (imports 100,000 vines representing 1400 varieties of grapes, exports cuttings to restore European vines destroyed by disease in 1870's-90's)...

Elisha Otis patents steam elevator... American Miners' Assn. is formed as early industrial union... John P. Charlton, Philadelphia, copyrights the postal card, first picture postal cards appear in 1890's... U.S. Army creates first efficiency boards to review qualifications of all officers serving in volunteer regiments... Coleman Sellers patents Kinematoscope (operates with photographs on rotating paddlewheel)... War Department adopts new regimental organization (provides for staff personnel of quartermaster, surgeon, chaplain, and band)... U.S. Sanitary Commission provides psychiatric care, social services for military personnel... Galena is U.S.' first regular ironclad warship... Secretary of the Interior: The Eighth Census, Manufacturers of the United States in 1860 (lists cotton goods industry as No. 1, lumber, boots and shoes, flour and meat, men's clothing, iron, machinery, wooden goods, wagons and leather, shows 140,000 manufacturing firms with total investment just over $1 billion, almost double that of 1850, to become 2nd only to Britain in industrial output).

Business Events

Writing Paper Manufacturers' Assn. is formed... Jay Cooke & Co. banking house is founded (sells over $1 billion in government bonds during 1861-65 with extensive advertising, publicity to fund Civil War, specializes in selling government securities in 1866-69, serves as financial agent for Northern Pacific Railroad in 1869-73, opens London office in 1871, loses place as leading U.S. investment house by 1871 to Drexel, Morgan &

Co., fails in 1873 when Northern Pacific defaults on obligations)...

After acting as agent since 1848 for family's 1761 business in Germany, Bavarian-born John E. Faber starts pencil factory, NY (operates plant with over 1000 workers by 1917)... Adolphus Busch, owner of brewer's supply store with brother in St. Louis since 1859, marries daughter of German-born brewer Eberhard Anheuser, full partner 1874 (introduces popular light-colored Budweiser beer in 1876 - U.S.' first beer marketed nationally, incorporates Bavarian brewery as Anheuser-Busch in 1879 - world's largest by 1980's)... John Wanamaker, brother-in-law open Oak Hall Clothing Bazaar, Philadelphia, as men's clothing business (guarantee money back to dissatisfied customers in 1865, operate largest U.S. retail clothing business by 1871 with advertising)...

Philo Remington takes over father's armory (incorporates in 1865 with capitalization of $1 million, makes agricultural equipment in 1867 - abandoned in 1887 for lack of marketing, starts making sewing machines in 1870 - abandoned for lack of sales organization, contracts in 1873 to make typewriters of Christopher Sholes - acquires ownership later, introduces typewriters at Philadelphia's 1876 Centennial Exhibition, forms Remington Standard Typewriter Co. as sales organization in 1881 to sell 1,200 machines, declares bankruptcy in 1886 - sales organization continues as independent typewriter business)... Schrafft candy business is started, Boston...

Van Camp canning operation is started, Indianapolis... Solomon Gump starts business, San Francisco, to supply mirrors to barrooms, bordellos (becomes luxury store specializing in Oriental goods, is acquired from family in 1969 by Macmillan Publishing - by 1980's with branches in Houston, Dallas)... Charles Krug Winery, oldest continuously operated in California, is first located in Napa Valley, currently owned by Mondavi family... Ansell N. Kellogg starts newspaper syndicate, WI, to provide local papers with articles... Zoheth Durfee obtains rights of William Kelley's patents to make steel (fails to acquire Bessemer's rights for U.S., erects experimental plant to make pneumatic steel with cousin William F. Durfee at Wyandotte, MI, in 1862 - production 1864, organizes with partners Kelley Pneumatic Process Co. in 1863 as first large-scale U.S. producer of steel, develops first significant laboratory in industry - dismantled 1865, acquires Robert Mushet's patent for Spiegileisen as re-carburizing agent in 1864, joins Alexander Holley, operator of 1865 steel plant in Troy, NY, with Bessemer's rights for U.S., to form Pneumatic Steel Assn. in 1866 to control basic patents for making steel)... Andrew Carnegie, while working for Pennsylvania Railroad, invests in Columbia oil business (-1865, after becoming disgusted with disorganized petroleum industry sells interests after earning $1 million).

1862

General Events

President Lincoln signs (May 20) Homestead Act (allows citizens to acquire up to 160 acres by paying $1.25/acre and settling on public land for 5 years)... Congress passes (July 1) Pacific Railway Act (-1869 with linkage, UT, of Union Pacific Railroad from East, Central Pacific from West)... Morrill Act grants (July 2) land to states for establishing agricultural, engineering colleges... Congress creates Bureau of Internal Revenue... Gail Borden patents concentrated fruit juice... U.S. issues greenbacks as first paper currency... U.S.S. Banshee is first steel-hulled ship to cross Atlantic... Commissioner of Agriculture, previously under Patent Commissioner in Department of Interior, is established with 45 employees (becomes department with 560 employees in 1889, operates with some 3,300 employees in 1901 and around 25,000 in 1930)... Edwin M. Stanton becomes Secretary of War (-1868, administers staff bureaus of adjutant general, quartermaster general, surgeon general, judge advocate general, chief of ordinance, commissary general, paymaster general, chief of engineers, chief signal officer and provost marshal general, approves reorganization of Army of Potomac, 150,000 men, into corps of divisions, brigades and regiments)... Agriculture equipment manufacturer, Richard J. Gattling, previously invented rice-sowing machine, wheat drill and steam plow, patents 10-barrel, rapid-fire gun (perfects weapon to fire 200 shots/minute by 1865, is adopted by U.S. Army in 1866 but ignored, is superseded by Hotchkiss gun of 1872 and Maxim's 1883 invention).

Business Events

F.A.O. Schwarz fancy toy store opens, NY... William Perry builds modern plant for assembling standardized sewing machines for Wheeler & Wilson Mfg. (uses accurate, specialized machine tools, jib and fixture design, and guages to produce some 30,000 machines yearly)... Alexander Holley, first U.S. steelmaker of note, goes to England to study naval armaments (sees converter at Bessemer's Sheffield plant, acquires U.S.' rights of patents for Erastus Corning, associates in 1864, starts Rensselaer Iron Works at Troy, NY, in 1865)... United States Brewers' Assn. is formed... Brown & Sharpe Co., RI, builds first universal milling machine, used by makers of hardware, tools, cutlery, locks, etc., within 10 years... Oil Creek Transportation Co. is formed to ship oil by pipeline from Oil Creek, PA, to Erie Railroad (fails in piping oil over long distance)... Gordon McKay, started shoe manufacturing firm in 1860 to operate with government contracts during Civil War, starts leasing shoe machines to other manufacturers... William S. Ladd organizes Oregon Steam & Navigation Co. to monopolize Columbia River traffic (starts Oregon Railroad & Navigation Co. in 1879)...

Alexander T. Stewart moves retail department store business from 1848 Marble Palace to larger Cast Iron Palace, builds U.S.' first real mansion after Civil War (evolves as world's largest retail business in 1870 with some 2,000 employees)... John Hancock Mutual Life Insurance Co. is started, Boston... San Francisco Stock Exchange is created to raise funds for mining ventures... Wheeler & Wilson Co. builds plant to build 30,000 sewing machines/year, produces peak of 174,088 in 1872.

1863

General Events

West Virginia is 35th State... President Lincoln proclaims (October 3) Thanksgiving Day as last Thursday in November... Brotherhood of Railway Locomotive Engineers forms as first railroad union - mostly a mutual insurance society (lists some 55,000 members in 1960s, is followed by Conductors' Brotherhood in 1868 - some 20,000 members in 1960s, Brotherhood of Railroad Brakemen, later called trainmen, in 1887 - some

190,000 members in 1960s, and Switchmen's Union of North America in 1906 - some 18,000 members in 1960s)... National Banking Act establishes system of federally chartered banks in parallel with state banks (-1913 when replaced by Federal Reserve System)... Congress establishes National Academy of Sciences to advise government on scientific research...

Congress approves free city mail delivery... Texas passes blue law to prohibit business activities on Sundays, repealed for most forms of retailing in 1985... Virginia Penny: The Employment of Woman (lists some 500 occupations open to women)... Illinois, Minnesota pass laws to fine, imprison strikers preventing others from working... First union of federal employees is started by NYC letter carriers... Alanson Crane patents fire extinguisher.

Business Events

Cornelius Vanderbilt, after cornering market on bear raiders Daniel Drew, "Boss" Tweed and other NYC officials selling short, gains control of New York & Harlem Railroad (in 1863 acquires control of Hudson River line from NYC to Greenbush across river from Albany, starts investing in New York Central stock - president 1867, consolidates system from NYC to Albany by 1869, invests in railroads to gain control, stop stealing, improve assets, and consolidate with others to build system with watered stock and pay huge dividends)... First National Bank of New York is established... James G. Batterson starts Travelers Insurance Co. in Hartford, CT (provides first U.S. accident, health insurance)...

Pennsylvania Railroad is first U.S. line to use steel rails... Milwaukie & St. Paul Railway, chartered 1852, reorganizes (builds first grain elevator in 1864, extends line to St. Paul in 1867, Chicago in 1873, and Seattle in 1909, is operated by government 1918-20, reorganizes in receivership 1925, 1935-38)... Thomas Durant, developer of Union Pacific Railroad in 1862, and madcap adventurer George Train devise Credit Mobilier, modeled on French organization, to finance construction of Union Pacific across plains to link with Central Pacific from California, exposed in 1872 scandal to reveal $23 million in unaccounted expenses for Union Pacific and $63 million in excess charges by Central Pacific... Al Reach, Philadelphia Athletics, is first baseball player paid regular salary... Eliphalet Dennison of Massachusetts label business patents new shipping tag (opens Chicago store in 1868, starts foreign sales in 1875, adopts plan to sell stock to executives in 1878)... Philip Armour starts grain and meat business in Milwaukie (starts Chicago meatpacking house in 1875)... With retirement of Isaac Singer, I.M. Singer & Co. is dissolved and replaced by The Singer Manufacturing Co. with Edward Clark as general manager under stipulation that neither Singer or Clark will be president while other partner lives (-1875 when Clark is president to 1888, starts plants in Scotland in 1867 and Montreal in 1873 - by 1965 factories in 29 countries)...

Levi P. Morton starts private banking house, NYC (develops business as one of most powerful on Wall Street with political connections)... After operating grocery store and brewery, San Francisco, since 1856, German-born Claus Spreckles starts Bay Sugar Refining to process cane from Hawaii (by 1884 monopolizes sugar industry on Pacific Coast, starts invasion of East Coast market in 1888-89 when American Sugar Refining invades his market, ends market war in 1890 with creation of Western

Sugar Refining with American Sugar)... First National Bank of Chicago is chartered with capitalization of $100,000...

First railroad dining cars appear on line between Baltimore and Philadelphia, cars with kitchens in 1868... John D. Rockefeller, Maurice Clark start Cleveland oil refinery to process naptha, kerosene from nearby Pennsylvania oil fields (after selling produce commission business acquires Clark's interest in 1865, forms Rockefeller, Andrews & Flager in 1867 with capitalization of $1 million when unable to get funds from banks for expansion of refinery business)... Forming partnership to create Union Iron Mills, Andrew Carnegie and partners from Keystone Bridge (builds Superior Rail Mill in 1864 and Pittsburgh Locomotive works in 1866, assumes management of Keystone in 1865 after rejecting promotion of Pennsylvania Railroad, moves headquarters to NYC in 1868, at age of 33 considers retiring in 1868 with income of $50,000/year)...

Saratoga Springs, NY, site of watering spa for dyspeptic tourists seeking the cure, holds U.S.' oldest horse race meeting, follows first cited horse race in 1734.

1864

General Events

Nevada is 36th State... Post Office introduces money order... London-born Samuel Gompers joins cigarmakers' union (participates in union affairs with free time after cigar-molding machine is first used in 1869 - local president in 1875 to promote business unionism by advocating improved working conditions and better pay instead of social change, serves as first president of American Federation of Labor for 1886-95, when defeated by Socialist, and 1896-1925)... U.S. Army organizes Quartermaster's Department into 9 divisions: animals, clothing & equipage, ocean and lake transportation, rail and river transportation, inspection, forage and fuel, barracks and hospitals, wagon transportation, and records and correspondence (requires public advertising, competitive bids for centralized purchasing by each division)...

Cigarmakers, iron molders form unions... "In God We Trust" is first minted on U.S. coins... Ulysses S. Grant becomes Commanding General of U.S. Army (-1869, uses war strategy of complete conquest of enemy forces and resources to overcome tactical impasse of rifled weapons)... Frederick Walton patents linoleum, ruled generic name in 1875... Railway mail service is started... Contract Labor Law permits employers to recruit foreign workers for U.S. jobs (-1968, results in formation of American Emigrant Co.)... First Japanese Ambassador to U.S. is received in San Francisco.

Business Events

R.R. Donnelly & Sons Co. starts Lakeside Press, Chicago (evolves as U.S.' largest printing business by 1980s)... Carlton & Smith advertising agency is started (employs advertising pioneer J. Walter Thompson in 1868)... Scottish-born Henry Chisholm, after operating brick and iron businesses, starts Cleveland Rolling Mill, pioneers City's steel industry... After working as traveling match salesman, Ohio's C.P. Barber starts Barber

Match Co. (installs machines in late 1860s to replace traditional hand labor, joins competitors in 1881 to form Diamond Match which acquires some 85% of U.S. market)... National Association of Wool Manufacturers is created... Yankee Joseph Perham charters Northern Pacific Railroad to build line from Lake Superior to Pacific (plans to sell one million people each a share of stock for $100, gets double the land grants awarded to Union Pacific and Central Pacific, is financed in 1869 by Jay Cooke & Co. to reach Bismark, ND, before funds are exhausted in Panic of 1873 which leads to demise of Jay Cooke & Co., is revived by Henry Villard in 1881 with support of J.P. Morgan)...

American Iron and Steel Assn. is created... First U.S. salmon cannery opens, CA... Federal charters are granted to Union Pacific, Central Pacific Railroads (provides subsidies of $48,000 for each mile of mountain track laid, $42,000 for intermountain track and $16,000 for track on level land, grants Central Pacific 12 million acres and $27 million in mortgage loans and Union Pacific 9 million acres and $24 million in loans)... Chicago & Northwestern Railroad is formed by merger of Chicago and North Western, Galena and Chicago Union railroads... After devising printed parlor games, such as The Checkered Game of Life, during Civil War when his railroad business was poor, Milton Bradley, partners start business to make, sell games (develops "The Wheel of Life" as scientific toy for showing moving images, reorganizes in 1878 as Milton Bradley Co.)...

After working with a circus and father peddling tinware, Jim Fisk is hired by Boston's Jordan & Marsh store to supervise its wholesale business (forms successful Boston syndicate to buy cotton with fall of New Orleans - squanders profits on New York stock market, opens NYC brokerage firm in 1866 - acts as undercover agent for Daniel Drew's operations, introduces Jay Gould to Drew in 1867, becomes officer of Erie Railroad in 1868 after joining Drew and Gould to defeat Cornelius Vanderbilt in stock battle)... Elgin National Watch Co. is started, IL (produces its first low-priced watch in 1880)... After first dry goods store in Portland, OR, failed to prosper, German-born Aaron Meier opens new retail business, joined by Emil and Sigmond Frank in 1870 to operate as Meier & Frank in 1875... Copper lode is found on upper Michigan peninsula, worked by Indians for centuries and white men since 1840s (results in Quincy A. Shaw, Boston investors forming Calumet & Hecla Mining to produce 50% of U.S. copper output in 1871).

1865

General Events

General Lee surrenders (April 8) to General Grant at Appomattox Court House, VA... Congress mandates free delivery of mail in larger cities... General Robert E. Lee becomes president of Washington College, named Washington & Lee later (-1870, starts "Student's Business School" for study of bookkeeping, business forms and procedures in 1868, proposes formation of commerce department in 1869 to study mathematics, bookkeeping, penmanship, commercial correspondence, geography, technology, commercial law, commercial economy, commercial history, modern languages - not implemented with death in 1870)... J.F., J.H. Gordon invent twine binder, patent in 1873)... James H. Nason, MA, patents coffee percolator... George Westinghouse patents rotary steam engine (invents air-brake for railroad cars in 1869 - 134 patents in 1880-90)...

Mild post-Civil War Depression begins (-1867)... Treasury Department creates Secret Service Agency to combat counterfeiting... Metallurgist James B. Elkington develops process, basically electroplating, for refining copper... First U.S. patent for oil stove is granted, follows use of oil and gas as fuels by China in 1000s... According to local papers, German-born clockmaker Jacob Brodbeck crashes, insufficient power, in testing airship with 2 counter-rotating propellers at San Antonio, TX... England's Henry Bessemer gets U.S. patent for steel-making process.

Business Events

National Association is created by 91 baseball clubs... With $100 saved from mining at Pike's Peak, John B. Stetson starts hat business, Philadelphia (achieves success with felt hat for wear in bad weather on frontier)... Edmund McIlhenny plants chili peppers for tobasco sauce on Louisiana's Avery Island (opens London office in 1872 for European business)... Ft. Wayne, IN, druggist Joseph C. Hoagland concocts Royal Baking Powder (uses picture of product in advertisements in 1870s, budgets $600,000/year for newspaper ads in 1890s as U.S.' largest advertiser of period)... Benjamin Altman opens dry goods store, NYC (opens Palace of Trade in 1876)...

William R. Grace retires from partnership in Peru chandlery business (leaves Peru affairs with brother Michael, liquidated around 1876, to visit Europe, starts W.R. Grace & Co., NYC, as agent for Peruvian business, trades arms to Peru for 1879-84 nitrate war with Bolivia and Chile, opens branch house in Chile in 1881, enters Peru's sugar industry in 1882 to operate almost 40,000 acres by death in 1904, acquires war bonds to gain property rights in Peru with Grace Contract in 1889 to receive concessions on guano and nitrate resources, assumes Peru's national debt in 1890 in return for concessions in silver mines, guano deposits and 5 million acres, starts New York & Pacific Steamship Co., becomes Grace Steamship Co. later, in 1891)... After serving as head of Union's Secret Service, Allan Pinkerton reopens private detective agency (opens branches in England and France, starts regular anti-union activities in 1877)...

Collis P. Huntington with Mark Hopkins, Charles Crocker and Leland Stanford create Southern Pacific Railroad (extend line to Los Angeles in 1876, reach New Orleans in 1884)... Henry P. Kidder reorganizes Boston banking house of John E. Thayer and Brother as Kidder, Peabody & Co. when Thayer retires (finances Atchison, Topeka & Santa Fe Railroad in 1870-88)... Union Stockyards, world's largest with 345 acres, is opened in Chicago by 9 railroads...

Daniel Drew buys small Connecticut railroad from Jay Gould to start alliance... San Francisco Examiner, San Francisco Chronicle newspapers are published... Samuel Van Syckel builds first oil pipeline, idea of Gen. S.D. Karns in 1860, in Pennsylvania to transport oil 5 miles (is acquired in 1877 by Standard Oil)... Philip D. Armour makes quick trip from Milwaukie to NYC to sell pork short (nets some $2 million, uses profits to start pork packing plant in 1868, pioneers use of waste products, moves to Chicago in 1875)...James Fisk, agent for Daniel Drew, sells run-down steamship line to Boston investors... First "Long-Drive" of Texas cattle is made to Sedalia, MO... First cold-storage facility in NYC is built... Tony Pastor opens Opera House to provide public entertainment, NYC (opens American Theatre in 1881 to present variety shows)... North Chicago Rolling Mill produces first U.S. railroad rails with Bessemer steel process... Former Sheriff William Butterfield starts business, CA, selling surplus goods of sailing ships (evolves as Butterfield & Butterfield auction business of San Francisco)...

Some 50 Chinese are hired as temporary workers by Union Pacific Railroad to replace Irish workers threatening to strike (uses professional labor contractors to recruit Chinese workers from Canton area to employ some 6,000 by 1866)... American Trading Co. of Borneo is granted land by Sultan of Brunei (fails to develop concession)... First U.S. artificial ice plant is built in New Orleans... After disposing of family's interest in Slaterville mills in 1849, Slater and Sons is incorporated with $500,000 by Horatio Slater to make broadcloth, doeskins and woolen goods (is operated by Horatio N. Slater, III in 1928, changes output to fine rayon products in 1934)...

Atlanta druggist John S. Pemberton starts selling "French Wine Cola - Ideal Nerve and Tonic Stimulant" to cure headaches, sluggishness, indigestion and hang-overs (registers trademark in 1885, mixes first Cocoa-Cola syrup with caffeine instead of cocaine in 1886)... Andrew Carnegie takes over Union Iron Mills with brother, partners... James J. Hill starts freight forwarding business in St. Paul, MN (contracts in 1867 to furnish oil to St. Paul & Pacific Railroad, starts Red River Transportation in 1870 to ship goods to Winnipeg, with partners purchases bankrupt St. Paul & Pacific in 1878 to revive and extend line to Montana by 1887 and Seattle by 1893)... Georgia Minstrels, first successful minstrel company in entertainment industry, is formed... Seth Milliken opens dry-good store, ME (expands into manufacturing, evolves by 1980s as billion-dollar business in textiles, stores, forest land).

1866

General Events

Congress authorizes (May 16) "Nickle coin"... Congress imposes (July 1) a 10% tax on all state bank notes to establish national currency... National Labor Congress meets in Baltimore with delegates from 50 trade unions and trade assemblies, 8-hour league and various reform societies (forms National Labor Union with William Sylvis as President - as President of Molders Union tried to establish cooperative foundries, is joined by Women's Sufferage Organization in 1868, records membership of some 600,000 by 1868, is joined by blacks in 1869, disintegrates in 1872 after unions drop out in 1871)... National Union of Business Colleges is created... Congress passes Mineral Land Act, first law to regulate extractive industries (enacts Mining Act and Timber Cultural Act in 1873, Desert Land Act in 1877, and Timber and Stone Act in 1878)... Hiriam Maxim patents, first of 122 U.S. and 149 British patents by death in 1916, curling iron (others: locomotive headlight, automatic sprinkler, fire extinguisher, electrical pressure regulator, and automatic machine gun)... Halcyon Skinner patents spelling machine... General strike for 8-

hour day is held in number of cities... Western Health Reform Institute is opened in Battle Creek, MI, by Seventh-Day Adventists (names Dr. J.H. Kellogg medical superintendent in 1876 who develops health foods and granola cereals to improve diet)... After 3 failures in 1857-58 merchant Cyrus W. Field completes laying trans-Atlantic telegraph cable, awarded gold medal by Congress in 1867 (is followed in 1956 by first telephone cable and first fiber optics cable in mid-1980s).

Business Events

Crane Co. starts pioneering medical department for employees... Henry Steinway builds Steinway Hall, includes retail business, warehouse, offices, and concert auditorium, in NYC (innovates by placing piano banks in major cities for pianists and by sponsoring touring artists, is acquired in 1972 by CBS)... German-born Jacob H. Schiff is licensed as New York broker (forms firm 1867-72, marries daughter of Solomon Loeb of Kuhn and Loeb banking firm in 1875, gets full partnership in 1885, finances Eastern railroads in late 1800's and industrial corporations in early 1900's)... Western Union absorbs 1865 United States Telegraph and American Telegraph enterprises with capital from Vanderbilts to form one national system (operates with 4 regional general superintendents supervising some 33 divisions with over 3,219 stations)...

Weed Sewing business is formed (hires Sharp's Rifle Mfg. to produce machines, starts own manufacturing in 1875 with processes, techniques borrowed from firearms industry)... Atlantic Storage Co. is founded (is acquired by Standard Oil in 1874 to become Atlantic Refining, is Atlantic Richfield in 1966)... National Board of Fire Underwriters is formed... After previously purchasing Central Overland California & Pikes Peak Express, Ben Holladay acquires Butterfield stagecoach business to create practical monopoly of Western stage business (later in year sells operation to Wells, Fargo express business for $1.5 million in cash and $300,000 in stock)... Charles Goodnight, Oliver Loving pioneer cattle trail from Texas to Denver, in period to 1886 over 10 million cattle roam western ranches employing some 40,000 cowboys...

Metropolitan Life Insurance Co. is formed... Thomas R. Bard, financed by Thomas Scott of Pennsylvania Railroad, discovers oil, CA (abandons project for lack of market, becomes wealthy after acquiring Spanish land grants with Scott in 1866-96)... Margaret L.A. Forge, hired in 1862 as bookkeeper by cousin Rowland H. Macy, becomes superintendent of his fancy dry goods business, NYC, recognized as first woman retailing executive... Ben Holladay acquires Oregon and California Railroad (is acquired after default in 1873 Panic by Henry Villard, agent for German bondholders)... Jack Daniel distillery, TN, is oldest registered in U.S.

1867

General Events

Nebraska is 37th State... Alaska is acquired (March 30) from Russia for $7,200,000 (results in fur industry becoming government monopoly)... Patrons of Husbandry is created as secret society for farmers (enrolls 858,000 members in Grange movement by 1873)... Horatio Alger: <u>Ragged Dick</u> (in first of 100 books to sell 20-25 million copies advocates success result of clean living, hard work, and good luck)... Thousands of workers march in Chicago to support new State law requiring 8-hour work day... Massachusetts is first state to pass factory inspection act, followed by NJ, WI in 1883... After perfecting machines for addressing newspapers and numbering tickets, Christopher Sholes, assisted by Carlos Glidden, devises a typewriter (obtains patent in 1868, sells rights to James Dinsmore, George Washington Yost for about $12,000, who resell rights to E. Remington & Sons for first production in 1873 - some 4,000 sold 1874-78)... Tenure of Office Act prevents President in removing appointed officials (-1926)... Gold is discovered, WY... Shoemakers form Knights of St. Crispin as national craft union... Miners' Union is formed by workers at Comstock Lode to protest cuts in $4 daily wage with declining profits (call strike in 1869, win 8-hour day in 1872)... New York builds elevated railroad for steam trains (-1871, leads to Chicago's elevated in 1893)... William D. Hunt, NY, and Lucien B. Smith, OH, independently patent ideas for barbed-wire fencing - impractical (is improved by Michael Kelly, NYC, in 1868 and Joseph F. Glidden, IL, in 1873).

Business Events

Baltimore merchant Johns Hopkins, wealth acquired as commission merchant, banker, shipowner, and stockholder of B. & O. Railroad, founds graduate-level university, modeled on German universities... Modern law firm of Milbank, Tweed, Hadley & McCloy is founded (evolves by advising Rockefeller interests to operate 300-member business with expertise in global finance in 1980's)... Chisolm Trail is pioneered by cattle rancher Jesse Chisolm from Canadian River, TX, to Central Kansas, used by over one million head by 1872... With retirement of Potter Palmer, his retail and wholesale dry goods business is acquired by Marshall Field and Levi Leiter, resigns in 1881 in belief that wholesaling not retailing was business to pursue, with partners to develop City's major department store... Mathilde C. Weil is hired by New York advertising business (starts own agency later to pioneer role of women in industry)...

Canning business is started in Portland, MA, by Burnham, formerly supplier of canned meats, provisions to Union Army 1861-65, and Morrill (starts with corn and meat products before adding lobsters, clams, and other items, introduces popular B & M Brick Oven Baked Beans in 1927)... Hungarian-born Morris Rich opens retail dry goods store in Atlanta, GA (evolves as Rich's Department Store)... Bavarian-born wholesale grocer Lewis Gerstle, broker Louis Sloss and partners acquire rights and privileges of Russian-American Fur Co. (form Alaska Commercial Co., acquire exclusive rights to hunt seals on Alaskan islands - must provide sustenance and schools for Aleuts, develop San Francisco-Alaska steamship line)...

In Philadelphia, Francis W. Ayer starts pioneering advertising business of N.W. Ayer & Son with father, bookkeeper and $25 (does $15,000 worth of business first year - U.S. leader by 1877 with branches in NYC, Boston, Chicago, and San Francisco, after soliciting ads for newspapers innovates by representing advertisers, mostly patent medicines, in 1875, pioneers market research in 1879 - some newspapers may have used readership surveys as early as 1824, publishes The American Newspaper Annual as reference book for advertisers in 1880, acquires National Biscuit Co. account in 1899 to create trademarks of Uneeda, Nabisco to pioneer packaged crackers, cookies)... Charles Pratt starts oil refinery on Long

Island (builds model tenement for workers, sells business to J.D. Rockefeller in 1874)... Samuel N. Inman opens cotton commission house in Atlanta, world's largest by 1890's... Physician and real estate investor Benjamin F. Goodrich acquires Hudson River Rubber business (with inducements from Akron moves business to Ohio in 1870 to escape competition)... Elisha Selchow takes over cardboard box business, NYC (as creditor acquires toy jobbing business, including trademark for game of Parcheesi, of Albert Swift in 1870, forms Selchow & Righter in 1880 with former employee of Swift to achieve success with Sliced Animal Puzzles and 1889 Pigs in Clover game)... Southern Pacific Railroad opens temporary hospital, first U.S. permanent company hospital in 1869... Air-chilling system of Dr. P. Henry of San Antonio is used on steamship <u>Agnes</u> to transport frozen beef from Texas to Florida (in 1879, after several failures, is followed by successful shipment of frozen meat from Australia to Britain with Gorrie's system)...

Cornelius Vanderbilt acquires control of New York Central Railroad by forcing drop in Central's stock prices when his Hudson River line is "unable" to deliver passengers to Central's depot in Albany from NYC (expands and consolidates system by acquiring 3 railroads with watered stock, acquires Lake Shore and Michigan Southern Railroads to reach Chicago in 1869, adds Michigan Central and Canadian Southern Railroads in 1875)...

In trial of competing horse-powered reapers, Champion, pulled by inventor W. Whitely of Springfield, OH, is declared winner (after building first reaper at age of 20 starts firm at 21 with Swiss-born machinist F. Fassler and funds from O. Kelly's California gold-rush fortune, produces more farm machinery by 1880 than all Chicago factories in world's 2nd largest plant under one roof - largest at Krupp works in Prussia, after losing $4 million from bad loan sells business to International Harvester in 1902 to pay creditors, dies broke in 1911)... After perfecting sleeping car in 1863, George Pullman forms Pullman Palace Car Co., Chicago (introduces dining car in 1868, chair car in 1875, vestibule car in 1887)... Amusement park opens outside Boston...

Pennsylvania Steel Co., designed by Alexander Holley, is built in Steelton as first significant Bessemer plant (adds rail mill in 1868 and laboratory in 1870)... With idea of Lloyd Tevis, Charles Crocker starts Pacific Union Express business as exclusive contractor for handling mail, bullion of Central Pacific Railroad (sells rights to Wells, Fargo, controlled by Lloyd Tevis, in 1869 for $5 million)... J.W. Power opens general store at Fort Benton, MT, to outfit miners for gold rush (develops Benton Transportation to monopolize upper Missouri River traffic in 1900's with stagecoaches, mule trains, and steamboats)... With contract from Hannibal & St. Joseph Railroad promoter Joseph McCoy develops Abilene, KS, as cattle boomtown, used as terminus by Kansas-Pacific Railroad for shipping cattle to Eastern markets... Retired merchants Abraham Kuhn and Solomon Loeb open NYC investing banking business, Kuhn, Loeb & Co. (finances Chicago & Northwestern in 1867 and Pennsylvania in 1885, take in Jacob Schiff as partner in 1885 - Otto Kahn in 1897, finance Chicago, Milwaukie & St. Paul road in 1885 - 12 more lines to 1929)...

Saratoga Springs, NY, hosts first running of Belmont Stakes... Amish start Eagle Shirt business in Quakertown, PA... Welch Foods is formed as

marketing arm of National Grape Co-operative Assn. in Concord, MA...
James Gordon Bennett, Jr., takes over father's New York Herald (boosts
circulation with Henry M. Stanley's expedition to find David Livingston
in 1879-81 and Nelly Bly's trip around the world in 1889-90, helps form
Commercial Cable in 1883 to handle European dispatches).

1868

General Events

Congress enacts (June 25) 8-hour day for government employees... Alabama,
Florida, Georgia, Louisiana, North Carolina, South Carolina are
readmitted to Union, Texas in 1870... China, U.S. sign treaty of commerce
and friendship (protects right of Chinese, Whites to migrate freely from
one country to another)... Trades Union Congress forms (evolves by 1980's
with 108 affiliated unions with some 11 million members)... Order of
Railway Conductors is formed... After working as telegrapher, Thomas A.
Edison is hired by Western Union's Boston office (invents automatic vote
recorder - abandoned with no market, applies for patent on stock ticker -
rejected as previously invented by Samuel S. Laws, resigns job in 1869 as
boss fed up with "flood of capricious inventions," forms partnership,
NYC, with electrical engineer Franklin Pope and James N. Ashley to make
stock tickers and telegraph equipment - purchased in 1870 by Gold & Stock
Telegraph Co., uses $40,000 from sale to start "invention factory")...

Territory of Wyoming is created... James Oliver develops new chilled-
steel plow for plains, patented in 1869... Massachusetts creates state
labor bureau... U.S.S. Wampanoag, designed by Benjamin Isherwood, is
launched as first Navy warship powered primarily by steam (despite
successful sea trials, operated at top speed of 17.75 knots as world's
fastest with innovative steam-propulsion system and hull design -
unequaled in performance by any steamship until 1879 and warship until
1889, is rejected for service in 1869 after political in-fighting among
admirals - claimed vessel would make life too easy for sailors used to
rigors of sailing ships, is converted to other uses)... First U.S.
sneaker shoe is developed, popularized by 1898 Sears Catalog.

Business Events

Libby, McNeill & Libby canning business is started to ship corned beef
from Chicago to Eastern cities... 1864 Carlton & Smith advertising agency
places ads in religious weeklies (branches into general and literary
magazines to pioneer field)... "Erie War" opens when Cornelius Vanderbilt
purchases stock in railroad controlled by Daniel Drew, Jim Fisk, and Jay
Gould in order to eliminate potential competitor for New York Central
line (suffers losses of $1-2 million when Drew, Fisk, Gould keep printing
new stock, after both parties bribe New York legislature negotiates peace
settlement - Erie reorganized with Gould as President, Fisk as Vice
President, and Drew as Controller until forced out when trapped by Gould
in bear raid)... American Merchant's Union Express Co. is formed by
rivals American Express and East's powerful Merchants Union Express,
William Fargo President (becomes American Express in 1873 to enter
financial field with money-orders in 1882 and travelers' checks in 1891,
operates 4,000 offices and 6,000 employees by 1904)... Manufacturer
Joseph Wharton helps form Industrial League of Pennsylvania as
protectionist lobby... John Dymond, New Orleans agent for NYC brokerage

house, buys first plantation - eventually owns over 10,000 acres to produce some 3 million pounds of sugar (starts movement in 1877 to form Louisiana Planter's Association)... Detroit meat packer builds early refrigerator railroad car (-1869, operates some 800 by 1885)...

Oliver W. Norton starts small plant in Chicago to make tin cans (with brother starts manufacturing tin cans in 1891, promotes use of cans for food preservation with business from Campbell Soup and Heinz, creates American Can in 1901)... Henry R. Towne becomes President of Yale Lock Mfg. (absorbs two competitors in 1878 and 1894, pioneers construction of cranes in 1878, reorganizes business as Yale & Towne in 1883, installs pioneering employee gain-sharing plan in 1884, promotes study of management in 1886 in address to American Society of Mechanical Engineers, employs some 5,000 workers by 1916 - 30 in 1868)... Saltry is started on Kodiak Island for salmon fishermen (becomes site for 2 canneries in 1878 to employ Chinese immigrants)... Underwood food business adopts Red Devil trademark, one of earliest used...

Hunkidori is introduced to U.S. market as pioneering "breath refreshener"... Cincinnati Red Stockings are formed as first professional baseball club (-1870, uses first uniforms)... Morgan Guaranty Trust, NYC, opens branch bank in Paris... Boston business interests form National Board of Trade as lobbying group... First U.S. commercial production of dynamite is started, San Francisco (is rejected by General Henry Du Pont as too dangerous)... Brigham Young founds Zion's Cooperative Mercantile Institution, Salt Lake City (advertises as "America's first department store")... Promoter Joseph McCoy stages Western extravaganzas, forerunners of Wild West Shows, in St. Louis and Chicago to sell Texas cattle to buyers... Strawbridge and Clothier retail business is started, Philadelphia (pioneers enlightened personnel practices)... Abram Hewitt uses first U.S. open-hearth process to make steel at Trenton works, NJ...

Deere & Co. is created to make farm implements... Studebaker Brothers Mfg. is formed in South Bend, IN, to make wagons, carriages (operates as U.S.' largest in 1870's - world's largest by 1900 with about 2,000 workers making some 75,000 vehicles/year)... John D. Rockefeller's refining business joins two other Cleveland refineries to acquire petroleum pipeline company and obtain preferential rebates for shipping oil from Erie Railroad (participates in forming Petroleum Producer's Association in 1869 to regulate prices, production of crude oil - ineffective by 1872)... F.M. Mowbray, UT, starts commercial production of nitroglycerin.

1869

General Events

Congress passes (February 24) Morrill Tariff to protect U.S. manufacturers... Public Credit Act requires (March 18) payment of government bonds in gold... Riots against Chinese workers are seen, San Francisco... Ives McGaffey, Chicago, patents "sweeping machine," first to use suction principle (is followed by J. Thurman's machine in 1899)... Colored National Labor Union is first national Black labor organization... William Semple, OH, obtains patent for chewing gum... Carbon paper is patented... Louisiana Lottery raises funds for economic development...

California workers riot against competing low-wage Chinese... Machine for washing clothes is invented... Labor unions hold national convention to seek ban on Chinese contract labor... Stuyvesant apartment building is first such structure built in NYC... Uriah Stephens, others organize Knights of Labor as small craft union of garment cutters (-1900, is succeeded by Terrence Powderly as Grand Master Workman in 1878 to become national labor organization, eliminates secret oath and rituals to appeal to Catholic workers in 1881, records over 70,000 members in 1884, after victorious strike against Jay Gould's Wabash Railroad in 1885 lists total membership of some 700,000 before dropping to around 100,000 in 1890 after unsuccessful walk-out against Gould's railroads and public outcry against anarchism of 1886 Chicago Haymarket riot)... Massachusetts creates pioneering Board of Railroad Commissioners to regulate industry... Charles Francis Adams, Jr., Henry Adams: A Chapter of Erie (exposes railroad scandals of Jay Gould, Jim Fisk).

Business Events

After serving as judge since 1859, British-born Thomas Mellon opens private bank, Pittsburgh (grants loan in 1872 to Henry C. Frick to develop coal and coke empire, advances $40,000 in 1872 to sons Andrew and Richard to start lumberyard - sold before Panic of 1873, accepts Andrew as partner in banking business in 1874 and retires in 1882 with Andrew in charge)... George P. Rowell publishes The American Newspaper Directory (as patterned on similar work in England provides circulation figures for advertisers)... California growers of deciduous fruit form association to obtain favorable railroad rates for shipping, fails within year...

Brewster & Co., New York carriage builders, adopt pioneering profit-sharing plan... Fruit merchant Joseph Campbell, ice-box manufacturer Abram Anderson start partnership in Camden, NJ, to can tomatoes, vegetables, and preserves (forms new partnership in 1891 with Arthur Dorrance to operate Jos. Campbell Preserve Co., introduces condensed soups of nephew J.T. Dorrance in 1897, becomes Campbell Soup in 1905)... Collis P. Huntington acquires control of Chesapeake & Ohio Railroad (builds Newport News, VA, as line's ocean terminus)... Charles E. Hires starts Philadelphia pharmacy with borrowed money (introduces soft drink with sassafras and herbs in 1875, promotes root beer at 1876 Philadelphia Centennial Exhibition, incorporates business in 1890 - sold to Procter & Gamble later, starts condensed milk business in 1896 - sold to Switzerland's Nestle in 1918)... Philadelphia retailer Marcus Goldman starts investment banking house, NYC (evolves as Goldman Sachs & Co. - U.S.' largest by 1980's with assets of $712 million)...

Manhattan retail store of R.H. Macy Co. adds departments of toys, silver and house-furnishings to those of dry goods, ready-made clothing, and menswear (adds books, stationery, soda fountain in 1870, groceries in 1873, china in 1874, women's and children's shoes in 1875, restaurant in 1878, and upholstery in 1880)... A.S. Cameron & Co., NJ, is one of first in U.S. to share profits with workers... With control of Erie Railroad, Jay Gould, Daniel Drew in collusion with Manhattan's "Boss" Tweed force Pennsylvania Bluestone Quarry to make them partners for access to Erie tracks (use same pressure to acquire interests in coal mines, railroads, ferries, etc.)... Dan Castello's circus is first to tour U.S. by train... George Westinghouse, Jr., patents air brake for railroad cars, (forms Westinghouse Air Brake Co., develops automatic brake in 1871 -

installed on most passenger trains by 1877 and required on freight trains by Federal Law in 1900)... J.P. Morgan's group wins armed battle for control of small New York railroad, Albany & Susquehana, over Jay Gould's side...

In seeking to win award from billiards supply house seeking an ivory substitute, NYC printer John W. Hyatt invents celluloid, world's first plastic (is used in late 1880's by Newark, NJ, Pastor Hannibal Goodwin for film, is introduced by George Eastman in 1889)... Jay Gould, Jim Fisk attempt to corner U.S. gold market, fail to bribe President Grant - Gould sells stock before market plunges on Black Friday... Construction of first transcontinental railroad is completed when tracks of Union, Central Pacific Railroads link in Utah... After successful operation during Civil War making arms, business of Francis A. Pratt, Amos Whitney incorporates (provides accurate guages, machine tools for large-scale production with interchangeable parts)... Donald McKay launches last clipper, _Glory_ _of_ _the_ _Seas_ (-1923, after voyages to San Francisco with grain, coal and lumber services Pacific whaling fleet, becomes floating cannery in 1911, floating refrigerated factory in 1913)...

Cornelius Vanderbilt's New York Central Railroad fights rate war with Jay Gould's Erie Railroad... Charles A. Pillsbury acquires share in uncle's small Minneapolis flour mill (forms C.A. Pillsbury & Co. in 1872 with father and uncle, builds innovative mill in 1879 to use Hungarian rollers in milling process, operates world's largest mill in 1883, after selling to English syndicate in 1889 becomes managing director)... H.J. Heinz, partner start business in Pittsburgh to make, sell horseradish (fails in 1875, restarts in 1876 with brother, cousin to make prepared foods)...

After seeing children chewing paraffin wax like candy, Thomas Adams, Jr., starts business with father to produce chewing gum on large scale (overcomes consumer resistance with different flavors and free samples with candy, introduces Black Jack licorice gum in 1870, forms American Chicle in 1899 with 5 competitors to control over 5 million acres of chicle land in Guatamala, Mexico, and British Honduras, sells to Warner-Lambert Pharmaceutical in 1979)... Albert Fink becomes General Superintendent of Louisville & Nashville Railroad (starts studies to determine real transportation costs of shipping goods, uses ton-mile as measure for unit cost - adopted later by all railroads as criterian for evaluating operations)... Wells, Fargo stagecoach business extends monopoly by taking over Charles Crocker's 1867 Pacific Union Express (loses control of operations to lawyer Lloyd Tevis and railroader Charles Crocker).

1870s

General Events

Japanese are recruited in Hawaii to work in California, some 200 by 1880... According to legend, C&O Railroad hires John Henry to drive spikes in building Big Ben Tunnel... West Coast tree-fallers use double-bit axes, two-men cross-cut saws seen in 1880's... Miners use Nobel's dynamite instead of black powder... Steam tractors appear on farms... Commercial process for tanning buffalo hides is developed (results in only some 1,000 buffalo left on range in 1886 from total herds of some 30 million)... Practical incubators, brooders for raising chickens are developed, followed by discovery in 1920's that eggs, broilers can be produced in confinement.

Business Events

Five NYC theaters present variety shows, new rage, with burlesques and musical comediettas... United States Hotel, residence of famous in 1870's-80's, opens in Saratoga Springs, NY (-1944)... Roll-top desk is built (provides lock on cover for security and cubbyholes for filing papers, records)... Carter's Little Liver Pills are made, NYC, as remedy for "headaches, dizziness, biliousness, torpid liver, constipation, and sallow skin".

1870

General Events

Congress passes (July 14) Internal Revenue and Tariff Act (although lowering some rates, removing some duties and eliminating excise taxes, maintains protectionist policy)... First federal trademark law is passed (grants first registered symbol to William Underwood & Co. of Boston for "Deviled Entrements")... First NYC subway line is opened to public...

Census shows population of 38.6 million, 9.9 urban and 28.7 rural, (lists 2,350,000 immigrants since 1861 and 14.6% of labor force as women with 930 in office jobs - some 386,000 women working by 1910)... James McPatrick devises first addressing machine... U.S., Britain sign treaty to suppress African slave trade... James Oliver forges cast-iron and steel plow... Machine for making pliable metal tubes is devised, used for toothpaste containers by dentist, CT, in 1892... Boardwalk is built at Atlantic City resort... First written contract between coal miners, operators is signed (provides sliding pay scale based on price of coal)... Metropolitan Museum of Art is founded, NYC (starts mail-order business in 1938 - 9 catalogs by 1988, operates with $6.98 million budget in 1970 - endowment 62.8%, membership 5.7%, gifts and grants 1.0%, city 29.2% and other 1.3%, forms Met's Business Committee and Corporate Patron Program in 1970s, with 2,200 employees operates in 1988 with budget of $65.5 million - endowment 16.6%, membership 14.9%, gifts and grants 15.4%, exhibitions 3.4%, merchandising 7.8% from publishing activities, educational programs and shops, admissions 10.1%, city 22.7% and other 9.1%).

Business Events

Pioneering prepared paint business of Sherwin-Williams is started, Cleveland (promotes products with money-back guarantee if not better than hand-mixed paints)... Scott's Emulsion, palatable form of cod liver oil, is prepared by New York druggist Alfred P. Scott, Samuel W. Browne (is viewed by 1895 Printer's Ink as world's largest advertiser)... Benjamin Babbit pioneers premium advertising in urging customers to exchange soap wrappers or labels for prizes... Andrew Carnegie starts Lucy Furnace to integrate production processes in making steel (despite ridicule of competitors hires chemist for product research, serves as Union Pacific director in 1871-72, forms new partnership in 1873 to build Edgar Thomson Works, by 1877 produces some 15% of U.S.' Bessemer steel)... After struggling with financially-troubled Hudson River Co. of New York, B.F.

Goodrich, granted loans from City for move, starts new rubber business in Akron, OH (reorganizes in 1880 as B.F. Goodrich Co. with first sound financing, followed in City by Goodyear Rubber in 1898, Firestone Tire & Rubber in 1900)... Northwestern, Rock Island, C.B. & Q. Railroads form "Iowa Pool" to share traffic between Council Bluffs, Chicago (-1885)... Will Cargill, brother build or buy grain elevators along Southern Minnesota railroad, financed by Milwaukee banks (buy elevators during Panic of 1873 to build grain empire, is sold to MacMillan family in 1916- $32 billion business by 1988)...

Chemist R.A. Chesebrough develops vaseline (starts business in 1875 to make vaseline, kerosene products)... William J. Palmer organizes Denver & Rio Grande Railroad... After working on Wall Street as office boy and clerk since 1862, E.H. Harriman opens brokerage house, buys seat on New York Stock Exchange with funds borrowed from uncle (repays uncle within year from business with such clients as Jay Gould, Commodore Vanderbilt, and August Belmont, starts investment banking firm in 1872, achieves first financial coup in 1874 by selling certain railroad stock short when "Deacon" White, renown speculator, attempts to corner market, loses profits to Astor interests during bear raid on Delaware & Hudson Railroad)...

John D. and William Rockefeller, Henry Flager, Stephen Harkness, and Samuel Andrews create Standard Oil Co. to operate world's largest refinery complex in Cleveland (acquire 5 large and 7 small Cleveland refining companies in 1871, join South Improvement Co., established 1871 by Thomas Scott of Pennsylvania Railroad, to pool oil shipments with other refineries - revoked by Pennsylvania Railroad after storm of protest from independent refineries and public, join other refineries in 1872 to restructure Petroleum Producers Assn. as National Refiner's Assn. - weakened by rise of new producers, acquire New York Central's oil terminal and shipping facilities in Manhattan in 1872)...

Potter Palmer opens Palmer House, Chicago's first luxury hotel... Arch Street Opera House opens, Philadelphia (operates as The Trocadero with burlesque shows in 1903-78)... Lyman Bridges' Chicago lumberyard use catalog to sell pre-fabricated structures for Western prairies... Pennsylvania Railroad President J. Edgar Thomson creates Pennsylvania Co. as holding enterprise, one of first in U.S.... James Phelan forms First National Bank of California (reorganizes later as Crocker First National)... After leaving Maine, William Deering starts agricultural implement business, IL, with partner Methodist Minister Elijah H. Gammon (acquires full ownership in 1879 to make twine binder of John F. Appleby, operates largest implement factory in 1880's with some 9,000 workers, joins competitors in 1902 to form International Harvester)...

Henry Hyde's Equitable Life is first office building with elevator... William D. Hoard starts county paper, WI (forms Wisconsin Dairyman's Assn. to pioneer State's industry, gets reduction in freight rates in 1873 and leases first railroad car to ship cheese to Eastern markets).

1871

General Events

After intense lobbying by Grangers and business interests, Illinois

Railroad Act forms (April 4) commission to set maximum rates for use of railroads and warehouses and forbid discrimination of corporations over small businesses, upheld by U.S. Supreme Court in 1877... Riots break out in Los Angeles, CA, against Chinese immigrants, lynch 15 workers in violence... Since not everyone can go to place of instruction, Methodists start pioneering correspondence educational program at Lake Chautauqua, NY (is adopted by business and correspondence schools)... Most of downtown Chicago is destroyed (October 8) by fire, results in 250 deaths and property damages of $196 million when purportedly Mrs. O'Leary's cow kicked over lantern (forces many displaced residents to move to Maxwell Street, starting its development as local pedestrian bazaar with push-carts, stalls, shops)... George Grant designs printing calculator...

Cattle drives to railroad collection points in Missouri, Kansas peak deliver some 600,000 head... U.S. whaling fleet of 33 ships is trapped, wrecked by ice off Northwest coast, AK... John C. Wilson devises first practical time-clock to record working hours of employees... Ralph Waldo Emerson: "If a man makes a better mousetrap, the world will beat a path to his door"... Industrialist Daniel Pratt founds Birmingham, AL (acquires Red Mountain Iron & Coal Co. in 1872 to develop City's iron industry - largest U.S. center for exporting pig-iron in 1898)... U.S. Supreme Court rules greenbacks, issued 1862, to be legal tender... Simon Ingersoll invents pneumatic rock drill... National Association of Professional Baseball Players is formed, NYC (-1876)... U.S. diplomatic mission, escorted by U.S. Navy's Asiatic Squadron, tries to open trade with Korea... Congress passes first U.S. Civil Service Act (-1875, creates commission to reform government personnel practices).

Business Events

Miriam Leslie becomes editor of <u>Frank</u> <u>Leslie's</u> <u>Lady's</u> <u>Journal</u> (develops publication as successful fashion magazine)... Alexander E. Orr, others reorganize NYC's produce exchange, becomes center for international grain trade... J.P. Morgan and Anthony J. Drexel of Philadelphia form Drexel, Morgan & Co. as investment banking business to challenge Jay Cooke's monopoly in financing operations of U.S. Government (-1893, participates in unsuccessful sale of $150 million of government bonds in 1873, forms syndicate in 1879 to sell New York Central stock overseas)... P.T. Barnum organizes circus as "The Greatest Show on Earth" (merges with James Bailey's circus in 1881, is acquired by Ringling Brothers in 1907)...

State insurance commissioners hold national conference in Manhattan to coordinate licensing, taxing policies (develop American Experience Table to establish uniform statistics for calculating risks)... New York Cotton Exchange is founded... Thomas Scott, Vice President of Pennsylvania Railroad, is President of four other railroads, Vice President of 12 more and Director for 33 other lines... C. Washburn's La Croix flour mill is U.S.' first to install innovative Hungarian process for milling flour with rollers... New Orleans Cotton Exchange is established (-1964)...

National Association, first professional baseball league, is formed by 10 teams (-1875)... Philadelphia and Reading Railroad acquires Philadelphia and Reading Coal & Iron Co. - by 1917 some 50% of State's total hard-coal output controlled by 4 railroads... H.C. Frick Coke business is started, PA, with Mellon financing (operates by 1880 with 1,000 ovens and 3,000 acres of land, is forced to accept Andrew Carnegie as partner in 1881)...

Aaron Montgomery Ward, after working for Marshall Field, starts small retail business in Chicago with partner (becomes official supply house of National Grange in 1872, issues first mail-order catalog, one page, in 1872, lists some 10,000 items in 240-page 1884 catalog - catalogs by Sears in 1888, L.L. Bean's outdoor wear in 1912, Swiss Colony's cheese business in 1926 and Harry & David's fruit business in 1936, generates annual sales of some $1 million by 1888)... Charles H. Fletcher purchases formula for Castoria, sold by Samuel Pitcher in 1868 (markets product as "pleasant and complete substitute for castor oil").

1872

General Events

National Labor Union forms National Labor Reform Party (nominates, February 22, David Davis for President and Joel Parker for Vice President)... First railroad branch of WMCA, founded 1851, opens to provide workers with recreation, entertainment (sponsors 118 branches by 1900)... Thomas A. Edison patents electric typewriter with single-element print wheel, used by IBM in 1961, for his ticker-tape machine... Engineer George B. Brayton designs two-cycle internal combustion engine (demonstrates model using coal gas for fuel at 1876 Philadelphia Centennial Exhibition)... Reformer Charles F. Adams, Jr., becomes first chairman of Massachusetts Board of Commissioners to oversee railroads (-1879, codifies legislation, becomes President of Union Pacific Railroad in 1884, is eased out in 1890 by Jay Gould, Russell Sage)... Income Tax is eliminated, revived in 1913 by Constitutional Amendment... Scottish-born David Boyle devises first U.S. ammonia compressor to produce ice for King Ranch, TX... Black inventor T.J. Marshall patents fire extinguisher... Former apprentice Terrence V. Powderly becomes President of Machinists and Blacksmiths National Union (is initiated into secret order of Knights of Labor in 1874, becomes Grand Master Workmen for 1879-93, advocates producers' cooperatives, trust regulations, currency reform, and abolition of child labor, lobbies for passage of 1885 Alien Contract Labor Law)... Congress passes law to forbid use of mails for "any scheme... to defraud, or for obtaining money or property by means of false or fraudulent pretenses"... First U.S. ski club opens at Berlin, NH.

Business Events

R. Hoe & Co., NY, starts pioneering formal apprenticeship program, followed by 12 others by 1910... Harry, Max Hart start Chicago retail clothing store (in 1879 are joined by brothers-in-law Levi Abt, replaced by Joseph Schaffner in 1887, and Marcus Marx in creating largest U.S. manufacturer of ready-made men's clothing - 38 factories in 12 states and 258 apparel stores in 1970's, launch industry's first national advertising campaign in 1897, introduce first tropical-weight suit in 1917 and first in U.S. with Dacron-Polyester and wool suit in 1953)...

German-born F.W. Rueckheim opens popcorn stand, Chicago (adopts name of Crackerjack in 1895, adds prizes to every box in 1912)... New York Central operates first electrically-lighted passenger car, followed in 1881 by first steam heating in cars to replace stoves, hot-water heaters... Cyrus H.K. Curtis starts publishing magazine People's Ledger (fails, starts Tribune & Farmer in 1879 with $2,000 loan from brother-in-

law, starts successful <u>Ladies'</u> <u>Home</u> <u>Journal</u> <u>and</u>   <u>Practical</u> <u>Housekeeper</u> in
1883, employs Edward W. Bok in 1889 as <u>Journal</u>'s editor, budgets $150,000
for advertising in 1890 and $200,000 in mid-1890's, acquires <u>Saturday</u>
<u>Evening</u> <u>Post</u> in 1897 - becomes world's largest-selling weekly, publishes
<u>Country</u> <u>Gentleman</u> in 1911)... Ellen C. Demorest starts the Women's Tea
Co. with Susan King (acquire clipper for China trade)...

Fur trader Norman W. Kittson, agent for Hudson's Bay 1861 steamboat line,
joins James J. Hill to combine steamboat operations on Red River (pledges
all assets with Hill, others in acquiring insolvent St. Paul & Pacific in
1878 to become wealthy)... Lewis Ginter starts tobacco business in
Richmond, VA (develops business with advertising to employ over 1,000
women making some two million cigarettes/day, sells interests to James B.
Duke's American Tobacco in 1890)... Samuel Noble starts Woodstock Iron
Co., AL (develops State's steel industry)... Louis Emery, Jr., owner of
Quintuple Oil in Pennsylvania, organizes independents as Oil Producers
Assn. to fight Standard Oil (organizes United States Pipeline in 1890 to
deliver oil of independents to Coast, establishes Pure Oil in 1890's to
market petroleum products of independent producers)... Enos M. Barton,
partner start Western Electric Manufacturing Co., Chicago, oldest U.S.
maker of electrical materials and appliances (reorganizes in 1881 as
Western Electric Co. with Bell patents)... National Refiner's Assn. forms
to regulate prices, production... Lyman Bloomingdale opens dry goods
store, Manhattan (joins Federated Department Stores in 1929, opens
gourmet delicatessan in 1948, opens first boutique in 1956 to serve
trendy "Bloomies")... U.S. railroads propose nationwide time zones to
eliminate confusion of scheduling trains, adopted by railroads in 1883...

The <u>Abilene</u> <u>Chronicle</u> requests all Texas drovers to go to other railroad
cities... In San Francisco two disheveled prospectors air tale of diamond
field discovery (start Great Diamond Hoax)... "Wild Bill" Hickok
presents "Grand Buffalo Hunt" extravaganza with Indians and Mexicans,
Niagara Falls... Gunpowder Trade Assn. is formed by industry
manufacturers to set prices, regulate production... Jay Gould is forced
out of Erie Railroad by insurgent stockholders with stolen, incriminating
records (after clearing $12 million by selling stock, starts partnership
with Russell Sage to acquire Western railroads)... Andrew Carnegie starts
building steel-rail rolling mill, designed by Alexander Holley (-1875, is
named Edgar Thomson Works after President of Pennsylvania Railroad,
employs Captain William R. Jones of Cambria Iron in 1873 as Master
Mechanic - General Superintendent of Daily Operations in 1889, appoints
William P. Shinn, former railroad manager, as General Manager to
coordinate operations for effectiveness with statistical data)...

New York <u>Sun</u> exposes Credit Mobilier scandal in financing Union Pacific
Railroad (reveals rake-off of some $23 million by T.C. Durant, Oliver
Ames and other stockholders, discovers Congressman Oakes Ames distributed
stock to congressmen to forestall investigation)... Daniel M. Lord,
Ambrose L. Thomas of New England open Chicago advertising agency (after
obtaining ads for Christian periodicals represent firms as clients in
1898 to realize $800,000 in billings, sell to former copywriter Albert
D. Lasker in 1912)... First Wisconsin paper mill is started by Kimberly,
Clarke & Co. to make newsprint from rags (evolves as one of world's
largest pulp and paper operations)...

German-born Frederick Weyerhaeuser starts Mississippi River Boom &

Logging Co., cooperative monopoly of logging operations in area (forms Chippewa Lumber & Boom Co. in 1879 in Wisconsin - world's largest mill, in 1900 purchases 900,000 acres of Far West timberland from James J. Hill's Northern Pacific Railroad for $5.4 million to start Weyerhaeuser Timber Co. in Tacoma, WA)... British-born Andrew Smith Hallidie, associates start cable-railway company, San Francisco (start service in 1873, is followed with City's 2nd cable line in 1877 by Mark Hopkins, Charles Crocker and partners, by Chicago line in 1881, Philadelphia line in 1883, and St. Louis line in 1886)...

Colonel Albert A. Pope starts manufacturing business in Hartford, CT, to make variety of products (sees British Smith & Starly bicycle at 1876 Philadelphia Centennial Exhibition, contracts with Weed Sewing Machine business in 1878 to make Columbia bicycle - start of U.S. bicycle industry, publishes Bicycling World in 1880 and The Wheelman in 1882 to promote use of bicycles, acquires Weed in 1890 to concentrate on making bicycles - operates 5 large plants with over 3,000 workers by 1898 to dominate industry, starts vertical integration in 1893, starts making electric cars in 1896, goes into receivership in early 1900's)... First U.S. borax is mined... Baker's Chocolate uses logo based in 1770 portrait of Viennese chocolate waitress.

1873

General Events

Coinage Act discontinues (February 12) dollar to establish gold-standard... Post Office issues (May 1) first one-cent postcards, use of picture postcards in 1898... Los Angeles becomes terminus for Southern Pacific Railroad, followed in 1884 by Santa Fe line to promote area to Midwesterners... After passage of Comstock Act to ban obscene materials from mails, morals crusader Anthony Comstock becomes Special Anti-Obscenity Agent for Post Office (creates New York Society for the Suppression of Vice, terrorizes publishers by arresting hundreds with questionable materials)...

Missouri miners form mine cooperative, pay royalty to owners for use of machinery (others: Cooperative Coal of Peoria, IL, and Summit Cooperative Coal & Mining of Bevier, MO)... Mark Twain, Charles Dudley Warner: The Gilded Age (encapsulates period of 1868-1900 with story of "Colonel" Sellers as seedy promoter with get-rich-quick schemes to highlight materialism, speculation, and corruption of era)...

Brotherhood of Locomotive Firemen and Enginemen is formed... Western farmers sell land when plagued by drought (starts consolidation of farms)... Black inventor Elijah J. McCoy patents first automatic lubricator for machinery... Joseph Glidden, Jacob Haish and Isaac Ellwood perfect barbed-wire in Dekalb, IL, to keep chickens from petunia patch (results in one patent to Glidden and Ellwood, acquired by supplier Charles Washburn of Washburn & Moen Mfg., MA, maker of women's hoop skirts, to produce 50 tons of fencing in 1874 and 44,000 tons in 1886, and other patent to Haish who loses rights on infringement suit in 1880)...

Thompkins Square Riot results when NY police charge radical labor meeting... Jesse, Frank and 5 members of James gang hold up first train near Council Bluffs, IA... Jacob Davis, Reno tailor, and Levi Strauss, proprietor of San Francisco dry goods store, patent pants with riveted pockets.

Business Events

Facing financial ruin in Panic, Lydia Pinkham and sons of Lynn, MA, concoct vegetable compound for female complaints with 19% alcohol (achieve success in 1880's with extensive advertising, reach yearly sales of $3 million in 1925, sell to Cooper Laboratories in 1968)... Austrian-born agriculturial equipment manufacturer John M. Kohler starts business, WI, making horse troughs for farmers (enters plumbing business with crude bathtubs in 1880's - exhibits bathroom fixtures in 1929 at Metropolitan Museum of Art, develops universal machine, powered by horses, for farm work - electrified in 1920's to eliminate need for storage batteries)...

Inventor-entrepreneur Hiram Maxim starts Maxim Gas Co. to develop gas lighting with partner (receives funds from NYC merchant A.T. Stewart, starts tinkering with electricity in 1876, creates United States Electric Lighting in 1878 to market inventions, applies for lightbulb patent in 1878 one day before Edison - loses court battle, provides first electricity for building in 1880 in lighting New York headquarters of Equitable Life Assurance)... Singer Sewing Machine business centralizes all U.S. manufacturing operations at large continuous-assembly plant to make standardized machines with interchangeable parts in Elizabethtown, NJ (builds large plant in Scotland, first there in 1867, in 1882 - by 1965 with factories in 29 countries)...

Swiss-born spice merchant Meyer Guggenheim, peddler and speculator during Civil War, starts lye business (sells out to invest in Hannibal & St. Joseph Railroad wanted by Jay Gould, uses profits from sale to start successful importing business in fine laces and embroideries, speculates with importing profits in 2 Colorado mines in 1881, with success enters smelting business in 1884 to dominate industry)... German-born Henry Villard is employed by German investors as financial agent for holdings in Oregon Steamship, Oregon & California Railroad, and Oregon Steam & Navigation Co. (organizes Oregon Railway Navigation in 1879)... Bessemer Assn. is formed by steel producers to share patents, territories... Minor C. Keith starts buying banana plantations, Central America (forms Tropical Trading and Transport business, London, to supervise banana operations, starts chain of stores, Costa Rica, to sell native products, merges interests with rival Boston Fruit in 1899 to form United Fruit, forms International Railways of Central America in 1912)...

Cornelius Vanderbilt builds New York Union Depot with underground viaduct, tracks for six railroads... Jay Gould purchases New York World to support schemes, causes (sells to Joseph Pulitzer in 1883)... Harper's Weekly illustrates "disassembly" line used in slaughter houses, created in Cincinnati and developed by Chicago packers... P.T. Barnum, self-styled "prince of humbug," opens Monster Classical and Geological Hippodrome, NYC, to house circus (becomes Madison Square Garden in 1879)... Big Bonanza mine is developed at Virginia City, NV, by 1874 makes 4 partners multi-millionaires... Adolph Coors, J. Schueler start brewery, CO, on trail to gold camps... William Sellers, manufacturer of machine tools, starts Midvale Steel with partner (increases business, employing 75 workers, to 400 in 5 years, sponsors pioneering research of

Frederick W. Taylor in 1880's to study work practices)... James E. Scripps starts Detroit _Evening News_, first U.S. tabloid (after brother starts Cleveland paper in 1878, builds chain of papers with philosophy of "God dam the Rich and God help the Poor," acquires United Press in 1907)... When Northern Pacific Railroad defaults on bonds, financial agent Jay Cooke & Co. declares bankruptcy (regains fortune and repays creditors by 1880's), starts 5-year financial panic with 10,478 firms to close by 1878 and over 20,000 failures by 1879 in global depression (forces 37 banks and brokerage houses to close on same day with Cooke, causes New York Stock Exchange, first time, to suspend trading for 10 days, results in 80% decline of membership in New York unions with use of blacklists, provides opportunity for Henry Clay Frick to earn $50,000 commission for selling small railroad - invested in coal-coke land).

1874

General Events

With pressure of Grange movement Wisconsin passes (March 11) Potter Law to regulate railroad freight rates, followed by Iowa on March 23... Massachusetts is (May 8) first State to adopt 10-hour law for women... Greenback Party is formed (November) in Indianapolis by mostly farmers who favor inflationary money over gold...

Social Democratic Workmen's Party forms to reform capitalism... Robert M. Green creates ice-cream soda, Philadelphia, followed by ice-cream cone at 1904 St. Louis World's Fair... As result of racial battles with Chinese workers, Cigar Makers International Union adopts first union label to identify its products, adopted by 5 other unions by 1890... Can opener is invented... James B. Eads builds steel bridge across Mississippi River at St. Louis (-1867)... H. Solomon introduces pressure-cooking process for canning foods, improved for mass production by A.K. Shriver of Baltimore... Black inventors Latimer, Brown patent railway car water closet... Franklin Wilson: _Wealth: Its Acquisition, Investment and Use_ (views work as form of worship)...

Socialists Labor Party is founded as product of 1864 International Workingmen's Association (starts Socialist Trade and Labor Alliance later to compete with American Federation of Labor)... Farms on prairies are devastated by hordes of grasshoppers (-1877)... After observing demonstration of phonautograph at MIT by Scott of France to produce sound waves, Scottish-born Alexander Graham Bell, applying theories of Oersted, Sturgeon, Faraday and Helmholtz, invents telephone to help deaf (demonstrates device in 1876)... Electric streetcar of Stephen Field is used in Manhattan (replaces horsecars of 1832)... NYC acquires old sloop-of-war for first academy for commercial mariners.

Business Events

R.H. Macy Department Store, NYC, holds first Christmas retail promotion... Seabury & Johnson business is created to make pharmaceutical plaster products with innovative India rubber base (evolves as Johnson & Johnson in 1885 to make individual surgical dressings with adhesive backing and carbolic acid antiseptic - idea from Sir Joseph Lister's speech in 1876, becomes world leader in medical supplies by 1980's)... Albert Fink: "Classification of Operating Expenses," _Annual Report_ of

Louisville & Nashville Railroad (aids in development of cost accounting)... Manufacturer Henry S. Parmlee sells first water-sprinkler system for fire protection... Bausch & Lomb optical business is started (supplies lens for first Kodak camera in 1888, obtains exclusive U.S. franchise from Germany's Zeiss Optical in 1888, patents iris diaphragm shutter in 1891)... Judge Thomas Mellon takes in son Andrew as partner in Pittsburgh banking business (retires in 1882 to leave business to Andrew, gives brother 50% in 1887, to continue family management of bank to 1967)... John T. Underwood joins father's business making typewriter supplies (acquires 1893 patent rights of Franz Y. Wagner's typewriter in 1895, makes first typewriters in 1897, builds complete plant in 1915 where 7,500 workers make 500 machines/day, merges with competitor Corona Typewriter in 1927)...

Wholesaler Isidor Straus, brothers lease department in R.H. Macy's department store, NYC, to sell china, glassware (after partnership with Macy acquire store ownership in 1893)... Standard Oil acquires NYC petroleum facilities of Erie Railroad to handle all petroleum shipments through City's ports (acquires largest refining companies in Philadelphia, Pittsburgh and New York in exchange for Standard Oil stock to control over 90% of total U.S. refining business by 1878, forces rival 1876 Empire Transportation Co., created by Pennsylvania Railroad, to capitulate in 1877, forms National Transit Co. in 1881 as combination of pipeline companies to fight attack of 1878 Tidewater Pipeline Co. on Standard's monopoly)...

Pennsylvania Railroad operates on some 6,000 miles of track, surpassed by only Britain, France... Albert Fink: The Fink Report on the Cost of Transportation (become basis for evaluation of rail operations by railroads)... With some $64 million acquired from Erie fraud, Jay Gould invests in Union Pacific (is forced out in 1882) and Kansas Pacific Railroad (sells later for profit of $10 million)... Western Railroad Bureau is created to stabilize rates between East-West railroads... Cooperative Barrel Mfg. is formed to supply flour barrels to milling business of Charles A. Pillsbury Co... R.H. Macy department store, NYC, creates mail-order department... Grand Union, world's largest hotel with 824 rooms, reopens in Saratoga Springs, NY, site of U.S.' biggest gambling resort, except for 1911 and 1912 bans on horse racing, from 1865-1930.

1875

General Events

Specie Resumption Act provides (January 14) for exchange of gold for legal tender in 1879... In treaty with Hawaii U.S. agrees to allow imports of Hawaiian products, mostly sugar, duty-free... Tariff Act raises (March 3) rates by 10%... U.S. joins international Universal Postal Union... "Molly Maguire's," secret Irish miners' group, is exposed when 14 leaders are tried for murdering mine owners, bosses (is abandoned with conviction and hanging of 10 leaders in 1876)... Pressure kettle is invented to provide reliable sterilization for canning... Oliver Dalrymple grows spectacular yields of wheat on land of Northern Pacific Railroad in Red River Valley, ND... Two Cornell University professors build U.S.' first practical electrical dynamo... First Kentucky Derby is held... Luther Burbank opens plant nursery, CA, to develop new strains of plants, vegetables, fruits.

Business Events

John F. Dryden renames 1874 Widows & Orphans Friendly Society as Prudential Friendly Society (provides first U.S. industrial insurance with idea from Britain, becomes Prudential insurance in 1878)... Bulliez ad agency is formed, specializes in newspaper advertising... James G. Batterson, founder of Travelers Insurance, starts New England Granite Works (uses labor-saving devices to increase productivity)... Frank Baldwin launches U.S. calculator industry, Philadelphia... Frank Peavey starts Minneapolis grain business (builds one of world's largest grain terminals in 1886, after extending operations to West Coast and shipping Oregon wheat to England starts Great Lakes steamship line)... After 1868 Corning Flint Glass business failed, Amory Houghton starts Corning Glass Works, NY (devises lightbulb for Thomas A. Edison in 1880, makes crafted Steuben glass in 1903, starts research laboratory in 1908 to develop Pyrex and Corning Ware)... German-born August Uihleim, brothers acquire 1874 Joseph Schlitz Brewery, founded in 1849 as Krug Brewery (uses advertising slogan "The beer that made Milwaukee famous" in 1894)...

Elegant 800-room Palace Hotel opens, San Francisco... Charles Goodnight blazes Goodnight Trail to herd cattle from New Mexico to Colorado (starts partnership in 1877 with John Adair of Ireland to develop J.A. Ranch, nearly 1,000,000 acres and 100,000 head of cattle, with systematized operations, forms first Panhandle stockmen's association in 1880 to combat cattle thieves and outlaws)... 1864 retail business of Aaron Meier in Portland, OR, becomes Meier & Frank (starts "Friday Surprise" sales every week in 1887, opens City's first women's ready-to-wear in 1893, starts Saturday night concerts in 1898, builds largest retail store west of Chicago in 1913 - first escalators on Pacific Coast, starts radio station in 1920, sponsors variety shows in 1932 to boost employee morale during depression, introduces charge-plate in 1946, opens first branch store in 1955 - first shopping center store in 1960, installs electronic data processing in 1963, sells ownership to May Co. in 1965)... The American Express adopts first U.S. industrial pension plan... Thomas Cusack starts Chicago outdoor advertising business (amasses assets over $26 million by 1924)...

Successful "99-cent" store opens in Watertown, NY (provides idea to F.W. Woolworth in starting variety business in 1879)... American Iron & Steel assn. is formed... Colonel Charles Conn starts musical instrument business in Elkhart, IN... Jay Gould acquires control of Atlantic & Pacific Telegraph business to compete with Western Union (develops new line as major system by 1877, starts to buy Western Union stock in 1877 which then absorbs Atlantic & Pacific, starts American Union with telegraph department of Union Pacific Railroad in 1877 when denied seat on Western Union's board by interests of Vanderbilt, Astor)... Southern Railroad and Steamship Assn. is formed by 24 Southern railroads to end ruinous rate battle, conceived by Albert Fink of Louisville & Nashville Railroad (inspires formation of Eastern Trunk Line Assn. in 1877)...

With $2,400 R.J. Reynolds starts small factory in Winston-Salem, NC to make chewing tobacco (markets 86 brands in 1887, sells most of interests to James B. Duke's American Tobacco in 1890, introduces Prince Albert pipe tobacco in 1907, regains tobacco business in 1911 with dissolution of American Tobacco by Supreme Court, introduces popular Camel cigarettes in 1913)... Michael Hickey stakes out gold claim on hill overlooking Butte, MT (after claim peters out is bought in 1882 by Marcus Daly's syndicate with George Hearst, discovering copper lode under claim form Anaconda Copper, world's largest producer of ore, in 1892, close in 1982 when prices fall)... New York Central train sets record of 37 hours in traveling to Chicago (drops to 16 hours by 1938)...

Pennsylvania Railroad employs chemist Charles D. Dudley to start laboratory to test, analyze materials from suppliers... Massachusetts wholesale butcher Gustavus Swift starts Chicago meat packing business (starts shipping dressed beef to East in 1877, uses refrigerator cars in 1881, installs continuous processing assembly in 1880's, starts building national network of branch operations in 1881, forms Swift & Co. in 1885 to open distribution centers in England, China, Hong Kong, Hawaii, Singapore, and Philippines, operates in 1912 with 30,000 workers in 400 cities, 4 continents)... John Wanamaker acquires old Philadelphia freight depot to start new retail store (opens Grand Depot in 1876 as large clothing store, uses most of first revenues for advertising, opens first store restaurant and starts mail-order business in 1876, starts specialty shops in 1877 to develop department store when local merchants refuse to lease spaces, promotes first "White Sale" in 1878, uses first full-page advertisements in 1879 - national advertising in 1882, starts mutual benefit association for employees in 1881, installs first department store soda fountain and elevators in 1882, acquires A.T. Stewart's old Cast Iron Palace in NYC in 1896 to open new store - abandoned 1954).

1876

General Events

Centennial Exposition opens in Philadelphia (displays telephone, bananas - a sensation, typewriter, mimeograph, casket and 2500 horsepower Corliss engine to symbolize power of technology)... Colorado is 38th State... U.S. wind-up alarm clock is invented by Seth Thomas Clock Co., CT... Alexander T. Stewart, New York's largest retailer, opens store in Chicago to challenge merchandising business of Field, Leiter & Co. (after price war liquidates business in 1882)... To eliminate dust causing his allergy, M.R. Bissel of Grand Rapids, MI, invents carpet sweeper with adjustable rotary brushes (leaves business to wife Anna with death in 1889, pioneers Shampoo-Master for home cleaning in 1950s, operates worldwide in 1980s with 1,600 employees)... Alexander Graham Bell patents telephonic device just hours before application of Elisha Gray for Western Union (forms Bell Association in 1877 with aide Thomas Watson, lawyer G.G. Hubbard, and leather merchant T. Sanders)... Charles F. Bush builds dynamo, several workable arc lamps... Congress passes law prohibiting merit assessment of government workers.

Business Events

William L. Douglas starts manufacturing shoes (advertises line of mass-produced, modestly-priced men's shoes with his picture, develops national chain of retail shoe stores)... After losing 1869-75 horseradish business in bankruptcy, Henry J. Heinz starts new business to make pickles, condiments, and prepared foods with brother, cousin (introduces ketchup, renames business H.J. Heinz Co. in 1888, advertises "57 Varieties" in

1896 - 57 selected as magical number, builds NYC's first electric sign in 1900, operates in 1919 with over 6,000 workers, no strikes, 25 branches and seed farms)... After working with Robison & Lake Circus since late 1850's, James A. Bailey tours Australia and South America with Cooper & Bailey Circus, formed after Civil War (after merging with Great London Circus to become 2nd largest after P.T. Barnum's Circus, forms Barnum & Bailey Circus in 1881, acquires Adam Forepaugh Circus in 1891 to tour world for some 8 years)...

Austin Corbin, associates form New York & Manhattan Beach Railroad (develop Coney Island as fashionable resort area)... U.S. operates some 11% of world's steel converters to produce 27% of world's output of Bessemer steel... U.S. National Baseball League is formed by teams in Chicago, Boston, Cincinnati, Hartford, Louisville, New York, Philadelphia, and St. Louis, followed by American Association in 1882-90 and American League in 1900... British Smith & Starly bicycle is exhibited at Philadelphia Centennial Exposition (launches U.S. bicycle industry)... C.C. Washburn, Charles Pillsbury organize Minneapolis Millers Assn., started informally in 1869... British-born Fred Harvey becomes restaurant manager for Topeka Railroad Depot (later manages all Santa Fe Railroad restaurants, employing "Harvey Girls," before becoming concessionaire for road's meal services handled by 47 depots, 15 railroad hotels, and 30 dining cars)...

Thomas A. Edison starts building industrial research laboratory, includes chemistry laboratory, electrical testing facility, machine shop and library, at Menlo Park, NJ (operates with team of specialists to invent telephone transmitter in 1876, phonograph in 1877, incandescent lamp in 1879)... Baseball player, manager Albert G. Spalding starts sporting goods business as side-line with brother and $800 (issues first catalog in 1876, joins business in 1877, issues baseball guide in 1878, capitalizes nationwide business in 1892 for $4 million)... Eli Lilly starts small business to manufacture drugs, Indianapolis (incorporates in 1881 to focus on prescription drugs instead of patent medicines, starts scientific division in 1886 and research library in 1891, forms botanical department in 1890 and biological section in 1914)...

George Hearst, partners acquire Homestake Mine in Black Hills (becomes industrial mining complex at site of perhaps world's richest mine to yield some $1 billion in ore)... Michigan Salt Assn. is formed... Vogue advertises St. Jacobs Oil as cure-all ointment for rheumatism (increases advertising expenditures to $600,000/year by 1881)... American Bankers' Assn. is formed... Canadian-born W.A. Burpee opens Philadelphia store to sell seeds, pigeons and poultry (becomes successful business with mail-order catalogs and truthful advertising, purchases large farm in 1888 to develop seeds and special varieties of vegetables, evolves by 1959 as world's "largest" seed-catalog and mail-order house, sells ownership to General Foods in 1970 - ITT in 1979)... Dutch-born Mary Ann Magnin, first woman in U.S. to own department store known as I. Magnin in 1880, opens lingerie shop for fashionable San Francisco ladies...

B.V.D. is registered as trade name for men's underwear... Edinburgh syndicate forms Prairie Cattle Co., pioneers such British operations in West (hires Murdo Mackenzie as manager, starts Texas headquarters in 1881 to supervise some 156,000 head of cattle on 5 million acres, CO, NM, TX).

1877

General Events

U.S. Supreme Court: Peik v. Chicago and Northwestern Railroad Company
(rules for Grange interests that state has power to regulate intrastate
and interstate traffic originating within its boundaries)... U.S. Supreme
Court: Munn v. Illinois (rules state has power to legislate warehouse
and intrastate rates to restrain railroads in gouging small or
independent merchants with high charges)... George B. Selden, patent
lawyer, develops two-cycle "gasoline carriage" (files for patent in 1879,
is granted 1895)... After 3rd wage cut is announced by Baltimore & Ohio
Railroad during Depression, first nationwide strike is started (July 14)
in 6 cities by Brotherhood of Locomotive Firemen and Enginemen (destroys
locomotives and battles anti-strike citizens, is supported by sympathy
strikes and violence by other unions - some two-thirds of rail lines shut
down, collapses with use of Federal troops and National Guard units -
results in placing of armories at major cities to make troops accessible
for future strikes and violence, adopts union resolution in 1877 to
forego future strikes for arbitration)...

Tombstone is settled, AZ, with discovery of silver in area... While
operating pottery business Frank Norton patents grinding wheel (sells
rights to Norton Emery Wheel Co. in 1885)... Charles B. Withington
invents wire bailer... Society of American Artists is formed by sculptor
Augustus Saint-Gaudens, fellow artists to promote mutual interests...
George Westinghouse, Jr., invents automatic telephone exchange, rejected
until other patents had expired... Elihu Thomson invents electric
resistance welding to automate one of blacksmith's most difficult tasks,
followed by carbon arc-welding of Russian N.V. Bernardus and Charles
Picard's oxyacetylene blowtorch in 1904... After some 10 years of
research, Thomas A. Edison patents phonograph (is followed in 1885 by
Graphophone of Alexander Graham Bell and Charles S. Tainter - produced by
Columbia Phonograph in 1896, and Gramophone of German-born Emile Berliner
in 1888 - produced by Victor Talking Machine in 1901).

Business Events

John Thompson founds Chase National Bank of New York (merges in 1930 with
Equitable Trust owned by John D. Rockefeller, Jr., merges in 1955 with
Bank of Manhattan, nation's 15th largest with 67 branches, to become
City's largest bank, loses lead to aggressive Citibank during 1970's)...

California grower William Wolfskill ships first lot of oranges to East by
railroad (takes 30 days for delivery)... Civil War profiteer, land
developer William Engemann builds Brighton Beach Hotel on Atlantic
seashore (starts development of Brooklyn ocean resort)... Union members
attack Chinese immigrants in San Francisco... Joel Tiffany patents first
successful refrigerator railroad car... Charles Francis Adams, Jr.:
Railroads: Their Origin and Problems, first comprehensive study of
railroads (recommends confederation of lines and government
regulation)...

Alexander Graham Bell, partners form Bell Telephone Assn. (extends
service from Boston to NYC and New Brunswick, NJ, over leased wires of

Western Union - fail to sell all patent rights to Western Union for
$100,000, employs Theodore M. Vail, General Superintendent of Railway
Mail Service, as General Manager in 1878 for influential contacts in
Washington, settles patent suit, one of over 600 against Western Union
who had hired Thomas A. Edison to develop another instrument, in 1879 to
acquire Western Union's 56,000 customers and all rights for $7 million,
reorganizes in 1880 as American Bell Telephone, starts American
Telephone & Telegraph in 1885 as subsidiary for operating long-distance
lines, reorganizes assets in 1899 as AT&T)... Quaker Mill of Ravenna, OH,
adopts Quaker Oats trademark, first breakfast cereal registered...

German-born David May starts retail business in Leadville, CO (evolves as
May Department Stores by 1978, with 148 stores, 17 major shopping
centers, trading stamp business, 70 catalog showrooms to achieve sales
over $2 billion, acquires Associated Dry Goods in 1986 and Filene's,
Foley's stores in 1988 spin-off of Canadian developer Robert Campeau's
purchase of Federated Dept. Stores to become 7th largest retailer with
sales of $10.3 billion)... Eastern Trunk Line Assn. is formed by
railroads to stabilize rates (names Albert Fink of Louisville & Nashville
Road as head of Executive Committee)... Asa Candler starts Atlanta drug
business (in 1886 buys part interest in patent medicine called Coca-Cola
from Atlanta pharmacist John Pemberton)...

L.C. Smith acquires business making guns (starts making typewriters in
1887, sells gun business in 1890 to focus on typewriters, merges with
Corona Typewriter in 1920 to form Smith-Corona)... Despite opposition of
Jay Gould and Collis Huntington's Southern Pacific, William B. Strong
starts developing Atchison, Topeka & Santa Fe Railroad (-1888, is removed
from office in 1889 by pressure of Boston's Kidder, Peabody investment
house to initiate reforms to consolidate system)... Samuel Colgate
introduces Colgate Dental Cream, world's largest seller for some 80 years
with extensive advertising and international sales organization, replaced
in 1950's by Procter & Gamble's Crest with fluoride... Anheuser Brewery,
St. Louis, starts using refrigerator cars to ship products... George
Eastman, bank bookkeeper, experiments with photographic equipment as
hobby (obtains patent in 1884 for paper-backed film and forms Eastman Dry
Plate & Film, introduces Kodak camera in 1888, employes research chemist,
one of first in U.S. industry, in 1887, introduces strip film for movies
in 1889)...

To prevent druggists substituting cheaper cough drops from open jars for
their product, Smith Brothers sell cough drops in packages with their
facsimiles as trademark (pioneers factory packaging)... Merchant-
entrepreneur Cyrus W. Field acquires large block of stock in NYC's
financially-troubled elevated railroad system (serves as president
without pay to establish operation, after participating with Jay Gould in
developing Wabash Railroad is ruined in 1887 when Gould takes over
Manhattan Elevated)... Calumet & Hecla Mining creates Employee's Aid
Fund.

1878

General Events

U.S. Supreme Court: <u>Hall</u> v. <u>Cuir</u> (finds railroad need not provide equal
accomodations to all passengers on basis of race)... Greenback Labor

Party is formed to lobby for more greenbacks, free coinage of silver, restrictions on Chinese immigration, and fewer working hours for labor (nominates last Presidential candidate in 1884)... Massachusetts lists 520 corporations, produce one-third of State's output, of some 11,000 manufacturing enterprises... Otis Elevator builds first high-speed elevator for commercial buildings...

Economic prosperity is revived (supports formation of some 62 new national, international unions by 1888)... Glass workers form union... Twine binder is invented, increases speed of harvesting... U.S. house committee sponsors study of European labor movement to determine causes of socialism and their implications for U.S. workers... D.A. Buck patents mass-produced, low-priced watch, Waterbury produces 500,000/year by 1888.

Business Events

A.H. Robins starts drug store business in Richmond, VA (as failing one-product business with Cascara, is revived in 1936 by E. Claiborne Robins)... First commercial telephone exchange is opened in New Haven, CT... Employee J. Walter Thompson acquires 1864 advertising business of William J. Carlton for $1,300 (-1916, expands business to acquire practical monopoly of magazine advertising, incorporates in 1896 as J. Walter Thompson)... German-born druggist Gerhard H. Mennen introduces corn-killer product for sore feet (introduces talcum baby powder in 1889 to enter skin product market)... Norwegian-born Simon Benson leaves Wisconsin logging to start lumber operation in Oregon (operates 15 camps by 1900, starts rafting lumber to his San Diego mill in 1906)...

Funk & Wagnalls publishing business is founded (issues first dictionary in 1885)... After bribery battle for votes in Congress, Collis Huntington of Central Pacific and Jay Gould of Union Pacific settle differences to buy Pacific Mail & Steamship Co., to coordinate interests in establishing virtual monopoly of railroad transportation for Western U.S.... James J. Hill, associates acquire bankrupt St. Paul & Pacific Railroad (organize St. Paul, Minneapolis & Manitoba road in 1879 -basis for Great Northern system in 1889)... Edward Clark, President of I.M. Singer sewing machine business, starts national network of regional sales offices with George Ross McKenzie to distribute products from world's largest sewing machine factory at Elizabethport, NJ... Horace Tabor, owner of Leadville store supplying miners in Colorado, grubstakes two miners with $17 in supplies (with one-third share of silver lode discovery, starts Leadville Smelter Supply Co., amasses some $9 million by 1881, acquires 175,000 acres of mining land, TX, and over 4 million acres of grazing land, CO, before bankruptcy in 1893 Crash)... Gold, silver are discovered near Tombstone, AZ...

Joseph Pulitzer acquires financially-troubled St. Louis Dispatch (merges paper with St. Louis Post to publish Post-Dispatch, acquires Jay Gould's New York World in 1883, starts New York Evening World in 1887, uses "yellow" journalism in 1896 to compete with William Randolph Hearst's Journal)... New England Telephone and Bell Telephone are created to replace Bell Telephone Assn. (are united in 1879 as National Bell by William H. Forbes and Boston investors - Forbes president of operation to 1907, reorganizes in 1880 as American Bell with capitalization of $10 million - American Telephone & Telegraph in 1899 with capitalization over $200 million, posts first yearly loss in 1988)... Machinist Frederick W.

Taylor is hired by Midvale Steel as common laborer - chief engineer 1884 (designs piece-rate wage system in 1881, starts pioneering studies of work to improve production methods in 1885)...

National Council of the Order of Sovereigns of Industry is formed, MA (introduces "Rochdale plan" of cooperatives to U.S.)... Pratt Coke & Coal business is started in Birmingham, AL - City's first large-scale industrial enterprise... Theodore M. Vail, superintendent of Post Office's Railway Service, is hired as General Manager of Bell Telephone (-1887 and 1902-1919, develops expanding system and integrates companies into efficient organization)... After being wiped-out speculating on Chicago Grain Exchange, John W. "Bet-A-Million" Gates, partner start successful business making barbed-wire (after series of consolidations, starting in 1889, forms American Steel & Wire in 1899, suggests formation of large steel combine in 1899 - implemented by J.P. Morgan as U.S. Steel without the "Plunger," after losing stock battle invests in 1901 Spindletop oil field discovery, TX)...

After managing Utah mine, Clarence Seamans returns to East to supervise sales of Remington typewriters handled by scale manufacturer Fairbanks & Co. as exclusive marketing agency (stays as manager in 1881 when Remington takes over marketing, acquires exclusive agency with partners in 1882 to sell all typewriters firm can make, purchases typewriter business in 1886 with partners when Remington & Sons need capital)... With support of Vanderbilts and J.P. Morgan, Henry Villard forms Edison Electric Light Co., capitalized at $300,000, as licensing agent for Edison's patents, replaced by Edison General Electric in 1888 and General Electric in 1892... German-born M. Berlitz starts business to train people in use of foreign languages.

1879

General Events

For first time since 1861, greenbacks are in parity with gold... Massachusetts adopts 10-hour day for workers, affirmed by U.S. Supreme Court in 1908... NYC passes law to regulate building of tenement houses (by 1900 lists 42,700 tenements to house 1,585,000 of City's total population of some two million)... Constantin Fahlberg discovers sacchrin as artificial sweetener, proposed for banning by FDA in 1977 - effective 1987... Henry George: <u>Progress</u> <u>and</u> <u>Poverty</u> (argues undertaxation of land basis for poverty, proposes single land tax as rents of landed proprietors exclude workers from free access to land)...

James Rilty, Ohio saloon manager, devises first U.S. cash register to reduce employee theft... After successes as lawyer and editor, Russell Conwell becomes Minister of Baptist Temple, Philadelphia (realizes fame on Chautauqua circuit with Acres of Diamonds lecture: "You Have No Right to Be Poor, It is Your Duty to Be Rich")... Safeguards on sale of diseased meats are removed from Chicago ordinance by business interests... Postal Act grants magazines second-class mailing privileges... California Constitution forbids employment of Chinese workers... After testing some 6,000 fibers, Thomas A. Edison invents incandescent lightbulb with carbonized cotton... After worker's mistake in printing feedbags, Scottish-born Robert Gair devises machine process to make cardboard boxes... Inventor George F. Bush demonstrates public arc lighting system in Cleveland, OH.

Business Events

Daniel Frohman organizes Madison Square Theater (sends touring companies throughout U.S. to present Broadway attractions)... Procter & Gamble introduces Ivory Soap to compete with expensive imported Castile soaps (develops floating soap in 1881 after mixing accident, produces 200,000 bars/day with continuous-process machinery)... Showman John E. Healy, "Texas Charlie" Bigelow use road show to sell liver pads (-1911, during tour concoct Kickapoo Indian Medicine, sponsor touring medicine shows in 1881 – operate some 150 at one time, present Kickapoo Spectaculars in late 1880s – early 1890s)... After centralizing management with franchised dealers, regional office network and sales organization, Cyrus McCormick incorporates as McCormick Harvesting Machine... Henry B. Plant with funds from express business buys two railroads (extends Southern Atlantic Coast Railroad line to Florida, develops village of Tampa as system's terminus, linked by his steamship line to Cuba, and winter resort in 1890's)... With idea from England, Joseph F. Knapp, President of Metropolitan Life Insurance since 1871, issues industrial life insurance... Jay Morton is employed by 1848 Chicago salt business (assumes control in 1885 on death of owner, becomes industry's leader as Morton Salt Co.)...

Jay Gould acquires control of Wabash, Missouri Pacific, St. Joseph & Denver, Missouri, Kansas & Texas and several smaller railroads (merges with Union Pacific to realize some $40 million in profits)... Custer Trail Ranch is started in Dakota Territory (revises business to operate as dude ranch in 1882, moves to Wyoming in 1904)... William J. Palmer starts Colorado Coal & Iron Co., first in State... After starting first branch in Chicago, Pabst of Milwaukee opens branch brewery in Kansas (establishes 30 more in 1881-94 to become a national brewer)... J.P. Morgan, associates acquire control of New York Central from William H. Vanderbilt (starts direct involvement in railroads)...

When employers reject idea, acquired from another store, to sell goods for 5 cents on open counters, Frank W. Woolworth opens The Great Five Cent Store in Utica, NY (fails due to poor location, opens Woolworth's Five Cent & Ten Cent Store in Lancaster, PA, in 1879 – by 1895 operates 28 stores with volume of $1 million, by 1900 59 stores, and by 1912 world's largest merchandising business with 596 stores)... Chicago speculator and packer Philip Armour succeeds in bear raid on pork (executes successful wheat deal in 1882, breaks wheat "corner" of Joseph Leiter in 1897)... Standard Oil Company of California is formed...

Finnish Sea Captain Gustave Niebaum starts Inglenook Vineyards in California's Napa Valley... Jordan Lambert, co-founder of Warner-Lambert business, introduces Listerine... Two brothers start selling paper bags from push cart, Philadelphia (evolves as Scott Paper Co.)... Land developer George C. Tilyou starts selling Coney Island real estate (promotes area as amusement park, opens Steeplechase Park in 1897, operates 8 other amusement parks later throughout U.S.)... Standard Oil of Ohio builds refinery in Galicia area of Poland, Ukraine (starts international investments of U.S. petroleum industry)... Chicago meat packer Philip D. Armour cans meat for export (opens Kansas City bank in 1879, acquires glue works in 1884, opens Armour Institute of Technology in 1893)... Harry G. Selfridge is hired as clerk by 1865 wholesale, retail business of Field, Leiter & Co., Chicago (becomes retail general manager in 1886 and junior partner in 1890, resigns in 1904 when denied senior partnership and rejected in expanding to Paris and London to retire, moves to London in 1906 - opens elegant store in 1909.

1880s

General Events

H.W. Seely invents electric fan... Manual training high schools appear in many major cities... Thomas A. Edison, financed by James Gordon Bennett of the New York Herald, tests air screws as lifting devices for vertical flight, unsuccessful... Land boom starts in Southern California (-1888)... Number of man-hours required per acre in wheat production drops, 75 before 1830, to 12... A section of Saratoga Springs, NY is designated for gambling activities (launches legalized gambling in U.S.)... J. Carpentier devises pneumatically controlled punch paper rolls to operate player pianos.

Business Events

Northwestern Knitting, Minneapolis, develops "itchless" underwear for men by weaving silk with wool (becomes Munsingwear in 1919)... Modern Schwarz Services International is started to advise breweries on how to make beer, CT... Several professional baseball teams are started by black players (leads to formation of Middle States League which folds in 1890).

1880

General Events

National Farmers Alliance is formed (helps form Populist Party in 1892)... Wabash, IN is (April) first town to be lit by electric lights with installation of Charles F. Bush's arc lamp system... Chinese Exclusion Treaty is signed (November 17) by China, U.S. (limits immigration of Chinese workers)... George Eastman patents roll film for cameras... Scientific American magazine is published... Case Institute for Technology is founded, Cleveland... Oregon State University establishes professorship in commerce (offers program in secretarial science in 1908)... First significant gold discovery in Alaska is found, followed by Klondike Rush in 1896-97, Nome in 1897-98, Fairbanks in 1902... James Wimshurst devises electrostatic generator...

Daniel E. Ryan: Human Properties in Growth (provides average measurements for average body for every age during juvenile years)... California State Board of Viticultural Commissioners is formed to help growers produce wine... U.S. Census shows population of 50.2 million, 14.1 urban and 36.1 rural (records 2,812,000 immigrants since 1871 - some 80,000 Jews in NYC to increase to 1,250,000 by 1910 with most from Russia)... Alexander Shapiro develops first gelatin process for duplicating machines, followed in 1881 by first wax stencil of Britain's D. Gestetner.

Business Events

German-born Anton Feuchtwanger creates first hot-dog, called also
Frankfurter or Weinie, in St. Louis (with no rolls provides patrons with
white gloves to keep fingers clean, uses buns when gloves not returned,
is introduced, along with beer, to ballparks by St. Louis Browns' owner
Chris von der Ahe in 1888, evolves as L.A. Garrett's double dog in
1988)... When Henry DuPont, head of family powder business 1850-89,
refuses to make dynamite as too dangerous, Lammont DuPont starts Repauno
chemical business to make new explosive... For first time in U.S.
retailing John Wannamaker's Grand Depot, Philadelphia, hires full-time
advertising copywriter... Henry Millis starts business bottling sparkling
cider, MA (after adding ginger ale, other drinks to line adopts brand
name of Cliquot Club)... Robert C. French starts spice company (perfects
mild mustard in 1904)... First commercial lighting system is installed on
steamship Columbia by Edison Electric Light Co., followed 6 months later
by installation of inventor Hiram Maxim's United States Lighting...

Private Los Angeles Athletic Club, City's oldest and one of most
prestigious, is founded by group called "Forty Thieves" (evolves by
1980's with interests in other famous clubs, 1,650 underdeveloped acres
near Mailbu, shopping centers, warehouses, vast collection of Western
art, and subsidiary making vitamins, food supplements)... Entrepreneur
Charles R. Flint acquires control of Maxim's United States Lighting
(fails to merge lighting business with Edison's company in 1882, starts
importing Brazilian rubber in 1884 - dubbed "Rubber King of America"
later, forms United States Rubber in 1892, purchases entire rubber output
of Belgian Congo in 1906)... With lucky petroleum find at Titusville, PA,
James M. Guffey starts oil business (evolves as largest producer in State
and one of U.S.' largest independents with wells in KS, TX, OK)...

After working as railroad telegrapher since 1877, James H. Rand becomes
bank teller (develops index filing system with "visible" dividers to
improve efficiency of clerks, starts Rand Ledger Co. to promote products
and other new inventions for processing and classifying information,
joins business with son's 1915 American Kardex in 1925 to become world's
largest maker of record-keeping supplies, merges with Remington
Typewriter in 1927)... After resigning from father's business making
quality mirrors, Jules S. Bache is hired by uncle's New York brokerage
house as cashier - Treasurer in 1881, Partner in 1886, and President of
J.S. Bache & Co. in 1892 (is accused of malpractice in 1893 - not proven,
handles reorganizations of American Spirits in 1895, Glucose Sugar
Refining in 1897, Distilling and Cattle Feeding Co., known as "Whiskey
Trust," in 1905, and Cosmopolitan Fire Insurance in 1906, after
pioneering middle-class market for stocks starts branch offices to
operate 7, including one in Liverpool, England, by 1905 - 37 branches,
800 employees by 1945)...

George Pullman starts building model industrial town for workers of
Pullman Palace Car Co. on Lake Calumet near Chicago (after lowering wages
without decreasing rents, requests National Guard to quell violent strike
in 1894, sells property after 1898 ruling by Illinois court company-
sponsored housing illegal)... Professors E.J. Houston, E. Thomson form
American Electric Co., CT... Southern Pacific Railroad links New Orleans
with Pacific Coast... Baltimore & Ohio Railroad forms relief association
to provide employees with insurance, 1882 charter revoked 1888... 11

Bessemer plants, 6 designed by Alexander Holley, operate in U.S.... After
conflicts on manufacturing policy (proposed production limit of 15,000
reapers/year) and patent rights, brother Leander McCormick is fired by
Cyrus (hires Louis Wilkinson as new manufacturing superintendent to use
armory practices to increase production to some 50,000 machines/year by
1884 and to train Cyrus McCormick, Jr.)... With backing of Baltimore &
Ohio Railroad, John G. Moore starts Mutual Union Telegraph (-1886 when
sold to Western Union by road to avoid bankruptcy)... John Wanamaker
opens Paris buying office for Philadelphia department store (starts
Bargain Room, forerunner of basement store, and introduces Spring sales,
opens offices in Berlin in 1888, Yokohama in 1909, and London in 1911)...

Alexander Graham Bell, two engineer-investors start Volta Laboratory to
perfect phonograph (resigns when venture is successful, leaves shares to
trust fund for research on deafness)... Jay Gould pressures Union Pacific
Railroad to buy his Kansas Pacific line, ousted from Union Pacific in
1884 (regains control in 1890)... After perfecting device in 1879 to make
arc lights profitable, inventor Elmer A. Sperry starts Sperry Electric,
Chicago, to make dynamos, arc lamps and electrical appliances (forms
Sperry Electric Mining Machine in 1888 to market his new cutting machine,
founds Sperry Electric Railroad in 1890 - sold to General Electric in
1894)... Jay Gould becomes largest stockholder in Western Union with bear
raid (pressures company to purchase his American Union Telegraph business
at inflated prices, forces Western Union employees to break strike in
1883)... Yale & Towne Mfg. adopts suggestion system...

Cattle barons build Cheyenne Club, Denver, as pleasure palace... 1822 Red
Swallowtail Line, last packet operation, discontinues transatlantic
service, followed by last packet ship in 1881... Mine owner George Hearst
acquires San Francisco _Examiner_ (with reluctance lets son take over in
1887)... Ambrose Swasey, W.R. Warner start machine tool business,
Chicago... Some 900 textile mills use almost 80,000 horsepower of energy
provided by dams on Merrimack River of NH, MA... Investment banker E.H.
Harriman becomes director of father-in-law's Ogdenburg & Lake Champlain
Railroad (acquires small Upstate New York railroad in 1881 with links to
New York Central and Pennsylvania Railroads, after rennovation sells line
in 1883 to Pennsylvania Railroad for substantial profit, joins board of
Illinois Central Railroad in 1883, out-maneuvers J.P. Morgan to acquire
Dubuque and Sioux City road in 1892, extends Illinois Central to New
Orleans by 1892, reorganizes Erie Road in 1893 with J.P. Morgan)...

With suggestion from Dr. John Shaw Billings, head of health statistics
division of U.S. Census Bureau, engineer Herman Hollerith designs
tabulating machine to use punched cards, first used to operate 1801
Jacquard loom, for counting census data, (obtains 3 patents in 1883 for
machines and punch-cards, rents machines to U.S. Census Bureau in 1890 to
compile population data - completes project in 2 years instead of
expected 10 for savings of some $5 million, sells machines to Canada,
Italy, and Austria in 1890 for census work despite opposition of
displaced clerks, incorporates business in 1896 as Tabulating Machine Co.
which evolves as International Business Machines in 1924)... 1879
National Bell Telephone reorganizes as American Bell Telephone (acquires
Western Electric, largest supplier, to serve 170,000 users by 1887 and
600,000 by 1900).

1881

General Events

First U.S. lawn tennis championship is held in Newport, RI... U.S. Supreme Court: <u>Springer v. United States</u> (rules income tax laws to be Constitutional)... Congress authorizes (March 3) central registration agency for trademarks... New Jersey authorizes financial aid for industrial schools, followed by Massachusetts in 1897 to fund textile schools, Connecticut in 1907 and New York in 1908... Manhattan YMCA graduates class of 8 typists... Federation of Organized Trades and Labor Unions is formed by U.S., Canadian unions... Dirt farmers form Farmers' Alliance (advocates anti-trust laws, government ownership of railroads, progressive income tax, and inflationary monetary policy, joins other groups to support People's Party, known as Populists, in 1890 national election)... Trade school for immigrants is started, Boston... James S. Brisbin: <u>The Beef Bonanza, or How to Get Rich on the Plains</u>...

Anti-Monopoly League is formed, NYC... Merchant Joseph Wharton donates some $100,000 to University of Pennsylvania to create first permanent collegiate school of business (follows attempts of University of Louisiana, University of Wisconsin, and Washington and Lee University, is followed by University of Chicago and University of California at Berkeley in 1898, Amos Tuck School at Dartmouth in 1900, and Harvard Graduate School of Business in 1908)... Charles H. Fitch: "Report on Manufacturing of Interchangeable Mechanism," Tenth U.S. Census ("coins" term of American System to describe assembly of interchangeable parts in making firearms)... British-born Frederick Marriott of San Francisco files patent application for steam-powered "aeroplane," first U.S. use of word (is rejected as impractical for having no gas to provide lift)...

William W. Browne creates Grand United Order of the True Reformers as mutual benefit society for freed slaves (charters first U.S. black bank in 1888, starts Old Folks Home in 1898, Westham Farm, and Mercantile and Industrial Association, by 1900 operates stores, hotels, newspaper, printing plant, and real estate office - $200,000 in revenue by 1901, declares bankruptcy in 1910 when bank fails).... School of Application for Infantry and Cavalry is started at Ft. Levenworth, KS (evolves as general training program for any position)... National unions gather in Pittsburgh to form Federation of Trades of Labor Unions (after failing to merge with Knights of Labor becomes American Federation of Labor in 1886 with former cigar-maker Samuel Gompers as President to advocate business unionism instead of political reform - 447,000 members in 1897 and over 2 million in 1904).

Business Events

Andrew Carnegie forms Carnegie Bros. & Co. to oversee various steel operations as limited partnership association, capitalized at $5 million (clears $2 million first year)... Jay Gould uses his New York <u>World</u> to manipulate stock prices of Manhattan Elevated (acquires controlling interest by 1886)... Charles E. Perkins becomes President of Chicago, Burlington & Quincy Railroad (advocates responsible decisions must be made at lowest practical level having closest contact wih customers, creates decentralized organizational structure in 1883)... California gold prospector Aaron Winters finds huge deposit of borax in Death

Valley, CA (sells claim to borax merchant who starts mining in 1883, uses 20-mule teams to transport borax)... John Wanamaker's Philadelphia department store starts insurance association for employees (sponsors profit-sharing plan in 1887 and First Penney Savings in 1888)...

Inventor Hiram Maxim visits Europe, advised by American in Vienna that he could make a pile of money by inventing something so Europeans could kill each other with ease (completes first drawings for first practical machine gun with 280 interchangeable parts and forms Maxim Gun Co. in 1882 - a merger later with rival Anglo-Swedish Nordenfeldt to acquire their strength in marketing, demonstrates gun at British factory in 1885 and for German Emperor in 1887 - adopted by British Army in 1891 and U.S. Army in 1915, starts developing steam-powered plane in 1891 to show possibility of flight before crash in 1894, obtains British citizenship in 1900 - knighted)... Atlanta International Cotton Exposition, U.S.' first international fair, is held (signals rebirth of Southern cotton industry - other regional industrial fairs in 1887 and 1895)... Captain Henry Metcalf develops managerial control system for Frankford Arsenal...

Merchant William Filene, sons start women's fashion store, Boston - by 1891 prominent fashion specialty store (introduce basement bargain sales in 1890's, form pioneering Filene Cooperative Management Assn. in 1898 to handle employee grievances)... After hawking tea, coffee from bright red wagon, Bernard H. Kroger is hired to revive Cincinnati Imperial Tea Co., (resigns in 1882 when denied one-third share of profits, starts Great Western Tea Co. in 1883 with partner, acquires partner's share in 1884 for $1,500, operates 4 stores by 1885 - first to place grocery ads, expands into mail-order and manufacturing in 1890's - first to operate a bakery, renames business Kroger in 1902 - first to operate a meat department, starts to acquire other chains in 1905 - by 1928 with some 5,200 stores and by 1980s operates 1,199 food stores and 560 drug stores to achieve highest sales in industry with volume of some $14 billion)...

Christian Brothers start making wine, CA... With backing of J.P. Morgan, German-born Henry Villard forms "blind pool" to acquire control of Northern Pacific Railroad (completes link to Pacific Coast in 1883, declares bankruptcy in 1884 after looting by construction company and insufficient traffic, is reorganized in receivership by J.P. Morgan in 1894)... American Association of Base Ball Clubs is formed (negotiates pact with National League in 1882, merges in 1891)... Joseph L. Hudson opens retail clothing store, Detroit (builds 8-story building in 1891 for J.L. Hudson Department Store, merges in 1969 with Minnesota retail business to form Dayton-Hudson Corp. - 339 stores and sales over $2.1 billion)...

James Buchanan Duke, manufacturer of chewing tobacco in Durham, NC, starts making cigarettes (acquires 2 Bonsack cigarette machines in 1884 and exclusive rights to machines in 1885, starts national advertising in 1885, spends some $800,000 on advertising in 1889, joins 4 competitors in 1890 to form American Tobacco to dominate industry)... Jay Gould controls 8 railroads, including Erie, to operate U.S.' largest rail network of 15,854 miles, 15% of industry's total mileage... Chicago department store partnership of Marshall Field, Levi Leiter is severed when Leiter leaves to focus on wholesaling (Marshall Field practices: courteous customer service with "Give the Lady What She Wants," personal shopping service, home delivery, and marked one-price policy, quality merchandise, cash sales)...

John Wanamaker acquires factory making Morris chairs to supply his department store business (acquires other supplier later)... Some 95% of U.S.' oil supply is produced by Pennsylvania fields... Ohio C. Barber, owner of 1864 Barber Match, creates Diamond Match with three competitors (acquires control of 85% of market, uses continuous automatic process to make 2 million matches, matchboxes/day)...

Henry P. Crowell acquires Quaker Mill at Ravenna, OH (promotes brand of Quaker Oats as first breakfast cereal, builds world's first mill in 1882 to produce oatmeal on continuous process, forms Consolidated Oatmeal in 1887 with other millers – replaced by 1887 holding company of American Cereal, joins competitors to form new American Cereal in 1891, forms Quaker Oats in 1901 as further consolidation of millers)...

British-born Samuel Insull is hired as Thomas A. Edison's secretary (is named Vice President of Edison General Electric in 1889, resigns in 1892 to become President of Chicago Edison when J.P. Morgan creates General Electric, innovates with central station operations and rate structures, expands utility service by acquiring central stations in Illinois and neighboring states).

1882

General Events

Congress passes (May 6) Chinese Exclusion Act (bans immigration of Chinese workers for ten years)... Congress authorizes (May 15) formation of Tariff Commission... U.S., Korea sign treaty of friendship, commerce... Strikes disrupt iron and steel industry and rail transportation... Despite warnings, first parade to honor Labor Day is held (September 5) by some 10,000 workers, NYC (becomes national legal holiday in 1894)... Thomas A. Edison's Pearl Street steam-powered central station, world's first power plant, starts supplying Manhattan with electricity... New York prohibits manufacture of cigars by family factories in tenement houses, ruled unconstitutional by U.S. Supreme Court... First U.S. hydro-electric power plant, designed by Thomas A. Edison, operates at Appleton, WI... 10-story Montauk Building, outer walls of traditional masonry, is erected, Chicago... Actors' Fund is created by P.T. Barnum, Edwin Booth, others to take care of needy actors... Library Bureau devises first vertical filing system...

Senate Committee on Education and Labor investigates relations between workers and companies... W.H. Vanderbilt: "The Public Be Damned," a response to reporter's question on consulting consumers about use of luxury trains... Naval engineer John Dolbeer patents donkey engine to skid trees, CA...

H.W. Seely invents electric flat iron... Congress passes first U.S. law on workmen's compensation for maritime industry... National Business College at Wheeling, WV, offers courses in bookkeeping, penmanship, business calculations, practical grammar, spelling, commercial law and commercial correspondence... Chinese Consolidated Benevolent Association is formed, San Francisco, by 6 Chinese companies, immigration and protection associations, to combat anti-Chinese activities, resolve community problems... James Bonsack, after working on invention since 1870's, patents machine to make cigarettes (processes 70,000 - 120,000 cigarettes/day)...

Atlantic Monthly: "The Political Economy of Seventy - Three Million Dollars" (attacks Jay Gould)... Boston theater is first in U.S. lit by electricity... California prohibits immigration of Chinese workers... Brookline Country Club, U.S.' "first," opens, MA, Long Island's Meadowbrook in 1883 (follows Myopia Hunt Club, MA, starting as baseball team in 1875)... John L. Sullivan knocks out Paddy Ryan, "American Champion," to become world's first heavyweight boxing champion (-1892 when defeated by "Gentleman Jim" Corbett, is first to make living as prize fighter).

Business Events

Frederick W. Taylor does detailed time studies of work in this time at Midvale Steel, starts evolution of scientific management (develops nucleus of planning department and experiments with functional foreman before resignation in 1890)... John A. Hillerich crafts baseball bat for Pete Browning of Louisville Eclipse team (with success starts making Louisville Slugger as Hillerich & Bradsby Co.)... After discovering Pennsylvania's largest gas well, J.N. Pew, E.O. Emerson build pipeline to Pittsburgh (form Sun Oil in 1890, operate pipelines and shipping, TX, and refinery, NJ, in 1901, discover oil, OK and LA, in 1909, open gas stations in 1920)... Hills brothers acquire retail business of San Francisco's Arabian Coffee & Spice Mills to start coffee business...

United Press news service is launched (-1897, is revived in 1907, declares bankruptcy in 1985)... While in high school, George S. Parker designs game "The Battle of Barrockburn" (designs "Banking" game in 1883, acquires Salem's Ives Co., owners of first U.S. board game "The Mansion of Happiness," in 1887, forms Parker Bros. in 1888, opens offices, NYC and London, in 1902, introduces fad of "Mah-Jongg" in 1924, markets "Monopoly" game in 1935, lists over 300 games in 1952, sells out to General Mills in 1968)... Dow, Jones & Co. is created by two newspaper reporters to distribute financial news (prepare first real index for stock price averages in 1884, publish Wall Street Journal in 1889, create Dow-Jones stock-market index in 1896, is sold in 1902 to Clarence W. Barron)...

Chicago Board of Trade rules "bucket shops", term used in 1870's to describe cheap bars, as dishonest brokerage houses in soliciting business with high-pressure tactics... Charles B. Manville starts making coverings for steam pipes and boiler installations at his Milwaukee plant (patents improved insulation material in 1886 to form Manville Covering Co., acquires competitor 1858 H.W. Johns in 1897, consolidates as H.W. Johns-Manville in 1901)... Buffalo Bill Cody, after appearing in Western melodramas on stage since 1872, presents his first Wild West Show at North Platte, NE... Joseph N. Pew forms Penn Fuel Co. to supply Philadelphia with natural gas (invents machinery to pipe gas over long distances)... When H.C. Frick visits Europe, Andrew Carnegie acquires control of his coke business (acquires Homestead Mills, Pittsburgh, in 1883, makes Frick chairman of Carnegie Brothers & Co. in 1889, acquires rival Duquesne steel business in 1890)... Samuel Sachs becomes partner in investment business of father-in-law Marcus Goldman (becomes major underwriter of public securities after Goldman's death, gains status by underwriting United Cigar and Sears, Roebuck in 1906)... With financial backing, developer Charles T. Yerkes acquires North Chicago streetcar line (builds Chicago Loop elevated and extends traction system with secretive financial manipulations and political bribery, after pressure sells holdings for some $20 million in 1899 to win control of London subway from J.P. Morgan)... Frank C. Ball and brother, makers of shipping containers for tin cans, start making glass containers (produce canning jars in 1885 when Mason's patent expires to acquire practical monopoly, move to Muncie, IN, in 1887 when granted $5,000 by City for relocation)... Alaska-Treadmill Gold Mining near Juneau is first large-scale mining operation in territory (becomes operation of 4 mines, employing 2,000 workers at capacity, and company city with boarding houses, a miner pays one-third of salary for room and board, gym, reading room, bowling alley, heated swimming pool and clubhouse)...

Charles A. Pillsbury Co. adopts profit-sharing plan... Union Assn. is formed as baseball league to battle National and American groups for market (-1884)... C.E. Kohl, George Middleton open Chicago's first dime museum (lease Olympic Theatre for vaudeville in 1884)... J. Cheek starts coffee business in Nashville, TN (names product Maxwell House for City's famous hotel)...

Meat packer Phillip D. Armour, Chicago, and George H. Hammond, Detroit, start developing network of branch houses, followed by Nelson Morris of Chicago and Cudahy brothers of Omaha in mid-1880's... Procter & Gamble registers trademark of man in the moon and 13 stars (after 1980 whispering campaign about trademark as satanic symbol, abandons company logo in 1985)... Standard Oil Trust, designed by lawyer Samuel C.T. Dodd to control 40 enterprises, is legally established by John D. Rockefeller, adopted as legal device in early 1890's by nearly 5,000 firms organized into 300 trusts (becomes largest producer of crude oil in 1892 with 25% market share, is dissolved by Ohio Supreme Court in 1892, is replaced by holding company of Standard Oil of New Jersey in 1899)... Cabot family of Boston start business to produce carbon black, filthiest substance known to man but needed for tires (after declining sales is reorganized in 1960 to diversify into metals and natural gas, flops by 1986 to put old-line family business in jeopardy in 1988).

1883

General Events

After losing business deal with leaky pen, insurance salesman Lewis E. Waterman invents "modern" fountain pen, resolves problem in maintaining constant, even flow of ink (evolves in 1935 with ink pen cartridge of Jif-Waterman and ball-point pen in 1938 by H. Biro, Hungarian journalist)... Oscar Hammerstein patents first practical cigar-rolling machine... Telephone service is started (March 24) between Chicago, NYC... G. Stanley Hall starts first U.S. laboratory for research in psychology at Johns Hopkins University... Charles Stillwell invents machine to make paper bags with flat bottoms (is improved by "Kraft" paper invention in 1910 and replaced by plastic sacks in 1979)... George Westinghouse devises system for piping gas over long distances...

Cowhands on 3 large ranches, Texas Panhandle, strike for wages of

$50/month (accept previous $30/month)... Lester Frank Ward: _Dynamic Sociology_ (opposes laissez-faire economy to favor state regulation)... Brotherhood of Railroad Trainmen is formed... Thomas A. Edison develops modern generator for electricity with carbon brushes... After U.S. tariff on cotton is imposed, many British cotton firms start branches in U.S...

Gold is discovered, ID (-1886)... Thomas A. Edison demonstrates electric railway at Chicago Railway Exposition... Warren Johnson invents electric thermostat (founds Milwaukee's Johnson Controls)... Congress passes Pendleton Civil Service Act (creates bipartisan commission to establish competitive examinations for employment, requires rules and regulations for personnel activities in government service)... Sidney Z. Mitchell installs pioneering incandescent lighting system aboard U.S.S. Trenton (-1885)... New York is first state to enact civil service law... Chelsea is built as NYC's first co-op apartment building (-1903, reopens in 1915 as hotel for artists, writers)... San Francisco Minstrels visit NYC (signals end of black-face shows)... John Joseph Montgomery tests gliders for flight (-1886).

Business Events

Canadian, U.S. railroads eliminate conflicting time systems (within months is adopted by 80 of largest cities, is supervised by Interstate Commerce Commission in 1918)... John Pitcairn, Pennsylvania railroad executive, and entrepreneur Captain John B. Forbes start Pittsburgh Plate Glass (operates 4 plants by 1890, introduce continuous ribbon method to make plate glass in 1924, safety glass for cars in 1928, heat-absorbing glass and curved windshields in 1934, produce first U.S. float glass in 1963)... Texas' oldest winery is started at Del Rio... Northern Pacific Railroad reaches Montana... French nobleman Marquis De Mores, bored with life of French aristocracy, starts meat plant on Little Missouri River in Dakota Bad Lands, tried to undercut Eastern packers by processing range-fed cattle to avoid transportation of live animals (-1887, develops town of Medora and commercial empire of some 9,000 acres and 10,000 head of cattle, loses fortune after starting Northern Pacific Refrigeration Car Co.)...

Benjamin Keith opens Gaiety Museum for public entertainment, Boston (opens Boston Bijou in 1885 with Edward Albee as vaudeville theatre - by 1914 controls some 400 theaters, forms United Booking Office in 1900)... Charles A. Coffin heads syndicate to purchase American Electric Co., CT (becomes Thomson-Houston Electric, merges with Edison General Electric in 1892 to form General Electric, Coffin President to 1913)... A.B. Dick starts Chicago lumberyard business (needing to duplicate daily records, starts mimeograph business with patent rights from Thomas A. Edison, sells lumberyard in 1887 to focus on making and selling duplicating machines, enters national market in 1890s)...

After working for Armour & Co. meat-packing business since 1877, German-born Oscar F. Mayer buys small meat market, sausage-making shop with brother (starts packing plant in 1888)... After selling Wyoming Ranch, larger than area of Connecticut, to Scottish Swan Land & Cattle Co., Alexander Swan becomes Manager (develops ranch to oversee 3.25 million acres, paying average dividends of 25% for 1883-85, declares bankruptcy in 1889 after swindling investors of some $500,000, is replaced by new manager, Scottish-born Finlay Dun, who returns business to solvency...

Brick layer John Merrick, former slave, and partners form fraternal insurance society of Royal Knights of King David (forms North Carolina Mutual's industrial insurance business in 1898 - by 1920's largest U.S. black-owned business with bank, loan association, insurance)... Springfield, MA, holds first U.S. bicycle show (evolves by 1894 with annual shows in Chicago, 225 exhibits and 100,000 admissions in 1896, and New York, 400 exhibits and 120,000 admissions in 1896)... Crane Co. starts large-scale production of copper-lined wood bathtubs (produces enameled tubs in 1893)... Pecos, TX, hosts riding, roping contest (follows fiestas in Old Spanish West and "rodeos" in late 1860's at Deer Trail in Colorado Territory, is followed by Payson, AZ, rodeo in 1884, Frontier Days' celebration at Prescott, AZ, in 1888, Cheyenne's first rodeo in 1897, Oregon's Pendleton Round-up in 1910, Canada's Calgary Stampede in 1912, and first successful Madison Square Garden rodeo, NYC, in 1922)...

Joseph Pulitzer, St. Louis newspaper publisher, buys Jay Gould's New York World to "fight all public evils and abuses"... Edward, O.W. Norton operate first "automatic line" canning factory... Abraham Abraham, Joseph Wechsler open store in Brooklyn Bridge area (reorganize in 1893 as Abraham & Straus)... Whitcomb L. Judson patents shoe-closure device with interlocking clasps (forms Chicago's Universal Fastener Co. with Col. Lewis Walker and Henry Earle, obtains 2 more patents in 1896, gets order for 20 mail pouches with device by Postal Service in 1896, hires Gideon Sundback, Swedish-born electrical engineer, in 1906 to perfect fastener - marketed in 1908 and patented in 1913, death of Judson in 1909 results in formation of Automatic Hook and Eye and Hookless Fastener in 1913 by Walker and Sundback, after first sales in 1914 and moneybelt product in 1918 sells popular tobacco pouch with fastener in 1919, after garment manufacturers reject fastener wins recognition with B.F. Goodrich's zippered rubber galoshes in 1923, adopts trade name of Talon in 1928, achieves general success after being featured in 1938 fashions of French designer Elsa Schiaparelli)... Ladies Home Journal is published... Northern Pacific links with railroad to Portland, OR.

1884

General Events

Coal miners of Hocking Valley, PA, strike over wages and working conditions (after violence lose public sympathy, capitulate after near starvation)... Anti-Monopoly Party forms to demand regulation of trusts, combines and monopolies (supports graduated income tax)... Gold is discovered, AK... Congress creates (June 27) Bureau of Labor in Department of Interior... World Industrial and Cotton Centennial Exposition opens in New Orleans (-1885)... 10-story Home Life Insurance Building, designed by William Le Baron Jenney, is built, Chicago, world's first with ingredients of "skyscraper" (uses steel skeleton instead of self-supporting masonry)... Levant M. Richardson, Chicago, patents ball-bearing rollerskate... King C. Gillette, inventor of safety razor in 1891: The Human Drift (proposes all of world's industries be merged into one gigantic corporation to eliminate social evils of competition)...

John Meyenberg, St. Louis, patents evaporated milk... Work is started to erect France's Statue of Liberty, New York Harbor, dedicated 1886... Financial panic ensues with scarcity of funds in money market for hectic

financing of railroads... Albany, NY, is first city to adopt civil
service law... German-born watchmaker Ottmar Mergenthaler patents
linotype machine... Union Assn. forms to play baseball, follows 7 clubs
of International Assn. in 1877... Croatian-born electrical engineer and
inventor Nikola Tesla is hired by Thomas A. Edison (resigns to start
Tesla Electric to do electrical research, develops arc lighting system in
1886, alternating current motor in 1888 - rights sold to George
Westinghouse, Jr., alternating current power transmission system in 1888
- denounced by Edison, high frequency current electrical generator in
1890, Tesla transformer in 1891, electrical radiations in 1896-98,
magnifying transmitter in 1897, and power transmission system without
wires in 1897-1905)... American Institute of Electrical Engineers is
formed primarily by telegraph technicians (results in group leaving in
1912 to form Institute of Radio Engineers, in formation by merger of
Institute of Electrical and Electronics Engineers in 1963)...

Dr. John H. Kellogg applies for patent on "flaked cereal and process of
preparing same."

Business Events

Samuel Sidney McClure forms pioneering U.S. newspaper syndicate...
Artemas Ward is hired as advertising manager, one of first, by New York
firm of Enoch Morgan's Sons, makers of Sapolio soap... Pennsylvania,
Baltimore & Ohio Railroads establish pension funds, provided by 14 roads
by 1908... Willamette Tent & Awning Business is started in Portland, OR,
to make sails, rugged outdoor garments (starts making ski apparel as
White Stag in 1929)...

La Marcus Thompson designs roller coaster, Russians use sleds in 1500s to
hurl down artificial slides of ice and snow on wood structures and French
replace runners with wheels in 1804, for Coney Island, follows one at
Mauch Chunk, PA... American Cottonseed Oil Trust is created (followed by
trusts in linseed oil in 1885, lead, sugar, whiskey, wire nails, plate
glass, and cordage in 1887, smelters and coal in 1889, starch in 1890,
wallpaper in 1892, leather in 1893)...

Edgar M. Bentley, Walter H. Knight start Cleveland's first electric
trolley car service... For first time, U.S.' iron production tops that of
England... D.E. Felt devises first commercial comptometer for new
National Mfg. Co. of Dayton, patent in 1887 (is acquired by John H.
Patterson and renamed National Cash Register in 1884, sells 64 machines
in 1885 - 5,400 in 1887 and 16,395 in 1890, is indicted for restraint of
trade in 1913 - overturned 1914)... George Eastman devises continuous-
process machinery to make film (introduces first commercial motion
picture film in 1884)... Small resort business opens on Waikiki Beach,
HI, followed by Beach's first hotel in 1901, plush Royal Hawaiian Hotel
in 1927, and Mauna Kea beach resort on Big Island in 1965)...

Five Ringling brothers start small circus in Baraboo, WI, with veteran
showman "Yankee" Robinson as partner (divides country with Barnum &
Bailey Circus in 1895, acquires Barnum & Bailey Circus in 1907 with death
of Bailey, acquires American Circus Corp., operator of five shows, in
1929)... During Depression, Jay Gould is forced to near bankruptcy by
Wall Street "bears" (is forced to sell Eastern railroads, uses settlement

to corner market held by raiders and recover losses, retires from Wall
Street in 1885)... Elegant Murray Hill Hotel, lit by electricity, is
opened, NYC... Alexander Winton starts Cleveland bicycle repair business
(forms Winton Bicycle in 1890, makes some 3,000 bicycles in 1893, builds
first gasoline-powered bicycle in 1895 and first automobile in 1896)...

Electrical engineer Frank Sprague, after working for Edison, invents
industrial electric motor (forms Sprague Electric Railway & Motor Co.
with E.H. Johnson and Edison, develops pioneering electric traction line
for Richmond, VA, in 1887, sells business to Edison General Electric in
1890).

1885

General Events

Contract Labor Law forbids (February 26) employers in contracting abroad
for immigrant labor, used to break strikes, in return for passage to
U.S... Post Office starts special delivery service for towns of 4,000 or
more... American Economic Assn. forms (argues state must contribute in
positive manner to maintain just progress for all citizens)... Postal
rates for second-class mailings are reduced, causes boom in magazine
publishing... Electric transformer is invented... W.L. Bundy invents
mechanism to clock working hours of employees... William S. Burroughs,
co-founder of American Arithmometer, devises improved adding and printing
machine, patent in 1888 for first commercial calculator (is used in 1910
by 175,000 businesses worldwide)... S.F. Bowser devises measuring pump
tank for merchants selling lamp oil, used later by gasoline stations to
pump fuel... Certain federal employees get 4 paid holidays/year, granted
to all per diem employees in 1887...

Alexander Graham Bell, Charles S. Tainter invent electric-powered
"graphophone" for sound reproduction... Federal law prohibits fencing of
public lands... During term of President Cleveland (-1889) Lt. Ainsworth
devises card index system for Bureau of Pensions... German-born Walter
Baron von Richthofen: Cattle-raising on the Plains of North America
(reveals wealth made in cattle business)...

American Machinist illustrates Edward Norton's automatic can-making
production line... Jay Gould's Missouri-Pacific Railroad is forced to
settle strike with Noble Order of Knights of Labor... Work is started,
Chicago, to build Marshall Field Warehouse, designed by Henry H.
Richardson as purely functional building (-1887)... William Dean Howells:
The Rise of Silas Lapham (portrays businessman hero as responsible
citizen who sacrifices material gain when necessary to do the "right
thing")...

Brotherhood of Ball Players forms as secret benevolent society to help
players in trouble, improve relations with club owners (-1890,, forms
league in 1889, strikes in 1890 to destroy American Assn.)... Kansas
closes borders to tick-infested cattle from Texas... Comedy team of Joe
Weber, Lew Fields tour U.S. (open NYC music hall in 1896)... Senate
negates canal across Nicaragua.

Business Events

Railroad financier Henry Villard designs elegant Hotel Villard for Portland, OR (is re-financed in 1888 and built in 1890 by businessman William S. Ladd -as Portland Hotel, leveled for parking lot in 1950's and re-designed as Civic Square in 1984)... Procter & Gamble finishes building model industrial complex, Cincinnati, to produce soap, cottonseed and salad oil, etc... Charles E. Perkins, President of the Chicago, Burlington & Quincy Railroad: "Organization of Railroads" (discusses in memorandum Road's new decentralized structure with Chicago headquarters of President and 3 Vice Presidents, advised by general staff with accounting and purchasing, to supervise 4 autonomous regional divisions, each with departments of transportation, traffic and legal)...

Citrus growers, CA, form Orange Growers' Protective Union as pioneering fruit-marketing cooperative (reorganizes in 1895 as Southern California Fruit Exchange - fails)... Moxie Nerve Food Co. of Lowell, MA, introduces drink to cure "paralysis, softening of the brain, and mental imbecility" (uses endorsements in 1920 to promote soda as "wicked good," continues in 1980s in New England)... Eastman Dry Plate & Film Co. of Rochester, NY, introduces Kodak camera with slogan, "You push the botton, we do the rest" (sells over 100,000 by 1889, sells Brownie box camera for $1 in 1900)...

George Westinghouse, Jr., forms Westinghouse Electric (develops business with Tesla's alternating current motor in 1887, refinances in 1891, forms patent pool in 1896 with General Electric, survives brief bankruptcy in 1907)... Robert Stuart, Canadian-born miller in Chicago, and Henry P. Crowell, founder of Quaker Oats, form Oatmeal Millers Assn. with others to compete with Akron's Ferdinand Shumacher, "the Oatmeal King" (start new pool in 1885 with Shumacher - loses mills to fire, form American Cereal Co. in 1888 with 7 largest millers, are forced out by Shumacher in 1897, regain control in 1899 with Shumacher out, diversify with animal feed in 1907 and pasta products in 1916)...

German-born James J. Speyer joins New York branch of family's Frankfurt banking business (becomes senior partner in 1899, is ousted from Southern Pacific in 1901 by J.P. Morgan and E.H. Harriman, handles number of railroad reorganizations as prominent international banking house, reorganizes Mexican railroad system in 1905, assists financing of Philippine railway in 1906, loses reputation during World War I from close ties with Germany, is black-listed by British in 1916, closes German branches in 1934 with rise of Nazi anti-Semitism, liquidates U.S. business in 1939)... Cuban Giants of Long Island are formed as pioneering professional black baseball team, followed by barnstorming teams in early 1900's, Negro National League in 1920, and Negro Eastern League in 1921... After operating as independent grain broker since 1874, Frank Peavey builds one of world's largest grain terminals, Minneapolis (innovates with concrete silo in 1899, becomes "Grain Elevator King of the World" by time of death in 1901)...

In this time, XIT, Texas ranch financed by English capital, operates over 10 counties with some 150,000 head of cattle (joins other ranching operations with British capital: Texas Land & Cattle Co. with more land than Long Island, Matador Land & Cattle Co., Ltd., with ranches in TX, MT, and Dakotas)... Flint Road Car Co., renamed Durant-Dort Carriage Co.

in 1886, is started, MI (becomes leading maker of horse-drawn vehicles with 14 plants in U.S., Canada to produce some 150,000 carriages, forms subsidiary companies to make parts for main assembly at Flint)... Henry Metcalf: _The Cost of Manufacturing and the Administration of Workshops, Public and Private_ (proposes management system of control with authority, information)...

Chemist Robert F. Lazenby formulates Dr Pepper soft drink in Waco, TX (advertises product in 1927 as drink for pep on discovering sugar provides energy, distributes product to South and Midwest in 1930's, introduces drink to national market in 1962, enters competitive New York market in 1970, introduces sugar-free drink in 1971, enters Europe market in 1976, achieves No. 3 market ranking in 1980, sells to Canada Dry in 1982, introduces caffeine-free drink in 1983, is acquired by Coca-Cola in 1986 for $470 million)... George Westinghouse establishes independent laboratory for inventor William Stanley with 14 patents (develops transformer in 1886 to make AC electricity practical, after conflicts with Westinghouse leaves 1890 to form Stanley Mfg., sold to Roeblings in 1899, and laboratory to develop AC motor, improves long-distance transmission of electricity in 1890s, sells lab to GE in 1903 after patent attacks by GE and Westinghouse, sells 32 patents to GE in 1906 for $32,000 and $12,000/year to run new lab to improve heating devices - designs thermos bottle).

1886

General Events

Knights of Labor strike Jay Gould's Missouri Pacific railroad system, ties up some 5,000 miles of track with over 9,000 strikers (submits to management terms when threatened with starvation, results in wage loss of $900,000 by workers and lost revenues of $3 million by company, contributes to demise of union)... In May between 40,000 and 60,000 members of Knights of Labor, anarchistic Black International, socialist unions and trade unions demonstrate for 8-hour day... U.S. Supreme Court: _Santa Clara County v. Southern Pacific Railroad_ (rules corporation, a person under 14th Amendment, cannot be deprived of profits or other rights)... Congress approves (June 29) incorporation of trade unions...

U.S. Supreme Court: _Wabash, St. Louis & Pacific Railway Company v. Illinois_ (holds state cannot regulate interstate commerce within its borders)... U.S.' "first" successful strike for 8-hour day is held in Chicago by butchers' union... Annual Winter Carnival is first held at St. Paul, MN, to ease tedium of grim winter... New York is first state to create permanent agency to mediate labor disputes... Henry James: _The Princess Casamassiona_ (predicts class war as inevitable)... Work is started in building hydro-electric plant, designed by Thomas A. Edison, at Niagara Falls (-1896)... Goldey Beacon School of Business opens in Wilmington, DE... President Cleveland recommends government should arbitrate industrial disputes...

Strike-breaking workers at Chicago's McCormick reaper plant are attacked by strikers (results in police action - 6 killed and some 12 wounded, results in further police action when meeting of some 1,300 strikers in Haymarket Square are disrupted by a bomb - 7 policemen killed and over 50 others wounded, results in conviction of 8 anarchists for starting riot)... R.R. Bowker: Economics for the People (states organizing, directing manager's major activities)... Amateur chemist Charles M. Hall (forms Pittsburgh Aluminum Co. in 1888 with Mellon financing - Aluminum Co. of America, Alcoa, in 1907) and Paul L. T. Heroult of France independently discover successful electrolytic process to make aluminum (results in first aluminum pots, pans in 1890)... Congress passes law to prevent foreign vessels carrying passengers between U.S. ports... First professional accounting association forms.

Business Events

The Sporting News is published by Spink family (focuses on baseball in 1887 to become game's bible, sells ownership in 1977 to Times Mirror, boosts circulation to 711,000)... Huckster Clark Stanley sells snake oil liniment, derived from medicine man of Moki Pueblo, AZ and TX, as cure for rheumatism... Procter & Gamble adopts employee stock acquisition plan, followed by 35 others by 1910... Jekyll Island off Georgia is acquired as secluded retreat by group of multi-millionaires, such as J.P. Morgan, William K. Vanderbilt, F.H. Goodyear, Pierre Lorillard, Vincent Astor and Marshall Field (develop island with "personal cottages," clubhouse and Sans Souci, precursor of condominium, for members without cottages)... For first time over one million shares of stock are traded on New York Stock Exchange in one day... Florida beaches are opened to Northern wealthy with construction of Florida East Coast Railway by Henry Flagler, Vice President of Standard Oil (extends line to Key West in 1908)... Johnson Wax business is started in Racine, WI, by carpenter Samuel Curtis Johnson (promotes wax products as gifts with his parquet floors (introduces "Glo-Coat" in 1932 as first one-step floor polisher to revive business, diversifies in 1956 with "Raid" bug killer)...

J.P. Morgan reorganizes Philadelphia and Reading, Chesapeake and Ohio railroads to rescue lines (fails to get railroad presidents in 1889 to form association to uphold Interstate Commerce Act and stabilize rates)... Harriet H. Ayer starts Recamier Mfg. to make, sell skin creams (advertises product with endorsements by famous women, starts first beauty column for New York World in 1897)... Thomas Fortune Ryan forms Metropolitan Traction Co., holding company for securities of operating companies (by 1900 acquires control over nearly all NYC lines)...

With funds from local barber Milton S. Hershey starts business in Pennsylvania making carmel candy (develops new process to make milk chocolate in 1890s, makes first U.S. candy bar in 1894)... After working as door-to-door book salesman since 1879, David H. McConnell starts California Perfume Co. to peddle products with books (becomes Avon business after World War II)... James H. McGraw, after working as subscription salesman, buys American Journal of Railway Appliances with borrowed money (moves business to NYC and purchases interests of partners in 1888 to start industrial and technical publishing empire, starts publishing books in 1909)... Sidney Z. Mitchell starts organizing 13 electrical utilities in Northwest (consolidates utilities in 1893 to eliminate wasteful competition, controls 10% of U.S. electrical operations by 1924)...

Arthur D. Little, Roger Griffin start independent chemical research laboratory in Boston to advise clients on chemical problems, paper technology (incorporates as Arthur D. Little in 1893 to become pioneer consulting business with chemists, engineers and managers, designs pioneering "pilot plant" experimental operation for United Fruit in 1911, transfers ownership to MIT in 1935)... St. Louis business of N.O. Nelson adopts profit-sharing plan for employees... La Marcus Thompson builds first true roller-coaster, Oriental Scenic Railway, at Atlantic City...

Wholesalers form National Butchers' Protective Assn. to fight large packing houses... Railroads adopt standard-guage track... Henry R. Towne: "The Engineer as an Economist" (urges study of management work at meeting of American Society of Mechanical Engineers - Captain Henry Metcalf discusses shop-order system of accounts and Oberlin Smith explains capital accounting)... First U.S. public roller-skating rink opens in Newport, RI... Stone Founders' National Defense Assn. forms to protect members against demands of labor, cited as first U.S. national organization of employers... Cosmopolitan magazine is issued for women...

First commercial incandescent community lighting system is tested near Pittsburgh... Diamond Crystal Salt is established in St. Clair, MI (-1987, after selling money-losing salt business for $65 million to world's largest salt producer, subsidiary of Dutch chemical enterprise, continues with specialty foods division)... German-born gardener William Radam patents "Radam Microbe Killer" in Texas as "purifier" of diseases (operates 17 factories by 1890, sells mixture, costs 5 cents/gallon, for $3/gallon, is forced out of business by 1906 Pure Food & Drug Act)... Atlanta pharmacist John S. Pemberton mixes first batch of medicinal drink (is reformulated later for first time in 1985 to have "more harmonious flavor") named Coca-Cola by bookkeeper Frank Robinson (forms Pemberton Chemical Co., sells part interest, complete ownership in 1891, to Asa Candler, Atlanta druggist bothered with headaches and dyspepsia)...

Richard W. Sears, railroad station agent at North Redwood, MN, buys consignment of pocket watches when not accepted by local jeweler (after selling timepieces by mail to fellow station agents, starts R.W. Sears Watch Co. to continue business, employs watch repairman Alvah C. Roebuck in 1887, issues first catalog in 1888 - first official in 1894, acquires interest of Roebuck in 1895 for $25,000 - returns as roving public relations ambassador in 1933, in order to focus on merchandising takes Julius Rosenwald as partner in 1895 to manage operations)... Scottish-born John T. Robertson, CT, turns gristmill into soap factory to make Bon Ami soap cakes, powder in 1913... Chas. A. Stevens opens, Chicago, to sell women's clothing (sells U.S.' first ready-made silk blouses and clothing for working women, after highly leveraged expansion to 29 stores declares bankruptcy in 1988 after entering glitzy haute couture market).

1887

General Events

Congress passes (February 4) Interstate Commerce Act (creates 5-member commission to supervise railroad freight rates, to stop discriminatory rates and pooling)... Post Office provides free delivery of mail to all communities of 10,000 or more... Reverend Hannibal Goodwin files patent application for celluloid photographic film, granted in 1898 after delays by challenges (results in suit by his business 2 years after his death against Eastman Kodak in 1902, is settled in 1914 for $5 million in damages)... Frank Sprague builds world's first complete electric railway system for Richmond, VA... L.S. Buffington designs 28-story "skyscraper," never built... Oil millionaire Charles Pratt creates Pratt Institute, Brooklyn, "for all classes of workers, artists, artisans, apprentices, and homemakers" (evolves as noted art-architecture-engineering school)...

Thomas A. Edison moves laboratories from Menlo Park to West Orange, NJ (with research team develops machinery to make cement, process for magnetic separation of iron from ore - failure, storage battery, dictating machine)... Thomas A. Edison develops peep-hole device to show series of pictures (devises Kinetoscope in 1889 to show moving images - first motion pictures with single camera by French physician F. J. Marey in 1880's)... German-born Emile Berliner invents Gramophone, replaces Edison's cylinders with records to form Gramophone Co. (is improved with spring-driven motor of Eldridge Johnson in 1896)... Department of Agriculture forms Forestry Division (evolves by 1988 with over 30,000 employees overseeing 156 national forests via 119 administrative units to earn $3 billion/year and spend $4 billion)... Player piano is invented, a hit in Western saloons.

Business Events

Elegant Grand Hotel, veranda one-eighth of mile long, opens on Machinac Island, MI, for wealthy summer vacationers (adds golf course in 1910 and swimming pool in 1920)... First oil-burning locomotive is tested on Altoona-Pittsburgh run, followed by first successful U.S. electric locomotive in 1895, first diesel-electric in 1925, and first gas-turbine-electric in 1948... English safety bicycle with chain-drive, two standard wheels appears in U.S. market, launches industry (uses brakes, pneumatic tires by 1890)... New York Life Insurance pioneers industry's branch office system (issues industry's first annual report for policyholders in 1896)... With funds from local merchants, farmers James Cannon starts cotton mill in Concord, NC (operates towel mill around 1906 and develops Kannopolis, world's largest unincorporated town, as model mill city with housing, schools, churches, dormitories for single women, and parks, uses trademark in 1916 to sell linen, towels)...

Andrew Carnegie starts building pioneering employee recreation center in Braddock, PA (-1895, contains theater, swimming pool, gymnasium, billiard room, bowling alley, photography facilities, classrooms)... Procter & Gamble adopts profit-sharing program for 400 wage earners, followed by John Wanamaker's department store in 1887 to cover some 3,000 employees... American Association of Public Accountants is formed, NY, to lobby for public accountancy laws (merges with other state groups to form national society, is replaced by American Institute of Accountants in 1916)...

Buffalo Bill Cody's Wild West Show introduces cowboys and Indians to Britain (continues on 7-year tour of 13 European countries, provides German military with innovations in loading, unloading trains)... Henry O. Havemeyer, brother form Sugar Refineries Co. as combination of 15 New York firms (dissolve trust in 1890, reorganize as American Sugar Refining in 1891 to expand with horizontal acquisitions to fight competition)... Stuyvesant Fish, director since 1877, becomes president of Illinois Central Railroad (forms decentralized organizational structure with headquarters in Chicago)... Adding machine, designed by William S. Burroughs, is made by Boyer Machine of St. Louis (patents workable machine in 1892 - English patent in 1895 before death in 1898, leads to Joseph Boyer's Burroughs Adding Machine Co. in 1905 - sales of $8 million in 1913 with 2,500 employees)... Self-taught chief engineer Charles M. Schwab becomes superintendent of Carnegie's Homestead Works (becomes general superintendent of Thomson Works in 1889, becomes president of Carnegie Steel in 1897 - world's first to have annual salary of $1 million, after being Carnegie's agent in negotiations with J.P. Morgan becomes first president of U.S. Steel in 1901 - resigns in 1903)... With savings as teacher S.H. Kress opens novelty and stationery store, PA (acquires wholesaler in 1890, opens first variety store in 1896 in Memphis, TN - by 1907 with 51 stores to gross $3 million, incorporates in 1907 as S.H. Kress Co., expands to 264 stores and some 22,000 employees by 1955)... Former British steel worker Harry M. Stevens starts business in Columbus, OH, to print and sell score cards for local baseball games (as one of sports' biggest concessionaires introduces German sausages in oblong rolls as "red hots" at NYC's Polo Grounds in 1900)...

Special Pennsylvania Limited train operates between Chicago, NYC (becomes Broadway Limited in 1902)... Fourteen local oil men in Findlay, OH, form Marathon Oil... James Coker, son start Carolina Fibre Co., first to make pulp from Southern pine... Huffy sewing-machine business is started (after developing line of bikes for children, acquires U.S. rights for Britain's Raleigh bicycles in 1982)... Modern Ingersoll Milling Machine business is started when Judge Jonathan Ingersoll purchases interest in machine tool firm for his son, aspiring professional baseball player...

After working for Pulitzer's New York World, William Randolph Hearst becomes editor of father's financially-troubled San Francisco Examiner (attacks City's bosses, Southern Pacific Railroad, and monopolies to achieve profits by 1890)... Chauncy Griggs starts St. Paul & Tacoma Lumber Co., WA... James Gordon Bennett's New York Herald starts Paris edition, becomes International Herald Tribune by 1980s... P.J. Towle, MN, originates Log Cabin syrup (offers $500 reward for evidence of impurity, is acquired by General Foods in 1927).

1888

General Events

Industrial Reform Party nominates (February 22) candidates for national election, also Union Labor and United Labor parties... Union Labor Party meets to support militant workers... Congress establishes (June 13) Department of Labor... Congress forbids return to U.S. of Chinese workers who have left the country... Congress investigates trusts... Congress passes first Federal labor relations law (establishes arbitration procedure, presidential board of investigation for railroads)... Congress grants letter-carriers 8-hour day (is extended in 1892 to cover laborers and mechanics of government and contractors, is followed by 1900 law to grant letter-carriers 6-hour day and 48-hour work week)... Colonel Jones starts breeding cattalo as hybrid of buffalos, cattle (flops as commercial venture)... Colored Farmers' Organization is formed in South... Nikola A. Tesla perfects alternating-current electric motor, manufactured by Westinghouse Electric... Belgium-born Leo Baekeland invents photographic dry plate for film processing (develops photographic paper, sells rights to Eastman Kodak in 1899)... Thomas A. Edison, associates issue pamphlet to warn public of dangers in using Tesla's AC electricity (attacks Westinghouse, Thomson-Houston electrical businesses as "patent pirates")... Edward Bellamy: <u>Looking</u> <u>Backward</u> (forecasts idealistic world of 2000 with no money as everyone uses so-called credit cards, work starting at 21 after education, and with retirement at 45)...

Business Events

Modern self-service merchandising is pioneered when Thomas Adams installs penny gumball machines on platforms of New York's elevated lines, followed by first coin-operated Coca-Cola cooler in 1936 and first automatic coffee dispenser in 1946... Los Angeles Chamber of Commerce is formed (promotes area throughout U.S. with displays by Hoosier Frank Wiggins at exhibitions, expands growth of City from 11,000 in 1880 to 50,000 in 1890 - over 2 million by 1930)... Hotel del Coronado opens for rich and famous across the bay from San Diego... Elizabeth B. Boit co-founds Harvard Knitting Mill, MA, to make women's underwear (operates with 360 employees in 1896, institutes profit-sharing plan in 1920)...

Lawyer Samuel P. Colt reorganizes National Rubber (joins formation of U.S. Rubber in 1892)... Theatrical agent Elizabeth Marbury is hired to represent author Frances Hodgson Burnett (forms American Play Co. in 1914)... Marc Klaw, Abraham L. Erlanger acquire Taylor Theatrical Agency (by 1895 operate 2nd largest booking agency with almost 200 theaters, join others in 1896 to form Klaw & Erlanger Theatrical Exchange to book acts for over 500 houses, maintain practical monopoly to 1910 when broken by rival Shubert brothers)... Arthur V. Davis joins Charles M. Hall's Pittsburgh Reduction Co. to produce first U.S. commercial aluminum (becomes president of Mellon's 1907 Alcoa in 1910)... With borrowed capital, Fuller E. Callaway starts 5-cent and 10-cent variety store, GA (develops business as department store and wholesale dry goods business, starts cotton manufacturing in 1900 - by 1920's with 12 mills, innovates as first in industry to sell directly to consumers, provides workers with housing, schools, churches, hotels, profit-sharing, group insurance, medical and nursing services, etc.)...

Burrelle's Information Services starts as business to clip articles for celebrities, later monitors publications for businesses and institutions (still extant)... Mum, first branded deodorant, is introduced, followed by Everdry in 1902 and Hush in 1908... Pawnee Bill's Wild West Show tours U.S., Europe (merges later with Buffalo Bill's extravaganza)... George P. Rowell publishes <u>Printers'</u> <u>Ink:</u> <u>A</u> <u>Journal</u> <u>for</u> <u>Advertising</u>... Waltham Watch Co., MA, devises transfer machine to feed parts to different lathes (is used in 1920's by Britain's Morris Motors, U.S.' Graham-Paige to produce automobile engine blocks with transfer machines supplying different work stations, leads to development of tape controls in 1950's for machine processing by U.S. Air Force to pioneer automation)... Edward Libbey's New England Glass Co. at Cambridge, MA, is closed by strike directed by Michael J. Owens (moves business to Toledo, OH, for cheaper fuel, hires Owens as foreman for glass plant - superintendent by 1890, sponsors experiments of Owens in 1898 to make glass bottles by machine, results in formation of Owens Bottle Co. in 1903 to make machines)...

Former Philadelphia merchant Meyer Guggenheim starts smelter operation at Pueblo, CO (abandons trading business and mining operations to concentrate on smelting after realizing ore processing more stable business, develops Philadelphia Smelting & Refining with sons to monopolize industry during 1890's in U.S., Mexico)... American Excelsior Co. is started to make packing material, mattress stuffing (still extant).   Using "blind pool," successful in his reorganizing Northern Pacific Railroad in 1881, Henry Villard with support of J.P. Morgan creates Edison General Electric, capitalized at $12 million, to consolidate 8 companies using Edison patents, ousted in 1891 with Morgan's formation of General Electric in 1892... Parker Pen, WI, starts business, world's largest pen maker by 1988... In extending Florida East Coast Railway, Standard Oil magnate Henry M. Flagler opens grand Ponce de Leon Hotel at St. Augustine for wealthy tourists... With rights from Edison Jesse H. Lippincott starts North American Phonograph (-1893 with receivership).

1889

General Events

Congress authorizes (February 20) Maritime Canal Co. of Nicaragua to build and operate canal across that country... North Dakota, 39th, South Dakota, 40th, Montana, 41st, and Washington, 42nd, become states... Kansas is first State to pass (March 2) anti-trust law (is followed by ME, MI, and TN, in 1889, SD, KY, and MS, in 1890, 5 more in 1891)... To raise new revenues, New Jersey passes (May) law to permit incorporation of "holding companies"... First International Conference of American States meets in Washington, DC, to form customs union, stymied by high-tariff industrialists... William Gray of Hartford, CT, patents coin-operated telephone (starts business in 1891 with Amos Whitney, Francis Pratt to install pay-phones in department stores)...

16-story World Building, world's tallest office structure, is erected, NYC, with steel-frame and masonry, followed in 1893-94 by Manhattan Life Insurance building with 20 stories... National Association of Letter Carriers is formed... Congress passes law to protect Alaskan salmon... Literary Digest: "The ordinary 'horseless carriage' is at present a luxury for the wealthy: although its price will probably fall in the future, it will never, of course, come into as common use as the bicycle"...

Angus Campbell devises spindle cotton picker... Actuarial Society of America is formed... Philadelphia merchant John Wanamaker becomes Postmaster General (-1893, introduces use of pneumatic tubes in postal service for handling mail - soon to replace use of cash children in retail stores, sponsors rural free delivery in 1893)... Singer Co. introduces electric sewing machine... After George Eastman creates tough, flexible celluloid film for rotating spool, Thomas A. Edison devises Kinetoscope cabinet, permits viewer to see moving pictures... Temporary social science organization forms (becomes American Academy of Political and Social Sciences in 1890)... Burger builds first tractor with oil engine...

Daniel Storer and William Hance, IL, patent bicycle with back-pedal brake... Oil wells are drilled offshore Santa Barbara, CA.

Business Events

Illinois Steel adopts pioneering social and recreational program,

emulated by others, including National Cash Register, in 1890-1910...
William Wright mixes first batch of Calumet baking powder in Chicago
laboratory-bedroom, acquired by General Foods in 1928... First public
coin-operated Gramophone is installed at San Francisco's Royal Palace,
followed in 1948 by Seeburg's modern juke box... Alfred Shook builds
Birmingham's first modern blast furnace, AL... Modern spice business of
McCormick & Co. is started, Baltimore... With funds from British
investors, world's largest flour operation is formed by merger of C.A.
Pillsbury & Co., Washburn Mill...

Henry R. Towne describes gain-sharing wage plan for employees, used since
1884, to American Society of Mechanical Engineers... Childs restaurant
chain is started (operates 106 places in U.S., Canada, by 1925)...
American League for Social Service creates "social secretary" function
(is used by industry to handle employee activities, results in first
conference of social secretaries in 1893)... Nicholas Gilman: Profit
Sharing Between Employer and Employee: A Study in the Evolution of the
Wages System (studies programs of French, English, and 32 U.S.
companies)... With technology for large-scale publishing, Frank A. Munsey
starts Munsey's Weekly (launches Munsey's Magazine in 1891, pioneers
achieving profits from advertising revenues rather than subscriptions,
after advertising for new subscribers in 1893 to save failing Weekly
breaks distribution monopoly of American News, starts acquiring
newspapers in 1901 with profits from Magazine - at one time operates 7
NYC dailies)...

Dutch-born Edward Bok becomes editor of Curtis' Ladies' Home Journal
(-1919, pioneers development of mass-circulation and general-interest
magazines, increases subscribers from 440,000 to 700,000 in 1892 and
1,750,000 in 1910 in advocating thrift, simplicity, conservation and
voluntarism for women, bans all patent medicine ads in 1892, starts
publishing plans in 1895 for more functional and attractive houses to
protest Victorian excesses, declares in 1907 that excessive materialism
is U.S.' greatest danger)... After operating Boston fruit commission
office since 1882, Andrew W. Preston starts banana importing business,
Boston Fruit, with 9 investors (becomes United Fruit in 1899)...

To resolve managerial conflict with Henry C. Frick, Andrew Carnegie forms
Carnegie Co., industry's largest with capitalization of $160 million
(acquires rival Duquesne steel business in 1890)... With idea for self-
raising pancake Charles L. Rutt, St. Joseph, MO, newspaper man, creates
Aunt Jemima pancake flour, first prepared food mix (names product after
catchy tune).

1890s

General Events

U.S. Naval Officer Bradley Fiske designs naval fire-control director with
motors, vacuum tubes, and synchronous motors, installed on most British,
U.S. war ships by end of W.W.I... Thomas A. Edison: "Treatise on
Economical Policy & Business" (opposes Sherman Anti-Trust Act as it
challenges legality of contracts made on basis of patent rights, proposes
minimum price guidelines by trade associations to correct abuses of too
much competition)... Henry Timken invents tapered bearing.

Business Events

To reduce production costs, National Cash Register creates Advanced Department, first firm to centralize welfare activities into one office to improve employee relations and quality of work, with welfare director, 3 aides to supervise employee social, recreational activities... Schuster's Department Store uses trading stamps to increase sales... W.W. Cole Show is started as a circus (-1981, merges later to form Clyde Beatty-Cole Brothers Circus)... Factories install electric motor drives to operate machinery... Men carrying sandwich signs with advertising messages appear on many city streets, electric signs in late 1890's and neon signs in 1920's.

1890

General Events

AFL establishes United Mine Workers... U.S. Supreme Court: Chicago, Milwaukee & St. Paul Railroad v. Minnesota (rules State cannot set fees to deny "a reasonable profit" to corporations as persons)... Wyoming, 42nd, and Idaho, 43rd, become States... Congress passes Sherman Anti-Trust Law (declares "illegal every contract, combination in the form of trust or otherwise, or conspiracy, in restraint of trade of commerce among the several States, or with foreign nations," leads to 23 anti-trust cases 1893-1903)... Congress passes (July 14) Sherman Silver Purchase Act (requires government to purchase 4,500,000 ounces of silver/month as backing for legal tender notes, is repealed 1893)... Congress passes (August 8) Original Package Act (upholds State's right to subject merchandise from outside the State to its own laws)... After strong complaints from Europeans on contaminated shipments of pork, Department of Agriculture is authorized (August 30) to inspect pork shipped to foreign markets...

Single Tax National League forms to promote single tax for all property... Congress passes (October 1) McKinley Tariff Act (raises tariffs to their highest level)... Congress passes Rivers and Harbors Act to restrict discharge of solid industrial matter into navigable rivers, followed in 1948 by water-pollution-control law... By accident, Wisconsin retailer Smithson creates ice-cream sundae by adding toppings when short of ice cream on Sundays... Ohio opens first State employment office, some 23 other states by 1915... Pasadena hosts first annual Rose Parade (sponsors first football game in 1902 as festival event - unsuccessful, revives football game attraction in 1916)...

St. Louis physician invents peanut butter in this time as health food, followed in 1903 by St. Louis' Ambrose W. Straub with patent for first peanut butter machine... AFL charters Retail Clerks National Protective Assn. (becomes Retail Clerks International later)... Last river packet on upper Missouri leaves Ft. Benton, MT, (reaches St. Louis in about 60 days after traveling some 3,000 miles)...

Congress establishes safety standards for coal mines... Deadwood, SD, sees last scheduled stagecoach service... William H. Stoats invents first mechanical coin-changer... American Academy of Political and Social Science: The Annuals, first issue on employment management... U.S. census records population of 62.9 million, 22.1 urban and 40.8 rural, and immigration over 5.2 million since 1881...

Black inventor W.B. Purvis patents a fountain pen... For first time value of agricultural production is equaled by manufacturing output, which doubles by 1900.-. In period to 1917 some 18 million immigrants arrive in U.S., two-thirds or more from Eastern or Southern Europe... Nation's wealthy is studied (reveals in report some one-half of U.S.' wealth held by 1% of families, is unchanged by 1914)... Carpenters achieve 8-hour day in 137 cities...

Jacob Riis: How the Other Half Lives (reveals inadequate living conditions of poor)... Wainright Building, designed by Lewis Sullivan as "Father of Modern Architecture," is built in St. Louis (-1891, contains all elements of structure, form for skyscraper)... N.O. Nelson Mfg. establishes model town for employees in Leclaire, IL... Captain Alfred Mahan: The Influence of Sea Power Upon History, 1660-1873 (argues strategic role of naval power key to success in international politics)... U.S. produces 9.3 million tons of iron/steel, No. 1 in world - 10.3 in 1900, 26.5 in 1910, 31.8 in 1913, 42.3 in 1920, 41.3 in 1930, and 28.8 in 1938 with Germany 2nd at 23.2.

Business Events

Antonio, Carlo Matranga of Sicily arrives in New Orleans (battle Provenzano brothers for city dominance, start rise of Mafia crime business in U.S.)... Twenty-seven firms, 312 by 1897, produce some 40,000 bicycles, peaks at 1.2 million in 1895... James C. Fargo, president of American Express, travels to Europe (on return, disgusted with lack of acceptance of letters of credit, directs Marcellus F. Berry to devise new financial instrument for traveling, issues first traveler checks in 1891 - $9,200 in first year to $6 million in 1901)... Volkman, Stollwerck & Co., NY, provides workers with pioneering vacation plan of one week/year...

Exclusive fashion house of Henri Bendel opens, NYC... Westinghouse Air Brake's foundry uses conveyor system with endless track (follows ceramic factory of ancient Athens where workers moved along production line to paint stationary vases)... After developing cash register and failing in competitive battle with National Cash Register, C.E. Skinner is hired as machinist by Westinghouse (is assigned to experimental laboratory, starts regular research laboratory in 1916)... James B. Duke, 4 competitors form American Tobacco Co. (evolves in 1890's with centralized headquarters, NYC, to supervise decentralized operations in controlling 62% of chewing tobacco market and 93% of cigarette market by 1900)...

Equitable Savings & Loan Assn., first such in Pacific Northwest, opens in Portland, OR (opens Washington branch in 1899 and Idaho office in 1910, avoids financial crisis in 1982 by selling to Benjamin Franklin Savings & Loan)... 1887 Sugar Refineries Trust dissolves, replaced by Henry O. Havemayer's American Sugar Refining in 1891... Lyman Stewart starts Union Oil Co., CA, followed by Standard Oil of California in 1913... Herbert H. Dow starts Midland Chemical, MI, to make bromine from local brines (operates first U.S. electrical chemical plant in 1892, becomes Dow Chemical in 1897)... James J. Hill creates Great Northern Railway, tracks parallel those of Northern Pacific (extends line to Seattle in 1893 with no land grants, assumes control of Northern Pacific in 1895 after bankruptcy in Panic of 1893, although blocked by Supreme Court in 1896 in joining 2 roads develops joint interests, starts Great Northern Steamship Co. in 1900 - folds in 1905)... After working for Armour & Co., Michael Cudahy starts packing house (evolves with 57 branches)...

Frederick W. Taylor, management pioneer, resigns from Midvale Steel to become general manager of Manufacturing Investment Co. (-1893, starts working in 1893 as independent consulting engineer to advise firms on systematizing shop management and lowering costs, works for Bethelehem Steel as consultant in 1898-1901, invests "high-speed" tool steel in 1899)... After sewing gloves Rose M. Knox and husband, former glove salesman, buy gelatin firm, NY (after husband dies in 1906, sells other businesses to focus on gelatin products, starts food column and experimental kitchen, provides employees in 1913 with 5-day work week, 2-week vacation, and time off for illness, triples value of business to $300,000 by 1915, at age of 92 is named America's foremost woman industrialist by Colliers in 1949)... Moses H. Cone forms selling organization for some 40 Southern mills (standardizes quality and improves styles)... Kate Gleason becomes secretary, treasurer of father's gear-cutting business (develops business as industry's leading producer before resigning in 1913 to develop suburban industrial real estate)...

World's largest glass-roofed arcade, prototype of modern shopping mall, opens, Cleveland, with shops, offices, and restaurants, anchored at each end by office buildings (is restored 1979)... Pioneering black-owned Georgia Real Estate Loan and Trust Co. is started in Atlanta, followed by Atlanta Loan and Title in 1891 and Union Mutual Insurance Assn., first in State chartered by blacks, in 1897... Oxford, Denver's oldest luxury hotel, opens.

1891

General Events

Supreme Court upholds Federal Income Tax adopted during Civil War... Congress approves (March 4) International Copyright Act... 11 Sicilians are indicted for murder of New Orleans' Irish Chief of Police (after rumors they are members of "Mafia" gang are killed by mob)... Nebraska passes (April 7) 8-hour day law... Convicts are used in Briceville, TN, as replacements for striking miners... Thomas A. Edison patents Kinetoscope picture machine (patents first significant radio device to send electrical signals without use of wire)...

To discourage flood of applications, Patent Office requires all inventors of perpetual-motion machines to submit models... Pioneering International Correspondence School is founded in Scranton, PA, followed by Chicago's American School of Correspondence and University of Wisconsin's extension division... Reformed Populace Party is formed by mostly farmers and workers (advocates government ownership of railroad, telegraph and telephone operations, free coinage of silver, graduated income tax, 8-hour day, popular election of senators, secret ballot, and government warehouses for grain, polls over one million votes in 1892 Presidential election)... E.G. Atcheson, PA, accidentally discovers carborundum while trying to make diamonds... Black inventor P.B. Downing patents street letter mailbox... Electrolytic process is developed for refining copper... Carriage & Wagon Workers' International Union is formed (is expelled from AFL in 1918 after jurisdictional dispute, disappears in 1920s with growth of United Automobile, Aircraft and Vehicle Workers).

Business Events

National Lead Co. is created by 25 makers of white lead products (introduces Dutch Boy paints in 1907)... After operating Boston advertising agency, Nathaniel C. Fowles starts pioneering full-time copywriting business (starts school of advertising, publishes how-to-do-it manuals on advertising)... Murdo McKenzie is hired by Scottish investors to operate 500,000-acre Matador Land and Cattle Co., TX (-1911, 1922-37)... Keuffel & Esser Co., oldest U.S. maker of slide rules, is started to make scientific instruments (abandons slide rule market in 1972 with appearance of pocket calculators)... Northwestern Consolidated Milling is formed by 1889 Pillsbury-Washburn company and 6 Minneapolis mills (is followed by 1892 organizations of Minneapolis Flour Milling, New York's Hecker-Jones-Jewell Milling by major mills and Sperry Flour, CA, by six mills)...

William Wrigley, Jr., partner start soap business (after adding baking powder to line give free chewing gum as promotional gimmick, contract with Zeno Mfg. in 1892 to produce gum, introduce "Spearmint" flavor in 1899 to focus on gum business, promote product with dictum: "Tell 'em quick and tell 'em often")... George Westinghouse, Jr., reorganizes 1869 Westinghouse Air Brake (starts Pittsburgh Meter in 1891, reorganizes and refinances 1886 Westinghouse Electric as Westinghouse Electric & Mfg. in 1893, joins General Electric in 1896 to form Board of Patent Control, acquires rights for Parson's steam turbine, declares brief bankruptcy in 1907-08)... George A. Hormel starts meat-packing business, MN (develops German canned ham process in 1927)... Leonidas, Alfred Merrit discover Mesabi range of iron ore, MN, acquired during 1893 Panic by John D. Rockefeller... Du Pont builds plant to test gunpowder for Army, Navy...

Frederick A. Halsey describes first "pure" wage incentive system for workers to American Society of Mechanical Engineers... Automatic Machine Co. develops first U.S. automatic vending machine to dispense postage stamps (follows use of such machines in Britain in 1880's to sell tobacco and snuff products, is followed by formation of Canteen Co. in 1929)...

American Railway Association is created... Engineering Magazine is issued (becomes Industrial Management in 1916)... Bartlett Arkell starts Beech-Nut Packing Co. with less than $10,000 to make hickory-cured hams (evolves by 1941 in baby foods to operate assets of $22.8 million with philosophy of welfare capitalism, is sold to Nestle in 1979 for $35 million)... James Stillman becomes president of National City Bank of New York (with backing of Rockefeller interests transforms bank from commercial operation to compete with Morgan and Schiff investment banks)... Wall Street Lawyer William N. Cromwell arranges voluntary agreement of creditors to save failing New York brokerage house - Cromwell Plan used to save many other businesses in distress (is retained by J.P. Morgan in 1896 to reorganize Northern Pacific Railroad - later U.S. Steel and Brazilian railroad for French and English interests, forms National Tube in 1899 as consolidation of 16 firms)...

Abandoning farming Henry Ford works as night engineer, $45/month, for

Detroit Edison Electric (builds first car, Quadracycle, in 1896)...
William Morrison, Des Moines, is "first" to build electric car in U.S...
The Stenographer reports 42 makers of typewriters, 89 by 1911.

1892

General Events

Ellis Island opens, New York Harbor, to process arriving immigrants
(handles over 20 million before closing in 1954)... Ohio Supreme Court
dissolves Standard Oil Trust (results in formation of Standard Oil Co. of
New Jersey as giant holding company in 1899, is dissolved in 1911 by U.S.
Supreme Court)... Congress passes (May 5) Geary Chinese Exclusion Act
(requires registration of all Chinese in U.S.)... Martial law is used in
Coeur D' Alene, ID, to quell labor violence of silver miners protesting
wage cuts (requires use of Federal troops)... First long-distance
commercial telephone service starts between Chicago, NYC... John
Froelich, IA, builds first practical self-propelled gasoline tractor,
precursor of John Deere models (is followed in 1901 by Dan Albone's 3-
wheel Ivel and in 1905 by first gasoline-tractor manufacturing business
of C.W. Hart and C.H. Pan, IA)... Employees of Boston Globe newspaper try
to start credit union... J.H. Northrup devises automatic loom... Black
inventor Sarah Boone patents ironing board... Black teamsters, White
scalemen and packers strike for 10-hour work day in New Orleans, ruled in
violation of Sherman Anti-Trust Act...

Socialist Party holds national convention... Andrew Carnegie's Homestead
Works, Henry Frick in charge while Carnegie visits Scotland, fights 5-
month strike of workers for union recognition (protects non-union workers
with armed Pinkerton guards, with defeat of Pinkertons calls in 8,000
National Guard troops - 20 killed and hundreds wounded, blacklists union
members throughout steel industry when operations resume with protection
of State Militia)... Trying to develop perfect billiard ball, J.W. Hyatt
invents ball bearing.

Business Events

Prestigious sporting goods business of Abercromie & Fitch opens in NYC
(expands to operate 9 retail branches nationwide before filing for
bankruptcy in 1976 - liquidation 1977)... 1869 Schoneberger & Noble
beverage business, inventors of cream soda, introduce celery tonic...
National Cash Register publishes pioneering N.C.R. magazine for
employees, followed by 4 firms in 1892-99, 8 in 1900-04, and 3 in 1905-
07... Thomas A. Edison and assistant W.K.L. Dickson, founder of Biograph
in early 1900's, build first motion picture studio in West Orange, NJ
(produce first practical movies in 1896)... Association for the Promotion
of Profit-Sharing is formed... Illinois Steel installs industry's first
safety department... Vogue is issued as fashion magazine for women,
acquired in 1909 by Conde Nast to become prestigious publication...

U.S. Rubber is created by merger of 10 Northeastern rubber firms (starts
horizontal integration in 1904 with purchase of General Rubber - by 1909
with rubber plantations in Sumatra, acquires Rubber Goods Mfg.,
combination of 20 businesses making consumer rubber products with U.S.'
rights for Britain's Dunlop tire, in 1905, creates development department
and starts central research function in 1912, introduces U.S. Keds in

1917, is acquired by DuPont in 1927 to appoint Francis B. Davis, Jr., of DuPont as President in 1929, installs multi-divisional organizational structure with central headquarters)... Elegant Italian Renaissance-style Brown Palace hotel opens in Denver...

Pattillo Higgins starts company to search for oil near Beaumont, TX (fails, starts new partnership with engineer Anthony Lucas, previously driller of deep wells, LA, for salt deposits, but fails, starts new partnership with Lucas, J.M. Guffy, and funds from Andrew Mellon to discover Spindletop in 1901 - land prices soar to almost $1 million/acre)... Patrick Calhoun, agent for J.P. Morgan, purchases bankrupt Richmond Terminal, basis for Southern Railroad system... Commerce Clearing House is started, Chicago, to provide lawyers with up-to-date legal information (is acquired by Quaker Oakleigh Thorne in 1907, issues reports to business on tax matters, government regulations)...

Clarence M. Woolley forms American Radiator with 3 competitors (survives 1896 Depression by invading European market - plant in 1895)... George Eastman reorganizes film business as Eastman Kodak (perfects daylight-load film, starts selling in foreign markets)... Carnegie Steel is formed as world's largest steel enterprise with capitalization of $25 million, Andrew Carnegie with over 55% of stock (after part ownership in Oliver Mining, expands and integrates production facilities during 1893-97 Depression)...

J.P. Morgan, Henry Villard form General Electric Co. by merging Thomson-Houston (arc lamps) and Edison General Electric (incandescent lighting), name Charles Coffin as president to centralize operations (obtains electrical genius Charles P. Steinmetz in merger, starts South African plant in 1890's - followed by General Motors and Ford in early 1900's, starts standardizing laboratory in 1895 which becomes research laboratory in 1901, to reduce litigation costs on patent infringement suits forms patent pool with Westinghouse Electric in 1896 - dominates rival with 62.5% share, starts forming product divisions in 1910-29)... After serving as executive with Edison and vice president of General Electric, British-born Samuel Insull becomes president of Chicago Edison Co. (innovates in utilities field with public relations, steam turbines, electric meters, open-end mortgages, mass marketing of stocks, and electrical power system with acquisition of various utilities)...

Independent theater producer Charles Frohman forms Empire Stock Co. to represent stage stars (joins others in starting Theatrical Syndicate in 1896 as central booking system for theaters)... George W. Perkins is hired by New York Life Insurance to supervise independent sales agencies (replaces agencies with branch offices to centralize control over sales force, rewards salesmen with bonuses and pension plan, and negotiates with Russia in 1899 to purchase their railway bonds)... Henry W. Oliver forms Oliver Iron Mining to develop Great Mesabi Range, MN (sells in 1901 to J.P. Morgan's U.S. Steel for $17 million - original investment $600,000)... Charles E. Duryea, brother Frank perfect first U.S. automobile in Springfield, MA (demonstrate car for public in 1893)...

Asa Candler incorporates soft-drink business as Coca-Cola (registers trademark with U.S. Patent Office, drops nostrum promotion to sell product as soda fountain drink, starts selling syrup to franchised bottlers, first unofficial in 1894, in 1899, patents modern Coke bottle

in 1919, retires, leaving control to family, in 1916 to be mayor of
Atlanta, fails to prevent sale of business financier Ernest Woodruff in
1917 to settle suit with U.S. for having too much caffeine in drink)...
Financier Jay Gould dies, leaves estate of some $125 million (causes
stock prices of Western Union, Manhattan Elevated, Missouri Pacific,
Union Pacific to rise).

1893

General Events

John L. Stephens, U.S. Ambassador to Hawaii, and powerful planters, led
by Sanford P. Dole, overthrow monarchy of Hawaii, declare Island U.S.
Protectorate (is rejected by President Cleveland, becomes territory in
1900)... Eugene V. Debs organizes millitant American Railway Union,
recognized as bargaining agent by Great Northern Railroad (enrolls some
50,000 members after successful strike against Great Northern in 1894,
declines in membership after 1894 Pullman debacle)... After lobbying by
property groups, Chicago limits height of buildings to 10 stories...

Western Federation of Miners organizes in Denver, CO (earns violent
reputation in winning higher wages and shorter hours, records dwindling
membership after losing copper strike on Michigan's Upper Peninsula in
1913-14, joins United Steel Workers in 1967)... Locomotive 999 of New
York Central's Empire State Express sets record of 112 mph, topped in
1955 with first 200 mph run by French electric locomotive... Cream of
Wheat breakfast cereal, first hot cereal since Indian mush in 1671, is
created at North Dakota flour mill... James F. Muirhead: United States,
first U.S. travel guide... Telephone lines link NYC, Chicago and
Boston... Financial Panic results when British investors sell U.S.
securities for gold, depletes reserves (-1897, forces 74 railroads into
receivership, 600 banks to close, and some 15,000 commercial houses to
fail)...

After lobbying by League of American Wheelmen, Department of Agriculture
creates office of Road Inquiry to develop roads for bicycling (becomes
Office of Public Roads in 1905)... World's Columbia Exposition is held,
Chicago, with naughty dances of Little Egypt as main attraction (exhibits
electric kettle - perfected in 1923 by England's A.L. Large with reliable
heating element, introduces cafeteria, Swedish invention, to U.S. - self-
service restaurants in NYC as early as 1885, gives demonstration of
psychological tests by psychologist Joseph Jastrow, exhibits world's
first filing system - previously records strung on threads during Roman
Empire era, demonstrates Ferris Wheel, 25 stories high with 36 cars
carrying 60 riders each, of inventor George Washington Ferris, shows use
of AC motor and power system of George Westinghouse)...

U.S. Supreme Court: U.S. v. Workmen's Amalgamated Council (rules Sherman
Anti-Trust Act applies to unions)... Railway Safety Appliance Act
requires all railroads to use air-brakes, automatic couplers... Lucania,
averaging 20 knots/hour, crosses Atlantic from East to West in record
time of just over 5-and-one-half days... H.D. Perky develops first ready-
cooked cereal, "Shredded Wheat," as breakfast food at Denver vegetarian
restaurant, starts Natural Foods Co. in 1895... U.S. Supreme Court:
Waterhouse v. Comer (rules any strike against interstate transportation,
communication industries as illegal)...

Business Events

Chicago's 1882 Spiegel's Furniture Store, developed business by supplying brothels with home furnishings, adopts policy of sales on credit (starts current mail-order business in 1903, is acquired in 1982 by West Germany's Otto Versand to become world's largest mail-order house by 1988)... Robert F. Dun, credit service pioneer, publishes Dun's Review as weekly report on business conditions... After observing use of batteries to power machine at Chicago Exposition, lawyer Isaac L. Rice acquires control of 1888 Electric Storage Battery Co., adopts trade name of Exide in 1900 (acquires over 500 related patents and rival firms to gross $1 million in 1895 and become virtual monopoly by 1897, is forced out of business in 1899)...

With debts over $125 million, Philadelphia & Reading Railroad declares bankruptcy (results in attempt of lawyer Isaac L. Rice and financial syndicate to rescue line by creating novel corporate holding company for road and its mining ventures, is forced aside by J.P. Morgan's syndicate to save railroad with Rice's innovative reorganization)... Elegant Waldorf Hotel opens, NYC (becomes Waldorf-Astoria in 1897)... After selling lumber, Frederick L. Maytag starts business in Newton, IA, to make and sell feeders for threshing machines (starts making washing machines in 1907, introduces electric washing machine in 1911, starts Mason Motor Car business in 1911 - fails, perfects gyrofoam agitator in 1922, diversifies with dishwashers in 1968 and microwave ovens in 1982)...

By accident Edward L. Doheny discovers high-quality oil near Los Angeles, site for 1,300 wells in 1913 (develops oil field in 1900 near Tampico to make Mexico world's 2nd largest oil producer)... Solomon D. Warfield organizes Seaboard Railroad, combination of 20 railways along Atlantic Coast from Maryland to Florida by 1900 (organizes International Cotton Mills in 1910)... George W. Crawford forms partnership with brother-in-law to develop natural gas fields (forms Ohio Fuel Supply in 1902, Lone Star Gas in 1909, Penn-Mex Fuel in 1909 - sold to Sinclair Oil in 1932, United Fuel Gas in 1916 for WV, KY, and OH, and Tropical Oil in 1916 for oil development in South America)...

After working as laborer, salesman, and sales manager, James A. Farrell becomes general manager of Pittsburgh Wire (maintains firm's solvency during Depression by being industry's first to develop foreign markets, becomes president of U.S. Steel Products in 1903 and U.S. Steel in 1911-32)... Mining engineer Frederick A. Heinze starts Montana Ore Purchasing Co. to operate smelter for independent mine owners (discovers copper lode in abandoned mine, purchases Rarus Mine with inheritance in 1895 to make millions, acquires another productive mine to discover more copper, battles Boston & Montana mining enterprise in 1900 on property rights - victorious with election of sympathetic judges, sells most of holdings in 1906 for $10.5 million to start United Copper, loses most of wealth in 1907 Panic)... After two discouraging years in teaching, Caleb D. Bradham, age 27, acquires corner drugstore on credit in New Bern, NC, (develops soft drink, "Brad's Drink," as mixture of kola-nut extract and "rare oil" to treat dyspepsia in 1898, patents drink in 1903 as Pepsi-Cola to evolve with syrup sales going from 20,000 gallons to over 100,000, starts franchising - million-dollar business by 1915, starts buying sugar in 1919 for inventory when price rises, declares bankruptcy in 1922 when unable to pay off bank loan with drop in sugar prices, reorganizes in 1923 as new Virginia corporation with underwriter Roy Megargel in control, after denied jobber's discount by Coca-Cola, is acquired in 1930 by Charles G. Guth with funds from Loft candy business, when unable to sell failing business to Coca-Cola in 1934 sells to James Carkner, associates for $600,000, achieves success by doubling size of bottles while maintaining price at 5 cents, stresses life-cycle styles in ads during 1950s to become 2nd largest in soft drink market).

1894

General Events

During year 750,000 workers go out on strikes... Jacob S. Coxey leads 400 people from Ohio to Washington, DC, to protest unemployment (advocates public works relief program of $500 million, abandons protest when leaders of Coxey's Army are arrested for trespassing on grass)... U.S. Supreme Court: <u>Regan</u> <u>v.</u> <u>Farmers'</u> <u>Loan</u> <u>&</u> <u>Trust</u> <u>Company</u> (rules judicial review of reasonableness of rates is Constitutional)... Congress declares (June 28) Labor Day as national holiday... 12,000 tailors in NYC strike to protest "sweat shops," piece-work... U.S., Japan sign (November 22) commercial treaty... Actors' Society of America forms as quasi-union to improve working conditions in theater productions...

New Yorker Augustus Sachett patents first plasterboard... George W. Cole invents 3-in-1 lubricant for use on his bicycle (distributes free samples with bikes as promotional device)... U.S. Supreme Court: <u>U.S.</u> <u>v.</u> <u>Debs</u> (sustains use of injunction against strikes, rules unions as monopolies by hindering trade)... C.B. King of Detroit patents pneumatic hammer... Underwriters Laboratories is started as 3-man research agency by insurance industry to test electrical wiring... Thomas A. Edison devises talking doll...

Henry Demarest Lloyd: <u>Wealth</u> <u>Against</u> <u>Commonwealth</u> (attacks Standard Oil Co., denounces laissez-faire economy and Social Darwinism, advocates nationalization of trusts)... Congress passes income tax bill, ruled unconstitutional by U.S. Supreme Court in 1895... Pennsylvania coal miners hold violent strikes to protest dangerous working conditions, followed by violent strike of 136,000 coal miners in Ohio... 500 miners at Cripple Creek, CO, strike to protest increase of hours without higher wages, suppressed by martial law... AFL repudiates socialism... Western Federation of Miners starts series of strikes for industrial unionism (-1904)... Workers at Pullman Palace Car strike to protest layoffs, reductions in wages of 25-33% with no decreases in rents in company housing and lower prices in company stores (is supported with general sympathy strike by American Railway Union, is suppressed after violence by use of 3,600 deputy marshals and U.S. troops to enforce injunction to maintain postal service, results in conviction of union leader Eugene V. Debs, defended by Clarence Darrow, for violating court injunction)... American Charles Jenkins, Louis Lumiere of France and Robert Paul of Britain independently perfect motion picture film projector... For first time since Civil War, U.S. shows a deficit, $61 million.

Business Events

George E. Haskell, William W. Bosworth start Beatrice Creamery Co. in

Beatrice, NE (achieve success with Meadow Gold Butter and other branded products, reincorporate in 1905 to start 5 more creameries, enter ice cream market in 1907, start advertising nationally, first in industry, in 1912, start diversification in 1964 - by 1980 Beatrice Foods with over 100 major brands, 9,000 products)... National Cash Register is one of first firms to install suggestion boxes to improve communications with employees (follows use of medieval Venetians who aired gripes, ideas with notes through slot in wall of Doge's palace)... Robinson-Danforth Commission business is started in St. Louis with $12,000 to make feed for animals (after acquiring interest of Robinson, loses mill by fire in 1896, introduces whole-wheat cereal, is endorsed by Dr. Ralston, health club president, in 1898, with success changes name of business to Ralston-Purina, opens research laboratory in 1916)...

C.H. Kramm starts Anchor Brewery near San Francisco (produces steam beer with bottom fermentation in 1896, is rescued in 1965 by Fritz Maytag of washing machine family to develop pioneering boutique brewery)... Henry G. Morris, Pedro Salom make Electrobats in Philadelphia, U.S.' first commercial production of electric cars... John Bigelow, Jr.: The Principles of Strategy (revised edition)... After death of Anthony Drexel, investment banking business is reorganized as J.P. Morgan & Co...

Thomas A. Edison opens Kinetoscope Parlor with peep-show machines in NYC, operated in vaudeville theater... Georgia Association of Life Insurers pioneers use of standard personal-history form... Octave Chanute: Progress in Flying Machines... After forcing North American Phonograph business into bankruptcy, Thomas A. Edison starts National Phonograph Co... Elwood Haynes with machinists Edgar and Elmer Apperson builds car in Kokomo, IN (produces cars in Kokomo to 1920's, pioneers automobile industry with some 1,500 manufacturers making over 3,000 different cars, trucks by 1980's)... Henry Flagler, with partner J.D. Rockefeller, Jr., builds luxury hotel to develop Palm Beach as resort area, FL (opens Royal Palm Hotel in Miami when his Florida East Coast Railway reaches City in 1896)...

Lifebuoy is introduced as household soap by Britain's Lever business, promoted as toilet soap in 1933... A cotton mill is first U.S. factory to be completely electrified (provides 22.5% of energy for industrial motors in 1899 - 48% in 1909)... William H. McElwain starts shoe business with $1,500 in savings and loan of $9,000 (develops quantity production methods to make low-priced shoes to revolutionize shoe industry with use of science, re-builds burnt-out factory in 1898 with capital from City's citizens, starts in 1902 to eliminate irregularity of employment in plants by designing planned flow of materials from suppliers to jobbers)...

Chicago meat packer Philip D. Armour diversifies with fertilizer business (starts soap works in 1896 and glycerin plant in 1897, makes soda fountain supplies in 1907, opens Argentina plant in 1915)... With assets of $2,500 John E. Tappan opens Minneapolis office to help local people prepare for financial disasters like Panic of '93 (manages assets of $153 million by 1939 - $34 billion in 1980s as unit of American Express with over 100 financial products and services, pioneers mutual fund investments, becomes Investors Diversified Services in 1949 to offer financial planning, insurance products, limited partnerships, and unit investment trusts).

1895

General Events

U.S. Supreme Court: <u>United States v. E.C. Knight</u> (holds Sherman Anti-Trust Act only covers monopolies in interstate trade)... Congress refuses (February 8) to pass a bill to reissue notes redeemable in gold (with Federal gold reserves down to $41 million forces President Cleveland to seek aid from Morgan-Belmont syndicate of bankers to sell bonds for gold, succeeds in stemming export of gold)... Cotton States and International Exposition opens in Atlanta, GA, to demonstrate progress of industrialization (shows moving pictures on screen)... Congress establishes first Isthmian Canal Commission to consider various routes for possible canal across Central America, others in 1897 and 1899... <u>The Aeronautical Annual</u> is published (- 1897)... John Richards lectures Stanford University engineering students on "works administration"...

Congress bans lotteries in interstate commerce, revived by first intrastate lottery, NH, 1964)... <u>Horseless Age</u> magazine is launched (proclaims new age of transportation)... Cornelius Vanderbilt builds "The Breakers," costs some $4 million, in Newport, RI, as "summer cottage"...

Woodville Latham demonstrates Pantoptikon, a combination of Edison's Kinetoscope and Magic Lantern... Militia is used to suppress strike of trolley railroad workers, Brooklyn... First U.S. Open Golf Championship is held at Newport, RI... Elwood Haynes, Kokomo, gets "first" traffic ticket for automobile speeding, Chicago, by bicycle-mounted policeman... Michael J. Owens patents machine to make bottles (develops automatic machine in 10 years)... Thomas Armat devises Vitascope to project Kinetoscope film on a screen (joins Thomas A. Edison later to form Vitascope Kinetoscope Co.)... After filing for first automobile patent in 1879, George B. Selden gets patent for essential features of modern gasoline-powered automobile (after legal controversy sells all patent rights in 1899 for $10,000 and royalties)...

American Society of Heating and Ventilating Engineers organizes... King Gillette devises safety razor... Frank Duryea, averaging 5 mph, wins first U.S. auto race, sponsored by <u>Chicago Times-Herald</u>... Dave Lennox invents modern house furnace... Washington, with near monopoly on Pacific salmon, agrees to stay out of Alaska waters if Alaska stays out of Washington's fishing grounds.

Business Events

National Association of Manufacturers is created, Cincinnati... Haskins & Sells accounting firm designs accounting system for Treasury Department... After being rejected in selling Dr. Kellogg's new coffee in 1891, ailing farm implement salesman C.W. Post creates Postum Cereal Food Coffee business (starts Postum Cereal Co. in 1896, introduces Grape Nuts in 1897-98 and Post Toasties in 1904, allocates $400,000 for advertising, $50,000 high budget for most firms, in 1899, leaves business to daughter who reorganizes in 1929 as General Foods)... Schwinn bicycle business is established... A. Sulka opens luxurious haberdashery in NYC (opens Paris branch in 1910)... Promoter Edward J. Pennington starts firm in Racine, WI, to make motor carriages (fails to make cars to perform as claimed, disappears from business when plan for $75 million Anglo-American Rapid

Vehicle Co. collapses)...

After being eased out of his Elliott-Lincoln business, inventor John Elliott and brother James, sons of ordained minister, form Lincoln Electric to build, repair electric motors with funds from Herbert H. Dow, future founder of Dow Chemical (incorporate in 1906, form employee committee to advise on operations, provide employees with life insurance in 1915, sponsor employees' association in 1919 to sponsor health benefits and social activities, provide 2-week vacations and piece-work pay system in 1923 - wages adjusted for changes in Consumer Price Index, start employee stock purchase plan in 1925 - key workers covered in 1914, start suggestion system in 1929 and bonus plan to improve productivity and cut costs in 1935, by 1980's is largest U.S. manufacturer of welding machines and electrodes - 2,600 U.S. employees and 600 foreign workers)...

B.F. Goodrich in Akron, OH, starts rubber industry's first research laboratory (pioneers vinyl products in 1926, develops first U.S. commercial process for synthetic rubber in 1939)... With loan from mother, William Randolph Hearst acquires New York Journal (starts circulation battle with Joseph Pulitzer's World in 1896 after pirating employees from World, in war of "yellow journalism" incites U.S. to fight Spain in 1897 to free Cuba, uses 1898 U.S. Maine's mysterious explosion in Havana's harbor as cause, claims victory over World by 1900)... J.P. Morgan wins battle with E.H. Harriman to reorganize Erie Railroad (uses Harriman's plan to revive line)...

First professional football game is played at Latrobe, PA... Hartford Rubber Works, later part of U.S. Rubber, produces pneumatic tires... American Express opens first European office in Paris (sponsors first escorted European tour in 1919 and world pleasure cruise in 1922, operates some 1,000 offices worldwide by 1970)... Frederick W. Taylor: "A Piece-Rate System, Being a Step Toward Partial Solution of the Labor Problem" (in presentation to Society of Mechanical Engineers, proposes job analysis and time studies to set standards for gain-sharing plans, discusses factory planning department of "functional foremen" to manage factory, do job evaluations, and hire, fire workers)... Salesman Thomas J. Watson, Sr., is hired by John Patterson's National Cash Register (attends training school for company indoctrination - required to dress in dark suits, white shirts, subdued ties and polished black shoes, after becoming top salesman by 1898 becomes branch manager in 1899, fired in 1913)...

Overall business of Oshkosh B'Gosh is started, WI (by accident introduces styled overalls for children in 1970's - 15% of sales in 1979 and 80% of 1985 volume of $162 million)... R.F. Outcault draws pioneering "Yellow Kid" comic strip for New York World (licenses derivative products in 1896 to create new business field, creates Buster Brown strip in 1902 for New York Herald, licenses rights for Buster Brown to variety of manufacturers at 1904 St. Louis World's Fair)... After operating bicycle repair shop in Dayton, OH, since 1892, Wilbur, Orville Wright start making bicycles (inspired by Otto Lilienthal's glider crash in Germany in 1896, build biplane in 1899, launch man-carrying glider experiments in 1900-01 at Kitty Hawk, NC)... Businessman Robert S. Brooking builds Cupples Station in St. Louis as private railroad terminal for industrial, commercial interests (becomes model for other cities)...

Thomas B. Gregory forms partnership by handshake with Harry J. Crawford to develop U.S. oil, gas properties - by 1932 with interests in over 2,000 wells (form Columbia Gas & Electric in 1926 to evolve with 55 affiliates in 257 cities)... Chicago clothier Julius Rosenwald acquires 25% interest in Sears, Roebuck (serves vice president and treasurer to 1910 - president to 1925, creates Advertising and Catalogue Department to merchandise products, builds efficient 40-acre mail-order plant in 1905, starts systematizing procedures and vertical integration - interests in 9 plants by 1906, 20 by 1908, and over 30 by 1918, opens firm's first branch mail-order office, TX, in 1906)... Frank B. Gilbreth starts contracting business (opens branches in New York, San Francisco and London, after developing methods to improve bricklaying uses camera in 1911 to film first time and motion studies)...

Studebaker Brothers, South Bend, make some 75,000 wagons, carriages during year with latest production technology... Field & Stream is published for hunters, fishermen... William K. Kellogg and brother John invent wheat flakes to provide patients bored with oatmeal at Battle Creek sanitarium, MI, with change in diet (lose technology and market to others, create corn flakes in 1902 - after buying out brother for $250,000 W.K. starts company in 1906 on urging of insurance executive Charles D. Balin to sell over one million cases in 1909)... Northrup loom allows for automatic replacement of bobbin and stop when threads break...

Emile Berliner tries to sell his gramophones through United States Gramophone (after W.C. Jones forms Berliner Gramophone as patent company takes over U.S. Gramophone to sell machines, made by Eldridge R. Johnson's plant, via regional firms in 1896, gives national distribution rights to advertising executive Frank Seaman's National Gramophone, because of patent suits by Edison-Bell Consolidated is acquired by Johnson in forming Victor Talking Machine with many foreign gramophone firms in 1901).

1896

General Events

Thomas A. Edison develops fluoroscope to experiment with X-rays... Lumiere brothers of France show movies in NYC... Utah is 45th State... Gold is discovered in Northwest Canada near Alaska (starts Klondike Gold Rush - over 18,000 prospectors in 2 years and around 100,000 in 3)... Post Office starts testing rural free delivery, adopted in 1902 when roads are improved... W.J. McGee, Smithsonian scientist, in Atlantic Monthly cites bicycle as "one of the world's greatest inventions"...

Harvey Hubbell, CT, patents electric light socket with pullchain... Community of Miami with less than 300 people is incorporated, FL... Auto race is won at Narragansett Park, RI, by 2 electric cars over 3 gasoline-powered Duryea racers, recorded top speed of 26.8 mph... New York passes first State law to license public accountants, followed by Pennsylvania in 1899 - all states by 1924... W.S. Hadaway invents electric stove...

Fanny M. Farmer: The Boston Cooking School Cookbook (is first to reach nationwide audience, stresses first uniform system of exact weights and measures for cooking, creates need for new kitchenware and implements)... Sault St. Marie Canal between Lake Superior, MI, is improved to handle shipments of iron from Mesabi Range, MN, to steel mills of OH, PA...

Milton Reeves, founder of Reeves Pulley in the early 1900's, designs variable-speed transmission for automobiles (is abandoned, re-discovered by "new" gearless transmission of Dutch firm in 1980's)... William Jennings Bryan presents "Cross of Gold" speech at Democratic National Convention to advocate free silver coinage... Samuel Langley, Secretary of Smithsonian Institution, successfully tests steam-powered model Aerodrome #5 (fails just days before Wright brothers to fly piloted plane in 1903)... Octave Chanute successfully tests biplane glider at Indiana Dunes on Lake Michigan... Thomas A. Edison shows first projected films at public showings in NYC, Paris and London...

After visiting Britian Elbert Hubbard, former soap merchant, creates pioneering Roycroft commune of craftworkers, NY, to start U.S.' arts and crafts movement (-1915, is followed by Gustav Stickley's profit-sharing guild in 1901 - bankruptcy by 1916).

Business Events

Frank Munsey, publisher of New York Sun, opens Mohican as one-stop grocery store, emphasizing floor space, large variety of products, some non-food, in departments, some self-service, although mostly cash-and-carry, and free delivery (fails to win acceptance of consumers)...

Dow Jones index to record stock trends is first published by Wall Street Journal, first industrial index in 1928 (registers over 100 on 1/12/1906, 381.17 on 9/3/1929 less than 2 months before Great Crash, 260.64 on 10/28/1929 after dropping 38.33 points, 41.22 on 7/8/1932 as Depression low, 500.24 on 3/12/1956, 1003.16 on 11/14/1972, 1209.46 on 4/26/1983, 1304.88 on 5/20/85, and over 1900 points before topping 2700 level in 1987, drops over 500 points on 10/19/87, hovers around 2000 in 1988)... Austrian-born Leo Hirschfield starts small candy shop, NYC (achieves success with Tootsie Roll, first U.S. hand-wrapped candy)...

Carlisle & Finch produce first electric toy train, follows crude tin pull-toy trains in 1830s-1840s and wind-up models in 1850's... Harrison Otis of Los Angeles Times forms Merchants and Manufacturers Assn. to oppose unionism (pledges members not to employ union workers)... S & W canning business is started... Harvey Firestone starts business in Chicago to make wheels (sells business in 1899 to competitor for $40,000 in cash, starts tire company in 1900 at Akron after inventing method to attach tires to rims)...

With stipulation their check would not be deposited for specified time period, Henry Rogers and William Rockefeller buy Anaconda Copper (form Amalgamated Copper to buy Anaconda for $75 million in Amalgamated stock, borrow $39 million with Amalgamated stock as collateral to cover check, sell Amalgamated stock for $75 million, using $39 million to retire loan and $36 million to divide in profits)... Scientific American shows testing apparatus used by Pope Mfg. to maintain strict quality control in making bicycles... John Wanamaker acquires old A.T. Stewart Department Store, NYC, to open branch of Philadelphia department store (closes 1954)...

First U.S. commercial motion picture exhibition is given at Koster &

Bial's Music Hall, NYC (uses Armat's Vitascope projector and Edison's Kinetoscope film)... The American Machinist gives detailed drawing of horseless carriage (inspires Henry Ford to build Quadricycle - re-sold later as "first" U.S. used car, sells first car in 1898 while still working for Detroit Edison Electric, resigns and starts Detroit Automobile in 1899 with backing of wealthy Detroit lumberman William H. Murphy)... Frederick W. Taylor is hired by Coleman DuPont of Johnson & Lorain Steel to install new cost and control system at several plants...

J. Lawrence Laughlin: The Elements of Political Economy (states manager should select factory site, control finances, buy materials, sell goods, supervise employees, etc.)... George Merrill, Jr., of Massachusetts is first in U.S. to buy gasoline-engine car, produced by Duryea... Adolph S. Ochs purchases ailing New York Times (revitalizes paper to attain national reputation for "all the news that is fit to print" by 1920)... After resigning from Standard Oil, Joseph S. Cullinan starts Petroleum Iron Works to make oil storage tanks (starts first Texas pipe line and refining business in 1897 - predecessor of Magnolia Petroleum, sells interest to form Texas Fuel Co. to participate in 1901 Spindletop Field discovery, reorganizes business as Texaco in 1902, resigns as President in 1913 when headquarters moves to NYC, starts Farmer's Oil Co. in 1914 - basis for 1916 holding company of American Republic Corp.)...

Thomas Sperry and Shelly V. Hutchinson start pioneering business to sell trading stamps to retailers wanting to increase sales with premiums (sell business to Beinecke family in 1928 - by 1967 with 8,000 full-time employees and 500 overseas to generate revenues over $300 million)... After running Centennial Brewery in Butte, MT, for 20 years, L.F. Schmidt starts Olympia Brewing near Seattle, WA (acquires 1884 Theodore Hamm Brewing of St. Paul, MN, in 1975, merges with 1883 Lone Star Brewery of San Antonio, TX, in 1976)... First race track for cars opens at Narragansett, RI.

1897

General Events

National Monetary Conference meets (January 12) in Indianapolis, IN, to design monetary system based on gold standard... U.S. Supreme Court in Trans-Missouri case rules railroads are covered by Sherman Anti-Trust Act... Dingley Tariff Bill protects (July 7) U.S. industry from exports... 90 cars run on U.S. roads - some 100,000 in 1906 and 1 million in 1913... Engineer Edwin S. Votey patents Pianola player piano (operates by holes on paper roll)...

U.S. annexes Hawaii (raises objections by Japan on future of some 25,000 Japanese on islands)... Black inventor J.L. Love patents mechanical pencil sharpener... Rufus Patterson patents machine to weigh, pack, stamp, and label smoking tobacco (becomes American Machine and Foundry with 45 plants, 19 research laboratories, 16,000-17,000 employees, and sales of $450 million by 1962)... J. Jones, using device from Gramophone's spring motor, invents speedometer... First Boston Marathon is held for amateur runners (grants privileges to top professional competitors in 1985 and awards cash prizes in 1986)...

Popular Science: "The energy necessary to propel the ship would be many times greater than that required to drive a train of cars at the same speed; hence as a means of rapid transit, aerial navigation could not begin to compete with the railroad"... Some 75,000 coal miners of United Mine Workers strike mines, OH, WV and PA (win 8-hour day, elimination of company stores)...

Boston is first U.S. city to operate electric underground railway... J.P. Morgan: "I owe the public nothing" (answers reporter's question on giving public explanation for Panic of 1897)... Harter, Bryan pioneer analysis of learning curve, used by Japanese after World War II to reduce production costs in competing with U.S.... Boston hosts U.S.' first major exhibition of arts and crafts... New Orleans' Storyville area becomes legalized brothel district (-1917).

Business Events

Sears, Roebuck advertises aluminum cooking utensils in mail-order catalog... When foremen at Simonds Rolling Mill Machine resign, they are replaced by functional foremen, advocated by Frederick W. Taylor... 1879 Bloch Bros. Tobacco Co. of Wheeling introduces West Virginia Mail Pouch chewing tobacco (advertises product in early 1900's on barns)... E.E. Calkins is hired as copywriter by advertising agency (innovates by enhancing eye-appeal of ads)... Pioneering Wanamaker Commercial Institute is started by Philadelphia department store to train young employees for promotion, graduates some 7,900 by 1909 (is emulated by Denver's Daniel & Fisher Department Store)... First working oil well off coast of California is operated... Publishing business of Doubleday & Co. is founded... Modern Shakespeare business making fishing equipment is started... First U.S. taxicab fleet, using 13 electric hansoms of Electrobat, is operated in NYC... National Cash Register opens French sales subsidiary... Accountants form national professional society...

Some 8 million bushels of wheat from West, Northwest are delivered to buyers by Philip D. Armour to block attempt of Joseph Leiter to corner wheat market... Emporium department store opens in San Francisco (follows Golden Rule Bazaar in 1850's)... J.M. Smucker starts cider business, OH (evolves with 29% of 1982 market in jams, jellies, and preserves with sales of $146.7 million)... New York cough medicine manufacturer, using Peter Cooper's discovery, creates gelatin dessert (becomes Jell-O business)... German-born Richard Wilhelm starts glue factory in Gowanda, NY (after buying old Peter Cooper Corp., becomes dominant firm in industry)...

69 mergers are made during year for total capitalization of $119.7 million (is followed by 303 in 1898 for $650.6 million, 1,208 in 1899 for $2,262.7 million, 304 in 1900 for $442,2 million, 423 in 1901 for $2,052.0 million, 379 in 1902 for $910.8 million, 142 in 1903 for $297.6 million, and 79 in 1904 for $110.5 million)... Joseph S. Cullinan builds first oil refinery West of Mississippi, TX... U.S. dynamite firms make agreements to allocate resources with French, British and German interests... After several years of experimentation, Francis E., Freelan O. Stanley make steam-powered automobiles in Newton, MA (-1925, screen customers to determine if appropriate for a Stanley Steamer)...

Steeplechase Park at New York's Coney Island opens... Studebaker Brothers, South Bend carriage makers, starts making electric cars (produce first commercial car in 1904, reorganize in 1911 to make just automobiles)... E.W. Scripps, M.A. McRae start forming chain of newspapers (operate 13 papers by 1914, reorganize in 1922 as Scripps-Howard)... Charles R. Flint creates National Starch (creates other consolidations, such American Woolen and American Chicle, to become known as "Father of Trusts")... Bicycle manufacturer Alexander Winton forms Winton Motor Carriage Co. (produces first cars in 1898, starts new business in 1912 to make improved diesel engines, liquidates car business in 1924 to concentrate on diesel line - sold to General Motors in 1930)... German-born Otto H. Kahn becomes partner in 1867 Kuhn & Loeb investment banking business...

Financial speculator Bernard Baruch earns some $40,000 on $200 investment in bearish sugar market - by 1900 a millionaire (starts industrial development business in 1903 to net some $700,000 by selling Amalgamated Copper short and some $7 million on coup with Texas Sulphur to give U.S. control of world market, amasses wealth of $22-25 million by 1929)... John T. Dorrance is employed by uncle's Campbell Preserve Co. (invents process to make condensed soup in 1899, sells some 6 million cans/year by 1904 with extensive advertising, places first national ad in 1905)... Charles R. Walgreen, Chicago, becomes registered pharmacist (acquires first pharmacy in 1902 when owner retires, operates 7 by 1916 as Walgreen Co. - 110 by 1927 and 493 in 215 cities and 37 states by 1939)...

Engineer Alfred P. Sloan becomes president of Hyatt Roller Bearing after father invests $5,000 in financially-troubled business (increases yearly sales under $2,000 to over $20 million by 1917)... Curtis Publishing acquires 1821 <u>Saturday Evening Post</u> for $100 in cash and $900 later (hires George Horace Lorimer as editor in 1899, focuses on business in portraying rich and powerful as role models and printing how-to-do articles, hires boy entrepreneurs, 47,449 by 1933, in 1899 to sell <u>Post</u>)... After previous attempts at mechanical piano players, Fourneaux of France shows "Pianista" at 1876 Philadelphia Centennial, Edwin S. Votey patents player piano, produced in 1898 by 1829 Aeolian Co., maker of parlor reed organs (is challenged in 1914 market by over 40 rivals to outsell pianos by 1919, ends 1932 with popularity of radios)...

Mining engineer Herbert Hoover is hired by British engineering firm of Bewick, Moreing and Co. to examine its mining properties in Western Australia (examines its coal and mines of Shansi, Manchuria and Mongolia in 1899, at age of 25 is chosen to reorganize its mining operations, 25,000 employees in China in 1901, is junior partner in 1902, ends partnership in 1907 to start consulting engineering business in NYC).

1898

General Events

U.S. Supreme Court: <u>Holden</u> <u>v.</u> <u>Hardy</u> (upholds Utah law limiting working hours in mining industry to 8)... Congress declares (April 25) state of war with Spain (-1898)... Erdman Arbitration Act provides (June 1) government mediation in railroad disputes (declares blacklists of union members illegal)... Augustus Herring makes successful powered glide flight of some 50 feet in Chanute-Herring Biplane... U.S. War Department grants Samuel Langley $50,000 to develop manned airplane... Danish-born Valdemar Poulsen invents magnetic recording of sound... One-minute vignette, "Triple-Creek Barroom," is first western film, followed in 1903 by 9-minute movie "The Great Train Robbery"   as first western with story... Slot machine is invented... War Revenue Act institutes first U.S. tax on legacies... Joe Smith, Charlie Dale form comedy team, NJ (-1950s after performing in Bowery saloons, vaudeville, burlesque, television).

Business Events

After sponsoring "Women's League" to provide classes in choral singing, physical culture, sewing, dancing and languages, Wanamaker Department Store, Philadelphia, starts "The Noonday Club" for male managers, buyers... Beeman's, minty-flavored chewing gum, is developed by Cleveland pharmacist, alleges cure for heartburn... Boston & Lowell Railroad operates first automatic central controlled signal system (follows use of first signals in 1849 by Erie Railroad)... "First" automobile dealer franchise, devised in medieval times by Catholic Church to license officials as tax collectors, is granted to William E. Metzger to sell steam-powered cars, 53,125 licensed dealers in 1927 (is followed in 1988 with first dealership corporation)...

Albert Lasker, son of German-born peddler who acquired wealth with interests in Galveston wholesale grocery firm, milling business, and banking, is hired as $10/week clerk by Chicago advertising agency of Lord & Thomas (earns $10,000/year as salesman in 1902 and $50,000/year plus 25% ownership in 1904, becomes head of copyrighting in 1905, acquires sole ownership of industry's largest advertising agency in 1912 with billings of some $6 million - $3 million in 1905, retires in 1918, returns in 1920 to acquire George Washington Hill's American Tobacco account in 1925, promotes Lucky Strike as No. 1 cigarette with hard-sell ads)...

N.W. Ayer & Son advertising agency is contracted by newly-formed National Biscuit Co., created by American Biscuit and Western cracker makers   to dominate 90% of U.S. cracker business, to promote pre-packaged crackers (introduces Uneeda brand with first million-dollar advertising program in 1899 to overcome traditional bulk purchases of crackers, achieves sales of some 10 million packages/month in 1900)... With sourdough starter from Europe, Larraburu Brothers Bakery is started, San Francisco, by family from Basque area of Spain (-1976, becomes world's largest baker of sourdough bread)...

Hess Family opens retail dry goods business in Allentown, PA, hotel (evolves as successful 37-store regional department store chain by 1980's with locations in communities of 100,000-200,000 not served by major stores)... Warner-Lambert introduces Euthymol toothpaste... Modern Union Carbide chemical business is founded... C.W. Post uses coupons to promote Grapenuts cereal... New York miller Thomas A. McIntyre forms United States Flour Milling Co. as a trust (after failing to acquire control of Northwestern Consolidated and Hecker-Jones-Jewell reorganizes as Standard Milling after receivership in 1900)...

With financing by J.P. Morgan's syndicate, Judge Gary organizes Federal Steel with capitalization of $200 million)... H.O. Keller of Reading, PA, is franchised to sell Winton cars, contests W.E. Metzer's Detroit dealership of steam cars as first franchise (is followed by first used-car dealer in 1902 in NYC)...

Pioneering Filene Cooperative Assn. is formed by Boston women's store to settle employee grievances (becomes "first" U.S. company union, establishes procedure in 1901 to handle employee wage disputes by arbitration)... American Institute of Social Service organizes to promote industrial betterment of employer-employee relations... James B. Duke, associates form Continental Tobacco with five plug tobacco companies (create American Snuff in 1900, Consolidated Tobacco and United Cigar Stores in 1901, operate some 150 factories by 1911)... William L. Murphy starts business to make folding beds with attachments for closet doors... Sieberling brothers form Goodyear Tire & Rubber to make bicycle tires (create labor department in 1910, sponsor welfare program in 1910-15 to provide health and insurance plans, social and athletic activities, stock purchase plan and housing, use "flying squadron" of roving workers in 1911 to eliminate need for temporary employees, operate by 1916 as largest U.S. rubber manufacturer with some 15,000 employees, sponsor Industrial Assembly in 1919 as company union - replaced by Rubber Workers Union in 1937, are ousted in 1921 after financial crisis to continue in field as Sieberling Rubber)... Consulting engineer Frederick W. Taylor is hired by Bethlehem Steel (-1901, introduces cost accounting system of railroads)...

When J.P. Morgan and Jacob Schift of Kuhn Loeb & Co., representing Vanderbilt interests, are unable to reorganize financially-troubled Union Pacific Railroad, E.H. Harriman acquires control (after detailed study, revives operation with Kansas-Pacific, Denver-Pacific and Oregon Short Line Railroads and with reconstruction program of $45 million, acquires Southern Pacific road in 1901 to generate net profits of some $42 million)...

Itinerate barber, land speculator Black Jesse Binga opens Chicago real estate office (charters bank in 1921-30, owns more property on State Street by 1926 than anyone else, loses fortune when bank is closed by state auditor, is convicted of embezzlement in 1933)... Scottish-born Donald Ross moves to U.S. (over next 50 years designs over 500 golf courses)... Travelers Insurance Co. issues first car insurance to protect against suits by horse owners...

Autocar Co. is started in Ardmore, PA, to make passenger cars (as one of first in industry drops cars in 1908 to focus on trucks).

1899

General Events

Thomas A. Edison develops alkaline battery for electric cars... U.S. Supreme Court: Addyston Pipe & Steel Company v. United States (holds negotiations between corporations to eliminate competition as violations of Sherman Anti-Trust Act)... Norwegian-born Johan Vaaler invents paper clip... Congress grants railway postal clerks annual 15-day vacation... Black inventor J.A. Burr patents a lawn mower... Thorstein Veblan: Theory of the Leisure Class (denounces business elite for "conspicuous consumption")... Newsboys strike Joseph Pulitzer's World and William Randolph Hearst's New York Journal to protest higher prices, supported by strike of newsboys from NJ to MA (lasts 15 weeks before papers concede defeat)... Lawyer Elihu Root becomes U.S. Secretary of War (-1904, reorganizes Army with management techniques and business methods, creates Army War College in 1901, forms Army General Staff in 1902-03)...

Cleveland U.S. Post Office uses Winton truck to collect mail...Black inventor G.F. Grant patents golf tee... Charles H. Duell, director of U.S. Patent Office: "Everything that can be invented has been invented"... Commercial travelers of Christian Commercial Men's Association of America form Gideons to place Bibles in hotels (becomes Gideons International in 1908 to solace "lonely men on the road").

Business Events

Vito Ferro, Mafia Don (evolves from 800 A.D. from either Arab term for union or Tuscan word for poverty or misery), lands in NYC (extracts money from new immigrants to build crime business)... Chicago Cardinals professional football team is formed (is oldest franchise when National Football League organizess in 1921)... Harley-Davidson motorcycle business is started (is acquired by Vaughn L. Beals, investors in 1981 to revive business, failing from Japanese competition, by stressing quality - most prestigious bike in Japan by 1985)... After troubles with new Winton car, James Ward Packard, maker of incandescent lamps, starts manufacturing quality cars (merges with Studebaker in 1954, closes Detroit plant in 1956)... 7 canneries form Columbia River Packers Assn. (evolves with Bumblebee label)... Siegel-Cooper Department Store starts pioneering employee insurance program...

Nicholas P. Gilman: Profit-Sharing Between Employers and Employees (after limited use of 37 plans in 1867-89, reports 21 plans in 1899)... After persuasion Coca-Cola licenses Benjamin Thomas, Joseph Whitehead of Chattanooga to operate bottling plant with syrup from Coca-Cola (expands licensing to other cities in 1901-03 - by 1909 with 379 franchises and some 1,000 in 1919)... California Fruit Grower's Association is assembled by 11 companies (evolves by 1916 with 6 more firms to account for 57% of canning and preserving activity in California as Del Monte)...

Eastman Kodak adopts profit-sharing plan (institutes benefit fund in 1911 and wage dividend in 1912)... Nicholas P. Gilman: A Dividend to Laborer, A Study of Employers' Welfare Institutions (warns on dangers of paternalism)... Speculators Thomas F. Ryan, William C. Whitney acquire rights from Selden to car patents of 1895 for $10,000 and royalties (leads to patent monopoly until broken by Ford in 1911)... Sidney W. Winslow joins with Gordon McKay and Goodyear Rubber to form United Shoe Machinery Corp. (evolves with 59 acquisitions and by leasing of machines to shoe manufacturers, is sold to competitor Thomas G. Plant's shoe business in 1910)... Charles W. Morse merges competitors to form American Ice Co. (is attacked in 1900 for corruption, NYC)...

Elbridge A. Stuart and T.E. Yerxa start Pacific Coast condensed milk business in Kent, WA (becomes Carnation Milk Products in 1916 and Carnation Co. in 1929 - by 1945 world's largest seller of evaporated milk)... Henry B. Endicott, George F. Johnson form Endicott-Johnson shoe business, NY (establish factories in rural areas with company housing and community facilities, allow workers to select hours of work and have direct access to management, adopt industry's first 8-hour day and 48-hour week in 1916, start profit-sharing plan for all workers in 1919)...

British interests incorporate American Marconi Co., NJ (operates 65 stations by 1914, reorganized in 1919 as Radio Corporation of America with patents, properties from General Electric, AT&T, Westinghouse Electric and United Fruit)... A.L. Dyke opens first U.S. auto parts store, St. Louis...

National Biscuit Co. uses Italian medieval cross as trademark for Uneeda crackers... P.J. Darlington: "Methods of Renumerating Labor," Engineering Magazine (discusses piece-work system)... Oscar Hammerstein opens Victoria Theater on New York's Seventh Avenue, followed by 13 more on 42nd Street by 1920 to create theater district... Detroit lumber dealer William Murphy, associates form Detroit Automobile Co. to finance Henry Ford in making cars (-1902, collapses when Ford builds racing cars and plans to build inexpensive cars for mass market, reorganizes with Henry M. Leland as production manager to make Cadillacs)... Adolph and Leonard Lewishon with Henry H. Rogers form American Smelting & Refinery (plan to either force Guggenheims out of business or take over interests, concede victory to Guggenheims in 1900-01 after bitter battle)...

American Brass is formed by 4 manufacturers (consolidates with Anaconda Copper in 1921)... After leaving plumbing-supply business, David D. Buick starts automobile factory, MI (-1902, is acquired in 1904 by Flint carriage maker William C. Durant, becomes one of 4 largest automobile companies by 1908 to compete with Ford, REO and Maxwell-Briscoe)...

Sicilian-born Ignazio Saietta, "Lupo the Wolf," lands in NYC (-1920, starts "Black Hand" terror of extortion in competing for territory with Camarra, Unione Siciliana, Chinese tongs)... White Star Line operates first U.S. steamship without sails... National Metal Trades Assn. organizes... Republic Steel is created... William Wood combines number of New England operations to form American Woolen Mills (becomes world's largest textile business)... After signing marketing agreement in 1894 United Fruit is formed by Minor Cooper Keith, holding key interests in land and railroads in Colombia and Panama, and Boston Fruit, operated by ship Captain Lorenzo Dow Baker and Andrew W. Preston, produce salesman and broker with banana plantations in Jamaica (issues first report in 1900 to reveal business owns and leases 250,000 acres in Colombia, Costa Rica, Cuba, Dominican Republic, Honduras and Nicaragua, employs 15,000 workers, owns 11 steamers and leases 30 more, and operates 117 miles of railroad, dominates Colombia's market with shutdown of Atlantic Fruit in 1920 and French company in 1921 to become known as "Octopus," is targeted for strike in 1928 by Colombian workers demanding United Fruit obey Country's labor laws - ended after martial law and killing of 68-80 strikers)...

Ransom E. Olds, backed by copper and lumber magnate Samuel L. Smith, starts Olds Motor Works in Detroit, MI, started making cars in Lansing, MI, in 1896 (-1904, after disagreement with Smith on what cars to produce starts Reo in Lansing with backing of local businessmen - part of General Motors in 1908 to become Oldsmobile)... W.H. Moore forms National Steel, industry's 3rd largest after Carnegie and Morgan's Federal Steel.

1900s

General Events

Elwood McGuire, IN, devises first practical lawnmower... Barber's pole trademark (symbolizes medieval tradition when doctors left scorned surgery to barbers) is used to identify barber shops (-1940s)... Term "sweetheart contract" is used to describe labor agreement favoring employer.

Business Events

Samuel A. Scribner creates the Columbia Amusement Co. (evolves to control all burlesque theaters between Boston, Chicago)... Steam-powered delivery trucks are used by Manhattan department stores (adopted by U.S. Postal Service in 1906 with trucks of White Motor Co.)... Tin-Pan Alley evolves in NYC as location for music publishers and composers of popular songs.

1900

General Events

Congress passes (March 14) the Gold Standard Act (establishes national banks with capital of $25,000 and over in towns of 3,000 or less to finance agrarian needs)... Congress establishes (April 30) Hawaii as a territory... U.S. Supreme Court: <u>Knowlton v. Moore</u> (rules War Revenue Act of 1898 with inheritance tax to be constitutional)... Reginald A. Fessenden transmits first human speech by radio waves... U.S. Department of Commerce and Labor: "The Betterment of Industrial Conditions" (summarizes use of personnel practices used in 1890s by 302 firms of 268,000 in manufacturing, reveals use of clubs, physical exercise programs, education, training and religious courses, social activities, housing, stock ownership programs, safety and health benefits, and financial aid programs)... U.S. Census is taken (counts population of 76 million, 30.2 urban, 45.8 rural, and 3,688,000 emigrants since 1891)...

U.S., Japan, voluntarily agree to stop Japanese immigration... AFL charters International Ladies' Garment Workers' Union... Otis Elevator patents escalator (demonstrates mechanism at 1900 Paris Exhibition, loses use of name "escalator" when ruled generic in 1949)... National Business Association is started by Booker T. Washington, others to assist blacks in developing small businesses... Elihu Root, Secretary of War, forms board to organize a War College to train staff officers for Army (is established 1901)... New York University, Dartmouth start business programs for undergraduate students... Some 20% of labor force is composed of children, ages 10-15... U.S. announces Open Door Policy to facilitate trade with China... To oppose anti-union employers and socialism National Civic Federation is formed by prominent business, public and union leaders, Mark Hanna president and Samuel Gompers vice president, to promote labor-management relationships (-1905)... Membership in American Federation of Labor is some 548,000 (lists some 1,494,000 in 1905, 1,562,000 in 1910, 1,946,000 in 1915, and over 4 million in 1920).

Business Events

Standard Oil declares first quarter dividend of $20 million, largest ever offered... Five Mack brothers, former wagonmakers, build first bus (introduce first hook-and-ladder fire truck in 1910, achieve success with heavy-duty truck in 1915)... Chicago's Lord & Thomas advertising agency forms a service unit (maintains records on how well ads perform for clients, uses wall chart to show due dates for various stages of different campaigns)... American League is created with baseball teams in Buffalo, Chicago, Cleveland, Detroit, Indianapolis, Kansas City, Milwaukee, and Minneapolis... Cleveland Chamber of Commerce creates industrial committee to study and improve personnel practices...

Edwin L. Shuey: <u>Factory People and Their Employees</u> (reports on attempts of firms to improve working conditions)... Inventor Elmer A. Sperry starts laboratory for electro-chemical research (-1910, invents gyrocompass in 1911 to use gyroscope toy, invented 1852, as compass stabilizer, follows foreign patent of Anchutz-Kampfe in 1908)... Filene's, Boston store for women, creates Welfare Manager's Office (in addition to providing medical and insurance plans, library lectures, bank, social, and recreational activities, adopts a profit-sharing plan in 1903, Saturday closings during summer in 1912, and paid winter vacations in 1924)...

Scottish-born James B. Forgan develops First National Bank of Chicago as major financial institution in Middle West... Newspaper publisher William Randolph Hearst acquires Chicago's <u>American</u> (operates 90 papers by 1935 - 10 by 1970s)... James J. Storrow, Jr. joins Boston investment house of Lee, Higginson & Co. (innovates with salesmen to promote small, individual accounts for investors)... After working with John G. McCrory, operator of a chain of 6 bazaar stores and 25-and-10-cent stores, since 1897, S.S. Kresge starts business with brother-in-law to operate McCrory Five & Ten Cent Stores in Detroit and Port Huron, MI (names business of 8 variety stores as S.S. Kresge & Co. in 1907, incorporates in 1912 to operate 85 stores, opens 25-cent to one dollar stores after World War I to grow faster than F.W. Woolworth's chain - some 600 stores by 1925, opens first K mart store in Detroit suburb in 1962 - U.S.' second largest retailer in 1977)...

After operating wholesale fruit business in New Orleans for United Fruit, Russian-born Samuel Zemurray, partner buy two tramp-steamers to ship bananas from independent plantations in Honduras (form Cuyamel Fruit in 1910 - by 1929 with 13 ships, sugar plantations and refinery, trades stock of company in 1930 for controlling shares in United Fruit)... Harry Stevens, director of catering for New York Polo Grounds is credited for putting hot dog with condiments in a bun, calls product "red hots" when customers shun ice-cream, peanuts in cold weather...

In defiance of Sherman Anti-Trust Act Andrew Carnegie incorporates new Carnegie Steel, capitalized for $160 million (using cost controls starts vertical integration into finished products to compete with Illinois Steel, National Tube, American Bridge and Morgan's Federal Steel and threaten competitors with market dominance)... After contracting in 1896 with Japanese steamship line, James J. Hill forms Great Northern Steamship Company in Seattle for trans-Pacific trade... International Time Recording Co. is formed to supply time clocks to industrial and

commercial businesses, becomes International Time Recording Co. later
after acquiring its competitors (is combined by Charles R. Flint in 1910
with his 1901 Computing Scale Co. and Tabulating Machine business,
founded by Herman Hollerith in 1896, to form Computing-Tabulating-
Recording Co. and become IBM in 1924)... Frederick W. Taylor, Maunsel
White perfect process for hardening tool steel (obtains patent - rights
to Bethlehem Steel, resigns from Bethlehem Steel in 1901 when new owner,
Charles Schwab of U.S. Steel, is not interested in Taylor and his work,
independently wealthy from steel process   retires from consulting work to
promote scientific management)... Eastman Kodak adopts profit-sharing
plan (establishes an employee stock-option plan in 1919)...

George Kleiser, Walker Forest start West Coast business in outdoor
advertising signs (still operates)... Frederick Weyerhaeuser, associates
form Weyerhaeuser Timber Company (acquires some 900,000 acres of
timberland in Western Washington from James J. Hill for $5.4 million,
starts real estate operation in 1970, owns 13 million acres of timberland
and employs some 40,000 U.S. employees by 1980s)... Willis R. Whitney,
MIT Professor, is hired by General Electric to organize research
laboratory (employs scientist Irving Langmuir in 1910 to do theoretical
research on gasses in a vacuum, employs some 400 scientific personnel in
late 20s... is followed by DuPont in 1902, AT&T in 1910-12, Eastman Kodak
in 1912, and Westinghouse in 1916 - 526 others by 1921 and over 1,600 by
1931)...

Although some firms use employment agents or employment clerks, B.F.
Goodrich Co. creates formal employment department in this time... 4,192
automobiles are produced, consisting of 1,681 steam, 1,575 electric, 936
gasoline cars...   James W. Packard starts Ohio Automobile in Warren
(changes name of business to Packard Motor Car and moves to Detroit in
1903)... With patent for attaching tires to rims, Harvey S. Firestone
forms Firestone Tire & Rubber (achieves success with tire order from
Henry Ford in 1906, introduces balloon tire in 1923, starts Liberia
rubber plantation with Ford in 1924, sells tire business in 1988 to
Japan's Bridgestone for $1.25 billion)...

U.S. financiers create Cuba Company with $8 million to develop Cuba's
railroads... U.S.' first auto show opens in NYC's Madison Square
Garden... George Verity starts American Rolling Mill in Middletown, OH
(with success becomes "dean of American Steelmakers," after losing $1.9
billion, some from recession but most from diversification - particularly
insurance, between 1982-86, struggles for survival in 1987-88)... After
riding gigantic Ferris wheel at Chicago's 1893 World's Fair, engineer
William E. Sullivan builds small portable model for fairs, carnivals in
Jacksonville, IL (5 wheels later incorporates Eli Bridge Co. in 1905 to
build amusement rides - 1,400 by 1988)... Pennsylvania Railroad forms
Pension Department.

1901

General Events

Bridgeport, CT, newspaper claims Bavarian-born tinkerer Gustave Whitehead
made sustained controlled flight of one-half mile at altitude of 20 feet
in heavier-than-air machine, Design 21, on August 14... Alva J. Fisher
devises first electric washing machine (replaces mechanical machines used

in England since 1830s and French industrial model from around 1840)...
Dr. Thaddeus Cahill builds electric typewriter (abandons business after
making 40 at unit cost of $3,925)...

Minnesota passes world's first optometry law (is designed to protect
public from exploitation by "traveling opticians" and "spectacle
peddlers")... Frank Norris: The Octopus (attacks monopoly of the
Southern Pacific Railroad for dominating California's politics and
economy)... Illinois, Michigan offer first college courses in general
marketing... A strike of Amalgamated Association of Iron, Steel and
Tinworkers is defeated by U.S. Steel after 5 months... National Bureau of
Standards is created to establish uniform, accurate measurements...
Alexander Anderson accidentally discovers puffed rice when rice explodes
during an experiment... Wilbur Wright presents paper on Kitty Hawk
experiments to Western Society of Engineers in Chicago (suggests Otto
Lilienthal's data on lifting effects of air pressure on wing surfaces in
error, joins brother Orville in building wind tunnel to obtain correct
data)...

Peter Cooper-Hewitt invents mercury vapor lamps... First state laws for
automobile registration are passed by New York (issues license plates in
1920), Connecticut (establishes first speed limit)... Hay-Pauncefort
Treaty is signed (November 18) by U.S., Great Britain (authorizes U.S. to
build, operate, and fortify a canal across Central American Isthmus,
acquires Congressional authorization in 1902 to obtain rights from French
Canal Co. - collapsed 1878-89 and revived 1894-1902, opens Panama Canal
in 1914)... President Roosevelt declares (December 3) in message to
Congress that trusts need to be regulated "within reasonable limits."

Business Events

Bergdorf Goodman store for elegance is opened in NYC as small ladies'
tailoring and furrier shop... H.J. Heinz food business hires social
secretaries to supervise personnel activities... First Pierce-Arrow car
is made by a business making bird cages, ice-boxes and bicycles (evolves
as a stylish, elegant auto before demise in 1938)... Colorado Fuel & Iron
creates Sociological Department with social secretaries to handle firm's
personnel activities, improve working conditions... U.S.' first
motorcycle, called Indian, is made by Henbee Manufacturing of
Springfield, MA (moves to England in 1953)...

Thomas F. Manville becomes president of father's H.W. Johns-Manville
insulation business (-1925, introduces some 1,300 new products despite
refusing to spend money on research)... Dennison tag, stationery business
of Massachusetts hires an advertising man (institutes merchandising
committee in 1906)... Frank Gerber, Sr., participates in forming Fremont
Canning (introduces line of strained baby foods in 1927 on urging of son,
promotes products with national advertising in 1928 - international
1962)... Edward A. Deeds designs plant with automatic equipment for
Shredded Wheat Company (-1902, forms Dayton Engineering Laboratory in
1909 with Charles F. Kettering - resigns in 1916 when Delco is acquired
by General Motors)...

Louis K. Liggett forms Drug Merchants of America as a central buying
agency for retail druggists (creates cooperative, named Rexall later,
with 40 druggists each paying $4,000 to build manufacturing facilities in

1902, helps form United Drug Co. in Boston in 1903 - President in 1904, organizes National Cigar Stands in 1906 and United Druggists Mutual Fire Insurance in 1908 as subsidiaries, starts Canadian subsidiary in 1909 - England in 1917, records 2,755 members in 1910 and 5,570 by 1914, is followed in 1944 by Justin M. Dart to build Dart Industries with Tupperware, West Bend kitchenware, and Duracell batteries - last Rexall store sold in 1978)...

Eugene Meyer, Jr. starts banking house and buys seat on New York Stock Exchange (meets mentor Bernard Baruch, achieves first financial coup in 1908 in winning stock battle with Guggenheims for control of Boston Consolidated Mining - by 1915 major figure in the copper industry, forms Allied Chemical & Dye in 1920 by merging five firms, is named to Federal Reserve Board in 1930, prepares bill to create Reconstruction Finance Corporation in 1932, acquires Washington Post in 1933, serves as president of International Bank for Reconstruction and Development in 1946)... After dealing in Kansas oil leases, Harry F. Sinclair acquires first operating well (leases land in 1905 in Indian Territories, OK, with stake from insurance claim after shooting off toe - soon wealthy after discovering Cushing field on unclaimed Creek land, consolidates oil properties as Sinclair Oil & Refining in 1916 - 56th largest enterprise in 1917)...

After touring National Cash Register, Massachusetts stationery manufacturer Henry S. Dennison starts suggestion bonus system (by 1906 sponsors factory clinic, employee cafeteria, library, social club and savings bank)... After returning to Seattle with $13,000 acquired in Klondike gold fields, Swedish-born John W. Nordstrom opens shoe store (hands business to three sons on 1930, operates 27 stores by 1963 with acquisition of Best's Apparel, enters California market in 1978 to become West Coast's largest fashion specialty retailer, evolves by 1987 with sales of $1.3 billion from 45 stores in 6 Western states as U.S.' leading fashion retailer, opens 55th store outside DC in 1988 to invade East Coast market)... Managers of vaudeville theaters are forced to show films after strike by performers...

Charles Reese is hired by DuPont to start chemical department... A battle for control of Chicago, Burlington & Quincy Railroad is fought by Edward H. Harriman of Southern Pacific and Union Pacific Railroads (is backed by Jacob Schiff of Kuhn, Loeb and Rockefeller's National City Bank) with James J. Hill of Great Northern and J.P. Morgan & Co. (results in counter-attack of Harriman's interests to take over Hill's Northern Pacific, is resolved with joint formation of Northern Securities to control Northern Pacific and Burlington lines with monopoly on traffic from Great Lakes to Pacific Northwest, is dissolved by U.S. Supreme Court in 1904 - control retained by Hill, Morgan)...

Thompson Products is started in Cleveland to mass produce precision parts for automobile, aircraft industries (provides funds in 1953 to scientists Simon Ramo, Dean Wooldridge to obtain Air Force contract to develop ICBM system, merges in 1958 to form TRW - sales of some $665 million in 1965)... James Dole starts company in Hawaii (opens first successful pineapple cannery on Islands in 1903, purchases Lanai Island in 1922 to make it world's largest pineapple plantation - later acquired by Castle & Cooke, is followed by Maui Pineapple in 1909 to become world's largest supplier of private-label pineapple brands with some 8,000 acres)...

Moana is first hotel on Hawaii's Waikiki Beach (is followed by Halekulani in 1917, Royal Hawaiian Hotel in 1927, Henry Kaiser's Hawaiian Village resort in 1959-60, Rockefeller's Mauna Kea Beach resort on Big Island in 1965 to develop tourist industry)...

Heublein restaurant business is opened in Hartford, CT (manufactures A-1 Sauce, acquires Smirnoff vodka in 1939 to evolve in value from less than $1 million to near $1 billion by 1970s)... King C. Gillette obtain patent for safety razor (starts Boston manufacturing business with associates in 1901, sells 168 razors in 1903 - 15 million in 1904, operates new plant in 1905, introduces first double-edged razor blade in 1928, diversifies with Toni, woman's home permanent process, in 1948)... White Motor Co. is created in Cleveland to make steam-powered cars (switches to gasoline cars in 1910)... Edwin Norton starts American Can Co. (follows with Continental Can in 1904)... After 8 frustrating years of efforts oil is discovered, strike called Spindletop (-1925 after producing 60 million barrels), near Beaumont, TX, by Pattillo Higgins, Captain Anthony F. Lucas, Australian mining engineer (results in 491 oil companies chartered by Texas first year, spawns formation of Guffey Petroleum with Mellon money - later named Gulf Oil when J.M. Guffey is discharged in 1907 for mismanagement)... Ezekiel Airship Manufacturing Company is started by Rev. B. Cannon, Texas sawmiller and Baptist minister, 12 others (fails to fly kerosene-powered plane in 1902 test)...

Thomas B. Jeffery, bicycle manufacturer, starts producing Rambler car at Kenosha, WI (-1916 when acquired by Charles Nash, closes for good in 1988)... Baldwin Locomotive Works starts new apprenticeship program... With $5,000 John F. Queeny creates Monsanto Chemical, saccharine first product (starts making aspirin in 1917 when German patent of Bayer expires, develops business with coal tar products after World War I, evolves as industrial enterprise with son Edgar as president in 1928 - assets of $12 million to $857 million by 1958, operates with assets over $1 billion in 1962 - U.S.' 5th largest chemical firm in with phosphates, aspirin, saccharin, nylon, acrylic fibers, and plastics)...

Sewall Avery forms U.S. Gypsum (develops business as one of industry's largest, becomes chairman of Montgomery Ward for 1931-55 to revive ailing retail business)... Charles M. Schwab, president of U.S. Steel, acquires Bethlehem Steel as personal venture (develops business by dropping unprofitable properties, discovering new raw materials, reducing costs, selling new products, and expanding during the Depression of 1907)... For first time value of U.S. exports passes value of British exports... To prevent Andrew Carnegie in dominating steel industry, United States Steel Corporation (includes Carnegie Steel - $250 million, Elbert Gary's Federal Steel, and later Rockefeller's Mesabi iron-ore range for $80 million - previously purchased for $420,000) is formed, Charles Schwab as catalyst, by J.P. Morgan & Co. (is capitalized for record $1.4 billion, is reconstructed in 1979 by David M. Roderick to close over 150 plants and facilities, to cut capacity by 30%, to eliminate some 100,000 jobs, and to acquire Marathon Oil - steel 32% of firm's revenues in 1981)...

Eldridge R. Johnson creates Victor Talking Machine business with Emile Berliner's patents (starts Victor Red Seal records in 1903 - Enrico Caruso's record first to sell one million copies, introduces Victrola in 1906, is acquired by Radio Corporation of America in 1925)... For first time trading on New York Stock Exchange exceeds (January 7) two million shares... Louisiana's first oil well is drilled in the Acadia Parish...

In largest single-day (May 9) decline on Wall Street since 1803, some prices drop by 20 points... National Cash Register creates labor department in this time to supervise employee activities... Britain's Price Waterhouse accounting firm employs U.S. staff of 24, NYC and Chicago (acquires U.S. Steel account in 1902, operates 11 offices in U.S., Canada, and Mexico with staff of 145 in 1911)... Joshua Lionel Cowen starts top-of-the-line toy train business, incorporates 1918 (is saved from bankruptcy with Mickey and Minnie handcar, license from Disney, in 1935).

1902

General Events

Congress creates (March 6) Bureau of the Census... Ida Tarbell: "History of the Standard Oil Company," McClure's Magazine (exposes practices of business giant)... George F. Baer, president of Reading Railroad, is forced to bargain with United Mine Workers after refusing to negotiate, arbitrate, or mediate in settling labor issues... Danish-born Valdemar Poulsen invents arc generator... American Automobile Association is formed in Chicago as federation of state organizations (with 800 accredited travel offices enrolls 27.5 million members in 1987)... A 23-week strike for union recognition is undertaken by some 140,000 United Mine Workers, John Mitchell president since 1898 (is settled in favor of miners, win 10% pay increase and 9-hour day, when president Roosevelt threatens to have Army take over mines)... Maryland passes first U.S. Workmen's Compensation Law, declared unconstitutional later... Arthur D. Little consulting business patents a process for making rayon...

George F. Baer: "The rights and interests of the laboring man will be protected and cared for - not by the labor agitators, but by Christian men to whom God in His infinite wisdom has given control of the property interests of the country and upon the successful management of which so much depends"... Flatiron building is built in New York as City's first skyscraper, world's tallest with 20 stories... Farmers' Educational & Coopertive Union and National Farmers' Union are formed... To make electric cars competitive with gasoline models, Thomas A. Edison invents alkaline storage battery... W.T. Stead: The Americanization of the World (discusses rise of U.S. in international markets).

Business Events

George Draper Dayton opens dry goods store in Minneapolis (founds Associated Merchandising Corporation in 1912 with other retailers for cooperative mass buying)... First formal DuPont research laboratory is created to improve its smokeless powder (starts next facility in 1903 to develop new products - unsuccessful so purchases existing firms in paints, pigments and dye stuffs after World War I with profits from gunpowder)... Grand Trunk Railway starts school to train apprentices in Battle Creek, MI... President of National Association of Manufacturers denounces 8-hour day as socialistic for restricting inalienable right of individual's use of time...

Boston's Filene specialty store for women starts building new store, soon world's largest (-1912, introduces "cycle building," Charge-A-Plate, college and high school boards, first minimum wage for women employees, and employee credit union by 1919 - prototype for others in U.S.)... Hamilton M. Barksdale, former general manager of Repauno Chemical, is hired by DuPont to develop administrative system (consolidates manufacturing activities and organizes three administrative departments to coordinate, evaluate and operate plants, becomes general manager in 1911)... Henry Leland is hired by lumberman William F. Murphy to manage 1899 Detroit Automobile while Henry Ford focuses on building, driving race cars (evolves as Cadillac Motor Car Co., produces first Runabout when Ford starts new automobile business)... Black John Mitchell, Jr., starts Mechanic's Savings Bank in Virginia with funds from fraternal society (fails in 1922 due to loan defaults by Mitchell's Repton Land, Unique Amusement and Bonded Realty businesses)...

Maggie L. Walker, executive treasurer of the Independent Order of St. Luke - a black fraternal society and cooperative insurance venture, publishes St. Luke Herald (starts St. Luke Savings Bank in 1903 - Consolidated Bank & Trust Co. in 1929-30, fails to develop St. Luke's Emporium as Richmond department store in early 1900s)... After operating 5 theaters and stock companies in Upstate New York, Russian-born Lee Shubert and brothers, sons of Lithuanian pack peddler, lease legitimate theater in NYC to defy monopoly of Klaw-Erlanger syndicate (form Shubert Theaters with producer David Belasco in 1905 to operate 13 theaters by 1906 and break monopoly by 1910, start battle in 1920 to fight B.F. Keith Circuit for control of country's vaudeville theaters - 75% acquired by 1924, form Shubert Theater Corp. in 1924 to operate 86 "first class" houses and 750 small theaters, acquire 6 London theaters in 1925, declare receivership in 1933 to continue as new corporation, to settle federal anti-trust suit sign consent degree in 1950 to break up monopoly)...

Atwater Kent Mfg. is created in Philadelphia by Arthur A. Kent to make small volt meters and home telephones (-1936 when closed, starts making radio parts in 1922 and radios in 1923 - by 1930 industry's leading producer with mass production of quality radios)... After working as research assistant for Arthur D. Little consulting business, George H. Mead returns to family's paper business to start firm's first chemistry laboratory (organizes Mead Pulp and Paper in 1905 to acquire Mead Paper from receivership, forms management, engineering and development company in 1919 and Mead Corporation in 1930 to consolidate operations - by 1963 with 41 plants in 17 states)... Association of Licensed Automobile Manufacturers is formed with rights to Selden's basic automobile patent of 1895 to force non-member car makers to pay royalties (rebuffs Henry Ford's membership, settles suit in 1911 after Ford's victory)...

Franklin motor car is produced in Syracuse, NY... After death of Eugene DuPont, five remaining partners in family powder business are unable to choose a successor (offer business to competitor Laflin & Rand, sell business to Alfred, general manager, and cousins Coleman, president, and Pierre, treasurer then president in 1915-19, for $12 million (appoint Alfred Moxham as head of development department for strategic planning, create an executive committee with Pierre as acting chairman)... Studebaker Co., South Bend builder of wagons, starts making electric cars (start manufacturing gasoline cars in 1904)... Standard Wheel creates Overland Automobile Division in Terre Haute, IN (shifts production of cars later to Indianapolis - until 1905 site for more car markers than

Detroit with Marmom the most famous, moves operations to Toledo in 1907 when acquired by John Willys during the Panic)... J.P. Morgan & Co. forms International Harvester, capitalized for $120 million (consolidates 5 firms, including McCormick and Deering, making agricultural implements with 80% of the market, forces dealers to sign exclusive contracts)...

J.P. Morgan & Co. form International Mercantile Marine with interests of White Star Line, Atlantic Transport Line, Dominion Line and part ownership of Britain's Leyland Line to operate 136 vessels (-1937, launches Titanic in 1912, reorganizes in 1914-15 after losing competitive battle with Cunard line, plans with Pan American Airways in 1937 for cooperative transatlantic travel)... J.C. Penney, partners open Golden Rule store in Kemmerer, WY (opens second in 1903, acquires partners' interests in 1907 for $30,000, operates 34 stores by 1912 in 8 Western states, changes name of business to J.C. Penney in 1913 - 71 stores by 1913, 127 by 1916, 177 by 1917, 475 by 1923, 1,586 in 1940 and 1,617 in 1956, forms corporation in 1924 - previously each store manager a partner, grants first credit in 1958, diversifies with full-line departments in 1963 to compete with Sears, abandons department store concept in 1983 to focus on specialty lines)... Macy's Herald Square store opens in Manhattan as world's largest retail outlet... Local investors start mining venture, becomes Minnesota Mining & Manufacturing and 3M later, in Two Harbors, MN (fails, develops improved, safe sandpaper to avoid bankruptcy in 1905)...

Miss Brisco, former teacher, is hired as welfare secretary by Joseph Bancroft & Sons, makers of cotton cloth in Wilmington, DE, since 1831, to supervise programs for improving working and living conditions, benefit plans and educational activities... Thomas Neal: "Rounding Out a Business," System (describes participative factory management at Acme White Lead and Color Works, Detroit)... Horn and Hardart Baking Co. opens U.S.' first self-service Automat cafeteria in Philadelphia, over 36, NYC, in 1930s-1940s with 1 cafeteria left by 1988 (in 1987-88 opens Dine-O-Mat, '50s-style diner chain, in NYC to pioneer new trend)... James B. Duke's American Tobacco sells all interests in Britain to Imperial Tobacco in return for Imperial's withdrawal from U.S., Cuba markets (is canceled by U.S. Supreme Court in 1911)...

J.P. Morgan & Co. creates International Nickel Trust to supply U.S. Steel with raw materials... Emil, Alex Dittler start business printing railroad schedules (print business cards, hotel directories, and contest tickets by 1970s, join Scientific Games in 1974 to develop near monopoly on instant game lotteries)... Basic concept for air-conditioning, saturating dry air with water to maintain desired level of temperature, is discovered by engineer Willis Carrier during cold, foggy night (obtains patent in 1906 - term "air-conditioning" coined in 1906 by North Carolina textile engineer Stuart Cramer, tests air cooling system in printing plant - later installed in cotton mills and first hospital ward in 1914, when employer Buffalo Forge drops engineering activities forms Carrier Engineering in 1915, develops centrifugal compressor for air-conditioning in 1922, installs system in first movie theater in 1922 - over 300 by 1930, first department store, J.L. Hudson of Detroit, in 1924, first multi-story office building in 1926 and Congress in 1928, develops central air-conditioning for buildings by 1939)...

Having lost wheat flake technology to Charles W. Post and others, John and Will Kellogg create Corn Flakes as new breakfast food (results in formation of Battle Creek Toasted Corn Flake Co. by Will, John more interested in being publicist and diet evangelist, with funds from Charles D. Balin, St. Louis insurance man)... Joseph S. Cullinan creates Texas Fuel, becomes Texaco later, to drill for oil in newly discovered Spindletop field in Texas... C.W. Post, others form Citizens' Industrial Alliance to oppose unionism, succeeded by National Trades & Workers Association as trade union substitute...

Former peddler Andrew Saks opens clothing store for men, NYC (-1923 when acquired by Gimbels)... Sakowitz family opens prestigious menswear store in Houston, TX (declares bankruptcy in 1985 after expanding to operate 17 high-fashion stores in TX, OK, and AZ in 1970s)... Glenn Curtiss starts business to make motorcycles (works as engineer in 1905 to build U.S. Army's first dirigible, is hired as director of experiments in 1907 by Alexander Graham Bell's Aerial Experiment Assn., starts first aircraft manufacturing business in 1909, starts military flying school in 1911, invents flying boat in 1912, designs first plane for transatlantic flight in 1913)...

Automobile racing is started on Florida beaches of Daytona with Ransom Olds and Alexander Winton clocking 57 mph (ends 1911 with Bob Burman's record of 141.732 mph in Benz car, is revived as racing business in 1959 with stock-car events)... Kansas school teacher and part-time salesman William Coleman acquires all rights to Irby gasoline lamp (after developing kerosene Coleman Lantern builds outdoor equipment business)... C.W. Hart, C.H. Pan build 4-wheel farm tractor (start first U.S. firm in 1905 to build tractors, introduce gasoline model in 1906, is acquired later by Oliver Corp.)...

Local tailor Matt Winn, investors buy 1875 Churchill Downs race track, KY, for $40,000, first profit in years in 1903 (despite law banning bookmaking discovers loophole to install parimutuel machines in 1908, as general manager and promoter increases purses from $6,000 and crowds of several thousand to purses over $100,000 and crowds over 100,000 by death in 1949).

1903

General Events

Congress creates (February 14) Department of Commerce and Labor, 2 distinct departments in 1913... Congress authorizes (February 14) creation of General Staff of Army, designed in 1901 by Elihu Root, Secretary of War, to centralize and coordinate activities (is formed with 2 generals and 42 junior officers over administrative, intelligence, military education and technical activities)... First Pacific cable links San Francisco, Manilla... Packard car is first cross-country from San Francisco to NYC, takes 52 days... Panama declares, November 4, independence from Colombia (is recognized November 6 by U.S., signs treaty on November 18 for canal)... Samuel Langley tests flying machine unsuccessfully... After developing propeller (copy wing in motion) and light-weight motor, world's first powered flight in heavier-than-air machine (design plane, costing under $1,000, from information provided in article by Otto Lilienthal, Samuel Langley, Octave Chanute) is made at Kitty Hawk, NC, by Orville, 120 feet in 12 seconds, and Wilbur Wright,

852 feet in 59 seconds...

G.C. Beidler, clerk in litigation office, invents photocopy process (obtains patent in 1906, introduces machine to market in 1907)... Congress creates Bureau of Corporations (establishes role of Federal Government in investigating corporate activities)...

International Brotherhood of Teamsters forms (elects Dan Tobin as president for 1907-52)... Western Federation of Miners starts series of strikes, CO (-1904)... Nevada passes incorporation law (provides for minimal supervision of stock ownership and operations, eliminates annual tax of other states)...

Elkins Act declares all railroad rebates to be illegal... Justice Department forms anti-trust division... Frank Norris: The Pit (exposes speculation on Chicago's wheat exchange)... U.S. Supreme Court: Champion v. Ames (declares Federal law banning interstate lottery tickets as legal)... W.E.B. Dubois: The Soul of Black Folk (insists blacks demand higher education and compete with whites for white-collar jobs)... Some 3,000 Chicago hotel workers strike for higher wages, better working conditions... Publisher William Randolph Hearst is elected to U.S. House of Representatives (receives support for Democratic presidential nomination in 1904).

Business Events

Thomas J. Watson of National Cash Register becomes head of used cash register business, secretly owned by N.C.R. (forces out most competitors in used market by undercutting prices)... Allen-Bradley industrial control business is started in Milwaukee with idea for rheostat control device of Lynde Bradley (designs futuristic computerized assembly line, not equaled by GM or Japanese, in 1985 to make different versions of a product in different lots)... Binney & Smith, founded 1864 as Peekskill Chemical Works, introduces Crayola crayons...

Gardner Cowles acquires major interest in Des Moine Register & Leader to start publishing empire (purchases Des Moine Evening Tribune in 1908 and competitors in 1924-37, starts broadcasting business in 1928)... Newspaper publisher William Randolph Hearst enters magazine field with Motor (adds Cosmopolitan in 1905, Good Housekeeping in 1911 and Harper's Bazaar in 1912)... Ross S. Sterling, owner of Galveston, TX, produce business, starts chain of feed stores to provide supplies for horses used at new oil discovery - soon a monopoly (develops small Texas railroad in 1906, acquires several oil field banks after Panic of 1907 - banks and feed stores finance each other, participates in forming Humble Oil in 1911 - partly acquired in 1919 by Standard Oil of New Jersey)...

As advised by Carl G. Barth and H.K. Hathaway, Tabor manufacturing business of Philadephia is first firm to install Taylor System of management (is adopted by Philadelphia's Link-Belt Engineering, founded by James Dodge, inventor of conveyor belt for assembly line, and 28 other firms by 1919)... After selling 3 barber shops, success with "cure" for baldness, and working as traveling salesman, Frank Phillips starts Anchor Oil business, OK (opens bank in 1905 to finance successful wildcatting ventures, starts Phillips Petroleum in 1917 with brother, starts research in 1917 to improve conversion of waste gas to gasoline - successful by

1930, expands with refineries, marketing division, and filling stations to sell "Phillips 66" in 1927, innovates by selling tires in stations in 1931, retires in 1949 after building industry's 9th largest firm)...

E. Richardson invents electric flat iron (starts Pacific Electric Heating in 1904 and Hotpoint Electric in 1911, merges with General Electric in 1918)... Everett G. Griggs, president to 1913, founds Pacific Coast Lumber Manufacturers Assn. (initiates first cooperative effort in area to standardize lumber grades, obtain better freight rates and develop larger markets)... Halsey and Stuart investment bank business forms (pioneers with informational advertising to sell municipal, railroad bonds to small investors, installs first private wire system in 1918 to link offices, innovates with training school for salesmen and radio advertisements, despite debacle of Insull empire collapse in 1931 becomes major U.S. investment business)...

Walter Dill Scott: The Theory of Advertising, first advertising textbook is Paul Cherington's Advertising as a Business Force in 1914... Albert Kahn, German-born industrial architect, designs new plant for Packard Co. (provides efficient flow of materials to assembly operations)... Potlach Lumber is started, ID, as subsidiary of Weyerhaeuser Timber... William Teller, Henry Brown: A First Book in Business Methods (pioneers development of general business textbooks, is followed in 1918 by Parks Schloch and Gross Murray with Elements of Business)... E.I. DuPont de Nemours Powder Co. absorbs other members of Gunpowder Trade Assn...

Financial panic is caused by wild speculation in securities... Leeds & Northrup Co. is started in Philadelphia to make electrical measuring equipment by Quaker Morris E. Leeds and Edwin Northrup, resigns in 1910 (starts profit-sharing plan in 1917, starts employee cooperative association, based on Filene's Association, in 1918 to sponsor athletic, education, sick relief, savings, and lunchroom programs, creates personnel activity in 1919-20 over objections from manufacturing function with advice from Robert Bruere, Ordway Tead from Bureau of Industrial Research, starts bonus plan in 1920 - informal activity in 1918, sponsors unemployment fund in 1922, group insurance plan in 1924, night educational program in 1925 and pension plan in 1926)... Auburn Automobile is started in Auburn, IN (is acquired in 1924 with Duesenberg Motor by Errett Cord)...

Herbert Hapgood: "System in Employment," System (describes use of traditional hiring methods before science of selection, shows need for employment records)... Neunst Lamp Co. forms employee group for consulting in advisory activities (pioneers development of company unions)... Frederick W. Taylor: "Shop Management," American Society of Mechanical Engineers (discusses role of functional foremen and need for centralized employment department for job analysis and evaluation)...

Henry Gantt: "A Graphical Daily Balance in Manufacture" (starts development of Gantt Chart - first published in 1918)... After two previous attempts, Henry Ford forms Ford Motor Co. with A.Y. Malcolmson, Detroit coal dealer, James Couzens, Malcolmson's secretary and later key manager, and banker J. Gray with machinists J.F., H.E. Dodge (after disagreement with partners over producing cars for rich or multitude introduces Model-T for mass market in 1908 to sell some 25 million by 1925)... National, American Leagues sign National Agreement as baseball treaty (sponsor first "World Series")...

After coup by militants, National Association of Manufacturers is transformed from international trade organization into anti-union society (while recognizing workers have right to organize, advocates independent unionism be suppressed and destroyed)... Automatic Vaudeville Co., chain of penny arcades, is started by furrier Marcus Loew with furrier Adolph Zukor and actor David Warfield (soon dissolves partnership to change arcades into nickelodeon theaters, introduces stage entertainment in 1906 to enhance movie programs, operates over 100 movie theaters by 1919, forms Metro-Goldwyn-Mayer in 1924)...

Harry Warner opens movie theater in New Castle, PA (is forced out of film exchange business in 1912 by General Film monopoly, moves operations to California in 1918, forms Warner Brothers in 1923 to produce movies, acquires Vitagraph, national system of movie exchanges, in 1925, produces first full-length movie with sound, assisted by Western Electric, in 1927, acquires movie theaters in 1928 - later chain over 500, is acquired by Kinney Services in 1969 and becomes Warner Communications in 1971)... William Harley, 3 Davidson brothers start business, WI, to make motorcycles (lasts to 1987 as only U.S. maker in market)...

Milton Hershey builds mass production plant at Hershey, PA, to produce chocolate candy (sells carmel business to American Carmel, employs some 1,500 workers at model plant town with housing, schools, churches, stores, banks, inn, golf course, amusement parks, zoo, football field, and dancing pavillion).

1904

General Events

North European steamship companies drop steerage rates for emigrants to $10... New York enacts speed law for cars (sets maximum speed in cities of 10 mph, 15 mph in small towns and 20 mph in country)... Broadway subway opens, NYC... International Typographical Union adopts 8-hour day... National Civic Federation sponsors conference on Welfare Work (proposes title of "welfare manager" be substituted for "social secretary")... Thorstein Veblen: Theory of Business (views economy as price system controlled by money interests with over capitalization by speculative earnings resulting in recurring crises, proposes in later works that production and distribution be controlled by engineers)... In Fall River, MA, 25,000 textile workers start protracted, bitter strike against mills (attracts national attention to deplorable working conditions)...

John Fleming devises two-element vacuum tube, perfected by Lee DeForest, others for transcontinental telephone line in 1915... National Child Labor Committee is formed limit use of child labor... Hudson & Manhattan Tube is built under North River to provide access to NYC... Glenn Curtiss designs first airplane engine... Public Franchise League is formed in Boston by reformers Louis Brandeis, Edward A. Filene and others as watchdog over municipal utilities...

Louisiana Purchase Exhibition is held in St. Louis (exhibits diesel engine, introduces ice cream cone, ice tea and hamburger)... When Dominican Republic declares bankruptcy, U.S. tax officials are sent to Island by President Roosevelt to collect custom revenues for European bankers... Dexter Kimball teaches works administration course at Cornell's Sibley College of Engineering... Quaker Elizabeth J. Magie patents Landlord game - never produced (is "played" by Charles B. Darrow before inventing game of Monopoly in 1931).

Business Events

First nickelodeon theater to show movies opens in Pittsburgh, over 1,000 throughout U.S. by 1906, 5,000 in 1907 and 8,000 by 1910 - first designed movie theater in 1914... William S. Farrish, partner start oil business in Texas to drill wells on contract and trade oil leases - by 1916 leading independent dealer (forms Gulf Coast Producers Assn. in 1916 to coordinate small operators, forms new Humble Oil & Refining in 1917)...

DuPont adopts pension and insurance plans for employees, followed by AT&T in 1913 and Sears in 1916... After amassing some $50,000 in garment industry, William Fox acquires Brooklyn nickelodeon theater (when NYC places nickelodeon theaters under police supervision in 1908 acquires vaudeville theaters to show movies and stage acts, organizes Greater New York Film Rental in 1912 to break monopoly of Edison's General Film Co. with court battle in 1915, forms Fox Films in 1915 to make movies in NYC, starts Hollywood studio in 1919, fails in 1929 to acquire Loew's MGM and Britain's Gaumont in building international movie empire, avoids receivership in 1935... Lena Himmelstein opens tiny Lane Bryant shop specializing in bridal, maternity clothes, NYC (becomes 175-store chain with sales of nearly $300 million in 1970s)... Colliers launches campaign against misleading advertising... Dr. Scholl starts business to make products for easing foot problems with arch-support device for shoes...

Butter Nut Boy is pioneering branded bread... Ladies' Home Journal prints series of articles to expose evils of patent medicines (contributes to passage of Pure Food & Drug Act in 1906)... George A. Stevens, Leonard W. Hatch: "Employers' Welfare Institutions," Third Annual Report of the Commissioner of Labor of New York (cites 110 firms trying to improve working conditions for employees)... With resources of family's flour milling machinery business Howard Marmon starts building Marmon cars in Indianapolis (-1932)... Associated Advertising Clubs of America is formed by local clubs, first seen in Chicago in 1894... Canadian-born John E. Kennedy, started advertising career as ad manager for Hudson's Bay department store in Winnipeg during 1890s, is hired as copywriter by Chicago's Lord & Thomas Agency (-1906, instead of fancy slogans innovates in ads by appealing to reason and intelligence of consumers)...

Carriage-maker William C. Durant acquires bankrupt Buick Motor (after failing to merge with rivals Ford, Maxwell-Briscoe and Reo - Ford and Olds wanted $3 million each in cash, forms General Motors in 1908)... Canadian-born J.L. Kraft moves to Chicago (invests savings in business to deliver cheese from wholesalers to retailers, forms J.L. Kraft Brothers & Co. in 1909, to eliminate spoilage of bulk cheese perfects method to make processed cheese in 1916, after court order shares rights with rival Phenix Cheese in 1921, merges with Phenix in 1928 - by 1931 with plants in 30 states and several foreign countries, is purchased by 1923 National Dairy Products in 1930)...

American Rolling Mill creates advisory employee committee, followed by Nelson Valve in 1907... Germany's M. Welte & Sohn introduces player piano to U.S. market, uses rolls of transcriptions by artists instead of usual mechanical perforations by score (evolves as technique for programming automated machines)... National Civic Federation, as recommended by William Tolman's League for Social Services, forms Central Welfare Department to advise members on programs for physical comfort, recreation, education, better working conditions, and financial plans for insurance and pensions... Some 700 trucks are registered in U.S., 3.4 million by 1929... Blenheim Ginger Ale is first produced, NC (still extant)... Charles Tilt forms Diamond T Motor Car Co. to build trucks... H.F.J. Porter, former associate of Frederick W. Taylor, helps firms form company unions (-1907)... Riverview Park opens in Chicago as amusement center (-1967)...

Russian-born Max Factor opens perfume, hair goods and cosmetics shop at St. Louis Fair (starts Los Angeles cosmetic business in 1909 - Paris branch and Hollywood make-up salon in 1935, operates in 144 countries with sales of $192.4 million in 1971)... Brookmeyer Econcomic Service is started as independent research organization... Some 40% of all manufacturing assets in U.S. are held by 318 firms... After retiring with wealth from produce business in 1901 and inheriting father-in-law's board seat on small North Beach savings bank in San Francisco to battle conservative directors, Amadeo Peter Giannini starts Bank of Italy, evolves later as Bank of America, to serve small businessmen, workers (opens first branch in San Jose in 1906 - 24 by 1918 with first statewide banking system, forms Bancitaly Corp. in 1919 to acquire stock in U.S. and European banks, acquires New York bank in 1919, acquires Bank of America of Los Angeles and its 21 branches in 1921 - 493 outlets in California by 1939, forms Transamerica Corp. in 1928)...

U.S. Supreme Court dissolves Hill-Harriman railroad combine in Northern Securities Company case (revitalizes Sherman Anti-Trust Act, establishes Theodore Roosevelt as trustbuster)... Charles W. Nash becomes general manager of Durant-Dort Carriage Works (installs belt conveyor to assemble carriages, becomes president of Buick in 1910 when William C. Durant builds General Motors, resigns from GM as president in 1916 when Durant returns as head)...

Reporter Ivy L. Lee starts publicity firm, pioneers field of public relations (is hired by New York bankers to convince property owners to provide right-of-way for new railroad line, is employed by Pennsylvania Railroad from 1906-14 to improve its image, is employed by John D. Rockefeller in 1915 to counter adverse publicity generated from 1913 Colorado "Ludlow Massacre," starts pioneering public relations firm in 1916 to advise public figures)...

Edward F. Hutton, later chairman of General Foods, starts Wall Street brokerage firm (after dynamic growth in 1970s-1980s is fined $2 million in 1985 on 2,000 counts of mail and wire fraud in check-kiting scheme, is rescued from financial losses of $90.3 million, in part from reckless spending, in 1987 by take-over of Shearson Lehman for some $1 billion)... Western Retail Lumbermen's Assn. starts insurance business, followed in 1909 by National Petroleum Assn. with National Petroleum Mutual Fire Insurance... Georgia farmers burn 2 million bales of cotton to prop up falling prices.

1905

General Events

U.S. Supreme Court: <u>Swift</u> & <u>Company</u> <u>v.</u> <u>United</u> <u>States</u> (indicts 17 leaders of Chicago's "Beef Trust" for violating Sherman Anti-Trust Act)... Samuel Gompers, president of AFL, denounces working wives, black workers... Benjamin Holt devises a crawler tractor (forms business in Peoria, IL, produces Caterpillar tractors in 1930s)...

Ole Evinrude, Fritz Ziegenspeck of Germany independently design first outboard motors for boats... Thomas W. Lawson: <u>Frenzied</u> <u>Finance</u> (exposes ruthless tactics used by Henry H. Rogers in forming Amalgamated Copper as trust)... J. Williams tests model helicopter, CT (fails with prototype in 1908)... New York forms Armstrong Commission to investigate insurance industry (recommends changes in actuarial and marketing practices, is followed by investigations of other states)... New York University presents first college advertising course... Charles Edward Russell: <u>The</u> <u>Greatest</u> <u>Trust</u> <u>in</u> <u>the</u> <u>World</u> (exposes practices of meat-packing industry)...

In this time Bavarian-born machinist and tinkerer Charles Fey devises Liberty Bell, first three-reel slot machine, in San Francisco... Industrial Workers of the World, called "Wobblies," is formed by "Big Bill" Haywood, former organizer for militant Western Federation of Miners, and other labor radicals in Chicago (expouses workers' revolution, acquires top membership of some 70,000 members as pioneering industrial union, achieves greatest victory in 1912 by winning strike of textile workers in Lawrence, MA, declines in 1912 after losing militant strike of textile workers in New Jersey, is attacked with 1918 prosecution of Haywood, members for conspiring to obstruct U.S. war effort, still exists)...

U.S. Supreme Court: <u>Lochner</u> <u>v.</u> <u>New</u> <u>York</u> (declares State law unconstitutional in limiting maximum working hours for bakers)... Control for supremacy of New York's Chinatown is contested by rival tongs On Leong, Hip Sing (ends with merger in 1906)... Joseph Pratt pioneers use of group therapy in treating tuberculosis patients... Society of Automobile Engineers is formed... Metropolitan Opera chorus strikes for higher wages, better working conditions.

Business Events

Public utility pioneer Ira C. Copley acquires first newspaper (forms Copley Press in 1928-47 to operate number of medium-sized, one-publisher papers in CA, IL)... "First" U.S. pizzaria opens in NYC (pioneers industry of some 36,000 parlors by 1986)... Arrow collar man advertising campaign is launched by shirtmaker (becomes cult icon in 1920s and mid-1980s)... Cudahy Packing introduces Old Dutch cleanser...

Oaks Amusement Park opens in Portland, OR (operates in 1980s as U.S.' oldest in continuous use)... Ira C. Copley forms Western United Gas & Electric through mergers (consolidates with others as Western Utility in 1921)... Sarah B. Walker, black entrepreneur, develops hair formula for black women (peddles product door-to-door in Denver in 1906, forms business in 1907, moves to Indianapolis headquarters in 1910, employs some 3,000 women agents giving treatments with house calls, forms "Walker Clubs" in 1913 for agents - cash prizes to clubs for community philanthropic work)... After designing alternating current transmitter in 1900-02 and forming American De Forest which evolves as United Wireless, Lee De Forest invents Audion amplifier to make transcontinental telephone service possible (invents triode in 1906 to provide foundation for radio broadcasting industry)...

Walter J. Kohler takes over family's 1873 plumbing business in Sheboygan, WI (builds planned company town on Lake Michigan in 1912, serves as governor 1928-30, refuses to bargain with AFL in 1934 as having provided employees with liberal benefits, needs National Guard to quell violence)... Arde Bullova works in father's 1875 small jewelry business (starts Swiss plant in 1919 to make watch movements, incorporates in 1923 as Bullova Watch, acquires subsidiaries in 1930s)... After previous failures in organizing themselves, citrus farmers form California Fruit Growers' Exchange as cooperative (achieve success with Sunkist brand in 1908 - 60% of U.S. market in 1980s)...

Israel Sack, Lithuanian emigrant, opens oldest continuous U.S. antique shop business in Boston (develops personal collection - nucleus of Metropolitan Museum's American wing in 1924, moves business to New York in 1933)... Samuel Prescott starts Boston Biochemical Laboratory to study, analyze, test food products (advises United Fruit in starting research laboratory in 1912-13)... Alaska Syndicate is formed by Guggenheim family, J.P. Morgan & Co., others to develop interests in copper and gold mines, canneries, railroads, steamships... Ex-Lax business is started, NYC, by Hungarian-born scientist...

Retail sales people in Boston area are given training course by Lucinda Prince (starts Union School of Salesmanship in 1908, Prince School of Store Service in 1911)... Henry L. Doherty starts business to provide utility companies with engineering, financial services (creates Cities Service in 1913 as holding company to operate 53 utilities)... Danish-born Charles E. Sorenson is hired by Ford Motor Co. as pattern maker (-1944, designs moving assembly line with William Knudsen in 1910-13)...

Russian-born impressario Sol Hurok arrives U.S. with $1.50 (-1974 after presenting great artists to U.S. audiences)... Chicago businessmen form first Rotary Club to do charitable work (spawns some 20,000 chapters, around one million members, in some 150 countries by 1980s, is opened to women by U.S. Supreme Court in 1987)... DuPont creates Operative Committee of departmental directors to coordinate current operations, permitting Executive Committee to make policy...

Sears opens Chicago mail-order plant (uses new machinery and gravity chutes to systematize handling of 100,000 orders per day, arranges work by simple repetitive operations)... Sime Silverman publishes Variety for show business... Lundsford invents Vicks VapoRub (evolves as Richardson family business to sell Clearasil Cream, Oil of Olay, NyQuil cold medicines, and Vidal Sassoon hair-care line in 1983, after threatened with take-over by Unilever in 1985 is rescued by Procter & Gamble)...

DuPont develops first practical production of visose rayon... Joseph Boyer starts Burroughs Adding Machine Co. in St. Louis (operates with sales of some $8 million and 2,500 employees in 1913)... Alonzo F.

Herndon, successful black barber, purchases mutual benefit society from 2 Atlanta ministers (becomes Atlanta Life Insurance as leading insurance business for blacks)... Riverview amusement park opens in Des Moines, IA... Automobile Gasoline Co. opens world's first drive-in gas station, St. Louis.

1906

General Events

Hepburn Act authorizes (July 29) regulation of rates charged by railroads, pipelines, and terminals... Pure Food and Drug Act prohibits (June 29) adulteration or mislabeled foods, drugs in interstate commerce... Samuel Gompers, AFL president, starts political activity to lobby Congress to exempt labor from anti-trust regulations... Upton Sinclair: The Jungle (exposes practices of meat-packing industry, inspires passage of Meat Inspection Act to bar diseased meat from interstate commerce - a federal grading service in 1927)...

R.A. Fessenden broadcasts first radio program of voice, music... University of Cincinnati starts pioneering cooperative educational program for engineering students... After strike International Typographical Union wins 8-hour day... National Society for the Promotion of Industrial Education organizes to prepare boys, girls for factory work... American Association for Labor Legislation forms (expresses concern about industrial diseases)...

University of Pennsylvania starts degree program in industrial medicine, first course in industrial hygiene at MIT in 1905... Skiing is seen on Mt. Hood, OR... Mill to make Cannon towels is built in North Carolina (creates Kannopolis as model mill city with housing, schools, churches, parks)... Chicago's last cable car makes final run... U.S. Supreme Court rules corporations must yield incriminating evidence in anti-trust suits.

Business Events

Canadian-born Alfred Fuller starts business in Boston to make brushes for household use, clears $42.15 in first week after selling door-to-door (advertises for salesmen in 1911 to recruit 260 dealers, paid 50% commission, and starts nationwide business - sales of $40,000 in 1910, $86,649 in 1916, over $250,000 in 1917, some $700,000 in 1918, $1 million in 1919, $12 million in 1924, and $109 million in 1960, hires first women in 1948 to introduce new cosmetic line, increases sales by 47% between 1953-67 while sales of Avon products with advertising and part-time women as independent contractors soar over 900%, starts national mail-order business and operates two retail stores in 1987 to improve market position)...

Claude C. Hopkins is hired as copywriter by Chicago's Lord & Thomas advertising agency (innovates with dramatic presentations, premiums and coupons)... Jacob Sapirstein peddles postcards from horse-drawn wagon (evolves as American Greetings by 1980s to operate $1 billion-a-year card and toy business)... Telimco places first ad to sell radios, priced at $7.50, in Scientific American...

Lever Brothers introduces Lux Flakes to soap market... Planters Nut &

Chocolate Co. is founded by Italian-born Amedo Obici, arrival in U.S. at age of 12 in 1889 to operate fruit and nut stand in 1896, and Mario Peruzzi... For first time Dow Jones index closes over 100 points... Carl Laemmle, after quarrel with wife's uncle to quit clothing business, moves to Chicago to invest in 5-and-10-cent store, enters nickelodeon business instead (starts producing cheap movies and forms service to distribute films of other producers, creates Yankee Films in 1909 to fight monopoly of Motion Picture Patents Co., renames business Independent Motion Pictures in 1910 to make 100 films in NYC)...

Stephen Birch participates in syndicate of J.P. Morgan, Guggenheim Exploration to acquire Alaska Copper (as managing director builds railroad, starts Alaska Steamship in 1907, forms Kennecott Copper in 1915 to oversee all enterprises - largest U.S. copper producer in 1940)... Boston speculator Jesse L. Livermore goes to NYC with $2,500 in savings from "bucket shop" operations (clears some $250,000 after selling stock of Union Pacific short - millionaire with speculations in Anaconda stock, tries to corner cotton market in 1908 - fails but regains $900,000, declares first bankruptcy in 1915 with debts of $2 million - repaid by 1917, nets some $100 million selling wheat short in 1925, after selling short declares 4th bankruptcy in 1934 - for first time fails to pay all creditors, opens New York office in 1939 as financial advisor to promote system to detect market trends, commits suicide in 1940 - estate with debts of $361,000)...

Hernand Behn, brother Sosthenes start sugar brokerage business in Puerto Rico (acquire control of Puerto Rico Telephone in 1914 when used as security for crop loan, form International Telephone & Telegraph in 1920 to raise capital for laying cable form Key West to Havana, start acquiring radio companies in Cuba and Puerto Rico in 1922, acquire AT&T's International Western Electric in 1925, acquire Mackey Co. and its Postal Telegraph System in 1928, expand operations to Spain, Romania, Vatican City, North and South America, and British Empire in 1920s-30s)... After working for Olds Motor Works since 1901, Roy D. Chapin starts independent automobile venture with Howard E. Coffin (forms Chalmers-Detroit Motor in 1908 with new financing, sells interest to Hugh R. Chalmers to start Hudson Motor Car in 1909 with Coffin and financing from Detroit retailer, introduces popular Essex car in 1919)...

Ford Motor co. opens sales branches in New York, Boston, Philadelphia, Buffalo, Chicago, Cleveland, and Kansas City... Halcomb Steel of Syracuse, NY, builds first U.S. electric steel furnace to serve automobile industry... Saloon keeper Tex Rickard, former Texas cowboy, rancher, town marshal and gambler, promotes his first ballyhoo lightweight title bout for $38,000, largest purse of time, between Battling Nelson and Joe Gans, NV (promotes first $1 million match in 1921 between Jack Dempsey, Georges Carpentier - Tyson bout in 1988 grosses over $65 million)...

Traveling animal show of Carl Hagenbach, acquired ownership from father in 1866, is acquired by Benjamin Wallace to form Hagenbach-Wallace Circus... Earl D. Babst becomes general counsel for National Biscuit Co. (-1915, develops trademark packaging to replace traditional bulk sales)... Gannett chain of small-town newspapers is started (becomes media empire after 1970 with Allen H. Neuharth operating 86 daily newspapers with circulation of 4.7 million, 6 television stations and 14 radio stations)...

Walter E. Flanders, machine tool salesman and mechanic, is hired by Henry Ford as production manager (-1908, instead of usual departments arranges machines by sequential operations to make Model-N cars, introduces interchangeable parts for large-scale production, uses static assembly line - workers move from car to car)... Henry Leland ships 3 Cadillac cars to England (amazes Royal Automobile Society by disassembling cars, mixing parts, then reassembling 3 new cars with interchangeable parts)...

Haloid Co. is formed in Rochester, NY, to make photographic paper (acquires rights to Xerox process in 1947)... General Electric markets first crude electric range... Civil Service Assembly of United States and Canada is created (becomes Public Personnel Association in 1958... Dr. Frank Fulton pioneers use of physical examinations for employees... Sears opens first branch mail-order office in Dallas, 2nd in Seattle in 1910 (provides customer credit in 1911, starts product testing laboratory in 1911, opens first retail store in Chicago in 1925)...

Honeywell Heating Specialties is started in Wabash, IN, to build water-heating equipment (acquires expertise in making automatic temperature controls through series of mergers, develops first successful electronic auto-pilot in 1941)... Standard Oil of Illinois is indicted under Elkins Act for accepting freight rebates, fined maximum of $29,240,000 in 1907.

1907

General Events

Congress passes (January 26) law to forbid corporations contributing to election campaigns for national office... Japan's laborers are excluded from entering U.S. by Presidential order... U.S. agrees to supervise Dominican customs until foreign creditors are paid... Oklahoma is 46th State... Chicago's Horace Mann High School starts pioneering part-time cooperative training program with businesses...

John L. Lewis works in Illinois coal mines (-1909, serves as AFL field representative in 1909 - international vice president in 1917 and acting president of United Mine Workers in 1919, serves as union president from 1920-60)...

Portland's first annual floral celebration is started, OR (evolves as Rose Festival)... Due to shortage of currency from wreckless, over-capitalizaiton of new enterprises, financial panic results when F. Augustus Heinze's United Copper fails and Knickerbocker Trust folds in market stung by insurance losses of 1906 San Francisco earthquake and fire (-1908, requires ability of J.P. Morgan, requested by President Roosevelt, friends to bring about recovery by importing some $100 million in gold from Europe, fails to stem ensuing Depression)... Jack London: The Iron Heel (expresses socialist views in attacking corporations)...

Perhaps first large-scale "social-scientific" study of public opinion is a survey of Pittsurgh, financed by Russell Sage Foundation... "Big Bill" Haywood, head of Industrial Workers of the World, and two union leaders are acquitted on charges of conspiracy to murder Idaho governor... After investing tetrahedron construction in 1902, Alexander Graham Bell, wife, and associates start Aerial Experiment Assn. at Hammondsport, NY (develop hydrofoil boats in 1908 - world speed record in 1919, make Canada's first plane flight in 1909).

Business Events

Ovorono, under-arm deodorant for women (men expected to smell), is created by Cincinnati surgeon, promoted by 1919 ad with "within the curve of a woman's arm" to avoid mentioning armpit... Henning W. Prentice, Jr., is hired in sales by Armstrong Cork (replaces secret "deals" between buyers and sellers in flooring business with published price list in 1920s, as president 1935-50 and chairman 1950-59 launches company's national advertising program to sell linoleum)... Thomas M. McInnerney starts department store in Rochester, NY (returns to Chicago in 1912 to manage City Fuel Co., acquires ice-cream maker Hydrox in 1914 as subsidiary - basis for National Dairy Products in 1923)...

Russian-born Louis B. Mayer from Canada acquires old burlesque theater in Haverhill, MA (develops Gordon-Mayer circuit of movie theaters as largest chain in New England)... Rockefeller interests send Cyrus S. Eaton to Manitoba, Canada, to acquire power plant franchises (continues project with Canadian money when Rockefeller's group drops venture during Panic, with success forms Continental Gas & Electric, forms Cleveland Trust in 1919 and United Light & Power in 1928 to serve 711 communities, invests in steel industry in 1925, buys stock in Samuel Insull's utility empire in 1928-29 which forces Insull to borrow funds in defense and declare bankruptcy in 1932, loses some $100 million in 1929 crash)...

Ford Motor Co. acquires Highland Park Race Track, MI, to build new plant (starts building branch assembly plants, modernizing assembly process in 1909 with logical arrangement of tools and use of time schedules)... Bullock's retail business is started, Los Angeles... Pike Place Market opens, Seattle (after fighting urban-renewal in 1970s, shows U.S.' highest per square foot sales in 1980s for 350 local farmers, fishmongers, bakers, butchers, artists, crafts people)... International Correspondence School at Scranton, PA, starts training programs for industry... B. Bendix starts business to make cars (-1909, starts Bendix Brake in 1912 and Bendix Aviation in 1929)...

Hurling Co. introduces pioneering electric washing machine... Axel Johnson devises first high-speed machine for making sanitary cans... American Messenger Co., named United Parcel Service in 1929, is started in Seattle by J.E. Casey, partner with $100, 6 messengers and 2 bicycles (operates nationwide system in 1980s with some 117,000 employees, sales over $300 million)... Scenes for "Count of Monte Cristo" are filmed at Santa Monica, CA (is followed by Biograph Studio at Los Angeles in 1909, by first Hollywood studio in 1911 - site later for others to avoid New York monopoly of General Film Co.)...

A "shopping center" is built in Baltimore... After selling public relations business in Atlanta for $25,000 (rejects trade for Coca-Cola franchises in Missouri, Kansas), superior specialty retail business is started in Dallas, TX, by Herbert Marcus - sole owner by 1927, with sister Carrie and husband Al Neiman (appoints Stanley Marcus general merchandising manager in 1932 - president in 1950, innovates with advertisements in <u>Vogue</u> - first store outside of New York to do so,

weekly fashion shows at hotels, "super spectacular fashion shows" to
launch seasons, fashion awards in 1938, extravagant "His/Her gifts" in
1960 Christmas catalog, halts expansion of 11 stores in 5 states to 21
stores in 11 states in 1985 to rethink merchandising strategy)... During
financial Panic E.H. Harriman loses some $100 million in personal funds
from losses on Union Pacific stock (results in dissolution of Harriman
Extermination League, an informal group of financiers)...

Bonwit Teller retail business is incorporated in NYC by Paul J. Bonwit
(opens apparel specialty shop for women in 1895) and Edmond D. Teller
(joins Bonwit in 1897)... Barnum & Bailey Circus is acquired by Ringling
Brothers (moves headquarters from Baraboo, WI, to Connecticut, starts
winter headquarters in Sarasota, FL, acquires   American Circus Corp.,
operator of Sells-Flato, Robinson, Hagenbach-Wallace, Sparks and Albert
G. Barnes shows in 1929)... After defeating Chicago rival Mont Tennes
becomes head of U.S.' gambling business (uses managerial techniques to
organize and systematize operations, acquires control of telegraph
service to monopolize track betting information, is squeezed out of
business in 1928 by Al Capone)...

Herbert Hoover starts mine engineering consulting business (grows with
offices in New York, San Francisco, Paris, etc., to advise on
administration and reorganization of large metallurgical, railroad and
mining enterprises)... Boston syndicate controlling AT&T is replaced by
J.P. Morgan & Co. (rehires Theodore N. Vail as president - retires in
1919, starts Western Electric Research Laboratories in 1907 - Bell
Telephone Laboratories in 1925, forms independent Bell operations into 10
regional divisions, establishes policy in 1908 that "Our business is
service," acquires 30% of Western Union in 1910 - forced by government to
divest in 1913, opens transcontinental telephone line in 1915, tests
transatlantic transmission from Paris to New York by radio telephone in
1915)... United Press, previously 1882-93, is formed as new syndicate
(-1985 when declaring bankruptcy)... President J.W. Van Cleve, National
Association of Manufacturers, asks members for $500,000 to fight
organized labor.

1908

General Events

Congress passes (May 28) bill to regulate child labor in District of
Columbia... Aldrich-Vreeland Act allows (May 30) banks to issue notes
backed by commercial paper and bonds of state, local governments... After
patents in 1869 to I.G. MacGaffey and H.G. Booth in 1901, James M.
Spangler patents electrically-driven suction sweeper, improves on David
Kenney's 1903 machine (sells rights to leather business of W.H. Hoover,
names business Electric Suction Sweeper, Hoover Co. later, to sell
appliances door-to-door, starts English business in 1920s - by 1950 with
operations in 107 nations with sales over $51 million)... Orville Wright
makes first plane flight exceeding one hour (is followed by first flight
over 400 hours in 1929 and over 1,200 hours in 1958)... Federal
Employers' Liability Act holds common carriers in interstate commerce to
be liable for injury or death of employees... Thorndike designs first
standardized achievement test...

Harvard Graduate School of Business Administration opens, some 30 such university programs by 1911 (after persuasion by Carl Barth adopts Taylor System as core course, requires students to take accounting, commercial law and commerce - becomes marketing in 1914)... Congress creates National Monetary Commission to review nation's financial structure... 47-story Singer Building is erected in NYC (is topped by 50-story Metropolitan Tower, 60-story Woolworth Building by 1913)... Northwestern University creates school of business...

U.S. Supreme Court: <u>Muller</u> <u>v.</u> <u>Oregon</u> (rules law limiting maximum hours women can work as Constitutional, hears sociological and economic facts by attorney Louis Brandeis)... Robert M. Yerkes, John D. Dodson of Harvard Physiological Laboratory are first researchers to study effects of stress on performance... U.S. Supreme Court: <u>Loewe</u> <u>v.</u> <u>Lawler</u> (outlaws secondary boycotts by unions, rules union in Danbury Hatter's case liable for damages under Sherman Anti-Trust Act - 83 further prosecutions of unions by 1928)... Chicago passes first local U.S. pasteurization law...

NYC law makes it illegal for women to smoke in public... Congress passes workmen's compensation law for certain civilian employees in federal government... First major application of job analysis is made with civil service jobs in Chicago... U.S. Supreme Court declares Section 10 of 1898 Erdman Act, outlawing "yellow dog" contracts in railroad industry, as unconstitutional... Yale's new Department of Business Methods offers "Commerce and the Commercial Policy in the 19th Century," "Corporation Economics," "Morals in Modern Business," "Problems in Business Management," "Trade Statistics," and "Forest Management abroad and in the U.S."... U.S. Federal Court sentences Samuel Gompers and all AFL officers for violating Court's injunction.

Business Events

Some 3 million catalogs of Sears, Roebuck are distributed to public, some 7.2 million in 1925... Building Owners and Manager's Association International organizes in Chicago... James Powers, former foreman with Herman Hollerith's 1896 Tabulating Machine Co., patents tabulating machine (organizes Powers Accounting Machine in 1909, contracts to tabulate 1910 census, starts Accounting and Tabulating Co. of Great Britain in 1914 with Prudential Assurance as major client)...

First electric home refrigerator is marketed, first practical home freezer in 1918... Fisher Body Co. is started by 6 brothers (with innovation and craftsmanship land Cadillac order in 1910 for 50 sedans, is acquired by General Motors in 1919)... Sears issues first Modern Homes catalog (-1940, using mass-assembly techniques in building construction, sells designs and construction kits for 22 models ranging from $650 to $2,500, sells over 100,000 before dropping business)... Walter P. Chrysler buys $5,000 Locomobile for study (joins Buick Motor in 1912 as works manager for $6,000 after rejecting offer of $12,000 by employer American Locomotive, becomes president of Buick in 1916)... First Model-T Ford is priced at $850, drops to $310 by 1926 after making 15 million...

Edison Laboratories creates Motion Picture Patents Co. with 7 major movie producers in attempt to control industry with film patents (forms General Film Co., "The Trust," in 1910 to establish production, distribution monopoly)... E.C. Sullivan takes over research laboratory of Corning Glass Works (develops Pyrex Glass)... H.L. Gantt installs Taylor System

at Joseph Bancroft & Sons Co. of Wilmington, DE, to improve operational
efficiency (pioneers in blending Taylor's managerial philosophy with
welfare work of employee benefits and services started in 1902)...

Essanay Co. is started in California by actor Gilbert Anderson, film
equipment distributor G.K. Spoor to make movies (pioneers movie business
in California, achieves success with Bronco Billy films)... Traveling
"Wild West" show with frontier pageantry, circus and vaudeville acts is
started by Miller Brothers' 101 Ranch, OK, with regular cowhands and
performers such as Tom Mix, Buck Jones, and Mabel Norman (declares
bankruptcy in 1931 after losing market battle to popular rodeos)... Two
brothers start Hupp Motor Car (-1941)... Owens Bottle Machine Co.
installs first glass-making machinery (is rejected by craft union of
glassblowers to ban members working in plants with such machinery, is
forced to disband local 300 in 1928)... Harrington Emerson proposes four
major staff offices, personnel, plant and machinery, materials, and
methods and procedures, for industrial organizations...

William C. Durant incorporates General Motors as holding company to
combine Cadillac, Oakland, Winton, Oldsmobile, 5 minor automobile firms,
3 truck companies, and 10 firms of accessories and parts (fails to
acquire Ford, Maxwell, Willys when J.P. Morgan refuses to finance
purchases, blunders in 1909 with purchases of Carter Car's friction
drive, Elmore Mfg.'s 2-cylinder and 2-cycle engine, and Heany Lamp - a
fraudulent device)... Wright brothers obtain $25,000 U.S. contract to
build a plane to fly at 40 mph, carry 2 passengers and fuel for 125
miles, and land undamaged... Henry L. Gantt: "Training Workmen in Habits
of Industry and Cooperation," presented to American Society of Mechanical
Engineers... Otto Zachow, William Besserdich build first 4-wheel-drive
car in Clintonville, WI... AT&T hires specialist in press relations...

Ernest W. Marland starts wildcatting venture, OK - by 1920 world's
largest independent petroleum operator (is forced out of business in 1928
by J.P. Morgan & Co. after refusing to economize)... Henry Ford starts
operations in Canada, Britain... After acquiring all U.S. producers of
photographic paper by 1898, George Eastman attempts to form international
cartel (is blocked by French law, is found guilty of violating anti-trust
laws in 1915 with control of 70-80% of U.S. market)... Mathematician Carl
Barth assists George Babcock to install Taylor System at Franklin Motor
Car Co. (-1912)... Paul Litchfield starts Goodyear Tire & Rubber Co.'s
research department (develops first practical airplane tire in 1910,
pneumatic truck tire in 1916, airplane disk brakes in 1932, and
"lifeguard" auto tire in 1935)...

Procter & Gamble scientists discover hydrogenation process (introduces
Crisco in 1911 to revolutionize cooking - Crisco Vegetable Oil in 1961,
Butter Flavor Crisco in 1983 and Crisco Corn Oil in 1986)... Champion
International builds paper mill on Pigeon River, NC (sparks war in 1987-
88 between TN and NC, environmentalists and workers on waste
pollution).

1909

General Events

Congress passes (April 9) Payne-Aldrich high tariff law... W.E. B. Du

Bois establishes (June 1) National Association for the Advancement of Colored People (advocates equality and equal opportunity)... I.C.C. prescribes general form for railroad balance sheets... G. Washington patents instant or soluble coffee... Congress passes corporate income tax (forces firms to maintain accounting records)... Frederick W. Taylor proposes to American Society of Mechanical Engineers that education consist of one week of classwork rotated with one week of field work...

Paper cup is introduced (follows first paper napkins in 1887)... Rose O'Neill copyrights "Kewpie Doll"... Strike of 30,000 members of International Ladies' Garment Workers' Union to gain recognition is suppressed by company, police brutality... Japanese strikers on Hawaii sugar plantations are indicted for inciting disorder... Government commission reports 6 men control tobacco industry with 86 firms worth $450 million... Former mining town of Reno relaxes residency requirements for divorce to attract unhappy socialites... Pittsburg labor conference declares war on U.S. Steel... First U.S. Aeronautic Show opens in NYC's Madison Square Garden... Congress passes copyright law to protect authors, composers... After all movie houses are closed in Manhattan as "immoral influence," New York creates State Board of Censorship to review films for exhibition... Supreme Court rules corporate director cannot legally profit from buying company's stock based on information concealed from other shareholders.

Business Events

Production is started at U.S. Steel complex, sprawling over five miles, at Gary, IN... O.F. Woodward acquires gelatin dessert business for $450 (promotes Jell-O as household name before selling to Postum Cereal in 1925 - General Foods in 1929)... General Electric markets first electric toaster, followed in 1927 by first pop-up toaster devised by Minnesota mechanic... Bishop family starts Pendleton Woolen Mills, OR... William Randolph Hearst starts International News Service for a.m. papers and National Press Association for p.m. papers (becomes INS in 1911, joins United Press Syndicate in 1957)... Belgian-born inventor Leo Baekeland creates first practical synthetic resin, Bakelite (starts General Bakelite Co. in 1910 to launch age of plastics, sells to Union Carbon and Carbide in 1939)... Ernest T. Weir starts Weirton Steel, WV (is forced to shut down in 1983 by owner National Steel - sold to employees)...

Conde Nast acquires Vogue, an obscure, high-society weekly journal (-1929, develops publication as arbiter of fashion by 1920s, acquires 1901 House and Garden in 1910 - becomes upper-class magazine for home decorating, forms United Publishing in 1911 to handle trade publications, acquires 1892 Vanity Fair in 1913 - merges with Vogue in 1936, introduces first foreign edition of Vogue for England in 1916, consolidates publications as Conde Nast Publications in 1922, introduces Glamour for young women in 1939)... Frank B. Gilbreth: Bricklaying System (proposes motion study to eliminate traditional waste)... After establishing credit unions in Quebec during early 1900s (follows movement in Germany during mid-1800s), first U.S. credit union is started in Manchester, NH, by Alfonse Desjardins, Msgr. Pierre Hevey (results in passage of first state law by Massachusetts on urging of Boston merchant Filene, charters 17 by 1911 and 75 by 1914, is followed by federal incorporation act in 1934)...

Remington Typewriter produces first noiseless typewriter (produces first electric typewriter in 1925)... Some 76% of manufacturing workers work 54-60 hours/week, 9% work over 60 hours/week... U.S. Steel creates surgical department... Columbia Theater is first Broadway house to present burlesque shows... Ohio railroad workers form mutual benefit society (becomes union later)...

Following maps in 1880s-1890s for bicycles, Andrew McNally, II prepares its first U.S. automobile road map... Glenn Curtiss and August Herring, previously collaborator with Octave Chanute and Samuel Langley, start first U.S. commercial aircraft manufacturing business (sell 5 planes in 3 years, after mass producing 5,000 Curtiss "Jennies" during W.W. 1 becomes U.S.' largest aircraft-manufacturer after War, merges with Wright Aeronautical in 1929 to create Curtiss-Wright)... Frederick W. Taylor obtains government contract to introduce management system at federal armories, rejected at Watertown Arsenal by strike of molders in 1911...

Frank A. Vanderlip becomes president of National City Bank of New York (innovates by hiring college graduates as future bank officers, opening Bank's first foreign branch office in 1914 and acquiring 1902 International Banking Corp. with 17 branches in 7 countries and 1912 American International with interests in 17 countries, with Bank largest in U.S. resigns in 1919 after battle with directors)... William Burns starts National Detective Agency, world's largest in 1920s...

Cy Elwell, recent engineering graduate, obtains $500 from Stanford University president David Starr Jordan to start wireless-telephone business in valley, basis for Federal Electric Corp. before acquisition by International Telephone & Telegraph... Studebaker in South Bend drops wagons to make just automobiles... Woolworth variety chain opens stores in Britain - world's largest merchandising business in 1912 with 596 stores... A.C. Gilbert forms Mysto Mfg. to make magic sets for children (after introducing chemistry sets, distributes some 30 million erector sets in 1915-30 so children can see how machinery works, acquires American Flyer model trains in 1939, liquidates business in 1967 for failure to adapt to changing market)...

After operating bargain basement in 1890s, Boston's Filene store for women institutes Automatic Bargain Basement with required reductions in prices if goods, some leftovers of manufacturers and other retailers, not sold in so many days... After one failure, Canadian-born Florence Nightingale Graham, former nurse and secretary, opens Elizabeth Arden beauty salon in Manhattan with loan of $6,000 for furnishings (opens 2nd in Washington, DC in 1914 with Boston and Paris by 1922 - 150 salons in 22 countries by 1929)...

Russian-born Joseph M. Schenck, operator of Manhattan amusement park with brother Nickolas, joins movie theater business of Marcus Loew (-1917, becomes chairman of United Artists in 1925 and forms 20th Century Pictures with Darryl F. Zanuck in 1933, is indicted in 1939 for perjury and labor racketeering case... Nickolas stays with Loew to take over 1924 MGM after Loew's death in 1927)... Charles F. Kettering, becomes director of GM research 1920, and Edward A. Deeds, resigns 1916 when United Motors acquires Delco, start Dayton Engineering Laboratories (develops farm lighting system, first practical electric self-starter for cars in 1911 - introduced in 1912 by Cadillac, automobile generator, high-octane aviation gasoline and ethel gasoline, synthetic lacquer, Freon, and two-cycle diesel engine, is acquired by General Motors with United in 1918)... Elon H. Hooker starts electrical-chemical business, attacked by environmentalist in 1979 for Love Canal disaster... Over 2 million Americans own stock... Wright brothers form million-dollar corporation to manufacture airplanes (obtain Army contract in 1910)... New York Times cites moving pictures as industry of $40 million/year...

Standard Oil gains control of Austria's petroleum industry, leaving only Romania in area as independent oil producer... Chicago's meat packers buy 2 Argentine packing plants to seek monopoly... Eureka Company of Detroit starts selling vacuum cleaners door-to-door... First black-run bank in Georgia is opened in Atlanta, followed by first chartered, Atlanta State Savings Bank, in 1913... After 1908 patent Sharp-Hughes Tool starts in Houston to make drills to penetrate rock, inherited by Howard Hughes in 1924.

1910

General Events

Mann-Elkins Act creates (June 18) commerce court to hear appeals from Interstate Commerce Commission (allows Commission to institute proceedings against railroad, telegraph and telephone companies)... Congress creates (June 25) postal saving system (-1984)... Mann Act prohibits (June 25) interstate transportation of women for immoral purposes... First mail carried by plane is flown from Albany to NYC by Glenn Curtiss...

Census counts population of some 92 million, 42 urban and 50 rural (lists some 8.7 million emigrants since 1900)... Preferential union hiring, grievance and arbitration boards are won by strike of International Ladies' Garment Workers' Union... First annual Pendleton Round-Up is held, OR... National Urban League forms (evolves with 113 affiliates by 1980s)... Victor Berger, WI, is first congressman elected on Socialist ticket... Robert Forest forms National Housing Assn. to improve deteriorating urban living conditions... Labor leader John Mitchell, clergy appeal for weekly holiday, declaring, "We don't care what the day is but we must have one day of rest"... "Weekend" becomes popular custom... Taft Commission on Economy and Efficiency in Government is formed to apply ideas, methods of efficiency movement (presents report 1912, results in reforms by 30 states during 1915-40)...

Congress permits creation of industrial banks for small savers... Fred Osius, Chester Beach and H. Hamilton invent first household electric motor for appliances... Nevada shuts down gambling industry (allows limited gambling up to $2 in 1915, passes wide-open gambling bill in 1931)... Physician Alice Hamilton pioneers industrial medicine with study of lead poisoning... Henry R. Seager, Columbia University, urges "a thorough-going organization of the country's labor market" with network of "cooperating labor bureaus," Wisconsin with 4 state-funded offices 1911-14... Norman Angell: The Great Illusion (argues war economic disaster for victors, losers).

Business Events

First Christmas club activity is started in Florida (pioneers bank savings clubs)... Gimbels opens department store at Herald Square, NYC (after purchase by chain of Batus, U.S. subsidiary of British-American Tobacco Co., is acquired by land developers in 1986 for over $150 million and liquidated - 39 stores close)... Cards showing champion women swimmers are used as premiums with packages of Panhandle Scrap Chewing Tobacco (-1915)... Western Clinic in Tacoma, WA, provides prepaid hospitalization plan for area's lumber industry, followed by plan for teachers at Baylor University in 1929, by first multi-hospital prepayment plan in New Jersey in 1933 as basis for "Blue Cross plans" in various states...

Publisher William Randolph Hearst starts King Features Syndicate to distribute articles to members... Henry P. Kendall becomes general manager of uncle's Plimpton Press (pioneers use of Taylorism - forms pioneering personnel unit to place new employees in suitable positions, buys hospital supply business, Lewis Batting Co., in 1912, revives troubled business with scientific management, product research and good working conditions - 13 plants and sales of $100 million in 1959, buys Rhode Island textile finishing business in 1915, improves performance by improving working conditions and decreasing weekly hours from 60 to 48 without lowering wages, buys first Southern cotton mill in 1916 to supply Northern plants, improves performance of each by building model mill village, reducing hours of work without loss of wages and eliminating night employment of women and children, incorporates as Kendall Mills in 1925)... General Electric starts creating product divisions in period to 1929... Bureau of Railway Economics is formed...

Carl Laemmle advertises Florence Lawrence as "Biograph Girl," pioneers movie star system... Benjamin Briscoe forms United States Motor Corp. with Maxwell-Briscoe, other firms (declares bankruptcy in 1912, is reorganized as Maxwell Motor Car to spawn Chrysler Corp. in 1925)... Chicago copywriter John E. Kennedy presents detailed plan for advertising research... Abe Plough markets nostrum for rheumatic fever (acquires bankrupt drug business in 1916, purchases company making St. Joseph Liver Regulator in 1920 to evolve as drug business with sales of $144 million, merges in 1971 with Scheering to operate with sales of some $2 billion in 1980s)... DuPont uses psychological tests to select personnel... Morris L. Cooke: <u>Academic</u> <u>and</u> <u>Industrial</u> <u>Efficiency</u> (applies scientific management to university administration)... Walter Dill Scott: "Psychology of Business," <u>System</u> (discusses worker motivation in pioneering article)...

Chicago's Consolidated Edison centralizes employment activities into one department... Continental National Bank absorbs Commercial National Bank of Chicago - soon one of U.S.' largest outside of NYC... Samuel Insull attempts rural electrification of Lake County, IL (-1913, represents first attempt to market electricity outside urban area)... Thomas A. Edison, partners form General Film Co., "The Trust," to absorb all U.S. licensed film exchanges and monopolize production, distribution and exhibition of movies (starts flight of independent studios to Florida, California, Mexico to avoid patent infringement suits, after eliminating 57 of 58 competitors ends in 1915 with legal victory of William Fox)... American Film Co., known as "Flying A," is started in Santa Barbara to make movies (-1920)... Enameled white bathtubs are marketed...

Remington Typewriter Factory at Illion, NY, is reorganized by Henry Gantt in accordance with guidelines of Frederick W. Taylor... Joyce C. Hall starts business in Kansas City as jobber of postcards (starts selling Christmas cards with "Hallmark" label in 1913, enters national market in 1923, evolves to operate some 20,000 card shops by 1980s - sales of almost $1 billion as world's largest in industry, diversifies in 1980s with specialty publishing, broadcasting, and crayons)... To save General Motors from financial disaster, William C. Durant borrows over $12 million from Boston, New York bankers (is removed from operating authority by syndicate and replaced as president by Charles W. Nash, former president of Buick, who appoints Walter P. Chrysler as president of Buick)... U.S. railroads use some 1,700,000 workers...

Term "scientific management" is reputed to have originated at meeting called by lawyer Louis Brandeis in home of H.L. Gantt to prepare for I.C.C. case on railroad rate increases (uses Harrington Emerson as expert witness to state that railroads can save some $1 million/day by adopting management principals)... Operation of Highland Park factory, designed by Albert Kahn with improvements from his 1905 Packard plant, is started by Henry Ford to make Model-T cars (uses time and motion studies, continuous conveyor belts and specialized machine tools in 1912)... Goodyear Tire & Rubber creates aeronautics unit to make first practical tires for airplanes (obtains Germany's Zeppelin patents in 1924 to build U.S.' first dirigibles for U.S. Navy in 1928 and blimps in 1930s, builds over 300 airships before sale of division in 1987)...

California becomes nation's leading oil producer with gusher of Lakeview No. 1 well near Los Angeles... Philip W. Drackett, wife start small chemical brokerage firm in Cincinnati (introduce Drano in 1923 to achieve success, create Windex glass cleaner in 1933)... Black-owned Mississippi life insurance business is started, followed in 1913 by North Carolina Mutual Life Insurance... Nearly a million cars are registered, over 2 million by 1915... Levitz furniture business is started, nationwide chain with 116 stores after W.W.II... Duncan Black, Alonzo Decker open Baltimore machine shop (patent world's first portable power drill with pistolgrip, trigger switch in 1917 to start new industry - worldwide leader in 1980s, expands with GE's small appliance business in 1984, bids $1.8 billion for American Standard, diversified manufacturer best known for pluming fixtures, in 1988).

1911

General Events

Charles F. Kettering, Delco, perfects 1899 electric self-starter of Clyde J. Coleman... Harvard forms Bureau of Business Research... 146 New York garment workers are killed in sweat shop during fire at Triangle Shirtwaist Co. (results in formation of New York Factory Investigating Commission to recommend new safety and health regulations)... Wausau Insurance Co., WI, introduces first U.S. workmen's compensation insurance... Andrew Carnegie founds Carnegie Foundation with $125 million "for the advancement and diffusion of knowledge"...

Circuit Court of Appeals rules Selden's patent for automobile is invalid and that Henry Ford did not infringe on its coverage (forces dissolution of patent monopoly)... U.S. Supreme Court upholds injunction against AFL in supporting molders' secondary boycott... DuPont Powder Company is judged in restraint of trade by U.S. Supreme Court (forces firm to divest itself of Hercules Powder, Atlas Powder)... U.S. Supreme Court upholds workmen's compensation law of Washington... Treaty allows limited immigration of Japanese workers...

Henry A. Gibson devises naval war game, pioneers U.S. decision-making simulations... Glenn Curtiss tries to patent the aileron (after legal battle with Wrights gets patent 1917)... New York closes failing Carnegie Trust Co... National Republican Club urges uniform nationwide regulatory laws for business to avoid "state regulatory socialism."

Business Events

Associated Advertising Clubs of America adopts slogan of "Truth in Advertising"... Sears introduces its first consumer credit program, "Easy Payment Plan" (introduces revolving charge plan in 1953)... 1899 Everleigh Club, Chicago's famous and elegant brothel (operated by 2 sisters using advertising, business methods), is closed by Mayor Carter Harrison, II... Frederick W. Hoffman: "Industrial Diseases in America," American Labor Legislation Review... Standard Oil is required by Supreme Court to divest itself of all subsidiaries (creates Standard Oil of New Jersey, named Esso in 1923 and Exxon in 1972-73, of California, Indiana, New York, and of Ohio)... H.K. McCann, formerly in Standard Oil's advertising department, starts advertising agency to serve new businesses created by break-up of Standard Oil... U.S. Supreme Court breaks up American Tobacco as R.J. Reynolds, Liggett & Myers, Lorillard and American Tobacco...

Custom-designed house car is built for T. Coleman DuPont (is followed in 1915 by "motorized bungalow" of Henry V. Joy, president of Packard Motor Co., and by several companies, such as Livabout and Caravan, to make house-car bodies by 1921, by Covered Wagon Co. of Arthur G. Sherman in 1929 and by Winnebago's first successful motor home in 1966)... After suffering wet feet during deer hunt, L.L. Bean designs Marine hunting shoe with rubber bottom, leather top (starts business with brother in dry-goods store at Freeport, MA, issues first mail flyer in 1912, although 90 of first 100 shoes returned fulfills guarantee of unqualified reliability, moves business from store's basement to new building in 1917, employs 25 people in 1924, starts operating store 24-hours/day in 1951, is succeeded by grandson, Leon Gorman in 1967 who continues tradition with modernization, becomes part of "preppie" look in 1980s, generates sales of some $253.7 million in 1984 - some 60 million catalogs/year and visits by some 2 million tourists as State's 2nd biggest attraction after Atlantic Ocean)...

Professional champion of bicycle racing Frank L. Kramer signs 10-year contract with promoter "Colonel" John M. Chapman to do exhibitions (-1922)... At age of 16 Sam Newhouse, high school drop-out, is put in charge of struggling Bayonne, NJ, newspaper acquired by lawyer to satisfy debt (buys first paper in 1922, with financial acumen and understanding of demographic trends builds $7.5 billion empire by 1987 to operate 26 major newspapers, 3 cable television networks, Random House Publishing, New Yorker, and Parade magazine, 35 Conde Nast publications including Glamour, GQ, Mademoiselle, Vanity, and Vogue - 28 others in Europe, and miscellaneous businesses)... Albert H. Wiggin becomes president of NYC's Chase National Bank (transforms business with less than $250 million in reserves to one of world's largest in 1935 with $2.5 billion by focusing on corporate accounts)...

Lawyer and politician Robert R. McCormick becomes president of Chicago's Tribune Co., part-ownership in 1914 with cousin Joseph M. Patterson (acquires 5 million acres of Canadian timber land in 1915-23 and builds 2 paper mills with towns, hydro-electric plants, railroads, and steamships, acquires Chicago radio station in 1924 - WGN for world's greatest newspaper)... General Electric is indicted in U.S. anti-trust suit (results in dissolution of GE's National Electric Lamp Assn. with 33 firms)... Charles C. Parlin is hired by Curtis Publishing Co. to manage new commercial research division... Frederick W. Taylor: The Principles of Scientific Management...

Tony Lama boot business is started in El Paso, TX... After attempting to start Little Motor Car Co., Chevrolet Motor Co. is started by William C. Durant, financed by J.J. Raskob and Pierre DuPont, and Louis Chevrolet, Swiss-born engineer and race car driver (with success swaps Chevrolet stock for shares of General Motors to win back control of GM in 1916)... Cessna is started in Wichita, KS, to make light aircraft... J.O. Eaton, associates start business to make truck axles, NJ (evolves as leading supplier of parts for cars and trucks, merges with 1883 Yale & Towne in 1966)... In this time automobile companies adopt franchise method to establish dealerships, first corporate dealership in 1988... Louis D. Brandeis: Scientific Management and Railroads...

First U.S. conference on scientific management meets at Amos Tuck School of Administration and Finance, Dartmouth College... Mercer T Head Race-About is first true U.S. sports car (-1914)... Thomas Ince is sent to Los Angeles by two ex-bookmakers, who had acquired movie studio after New York ban on horse racing, to manage their operations (produces movie/week by 1913, stars William S. Hart in westerns to 1925 - within few years earning $2,025,000)... Standard Oil of New Jersey launches global marketing program, followed by Coca-Cola in 1940s...

Arthur D. Little consulting business designs "pilot plant" experimental operation for United Fruit... Frank B. Gilbreth, others form Society to Promote the Science of Management (becomes Taylor Society in 1915, merges with Society of Industrial Engineers in 1936 to form Society for the Advancement of Management)... New York Edison starts commercial school for new employees... Frank B. Gilbreth: Motion Study: A Method for Increasing the Efficiency of the Workman... Philadelphia Rapid Transit starts "cooperative welfare plan"... Pantasate Co. adopts first U.S. group life insurance plan... Vocational Bureau of Boston studies human factors in organizations... Harrington Emerson: Efficiency as a Basis for Operation and Wages...

Austrian-born Nathan Ohrbach opens Bon Marche as specialty shop for women, Brooklyn (closes 1986)... Dennison stationery business, MA, adopts "Management Industrial Program," provides stockholders with non-voting stock and managers with voting stock and profit-sharing plan (provides first U.S. employer unemployment insurance in 1916, creates employment office in 1919, starts employees' committee in 1919, employs business historian in 1920)... Frank B. Gilbreth is first to use camera to film time and motion studies... Anthony Overton, black entrepreneur, moves Hygienic Mfg. making baking powder, extracts and toilet preparations, from Kansas City to Chicago (introduces cosmetic line of High Brown products later)...

Glenn L. Martin starts business in California to make airplanes (merges in 1917 to form Wright-Martin Aircraft, starts new airplane manufacturing business in 1918 - designs first plane for mail service, designs B-10 Bomber, first twin-engine and all metal plane, in 1932 and B-26 Bomber to operate largest U.S. airplane manufacturing firm by World War II)... Brazilian Trade Corp. is first U.S. firm to acquire trade concession in Brazil... Chicago, NYC are linked by biweekly car service... DuPont creates Efficiency Division and Prevention of Accidents Commission as staff functions...

Oregon apple growers near Hood River form Apple Growers' Assn. as cooperative, Diamond Fruit Growers in 1964 (adopts Diamond trademark, used since 1909, in 1912)... After marriage British-born Vernon Castle, former stooge for comic Lew Fields, and wife, Irene, began career as professional dancers (after debut at Paris' Cafe De Paris during honeymoon popularize Castle Walk, Boston waltz, fox-trot, devised by Harry Fox for 1913 Ziegfeld Follies, hesitation waltz, and turkey trot to make dancing fashionable, with success spawn books, records, dresses, hats, candy, beauty cream, shoes, cigars, and Castle Bob hairstyle before W.W. I).

1912

General Events

New Mexico is 47th State... Congress authorizes (August 24) Parcel Post System... Radio Act grants limited authority to Secretary of Commerce to regulate broadcasting, followed by Federal Radio Commission in 1922... Government adopts 8-hour work day for employees on public contracts... H.S.J. Porter, others create Efficient Society to improve productivity of individuals, society... Vogue encourages women to "paint" their faces... Massachusetts enacts first state minimum wage law (covers women, minors)... Arizona is 48th State... Congress investigates strike at Watertown Arsenal on urging of organized labor opposed to Taylorism (bans use of stopwatch and other features of Taylor's wage system in government installations)... Congress creates U.S. Commission on Industrial Relations... National Safety Council is formed...

Juliette Low forms Girl Scouts (evolves with $22 million budget, 672,000 adult volunteers and paid staff of about 5,000 in 1987 as one of U.S.' best managed organizations)... For first time liquidified petroleum gas is used for cooking, heating on Pennsylvania farm... Successful violent strike for higher wages is held in Lowell, MA, by thousands of mill workers, supported by Industrial Workers of the World with "Big Bill" Haywood and Elizabeth Gurley Flynn (receives public support after observing tactics of mills)... Institute of Radio Engineers forms.

Business Events

Arthur Murray starts giving dancing lessons (sells chain of 500 studios for $5 million in 1952)... When idea was rejected by employer, Edward G. Budd starts business to make all-steel auto bodies (becomes exclusive supplier of car bodies for new Dodge automobile firm in 1915, builds first stainless steel airplane in 1931 and stainless steel pioneer Zephyr for C.B. & Q. Railroad in 1934)... Lawyer Ogden M. Reid becomes managing editor of father's New York Tribune, increasing circulation from 50,000 to 142,000 by 1921 (names wife Helen advertising director 1922-47, acquires New York's Herald and its Paris edition in 1924, sells papers to John J. Whitney in 1958 - closed by City-wide strike of 1966)... United States Chamber of Commerce is formed, over 4,000 associated groups in 1982... First permanent group of women in advertising is formed, NYC (follows Women's Publicity Club of Boston)... NYC delicatessen owner Richard Hellmann sells prepared home-made mayonnaise in glass jars...

California Associated Raisin Co. is formed as a growers' cooperative (adopts Sun-Maid trade name in 1915)... Home electricity is used by only 1/6th of all U.S. families, some 2/3rds in 1927... In this time Ford Motor Co. operates a work standards or time study department... First Better Business Bureau is formed by local businessmen, Minneapolis, to protect consumers, 167 autonomous bureaus in U.S. by 1983... Oil is discovered in Oklahoma (is followed by strikes in KS in 1915, TX in 1917, 1918 and 1920, OK in 1918, Long Beach, CA, in 1921, and East Texas in 1927)... With appearance of personnel departments in industry Meyer Bloomfield, Director of the Vocational Bureau of Boston, and others form Boston Employment Managers' Assn. to pioneer field of personnel administration...

First film comedy of Mack Sennett's Keystone Co., financed by bookies, is produced... British-born C.E.K. Mees, idea from Germany's Bayer Chemical, designs research laboratory for Eastman Kodak, model for other U.S. firms... With fortune acquired from acetylene lamps, sells business just as electric headlights are introduced, Carl Fisher of Indiana starts developing Miami Beach... James S. Kemper writes "first" automobile liability insurance (founds Lumberman's Mutual Casualty in 1912 to provide workmen's compensation coverage and manufacturers' public liability insurance, innovates with salaried sales agents)...

Edwin E. Pratt: "A New Industrial Democracy," The Annuals... Packard Piano Co. adopts employee representation plan... After cleaning toilets in steel mill and working as chief chemist for American Linseed, O.E. Eisenchimal, eccentric emigrant from Vienna, starts vegetable oil business, Scientific Oil Compounding (locates plant on Indiana-Illinois state line in case anyone wants to see license, hires only women as executives - men as plant employees, provides employees with breakfast and lunch, cosmetics, candy, clothing, book allowances, tank car of linseed oil for speculation, and slack time for ping-pong and poker)...

Commonwealth Edison of Chicago uses job studies of E.O. Griffenhangen to provide information for job classifications, job ratings, and changes in employment and jobs... Equitable Life writes pioneering group life insurance plan for Montgomery Ward employees... U.S. Rubber adopts employee stock-purchase plan (installs pension plan in 1917 for aged and infirmed workers)... Samuel Insull creates Middle West Utilities as holding company for stock in other utility companies (becomes president of Chicago's People Gas in 1919, builds pyramid group of utilities by 1930 to serve some 4.5 million customers in 5,000 communities in 32 states and produces 10% of U.S.' electric power with assets of $2.5 billion, is forced into receivership in 1932)... International Morrison-Knudsen construction business is started with $600, followed in 1914 by

Henry J. Kaiser's construction business... Adolph Zukor, former partner
of Marcus Loew, starts Engadine Co. with others to purchase U.S. rights
for French film starring Sarah Bernhardt (starts Famous Players Co. with
Daniel Frohman during year to launch studio system)... Walter P.
Chrysler is hired as works manager by Buick division of General Motors
(introduces new production processes, becomes president in 1916, resigns
in 1920 after differences with William C. Durant)...

Former copywriter Albert D. Lasker acquires Chicago advertising agency of
Lord & Thomas (acquires American Tobacco account of George Washington
Hill in 1923, develops mass advertising techniques to make Lucky Strike
U.S.' largest selling cigarette)... Universal movie business is started
by Carl Laemmle's Independent Motion Pictures, several small movie
studios, followed by Warner Brothers in 1923, Columbia Pictures and
Metro-Goldwyn-Mayer in 1924, Radio-Keith-Orpheum in 1928, Twentieth-
Century Fox in 1935 and Republic for "B" movies in 1935...

Royal Dutch Shell starts U.S. subsidiary to compete with interests of
John D. Rockefeller... William H. Hodkison, other film distributors form
Paramount Pictures to distribute feature motion pictures of Adolph
Zukor's Famous Players studio and Lasky Feature Play Co. (are merged in
1916 as Famous Players - Lasky Corp., retains name of Paramount for
distribution and theaters, by Adolph Zukor, acquires some 600 theaters in
1916-19 when independent theaters form National Exhibitors Circuit,
operates some 1,300 theaters and 500 subsidiaries as Paramount by 1932,
flirts with bankruptcy in 1936)... Clarence Walker Barron, owner of The
Wall Street Journal, appoints himself as editor (increases circulation
from 7,000 to 52,000 in 1928 as paper goes from 4 pages to 20).

1913

General Events

16th Amendment for graduated income tax is adopted... Congress passes
(October 3) Underwood Simmons Tariff Act, first tariff reform since Civil
War (lowers duties on 958 items)... Owen-Glass Federal Reserve Act
creates (December 23) board to oversee 12 regional Federal Reserve
Banks... Some 150,000 garment-workers in Boston, New York strike to win
reduced hours, higher wages and union recognition... C.O.D. mail service
is started... U.S. railroads propose nationwide time zones to eliminate
confusion in scheduling trains... Some 9,000 miners at Calumet and Hecla
mines, 1864-1968, strike on Michigan's Upper Peninsula for $3.50/day and
shorter hours (-1914, after damage and violence requires National Guard
and strike-breakers from New York's Waddell-Mahon Detective Agency to
break strike, union)...

Grand Central Terminal opens, NYC (records peak traffic in 1946 by
handling over 65 million railroad passengers)... NYC's Woolworth Building
with 60 stories is world's tallest, topped by Chrysler Building in 1930
with 77 stories, Empire State Building in 1931 with 102 stories, World
Trade Center in 1972 with 110 stories, and Chicago's Sears Tower in 1974
with over 110 stories)... Automatic bread-wrapping machine is invented...

House's Pujo Committee reports 118 seats on Boards of Directors of 34
banks and trust companies, 35 seats on Boards of 10 insurance companies
and 193 seats on Boards of 68 non-financial firms are held by members of

House of Morgan (holds 314 directorships in 112 corporations with assets of $22 billion), First National City Bank, First National Bank and Bankers' Guaranty Trust Company... Lincoln Highway Assn. forms to promote a coast-to-coast highway... Charles A. Beard: An Economic Interpretation of the Constitution of the United States (shows founding fathers with interests in money, public securities, manufacturing, trade, shipping)...

U.S. is world's leading debtor nation, again 1985 (is leading creditor in 1917)... U.S. Department of Labor is created as distinct organization with Bureau of Labor Statistics and Conciliation Service... California passes Alien Act to bar Japanese from owning land or leasing land longer than 3 years... Rockefeller Foundation is created by John D. Rockefeller with over $182 million to promote well-being of mankind throughout world... William M. Burton obtains first patent on cracking process to convert petroleum into gasoline (sells rights to Standard Oil)...

After formation of 2 AFL unions in 1896 and 1900 for vaudeville actors, Actors' Equity Assn. forms to improve working conditions and fight large booking agencies (shows compatibility of artists with trade unionism movement by shutting down Broadway in successful 1919 strike)... Silk workers of Paterson, NJ, strike to protest use of new machines, loss of wages and unemployment (lasts 5 months with support of Big Bill Haywood's Industrial Workers of the World until defeated by police, loss of strike funds and hunger)... Beta Gamma Sigma is formed as a nationwide honorary society for college students in business...

American Association of Public Employment Offices is formed... Mellon Institute is formed by University of Pittsburgh to do industrial research... With some 350,000 playing the game in U.S., amateur golfer Francis Ouimet, U.S., wins U.S. open to beat British professionals Harry Vardon and Ted Ray, over 2 million U.S. golfers by 1923.

Business Events

After rejecting Phoenix, AZ to make movies, Cecil B. De Mille uses the Barn, first major film studio in Los Angeles, to make "The Squawman," first feature film shot in Hollywood... Hudson exhibits first sedan car at National Automobile Show... Domelre produces first practical electric refrigerator in Chicago... Portland Knitting Co., OR, devises wool trunks for rowing club, becomes Jantzen swimsuit business in early 1920s (as one of first in industry diversifies in 1938 with full range of dressy wear, merges in 1979 with 1916 Blue Bell clothing firm, NC, specializing in rough-and-ready clothing)...

After 1911 break-up of American Tobacco by U.S. Supreme Court, R.J. Reynolds launches Camel cigarettes with massive advertising campaign (captures 50% of market by 1921, loses market leadership to American Tobacco's Lucky Strike in 1926)... Kimberly-Clarke paper business, WI, adopts strategy to concentrate resources on chemical processing of wood (develops Cellucotton during World War I for absorbent bandages which becomes Kotex Napkins in 1920)... Gulf Refining is first in industry to open drive-in automobile service station, Pittsburgh, gasoline usually sold at stores selling groceries, hardware, drugs, etc., until 1920s...

Ford Motor Co. develops modern assembly line, designed by Danish-born engineer William S. Knudsen, with magneto coil sub-assembly, adding assemblies for engines and transmissions later (produces some 260,000 cars with 13,000 employees - other 299 U.S. car makers using 66,000 workers to produce 286,000 cars)... Arthur V. Davis of Alcoa admits to House inquiry that aluminum industry is governed by international agreement...

A&P grocery chain experiments with high-volume, low-mark-up "Economy Stores" (tries again with "Golden Key" stores in 1965, "A-Mart" in 1969, "Warehouse Economy Warehouse Outlets" in 1971 and "Futurestores" in 1984)... After graduating from University of California and Oxford, J. Paul Getty leases Oklahoma land, apparently barren, to drill for oil (acquires first million by 1916, after fancy living starts new business in 1919 with father to buy and sell oil leases and drill wildcat wells, acquires fortune of $3 million during 1920s to build Getty Oil)...

Meyer Davis' band is hired by Bar Harbor hotel, MA, to play sweet music for socialites (evolves to operate 89 orchestras with over 1,000 musicians by 1941)... Modern Cummins Machine Works is started in Columbus, IN, as auto repair business by William G. Irwin (finances inventor Clessie L. Cummins in 1919 to perfect Rudolf Diesel's engine built for pumps and agricultural equipment, acquires license in 1919 to build Huid oil-burning engines, receives Sears contract in 1920 to make Huid engines - canceled 1922 as engine not successful, after tests with shrimp boat and yachts perfects light-weight diesel boat engine by 1929, sets diesel speed record of 100.755 mph in 1931, sells diesels to truckers in 1932 - sales over $5 million with $1.7 million in backorders in 1939)...

In this time Leitch Plan of Industrial Democracy is adopted by Packard Piano Co., Printz-Biederman Clothing Co... Magnus Alexander at General Electric does empirical study of labor turnover costs, published 1917... Chicago's Martin Beck opens Palace Theater, NYC (becomes mecca for vaudeville artists)... U.S. Rubber creates research laboratory, followed by Standard Oil of New Jersey in 1919... British-born Charlie Chaplin signs movie contract for $150/week with Mack Sennett (earns some $1 million/year within 4 years)... National Association of Canners creates central laboratory... Brillo Pad is introduced to market... National Association of Corporation Schools is formed... Hugo Munsterberg: Psychology and Industrial Efficiency (analyzes jobs by mental, emotional requirements)...

Elizabeth Otey: Employers' Welfare Work... Harrington Emerson: The Twelve Principals of Efficiency... AT&T establishes pension plan... Edward Bernays is hired as publicist by Metropolitan Opera (-1917, starts pioneering public relations agency after W.W.I.)... Dan O'Connor, Westinghouse engineer, develops Formica as insulating material (joins Herb Faber to form Formica Corp., devises laminated sheets in 1920s)...

After 3 failures, black entrepreneur Herman Perry, Atlanta, starts Standard Life Insurance (borrows funds from insurance business in 1917 to start Service Co. to oversee commercial and industrial enterprises - 11 by 1925 in construction, printing, farm bureau, pharmacy and philanthropy, opens Citizens Trust Bank in 1921 as depository for enterprises and facility for local blacks, forms holding company in 1922, employs over 2,500 in 1923, after failing to pay loans to service subsidiaries is taken over in 1925 by Southern Life)... Clorox liquid bleach is first sold to commercial laundries and breweries, consumers in 1918...

Advertising salesman Edward J. Noble acquires stock and trademark of Life Savers (adds fruit drops in 1924, joins Louis K. Liggett, founder of United Drug in 1903, in forming United, Inc. in 1928 with Sterling Drug, Bristol-Myers, and Vicks - dissolves 1933, merges with Beech-Nut Packing in 1956 - 1958 sales of $122 million).

1914

General Events

Tent colony of Colorado miners striking against Rockefeller properties is attacked (April 20) by National Guard, killing 11 women and 2 children (results in formation of Colorado Coal Commission by President Wilson to investigate "Ludlow Massacre" and in public outcry against Rockefeller family, interests)... Archduke Francis Ferdinand, Crown Prince of Austria, is slain (June 28) in Sarajevo (ignites World War I)... U.S. signs (August 5) treaty with Nicaragua to build canal across its land...

Treasury Department creates Bureau of War Risk Insurance to cover merchant ships and crews... U.S. Open is won by Walter Hagen, first professional golfer to make living from sport... Picture Palace for showing feature movies opens on Broadway with carpeting, soft seats, chandeliers, orchestra, organ... Although no unfair competitive practices had been uncovered, Government forces International Harvester to sell 3 divisions during W.W.I. with consent decree (is acquired by Tenneco in 1984 to avoid bankruptcy, continues in 1985 as Navistar truck business)... Federal Trade Commission is created (replaces Bureau of Corporations)... American Society of Composers, Authors and Publishers is formed by Victor Herbert, John Philip Sousa, others (win royalties in 1941)... Clayton Anti-Trust Act restricts (October 15) use of injunctions in labor disputes, makes picketing legal, bans firms buying stock of competitors to lessen competition, bans price discrimination, tie-in agreements and interlocking directorates, exempts unions and farm coopertives from Sherman Anti-Trust Act, and prohibits mergers that might reduce competition or tend to create a monopoly...

Agricultural Extension Service is formed to distribute new technologies to farmers... Curtiss Jenny, biplane with front engine, is designed by Glenn Curtiss (evolves as principal civilian aircraft in 1920s)... Federal League is formed as new major baseball organization by striking players from American League (-1915)... Congress creates Commission on National Aid to Vocational Education (enacts National Vocational Education Law in 1917)... Congress passes law to set maximum 8-hour day, 48-hour work week for women employed in District of Columbia (is declared unconstitutional in 1923)...

Sydney Hillman becomes president of Amalgamated Clothing Workers (-1946, innovates with cooperative housing, social activities and banking services)... New Jersey sets minimum wage for women at $9/week... Arizona adopts old-age pension system, declared unconstitutional by State's Supreme Court.

Business Events

Ford Motor Co. installs first automatic conveyor belt for assembly line
to make cars with specialized machines (reduces production time to make
1 car from 12 hours, 8 minutes to 1 hour and 33 minutes, increases annual
output of Model-T cars from 300,000 to some 2 million in 1923, prices
lowered by some 60%, to achieve market share of 48% - 9.4% in 1908, 20.3%
in 1911, and 39.6% in 1913)... Modern Booz, Allen & Hamilton
international management consulting firm is founded by Edwin G. Booz
(evolves as largest management consulting business in world after W.W.II
with "department store" approach to offer wide-range of specialty
services, after declining business in 1970s is revived by specializing in
government work - sales of $340 million in 1987 up 19% from 1977)...

George Bunting concocts first batch of sunburn remedy, renamed Noxzema,
at his Baltimore pharmacy (launches Cover Girl line of cosmetics in 1962
and Clarion treatments for sensitive skin in 1986 to become industry's
leader with revenues of $439 million)... Frank B. Gilbreth, pioneer in
scientific management, quits Taylorism when methods do not work at New
Jersey Hermann, Aukan Co. (concentrates on developing motion studies)...

Henry J. Kaiser starts construction business to handle highway projects
in British Columbia, Washington, Idaho and California (completes $20
million road building program for Cuba in 1927-30, levies for Mississippi
River in 1927-30 and Southwestern pipeline project with Bechtel
Construction in 1930-33)... Charles E. Merrill starts brokerage business
(makes first fortune underwriting chain stores, acquires Pathe Exchange
Motion Picture Co. in 1920)... When father dies, Marjorie M. Post takes
over Post Cereal Co. (-1922, expands business to create General Foods in
1929)...

Black engineer Archie A. Alexander starts contracting business with white
partner (starts engineering firm in 1929 with white partner to achieve
success with government contracts)... Herman Brown becomes partner of
Brown & Root construction business, president 1929-62 (develops business
with government contracts as one of world's largest with subsidiaries in
hotels, oil and gas properties, paper mills, mines, real estate, office
buildings, dude ranch)... Association of National Advertisers is
formed... After leaving Henry Ford H.E., J.F. Dodge start automobile
business (-1928 when acquired by Chrysler)... M.N. Zimmerman makes first
in-depth study of chain store distribution for Printer's Ink.. 1916
Kiwanis International service organization is started as Benevolent Order
of Brothers by business, professional men (evolves by 1980s with some
300,000 members, after court challenges accepts women members in 1986)...
Harry, David Holmes assume operation of father's pear orchard near
Medford, OR (sell fruit by mail-order in early 1930s, launch successful
Fruit-of-the-Month Club in 1937)...

American Audit Bureau of Circulation is created, followed by associations
in France in 1922, Switzerland in 1925 and Britain in 1931... Alexander
H. Church: The Science and Practice of Management (identifies functions
of management as design, operation, equipment, comparison and control)...
With labor turnover of 380% Henry Ford grants workers on assembly line a
$5 wage, $6/day in 1919, for 8-hour day as reward for enduring drudgery
on production line (also provides profit-sharing plan - bonus given only
if saved or invested, hospital, English Language School, and employment

for handicapped, starts operation of Sociological Department to combat labor turnover and signs of unionism)... 41 U.S. companies operate with two or more plants in foreign countries...

Louis D. Brandeis: <u>Business - A Profession</u>... Fire destroys film department of Edison Laboratories (abandons Kinetophone project to synchronize film and sound)... Manhattan's National City Bank opens branch in Buenos Aires, Argentina (develops educational program for Bank's foreign service)... Selig Grossinger buys small ramshackle farm in Catskill Mountains to recover health in running small NYC restaurant (accepts boarders when farming doesn't pay, adds rooms in 1915 to start resort business, acquires nearby hotel in 1919 - then lake and woodlands, forms Grossinger Hotel & Country Club by 1929 - over 500 rooms with public relations agent to pioneer loose confederation of some 1,000 resorts in area known by Jewish clientele as Borsch Belt for beginning performers, is sold in 1986 to Servico for conversion as "yuppie" paradise)...

Oscar, David Sunstrand invent 10-key adding, listing calculator... Texaco introduces charge card... Lillian Gilbreth: <u>The Psychology of Management</u> (pioneers study of human factor in management)... Swedish-born miner Carl Wickham starts bus service, MN (operates fleet of 18 buses in 1918 as Mesaba Transportation, sells of ownership in 1925 to join Ralph Budd, president of Great Northern Railroad, in new bussing venture - Greyhound in 1930)... Baltimore's Henry Sonneborn & Co., maker of men's ready-to-wear clothing, forms employee benefit society, patterned on Filene's association (adopts techniques of scientific management to become one of first to implement both managerial philosophies)... Chalmers automobile business introduces Saxon car to compete with Ford Model-T (flops)...

White Motor of Cleveland establishes "shop forum"... Miner Chipman uses attitude survey to gather employee opinions for Secretary of War on use of Taylor System at Watertown Arsenal... U.S. Circuit Court of Appeals upholds patent claims of Wright Brothers (receive 20% royalty on every plane sold in U.S., continue patent war with Glenn Curtiss to 1917)...

World's first "regular" air service is started by St. Petersburg-Tampa Airboat Line... When all Wright, Curtiss pusher biplanes are grounded after an accident, U.S. Army orders new planes from Los Angeles plant of Glenn Martin, former automobile dealer... After being fired by National Cash Register, Thomas Watson becomes president of 1910 Computing-Tabulating-Recording (forms engineering laboratory, enters Canadian market in 1917 with formation of International Business Machines, develops first synchronized time system in 1919 and first printing calculator in 1920, acquires Pierce Accounting Machine in 1921, incorporates business as IBM in 1923, introduces first completely self-regulating time system in 1924, acquires Electronic Typewriter in 1930s - introduces its first electric typewriter in 1935, develops its first electronic calculator in 1946 and large-scale electronic calculator in 1948, presents its first electronic data processing system in 1952)...

F. Donaldson Brown is hired as assistant by DuPont treasurer's office (develops technique for calculating return on investment, becomes treasurer in 1918)... Raggedy Ann Doll is introduced, one of earliest licensed products in toy industry... After operating largest New England chain of movie theaters, Louis B. Mayer starts Boston film distribution agency (organizes Metro Pictures with others in NYC in 1915, resigns to start Louis B. Mayer Pictures in 1918 to make movies in Culver City, CA, sells production business to theater operator Marcus Loew in 1924 in forming Metro-Goldwyn-Mayer, MGM)... Tinker Toys appear in toy market, Lincoln Logs in 1916... Commonwealth Edison adopts "first" industrial job evaluation plan.

1915

General Events

John Dewey: Schools of Tomorrow (urges learning of skills rather than information)... U.S. bankers arrange $500 million loan to British, French... Union of steel workers strikes to win 8-hour day, other concessions in East Youngstown, OH... U.S. Coast Guard is created to prevent contraband trade, assist vessels in distress... Wireless service is established between U.S., Japan... La Follette Seaman's Act improves working conditions for merchant seamen... Major General Leonard Wood starts experimental camp to train new Army officers, model for similar training schools... Willford I. King: The Wealth and Income of the People of the United States (shows 1.6% of population with 10.8% of U.S.' wealth in 1890, 19% by 1910)... American Society of Safety Engineers is formed... Carnegie Institute of Technology creates Division of Applied Psychology... Thomas A. Edison designs war game to simulate submarine warfare... Dartmouth's Amos Tuck School of Administration offers first university course in employment management...

First doctoral dissertation on management is written at Columbia University in field of political science... Anarchist Emma Goldman, New York garment workers start communal colony at Stelton, NJ... Charles Henderson: Citizens in Industry (discusses industrial democracy)... U.S. Justice Department rules baseball leagues do not violate Sherman Anti-Trust Act... National Board of Review, formally National Board of Censorship, is created by NY to monitor exhibitions of movies.

Business Events

Henry Ford produces his one millionth car... "Jitney" cars are used for intracity, intercity transportation... After opening beauty salons in Melbourne in 1902 and London in 1908, Polish-born Helene Rubinstein opens salon in NYC (by 1917 with others in Philadelphia, New Orleans and San Francisco)... Carl Laemmle starts movie operations of Universal on ranch near Los Angeles (charges visitors 25 cents to watch production of silent movies, evolves as Universal Tours in 1964 to. handle as many as 30,000 tourists/day)... After purchasing cousin Coleman's stock Pierre DuPont becomes president of DuPont over bitter objections of cousin Alfred (serves as chairman 1919-40)...

After disagreements with father over national advertising, James H. Rand, Jr. forms American Kardex with borrowed $10,000 to compete with father's Rand Ledger Co. of late 1800s (opens German factory in 1921, creates Kardex Institute in 1922 as non-profit organization to improve business records, merges with father's business in 1925 to operate Rand-Kardex)... "The Penalty of Leadership" ad, designed by Theodore F. MacManus for Cadillac, is printed in Saturday Evening Post with no mention of product, viewed by some as perhaps greatest ad with soft sell approach...

Lawrence L. Frank, Theodore Van de Kamp start Los Angeles potato-chip stand (evolves by late 1920s as Van de Kamp's Holland Dutch Bakers, starts selling frozen entrees in 1959 before acquisition by Pillsbury)... Classic Coca-Cola bottle, viewed by some as perfect package, is designed by Root Glass, inspired by shape of cocoa bean... National Association of Teachers of Marketing and Advertising is formed... Trailmobile designs first 4-wheel trailer, pulled by Model-T Ford... U.S. Steel, J.P. Morgan & Co. acquire Midvale Steel, Remington Arms to form armament trust... Isaac M. Rubinow: Standard Accident Tables (provides basis for compensation rates)...

R.H. Macy retail business creates staff planning department (studies such problems as employee bonuses, traffic, departmental locations, design of fixtures)... After 1914 Ludlow Massacre John D. Rockefeller's Colorado Fuel & Iron Co. starts program of employee representation... System: "What Are Your Men Thinking About?" (gives results of employee attitude survey)... Cheney Brothers Silk Mfg. employs first full-time psychiatrist in U.S. industry...

Alfred Mellowes designs electric refrigerator (is produced by Guardian Refrigerator, is acquired in 1919 by General Motors to become Frigidaire)... Robert S. Hoxie: Scientific Management and Labor... Ford W. Harris designs first economic lot-size model... John D. Rockefeller borrows Ivy Lee, public relations expert, from Pennsylvania Railroad to handle adverse publicity from 1914 Ludlow Massacre, CO (advises Rockefeller to tell the truth)...

Professor Huebner writes first U.S. textbook on insurance... American International is founded to invest capital in foreign markets... Horace B. Crury: History and Criticism of Scientific Management (records 60 uses of Taylorism and 200 of Emerson's system by 1912)... Sir Thomas Lipton introduces pre-packaged tea to U.S. market (follows invention of tea-bag by Thomas Sullivan, NYC, in early 1900s)... Original Celtics basketball team is formed in NYC by semi-professional basketball players, followed by formation of National Basketball League in 1937...

Pepsodent toothpaste is created (is advertised in 1919 for having Irium by Albert Lasker's Lord & Thomas advertising agency of Chicago to become common household product)... French-born Charles Bedaux devises wage system to reward workers for increasing productivity... Ohio Oil opens Elk Basin oil field in Wyoming, MT... Portland Cement Assn. starts small research laboratory... Alfred Knopf starts quality publishing house (is acquired by Random House in 1960, by RCA in 1966, by Newhouse Publications in 1980)...

Pioneering Guaranty Securities Co. is started in Toledo to finance consumer installment purchases of Willys - Overland cars, followed by General Motors Acceptance Corp. in 1919 and Ford Universal Credit Corp. in 1928... National Retail Dry Goods Assn. creates central education department to train clerks... Meyer Bloomfield: "The New Profession of Handling Men," The Annuals (discusses organizational role of employment department)...

7 brothers start Jacuzzi family business to develop pitched propeller for government contract (develop water-injection pump in 1926 and whirlpool bath in mid-1960s, is acquired in 1979 by Walter Kidde & Co., New Jersey

conglomerate)... J.P. Morgan investment banking house is contracted by Allied governments to centralize purchases of U.S. war supplies (appoints Edward R. Stettinus to allocate and supervise British and French purchasing of over $3 billion in goods by end of war)...

Chinese merchants in San Francisco start China Mail Steamship Co. (-1923 when ended by bankruptcy)... H.S. Dennison, others: Profit Sharing: Its Principles and Practice (views traditional profit-sharing as idealistic, advocates bonus plan for managers, foremen as workers not sufficiently informed, responsible for effective participation)... Tennessee Baptist Minister Samuel M. Skaggs opens Skaggs Cash Store in American Falls, ID (incorporates in 1926 as Safeway Stores with financing of broker Charles Merrill)... John T. Underwood builds world's most complete typewriter plant (produces 500 machines/day with 7,500 workers, merges with competitor Corona Typewriter in 1927)... Lincoln Electric forms employee committee to advise on operations (provides employee life insurance in 1914, starts employees' association in 1919 with health benefits and social activities, provides two-week vacations and piece-work pay system in 1923- wages adjusted for changes in Consumer Price Index, starts employee stock ownership plan in 1925, starts suggestion system in 1929 and bonus plan to increase productivity in 1935).

1916

General Events

Keating-Owen Act bars (September 1) goods made by child labor from interstate commerce... Congress passes (September 7) Workmen's Compensation Act to cover some 500,000 Federal employees... Union of National Vaudeville Artists is formed... Carmel-by-the-Sea incorporates, CA (adopts zoning law in 1929 to subordinate business, commercial activities to residential living)... Bureau of Labor Statistics launches study of welfare work by U.S. business (-1917, reports only 431 firms so involved)... Edwin Northrup invents induction furnace... Jamaican-born Marcus Garvey creates Universal Negro Improvement and Conservation Assn. in Harlem, NY, to instill racial pride, to acquire economic power (sponsors 30 branches by 1919 in advocating racial purity, separatism and racial solidarity, organizes Black Star Line in 1919 - collapses in 1927 with faulty ships and mismanagement, develops chain of restaurants and grocery stores in 1920s, announces plans in 1924 for "back-to-Africa" colonization, is deported in 1927 as undesirable alien after conviction for defrauding stockholders)...

Congress authorizes construction of two nitrate plants and dam at Muscle Shoals, Tennessee River in Northern Alabama (starts debate over Government's role in river navigation, public power, flood control, agricultural conservation, regional planning, use of natural resources)... Congress authorizes U.S. Shipping Board to develop ship building program... Congress passes Federal Child Labor Law, declared unconstitutional in 1918... Council of National Defense is created to oversee procurement of war materials...

War Industries Board is established to control prices, coordinate procurements... U.S. Supreme Court declares Federal Income Tax constitutional... Congress passes Federal Farm Loan Act (establishes land bank for extending credit to farmers)... South Carolina enacts bill to limit working age of children in mills, mines and factories to 14 (is followed by similar laws in 37 states by 1919 to ban use of child labor in manufacturing - 19 states restrict working hours of women)... American Association of Collegiate Schools of Business organizes to set accreditation standards, encourage research, provide "professional" aura to business education... Rural Post Roads Act provides $75 million for building state roads, followed by 1921 act to develop national highway system... University of Washington starts Bureau of Industrial Research, followed by Industrial Research Department at University of Oklahoma in 1917...

Robert S. Brookings starts Institute for Governmental Research (leads to creation of Government's Bureau of the Budget in 1921)... Congress creates U.S. Tariff Commission to do research on changing tariffs, expanding foreign trade (becomes International Trade Commission in 1974 to issue quasi-judicial recommendations after determining impacts of foreign imports on U.S. business)... Congress passes legislation whereby U.S. cargo-liner business would be regulated by shipping "conferences" of carriers to set common rates, schedules... American Federation of Teachers organizes...

To prevent nationwide strike Adamson Act grants railroad workers 8-hour day, time-and-a-half for overtime... Some 4,000 waterfront workers strike in San Francisco in first united West Coast support for 8-hour day, joined by steelworkers to fight Law and Order Committee of merchants... President Wilson demands railroads grant workers 8-hour day... U.S. reports 100% increase in food prices over 1915... With over 30 film companies in area, Jacksonville, FL, starts discouraging filmmakers, forcing many producers to flee to Hollywood, CA... Carnegie Institute of Technology forms Bureau of Salesmanship Research with Walter Dill Scott in charge.

Business Events

Nathan, Ida Handwerker open Coney Island food stand (becomes Nathan's Famous Hot Dogs with franchised stands throughout Northeast)... Otto Schnering starts Curtiss Candy Co. in Chicago (introduces popular Baby Ruth candy bar with industry's first national advertising in 1920)...

Sears institutes employee pension and insurance plan... After customer complaints about contaminated sandpaper, 1902 Minnesota Mining & Manufacturing business starts research laboratory with budget of $500 (expands to 6,000 scientists and engineers by 1988 to create over 200 new products/year for line of some 60,000 items - sales of $9.4 billion in 1987)... Mass production of enameled cast-iron fixtures is started... Eugene G. Grace succeeds Charles M. Schwab as head of Bethlehem Steel (-1957, expands operations with over 30 acquisitions to become world's 2nd largest steel producer)...

Floyd L. Carlisle forms syndicate to create St. Regis Paper Co. (forms Niagara Hudson Power in 1930s to purge utility industry of evils)... Henry Crown joins brother's Chicago steel brokerage business (reorganizes operation as Material Services Corp. to supply building projects in 1919 - president in 1921 to dominate City's construction field with political connections in 1920s, survives Depression with governmental contracts)... French-born Charles Bedaux starts efficiency engineering business to advise firms on improving productivity... Alan Ryan tries to corner market in stock of Stutz Motor Co. (acquires control in 1920 after catching number of speculators selling short, settles with shorts for $1.6 million and is expelled from New York Stock Exchange, declares bankruptcy in 1932 with assets of $643,000 and liabilities over $32 million)... Eli Lilly pharmaceutical business creates employment office (starts industrial medicine department in 1917, pension plan in 1920, cafeteria in 1924 and health insurance in 1927)... Model-T touring car is priced at $360, $850 when first introduced... Henry Ford starts building super plant at River Rouge in Dearborn, MI (-1927, is designed as integrated system of mills, forges, docks, assembly plants to transform raw materials into automobiles)... National Industrial Conference Board is created by business interests for research, public relations and lobbying... Henry Ford Trade School opens to provide workers with high school education... First convention of National Federation of Business and Professional Women is held... Groceterias appear during this time, CA...

Chesebrough-Ponds introduces Cutex, first liquid nail polish (follows 1911 liquid cuticle remover)... Frank, Lillian Gilbreth: <u>Fatigue Study</u>... When New York Central is forced by ICC to divest itself of run-down New York, Chicago & St. Louis Railroad, Nickle Plate Line is acquired by 2 Van Swearingen brothers, Cleveland real estate developers (acquire Toledo, St. Louis and Western, Lake Erie and Western lines in 1922 to operate over 1,700 miles of track, acquire Erie and Pere Marquette roads in 1923, build Cleveland Terminal with office buildings and hotel in 1924 and acquire more lines to operate system in 1925 with 9,245 miles of track and $1.5 billion in assets, are forced in 1930 to borrow money with properties as securities from J.P. Morgan & Co. to pay Cleveland bankers, default on payments in 1935 - one brother's estate valued at $3,068 and other with debts of some $80 million)...

"Inventor" Louis Enricht announces substitute for gasoline that can be made for penny/gallon (amasses fortune until fraud discovered)... After helping to extend Chicago Rock Island & Pacific Railroad into Indian Territory in 1899, working for Southern Pacific and supervising large stone quarry Warren Bechtel starts construction business in Oakland, CA (-1936, assists in building Hoover Dam in 1931, grows with brilliantly intuitive Steve Bechtel, Sr., in 1936, forms Bechtel-McCune in 1937 to design build petroleum refineries and chemical plants, builds ships during W.W.II, resigns in 1961 to let Steve, Jr., transform business into engineering and management services)...

Railroads handle some 77% of intercity traffic... Homemaker Nell Q. Donnelly sells "dress aprons" to George B. Peck dry-goods store in Kansas City (forms Donnelly Garment Co. to gross some $3.5 million/year in 1930s)... Allan, Malcolm Loughead start Lockheed Aircraft in California to build flying boat (is acquired by Detroit Aircraft in 1929, is acquired in 1932 by syndicate of Robert E. Gross)... Dennison Company, MA, sponsors first U.S. employer unemployment insurance system (-1929 when funds are exhausted)... New Machine Society is formed by H.L. Gantt, others to promote scientific organization of society by engineers... Frank Conrad, Westinghouse engineer, starts transmissions by wireless set at Wilkinsburg, PA (plays recorded music during "broadcasts" to fellow ham operators in early 1920s)... Pacific Aero Products is organized in Seattle with Navy contract to make sea planes (changes name to Boeing

Airplane in 1917 to make single-engine sea planes, receives   mail service
contract in 1919 to serve Seattle and Victoria, BC, obtains one of first
military contracts in 1921 for making fighter planes)... National Society
for the Promotion of Industrial Education meets... Minnequa Steel Works
starts employee representation plan... William C. Durant combines
suppliers of roller bearings, rims, brakes, radiators, horns, ignition
and lighting systems as United Motors (appoints Alfred C. Sloan, Jr., of
Hyatt Roller Bearing as president, merges with General Motors in 1916)...

Sinclair Oil business incorporates (constructs pipeline from Oklahoma to
Chicago and builds 2 refineries, operates with some 7,900 employees in
1938, records gross income of $77.5 million - $523 million in 1951 with
some 15,000 filling stations)... After resigning from General Motors on
return of William C. Durant, Charles Nash buys ailing Thomas B. Jeffery
Co. in Kenosha, WI (starts Nash Motors to build Rambler cars for upper
middle-class market, acquires Lafayette Motors of Indianapolis in 1919 to
build luxury cars - folded 1924, buys bankrupt Mitchell Car of Racine to
build successful light, medium-priced cars, merges with refrigerator
business in 1937 to form Nash-Kelvinator)...

Clarence Saunders opens pioneering King Piggly Wiggly self-service store,
also used by several merchants in Southern California, in Memphis, TN
(opens 9 stores first year, obtains patents in 1917 on layout, fixtures
and fittings, operates some 1,200 stores, 550 franchised, in 29 states by
1922)... During this time Victor "The Count" Lustig peddles perpetual-
money machine to investors, acquires fortune before hoax revealed (is
successful later in selling Eiffel Tower twice to gullible Paris junk
dealers)... Endicott-Johnson is first business in shoe industry to adopt
8-hour day, 48-hour work week...

J. Walter Thompson Advertising Agency is acquired by Stanley Resor's
syndicate (commissions study Population and its Distribution to pioneer
use of demographics in research, creates director of research in 1922,
eliminates small accounts to triple business during 1920s - world's
largest by 1927 with staff of 432 and annual billings of $23 million,
opens London office in 1923-23, goes worldwide in 1929-33 to service GM
accounts)... After emigrating to U.S. penniless at age of 13 to become
wealthy glove manufacturer, Samuel Goldwyn starts Goldwyn Pictures (joins
1924 formation of Metro-Goldwyn-Mayer, resumes business later as
independent studio)... Pittsburgh steel mills plan to import Southern
Negroes to ease severe labor shortage...

With 2,476,920 shares of Standard Oil stock at $2,000 each, J.D.
Rockefeller is first in business to become billionaire... Henry Ford
awards women workers equal pay of $5/day... Retail Research Association
is formed by 18 leading department stores, including Filene's, F&R
Lazarus, J.L. Hudson, L.S. Ayres and Dayton, to develop new uniform
system of accounting records for comparing performances (results in
formation of Associated Merchandising Corporation in 1918)... First U.S.
pro golf tournament is held on Siwanoy Course at Bronxville, NY... Debt-
ridden Judge Bingham marries Mary Lily Flagler, U.S.' richest woman (with
$5 million from wife's estate in 1916 buys Louisville's Courier-Journal
to build publishing empire, after dissension among grandchildren is sold
by family to Gannet chain in 1986).

1917

General Events

Immigration Act (February 5) requires emigrants to pass literary tests, bans Asian workers except Japanese... Smith-Hughes Act (February 23) creates Federal Board for Vocational Education (provides matching funds to states for trade, agricultural schools)... Congress declares (April 12) war against Germany (declares war against Austria-Hungary on December 7)... Upton Sinclair: King Coal... 3 cents is required for first class postage, 2 cents in 1919, 3 cents in 1932, 4 cents in 1958, 5 cents in 1963, 6 cents in 1968, 8 cents in 1971, 10 cents in 1974, 13 cents in 1975, 15 cents in 1978, 18 and 20 cents in 1981, 22 cents in 1985 and 25 cents in 1988... University of Washington opens School of Business Administration... Federal Trade Commission: Uniform Accounting...

After operating mine engineering business since 1907, Herbert Hoover becomes U.S. Food Administrator (creates Sugar Equalization Board to regulate industry and U.S. Grain Corp. to centralize, stabilize purchase and distribution of food for allies and U.S.)... Chicago is first city to create movie censorship board, followed by all major cities by 1928 (closes last U.S. board in 1981)...

In this time Dramatist Guild forms in NYC for collective action against Broadway producers... U.S. takes over railroads (-1920)... U.S. Supreme Court upholds Washington's Workmen's Compensation law (legalizes laws of some 30 states)... Federal Trade Commission starts series of conferences for voluntary elimination of unfair competitive practices... Some 1,200 strikers of Industrial Workers of the World are deported during strike of Arizona Copper Mines... U.S. Supreme Court: Hitchman Coal Company v. Mitchell (upholds "yellow dog" contract)... The Journal of Applied Psychology is published (follows similar German magazine in 1907)...

Job instruction training is used at U.S. Navy shipyard... President Wilson creates mediation commission to assist in resolving labor disputes... United States Fuel Administration is created to place coal production under governmental control (requires cooperation of coal, petroleum and railroad industries)... U.S. Army uses merit ratings to evaluate trainee officers... Permission is granted to War College Division of general staff to produce training films (turns out 57 by 1918)... Council of National Defense forms War Industries Board to set production priorities... Some 50,000 workers from 25 unions return to work after striking for higher wages... Committee on Classification of Personnel is formed by Army's Adjutant General's Office (results in Army Personnel Program)... American Psychological Assn. creates Committee on Psychological Examination of Recruits to prepare 2 mental-ability tests (assists Army with first personnel research to develop Alpha-Beta test)... U.S. Shipping Board uses new U.S. Employment Service as sole supplier of shipyard labor.

Business Events

Color Association of the United States issues annual forecasts on standard shades for apparel, interiors... National Restaurant Assn. organizes, some 10,000 members operating 125,000 establishments in 1987... Frederick B. Rentschler starts Wright Aeronautical Corp. (starts

Pratt & Whitney Aircraft in 1925 as independent venture, merges Pratt & Whitney with Boeing, other companies in 1928 to form United Aircraft and Transportation, after Boeing's required divesture in 1935 becomes independent United Aircraft)...

Hugh R. Cullen starts wildcatting for oil (operates some 350 producing wells in mid-1950s, dies in 1957, gives away some 93% of $250 million fortune)... After acquiring Columbia Trust in 1914 as youngest U.S. bank president and heading collateral loan business of father-in-law (resigns after scandal at Columbia Trust), Joseph P. Kennedy becomes assistant general manager at Bethlehem Steel (works for Boston investment bankers Hayden, Stone & Co., in 1919-24 to learn skills in handling stocks, starts private investment business in 1922)...

While pre-med student at Columbia University, Armand Hammer aids father in acquiring control of Good Laboratories, becomes part of Allied Drug & Chemical Co. in 1920 (achieves success in 1918-19 with use of ginger extract as legal substitute for alcohol - corners world market in ginger, meets Lenin in 1921 while delivering medical supplies needed for Typhus epidemic in U.S.S.R. and collecting debt for father, on "urging" of Lenin to help revive Soviet economy obtains concessions to trade minerals for U.S. grain, acquires manufacturing permit in 1925 to start country's largest pencil factory, with permits canceled by Stalin flees U.S.S.R. in 1930 with enormous cache of art treasures)...

Lawrence Valenstein opens NYC art studio (after advertising assignments evolves as Grey advertising business to pioneer Jewish role in industry)... After first model in 1907, Ford Motor Co. starts making world's first mass-produced tractor (-1928), and trucks... American Association of Advertising Agencies organizes with 111 members... Sears starts developing centralized, functionally departmentalized organizational structure (-1924)... Goodyear pioneers development of pneumatic tires for heavy trucks (by 1920 replaces solid tires on most trucks)... Converse devises high-top canvas basketball shoe, promoted by use of U.S. Olympic Team in 1930... International Association of Lions Clubs forms as service organization for businessmen... American Institute of Planners forms...

Griesedieck Brewery is started in St. Louis (pioneers regional expansion in 1935 with acquisition of Falstaff)... Branch Rickey becomes general manager of St. Louis Cardinals (pioneers farm system to develop new baseball players)... Management consulting firm of Frazer and Torbet forms to advise businesses on corporate, industrial reorganization (advises Sears in 1920s on planned reorganization, is absorbed later by McKinsey & Co.)... During W.W.I Scott & Fetzer business organizes to make flare pistols (starts making Kirby vacuum cleaners in 1920s, starts diversification program in 1964-73, acquires World Book business in 1978 to revive sales by appointments with home buyers)...

Johnson floor business in Racine, WI, sponsors employee profit-sharing plan (adopts pension, hospitalization programs in 1934)... Cowboy Tom Mix is hired by ex-nickelodeon operator William Fox to make western films (-1935, earns $17,500/week by 1925)... Promoter Hubert Eaton is hired by Los Angeles cemetery (establishes Forest Lawn's Memorial Park as known landmark)... First Sunday baseball game is played in NYC, both managers arrested for violating City's Blue Law... In addition to operating beauty salons in London, New York, Philadelphia, New Orleans, and San Francisco, Helena Rubenstein starts wholesale business in beauty products (trains saleswomen to show customers how to use her products for individual skin requirements, introduces line of medicinal products in 1920 to treat acne and other skin problems)... Distributor Adolph Zukor pioneers block-booking of movies (forces theaters to buy unpopular films to show popular movies)... U.S. Steel is ranked first of all corporations by value of assets, followed in order by Standard Oil of New Jersey, Bethlehem Steel, Armour, and Swift (is followed by 1957 listing of Standard Oil of New Jersey, General Motors, U.S. Steel, Ford Motor, and Gulf Oil, and in 1982 by Exxon, General Motors, Mobil, IBM, Texaco - U.S. Steel 14th)...

Henry L. Gantt, Russian-born Walter N. Polakov use Gantt charts to assist shipyards in increasing production of patrol vessels... Pappy Chalk starts first international plane service between Florida and Bahamas (becomes booming business during Prohibition-Era in ferrying bootleggers to Islands, contributes to development of Bimini as tourist resort)... Society of Industrial Engineers is formed... Clarence Salyer, unschooled Virginia mule skinner, starts farming 80 acres in San Joaquin Valley, CA (evolves by 1981 to operate 65,000 acres with assets over $50 million)... A study of largest industrial enterprises reveals 278 to have assets of $20 million or more - 30 in mining, 7 in petroleum, 5 in agriculture, and 236 in manufacturing with 39 in primary metals, 34 in food products, 28 in transportation, 24 in machinery, 24 in petroleum and 21 in chemicals... Robert Dickinson: "Scientific Management and Hospital Organization"...

Curtis Publishing Company starts to standardize office work... After leaving Cadillac because of William C. Durant, Henry Leland starts Lincoln Motor Co. with son (builds 6,500 Liberty ships, is acquired in receivership by Henry Ford in 1929 to diversify product line)... In this time a group of naval architects, led by team from Bethlehem Steel, develop prefabricated ship construction... Aluminum salesman uses steel wool pads impregnated with soap as free premiums for buyers of cookware, named S.O.S. by wife...

After producing over 5,000 airplanes during World War I, Curtiss Aeroplane and Motor is acquired by automobile pioneer John Willys (is forced out in 1920-21 with collapse of auto empire - Clement Keys in charge, merges Curtiss with 1917 Wright Aeronautical to form Curtiss-Wright in 1929, is acquired in 1940 by Floyd Odlum's Atlas Corp.)... Standard Oil of New Jersey institutes employee representation plan, developed by Clarence J. Hicks... American Stainless Steel is formed, Pittsburgh, with patent rights from Britain's Harry Brearley... 61 shipyards, 37 for steel and 24 for wooden ships, operate 211 ways, 1,284 ways by U.S. yards in 1918 with Hog Island near Philadelphia world's largest with 50 ways in using mass-production with prefabricated and standardized parts.

1918

General Events

William I. Thomas, Floran Znaniecki: The Polish Peasant in Europe and America (pioneers social science use of term "attitude" as purely mental state - basis for attitude surveys in late 1920s)... Forest R. Moulton heads of Ballistics Branch in Office of the Chief of Ordnance (introduces numerical techniques of astronomy in decision-making)... U.S. Patent Office refuses to consider all applications for perpetual-motion schemes... Federal Reserve System leases telegraph lines to settle payments between banks...

Germany signs (November 11) armistice treaty... Wisconsin dentist creates Anacin... Post Office, Army start air-mail service on experimental basis between NYC, Washington, abandoned (tries service between Chicago and Cleveland, New York and Chicago in 1919, starts transcontinental flights and international air-mail to Canada in 1920, flies regular air-mail service in 1924)...

Webb-Pomerene Act exempts U.S. cartels in international trade from anti-trust legislation (spawns some 45 export associations by 1936)... M.L. Cooke: <u>Are Cities Awake?</u> (advocates better management of city government by scientific management, harmonious cooperation of labor and management by participation in decision making)... U.S. Department of Labor forms Division of Negro Economics to improve race relations... National War Labor Board is formed to resolve employer-employee disputes with mediation, conciliation services (results in creation of many "works councils" with employee representation in factories)... Bernard Baruch becomes chairman of War Industries Board (when automobile makers refuse to curtail production of cars, stops rail service to plants and seizes stockpiles of steel to force compliance)... Congress adopts four 1883 standard time zones of railroads for nation (adopts first daylight savings time - ended 1919, adopts daylight savings time year-round during World War II, is legalized by federal law in 1966)...

General John J. Pershing commands American Expeditionary Force in France (operates with headquarters staff of military intelligence, purchase, storage and traffic, and war plans - each linked with similar General Staff activities at War Department, commands Army divisions of 979 officers and 27,082 men - 12,000 considered limit for effective command by British, French, and German generals)... U.S. Federal Food Board prosecutes grocers refusing to label food...

War Industries Board declares moving pictures an "essential industry"... Government employees are granted 8-hour day... Chinese waiters in Chicago form Man Sang (People's Livelihood) Association to obtain higher wages, better working conditions... Booth Tarkington: <u>The Magnificent Ambersons</u> (describes effect of industrialism on feudal Midwest)... Mary Parker Follett: <u>The New State: Group Organization the Solution of Popular Government</u> (advocates individual's potential is achieved through group experience)... Teachers Insurance and Annuity Assn., College Retirement Equities Fund form to manage pensions of college staff, U.S.' oldest and largest, $60.7 billion in 1987, private pension system.

Business Events

Bethlehem Steel forms company unions (adopts welfare, pension, vacation, health, stock purchase and safety plans)... General Motors institutes cash-bonus plan for executives, ends mid-1980s... By this time all U.S. A & P grocery stores are converted to cash-and-carry... Former newspaper reporter George H. Williamson opens candy shop, Chicago (creates Oh Henry! candy bar)... Edsel Ford becomes president of Ford Motor Co.

(-1943)... Swiss-born Camille Dreyfus forms American Cellulose and Chemical (pioneers "Celanese" yarn in 1924, renames company Celanese Corp. with stock issue underwritten by J.P. Morgan's investment banking house, records growth of some 700% by 1939 and 233 patents, starts Mexican operation in 1944)...

After receiving law degree and starting paper with 25 cents, Robert Abbott's Chicago Defender records circulation of some 125,000 (encourages Southern readers to travel North for work, starts printing press in 1921 when white firm stops supplying paper during riots of 1919, dies in 1940 as probably City's first black millionaire)... Russian-born William, Ida Rosenthal open dressmaking business in NYC (pioneer development of modern brassiere, follows 1910 device by corsett manufacturer for opera singer, by Ida for women tired of boyish look with 1916 Caresse Crosby bandeau, found Maidenform Brassiere in 1923 to become major business by 1930 in women's undergarment industry - sales of $100,000 in 1927 and over $30 million by 1958)...

To battle sales slump Ford dealer Walter J. Jacobs starts small rental car business with 12 Model-T Fords (is acquired in 1923 by John Hertz, owner of Yellow Truck and Coach Mfg. to develop business by leasing trucks - topped for first time in 1958 by car rentals, is acquired as Hertz Drive-Ur-Self system by General Motors in 1925-53, uses rudimentary charge-card service in 1926)... Associated Merchandising Corp. is formed as cooperative buying group by Detroit's J.L. Hudson department store, Filene's of Boston and 17 other large independent department stores (serves 31 department stores by 1970s)...

Conrad Hilton acquires Mobley Hotel in Cisco, TX, when unable to buy local bank for expanding family's banking business (ac quires Ft. Worth's Hotel Mellia in 1918 and Waldorf Hotel in Dallas in 1920, continues to buy and sell hotels during 1920s-30s, forms Hilton Hotels in 1946)... Jersey Standard forms personnel units, company unions...

To protect investment of DuPont in General Motors, J.J. Raskob, business associate of Pierre DuPont, becomes GM treasurer... Mary Parker Follet: The New State: Group Organization the Solution of Popular Government (pioneers use of group process approach in solving management problems)... Industrial Management presents first published Gantt Chart (follows use of progress and performance charts before W.W.I by consultant Henry Gantt at General Crozier's Frankfort Arsenal)... Leeds & Northrup Co. sponsors company union, modeled on Filene's association... Dutchess Bleachery, NY, starts employee representation plan... F.C. Henerschott, F.E. Weakly: The Employment Department and Employee Relations (is based on course given at LaSalle Extension, University of Chicago)...

Navy patrol vessels are produced on assembly line, designed by William S. Knudsen of Ford Motor Co... When military contracts are canceled, DuPont starts program of rapid diversification into artificial leather, chemicals, dye stuffs, paints and varnishes, and textiles (requires formation of decentralized, multi-divisional organizational structure with central headquarters for administrative control to implement strategy)... General Electric Employee's Mutual Benefit Association participates in forming employee representative plans for collective bargaining (adopts GE Employee's Security Program in 1923)... Yugoslav-born restaurateur Marcus Nalley starts Nalley's Fine Foods in Tacoma, WA, with potato chips - adds mayonnaise and pickles by 1930 and canned-meat during W.W. II (after death in 1962 is acquired in 1966 by conglomerate W.R. Grace & Co. and in 1975 by Curtice-Burns Foods, NY, to become leading regional brand, Pacific Northwest, by 1980s)... After 22 days 2 Goodyear trucks complete first transcontinental run from Boston to San Francisco.

1919

General Events

18th Amendment for Prohibition of Alcohol is ratified (January 29), followed by Volstead Act (October 28) to enforce Prohibition in 1920 (results in 219,000 speakeasies, ends 1933 after arrest of some 300,000 law breakers)... First daily air-mail service is started (July 1) between Chicago, NYC... Lt. Commander Albert C. Reed, 6-man crew in Curtiss flying boat make first Atlantic crossing by plane from Newfoundland to Lisbon via Azores... Michigan, Montana are first states to pass equal pay laws for women...

American Farm Bureau Federation is formed... American Catholic bishops urge social reconstruction program (urge minimum wage, social security, unemployment compensation, old-age insurance)... Women's Press Club organizes in Washington (admits men as members in 1971, after changing name to Washington Press Club merges with male-dominated National Press Club in 1985)...

Some 350,000 steel workers in U.S. strike for 8-hour day, right to organize (-1920)... Communist Party forms in Chicago, membership of some 100,000 during Popular Front era of 1935-39... 1,117 of Boston's 1,544 policemen strike (are replaced with new officers by Governor Coolidge: "There is no right to strike against the public safety by anybody, anywhere, any time")...

Father Divine, charismatic black evangelistic leader, becomes national figure in this time (advocates racial and economic equality, black business, black responsibility)... Acting President John L. Lewis, United Mine Workers, closes over 70% of bituminous mines and nearly 100% of anthracite pits with strike (continues strike despite court order to desist and is held in contempt, orders miners to work when U.S. Government enters situation, results in formation of Presidential arbitration commission)... Oregon is first state to levy tax on gasoline for road construction, adopted by all states by 1929... After conflict between members of American Legion and Industrial Workers of the World in Centralia, WA, 4 members of Legion are killed (results in murder of 5 jailed union members)... Labor conference urges adopting 8-hour, 48-hour week... Popcorn is sold in movie theaters... Railway workers strike for higher wages, government ownership... Congress passes bill to ban railway strikes... North Dakota places mines under martial law...

U.S.' first municipal airport opens in Tucson, AZ... Glenn Plumb, counsel for railroad unions, calls for creation of public corporation, one-third of board appointed by U.S. president, one-third selected by technical and management staff and one-third elected by employees, to operate U.S.' railroads with profits shared equally by employees and government (despite opposition of Samuel Gompers is supported by AFL in 1920)...

United Mine Workers adopt resolution for nationalization of coal industry... With representatives of labor, capital, and public President Wilson's National Industrial Conference proposes "right of wage earners to organize in trade and labor unions, to bargain collectively," and "to be represented by representatives of their own choosing," not endorsed by employer group.

Business Events

Engineer William F. Rockwell, after starting Boston's Scovill & Co. in 1913-15 as consulting engineering service, starts Wisconsin Parts Co. (after acquisition by Timken - Detroit Axle in 1928, becomes president of business in 1933-40 and chairman 1940-53 before creation of Rockwell International in 1967)... Paul Hoffman acquires Studebaker's Los Angeles dealership (after achieving sales of $1 million/year becomes Studebaker vice president of sales in 1925, acquires corporation from receivership in 1933 - president 1935-48 and chairman 1948-56)... Sid Richardson (discovers Keystone oil field later in West Texas), Clint Murchison join forces to trade cattle, play poker, deal in oil leases...

After serving in American Ambulance Corps, Walt Disney works at Kansas City art studio (co-starts Iwerks-Disney Commercial Artists in 1920 to do illustrations for advertisements, works for Kansas City Film in 1920 as cartoonist, creates Laugh-O-Gram Films in 1922 with Ib Iwerks - bankruptcy in 1923, moves to Hollywood in 1923 to do cartoons with brother Roy, contracts with Universal Studios in 1926 to do Oswald the Rabbit cartoons, produces "Steamboat Willy" with Mickey Mouse in 1928)...

Bruce Barton, Roy Durstine and Alex Osborn open NY advertising agency with borrowed $10,000 (acquire part of GE account in 1920, GM in 1922, Dunlop Tire and rest of GE in 1923, and part of Lever Brothers account in 1924, are joined in 1928 by George Batten)... Pitney Bowes business to make postage-meter machines is started (introduces metered mail in 1920)... Macy's Department Store in NYC starts executive training program... Austrian-born Edward L. Bernays, nephew of Sigmund Freud, starts pioneering public relations firm, publisher Horace Liveright first client...

Ex-convict Charles Ponzi, formerly peddler and waiter, launches "fool-proof" scheme to make money with $150 cash (pays eager investors 50% interest in 45 days - 100% in 90 days, uses funds to buy international postal coupons in one country where rate is low and sell for higher price in another country, after paying almost $10 million in new money on due accounts, is exposed as fraud and returned to jail)...

Robert Woodruff's, president 1923-1955, syndicate acquires control of Coca-Cola for $25 million, sales of $32 million in 1920 (promotes soft drink as national custom in 1920s to increase profits from $4.5 million to $13 million by 1938, after innovating with take-home carton in 1920s introduces retail cooler in 1930, promotes Coca-Cola as international drink after W.W.II - profits of some $400 million in 1977)... H.L. Gantt: Organizing for Work (observes business needs to accept social responsibilities)... International General Electric, Gerald Swope president, is formed as subsidiary to manage firm's foreign operations...

R.S. Reynolds, Sr., with backing of Reynolds Tobacco, founds U.S. Foil Co. to roll tin, lead packaging materials (forms Reynolds Metal in 1928 as subsidiary, expands fabrication of aluminum in 1938 to challenge Alcoa's monopoly after seeing Germany's production of metal, gets $15.8 million from U.S. in 1940 to build aluminum plant in Alabama, opens bauxite mines in Jamaica in 1950 and British Guiana in 1952, forms Reynolds Aluminum in 1955, acquires British Aluminum in 1959 to operate 61 plants by 1961)...

Seats on New York Stock Exchange sell for $60,000-110,000, around $500,000 in 1929... Less than 10% of U.S. cars are closed (changes to 43% by 1924, 82.8% by 1927)... Fanny Farmer candy business is started (evolves to operate 325 shops in 23 states by 1980s)... H.L. Gantt writes series of articles on impending economic catastrophe (predicts crisis of over-production due to increasing efficiency, indicates government intervention is required to handle crisis)... Horace Moses starts Junior Achievement Program, MA, to involve young people in free enterprise...

"Fatty" Arbuckle is first movie star to sign $1 million contract, ruined by 1921 scandal trial... H.L. Gantt, W.N. Polakov, Harrington Emerson and other engineers submit "Declaration of Principles" to President Wilson (as business acquires wealth without rendering commensurate service to society, recommend selected industries be socialized to supply necessary commodities and services)... New York Daily News is first successful U.S. tabloid... Bank of North Dakota is first state owned, operated bank... U.S. firms acquire oil concessions in Venezuela (evolves by 1928 where over 35 firms control over 50% of country's production - Jersey Standard leader)... Oliver Smith, CA, invents mechanical rabbit for Greyhound racing... Andrew Carnegie dies, leaves estate of some $30 million - $20 million to Carnegie Foundation (during lifetime donates over $350 million to charity interests, lists charity priorities as universities, libraries - 1,946 in U.S., hospitals, parks, concert and meeting halls, swimming baths, churches)...

William Randolph Hearst acquires San Francisco Call (supervises 13 papers, 6 magazines, International News Service and King Features Syndicate with final approval on all important decisions, incorporates 90 newspapers as American Newspapers in 1935 with assets of $197 million)... Director D.W. Griffith and actors Charles Chaplin, Mary Pickford, and Douglas Fairbanks create United Artists movie studio to make, distribute their films, acquired by Transamerica in 1967... General Motors Institute is created to train engineers for GM, industry, divested by GM in 1982 as independent educational institution...

Metropolitan Life Insurance starts pioneering counseling program to help New York employees with business, personal problems... Bernard MacFadden publishes True Story Magazine as first-person, confessional publication (acquires circulation of some 850,000 by 1924 - even with Good Housekeeping, challenges lead of Ladies' Home Journal in 1927 in selling some 2 million/issue)... National Industrial Conference Board: Works Counsels in the United States (describes use by 225 firms)... Personnel magazine is published...

After football games played in early 1900s by 13 steel mill towns, OH and PA, organized professional football is started with formation of Green Bay Packers by Frank Peck, owner of Indian Packing Co., and Curly Lambeau with $500 (are joined by Staley's Bears of George Halas with sponsorship of Staley Starch Co. in Decatur, IL, results in formation of American Professional Football Assn. at Canton, OH, in 1920 by Lambeau and Halas with teams from Canton, Cleveland, Dayton, Akron, Massilon, Rochester, Rock Island, Chicago, Decatur, Hammond and Muncie - Jim Thorpe president, is reorganized by promoter Joe F. Carr in 1921 as National Football League with each franchise costing $50)...

General Motors forms GM Export Co... Industrial conference is held to reduce industrial conflicts... James O. McKinsey joins 1917 consulting firm of Frazer and Torbet (-1925 advises Sears on reorganizing in 1920s)... Joseph P. Kennedy acquires control of New England chain of 31 theaters (obtains rights to show British films, acquires Film Booking Office in 1926)...

American Express sponsors tour of Europe for travelers (advertises its first world pleasure cruise in 1922)... Charles S. Davis forms Borg-Warner as combination of 15 makers of automobile parts... Robert E. Wood, former brigadier general of Army's Quartermaster Corps, is hired by Montgomery Ward as new general merchandise manager (-1924, devises strategy, pioneered by J.C. Penney for automotive age, to develop chain of stores in small towns, resigns when plan is rejected to join Sears in 1925)...

Milwaukee magazine publisher Alfred Lawson starts airline, builds first true passenger airliner (declares bankruptcy after becoming over-extended)... Scott Co. forms in Philadelphia to provide pioneering consulting services in psychology, personnel to business... With government urging Owen D. Young of General Electric organizes Radio Corporation of America by acquiring assets of British-owned American Marconi and pooling patents of General Electric - forced to divest by government in 1930, Westinghouse - forced to divest interests in 1930, AT&T - dropped out in 1926, and United Fruit in return for stock...

Pennsylvania Hotel, world's largest with 2,200 rooms, opens in NYC... National Association of Motion Picture Industry agrees to submit films for censorship... Hobart introduces Kitchen Aid food mixer... After informal arrangements since 1907, florists form FTD, Florist Transworld Delivery, to aid each other with billings on out-of-town orders.

1920s

General Events

Cletus Killian invents digital device for automatic machine control (is denied patent as Patent Office viewed such machines as impossible, receives patent in 1960 two years before death).

Business Events

Many firms employ secretaries in centralized typing pools... Members of roving Williamson gang visit communities to sell homeowners on various home repair scams (still extant)... A.O. Smith automobile plant in Milwaukee, WI, uses self-acting equipment and automatic transfer machines... With Henry Ford's approval, tough Harry Bennett takes over firm's police force, known as Service Department (with underworld

connection uses hoodlums to intimidate employees and fight unions)...
Some 300 cigar factories operate in Ybor City near Tampa, FL (before
mechanization in 1920s and layoffs employ 30,000 workers who pool
resources to hire readers - listen while working, build hospitals and
clubs with cafes, ballrooms and theaters, and form mutual aid societies,
is revitalized in 1972 with old plants as shops and restaurants).

1920

General Events

For first time more workers are employed in manufacturing than
agriculture... 23.9% of labor force are women (expands to 25.4% in 1940,
29.1% in 1950, 34.8% in 1960, 42.6% in 1970, 51.1% in 1980)... Esch-
Cummins Transportation Act creates (February 28) labor board to handle
disputes of workers... U.S. Supreme Court: United States v. United
States Steel Corporation (rules large corporation is not necessarily an
illegal monopoly)... Merchant Marine Act (June 5) continues wartime
Shipping Board to sell fleet to private owners, operate all vessels not
sold)... Some 5 million workers are members of AFL (dwindles to 3,444,000
by 1929)... James Smathers devises pioneering electric typewriter...

Wharton School, University of Pennsylvania, presents labor management
course... Whiting Williams: What's On the Worker's Mind: By One Who Put
on Overalls to Find Out (pioneers field of industrial sociology)...
Samuel Gompers, president of AFL, supports labor-saving machines if they
don't replace intelligence... When inflationary prices of post-war period
collapse after consumers stop buying, economic slump evolves, followed by
1921 recession... Harvard's Graduate School of Business offers industrial
management program...

Kansas Court of Industrial Relations is first U.S. tribunal for
compulsory arbitration, declared unconstitutional in part later...
Population census shows total population of 105.7 million, 54.2 urban and
51.5 rural (shows immigration of some 5.7 million since 1911)... National
Bureau of Economic Research is created... U.S. Supreme Court bans "open-
price" planning by competitors in an industry to share information on
market conditions...

Federal Power Commission is created to regulate power plants... Professor
Prescott of MIT is employed by Joint Coffee Trade Publicity Committee to
study chemistry of roasted coffee beans... First U.S. Junior Chamber of
Commerce organizes in St. Louis (evolves with some 7,400 chapters by
1980s)... U.S. Army's general staff reorganizes with G-1 for personnel,
G-2 for military intelligence, G-3 for operations and training and G-4
for supply - War Plans Division to do strategic planning in
coordination with G-3...

With 2 million jobless AFL campaigns for 2-year ban on immigration...
50,000 workers shut-down 25 railroads with strike... Brookwood College
for adult education opens in New York with funds from labor unions...
U.S.-funded study recommends "Super-Power" for Northwest with
interconnction of private electric utilities to launch new industrial
revolution... With 1913 as 100, U.S.' index of annual manufacturing
production is 122.2, world's 2nd highest, 148 in 1925 (2nd), 148 in 1930
(4th), 140.3 in 1935 (4th), and 143 in 1938 (5th)... Second Industrial

Conference recommends creation of National Industrial Board and system of regional conferences to assist in voluntary arbitration of labor disputes (favors employee representation in form of shop organization, opposes company unions).

Business Events

After "Big Jim" Colosimo is killed, nephew Johnny Torrio takes over his crime empire in Chicago (-1925, competes for market share in Chicago beer wars with O'Banion on North Side, O'Donnell brothers on West Side, and "Terrible" Genneas of South Side, forms all-Chicago underworld council to coordinate activities and maintain peace)... After squabbling with partners, Couzens and Dodge brothers, resigning as president of car business in 1918, announcing plans to start new family-owned car business, and settling disputes to buyout partners for $105 million on their original investment of $33,000, Ford Motor Co. is incorporated by Henry Ford, 55.3%, wife Clara, 3.0%, and son Edsel with 41.7% of shares... 8MK, later WWJ, in Detroit is U.S.' first commercial radio station to do daily broadcasts... After operating restaurant in Portland, OR, Simon C. Barry invents machine to make soft ice cream (markets Siberian Soft Ice Cream machines, operates 99 outlets in Pacific Northwest by W.W.II, loses market to rivals after war)... Taggart Baking of Indianapolis introduces Wonder Bread (is acquired in 1925 by Continental Baking to become pioneering national brand)...

H.L. Hunt borrows $50 before heading to oil boom in El Dorado, AR (after making and losing a fortune heads for Tyler, TX, with $108, borrows funds in 1930 to buy center of East Texas field from "Dad" Joiner for $30,000 in cash and payment of $1.2 million if oil discovered - richest find of its time, starts Hunt Oil in 1936 - largest independent by World War II, moves to Dallas in 1938 to acquire interests in oil and gas, real estate, silver, sugar, cattle, horses and electronics before death in 1974, leaves estate of some $4 billion)...

Mining engineer and consultant Herbert Hoover, president of Confederated American Engineering Society, sponsors study of waste in industry (issues Waste in Industry in 1921 to castigate inefficiencies of U.S. management for slack production, unemployment)... William A. Fairburn, head of Diamond Match since 1909, contracts with Ivar Kreugar of Sweden to distribute matches of his Swedish international cartel to forestall its entry into U.S. market (when cartel collapses in 1932 acquires 90% of U.S. market by 1937)...

Donald Douglas starts aircraft business with $600 to build plane for first non-stop transcontinental flight (fails, starts Douglas Co. to build torpedo boats for U.S. Navy, forms Douglas Aircraft in 1928 to build transport planes)... After leaving Buick because of W.C. Durant, Walter Chrysler is hired by banks to rescue failing Willys-Overland automobile business (is re-acquired later by John Willys to build popular Overland car) and Maxwell (is reorganized in 1921 to become Chrysler Corp. in 1925)... Wall Street is bombed (inflames public fears of radicals, communists)...

Francis M. Lawson: Industrial Control, field's first textbook... With $100,000 from Bank of America, Harry Cohn, former pool hustler, shipping clerk, vaudeville actor, trolley conductor and song plugger, forms C.B.C.

Film Sales Co. with brother Jack and Joe Brandt (becomes Columbia Pictures in 1924 - production chief of California operations in 1932 with Jack in charge of finances in NYC, develops business as one of profitable major studios in 1930s, dies controversial figure in 1958 with estate of some $14 million)...

After working as candy salesman and failing as candy maker twice, Frank Mars, son of Pennsylvania grist mill operator, starts new candy business near Minneapolis (after introducing Snickers in 1921, creates popular Milky Way bar in 1923 - sales jump from $72,800 to $792,900 within one year, moves plant to Chicago in 1929, introduces Three Musketeers bar in 1932)... Ordway Tead: <u>The</u> <u>Labor</u> <u>Audit:</u> <u>A</u> <u>Method</u> <u>of</u> <u>Industrial</u> <u>Investigation</u>... After organizing Chicago American Giants in 1911 as barnstorming baseball team, Rube Foster forms Negro National League... Sears adopts time-payment plan for customers... Tanners' Council starts production research program...

As result of Volstead Act on prohibition, American Institute of Baking acquires research laboratory of brewing industry ... Ordway Tead, Columbia instructor of one of first courses in personnel and Henry Metcalf, vocational counselor in government personnel work: <u>Personnel</u> <u>Administration</u> (pioneers field's textbooks)... Aeromarine West Indies Airways is formed by automobile dealer to deliver mail between Key West, Havana (-1923)... Gambler, financier Arnold Rothstein organizes NYC's bootleg business by special territories to prevent cut-throat competition among mobs... Financier Eugene Meyer, Jr., creates Allied Chemical & Dye Corp. as merger of 5 firms, each specializes in different field of chemical industry (earns nearly $212 million in 1920-30 with $134 million in dividends, survives Depression not missing dividend)...

J.C. Shaw devises sensing device, controlled by servomechanism, to operate electro-mechanical duplicating system for metalworking... Eastman Kodak employs university recruiter to interview, select new chemists... Henry Ford acquires coal fields in Kentucky, West Virginia (purchases railroads for delivering coal to Detroit)... Personnel Research Federation organizes... Pittsburgh's KDKA, owned by Westinghouse Electric, is first licensed radio station (is followed by 600 by end of 1922)... Harvard Knitting Mill adopts employee profit-sharing plan (-1927)... Haldeman-Julius Co., KS, prints first Little Blue Books for popular reading... Elgin Watchmakers College is started, IL (-1960)...

Christian K. Nelson creates chocolate-covered ice cream bar at Iowa ice cream store (forms partnership with Russell Stover to market Eskimo Pies, obtains patent in 1922, is acquired by United States Foil Co. of R.J. Reynolds in 1924)... Former Iowa bicycle builders Fred, August Duesenberg start making racing cars (use first straight-engine and hydraulic brakes - invented 1918 by aviation pioneer Malcolm Loughhead, is acquired in 1924 by Errett Cord along with Auburn Automobile)... After losing some $30 million (drops GM's ventures in tractors, farm machinery) in effort to maintain price of General Motors stock, William Durant sells GM shares to DuPont-Morgan syndicate (replace Durant as president with Pierre DuPont - Alfred P. Sloan, Jr. as executive vice president)...

Marcus Loew acquires Metro, small independent movie company, to produce films for his chain of some 100 theaters (acquires film production companies of Samuel Goldwyn and Louis B. Mayer to form Metro-Goldwyn-

Mayer in 1924)... Several Chicago White Sox baseball players are indicted for conspiring with gamblers to fix 1919 World Series (results in appointment of Judge Kenesaw Mountain Landis as first baseball commissioner to restore public confidence in sport business)... Shell opens new oil field in Long Beach, CA... First U.S. international air-mail contract is given to Eddie Hubbard to deliver between Seattle and Victoria, British Columbia... C.L. Griggs of Price's Branch, MO, creates popular orange drink of Howdy (sells another drink as Bib-Label Lithiated Lemon-Lime Soda, after 6 tries names new drink 7-Up)...

168 banks are closed during year, 505 in 1921, 367 in 1922, 646 in 1923, 775 in 1924, 618 in 1925, 976 in 1926, 669 in 1927, 499 in 1928, 659 in 1929, 1,352 in 1930, 2,294 in 1931, 1,456 in 1932, and 4,004 in 1933... Alfred P. Sloan, Jr., submits objectives for reorganizing General Motors to Chairman Pierre duPont: to identify functions as they relate to each other and central organization, to determine status of central organization in coordinating parts, and to centralize control of executive functions with chief executive as styled on DuPont's new structure (is approved with corporate headquarters and advisory staff to plan, coordinate and control decentralized divisions, completes organizational changes by 1924)...

When wife is unable to bandage cuts, Earl Dickson, Johnson & Johnson, devises first band-aids (leads to assorted sizes in tin boxes in 1938, sheer Band-Aids in 1958, and clear bandages in 1980s)... Dan Field, dean of NYC matchmakers in 1980s, opens Field's Exclusive Service to arrange marriages.

1921

General Events

Iowa is (April 11) first State to impose cigarette tax... Emergency Quota Act permits (May 19) entry on basis of nationality in U.S. as of 1910 (sets total immigration of 357,000, starts competition of liners for tourists)... Congress passes (May 27) Emergency Tariff Act... Congress passes (June 10) Budget and Accounting Act to create Bureau of Budget (requires president to submit annual budget, used by English Government since late 1700s, to Congress, is transferred to White House in 1939, is reorganized as Office of Management and Budget in 1970) and General Accounting Office... August unemployment figures show 5,735,000 workers idle...

Revolutionary CD-12 engine, re-designed by Arthur Nult of Curtiss Airplane, is tested at 393 mph (replaces W.W.I automobile engine used in airplanes)... Some 5 million workers are registered as members of AFL, drops to some 3.4 million in 1929... As sign of times New York Central cuts wages of some 43,000 workers by almost 23%... Herbert Hoover presides over national conference on unemployment, reaching over 5.7 million (recommends job programs and cuts in prices)...

U.S. Supreme Court: <u>Duplex Printing Press Company</u> <u>v.</u> <u>Deering</u> (rules Clayton Act did not legalize secondary boycotts or protect unions against injunctions in being conspiracy in restraint of trade)... Psychological Corp. forms as non-profit research organization... Post Office pilots fly mail from San Francisco to New York in record time of 33 hours, 20 minutes...

Lenin's article, "Scientific Management and the Directorship of the Proletariate," is published in U.S. (urges Soviet leaders to study work of Frederick W. Taylor)... Major strike of coal workers is supported by "Triple Alliance" of union miners, dockworkers and railwaymen (collapses during strike)... 8 million women are working, some 87% in teaching and secretarial work... 9.3 million cars are registered, 23.1 million in 1929...

Herbert Hoover becomes Secretary of Commerce (-1928, to initiate local and state actions sponsors some 250 conferences to educate participants on problems, creates Division of Simplified Practices to standardize dimensions of staple goods, reorganizes Bureau of Foreign and Domestic Commerce into 15 commodity units to promote sales, provides manufacturers with monthly reports on supplies of raw materials and economic trends, encourages steel industry to adopt 8-hour day in 1923 without using legislation, creates Business Cycles Committee in 1923 to improve information for decision makers, sponsors Railway Labor Act to endorse collective bargaining and Air Commerce Act in 1926).

Business Events

Freida Loehman opens clothing shop in Brooklyn to sell excess inventories of brand-name apparel at discount prices (pioneers field of off-price retailing, is acquired by Associated Dry Goods in 1983 and May Department Stores in 1986, by mid-1980s operates with over $200 million in sales from chain of 82 stores in 26 states - 4th largest in bargain retailing industry)... After operating Great Lakes ship chartering business since 1916, Daniel K. Ludwig acquires first oil tanker (avoids bankruptcy in 1933 by selling collier to whaling syndicate, forms National Bulk Carriers which evolves as one of world's largest multinational firms - U.S.' largest in shipping and 3rd in world after W.W.II, obtains bank loan in late 1930s to acquire surplus W.W.I dry-cargo vessels for conversion into tankers, pioneers industry's use of charters - basis for largest private fleet by 1960s)... Julius Rosenwald, president of Sears, pledges $21 million of personal wealth to assist Sears during post-War Depression (exhibits mail-order merchandise in showrooms to stimulate sales - a success, adopts centralized, functionally departmentalized organizational structure by 1924)...

After wheeling and dealing with Sid Richardson, Clint Murchison starts new partnership with Ernest R. Fair to drill for oil (after near bankruptcy strikes it rich, sells out for $5 million in 1927 to retire)... Royce Hailey's Pig Stand in Dallas serves barbecued sandwiches to drivers, pioneers drive-in service... Despite opinions of experts that it couldn't be done, geologist Wallace E. Pratt, using first seismic surveying, discovers famous Mexia oil field in Central Texas (establishes Standard Oil of New Jersey as profitable operation)... Betty Crocker, modeled on Nabisco's Blue Bonnet Sue and Quaker Oats' Mama Celeste, is created by Washburn Crosby, millers of Gold Medal Flour, to answer inquiries from women (becomes company symbol in 1925, is acquired in 1928 formation of General Mills, is used as brand for 140 products by 1980s)... Minnesota Cooperative Creameries Assn. is formed as shipping agency by small, farmer-owned dairy cooperatives (uses Land O' Lakes brand in 1924)...

Charles F. Mitchell becomes president of New York's National City Bank, Citibank in 1950s (-1933 when forced to resign, transforms Bank into diversified financial services corporation by pioneering modern retail banking with individual accounts in 1928, branch banks in 1929, and trust business, is attacked by Senate Banking Committee in 1932 for role in 1929 Crash, is indicted in 1933 for tax evasion - acquitted, after operating investment business becomes chairman of Blyth & Co., West Coast investment business, to develop it as leading underwriter, is prosecuted in 1950 for role in anti-trust suit - dismissed)...

Billy Ingram opens first White Castle restaurant, specializes in hamburgers derived from meatballs sold at carnivals, in Wichita, KS, spawns Milwaukee's White Tower chain in 1926, White Diamond, Royal Castle and White Crest (with no francises expands to 119 places by 1931 and around 200 in intercity areas by 1960, markets frozen hamburgers in grocery stores in mid-1980s)... David Sarnoff becomes general manager of Radio Corporation of America (after success manufacturing radios becomes executive vice president in 1922, launches National Broadcasting Co. in 1926, acquires 1901 Victor Co. in 1927 to produce records and Victrolas, becomes president in 1930-47 and chairman for 1947-71)...

Atlantic City holds first Miss America contest to extend tourist season... Christy Walsh, "first" modern business agent for athletes, is hired by Babe Ruth to handle his non-baseball commercial ventures... F. Donaldson Brown, treasurer of DuPont since 1918, becomes GM'S vice president of finance (-1937, designs information procedures to control operating divisions by 1922, uses ingredients of planned program budget system)... 88 airlines operate in U.S. (jumps to 129 in 1923 - only 17 of first 88 survive)... National Institute for Commercial and Trade Organization Executives is formed by U.S. Chamber of Commerce to prepare administrators for new fields...

Bran gruel is accidentally created by unknown health clinician in Minneapolis (becomes Wheaties in 1924, introduces first box-top premium in 1931)... Personnel Research Federation is created as clearing house for information on studies of personnel activities... Henry Ford is forced to pay $75 million bank loan (cancels all orders for materials and supplies, closes all factories, ships 125,000 cars to dealers for cash - either pay or lose franchise, after acceptance by almost all of 17,000 dealers starts production again when inventory is depleted)... DuPont is reorganized with 5 autonomous divisions, cellulose, paint, purolin, dyestuffs and explosives, and administrative headquarters with general executives, staff specialists and accounting, statistical offices...

Avid sportsman Eddie Bauer starts small shop in Seattle to string tennis rackets (obtains patent for quilted goose-down jacket and sleeping bag in 1936, issues first mail-order catalog in 1945 with outdoor gear and clothing - almost 100% of total business by 1953, sells to General Mills in 1972)... Charles A. Cannon becomes president of father's 1887 Cannon Mills (innovates with national advertising, trademark, pastel colors, clear wrappings and style shows, extends towel line with sheets, hosiery, bedspreads, draperies, decorative fabrics and blankets, operates 17 plants with some 24,000 workers in 1971)...

Ford Motor Co. produces some 55% of U.S. automobiles, declines to around 30% by 1926... Some 20,000 businesses fail during year... John Robert

Powers starts finishing school for young ladies in Boston (pioneers international modeling business in 1980s)... Dwight T. Farnham: <u>American</u> <u>vs.</u> <u>Europe</u> <u>in</u> <u>Industry:</u> <u>A</u> <u>Comparison</u> <u>of</u> <u>Industrial</u> <u>Policies</u> <u>and</u> <u>Methods</u> <u>of</u> <u>Management</u>... Despite previous failure in 1880, Montgomery Ward opens outlet stores (operates 37 by 1927 and some 500 by 1929, starts mail-order agencies in small towns in 1926)... <u>Administration</u> is first general business magazine...

Eddie Rickenbacker, former ace pilot during W.W.I and racing car driver, starts automobile business, bankruptcy in 1926... Danish-born William S. Knudsen, head of Ford's Highland Park plant, is fired after conflicts with Henry Ford (joins General Motors, becomes general manager of Chevrolet in 1924, instead of imitating Ford's assembly process with single-purpose equipment installs decentralized production system with general-purpose machines for continuous change and expansion by 1929, becomes GM president in 1937)...

After leaving GM William C. Durant raises $7 million to start Durant Motors (-1933, acquires Goodyear plant for production and GM's Sheridan Motor Car Division in 1921, collects firms making parts, introduces Star Automobile - later Flint Car, liquidates business in 1933)... First Radio Shack store opens... Clarence Walker Barron, owner and editor of <u>The</u> <u>Wall</u> <u>Street</u> <u>Journal</u>, starts weekly investment newspaper... Although bargain haven for local buyers since early 1900s, Flemington, NJ, sees its first factory outlet store (evolves by 1988 as village of 4,000 with 125 factory outlets to serve some 35,000 regional, national shoppers/week).

1922

General Events

Capper-Volstead Act permits (February 18) farmers to buy, sell cooperatively without being subjected to anti-trust laws)... Professional baseball is ruled immune from federal anti-trust legislation... In Herrin Massacre, 20 guards and strike-breakers are killed by coal miners, IL... All major ports on West Coast are shut down by strike of International Longshoremen's Association, broken by companies moving 1,500 strike-breakers from port to port...

War, Navy Departments create interservice industrial planning agency... Oil pollution is studied in Texas Gulf area, followed by others to 1926... John D. Rockefeller, Jr., others create Industrial Relations Counselors to advance knowledge and practice of human relations in industry, commerce, education and government...

United Mine Workers call nationwide strike, joined by some 100,000 non-union workers (-1923, achieve best contract in 1924 with $7.50/day and improved working conditions)... Interior Secretary Albert B. Fall, bypassing competitive bidding, leases Naval Oil Reserve at Teapot Dome, WY, to Harry Sinclair's Mammoth Oil and leases Elk Hills reserve in California to Edward L. Doheny (results in Congressional investigation and indictments of Fall, Sinclair, and Doheny in 1924 for bribery and conspiracy - only Fall, first Cabinet member jailed, convicted)...

Congress adopts protectionist tariff... U.S. Supreme Court: <u>United</u> <u>Mine</u> <u>Workers</u> <u>v.</u> <u>Coronado</u> <u>Coal</u> <u>Company</u> (declares union innocent of violating

Sherman Act, reverses position in 1925 to hold union's strike an illegal restraint of interstate commerce)...

After strike of 2 months, railway shipmen return to work... Princeton University's Department of Economics and Social Institutions forms Industrial Relations Section... 600 commercial radio stations operate in U.S.

Business Events

After developing pioneering baking mix for corn muffins in New Brunswick, NJ, McCollum creates pie crust mix after testing various recipes at church suppers and service club dinners (is followed in 1929 with gingerbread mix by molasses business of Pittsburgh's Duff Co. - markets various cake mixes in 1930-36, by Armed Forces with various mixes in 1943, and by Pillsbury's hot roll mix in 1947 - first cake mix in 1948)... T. Claude Ryan forms Los Angeles - San Diego Airline (starts Ryan School of Aeronautics in 1928)... With $86,000 Henry R. Luce, Briton Hadden create Time for college-educated men and women (issue magazine in 1923 - 12,000 circulation to 107,000 by 1925 and 2.5 million in 1960, introduce Fortune in 1930, Life in 1936)... James O. McKinsey, pioneering management consultant: Budgetary Control... AT&T's WEAF station airs first regular radio commercial (serves 25 sponsors by 1923)...

Ad agency of playboy Gerald Lambert devises "Halitosis" ad campaign, prevents bad breath, to promote Listerine of father's Warner-Lambert business as antiseptic mouthwash (revives sluggish sales in 5 years on annual ad budget of $5 million to net over $4 million, is followed by use of warnings about "BO" in Lifebuoy ads of 1933)... Control of Stutz auto company, started in Indianapolis to make racing car, is acquired by Bethlehem Steel tycoon Charles M. Schwab (-1935, achieves success with sporty Stutz Bearcat during 1920s)...

T.P. Wright, general manager and chief engineer for Curtiss Airplane, starts pioneering studies on variations of cost with cumulative production quantities (publishes report in 1936 on progress function)... Wholesale bakers create Quality Bakers of America Cooperative to compete in market with baking giants... A.E. Stouffer opens small stand-up dairy counter in downtown Cleveland (becomes restaurant chain in major cities by 1950s, launches line of frozen dishes in 1954 to sell some 300 million packages/year in 1980s)...

Stock of Piggly Wiggly Stores, self-service chain of 550 operations owned by Clarence Saunders with some 650 independent stores, is listed on New York Stock Exchange (results in bear raid by speculators selling short as price drops from $50 to $40 when troubles of several independent stores start rumors of failing chain, triggers counter attack by Saunders with personal funds and loan of $10 million-plus to buy stock sold short, drives price to high of $124 before Exchange suspends further trading in 1923 to give shorts time to find stock and avoid corner, forces Saunders out of business later in year when unable to pay debts acquired to corner stock, starts new chain of stores in 1928)... After selling newspapers since 1908 and dropping out of school after discovering he could make more money selling than his teachers, W. Clement Stone, born 1902, starts insurance business Combined Registry Co. in Chicago (develops insurance empire worth some $300 million by 1960s as true believer in Horatio Alger

gospel)... Metropolitan Life Insurance builds pioneering apartment
housing complex in NYC's Queens... Harvard Business Review is
published... Promoter Ivan Gates starts daredevil Gates Flying Circus
with Clyde "Upside-down" Pangborn, followed by daredevil auto shows,
i.e., Joey Chitwood...

Country Club Plaza opens near Kansas City as first U.S. planned shopping
center, followed by Suburban Square at Ardmore, PA, in 1928 and Highland
Park Village in Dallas in 1931... R.H. Macy, founded 1858, becomes
publicly owned company (goes private in 1985 with U.S.' largest leveraged
buyout of $3.5 billion, in losing 1988 battle for Federated Department
Stores, 650 outlets, to Canada's Campeau adds Federated's I. Magnin chain
and Bullock stores, $1.1 billion, to operate 96 department and specialty
stores in 14 states)... Some 300 firms are in tire market, 26 left by
1935... William Clark: The Gantt Chart: A Working Tool of Management
(is translated into 8 languages, is used by USSR in formulating 5-year
plans)...

A.O. Smith Corp. designs production line to assemble 10,000 automobile
frames/day... First U.S. oil development in Middle East is undertaken in
Iraq by consortium of Jersey Standard, 6 other oil companies with
assistance of U.S. State Department... Retired Signal Corps General
George Squier starts Wired Radio, Inc., to compete with wireless radio
(becomes Muzak in 1934 to provide programmed music over phone lines for
restaurants and hotels)...

George S. Radford: The Control of Quality in Manufacturing... DeWitt,
Lila Wallace publish compact magazine Reader's Digest (issue British
edition in 1938 - 39 editions in 15 languages by 1980s, start Condensed
Book Club in 1950 and take first ads in 1955, achieve 1973 circulation of
18 million with 12 million more in 16 languages)...

William Black starts nut stand on Time Square, NY (evolves as Chock Full
O'Nuts, lunch-counter chain and coffee business with sales over $100
million by 1982)... First National, a circuit of exhibitors, starts
producing movies to control increasing production costs from star system
(pioneers industry tend of vertical integration)... 263 aircraft are made
in U.S. during year, some 21,000 in 1918... With funds from Henry Ford,
William D. Stout starts business to build new aircraft to carry loads for
great distances (-1925 when acquired by Ford)...

Stations WJZ in NYC, WGY in Schenectady form first radio "network"...
Gerard Swope becomes president of General Electric (-1939 and 1942-44,
sells interests in power companies to focus on consumer products - some
50% of business by 1930, establishes employee securities program in 1923,
proposes unemployment insurance plan to workers in 1925 - rejected but
accepted after 1929, introduces 5-day work week in 1931, proposes
stabilization program for industry in 1931 with national trade
associations functioning under federal regulation, recognizes CIO union
in 1935)...

Retired farmer George J. Mercherle starts State Farm Mutual Insurance,
IL, to provide protection for farm vehicles (evolves as world's largest
automobile insurance business by 1940s and as largest U.S. insurer of
property and casualty in 1980s - some $11 billion/year in premiums)...
Bethlehem Steel acquires Lackawanna Steel (acquires Midvale, Cambria in

1923 and Pacific Coast Steel in 1929)... The Journal of Personnel Research is published (becomes Personnel Journal in 1927)... Gray Motor Co. is started (-1926)... Laurence Marshall starts Raytheon Co. (evolves to make radar, Hawk missle, microwave ovens, etc.)... Moses L. Annenberg publishes Daily Racing Form (achieves near monopoly of information on 29 tracks by 1930)... With 8th-grade education, Fred Meyer opens grocery store in downtown Portland, OR (opens world's first self-service drug store in 1930)... Juan Trippe, Navy pilot in World War I, starts Long Island Airways to carry socialites to resort areas (starts Colonial Air Transport in 1924, operates first air-mail contract between NYC and Boston, after stockholder conflict sells out in 1927)...

AT&T starts radio station WBAY in NY (starts radio network in 1923, drops radio activities in 1924, sells all plants outside of U.S. to International Telephone & Telegraph in 1924, introduces commercial telephotograph service and develops synchronized sound-action system for movies in 1925, starts commercial telephone service with London in 1927 - all major cities by 1929, demonstrates feasibility of long-distance television in 1927)... Will H. Hays, industry leaders form Motion Picture Producers and Distributors of America to regulate movie morals...

National Safety Council, National Association of Corporation Training and National Association of Employment Managers merge to create National Personnel Association... James Dole buys Hawaii's Lanai to grow pineapples, becomes part of Castle & Cooke later (develops paternalistic community for plantation, builds island's first hotel for tourists in 1988)... Local Minneapolis barber starts chain of hair salons, U.S.' largest with some 500 places in U.S., Canada, Mexico, and Puerto Rico in fragmented market with 1988 sales of $192 million (acquires Fathers Mustache barber shops in 1984 and Essanelle Salons in some 60 department stores).

1923

General Events

Intermediate Credit Act (March 14) authorizes Federal Reserve to aid credit banks in financing agricultural cooperatives... U.S. Supreme Court: Adkins v. Pilgrims Hospital (rules District of Columbia's minimum wage law for women, children to be unconstitutional)... After pressure by President Harding, U.S. Steel adopts 8-hour day... Nevada, Montana are first States to adopt old-age pensions... Lts. J.A. Macready, Oakley Hall make first non-stop transcontinental flight in 26 hours, 50 minutes... New York repeals enforcement of Prohibition (encourages bootlegging, speak-easies, such as Stork Club and "21," moonshining, etc.)... Col. Jacob Schick patents electric razor, first sold 1931... John B. Tytus devises continuous hot-strip rolling of steel... Farm foreclosures, bank failures occur with slump in hog market...

Edward Stinson makes all-night, non-stop flight from Chicago to Long Island in Junker monoplane... Lee de Forest develops Phonofilms to produce sound movies (produces 2 short films and feature film by 1927)... Jefferson Caffery is named counselor to U.S. Ambassador to Japan (urges Japan to buy more U.S. products as 44% of their country's exports in 1922 go to U.S.)... Plans are announced for labor college in NYC... U.S. and Germany sign (December 18) commercial treaty... Open Market Investment

Committee is formed to advise Reserve bank and board on moderating swings of inventory cycle.

Business Events

Floyd Odlam forms Atlas Corp. with $40,000 (evolves as No. 1 U.S. investment trust during 1930s with over $120 million by acquiring bankrupt utilities, movie companies and stores, acquires Curtiss-Wright in 1940)... Romanian-born Meyer Bloomfield, industrial relations pioneer, starts labor relations consulting business... Victor Emanuel, partner acquire father's utility business (sells 14 utilities to Sam Insull in 1926, invests in English stock market in 1927-34, acquires Cord Corp. in 1937 to develop conglomerate after W.W. II)...

With backing of local people, J. Spencer Love starts textile plant in Burlington, NC (opens first plant to weave rayon, cotton bedspreads in 1924 and 2nd plant in 1925 to make rayon dresses, operates 22 plants by 1937 as world's largest weaver of rayon fabric, as Burlington Industries operates 135 plants in 1972 with 84,000 employees in U.S., 10 countries to achieve sales of $1.8 billion)...

Eli Lilly pharmaceutical business of Indianapolis starts commercial production of insulin to establish itself in industry (enters agricultural market in 1954 to use resources)... Fashionable clothing business of Saks family, founded in late 1800s, is acquired by Gimbel Brothers department store chain, incorporated in 1922 with stores in Milwaukee, Philadelphia and NYC (opens Saks Fifth Avenue in New York for wealthy in 1924 - 49 stores nationwide by 1987, acquires Pittsburgh Kaufman & Baer Department Store in 1925)... Hassenfeld Brothers is started in Pawtucket, RI, as fabric-remnants distributor (evolves by 1986 as world's No. 1 toy company with sales of $1.2 billion)... Air-O Mix of Delaware sells Whip-All, first portable electric beater... John O. Young (-1934), Raymond Rubicam (-1944) start advertising agency (achieve success with Postum and Jell-O in 1926, becomes U.S.' largest independent agency in 1979)... Walter Dill Scott, Robert Clothier: Personnel Management: Principles, Practices and Point-Of-View (provides first behavioral treatment of subject)... Commander Eugene F.M. McDonald, one-time Arctic explorer, starts Zenith Radio (-1958)... American Management Assn. organizes (assimilates National Personnel Association)...

A.C. Nielsen Co. is started to do performance surveys of industrial equipment and product evaluation surveys (does consumer surveys in 1933)... Royal Little starts Special Yarns business in Boston (becomes Textron in 1944)... Willys Overland introduces colored "Red Bird" car (is followed in use of color by General Motors in 1924 with multiple-colored models, by Hoosier Kitchen Cabinets in 1924, by Crane Co. with color schemes for bathroom, by colored refrigerators and Pepperell Linen in colors by 1928)... Assets of Ford Motor Co. are valued as $536,351,939 - almost one-third in cash, some $100,000 in assets when first organized in 1903...

Hydrox merges with Pittsburgh dairy to form National Dairy Products (acquires Kraft-Phenix cheesemakers in 1930, becomes Kraftco in 1939 and Kraft, Inc. in 1976 to operate 170 plants in 130 countries to make products with 850 brands - sales of $6.4 billion in 1979)... Crystal Palace opens in San Francisco, forerunner of supermarket... Procter &

Gamble guarantees employees 48 weeks of work/year (is followed by 1935 plan of Nunn-Bush Shoe to guarantee 52 weeks/year)... Charles Norris: Bread (discusses role of women working in business)...

After developing process to freeze fish for U.S. Bureau of Fisheries (notices freezing of rabbits, ducks and game by Eskimos on U.S. biological expedition to Labrador in 1916), Clarence Birdseye is employed by Atlantic Coast Fisheries to commercialize process (forms General Seafoods in 1924, perfects freezing process by 1925, is acquired by Postum in 1929)... Russian-born Igor Sikorsky starts Sikorsky Aero Engineering on Long Island (builds first commercial plane in 1928, is acquired by United Aircraft & Transport in 1928 - part of United Aircraft in 1934, develops first U.S. practical helicopter by 1940)...

Jackson mills of Nashua Mfg., NH, builds new factory to ensure continuous flow of textiles from raw materials to finished goods... Standard Oil of California is one of first industrial firms to make public statement on employer-employee relations... E.K. Hall becomes Vice President in Charge of Personnel Relations for AT&T, first in business with title.

1924

General Events

Child labor amendment is sent (June 2) to states for ratification, abandoned 1950 with 10 states short... Communist-oriented Workers' Party nominates William Z. Foster for president... Jay David Houser, headed consulting group after World War I doing consumer attitude surveys for utilities, is named Wertheim Fellow by Harvard (discovers by interviews with business executives that few have accurate information on employee morale, publishes What the Employer Thinks in 1927 with determinates of employee morale)... After 57 shops 2 of 4 U.S. Army seaplanes, Douglas World Cruisers, complete first round-the-world flight in 175 days...

J.R. Commons: Legal Foundations of Capitalism... H.F. Dodge, H.G. Romig and W.A. Stewart at Bell Telephone Laboratories pioneer statistical inferences, probability theory... After death of Samuel Gompers, William Green of United Mine Workers becomes new president of American Federation of Labor (-1952)... Taylor Society sponsors first formal meeting of college professors to determine basic knowledge and appropriate management courses for college curricula... Congress creates Inland Waterways Corp. to supervise government-owned canals and improve riverways... As suggested by Herbert Hoover, Secretary of Commerce, Stanford University develops school of business administration, modeled on Harvard's program... Army Industrial College is created to prepare officers in planning for industrial mobilization... Macy's first annual Thanksgiving Parade to start holidays is held in NYC... U.S. Supreme Court upholds NY law forbidding late-night work for women...

Toastmasters International, 6,500 clubs in 50 countries in 1987, is started in Santa Ana, CA, to help people learn communications skills for career advancement (accepts first women members in 1973 - 45% of 1987 membership).

Business Events

Sweden's Electrolux introduces canister vacuum cleaner to U.S. market...
James O. McKinsey: <u>Managerial</u> <u>Accounting</u> <u>and</u> <u>Business</u> <u>Administration</u>
(stresses sound organizational planning)... Mrs. O.H.T. Belmont, doyenne
of New York society, is persuaded to endorse Ponds cold cream in exchange
for charity donation... IBM adopts pioneering employee self-regulating
time system... U.S. Chamber of Commerce: "Principles of Business
Conduct"... International Harvester introduces Farmall tractor, model for
other manufacturers... Richard L. Simon, Max L. Schuster start book
publishing business... Racing car of business Fred and August Duesenberg
and Auburn automobile is acquired by tycoon Errett Lobban Cord
(introduces Duesenberg's elegant uncompromising car in 1926 and Cord
automobile in 1929, liquidates Auburn-Cord-Duesenberg business in
1937)... Sears starts radio station, WLS for world's largest store, in
Chicago... Ford Motor Co. produces its 10 millionth car... Alfred P.
Sloan, Jr., becomes president of General Motors (-1929), Pierre DuPont is
chairman... Merrill R. Lott devises one of first job evaluation methods
using job characteristics...

Stanley Slotkin, after quitting high school to earn some $10,000 in
running bicycle business with 5 employees, starts Abbey Rents in Kansas
City when chair rental business refuses to pay for damages to his pants
(expands business to make some $2 million/year after going public in
1962)... After death of father, Howard Hughes, Jr., inherits 1909 Sharp-
Hughes Tool while freshman at Cal Tech (nets $2 million in first year,
starts producing successful movies in 1926-32 to use spare time)... First
singing commercial on radio advertises Wheaties...

General John Carly, Bell Telephone, makes first coast-to-coast radio
broadcast... National Automobile Show is held (fails for first time to
exhibit any electric or steam models)... Walter Shewhart, Western
Electric, devises quality control chart (pioneers new field of quality
control in 1930s)... Kimberly-Clarke markets Kleenex tissues, used at
first to remove cold cream (follows use of nose-paper by Japanese in
1600s, adds "pop-up" feature in 1929)... Frank W. Epperson patents
Epsicle, frozen confection or ice lollypop (is acquired in 1929 by small
company that renames treat Popsicle)...

William H. Mason, former associate of Thomas A. Edison, starts Mason
Fiber Co., MS, to utilize sawmill waste in making "pressed wood" (renames
business Masonite Corp. in 1928)... Vincent Bendix starts Bendix
Engineering Works to make novel French brake... Marcus Loew, head of
theater chain, combines Metro studio, Goldwyn Picture Corp., and movie
business of Louis B. Mayer as Metro-Goldwyn-Mayer (is managed by Nickolas
Schenck in NYC after death of Loew in 1927, Mayer West Coast production
chief, to fight off take-over attempt of William Fox to build
international movie empire)... Employee productivity is studied at
Western Electric's Hawthorne plant in Chicago by National Research
Council, MIT and Elton Mayo with Harvard associates...

Julius Stein, former ophthalmologist by training and part-time musician,
starts Music Corporation of America to arrange "one-night" bookings for
bands (opens Hollywood office in 1937 to become all-purpose booking
agency, evolves as billion-dollar entertainment empire with Universal
Studios and Decca Records)... Former bush pilot starts Wien Air Alaska...

Henry Metcalf presents pioneering executive development program in NYC...
Pittsburgh steel industry reports 8-hour day increases efficiency and
improves employee relations... Electric Industry Assn. forms... Sumner
Redstone, billionaire businessman by 1988 (starting with drive-in movie
theaters in New York, New England builds National Amusements theater
chain with 425 screens, adds Viacom, one of U.S.' largest media firms, in
1987 for $2.8 billion) is born.

1925

General Events

Engineer Vannevar Bush, MIT, devises first "modern" computer with
electric motors, thermotubes, and electronic storage... AT&T sends photo
by wire to 3 cities simultaneously... AT&T creates Bell Laboratories (by
1986 operates with some 20,000 employees, 2,769 with doctorates, at 19
facilities - 21,000 patents and 7 Nobel Prizes)... In this time (-1929)
chlorofluorocarbons appear in coolants (leads to warning by scientists in
1970s on dangers to ozone, U.S. bans on use in spray cans, and 1986
Montreal Protocol to reduce worldwide use by 35% by 1999)...

Asa Randolph secretly organizes Brotherhood of Sleeping Car Porters,
recognized by 1935 contract with Pullman Palace Car Co... Kelly Act
grants authority to Postmaster General to let air-mail contracts by
private bidding (results in cancellation of contracts in 1934 after
collusion by airlines)...

Warner W. Stockberger is made personnel director by U.S. Department of
Agriculture, first to hold position in government... Pioneering
Westchester County Parkway opens for automobile traffic, NY... President
Calvin Coolidge: "The Business of America is Business," speech to
American Society of Newspaper Editors...

AFL convention endorses resolution to cooperate with ownership and
management... Robert Brooking: Industrial Ownership: Its Economic and
Social Significance (proposes management is trustee for public)...
In this time social workers, psychologists use group work to resolve
personal problems... Russian-born Vladimir Zworykin, RCA director of
electronic research in 1929-42, obtains patent for iconoscope,
successfully demonstrates television in 1933... Giant Power Survey Board:
Giant Power (proposes statewide electrical energy plan of M.L. Cooke to
integrate PA's utilities, use coal resources and latest technology)...

Term "mass production" is first used in article by Henry Ford for
Encyclopedia Britanica... 32 playwrights sign basic agreement in secret
meeting to seek just royalties from Broadway producers... Bruce Barton:
The Man Nobody Knows (portrays Christ as "World's Greatest Salesman" and
first-rate manager in selecting 12 mediocre men to conquer world).

Business Events

Filene's, women's specialty store in Boston, pioneers branch stores in
suburban areas with place in Wellesley, MA... Standard Oil of New Jersey
adopts 8-hour day for workers in oil fields... International Match Co.,
NY, contracts to manufacture all matches for Poland... Walter G. Beech

founds Travel Air Mfg. to make small planes (merges with Curtiss-Wright in 1930, forms Beech Aircraft in 1932)... James O. McKinsey, formerly with 1917 consulting business of Frazer and Torbet, starts management consulting business, international operation in 1980s... George Washington Hill succeeds father as head of American Tobacco (promotes Lucky Strike, introduced 1916, as No. 1 cigarette with mass advertising)... Howard E. Coffin starts National Air Transport, evolves as United Airlines in 1934... A&W root beer business is started, pioneers franchise system in fast-food industry with one of first to J. Willard Marriott in 1927...

After selling bus holdings of 1916 Mesaba Transportation, Carl Wickman and Ralph Budd, president of Great Northern Railroad, start forming unified bus system with local and regional lines, including Michigan Greyhound operation of Frank Fageol (rename Northland Transportation as Greyhound Corp. in 1930, after falling revenues from deregulation of airlines in 1978 and buses in 1982 is sold by holding company to Texas investor group in 1987 for $325 million - acquires ailing No. 2 Trailways for $80 million in 1987)... While on sick leave from selling insurance, Clinton Odell starts Burma-Shave brushless cream business (posts rhyming highway signs in 1929 until banished by 1965 Highway Beautification Act)... Table Supply Co. is started in Miami (evolves as modern chain of Winn-Dixie Stores)...

Minnesota Valley Canning adopts Green Giant trademark... Carbide and Carbon Chemical Co. experiments to fractionate natural gas (results rapid continuous-flow-process production with dairy industry)... In years to 1931 5,846 mergers are recorded, increasing share of U.S.' output by 100 of largest manufacturing firms from 36% to 44% - 70% in 1943... Stanley Steamer automobile business declares bankruptcy...

Roadside establishment at San Luis Obispo, CA, advertises lodgings as Mot-el Inn (replaces tourist courts or camps, some 2,000 by 1926, by 1946, evolves with first Holiday Inn in 1952 and first Howard Johnson's motel in 1954 - some 60,000 motels by 1960)... Two days after playing last college football game with Illinois, gridiron star Red Grange signs contract with promoter and agent C.C., "Cash and Carry," Pyle (handles all personal product endorsements of Grange for some $100,000) and joins Chicago Bears pro football team to play 10 exhibition games in 17 days (guarantees Grange 50% of all gate receipts - 40% to Pyle, establishes professional football as popular sport... John Hertz starts Yellow Cab Co...

Some 588,000 miners work to produce 520,000,000 tons of coal (drops to 208,000 in 1981 to mine 774,000,000 tons)... After 8 years of research Pittsburgh Plate Glass develops process for making window glass vertically in continuous ribbon... National Association of Foremen organizes (evolves as National Management Association)... Great Western Building and Loan Assn. of Los Angeles is first mutual bank to open in California (with assets of $3 million is acquired in 1946 by Adolph Slechta - $8 million in assets by 1948 and $12.9 million in 1949 to become State's 2nd largest in 1953, is acquired in 1955 by investment house of Lehman Brothers for $10 million - assets of $130 million in 1956)... Harold Ross starts New Yorker magazine, profits every year after 1928... Pratt & Whitney, machine-tool concern with surplus cash and few work orders, develops new airplane engine (tests Wasp engine with twice power of Wright's Whirlwind in 1926)...

James H. Rand, Sr. and Jr., merge businesses to form Rand-Kardex, office supply business with 210 patents and over 4,000 products (merges with Remington Typewriter in 1925 to form Remington-Rand)... All AT&T operations outside of U.S. are sold to International Telephone & Telegraph of Sosthenes, Hernand Behn with telephone holdings in Puerto Rico and Cuba... Robert Lehman becomes principal partner of family's investment banking business, started by 3 brothers in 1850 at Montgomery, AL, as commodity business (switches investments from traditional industrials to finance new ventures, such as consolidating Keith-Albee, Orpheum theater chains in 1928 to form nation's largest vaudeville circuit, Pan-American World Airways, Aviation Corp., holding company of airlines that becomes American Airlines in 1929, Allen B. DuMont Laboratories, television pioneer in late 1930s, Continental Airlines in 1941, Kerr-McGee petroleum business in 1948, and conglomerate Litton Industries)...

Robert E. Wood, former general merchandise manager for Montgomery Ward since 1918, is hired by Sears as vice president for real estate and retail stores, president 1928 and chairman 1935-54 to make Sears No. 1 retailer, (opens 8 retail stores first year, operates 192 in 1928 to Ward's 244, some 300 in 1931 to Ward's 610, 724 in 1958 to Ward's 544, and 864 in 1979 to Ward's 419)...

Pioneering U.S. pizzeria opens in New Haven, CT... Learning curve phenomenon is first observed at manufacturing operations of Wright-Patterson Air Force Base, OH (is reported first in 1936 by T.R. Wright, manager of Buffalo plant of Curtiss-Wright in "Factors Affecting Cost of Airplanes," Journal of Aeronautical Science)...

Walter P. Chrysler forms Chrysler Corp. with reorganization of Maxwell and Chalmers car companies, industry's 5th in 1926, 3rd in 1929, and 2nd in 1933 (acquires 1915 Dodge car business in 1928)... Remington Typewriter introduces first commercial electric typewriter... E.L. Degolyer, U.S. pioneer in science of geophysics, creates Geophysical Research to design and make seismic equipment and conduct seismic explorations in finding new locations for oil wells (discovers first field in 1926)... After working with evangelist Billy Sunday, George F. May starts production control consulting business in Chicago (evolves as international management consulting firm)... General Motors plans strategy of annual model changes (implements with 1932-33 models)... With $500 Howard Johnson buys money-losing drug store in Quincy, MA...

Clarence Birdseye perfects process to freeze foods (starts business with financing from J.P. Morgan & Co., is acquired in 1929 by Postum)... 1896 Postum Cereal Co., which introduced popular Post Toasties in 1907 and 40% Bran Flakes in 1922, acquires Jell-O dessert business (in 1926 acquires Swans Down cake flour from Igleheart brothers, Minute Tapioca Co., developer of pre-cooked instant rice for armed services during W.W. II, and Franklin Baker coconut business, in 1927 acquires businesses of 1887 Log Cabin maple syrup and Walker Baker Chocolate, in 1928 acquires LaFrance laundry products, Calumet Baking Powder and Maxwell House Coffee of Cheek-Neal Co., reorganizes in 1929 as General Foods with acquisition of Birdseye Frozen Foods, acquires rights in 1933 to decaffeinated coffee developed by German coffee merchant - names brand Sanka, acquires Gaines in 1943 with revolutionary dry dog food, acquires Perkins Products, makers of Kool-Aid, in 1953, Good Seasons salad dressings in 1954, S.O.S. cleansing pads in 1957 - spun-off in 1968 by order of FTC, and Open Pit barbecue sauces in 1960, introduces freeze-dried instant coffee Maxim in 1964 to U.S. market, acquires Burger-Chef, Indianapolis-based chain of some 700 fast-food eateries, in 1967 - 1,200 by 1970s, in 1970 acquires franchised door-to-door skin care business of Viviane Wood - sold 1975, Atlee Burpee business in garden products, and Kuhner preschool toy business - sold 1974, operates 3rd largest U.S. food business in 1979 with sales over $5 billion, is acquired by Philip Morris business in 1985 for $5.7 billion)...

With failure of black Herman Perry's Standard Life Insurance and businesses in Atlanta, 2 blacks acquire pharmacies from empire to build 5-store chain of Yates and Milton Drugs... Fred Cole starts Cole swimwear business in California, one of largest by 1980s... Henry Ford acquires control of Stout Metal Airplane Co., previously Ford Air Transport to ferry parts between plants (wins mail contracts for Detroit-Chicago and Detroit-Cleveland, starts Stout Air Services in 1926 to carry cargo, passengers between Detroit-Grand Rapids - Cleveland in 1927, turns over airline to Stout in 1928 to build sturdy Ford Tri-Motor plane, the "Tin Goose," makes 198 before dropping venture in 1932-33).

1926

General Events

AFL plans to unionize auto industry... Radio picture service is opened between NYC, London... After 165 days strike of anthracite miners is settled... President Coolidge signs (February 26) Revenue Act to reduce income taxes, surtaxes and other taxes... Air Commerce Act gives (May 20) Department of Commerce control over licensing of aircraft and pilots, establishes airports)...

Mail service is started between Chicago, St. Louis by pilot Charles A. Lindbergh for Robertson Aircraft (evolves as American Airlines)... Robert H. Goddard tests first liquid fuel rocket... Railway Labor Act creates National Railroad Adjustment Board with members from carriers and unions to settle disputes (requires employers to bargain with employees, prohibits discrimination against union members, provides grievance and arbitration procedures, "cooling off" periods, fact finding and mediation)...

Williamsburg, first settled, VA, in 1632, is restored with Rockefeller financing to original Colonial appearance (pioneers evolution of theme parks)... American Arbitration Assn. is formed... Harry Lipsig opens law office, evolves by 1988 as U.S.' largest personal-injury, product-liability firm by winning 95% of cases.

Business Events

Purolator currier service is started by Brady family, acquired by Emery Air Freight in 1987 for $323 million... While carrying airmail Western Air Express starts scheduled passenger service between Los Angeles, Salt

Lake City (merges in 1930 with 1929 Transcontinental Air Transport to launch coast-to-coast air as Transcontinental & Western Air, T.W.A. and TWA in 1950 as Trans World Airlines)... Thorndike Deland opens pioneering headhunting office in NYC to recruit executives for retailers (becomes sideline for management consulting firms of McKinsey & Co. and Booz Allen & Hamilton)... First U.S. truck concrete-mixer is operated... Independent Grocers' Alliance, IGA, organizes to do purchasing for members, 3,000-odd stores in 1988 as U.S.' 4th largest food retailer... Goodyear Tire & Rubber starts making tires for Sears, Roebuck...

After 11 years selling groceries to Idaho farmers, Samuel Skaggs, assisted by broker Charles Merrill, incorporates business as Safeway Stores (acquires some 1,400 grocery outlets of Pacific Northwest chain of MacMann in 1931, operates 2,338 grocery stores worldwide as U.S.' largest in 1986 when $4.25 billion leveraged buyout is engineered to avoid hostile takeover)... Despite waiting list of some 50,000 buyers for Model Ts, Henry Ford shuts down automobile production to fight GM's Chevrolet in low-price market (retools for new Model A car at cost of some $250 million)... Former advertising man Harry Scherman starts Book-of-the-Month Club... After acquiring radio stations of AT&T, RCA creates National Broadcasting Co. to operate Red, Blue networks - Blue basis for ABC in 1943... Modern Slater food service management business is started by John Slater on taking over operation of fraternity's dining room...

After working as broker's clerk in 1904, speculating to earn first success with some $30,000, roaming world, marrying daughter of well-to-do California businessman, and working for Wall Street brokerage firm as office manager after W.W. I, Bernard E. Smith, "Sell-Em Ben," buys seat on New York Stock Exchange with $150,000 from personal funds and loans from rich clients to trade for himself (is forced to sell interests in 1929 at great loss, sells short in 1930 to become leading bear raider of decade, invests profits in Canadian and Alaskan gold mines - price to rise from $20 to $35.30/ounce by 1934)... In gaining 30% of automobile market of General Motors passes Ford for first time...

Ford workers are granted 8-hour day, 5-day work week... American Basketball League is formed (-1931)... Some 449 million shares of stock are traded on New York Stock Exchange during year (climbs to 576 million in 1927, 920 million in 1928 and 1.24 billion in 1929)... American Home Products is started (hires Alvin Bush as chairman in 1934, diversifies by acquiring 34 drug, food companies to pioneer conglomerate movement with 60 firms by 1948, beats rivals in 1988 to acquire A.H. Robins, $5 billion health care business in Chapter 11, for some $3.2 billion in AHP stock)... Associated Telephone Utilities is formed to serve subscribers in Wisconsin and Long Beach, CA (evolves as General Telephone & Electronics in 1951)... Cannon introduces colored towels with decorative designs (uses professional designer from Macy's to advise on motifs)... In this time J. Walter Thompson agency advertises Fleischmann's Yeast as source of vitamins and natural laxative to overcome staid image of product as "Soul of Bread" (increases sales by some 130% from 1923 to highlight innovative advertising in 1920s)...

Corning Glass invents "ribbon" machine to replace traditional hand-blowing process in making glass... Mill owners form Cotton Textile Institute as national trade association to revive industry with economic stabilization, voluntary self-regulation (is opposed by members refusing to accept production and pricing policies until adoption of NRA codes in 1933)... "Union-Management Cooperation in the Railway Industry" is subject at meeting of Taylor Society (discusses success of Baltimore & Ohio plan)... Sophie Haas, later Gimbel, is employed by Saks Fifth Avenue in Salon Moderne (becomes pioneering U.S. fashion designer with Gilbert Adrian and Edith Head dressing film stars)... General Motors establishes group insurance plan for workers (also provides employee's savings and investment plan, preferred stock subscription plan, several recreational and educational plans)... Montgomery Ward exhibits merchandise shown in mail-order catalogs (starts retail stores when customers want to buy displayed goods - 517 by 1929 and 610 by 1931)...

Charles D. Dickerson starts Northwest Airlines... Varney Airlines gets air-mail contract for Elko, NV, to Pasco, WA, (obtains contract in 1929 to serve Portland, Seattle, and Spokane, is absorbed in 1930s by Boeing's United Aircraft and Transport - United Airlines in 1934)... After winning government contract for transcontinental mail service, 1917 Boeing Airplane Co. forms Boeing Air Transport to carry passengers from Chicago to San Francisco (after 1934 anti-trust suit divests subsidiary which becomes independent United Airlines)... Santa Fe Railroad starts daily service between Los Angeles, Chicago... Vitaphone features music in first talkie... Check radioed from London is cashed in NYC, first in history... Investor Joseph P. Kennedy acquires control of Film Booking Office (moves operation to Hollywood, acquires control of Keith-Albee-Orpheum theater chain in 1927, leaves stock market before Crash, acquires wealth during 1929-33 by selling short)...

After bankruptcy of car business Edward V. Rickenbacker organizes Florida Airways (after selling airline to Juan Trippe buys control of Indianapolis Motor Speedway in 1927 - president to 1945, joins General Motors in 1928 as assistant sales manager of Cadillac, becomes vice president of GM's new Fokker Aircraft division in 1929-32)...

Accountant C.R. Smith becomes assistant treasurer of Texas-Louisiana Power (becomes head of utility's Texas Air Transport carrying mail between Dallas, Brownsville and Houston, becomes vice president of Southern Air Transport, consolidation of airlines in area, after acquisition by Aviation Co. in 1929 becomes vice president of new American Airways in 1930 - president of new American Airlines in 1934-42)... William S. Paley, vice president of father's Congress Cigar business, negotiates radio advertising contract - success despite opposition of father and uncle (purchases United Independent Broadcasters, network of 12 stations, in 1927, forms Columbia Broadcasting System in 1928 to operate 70 stations in 1930 and 114 in 1940, starts raiding NBC shows for talent in 1935)...

Jack Frye, after operating flying school and air taxi service, becomes president of Aero Corp. of California (in 1927 starts regular service between Los Angeles, Tuscon and El Paso to evolve as Standard Air Lines in 1929, becomes vice president of Western Air Express in 1930, after 2nd merger in 1930 to form Transcontinental and Western Air starts Transcontinental's first passenger service in 1930 - mail service in 1931, becomes president of T.W.A. for 1934-47)... "Cash and Carry" Pyle forms American Football League, Red Grange star attraction (-1926)...

Lawyer William M. Allen assists in creating Boeing Air Transport (serves as president 1945-70 to make Boeing world's No. 1 manufacturer of planes)... DuPont budgets funds for research, mainly in chemical physics (hires Harvard's Wallace H. Carothers as head of "pure" science laboratory, patents nylon in 1937)... Henry Ford: <u>Today</u> <u>and</u> <u>Tomorrow</u> (advises manufacturers to scrap warehouses to minimize flow of materials, to use small plants for efficiency, staff new operations with new people, use profits to raise wages and lower prices and pay according to ability, advocates flexibility in assigning workers to jobs, asserts overseas producers can only undersell U.S. firms when domestic prices are "stupidly high," and predicts competition will force reorganization and replanning of these firms).

1927

General Events

McNary-Haugen bill requires (February 11) Government to purchase agricultural surpluses for resale in world market, vetoed by President Coolidge... Federal Radio Commission is created (February 23) to regulate new industry... In <u>Spirit</u> <u>of</u> <u>St.</u> <u>Louis</u> Charles A. Lindbergh is first to make solo flight from NYC to Paris, covers 3,600 miles in 33.5 hours...

Harvard Business School is first university to offer course in business history... Massachusetts is first state to require auto insurance... Federal Trade Commission finds Adolph Zukor, Jesse Lasky guilty of film trust conspiracy... Television broadcasts are tested successfully in NYC... Fox Studios exhibits Movietone to synchronize sound with moving pictures (licenses process to MGM, Paramount, United Artists in 1928)...

Army Air Corp officers Lester Maitland, Albert Hengenberger in Fokker Trimotor complete first flight of some 2,400 miles from California to Hawaii in 25 hours, 50 minutes... Editor William White: "The real revolutionist is advertising man, whose stimulation of mass desire and demands results in mass production and buying... Could I control advertising publications of this country I would control entire land"...

U.S. Supreme Court rules bootleggers must file income tax returns... After 1924 study at Western Electric's Hawthorne plant in Chicago proves inconclusive in determining effects of lighting on production, pioneering research study, funded by Rockefeller Foundation, is started by Elton Mayo, Friz Roethlisberger of Harvard Graduate School of Business to investigate effects of employee behavior on productivity (-1932)...

Governor Benjamin Strong reduces Federal Reserve discount rate to help friend, Governor Norman of Bank of England (causes fall in prices of secondary stocks)... McFadden Banking Bill regulates branch banking (permits national banks to start branches within their municipal territories, is followed by 1970 act to allow banks to have consumer-finance, business-loan offices in other states and 1982 act to permit acquisitions of ailing banks in other states... of some 15,000 banks in 1984 Citicorp largest with 947 offices in 40 states, 11 banks in Canada and about 300 in Britain)... Nevada establishes residence of 3 months, 6 months since 1915, as legal requirement for divorce (adopts device used by Indiana, Dakotas in 1800s to improve business)...

Goodyear Tire & Rubber patents synthetic rubber... Commander Richard E.

Byrd, crew fly first official transatlantic air mail to France... John D., Mark D. Rust of Texas invent mechanical cotton picker (demonstrate machine in 1936 to prove it can pick 100 times faster than field hands - harvests 10% of 1949 crop and nearly 90% in 1969).

Business Events

Remington-Rand is created by merger of 1886 Remington typewriter business, 1925 Rand-Kardex, 1909 Powers Accounting Machine Co. and other firms (merges with Sperry Gyroscope to create Sperry-Rand in 1955)... Lux uses testimonials of Hollywood stars to advertise toilet soap... Perkins Products, mail-order purveyor of flavorings, spices and other household products of Hastings, NE, creates Kool-Aid powdered beverage business (with success moves to Chicago in 1931 to concentrate on drink business)... J. Willard Marriott, partner open franchised A&W Root Beer stand in Washington, DC (opens 2nd 1927, drops root beer business in winter of 1927 to open first Hot Shoppe with Mexican food - 7 units by 1932, forms airline catering division in 1937)...

"Seven Group" is organized, NYC, as informal alliance of criminal gangs, Arnold Rothstein and Johnny Torrio key figures (establishes connections with mobs in other cities)... Present Lockheed Aircraft business is started by John K. Northrop, others (resigns in 1928 to do research on all-wing aircraft, after forming Avion Corp. in 1930, acquired by United Aircraft and Transportation, starts Northrop Corp. in 1932 to design and build military airplanes)... American College of Life Underwriters organizes to establish certification procedures for members... Commercial telephone service is started between NYC, London, extended to major European cities by 1929... Gail Borden business introduces homogenized milk to U.S. market...

1853 Seth Thomas Clock Co. makes first electric clocks (merges with Western Clock of Illinois in 1931 to form General Time)... American Railway Express, airlines start air express service... Gerald Gidwitz starts Helene Curtis cosmetic business to supply beauty salons (enters consumer market in 1940s)... Wildcatter "Dad" Joiner discovers East Texas oil field (sells rights in 1930 to H.L. Hunt, former gambler)...

Wildcatter and gambler Clint Murchison develops oil and gas field in West Texas (forms M&M Pipeline to carry oil to railroad, after capping gas wells as of no value creates first U.S. market for natural gas in 1928 when people of Wink, TX, agree to buy product at bargain prices, forms Southern Union Gas in 1929 to supply gas to Albuquerque, starts American Liberty Oil in 1930 with partner and $200, selling to partner in 1947 for $6 million after clearing some $415 million, and starts new partnership with old friend Sid Richardson, others to build oil pipeline from East Texas field to Tyler refinery, sells producing oil fields to ARCO in 1934 - retains 4.4 million barrels on gamble oil prices will rise to net some $5 million, gambles in 1938 in selling oil leases with stipulation that he would receive 50% ownership when buyer's investment has been paid - successful when prices rise)...

Harley Earl, designer of custom auto bodies for Hollywood movie stars, is hired as consultant by General Motors to design La Salle car (becomes head of GM's styling section with success - first in industry, retires in 1959)... Automobile industry is composed of 44 firms, 102 in 1923...

Procter & Gamble pioneers product management system in assigning specific manager responsibility for Camay soap business... Upton Sinclair: <u>Oil!</u> (describes abuse of power by petroleum firms)...

Joe C. Thompson starts modern Southland grocery business, TX, to sell milk, eggs, bread at chain of ice houses (adds gasoline pumps in early 1930s - flops, revives idea in 1963 - success in mid-1970s with bargain-rate gas at chain's 7-Eleven stores, evolves as 12th largest U.S. retail business by 1987 with 8,202 convenience stores, 4,102 licensed, in 49 states and 11 foreign countries)...

Kaiser Paving Co. obtains contract for 200-mile highway in Cuba, its first major construction project outside U.S. (-1931)... Abe Saperstein organizes Harlem Globetrotters as touring basketball team (plays first game in Hinckley, IL, is acquired in 1967 on death by Metromedia)... Jersey Standard is formed as holding company with central headquarters, including coordinating and budgeting departments, to oversee operating activities (is implemented by World War II)...

AT&T makes television transmission between NYC, Washington (is followed by Atlantic transmission in 1928 by John Baird of Scotland, regular BBC transmissions in 1930 and by France in 1935)... During week of December 3rd more shares of stock are sold than during any previous week in history of New York Stock Exchange... Macy's establishes Bureau of Standards, probably first formal product testing activity of any U.S. retail store... Warner Brothers produces first "talkie" feature, <u>Jazz Singer</u>, with Al Jolson (revolutionizes movie industry)... New York Stock Exchange expands for world trading... General Motors declares dividend of $65,250,000, world's largest... Average U.S. wages are highest in world at $1,280/year...

First woman buys seat on New York Stock Exchange... With backing of Lehman Brothers Juan Trippe, others form Aviation Corp. of America with capitalization of $300,000 (joins Pan American Airways of 1927 to form holding company of Atlantic, Gulf and Caribbean and New York Airways - Pan Am operating business with Trippe president (to avoid crowded competition in domestic market starts service with mail contract for 90-mile route between Key West and Havana with Fokker Trimotors - service to Panama by 1929, adds Grace Airways, Panagra, and New York, Rio and Buenos Aires lines in 1929, serves first in-flight meals in 1929 and hot meals in 1936, acquires 2 Alaskan lines in 1932 and China National Aviation in 1933)...

With savings from odd jobs Milton J. Petrie opens hosiery store, Cleveland, builds chain to sell moderately priced young women's clothing (goes bankrupt in 1937, finds niche after W.W.II with shopping-center stores selling simple, trendy clothes to young women - 1,600 stores by 1988)...

Clifford Ball starts airline, becomes Pennsylvania Airlines in 1930 (absorbs 1929 Kohler Aviation in 1934 and 1934 Central Airlines to form Pennsylvania-Central in 1936)... William Randolph Hearst hires Merryle Rukeyser as financial columnist to "humanize and simplify" coverage of business and finance, syndicated to nearly 200 papers for over 30 years.

1928

General Events

Communist-dominated Workers' Party nominates William Z. Foster for President... Merchant Marine Act provides (May 22) subsidies to private shipping companies... Muscle Shoals Bill gives (May 25) government control of Tennessee hydroelectric system... General Electric demonstrates TV broadcasts to home receivers... U.S. passes (May 27) record peacetime budget of $4.5 billion... Some 65,000 students are enrolled in business courses at 89 universities, colleges... Brookings Institute for Government Research is formed as merger of 1916 Institute for Government Research, 1922 Institute for Economics and 1924 Graduate School of Economics and Government... Fourth International is formed in NYC by Communist supporters (follows first in 1864 at London, 2nd in 1889 at Paris, and 3rd in 1917 in Russia)...

Federal Trade Commission investigates holding companies (completes 96 volumes in 1934-35 to report state regulations ineffective)... Teleprinters, teletypewriters are used in U.S., Britain, Germany... William T. Foster, Wadill Catchings: Road to Plenty (predicts possibility of economic woes, advocates increases in total payrolls to stimulate effective purchasing power and increases in spending by Federal Government to offset inability of business to encourage demand)...

Stuart Chase, F.J. Schlink: Your Money's Worth (attacks advertising as dishonest, proposes consumer testing service to gather objective product information - impetus for consumer-education groups and consumers' movement in the 1930s)... Edwin Link, father of simulator technology, uses organ bellows and suspended box to duplicate motion of airplane in flight, evolves with use by airlines to train pilots with advance flight simulators and Disneyland's Star Tours ride in 1987.

Business Events

4,790,270 shares are traded (March 28) on New York Stock Exchange, 4,820,840 on May 16, some 5 million on June 12, 6 million on November 16, and 6,954,000 on November 23... Studebaker acquires Pierce-Arrow automobile business... Colgate and Palmolive-Peet businesses are consolidated... Helena Rubinstein incorporates retail, wholesale cosmetic business (opens elegant NY salon for health and skin care in 1936, opens salon in Rio de Janerio in 1940)... After failing in storage battery business twice, Paul D. Galvin start Galvin Manufacturing Corp., becomes Motorola later, to make radios (acquires success with car radios in 1932, Bill Lear is chief engineer, portable radios and "Handi-Talkies" in W.W. II, as $6.7 billion electronics giant in 1988 is U.S.' largest supplier of semiconductors)...

Pioneering open-end (others of time as "closed-end" types with Goldman Sachs Trading Corp. in 1928-29 as largest with $330 million) Mutual Investment Fund in industrial and power securities, becomes Wellington Fund in 1935, is created by Walter L. Morgan (creates Wellington Corp. in 1929 to provide fund and clients with administrative and investment advisory services, starts retail selling organization in 1931, operates in 1934 with assets of some $500,000 - $1.6 billion of resources and 350,000 shareholders by 1960s)... Fleers Corporation of Philadelphia invents Double Bubble gum...

William Dreyer starts ice cream business in California (invents Rocky Road flavor, is acquired by new owners in 1977 to go from some $6 million in sales to $84 million in 1984 by advertising quality product and exploiting market between supermarket and super-premium brands)... George Eastman exhibits first color motion pictures... T.C. Fry: <u>Probability</u> <u>and Its Engineering</u> (discusses queueing theory)... "Steamboat Willy," featuring Mickey Mouse, is first film production of Walt Disney (produces "Snow White" in 1937 as first animated feature film)... Philosophy of slain gambler Arnold Rothstein, underworld must operate like big business and develop image of respectability, is implemented in NYC by Frank Costello, "Lucky" Luciano and Meyer Lansky, Bugsy Siegel an aide...

Beverly Wilshire Hotel opens for rich and famous in Beverly Hills, CA... Ralph C. Davis: <u>The Principles of Factory Organization and Management</u>... A.P. Giannini forms Transamerica Corp. as holding company for interests in real estate, insurance, and other financial adventures (on traveling to Europe in 1931 puts New York banker Elisha Walker in charge - starts dismantling empire, returns to regain control with people crusade, survives 1930s by financing U.S. dam projects in West)... After starting as small group of 4-5 stores to do cooperative buying, Ace Hardware incorporates in Chicago (grows to chain of 41 stores in 1934, about 3,000 in 1967 and over 5,000 outlets in 1988)... U.S. Navy contracts Goodyear Zeppelin to build rigid airships <u>Akron</u>, is destroyed in 1922 storm, and <u>Macon</u>, crashes in 1935 with wind gust (flies 168 blimps during W.W.II, builds 4 largest blimps, 403 feet, in late 1950s, plans YEZ-2A, world's largest at 425 feet, for flight in 1992)...

David Sarnoff of RCA, Joseph P. Kennedy create Radio-Keith-Orpheum Corp. RKO, to produce and distribute movies with interests from RCA, American Pathe and Kennedy's Keith-Albee-Orpheum theater circuit and Film Booking Office... Clement M. Keys creates North American Aviation as holding company of various aircraft manufacturing companies and airlines (develops Transcontinental Air Transport for combined air-rail service between New York and Los Angeles, merges with Western Air Express in 1930 for all-air service between New York, Los Angeles)...

To supplement regular canning business, Gerber produces strained baby foods for grocery stores with national advertising to replace traditional liquid diets sold by pharmacies on prescription (goes international 1962, by 1988 sells 187 varieties of baby food, 71% of market, along with 116 day-care centers and insurance after divesting trucking, toy and furniture businesses)...

Thomas E. Braniff, insurance business owner, finances airline operating between Oklahoma and Tulsa (sells business to Universal Aviation in 1929, starts Braniff Airways in 1930 to operate between Texas and Chicago)... Borg-Warner is formed by 4 automobile parts firms (develops new process in 1930 to make truck wheel hubs - wins patent infringement suit with Budd Wheel, diversifies with Norge Division to sell washing machines in 1932, flat irons in 1933 and stoves in 1934, designs and produces amphibious tank in 1941 for Army, develops automatic transmission for cars in 1948, forms Borg-Warner Acceptance Corp. in 1952, acquires York Corp. in 1956 to develop air conditioning for cars, acquires manufacturer of giant pumps in 1957, records sales of some $600 million in 1958)...

Donald Douglas starts Douglas Aircraft business (introduces DC-1 in 1931, DC-2 in 1933 before making popular DC-3 for airline commerce in 1935)... Revere Copper and Brass is created by merger of 6 firms, including Taunton-New Bedford Copper from Paul Revere's foundry in early 1800s (-1982)... Richard B. Franklin, Carroll B. Larrabee: <u>Packages that Sell</u>... Bechtel, Kaiser form first significant U.S. joint construction venture to supply rock ballast for Western Pacific Railroad... National City Bank of New York is first commercial bank to grant personal loans (starts branch offices in 1929)...

Horatio N. Slater, III, descendent of Samuel Slater, starts Slater Mfg., SC, as first U.S. mill to make rayon cloth... "Cash-and-Carry" Pyle promotes 3,422-mile transcontinental "Bunion Derby" foot race with accompanying side show (despite $360,000 in prize money for some 2,000 men and women runners, flops)... Nelson Doubleday becomes head of family's publishing business (adopts strategy of mass production for distribution of inexpensive books to mass market, develops chain of 26 retail stores, acquires Literary Guild of America in 1934 - by 1947 largest U.S. publisher, is acquired, excluding New York Mets baseball franchise, in 1986 by West German communications conglomerate of Bertelsman AG for some $500 million)...

Stockbroker Charles Merrill, Lingan Warren start MacMann grocery chain in Pacific Northwest (merge 1,400 units with Safeway after acquiring controlling interest in 1931 from founder Samuel M. Skaggs)... Daven Corp., NJ, announces home television sets for sale at $75... Seat on New York Stock Exchange sells (October 10) for record $450,000, $550,000 on November 23rd... While serving as president of Sego Milk Products, Stoddard Lumber, Utah Construction and Amalgamated Sugar, Mormon Marriners Eccles becomes president of First Security Corp. with 26 banks in Utah, Idaho and Wyoming (manages finances so no depositors lose money with Crash of 1929, becomes Assistant Secretary of Treasury in 1933 and chairman of Federal Reserve Board 1934-48)...

After being forced out of chain of self-service Piggly Wiggly stores, Clarence Saunders starts new grocery chain called Clarence Saunders, Sole Owner of My Name (after becoming millionaire for 2nd time declares bankruptcy in 1930)... Pitcairn Aviation starts mail service between New Brunswig, NJ, and Atlanta (becomes Eastern Air Transport in 1930 with extended service)... WGY of Schenectady, NY, broadcasts first scheduled television in U.S... Although viewed by Henry Ford as immoral, son Edsel starts Ford's Universal Credit Corp. to assist buyers in purchasing cars... Lew Hahn, head of Hahn Department Stores, starts acquiring other department stores, such as Bonwit Teller, Brooks Brothers and Jordan Marsh, to create Allied Stores - 165 stores and sales of $1.9 billion by 1977 (is acquired in 1986 by Canadian developer Robert Campeau who sells most of Allied's store divisions to foreign buyers to pay debt)...

Coca-Cola enters international market by sending 1,000 cases of "official soft drink" with U.S. team to Amsterdam's Olympic Games (acquires licensed rights for 1988 Calgary games for $300 million)... First gambling ship off Southern California coast anchors just outside 3-mile limit... Coast to Coast hardware chain starts, expands nationwide after W.W. II with some 1,450 stores by 1988... After shutting down production to re-tool, Ford Motor makes Model A cars to compete with popular Chevrolets (-1931)...

GE's WGY in Schenectady, NY, gives first television schedule... While working in family's china factory, Chicago, Jim Warsaw makes souvenir ashtrays with logo of Chicago Cubs baseball team to sell in Wrigley Field, license from Chicago Bears in 1938 (as Sports Specialties pioneers market in 1988 of hundreds of rivals selling licensed wares of sport teams)... Rapid Air Lines forms (-1929)... After working a grain and hay business when he was 19, Charles Sammons, 1898-1988, enters insurance field, TX (forms Reserve Life Ins. in 1938, forms Sammons Enterprises in 1962 to manage various firms to become billionaire).

1929

General Events

Federal Reserve Board forbids (February 2) member banks to grant loans to anyone using money to buy stock on margin... On March 26 some 8.2 million shares of stock are traded on New York Stock Exchange... Congress meets (April 15) in special session to resolve nation's economic problems...

Agricultural Marketing Act establishes (June 15) federal farm board to aid farmers' cooperatives, sell agricultural surpluses at more stable prices... On September 3rd, Dow Jones Industrial Average reaches all-time high of 381.17 (drops to 260.64 on October 28 after falling 38.33 points and low of 41.22 on July 8, 1932)... On October 24, Black Thursday, some 13 million shares are sold on New York Stock Exchange (results in futile attempts by wealthy investors, such as House of Morgan and John D. Rockefeller, to stem decline of prices and in sales of 16 million shares on following Black Tuesday - stock losses of $30 billion by November 13)... U.S. farmers form $50 million cooperative marketing association... Bell Laboratories demonstrates system to transmit television pictures in color...

Consumers Research, initiated by Stuart Chase, launches consumer movement with 1,200 members (expands to 25,000 members in 1931 and 45,000 in 1933)... New York, Oklahoma adopt extensive programs of old-age benefits... Tombstone, AZ, celebrates first annual Helldorado Celebration to rejuvenate mining community... Philadelphia Savings Fund Society's building is built, first in U.S. to reflect international style of architecture with steel frame, glass-curtain walls...

Some 500,000 U.S. tourists visit foreign countries... Battelle Memorial Institute is created to do industrial research, education with funds from iron-and-steel fortune... Trade Union Unit League is formed with assistance of Communist supporters... 6.21 mile Moffat Tunnel beneath Continental Divide opens (allows skiers from Denver to reach nearby slopes, first ski trains in 1938)... Abbott Payson Usher: A History of Mechanical Inventions (studies technology as human enterprise)... After planting tulips in 1927, Holland, MI, sponsors first annual spring tulip festival, attracts some 500,000 tourists yearly in 1980s.

Business Events

Henry Ford creates 240-acre Greenfield Village in Dearborn, MI, pioneering theme park with settings and buildings of 1600s-1800s... Delta Airlines is started in Monroe, LA (by 1940 expands across South and moves headquarters to Atlanta, GA)... Steelmaker Tom Girdler, financier Cyrus

Eaton create Republic Steel... Henry Ford acquires Lincoln Motor Car Co. from receivorship (ousts Henry Leland)... Howard Ahmanson, pioneer of U.S. savings and loan industry, avoids 1929 Crash by selling stocks early and retaining father's National Insurance Co. (specializes during 1930s in insuring foreclosed properties, after W.W. II builds Home Savings & Loan Assn. by intricate acquisitions in Southern California as nation's largest)...

Transcontinental Air Transport starts first continental air service with rail connections, uses flight attendents between NYC, Los Angeles (takes 36 hours with 7 stops with $351.94 for one-way ticket)... Ford Motor Co. contracts to build plant in Soviet Union to produce 100,000 cars/year... Ross McIntyre consolidates his Twentieth Century stores with 4 other chains to operate MacMarr stores with 400 outlets in 5 western states (merges with Safeway chain in 1931)...

General Motors acquires Opel AG, Germany's largest car maker... Northland Transportation, Greyhound Lines in 1930, acquires fleet of double-decker buses (takes 5 days, 14 hours to travel from San Francisco to NYC)... To bolster economy Ford Motor Co. increases wages from $6 to $7/day... 400 U.S. business leaders form council to foster trade... Largest U.S. bank merger of $2 billion is made by National Bank of Commerce, Guarantee Trust... Universal Airlines shows movies on scheduled flight between Minneapolis, Chicago... 1884 Willamette Tent & Awning business in Portland, OR, starts making ski apparel as White Stag... Arthur G. Sherman starts Covered Wagon Co. to make mobile homes, sells some 32,000 of market's 200,000 by 1936...

In order to expand 1925 small ice cream business, Howard Johnson, lacking capital, sells franchises for use of name, supplies (expands to 25 restaurants by 1935 and 100 along East Coast by 1940, opens first motel in 1954, evolves with 350 restaurants, 68 turnpike restaurants and 125 lodges and hotels when acquired in 1980 by Britain's Imperial Group, is acquired in 1985 by Marriott Corp. and Prime Motor Inns for $314 million in cash)... William Benton, Chester Bowles start advertising agency... Willamette-Ersted Co., Hyster later, is started in Portland, OR, to make materials-handling equipment...

After reviving bankrupt Portland-Tillamook Stage Line and selling in 1928 to Southern Pacific's trucking firm, Consolidated Truck Lines is started in Portland, OR, by Leland James, others to combine small trucking operations into integrated system (operates 85 trucks in 1930 over 1,836 miles of road - 7,700 miles in 1939 as Consolidated Freightways, produces first Freightliner trucks in 1940 - sold to Mercedes Benz in 1981, launches CF Air Freight Service in 1970, evolves as industry leader by 1979 to operate 267 terminals in 47 states and Canada)... Wisconsin Cheese Producers' Federation organizes with 299 members to market non-perishable products throughout U.S...

Aviation Co. is organized with $40 million from Lehman Brothers, Harriman interests (acquires 80 subsidiaries with 9,000 miles of air routes, consolidates lines in 1931 as American Airways, American Airlines in 1934, is acquired by E.L. Cord of Century Airlines in 1933 and by Victor Emanuel in 1937)... Woolworth's variety business starts national advertising campaign... Kelvinator sells refrigerators for $175... Dutch-born A.L. van Ameringen, William T. Haebler of U.S. start International

Flavors & Fragrances to develop smells, tastes for cosmetic, food industries... Grumman Aircraft Engineering Corp. is started on Long Island as repair business for amphibious aircraft (evolves as giant aerospace business)...

AT&T is first corporation to record annual revenue over $1 billion... Aluminum furniture is introduced to market... Filene's of Boston, Abraham & Straus of New York and F. & R. Lazarus of Columbus, OH, form Federated Department Stores (pioneers trend whereby 60% of 4,221 department stores by 1929 in chains, after bidding war sells 650 department and specialty stores in 36 states to Canada's Campeau Corp. in 1988 for $6.58 billion, sells I. Magnin and Bullock stores to rival R.H. Macy for $1.1 billion, promises Filene's and Foley's to May Department Stores)... New York Curb Exchange, forerunner of American Stock Exchange, is formed from Curb Market...

National Steel is formed by Weirton Steel, Great Lakes Steel and part of M.A. Hanna Co... Harlan Sanders opens filling station, KY (provides meals for hungry travelers as side line, with success opens restaurant - endorsed by critic Duncan Hines in 1939, develops new method of cooking chicken with pressure cooker in 1939)... French-born Raymond Loewy starts industrial design studio to style products for business clients (designs Hupomobile in 1934, Greyhound Scenic Cruiser in 1940, Pepsodent toothpaste tube with elegant look in 1945, International Harvester logo in 1946, post-War Studebaker car and Exxon emblem in 1950s)... McGraw-Hill publishes _Business Week_, generates revenues of $100 million in 1980s...

Charles Atlas, nee Angelo Siciliano of Brooklyn, and Charles Rollman incorporate to merchandise physique-building program of isotonic exercises... Johns Manville insulation business adopts collective bargaining (adopts 8-hour day and 40-hour work week for management, starts surveying employees' attitudes, publishes annual and semi-annual financial reports to stockholders in 1938)... U.S. produces over 4.5 million cars, France 211,000, Britain 182,000 and Germany 117,000...

After introducing German process for canning ham in 1927, Jay Hormel becomes president of family's Minnesota packing business (-1954, after strike recognizes independent union in 1933, promotes new chili con carne product in 1935 with Mexican dancers, introduces Spam in 1937 to produce 3-4 million cans yearly in 1980s - by 1940 some 70% of urban Americans using canned meats after 18% in 1937, introduces special wage plan in late 1930s to reward productivity with fewer hours - model for packing industry, starts joint earnings plan for employees in 1938 to supplement regular income with stock dividends)... Boeing builds 80A trimotor biplane for transcontinental passenger flights by its United Airlines...

General Motors acquires Fokker Aircraft, becomes General Aviation Corp. and absorbed by North American Aviation in 1933 (also purchases 24% interest in Bendix Aviation and acquires Allison engineering business, originally machine shop making parts for racing cars)... Chicago accounting firm of Frazer & Torbet is hired to revamp management structure of Sears, Roebuck (recommends 4 territorial officers and 33 district managers - scrapped in 1932, while continuing mail-order business as functional organization starts territorial decentralization for retail stores in 1935-48)...

Walt Disney licenses Mickey Mouse emblem to tablet manufacturer for $300, pioneers licensing industry of some $5 billion in 1985 (forms licensing activity in 1932, licenses Mickey Mouse Watch in 1933 - some 1,600 licenses for nearly 8,000 items by 1985)... After seeing game of rank-and-file numbers at Georgia carnival, Edwin F. Lowe devises game of Bingo (starts making and distributing contest cards popular with church fund-raising, is used in 1951 to help save town of Renovo, PA)... Wisconsin Aluminum Foundry sells All-American Pressure Cookers... U.S.' share of world manufacturing output is 43.3%, 31.8% in 1932, 35.1% in 1937, and 28.7% in 1938... Gorst Air Transport forms (-1935), as does Curtiss Flying Service (-1932), United States Airways (-1934) and Southwest Air Fast Express (-1938).

1930s

General Events

California Agricultural Experiment Station and Bureau of Agricultural Engineering develops combine for harvesting sugarbeets (harvests 7% of 1944 crop and 100% in 1958)... Mississippi starts "Balance Agriculture with Industry" program for economic growth (becomes prototype for other southern states).

Business Events

Socony Vacuum and Sears start formal management training programs... Henry Ford builds 3 plants to process soy beans (pioneers U.S. industry)... Walter Rautensterauch develops break-even chart.

1930

General Events

President Hoover (March 7): "Prosperity is just around corner"... Public Buildings Act grants (March 31) $203 million for construction projects... Congress appropriates (April 4) some $300 million in federal aid to states for road construction... Despite opposition of 1,028 economists, President Hoover signs (June 17) Hawley-Smoot Bill to raise duties on imports by up to 50% (results in retaliatory measures by other nations to protest prohibitive duties and decline of U.S. exports by 2/3 in 1932)...

Thomas Edison tests first U.S. electric passenger train is between Hoboken and Montclair, NJ... Due to rising unemployment State Department prohibits (September 9) immigration of almost all foreign workers... President Hoover asks (December 2) Congress for $150 million to ease unemployment with public construction (receives $116 million)... NYC installs traffic lights, devised in 1923 by black businessman Garrett A. Morgan... Labor leaders lobby Congress to ban all Soviet imports...

President Hoover establishes Committee for Unemployment Relief... At MIT Vannevar Bush completes building differential analyzer to solve differential equations (stimulates international interest in analog computing)... U.S. Patent & Trademark Office is permitted to patent new plants produced by grafts, cuttings or other asexual methods... By accident Lawrence Hyland, Naval Research Laboratory, discovers radio shortwaves react to presence of airplanes (launches U.S. radar research – practical in 1940 with magnetron)... Unionism is seen on rodeo circuit as professional contestants seek more prize money... Harvard creates Department of Industrial Research, pioneers new field of industrial sociology...

William Foster: "Russia will eclipse the U.S. industrially in 15 years or sooner"... U.S. Supreme Court: Texas and New Orleans Railroad v. Brotherhood of Railroad Clerks (rules railroad must stop using company union to interfere with employees' rights)... Congress passes Airmail Act to develop coordinated airline systems by eliminating small, under-capitalized carriers (promotes passenger- travel by paying carriers for space instead of pounds carried, results in formation of new lines by mergers to end intense competition for airmail contracts)...

President Hoover proposes relief program with federal leadership for national voluntary effort... Paul Rowe invents phone-answering device, not commercial until 1960s... AFL: "Labor's Principles of Scientific Management" (urges acceptance of approach)... C.W. Kelsey, pioneer automobile inventor, invents rotary tiller.

Business Events

NYC's private Bank of the U.S., some 60 branches and 400,000 depositors, closes (results in indictments of 3 officers for misuse of funds – guilty), one of some 1,300 since Fall of 1929 to close... After merger Transcontinental and Western Air, T.W.A., drops rail connections on coast-to-coast flights (cuts time from 36 to 18 hours by 1934, becomes Trans World Airlines, TWA, in 1950)... "21" Club opens in Manhattan as speakeasy, nightclub after Prohibition ends... Investment broker Charles E. Merrill retires to focus on underwriting and personal banking (starts brokerage business in 1940)... Robert A. Pinkerton, II succeeds father as president of detective agency business (-1967, expands operations to provide security personnel for industry and staff to handle sporting events, political conventions and trade fairs – only 5% of business from insurance investigations by 1967)...

William Zeckendorf sells first real estate property (joins 1922 Webb and Knapp real estate business of NYC in 1937 – president in 1947 to increase holdings from $50 million to $100 million, starts construction subsidiary in 1952, after operating as Manhattan's leading land developer declares bankruptcy in 1965 on loans at interest rates as high as 24%, declares personal bankruptcy in 1968)...

Standard Oil of Indiana starts pioneering program to lease gas stations to managers... Cincinnati Milling Machine develops tracing device to duplicate contours for milling... Crossley introduces rating system to determine number of listeners for radio programs... American Tobacco is required by FTC to stop using testimonials of endorsers not having used product... Game of Monopoly, akin to unpatented Landlord's game of Quaker Elizabeth J. Magie in 1904, is devised by unemployed Charles Darrow (after rejection by Parker Brothers and Selchow & Righter game businesses makes and sells game to prove marketability, is acquired by Parker in 1935 to sell some 20,000 sets/week – some 80 million in 27 countries by 1980s)...

Richard Whitney becomes president of New York Stock Exchange, convicted
in 1938 for irregular stock transactions... A.P. Giannini forms Bank of
America to consolidate banking interests in California, New York, and
Europe (opens London branch in 1931 - 124 branches in 78 countries by
1972, operates with assets of some $6 billion in 1939, retires 1945)...
Merchandise Mart, world's largest commercial building, is built for $32
million in Chicago by Marshall Field department store as warehouse,
wholesale center, acquired in 1945 by Joseph P. Kennedy for $13
million...

After suggestion for supermarket store to Kroger management is rejected,
first true supermarket grocery store, King Cullen Grocery Company Store,
is opened in Queens, Long Island, by Michael Cullen with wholesaler
grocer Harry Socoloff (lures customers with screaming ads of low prices,
is followed in 1932 by Big Bear Store in Elizabeth, NJ, to gross over
$31,000 first day - some $3.873 million in year, in 1933 by Albers
Supermarkets in Cincinnati and Kroger's Pay 'N' Takit stores later - 94
U.S. supermarkets in 24 cities in 1934, 1,200 in 85-odd cities in 1936
and some 33,000 by 1960)...

Industrial Employment Code is drafted to set first standards for
personnel administration... Fred Meyer, operator of local grocery
business in Portland, OR, since 1922, opens world's first self-service
drug store (opens suburban grocery store with parking lot in 1931 - chain
of 69 retail super-stores by 1970s with sales over $1 billion, is
followed in 1934 by super-drug store of Chicago's Walgreens at Tampa, FL,
to pioneer modern drug store selling plethora of goods)... Henry J.
Kaiser provides shipyard workers with health program (provides prepaid
medical service to construction workers on Southern California aqueduct
project, provides coverage to all employees in 1942)...

General Motors announces plans to enter radio industry... World's largest
bank is formed by merger of Chase National with Equitable Trust,
Interstate Trust... Chrysler introduces Plymouth car to compete with
Ford, Chevrolet... First U.S. commercial television is announced in
Chicago by _Daily News_' radio station, Libby McNeill & Libby food business
(states sets will be available from Western Television of Chicago)...
James Dewar, driver of horse-drawn poundcake wagon, creates cream-filled
snack bar called Twinkie (is produced by Continental Baking to sell over
30 billion by 1985)... To provide employment Hershey chocolate business
transforms industrial town of Hershey, PA, into campus setting with
community buildings, hotel, school, office building, sports arena and
football stadium (is targeted in 1937 for CIO sitdown strike in demanding
closed shop - broken-up by club-wielding farmers, is organized by AFL in
1940)... Robert Trent Jones designs his first golf course, over 450
throughout world by 1982... First National Management Conference is held
to discuss, analyze management efficiency, conservation...

Detroit Edison makes last electric car for special order... Auto Ordnance
Co. develops first U.S. commercial food dehydration-freezing process...
On recommendation of Charles F. Kettering, General Motors acquires Winton
Engine Co. and Electro-Motive Corp. for work in developing diesel engine
for locomotives... Richard G. Drew devises strip of transparent
cellophane (introduced by DuPont in 1924) with stickum for Minnesota
Mining & Manufacturing (names product Scotch Tape - used first by mostly
bakers to seal packages)... Geophysists John Johnson, Everette Degolyer

start Geophysical Service in Dallas, TX (after diversification in electronics during World War II becomes Texas Instruments in 1951)...

Goodyear Tire & Rubber adopts 6-hour day... United Airlines uses first women flight attendents on service between San Francisco, Chicago... Airplane ticket from Los Angeles to New York costs some $300... With 15,700 outlets A & P grocery business is largest U.S. chain, rescued from financial woes in 1979-80 by West German conglomerate... Samuel Zemurray swaps stock of 1910 Cuyamel Fruit to gain control of ailing United Fruit (revives business in 1938 with Costa Rican contract, evolves by 1946 with 83,000 employees and 116,000 acres in bananas, 96,000 in sugar and 48,000 in cacao, engineers overthrow of Guatemala's government in 1954 with CIA asssistance to forestall expropriation of plantations, is acquired by AMK Corp. in 1969 to form United Brands)...

Louis B. Mayer, MGM's production head, is highest salaried person in U.S. with almost $1 million (-1937)... Robertson Airplane Service forms (-1933), as does Bowen Air Lines (-1936) and Gilpin Lines (-1934)... Rapid Air Transport forms, joins 1932 Hanford Tri-State Air in 1933 to form Hanford-Rapid Air and Mid-Continental in 1938.

1931

General Events

U.S. Treasury Department predicts (May 2) billion-dollar deficit... Kansas farmers produce (July) bumper crop of wheat, prices collapse (results in some counties granting tax moratorium to aid farmers)... U.S. contracts to build 90 Soviet steel plants... Clyde Pangborn, Hugh Herndon make first non-stop flight over Pacific, cross 4,400 miles from Tokyo to Seattle in 41 hours... Some 827 banks closed in September and October... MIT starts Sloan Fellowship Program as first university resident management development program for business executives, followed by Harvard in 1943, Western Ontario of Canada in 1948, University of Pittsburgh in 1949... Davis-Bacon Act requires construction firms with over $2,000 in government contracts to pay prevailing wages to workers... Airline Pilots Association forms as union... Out-of-work architect Alfred Butts invents Lexico word game (becomes Scrabble in 1947-49)... California is first state to pass "fair trade" law (allows producers to set minimum retail prices for goods)...

Wiley Post, Harold Gally of Australia make first flight round-the-world in single-engine plane, finish 8 days, 15 hours and 51 minutes later... Some 30 experimental television stations operate in U.S... Nevada passes wide-open gambling bill (results in opening of Bank Club in Reno by Bill Graham and Jim McKay, gambling operators in mining camps of Tonopah and Goldfield) and 6-week divorce law for non-residents - at 3 months until Arkansas and Idaho entered market in 1930.

Business Events

George Gallup, professor of advertising and journalism at Northwestern University, makes pioneering market survey of magazine readership for Gardner Cowles, Jr., of Des Moines, hired by Young & Rubicam ad agency in 1932-48 to do market research... Coca-Cola launches ad campaign to promote soft drink for all seasons (creates modern image of Santa

Claus)... T.W.A. starts first air-freight service by shipping livestock from St. Louis to Newark... DuPont announces plans to develop synthetic rubber... Charles Lindbergh starts Pan Am's service to South America... After victory over traditional "Mustache Petes" in Castallammarse War Salvatore Maranzano becomes "Boss of Bosses" of NYC's crime business (creates 5 crime families, Gambino, Genovese, Lucchese, Bonanno and Columbo, to divide City's market - lose power in mid-1980s with competition from some 22 non-Mafia mobs, mostly minorities plus those from Colombia and Jamaica, in NYC-New Jersey area, is slain later in year by "Lucky" Luciano and Vito Genovese)...

Atwater Kent, country's leading producer of quality radios, starts private relief program to assist former employees (closes business in 1936)... After building pyramid public utility empire to serve some 5,000 communities in 32 states, London-born Samuel Insull borrows some $48 million to block stock raid of Cleveland's Cyrus Eaton, others (flees to Europe when empire enters receivership in 1932, after return by force in 1934 is acquitted of charges)... Walter Shewhart: _Economic Control of Quality of Manufactured Product_ (pioneers field of quality control)...

In response to letter from Transcontinental & Western Air, Douglas Aircraft designs DC-1, built as prototype commercial airplane with 2 engines to compete with United Airline's Boeing trimotor plane (produces DC-2 in 1933 for Jack Frye's T.W.A., develops DC-3 in 1935 for C.R. Smith's American Airlines to make commercial air travel feasible)... James D. Mooney, Alan C. Reiley: _Onward Industry_ (proposes principles for studying different organizations)... Eastman Kodak starts program of unemployment insurance... B.F. Goodrich tire business develops first tractor tire for Florida farmers... John Sloan of Chicago devises modern pinball machine, marketed as Ballyhoo by In and Outdoor games (introduces first electric machine in 1933, after operating video games in late 1970s sells arcade-game division of Bally in 1988 when video craze cools)...

Henry S. Dennison: _Organization Engineering_ (proposes using groups to build total organization structure)... After operating San Diego flying service since 1922, T. Claude Ryan starts Ryan Aeronautical to make airplanes (evolves as first volume producer of monoplanes, devises Navy's first jet plane and world's first Vertijet, is acquired by Teledyne in 1969)...

Ted Hustead, 28-year-old Nebraska pharmacist, opens Wall Drug Store, SD, with $3,000 (advertises free ice water and coffee for 5 cents to attract curious travelers - some 20,000 customers on busy summer day)... Confederation of construction firms, "Six Companies," is formed by Henry Morrison, Henry J. Kaiser, Stephen D. Bechtel, and others to build Hoover Dam with 1,200 men, largest contract awarded by U.S. for $48.9 million (-1935 after 21 months, 18 months ahead of schedule, build structure with volume larger than Egypt's biggest pyramid built by some 100,000 workers in 20 years)... Bank of America opens branch office in London (by 1972 operates 124 branches, 84 subsidiaries in 78 countries)... Warren Wright inherits Calumet Farm business breeding trotting horses, KY (develops operation as leading stable for breeding thoroughbreds)...

As result of financial difficulties, Sewell Avery, president of U.S. Gypsum, becomes chief executive of Montgomery Ward (adds 178 new stores from 1935-42)... After buying rights for French shampoo tint called

Clairol, Lawrence Gelb starts hair-coloring business, successful with imaginative advertising campaigns (is acquired in 1959 by Bristol-Myers - sales of some $500 million in 1980)... With $35,000 acquired from variety of small businesses, including bankrupt orange-juice bottler, Norton Simon starts business packing inexpensive canned goods (sells to Hunt Brothers Packing in 1943 to net $3 million, reacquires business to develop Hunt Foods & Industries with interests in 27 other companies, such as McCall Corp., Canada Dry, Knox Glass, Evans Products, Swift & Co., and American Broadcasting-Paramount Theaters)...

After suggestion by insurance broker Carl L. Odell in 1930 to General Wood of Sears, Allstate Insurance is created to issue car insurance - first time insurance handled by general merchandising business (realizes first million in premiums in 1936, in 1939 pioneers rating plan for different types of risks, in 1947 decentralizes organization to zones and regions, enters Canadian market in 1953 - Europe and South America in 1959, starts group life, health insurance programs in 1958, adopts innovative no-cancellation policy in 1960, creates Allstate Motor Club in 1961, operates countrywide in 1987 with over 50,000 employees at 5,860 locations)...

To maintain employment General Electric introduces 5-day work week (recognizes CIO Union of Electrical Workers in 1936 after strife)... TWX telegraph printing system goes national, Britain's Telex in 1932... Procter & Gamble adopts marketing strategy to pit brands against each other, reorganizes 1987 to adopt catagories to coordinate competing brands in same market... Varney Air Service starts (1934)... To avoid U.S. regulations, John R. Brinkley of Del Rio, TX, opens radio station XER in Ciudad Acuna, Mexico, as first of border radio-blasters (-1941 when closed by Mexico after U.S. pressure, advertises patent medicines, pioneers development of radio evangelists and country music market).

1932

General Events

President Hoover signs (January 22) bill to fund Reconstruction Finance Corp. with $500 million and authorization to borrow $2 billion... Glass-Steagall Banking Act authorizes (February 27) Federal Reserve System to expand credit (bars banks in trading stocks, securities)... U.S. debt passes (April 13) $2 billion, highest peacetime mark... Relief and Reconstruction Act extends (July 21) loan limits of Reconstruction Finance Corp. by $3 billion... Federal Home Loan Bank Act authorizes (July 22) regional banks to lower home mortgage rates... Controller of Currency declares (August 26) moratorium on foreclosures of first mortgages...

Unemployment rises to some 11 million in August... U.S. National Labor Committee starts drive to end child labor... Engineers form Technocracy, Inc. to propose depressed economy be turned over to those technically trained to save nation (-1933 when abandoned as lost cause)... Manhattan's Palace Theater, once mecca for vaudeville acts, starts showing movies... Bread lines are seen in major cities... Communists urge unemployed to march on Ford River Rouge plant (clash with Dearborn police and Ford's security force led by ex-boxer Harry Bennett)... Russian-born David Dubinsky becomes president of International Ladies' Garment

Workers' Union (-1966, retires $1 million debt by 1934, sponsors low-cost housing in New York, develops 850-acre resort, obtains 35-hour work week in 1935, employer-funded vacations in 1937, health and welfare fund in 1937, retirement fund in 1943 and severance pay in 1950)... Average wage drops 48% from 1929...

Norris-LaGuardia Act allows workers to organize unions, restricts use of injunctions against labor activities, and declares yellow-dog contracts unenforceable... Adolph A. Berle, Gardiner C. Means: The Modern Corporation and Private Property (reveals in pioneering study most corporations run by managers instead of stockholders)... U.S. unemployment reaches 13.7 million by year's end, some 30 million worldwide... W.H. Carothers of DuPont synthesizes polyamide (leads to nylon in 1936)... Organization of Amana Colonies in Iowa is divided into Amana Church Society for spiritual matters and Amana Society to oversee business activities (sells Amana refrigeration in mid-1960s, abandons Amana name monopoly with Iowa Supreme Court decision in 1982)... Wisconsin is first state to pass unemployment insurance act... Carl C. Magee patents parking meter, first installed by Oklahoma City in 1935.

Business Events

Some 5,000 banks are closed during year... Edwin Land, Harvard drop-out, forms Land-Wheelwright Laboratories to perfect 1929 polarizing process (obtains basic patent in 1934, licenses rights to Eastman Kodak in 1935 for camera filters)... Edward Rickenbacker resigns as GM's Vice President of Fokker Aircraft Division to become Vice President of American Airlines (is hired by GM in 1933 as vice president of its new North American Aviation, becomes general manager of subsidiary Eastern Airlines in 1935, heads group of investors to take over Eastern in 1938 when GM is forced to leave airline business, operates Eastern as President to 1953 and Chairman to 1963, earns reputation for efficiency and poor customer service)...

After quarreling with father, founder of Mars, Inc. making Milky Way and Snickers, Forrest Mars, Sr., goes to England with $50,000 from father (builds billion-dollar candy and pet food business by 1980s)... Elmer Doolin starts Frito snack-food business with $100 and corn chip recipe...

American Automatic Typewriter devises automatic typewriter, uses technology of player piano, for repetitive letter writing... Daniel Starch starts market research business... Herman W. Lay starts business distributing potato chips in Nashville (merges with Frito business in 1961)... Jay Stirling Getchall creates ad to compare Plymouth car to unnamed cars of competitors (increases Plymouth's market share from 16% to 24% in 1933)...

Robert R. Young acquires New York brokerage house (purchases seemingly worthless stock to make business profitable, acquires bankrupt Allegheny Corp. in 1937)... Inventor Abram N. Spanel, holder over 2,000 patents, starts International Latex business to make bras, girdles (becomes Playtex later)...

Storyboarding technique, series of sketches of key movements in movie action sequence, is developed at Disney Studios (starts Disney Art School)... Allan Mogensen develops work simplification in this time as technique to improve productivity...

For first time since 1927 Ford Motor Co. records net profit... Myron C. Taylor, operator of textile mills and financier (associated with House of J.P. Morgan), becomes chairman of U.S. Steel (-1938, reorganizes structure with general staff - modeled on General Motors, starts collective bargaining with Steel Workers Organizing Committee in 1937 - first in industry)... Charles P. McCormick, president of Baltimore spice business, creates junior board of directors, with young executives... Marmon Motor Car Co. declares bankruptcy, as does Franklin, Moon, Pierce-Arrow, Kissel, Gardner, Auburn, Peerless, Stutz, and Duesenberg - Cord-Reo survives as truck manufacturer in 1936)... Grade-school drop-out William P. Lear starts Lear Aviation (evolves as $40 million operation by end of World War II, popularizes private executive jet planes in mid-1950s)... Ford Motor Co. uses cast steel instead of forged steel in making V-8 crankshafts... Beech Aircraft to make small planes is started in Wichita by Walter, president, and Olive, wife and former secretary as financial officer - president in 1950 to start diversification (with sales of some $60 million is acquired in 1980 by Raytheon)... Magical F.A.O. Schwarz toy store opens in NYC at new Fifth Avenue, 58th Street location (evolves as 22-store chain by 1986)...

To fill in for sick uncle, Samuel J. Popeil starts career hawking household gadgets with store demonstrations (starts business in 1939 to make gadgets and train demonstrators)... Russian-born Maurice Greenberg starts Connecticut Leather to sell leather supplies to shoemakers (starts selling toys in 1954 and plastics in 1960, becomes conglomerate of Coleco in 1960s with management by sons, avoids bankruptcy in 1978 with ColecoVision, launches fad of Cabbage Patch Dolls in 1983 - revenues of some $510 million, buys Selchow & Righter, owner of Scrabble and Trivial Pursuits games, in 1986, declares bankruptcy in 1988)...

After working in Seventh Avenue dress house in 1923 and as salesman for nail polish distributor in 1930, Charles Revson, born in 1906 as son of cigarmaker, borrows $300 from loan shark at interest rate of 24% to start Revlon Nail Enamel with brother Joseph and chemist Charles Lachman (grosses $4,000 first year, introduces innovative color-coordinated beauty products in 1939, introduces first liquid make-up in 1950 and chic lipstick cases in 1954)...

After attending University of Georgia and injuring shoulder playing football, Louis E. Wolfson returns to family's junkyard business in Jacksonville, FL (several years later borrows $10,000 to start Florida Pipe & Supply with father and older brother to buy discarded pipe and building materials from Penney Farms, home for retired ministers started by J.C. Penney, sells pipe, costing $275, for $100,000, during World War II buys and sells government surplus before dissolving business worth $2.5 million in 1949 to become corporate raider in 1950s)... Inventor Wally Byam designs Airstream trailer (starts business making modern mobile homes for travelers)...

1933

General Events

Jobless figure reaches (January 31) 15 million... President Roosevelt

(March 4): "The only thing we have to fear is fear itself"... President Roosevelt declares (March 5) 4-day "bank holiday" to stop run of depositors on banks, (summons Congress to special session)... Emergency Banking Act gives (March 9) President broad powers over banking transactions, foreign exchange... Economy Act reduces (March 20) salaries of federal employees... Civilian Conservation Corps is formed (March 31) to provide work for young men, handles over 2.5 million by 1941-42... U.S. goes (April 19) off gold standard... Federal Emergency Relief Act authorizes (May 12) immediate grants for relief projects... Agricultural Adjustment Act provides (May 12) relief to farmers with parity prices and subsidies...

Tennessee Valley Authority is created (May 18) as public corporation, David Lilienthal dominant director, to serve some 700,000 users with 138 power stations... Federal Securities Act requires (May 27) Federal Government to approve all issues of stocks and bonds (requires underwriters to provide public with information on corporations)... U.S. Employment Service is formed (June 6)... Homeowners' Loan Corp. provides (June 13) money for mortgages and repairs, some one million loans by end in 1936... National Industrial Recovery Act forms (June 16) Public Works Administration and National Recovery Administration (requires industries to establish codes for fair trade, is declared unconstitutional in 1935)...

Farm Credit Act and Banking Act of 1933 (creates Federal Bank Deposit Insurance Corporation to protect depositors) are passed (June 16)... National Labor Board is created (August 5) by Presidential order to enforce right of organized labor to bargain collectively... Civil Works Administration is created by Presidential order, provides jobs for some 4 million by end of 1934... Detroit defaults on debt of $400 million... New Radio Workers' Union administers welfare program of Philco's Philadelphia plant (pioneers movement in 1930s with unions handling benefit and recreational activities)... New Jersey is first state with multihospital prepayment health plan (starts evolution of "Blue Cross Plans" in other states)...

Heywood Broun, others form American Newspaper Guild as union... Australian-born Harry Bridges organizes International Longshormen's Association in San Francisco (strikes for recognition in 1934 - supported by first U.S. general strike, joins CIO in 1937, is ordered deported in 1942 - invalidated by Supreme Court, indicted and convicted in 1949 for perjury in swearing during naturalization not member of Communist Party - overturned by Supreme Court in 1953)... U.S. sues IBM for violating Sherman Anti-Trust Act in controlling some 80% of market in keypunchers, sorters, and accounting machines used in tabulating data... Buckminster Fuller designs futuristic, aluminum-skinned, three-wheel front-wheel drive Dymaxion car to carry 11 people (cruises at 120 mph and averages 22 mpg, abandons project when prototype is involved in fatal collision - attacked as folly by papers although other car at fault)... U.S. resumes trade with Soviet Union...

AFL fails to organize auto industry (is organized by United Auto Workers in 1935 which joins CIO in 1936, is ousted from AFL in 1938)... After no rain for 18 months topsoil from Oklahoma to South Dakota is swept by severe winds to create "dust bowl" (results in some 300,000 refuges migrating to California next 4 years)...

Elton Mayo: <u>The</u> <u>Human</u> <u>Problems</u> <u>of</u> <u>an</u> <u>Industrial</u> <u>Civilization</u>... To stop hoarding of gold President Franklin Roosevelt orders surrender of all private stores of gold to Federal Reserve Banks... After failures by Actors' Equity Association to organize actors in movie industry in 1920s, Screen Actors' Guild is formed as union... Cookies made by Girl Scounts in demonstrating new oven are bought by passers-by (starts annual Girl Scout program in 1934 to sell cookies to raise money for movement - some $200 million in sales by 1980s)... F.J. Schlink, Arthur Kellett: <u>1,000,000</u> <u>Guinea</u> <u>Pigs</u> (attacks misleading advertising of drugs, cosmetics)...

As Secretary of Labor Frances Perkins is first woman cabinet officer (-1945)... 18th Amendment on Prohibition is repealed (December 5) by 21st Amendment (results in many speakeasies, such as Sherman Billingsley's Manhattan Stork Club, becoming nightclubs, in some 750 breweries - in 1960s top 10 with about 50% of market and only 2 of 42 left in 1980s with almost 50%, and in shift of underworld interests to other activities for new revenues: numbers, gambling, loan sharking, labor racketeering - unions of teamsters and stage employees)... Some 2 million workers are members of AFL... By end of year 4,004 banks are closed, 25% of labor force is unemployed and 31% of country's production is shut down...

Dr. Francis E. Townsend announces plan to cure Depression (proposes all over 60 years of age to receive $150/month if they spend it)... Dorothy Day, social visionary, and French philosopher Peter Maurin start Catholic Worker Movement in NYC to aid poor... First recorded "sit-down" strike is held by packing house workers at Hormel plant in Austin, MN... United Mine Workers starts organizing drive (records membership of some 578,000 in 1936, around 500,000 in 1920 and 150,000 in 1932)... After number of successful strikes membership in Amalgamated Clothing Workers rises from 75,000 to near 125,000...

Fred Osius of Miami, FL, gets patent for food blender (with financial backing from orchestra leader Fred Waring in 1936, becomes pioneering food processor in 1937 as Waring Blender)... Diego Rivera: "Detroit Industry" (bases cycle of frescos on Detroit's Ford Rouge Plant)... President Roosevelt forms National Planning Board for use of natural resources, National Resources Board in 1934 and Natural Resources Committee in 1935.

Business Events

1884 NCR introduces "itemizing" cash register... Starting with one small delivery truck in Asbury Park, NJ, Leon Hess transforms father's ailing coal yard and gas station into U.S.' 13th-largest oil business, 173rd-largest company, by 1987... Business leaders form U.S. Business Advisory Council to help with economic recovery... Lawyer Leonard H. Goldenson joins Paramount Pictures to reorganize firm's New England theaters (supervises some 1,700 houses throughout U.S. in 1938, becomes president of United Paramount Theaters when movie firm is forced by 1949 Supreme Court ruling to separate production and exhibition businesses)...

William Paley, head of Columbia Broadcasting System, organizes industry's first news service... After death of parents, grape growing business near Modesto, CA, is transformed to make wine by Ernest, Julio Gallo with some $5,900.23 and recipes from public library (start bottling Gallo wine in

1938, introduce Thunderbird fortified wine in late 1950s, sign FTC consent order in 1976 on charges of unfair competition in punishing distributors for handling other brands - set aside 1983, introduce wine cooler Bartle & Jaymes in mid-1980s to become No. 1 in 1986 market with over 100 rivals, sue brother Joseph in violating trademark rights by selling cheese - countersuit for 1/3 of father's estate, operate with divided kingdom, Ernest over marketing and Julio over production, to achieve 21.6% of U.S. wine market in 1986 with 115 growers and estimated sales of some $1 billion as world's largest wine business)...

Durant Motors, founded 1921 by William C. Durant, creator of General Motors in 1908, is liquidated (declares bankruptcy in 1935 with debts of $914,000 and assets of $250, opens New Jersey supermarket in 1935, promotes chain of bowling alleys for family recreation in 1940, stymied by W.W. II, before death in 1947)... IBM acquires Electronic Typewriter (produces first commercially successful electric typewriter in 1935)...

Procter & Gamble introduces Dreft, first synthetic detergent... American Trucking Assn. is formed... 1912 Paramont Pictures declares bankruptcy (illustrates failure of some 5,000 of estimated 16,000 movie theaters from high costs, low attendance)... Chicago Bears and New York Giants play first World Championship football game, each winning player gets $210 - $36,000 in 1986... Paul Hoffman, vice president of sales, and partners rescue Studebaker from receivership (advertises in 1938 with union funds)... Danish-born A.C. Nielsen develops retail-sales index for druggists... Laboratories of U.S. manufacturers employ some 10,900 researchers (climbs to 28,000 in 1940 and 45,900 in 1946 - Britain with some 1,724 in 1933, 4,505 in 1938 and 5,200 in 1945-46)...

After fleeing Russian Revolution in 1917, Rudolph Kunett, family friend of Smirnoff family (makers of vodka since 1818), enters U.S. (opens vodka factory in 1934, with scant success sells business in 1939 to Heublein family, operators of factory - restaurant in Hartford, CT, since 1901, for $14,000 and royalties, achieves success with sales in Carolinas from likeness to moonshine, grows from under $1 million business to nearly $1 billion by 1970s)... After experimenting with small car for military reconnaissance, U.S. Army asks Bantam, Willys and Ford to build new car (awards contract to Willys, originally Overland in 1903, for its "jeep" - original design discontinued 1986)... First U.S. drive-in theater opens in Camden, NJ, over 5,000 others by 1956...

William Albers, former Kroger president, starts Super Markets in Cincinnati... Topps Chewing Gum Co. gives baseball cards with bubble gum (follows promotions of cigarette-makers with baseball cards in 1880s)... After operating gasoline station, wildcatter Glenn H. McCarthy starts successful petroleum business, becomes Shamrock Oil... President Walter Teagle, Standard Oil of New Jersey, delegates authority to independent operating units (creates coordinating committee at corporate level to define goals and policies, review budgets and to evaluate performances of operating units)...

National Association of Manufacturers launches promotional campaign for open shop... Successful regional Alaska Airline of 1980s is started with float plane on Northern frontier (survives deregulation of 1978 by expanding with West Coast routes to serve 30 cities)... Wheaties, created in 1921 and introduced in 1924, starts advertising baseball games (adopts slogan "The Breakfast of Champions" in 1933, puts pictures of players on boxes in 1934, sponsors first televised commercial sports broadcast in 1939)... Brunswick, makers of pool equipment, hires pool shark Willie Mosconi, age 19, to barnstorm Midwest to demonstrate its products for $600/mo... Crown Publishing is started by Nat Wertels, partner (is sold in 1988 to S.I. Newhouse media empire for some $100 million, nearly 50% of market held by multinationals, to create world's biggest trade - publishing company with Random House, Knopf, Times Books, Ballantine Books and smaller houses)... First annual gift show with new products for retailers opens in Portland, OR, evolves as traditional opening for gift show circuit.

1934

General Events

Gold Reserve Act fixes (January 30) value of gold at $35/ ounce... Dollar is devalued to 59.6 cents... By Presidential order Export-Import Bank is created (February 2) to encourage foreign trade with short-term credit loans... Federal Emergency Relief Assn. funds (February 15) new programs in public works and relief... Cotton Control Act replaces (April 21) voluntary compliance with quotas... Severe dust storms hit (May 10-11) Texas, Oklahoma, Arkansas, Kansas, and Colorado (creates "the dust bowl")... Securities Exchange Commission is created (June 6) to regulate industry (prohibits manipulation or deception in trading stock)...

Corporate Bankruptcy Act allows (June 7) bankrupt firms to reorganize if 2/3 of creditors approve... Reciprocal Trade Agreement Act is passed (June 12) for negotiations with other countries... Federal Communications Commission is created (June 19) to supervise industry... Federal Housing Administration is created (June 28) to ensure loans for home building and repairs... Federal Farm Bankruptcy Act puts (June 22) moratorium on farm mortgage foreclosures... President Roosevelt nationalizes (August 9) purchases of silver at 50.01 cents/ounce... Utopian Society organizes in Los Angeles (claims profit root of all evil)... 8 people are shot in Rhode Island as 3,000 textile workers battle troops... 50 people are shot as police fire on striking truckers, MN... Some 10.8 million are unemployed in October...

When Kohler plumbing business in Wisconsin refuses to bargain with AFL, 2 strikers are killed and 40 injured during riot with National Guard (forms Kohler Workers Assn. as company union to defeat AFL in National Labor Relations Board election)... Black-McKeller Bill, part of Airmail Act, decrees no airline can be part of company that builds planes (forces Boeing to divest itself of United Airlines, starts building planes for transoceanic travel in 1936, introduces Stratoliner with pressured cabin for high altitude flight in 1939)... Railroad Retirement Act, first U.S. law governing pensions, is passed...

After successful strikes in organizing drive, International Ladies' Garment Workers' Union records all-time high of 200,000 members - some 40,000 in 1933... Southern Tenent Farmers' Union forms in Alabama (achieves recognition with successful strike in 1935 by some 5,000 cotton-pickers, records membership of nearly 31,000 in 1937, drops out of CIO's United Cannery, Agricultural, Packing House and Allied Workers in 1939, becomes National Farm Labor Union in 1947-49, becomes National

Agricultural Workers' Union before absorption by Amalgamated Meat Cutters' Union in 1960)...

New York approves first non-profit Blue Cross Plan with hospital coverage for workers (extends coverage of New Jersey's 1933 plan to wives and children of employees, expands in interstate coverage when enrolling GM employees in local plans at different plant locations in 1941, forms national association in 1948, provides first mass enrollment for uniform hospital service and benefits in 1950 for over 300,000 workers and families in steel industry, covers federal employees in 1959)... IWW holds "sit-down" strike at Hudson automobile plant...

Congress places controls on cotton and sugar production... Amos L. Beatty becomes chairman of government's Petroleum Planning Committee (formulates "Quotas of Commerce" concept to limit production by denying admission of petroleum into channels of interstate distribution)... Reciprocal Trade Agreements Act is passed (-1962, leads to 29 pacts by 1947)... First U.S. regular ski area, called Gilbert's Hill, opens at Woodstock, VT... Federal Communication Commission starts investigating AT&T as "world's biggest monopoly," dropped just prior to W.W. II... Society for Advancement of Management is formed by Society of Industrial Engineers, Taylor Society... U.S. Employment Service starts occupational-research program... Copeland Act penalizes government contractors receiving kickbacks of wages from employees... Secretary of Labor Frances Perkins sponsors first National Labor Legislation Conference to develop appropriate laws for labor relations...

All airmail contracts with private airlines are canceled by government as result of their collusion on pricing (cancels specified airline routes, uses Army Air Force to fly domestic mail, after 78 days reopens contracts to commercial lines on bid basis after 10 Air Force pilots die carrying mail)... U.S. joins International Labor Organization... Lewis Mumford: Technics and Civilization (with The Myth of the Machine, 1967 and 1978, attacks society for failure to integrate technology with humane way of life)... International Longshoremen's Assn. closes West Coast ports over 2 months in "Big Strike" to protest "gang bosses" and blacklisting - general strike in San Francisco with use of National Guard (is settled with recognition as bargaining agent and arbitration).

Business Events

Ford Motor Co. restores $5/day minimum wage... Washeteria, pioneering laundromat, opens in Ft. Worth, TX... American Airlines starts sleeper plane service between Chicago, NYC... Union Pacific's new streamlined diesel train sets record of 14 hours, 32 minutes from Los Angeles to NYC... "Lucky" Luciano, NYC's "Boss of Bosses," forms nationwide syndicate La Cosa Nostra with 25 "family" bosses to organize U.S.' crime business...

Eli Lilly pharmaceutical business in Indianapolis opens London subsidiary... Frederick Rentschler becomes head of United Aircraft, off-shoot of Boeing divesture, to manufacture engines, etc. (supports work of Igor Sikorsky to develop helicopter - first successful test in 1940)... Florence Nightingale Graham, owner of Elizabeth Arden beauty salon business, opens deluxe health resort in Maine (opens fancy winter resort, Main Chance, in Phoenix, AZ, in 1945)... Joseph P. Kennedy forms Somerset

Importers (with control of good Scotch stockpiles liquor as "medicinal" for end of Prohibition)...

Beardsley Ruml becomes treasurer of R.H. Macy retail business in NYC (-1945, creates new system of accounting and cash-time plan)... After consolidating 4 independent airlines with Boeing's former United, William A. Patterson becomes president of new United Airlines (-1966)... C.R. Smith becomes president of new American Airlines, American Airways in 1930 (-1942, creates 5-year plan to focus on passenger service instead of mail contracts, sells transportation as product, contracts with Douglas Aircraft for revolutionary 21-passenger DC-3 in 1936)... When unable to obtain reproductions of patents Chester F.L. Carlson experiments with electrostatic copies (produces first in 1938)... William J. Levitt builds first housing development of 200 houses, some 2,000 more in next 7 years (mass produces 2,350 housing units for Navy at start of W.W. II)...

Proprietary Association formulates ethical code for over-the-counter drugs... National Airlines is founded... After forcing government through Independent Air Transport Operator's Association to revise procedures for letting airmail contracts, Thomas E. Braniff's airline of 1930 obtains first airmail contract, forced out of Mexican and South American markets by Pan American in 1947... Auctioneer Leslie Bohn starts sidewalk stock market in Waynesboro, PA, as forum for trading shares in local enterprises...

Philip Wrigley starts annual income insurance plan for employees (guarantees income for definite period of time, starts gradual retirement plan in 1950 to allow employees to continue working after age of 65 with reduced workload)... Mutual Broadcasting System is started with 2 radio stations... In this time Farmers' Market complex develops in Los Angeles... Wall Street financiers urge ex-Marine Major General Smedley D. Butler to lead march of 500,000 fascists to take over Washington (refuses)... Hinky Dink's restaurant is opened in Oakland, CA, by Victor J. Bergeron, "Trader Vic," with $525 loan and 2 barrels of beer (starts Trader Vic chain of 21 exclusive restaurants after W.W. II)... Chrysler introduces streamlined "Air Flow" car... First Boston Corp. is created when Chase Manhattan, First National of Boston are required by Glass-Steagall Act to divest investment banking activities (acquires Mellon Securities and industrial clients in 1946)...

Henry J. Kaiser, others create Columbia Construction Co. to build Bonneville Dam on Columbia River (-1938)... Pittsburgh Plate Glass Co. invents safety glass... U.S. Rubber develops new yarn of "Lastex"... Cooper's Underwear of Wisconsin, becomes Jockey International later, designs cotton briefs for men (is introduced by Marshall Fields' Chicago store in 1935 on cold winter day - stock sold out by noon)... Helen Richey is hired by Central Airlines as first woman pilot on scheduled airline, forced to resign by union pressure... James A. Ryder starts truck-leasing business with $35 down payment on $200 used Model-A truck (evolves as industry's largest with 1980 revenues of some $1.8 billion)... Malcomb McLean starts truck business in Red Springs, moves to Winston-Salem, NC, in 1947 (evolves by 1980s as U.S.' 5th largest trucking concern, files for bankruptcy in 1986 as another victim of truck deregulation to idle some 9,800 employees and 9,000 rigs in 45 states)...

Martha Phillips rents space for dress business, nothing under $100, on

12th floor of Manhattan building - $25 million-a-year business in 1980s as Martha, Inc. (opens Palm Beach store in 1945, Bal Harbor shop, FL, in 1965 and Park Avenue Salon in 1966)... Western Family grocery supply business is started in San Francisco, moves to Portland, OR, in 1983 (grows from sales of $135 million in 1980 to over $200 million in 1988 to supply 2,600 products to customers, including 90-store Japanese retail grocery chain and east Coast grocery wholesalers, with headquarters staff of 37)... Varney Speed Lines starts, becomes Varney Air Transport in 1935 and Continental in 1937... Silk plant, NJ, is first fined for violating NRA codes.

1935

General Events

Emergency Relief Appropriation Act provides (April 8) some $5 billion for immediate relief and employment (creates Works Progress Administration under direction of Harry Hopkins - employs some 8,500,000 by 1943 for $11 billion)... Rural Electrification Administration is created, May 11 (establishes lending agency in 1936 to favor non-profit cooperatives)... U.S. Supreme Court: Schechter Poultry Corporation v. United States (rules 1933 National Recovery Act unconstitutional)... National Labor Relations Act gives (July 5) employees right to join labor unions (formulates unfair labor practices for employers, is upheld by U.S. Supreme Court in 1937)... Congress passes (August 23) Banking Act of 1935 to revise operations of Federal Reserve System...

Public Utilities Act requires (August 26) public utility companies to register with Securities and Exchange Commission... Washington, Brazil sign (February 2) trade accord... Martial law is declared in Omaha to quell rioting strikers... Some 18,000 musicians obtain work in Federal arts job relief program...

After $90 million in pay raises, some 40,000 miners return to work after 4-day strike... Despite plea of Britain for embargo, U.S. firms sell oil to Italy... Washington signs (November 15) trade treaty with Canada... Boston retailer Edward Filene launches Consumer Distribution Corp. to develop consumer cooperatives, particularly cooperative department stores... After world tour Walter Reuther becomes local president of United Automobile, Aircraft, Agricultural Implement Workers of America (wins union recognition from GM with sit-down strikes in 1936-37, becomes president of United Automobile Workers in 1946, president of CIO in 1951 and vice president of AFL-CIO in 1955-68)...

August Bowmer starts Ashland's Oregon Shakespearean Festival with boxing matches to defray costs of plays (by 1980 attracts over 300,000 play-goers annually on budget of $5.5 million, starts Portland subsidiary in 1988)... While driving through Iowa countryside John D. Atanasoff creates first electronic digital computer, with binary code, nonracheting logic, serial calculation and regenerative memory (starts work in 1937, completes basic design in 1939, builds electronic calculator in 1941 with Clifford Berry, provides ideas for John Mauchly, J.P. Eckert in building ENIAC in 1946)...

U.S. Department of Agriculture scientists develop synthetic insecticide, DDT in 1939 by Swiss chemist... Some 8% of U.S.' income goes to recreation... First Welcome Wagon activity, representing local business interests, to greet new community residents is started... Social Security Act is passed, August 14 (grants pensions to retirees at age of 65 in 1942, provides financial aid to families with dependent children, from $21.3 million to 534,000 applicants in 1936 to $7 billion for 11 million recipients in 1981, and blind and aged, and establishes unemployment insurance system - Britain in 1911 and Germany after W.W. I, is declared constitutional by U.S. Supreme Court in 1937)... Neutrality Act forbids shipment of arms, munitions to belligerents... After AFL convention ignores issue of industrial unionism, John L. Lewis of United Mine Workers and leaders of 8 unions form Committee for Industrial Organization (are expelled from AFL in 1937 to form Congress of Industrial Organizations, merge in 1955 to form AFL-CIO)...

Annual Orange Bowl and Sugar Bowl post-season football games are started, followed by Cotton Bowl in 1937... Yale Professor Thurman Arnold becomes head of Justice Department's Anti-Trust Division (-1943, launches aggressive campaign against monopolies, plans case against Alcoa to redefine monopoly with market structure and potential power instead of mere size)... Edwin Armstrong demonstrates FM radio, patents in 1933 (perfects device by 1939)... Motor Carrier Act grants authority to Interstate Commerce Commission to regulate trucks (uses railroad regulations for guidelines)... After organizing long-haul drivers in 1933-35 despite violent resistance of trucking companies and auto manufacturers, James Hoffa, age 21, becomes business agent for Detroit local of Teamsters Union (becomes negotiating chairman for Central States Drivers Council in 1940 - vice president in 1941, president of Michigan Conference of Teamsters in 1942 and trustee to audit union books in 1943).

Business Events

TWA uses "air hostesses" on flights of 14-passener DC-2 planes... Gardner Cowles, Jr., and brother purchase Minneapolis _Star_ for $1 million to form publishing empire with father's Des Moines _Register_ (launch _Look_ photo magazine in 1937 - dropped in 1971 from TV competition)... Henry Steinborn develops Capitol News Agency in Chicago in this time to distribute tip sheets to gamblers (evolves as City's secondary distributor to handle publications not socially acceptable)... IBM issues _Think_ for employees, customers... Harwood Cochran starts Overnight Transportation in Richmond, VA, as less-than-truckload business with 2 used trucks (evolves as market's largest non-union firm with some 4,000 trucks before 1986 acquisition by Union Pacific Railroad for $1.2 billion)... IBM contracts to process data for Social Security Agency, largest government operation of time, to survive Depression... Promoter Leo Seltzer flops in promoting world's first roller-skating marathon in Chicago (with rules devised by sportswriter Damon Runyon creates Roller Derby, grows in popularity by 1948 only to decline by 1958, is revived as TV attraction by son Jerry on 40 stations in 1961 - some 20 million viewers in 1973)...

While teaching chemical engineering at California Institute of Technology, Arnold O. Beckman creates Beckman Instruments (invents non-clogging ink and meter to measure acidity in lemon juice to develop business with sales of some $618 million, in 1982 sells business to Smith Kline for $1 billion, with wealth provides research funds to scientists -

$75 million alone in 1985 to rank 2nd only to Ford Foundation in philanthropy)... Boeing makes first B-17, Flying Fortress (is produced on assembly lines of Douglas, Vega and Boeing during W.W. II to make 12,737 planes)...

Harold S. Smith and father, former game operators at amusement parks and fairs, open Harolds Club in Reno (promotes gambling for middle-class spenders)... After making 150 prefabricated motor homes with General Electric, Gunnison Magic Homes is started in New Albany, IN, to pioneer prefabricated house manufacturing business (uses "first" conveyor system to build homes)...

After selling low-cost insurance policies door-to-door in Chicago, John Donald MacArthur acquires near-bankrupt Bankers Life & Casualty Co. with $2,500 (develops firm in 5 years with assets of $1 million - multi-billion-dollar business on death in 1976)... Statistician George Gallup starts American Institute of Public Opinion to pioneer polling industry (uses scientific sampling techniques, development of early 1930s, gains success by predicting right outcome of 1936 election)... Twentieth-Century Fox movie studio, Darryl F. Zanuck in charge, is created by merger of J. Schenck's Twentieth-Century and Fox Film Corp... Mademoiselle magazine is published for young women...

Parisian-born Germaine Monteil, former haute-couture designer, starts cosmetic and skin-treatment business, acquired in 1968 by British-American Tobacco for $36.5 million... Howard Hughes starts Hughes Aircraft to build experimental planes (sets transcontinental record in 1935 of 9 hours and 27 minutes, sets round-the-world record of 3 days, 19 hours in 1937 only to contract bone disease from use of oxygen, acquires control of Trans World Airlines in 1936-39 - sold in 1966 for $546 million after losing control in 1961 law suit, develops Hughes Aircraft with government contracts during W.W. II, while test-piloting experimental plane in 1946 makes crash landing, injuring lungs and rendering him susceptible to bronchial infections - designs new hospital bed, is investigated by Senate in 1947 for irregularities in government contracts - tests "Spruce Goose" to prove it could fly, acquires control of RKO Pictures in 1948 - sells in 1972 for $150 million, develops first radar-guided air-to-air missile in 1949, starts developing hardware for CIA in 1949, starts avoiding publicity in 1952 - no public photographs after 1957)...

Associated Press launches Wirephoto, first successful service to transmit photographs by wire... Ralph C. Davis: Business Organization and Operation (is first American to identify management functions)... Roto-Rooter drain-cleaning service is started in Iowa (after winning court case by plumbers evolves nationwide by 1980s with franchises in almost every county)... With only 6 years of schooling S.B. Fuller, first black member of National Assn. of Manufacturers, starts peddling soap door-to-door in Chicago, sells cosmetics later (by 1963 operates business with over 3,000 sales reps in 38 states and controls 8 other corporations including department store and chain of newspapers, survives bankruptcy in 1968 after civil rights advocates, blacks boycott stores, products for urging blacks to develop themselves by working harder, showing more initiative).

1936

General Events

German dirigible Hindenburg completes first scheduled transatlantic flight to Lakehurst, NJ (explodes there in 1937 during landing to end commercial airship transportation)... Washington reports (January 6) 5-year peak in industrial output... Robinson-Packman Act prevents (June 20) stores from engaging in price-cutting and other practices intended to eliminate competition and establish monopolies (results in independent groceries forming cooperatives grocery chains)...

Congress establishes (June 26) U.S. Maritime Commission to regulate industry with Merchant Marine Act... Atomic power is used in New Jersey to cure cancer in mice... Police disperse some 2,500 striking Mexican citrus fieldhands, CA... Secretary of Interior Harold Ickes dedicates pioneering automated farm in Virginia... For first time in 10 years imports exceed (October 4) exports...

Washington reports (November 8) business at highest level since 1930... Seven GM plants in Flint, MI, are closed by sit-down strikers seeking union recognition... Charles "Lucky" Luciano, operator of $12 million-a-year NYC prostitution ring since 1933 and overboss of U.S. crime, is found guilty of prostitution charges (although deported to Italy in 1946 maintains ties to underworld with meetings in Havana)...

Steel Workers Organizing Committee, renamed United Steelworkers of America in 1942, is headed by Scottish-born Philip Murray (becomes head of CIO in 1940 on resignation of John L. Lewis)... American Guild of Musical Artists is formed as union...

Movie "Modern Times" depicts work on assembly line and life of mass production society... After 5-week strike, first large "sit-down," Goodyear Tire & Rubber recognizes CIO's United Rubber Workers (initiates unionization of Akron rubber industry)... C.C. Furnas: Next 100 Years (pioneers study of forecasting)... Muzafer Sherif: The Psychology of Social Norms (pioneers study of group behavior)... Senate LaFollette Committee investigates violations of basic rights of workers by large employers... United Automobile Workers affiliates with CIO, recognized by General Motors and Chrysler in 1937 - Ford 1941... Anti-Strike-Breaking Act prohibits transportation of strike-breakers in interstate, foreign commerce...

Walsh-Healey Act requires any government contractor over $10,000 to adopt prevailing wages, hours and working conditions for employees (establishes requirements for child and convict labor)... Directors' Guild of America is formed as union (authorizes first strike in 1957)... U.S. tax laws are amended to permit corporations to make tax deductions for contributions to charitable causes... Consumer's Union is formed as non-profit organization by striking employees of Consumers Research, founded 1928, to evaluate products for protection of public (issues Consumer Report to give results of tests)...

Delta Development, secretly owned by county district attorney Leander Perez, acquires mineral rights for Plaquemines Parish, LA (acquires millions and political power, lasting to 1980s, from leases on discovery of oil, gas fields)... U.S. indicts Teamsters Union for trucking racket... Maritime Commission takes over Dollar Steamship Co., largest on Pacific Coast in 1902 (-1952).

Business Events

Homer Laughlin China, WV, introduces art deco Fiestaware (becomes basic dinnerware of U.S. until discontinued in 1972 - popular again in 1986)... Nash Motors and Kelvinator Refrigerator business merge (names George W. Mason of Kelvinator as replacement for retiring Charles W. Nash)... Former barnstorming pilot, Robert F. Six acquires part ownership in Southwest Division of Varney Speed Lines with airplane service to El Paso and Pueblo, CO (names company Continental Airlines in 1937 and moves headquarters to Denver - Los Angeles in 1963, stuns industry in 1962 with economy fare for Chicago - Los Angeles route, operates during peak year of 1982 to serve 86 domestic and 24 foreign cities)... After selling car for $300 Bob Wian buys old diner in Glendale, CA (achieves success with Big Boy double-deck hamburgers, sells franchise rights to Elias brothers in 1952 - over 800 places worldwide by 1986)... Trade publication Super Market Merchandising is issued...

Professor Charles L. Jamison, University of Michigan, invites management educators to form association to advance science of management (evolves as Academy of Management in 1941, over 6,000 members by 1980s)... First drive-in bank opens in South Bend, IN... Journal of Marketing is published... Oscar Johnson with Edwin, Roy Shipstad presents first Ice Follies show... Henry R. Luce publishes Life magazine (ceases weekly publication in 1972 after competition from television)... Portland-based Sprouse-Reitz, OR, is first U.S. variety chain to use self-service (after starting as Tacoma, WA, wholesale supplier in 1909 enters retail trade in 1918, changes policy of "nothing over 15 cents" in 1920 to "nothing over 49 cents," sells aluminum cookware in 1920s - resisted by customers for causing cancer, operates 321 variety stores in 11 states to gross over $200 million annually by 1986)... Ellery J. Chun designs first Hawaiian "Aloha Shirt" with striking colors (is styled in 1980s by high-fashion designers from Italy, Japan, and France to produce dazzling prints)...

Failing aircraft business of Clyde Cessna is acquired by nephew Dwane L. Wallace (maintains business by winning air races until W.W. II when military orders for trainers provide base for success in 1950s - leader of industry with some 600 dealers, introduces pioneering corporate jet plane in 1971)... Owens-Illinois produces glass blocks for building purposes... Edward Uhlan starts Exposition Press (evolves as one of nation's leading vanity presses in 1970s)... Ford Foundation is created to provide continuity of ownership for Ford Motor Co...

IBM introduces new management approach whereby employees consult with supervisors in formulating production goals... Union Pacific Railroad, W. Averill Harriman chairman, opens Sun Valley ski resort, ID (operates first U.S. chair-lifts for skiers, is acquired in 1977 by Earl Holding of Sinclair Oil and Little America hotel chain to operate ski-lifts, Sun Valley Lodge, Sun Valley Inn, 2 ice rinks, restaurants and condominiums)... After failing to recover $30,000 loan to friend importing canaries from Germany's Harz Mountain region, Max Stern sells collateral of some 2,000 singing birds in New Orleans (starts Hartz Mountain pet business, is saved from financial troubles by son Leonard in

1959 to achieve sales of some $150 million by 1973 with 1,200 products - 60 in 1959, evolves as world's largest seller of pet foods and supplies in 1982)...

John Mecom borrows $700 from mother to start oil-drilling business in Texas, Louisiana, Columbia and Mideast (files for bankruptcy in 1970 after overly ambitious drilling created cash-flow bind, recovers after 1973 Arab oil embargo to buy back property cheaply, dies in 1981 after creating empire with interests in oil fields, hotels, ranches, and other ventures with annual revenues of some $300 million)... After polling voters by telephone Literary Digest predicts Alf Landon will be elected president by landslide (is forced out of business with election of Franklin D. Roosevelt)... After losing fortunes in 2 retail grocery businesses to bankruptcy, Clarence Saunders starts Keedoozle as fully-automated store (due to mechanical problems abandons project prior to W.W. II, returns to concept in 1948 and sells 12 franchises before canceling project in 1949, starts Foodelectric before death in 1953)...

Lew Wasserman joins Julius Stein's Music Corporation of America as national director of advertising and promotions (becomes agent in 6 months with Kay Keyser as first client and president of MCA's Hollywood agency in 1946)... Moses L. Annenberg, publisher of Daily Racing Form, revives failing Philadelphia Enquirer... Standard Oil of New Jersey liquidates Mexican subsidiary (acquires Venezuelan concession in 1937)... Texas oil man Clinton Murchison acquires nearly-bankrupt Reserve Loan Life Insurance of Indiana to diversify interests (adds 4 others to consolidate in 1955 as Life Companies with assets over $130 million)...

Spanish-born Prudencio Unanue Ortiz starts Goya Foods in Secaucus, NJ, to import Moroccan olive oil and sardines for New York's Spanish community (starts marketing products for Puerto Ricans and Cubans after W.W. II, advertises to Anglos in 1979, enters Mexican-American market in 1981 with taco sauce and bean dip to become U.S.' largest purveyor of Hispanic foods, sells over 700 products for sales of $265 million in 1987)...

Stock-market forecaster Arnold Bernhard starts Value Line Investment Survey, world's largest investment advisory service in 1987 with some 134,000 subscribers... After 1935 inaugural flight Pan Am's China Clipper starts regular passenger, $1,438.20 round trip, and mail service to Manila, stopping at Midway Island for refueling and hotel - "first" operated by airline (extends service in 1937 to Hong Kong and Auckland, with financial problems sells Pacific routes to United Airlines in 1985 for $750 million).

1937

General Events

U.S. Supreme Court: West Coast Hotel v. Parrish (reverses previous decision to uphold minimum wages for women)... President Roosevelt signs (August 18) Miller-Tydings rider to an appropriation bill (allows some fixed-pricing to halt destructive price-cutting)... 40,000 workers return to work after San Francisco dock strike... Union of rubber workers closes Firestone plants in Akron... AFL denounces sit-in strikes as illegal in siezing properties... CIO promises to purge itself of Communists... Some 65,000 workers strike Chrysler... Movie industry averts strike by granting Screen Actors Guild closed shop and benefits for extras and bit players... John L. Lewis, president of UMW, orders strikes to halt coal deliveries to steel mills... Philadelphia court rules sit-down strikes illegal... Rail unions win pay raise of 44 cents/day... Washington reports (October 3) Federal Government paid 14% of U.S. income in 1936...

NLRB rules Ford guilty in violating labor laws... Timberline Lodge on Mt. Hood, OR, is dedicated (opens for skiers in 1938, provides base for ski boom in 1950s-1960s... Howard Aiken, Harvard graduate student, conceives and begins construction of first all-purpose digital computer (completes Mark I in 1943 with assistance of IBM)... Artificial sweetener cyclamate is discovered, banned by FDA in 1970... According to Gallup Poll $30 is estimated required amount to pay weekly expenses for family of 4 (rises to $43 in 1947, $72 in 1957, $101 in 1967, $177 in 1977 and $296 in 1982)... While teaching at University of Chicago, Ludwig von Bertalanffy develops general systems theory... Stock market decline signals serious economic recession... DuPont patents Nylon, discovered by Wallace H. Carothers (shows first hosiery at 1939 New York World's Fair - 64 million pairs sold first year, is used during War for tents, parachutes, uniforms, rope, surgical thread and tires, in Europe's post-War black market sells for $3,000-$4,000/pair, loses patent rights in 1961)...

American Engineering Council research report is published by National Bureau of Casualty & Surety Underwriters as first emperical study of safety and production... U.S. Supreme Court: NLRB v. Jones and Laughlin Steel Corporation (declares National Labor Relations Act of 1935 constitutional)... American Medical Assn. creates Council on Industrial Health... 10 people are killed, 80 wounded in Memorial Day clash of police and members of Steel Workers' Organizing Committee outside Republic Steel plant at South Chicago...

Ludwig Mies van der Rohe, former director of Germany's Bauhaus design institute in 1930, becomes director of Architecture Department, Illinois Institute of Technology (pioneers international style of architecture in U.S.)... Walter Reuther, other leaders of United Automobile Workers are beaten during "Battle of the Overpass" by thugs of Harry Bennett's Service Department at Ford Motor when attempting to distribute union materials on footbridge into River Rouge plant (although Edsel Ford favors negotiations, is overruled by Henry Ford until government pressure in 1941 forces acceptance of union)...

AFL boycotts Japanese imports... Raymond Moley: Industrial Leadership (discusses management responsibilities)... U.S. Department of Interior: Technological Trends and National Policy (pioneers technical forecasting)... First U.S. outdoor historical drama by community for tourists is presented in Virginia on "The Lost Colony" of Roanoke Island... George Stibitz of AT&T builds first binary calculator... After 44-day sit-down strike, CIO's United Auto Workers is recognized by General Motors (signs contracts with GM, Chrysler).

Business Events

Ford Motor Co. produces 25-millionth car... Victor Emanuel, after investing in English stock market 1927-34, acquires Cord Corp. (builds subsidiary Aviation Corp. with Consolidated Vultee Aircraft to produce over $4 billion of equipment during W.W. II, shifting from aircraft to consumer products obtains Crosley Corp., maker of small cars, refrigerators, ranges, radios and television, in 1945, sells Consolidated to Atlas Corp. in 1947, acquires Bendix Home Appliances in 1950 and Horn Mfg., maker of farm equipment, in 1951 to build AVCO Corp. as pioneering conglomerate)... Ray A. Kroc, while paper-cup salesman for Lily-Tulip Co. (convinces Walgreen drug store business to sell drinks in cups "to go"), discovers mixer that can make 6 milk shakes at one time (acquires exclusive distributorship for "multi-mixer" in 1938, while selling mixers visits McDonald's restaurant in 1954 in San Bernardino, CA)... Bendix Home Appliance demonstrates first automatic washing machine at Louisiana County Fair... D.R. Miller, wife start Carson & Barnes Circus (operates in 1980s with 1 Big Top, 80 brightly-painted vehicles, 250 employees and assorted animals to tour 20 states from home base in Paris, TX)...

Hamilton Mfg., WI, acquires designs for first U.S. commercial clothes dryer from J. Ross Moore... Margaret Rudkin starts Pepperidge Farm bakery business to make preservative-free whole wheat bread, acquired by Campbell Soup in 1961... Kitchen Aid of Hobart Mfg. makes first electric coffee grinder... IBM employs over 10,000 workers, 3,953 in 1926 (increases to over 22,000 in 1946, some 28,000 in 1949, 94,000 in 1959, 149,834 in 1964, 258,622 in 1969, 354,936 in 1981, and 390,000 in 1984)... After operating movie theater Maurice, Richard, McDonald brothers open restaurant in Pasadena, CA, (open 2nd in San Bernardino in 1939 – visited by Ray Kroc in 1954)... Publisher William Randolph Hearst is forced out of financially-troubled empire by creditors (is revived in 1942 by William Randolph, II)... Edwin H. Land creates Polaroid Corp. to make non-glare sunglasses, camera filters (designs enterprise in image of Plato's Academy to bring science and technology together to satisfy human needs, innovations and not profits the goal)...

A&P converts small "economy store" into supermarket operation, first of its some 4,000 by early 1950s... Ex-clerk David Schwartz starts Jonathan Logan business, NYC, to manufacture garments for women (evolves with modern management methods to operate 12 divisions, 18 plants before going public in 1959, becomes largest on Seventh Avenue in 1980s with sales of some $80 million in ladies' overwear)... Leslie Combs starts thoroughbred breeding business, eventually 2,000 acres as Spendthrift Farm, outside Lexington, KY (realizes success in 1955 with Nashua, sells shares in 1983 to create first publicly-owned horse breeding business)... Food Marketing Institute sponsors supermarket industry's first convention...

Hormel Packing, MN, adopts guaranteed annual wage for employees... Los Angeles hydrographer Dave McCoy builds rope tow for skiing on Mammouth Mountain, CA (operates 3 ski tows in 1946 to handle up to 350 skiers/weekend – in 1950 handles 1,800 skiers/hour, starts his first chair lift in 1955 with borrowed money, develops ski business as U.S.' biggest by 1980s with 1,330 acres, 23 chair lifts, some 1,400 winter employees to handle 14,000-17,000 skiers/weekend)... Council on Personnel Administration forms... American Marketing Society, National Association of Marketing Teachers form American Marketing Association... Alfred P. Sloan, Jr., becomes chairman of board of General Motors (-1956, develops business to produce some 40% of U.S. cars and 35% of world output, is replaced as president by William S. Knutsen to 1940)... National Basketball League forms in Midwest towns (merges in 1949 with 1946 Basketball Association of America to form National Basketball Association)... Masters opens U.S.' first discount store in NYC loft building... Joseph Scanlon devises plan whereby firm and employees would share in savings from reduced labor costs...

John Ringling North, nephew of last Ringling brother, takes over management of debt-ridden Ringling Brothers and Barnum & Bailey Circus (-1943 and 1947-67, rescues business with modernization, collapses Big Top in 1950s to present shows in air-conditioned arenas)... Robert Young, supported by Allen Kirby, heir to Woolworth fortune, acquires control of Allegheny Corp., bankrupted railroad empire of Van Swearingen brothers, from George Ball of Muncie, manufacturer of canning jars... Sylvan N. Goldman, operator of Standard Food Stores based in Oklahoma City, invents shopping cart (gives store demonstrations so customers will use new-fangled device, obtains patent in 1940, evolves with VideOcart in 1988 with advertising)... J. Willard Marriott, owner of chain of Mexican food restaurants, starts airline catering business (operates 90 flight kitchens by 1985).

1938

General Events

Washington reports (January 1) at least 7.8 million, 20% of labor force, are jobless... 36 million people are covered (January 2) by Social Security... U.S. stops (March 27) buying Mexican goods in retaliation for seizure of U.S. oil companies on March 18... Revenue Act is passed (May 27) to reduce corporate taxes in stimulating economy... Congress passes (June 22) Chandler Act to amend Federal Bankruptcy Act of 1898 (sets up procedures to avoid liquidation)... Congress establishes (June 23) Civil Aeronautics Authority to regulate growing industry... Food, Drug and Cosmetic Act requires (June 24) detailed disclosure of ingredients...

President Roosevelt signs (June 25) Fair Labor Standards Act (sets minimum wage at 40 cents/hour and maximum work week at 44 hours, drops to 40 in 3 years, for business in interstate commerce)... John L. Lewis is first president of Congress of Industrial Organizations, CIO (-1940, resigns when Roosevelt is elected for 3rd term)... President asks capital, labor to cooperate on recovery... First nylon-based tooth brushes are sold, NJ... Akron police disperse Goodyear strikers, one of over 150 unauthorized stoppages in past 2 years... Justice Department sues major Hollywood studios to seek divesture of theater chains (forces studios to accept consent decree in 1948 and split production and theater operations)... By accident, while experimenting with flourocarbon gases in DuPont laboratory, Roy Plunkett discovers Teflon (obtains patent in 1941, is used by bakeries after W.W. II, is introduced to retail market by Macy's in 1960)...

U.S. Supreme Court rules management can hire "permanent replacements" for striking workers... H.S. Dennison, Lincoln Filene, others: Toward Full Employment (proposes taxation scheme to increase consumption and decrease savings)... University of Chicago offers U.S.' first program in hospital administration... Railroad Unemployment Insurance Act is passed... Congress creates Federal Maritime Labor Board... United Electrical & Radio Workers, James Carey president, signs labor contracts with RCA and GE... President Roosevelt's Executive Order 7916 requires all administrative branches of government to establish personnel offices... CIO's Steel Workers Organizing Committee is recognized by U.S. Steel, first in industry, as bargaining agent (signs contract for 10% wage increase, 8-hour day and 40-hour week, is followed by other steel firms in 1941 with pressure from National Labor Relations Board)... NYC issues last taxi medallion of 11,787, traded for around $140,000 in 1988 (spawns informal fleet of 40,000 limousines and gypsy cabs to compete in market without licenses).

Business Events

General Motors starts mass producing diesel engines... Aramco discovers first commercial oil in Saudi Arabia... Colonel George L. Artamonoff is becomes president of new Sears International, Inc. (founds Sears of Cuba and plans Latin America expansion)... In Seattle 22 mountain climbers pool resources to form Recreational Equipment, Inc. as outdoor gear co-op (grows with membership over 1,000 after W.W. II, some 85,000 in 1966 and more than 300,000 in 1972 - 2-millionth member in 1987, opens first store outside of Seattle in 1975 - by 1987 17 stores in 10 states and 2 on East Coast, operates in 1987 with 1,500 employees as $50 million business)...

After defending itself against several organizing drives by unions in 1937, Sears launches employee attitude survey program, evolves as industry's largest (hires Houser Associates to do "morale surveys" of some 37,000 employees in 1939-42, forms personnel research department in 1939, with survey programs suspended 1943-46 experiments with non-directive interviewing to assess employee attitudes, starts "organizational survey" program in 1946, designs Employee Inventory questionnaire in 1951)... For first time U.S. business spends more advertising dollars on radio than magazines... Owens-Corning fiberglass business is founded... Physical fitness pioneer Vic Tanny starts weightlifting gymnasium Santa Monica, CA (develops business as chain of health spas by 1961 to gross some $35 million in encouraging use by women, shortly afterward declares bankruptcy from over-extended finances and unpaid taxes)... Eastern Airlines and Douglas Aircraft are created with financing from Laurance Rockefeller...

Automobile manufacturers use dealer relations boards (adopt independent umpires in 1955 to settle disputes)... Charles McCormick: <u>Multiple Management</u> (discusses successful role of younger executives on junior board of directors in family spice business - later participation by executives on sales and factory boards)... U.S. aircraft industry produces some 3,600 planes during year, makes 8,300/month by 1943... La Pointe Steel Co. is saved from bankruptcy by union-management productivity plan, designed by Joseph Scanlon to share results of decreased costs with workers... Tim McCoy forms last major Wild West Show (-1938)... Sylvania introduces commercial fluorescent lighting (follows development by General Electric which withholds innovation to protect market position in light bulbs)...

When Henry Ford suffers stroke, Harry H. Bennett, former ex-boxer who is director of personnel and plant security, gradually assumes power over company, ousted with cronies when Ford is replaced by Henry Ford, II in 1945... Chester I. Barnard: <u>The Functions of the Executive</u> (defines organization as "system of consciously or coordinated activity, in which executive is most strategic factor," proposes functions of executive as communications, motivation of effort and formulation of goals)... After stopping tractor production in 1928 and reaching informal agreement with Irish-born designer and engineer Henry Ferguson, Ford Motor Co. produces new light-weight tractor to sell for $300-350, pays Ferguson some $10 million later on patent infringements...

After 4 years of effort, Chester F. Carlson, son of Swedish immigrant barber, and aide Otto Kornei, German refugee physicist, develop duplication process of electrophotography (obtains first patent in 1940, after rejections for financing by U.S. Army Signal Corps and IBM obtains financial support for development in 1944 from Battelle Memorial Institute in return for 75% of royalties, sells all rights for Xerography to 1906 Haloid business of Joseph R. Wilson in 1947)... After failing with bingo parlor Bill Harrah achieves success with new casino in Reno... CBS starts record division by acquiring small outfit for $700,000 (produces first LP record in 1948, with profits of $162 million in 1986 sells to Japan's Sony in 1987 for some $2 billion)... First annual Premium Incentive Show opens, NYC, exhibits products for consumer "premiums" and corporate gifts, industry of some $6.5 billion by 1988 (leads to Tiffany division, perhaps U.S.' oldest, to serve corporate clients - 27,454 by 1988)... Curtis L. Carlson starts selling Gold Bond trading stamps to retailers in Twin Cities, MN (by 1988 runs $4-billion-a-year conglomerate with Radisson Hotels, TGI Friday restaurants and Ask Mr. Foster Travel).

1939

General Events

President Roosevelt submits (January 5) budget of $9 billion, $1.319 million for defense, to Congress... U.S. Supreme Court: Tennessee Electric Power Company v. Tennessee Valley Authority (rules competition of TVA with private utility companies as constitutional)... U.S. Supreme Court: National Labor Relations Board v. Fansteel Metallurgical Corporation (rules sit-down strikes are illegal)... President Roosevelt signs (April 3) Administrative Reorganization Act to examine and reorganize executive agencies...

New York World's Fair opens (April 30) as "The World of Tomorrow" (-1940, shows Westinghouse's first all-electric kitchen, exhibits DuPont's nylon stockings - sold at retail in 1940 and produced for civilians in 1945, provides first public demonstration of television)... CIO suspends 2 teacher unions for communist activities... U.S. cancels (July 2) 1919 Trade Treaty with Japan... Stocks climb (September 5) with war boom...

AFL proposes (October 11) boycott of goods from belligerents and opposes U.S. entry into war... Neutrality Act of 1939 is signed (November 4)... California Physicians Service introduces first Blue Shield Plan for medical care... Business Week lists 22 national consumer groups in survey... War Resources Board is created, Edward Stettinus chairman... General Lesley McNair designs prototype of new army division for flexibility by eliminating all extra units and pooling specialists (creates triangular division of 3 regiments, some 5,000 each by 1943, to replace square divisions of 4 regiments, plans units larger than divisions, corps and armies, to operate as "task forces" by assembling required standardized units for special missions, places all troops not in divisions in permanent units of smallest size for interchangeability as required by situation)... Polyethylene is invented... First annual NCAA Basketball Tournament is played, first televised in 1954...

German-born Kurt Lewin develops action research, introduced in 1930 article by Lewin, R. Lippit, and R.W. White, at Harwood Manufacturing, followed by work of William Whyte, Edith Hamilton in 1945-46 at Chicago's Treemont Hotel... U.S. Department of Labor: <u>Dictionary of Occupational Titles</u>... George Stibitz, Bell Telephone Laboratories, devises Complex Number Calculator, first electrical digital computer... Historian Arthur Schlesinger, Sr., predicts postwar waning of liberalism in 1962, give or take 2 years (predicts conservative era to start in 1978 and end in 1990s)... Joint Conference Board, members from unions and construction firms, forms to promote harmony in Toledo's fractious construction industry... San Francisco opens world's fair... U.S. is world's No. 1 in producing chemicals.

Business Events

1923 A.C. Nielsen Consumer Testing Service opens English office, Canadian office in 1944 (starts Nielsen Radio Index in 1942 to provide advertisers with ratings of listeners for various radio shows, after Crossley drops out of radio ratings in 1946 acquires major competitor C.F. Hooper in 1950)... NBC airs first televised pro football game at Ebbets Field, Brooklyn... Bank of Basel opens branch in NYC to provide depository for European funds... Standard Oil of California obtains oil concession for all of Saudi Arabia for $1.5 million in gold, annual payments of $750,000 and royalties... T.A. Peterman acquires Oakland's Fageol Truck & Coach Co. from receivership, becomes Peterbilt truck-building business...

J. Walter Thompson ad agency forms consumer panel of 5,000 families to provide data on spending habits... Some 63,000 workers are employed in aircraft and parts industries (peaks at 1,345,000 during war before dropping to 237,000 in 1946)... Wildcatter H.E. Chiles with 2 trucks starts oil field supply business of Western Company of North America (bluffs way through 1960s financial crisis by persuading customers Western is awash in cash with fleet of new cars for salesmen, acquires Texas Rangers baseball franchise in 1980, is forced to sell team in 1986 to survive oil recession)...

American Export Airline is created by American Export Steamship Co... Accountant R.N. Elliott writes series of articles on use of Wave Principal in understanding fluctuations in stock market (theorizes investor psychology, swinging from pessimism to optimism in more or less rhythmic cycles, driving force of changes on stock market, is neglected until revived by Robert R. Prechter in 1979 with accurate predictions on movements in stock market)... After success in England as builder and mortgage banker, Polish-born Mark Taper moves to U.S. to retire (starts business in Southern California as building developer, acquires first saving and loan association in 1950 to develop business as largest publically-owned association with $2 billion in assets)... Joseph A. Albertson, former Safeway manager, opens supermarket in Boise, ID (evolves to operate 396 units by 1980 with centralized management information system and decentralized merchandising responsibility)...

Crosley Corp., manufacturer of radio and television equipment, introduces compact, lightweight car to market (-1945 when acquired by AVCO)... L.F.

Skaggs, Sr., son of Tennesse Baptist Minister Samuel M. Skaggs who started Skaggs Cash Store in 1915 - incorporated as Safeway in 1926, acquires 4 Payless Drug Stores in Salt Lake City... After borrowing $20,000 James Rouse opens real estate business (starts Rouse Co. in 1966 to revitalize urban areas of Boston, New York, Baltimore, San Francisco, Milwaukee, and St. Louis, retires in 1979 from firm with some $700 million in assets - financial difficulties in 1987-88)... Robert de Graff starts Pocket Books to publish 25-cent paperbacks (-1957, sells test run of 100,000 paperbacks in first week... by 1960 U.S. paperbacks outsell hard-back books)...

Harold Oltz, Hammond, IN, paper-maker, sells patent rights for machine to freeze, dispense soft ice-cream to John McCullough, manufacturer of ice-cream mixes (results in first Dairy Queen drive-in by Jim Elliott, Moline, IL, is franchised by McCullough and Harry Axene in 1940s - some 3,750 outlets by 1969)... To hedge against possible inflation, interior decorators Bertha, Nealey and Ruth Bigelow start tea business (introduce Constant Comment tea as first product in developing Bigelow as international business)... Henry J. Kaiser creates Permanente Cement to supply cement via 9.6-mile conveyor belt, world's longest, to construction site at Shasta Dam, CA...

William Hewlett and David Packard, Stanford engineering students, are encouraged by engineering professor Frederick Terman to start business making audio oscillators in Palo Alto garage, sales of some $4.25 billion in 1980s from electronic products (starts development of area, evolves as Silicon Valley with Varian Associates in 1948, Fairchild Semiconductor in 1957 to sire 38 other firms, and some 2,000 high-tech firms by 1980s before recession in 1985)... Canadian-born Nathan Cummings acquires ailing Baltimore coffee and tea business (develops business through internal growth and acquisitions, such as Sarah Lee and Fuller Brush, to become Consolidated Foods)...

J.C. Penney retailing business adopts retirement and profit-sharing plans for employees... First conference of Negro Newspaper Publishers Association meets... F.J. Roethlisberger, W.J. Dixon: Management and the Worker (discusses Hawthorne studies)... After spending 5 years working for Glenn L. Martin Co. in Baltimore as project engineer, James S. McDonnell raises some $165,000 to start aircraft business in St. Louis with objective of providing maximum service possible to U.S. Government in design and manufacture of airplanes...

Carl Kiekhaefer starts business repairing defective outboard motors (makes outboard motors as Mercury Marine by 1947)... Charles E. Wilson replaces Gerard Swope as head of General Electric (-1942 and 1944-50, consolidates product diversification of Swope, leads to product decentralization of Ralph Cordiner in 1950-63 and coordination of centralization-decentralization by Fred Borch in 1963-72 with strategic business units)... IBM records sales of $40 million, $140 million in 1945... General Electric introduces first refrigerator with dual controls for freezer compartment... Packard car costs $888...

Pan Am pioneers transatlantic passenger service with Dixie Clipper to Lisbon in 23 hours, 52 minutes (plans route in 1941 from NYC to Cairo via Puerto Rico, Trinidad, Natal, Liberia, Nigeria and Khartoum - later to India and China)... U.S. produces 5,856 planes, 12,804 in 1940, 26,277 in

1941, 47,836 in 1942, 85,898 in 1943, 96,318 in 1944, and 49,761 in 1945.

1940

General Events

President Roosevelt submits (January 3) budget of $8.4 billion, some $1.8 billion for defense... President Roosevelt establishes (May 25) Office of Emergency Management... Export Control Act restricts (July 2) exports of any materials vital to defense... U.S. bans (September 26) exports of scrap steel and iron... Office of Production Management is created (December 20), William S. Knudsen of General Motors head... Bell Aircobra breaks 600 mph barrier... Federal Communications Commission develops rules for television... U.S. debt reaches $43 billion... 40-hour work week is established... John Mauchly and John Eckert, graduate students at University of Pennsylvania's Moore School, design computer (obtain Army contract in 1943 to build ENIAC, Electronic Numerical Integrator and Computer, obtain first commercial customers for ENIAC in 1943, test ENIAC in 1945)... James Caesar Petrillo becomes president of American Federation of Musicians (-1958, strikes 27-months in 1941-43 against record companies to win royalties on all sold)... Bell Relay computer, designed by George Stibitz of Bell Laboratories, is demonstrated at Dartmouth College... Government does 70% of its own research (funds 70% in non-government facilities by 1944)... Some 9 million workers are union members (increases to some 15 million in 1945)...

MIT creates Servomechanisms Laboratory to develop remote control systems for artillery (evolves during war into Whirlwind computer project to program numerically controlled tool machines, develops first equipment in 1951, demonstrated 1952, to become center for automated machine tools)... Population census registers some 131.7 million people, 74.4 urban and 57.3 rural... President Roosevelt is re-elected for 3rd term (results in resignation of John L. Lewis as president of CIO in protest)... Congress taxes excess profits... Survey shows U.S. industry employs some 150 mathematicians... Less than 100 airports are operated in U.S. (increases to 865 by 1943)...

U.S. Army's Benjamin Davis is first Negro to become Brigadier General... Pennsylvania Turnpike opens for traffic between Harrisburg and Pittsburgh... Foreign investment in U.S. is $8.1 billion, $7.7 billion in 1950, $20.7 billion in 1974, and $89.9 billion in 1982... National Defense Advisory Commission, GM president William S. Knudsen chairman, is formed to assist European friends with production and distribution of military supplies (sponsors Production Requirement Plan in 1941, designed by David Novick, to set priorities for allocation of resources to allies - mandated for U.S. after Pearl Harbor, and Controlled Materials Plan in 1942, Federal Government's first programmed budget with goals and elements cutting across traditional service lines)...

31.1% (17.6% in 1900s) of labor force is in white-collar sector (some 2.9 million in professional and technical jobs - more than doubles by 1964), 40.0% (35.8% in 1900) in blue-collar sector, 11.7% (9.1% in 1900) in service sector, and 17.4% (37.6% in 1900) in agriculture (evolves by 1980 with 52.2% in white-collar work, 31.7% in blue-collar, 13.3% in service, and 2.8% in agriculture)... Civil Service Act is amended to establish policy of federal employment without regard to race or religion (covers some 200,000 jobs with examinations and pay scales in 26 federal agencies)...

War Production Board is created (establishes War Manpower Commission which devises Training within Industry Program to improve productivity)... Investment Advisors Act limits some of widespread abuses of 1930s (grants FCC control over registration)... U.S. Supreme Court: Apex Hosiery Company v. Leader (rules sit-down strikes not illegal)... First freeway, Arroyo Seco, in Los Angeles system opens (evolves by mid-1980s with clogged traffic)... Vannear Bush informally organizes several scientists to utilize science for possible war (evolves as U.S. Office of Scientific Research and Development in 1941)... War Department's Adjutant General's Office forms Personnel Procedures Section... U.S. funds MIT's Radiation Laboratory to work on compact microwave radar transmitters, receivers and detectors... Congress authorizes doubling of Navy's combat fleet, 7,800 combat aircraft and Army of some 1 million.

Business Events

After building successful candy and pet food business in England, Forrest E. Mars, Sr., starts new candy business in Newark, NJ, to compete with father's candy business (creates unmeltable M&M candies for servicemen, creates Uncle Ben's pre-cooked rice in 1940s, takes over father's faltering business in 1964 to develop $5 billion operation in 1987)...

Boeing 307 Stratoliner is first pressurized commercial aircraft... After working for Benton & Bowles ad agency as account executive, Ted Bates starts agency with his previous accounts of Wonder Bread, Colgate Dental Cream... Annual U.S. automobiles show exhibits of cars of General Motors, Chrysler, Crosley, Graham-Paige, Hupp, Hudson, Ford, Nash, Packard, Studebaker and Willys...

In order to entertain customers while they wait in line at popular Chicken Dinner restaurant, Ghost Town, early U.S. theme park, opens at Knott's Berry Farm at Buena Vista, CA, started in 1920s as berry farm by Walter Knott, developer of boysenberry hybrid in 1930s (opens Fiesta Village after success of Ghost Town, Roaring 20's in 1975, Knott's Airfield in 1976, Kingdom of Dinosaurs and Camp Snoopy in 1983, operates 165 rides, attractions, live shows, restaurants and shops on 150 acres in 1987)...

Case Clothes is started, CT, to sell men's clothing on high-volume, no-frill basis (is acquired in 1946 by United Merchants to develop national chain of Robert Hall Clothes - bankruptcy in 1977)... Merrill, Lynch and Co. is merged with E.A. Pierce & Co. and Cassatt & Co. by Charles E. Merrill to form new brokerage business (is joined by Fenner and Beane in 1941 to create Merrill, Lynch, Pierce, Fenner and Beane as world's largest brokerage house with 71 partners and offices in 93 cities - 107 partners in 1956 at 116 offices in 106 cities with over 4,600 employees (issues Investor's Reader, launches program in 1941 to "Bring Wall Street to Main Street," starts sales training program - model for other Wall Street houses, presents "How To Invest Show" for middle class investors in 1955)...

With grant from Enterprise Associates, R.S. Morse forms National Research Corp. in Boston area (as result of research on freezing concentrated orange juice creates Minute Maid Co. in 1945, sells to Coca-Cola in 1960)... Jack M. Eckerd buys 2 drug stores from father (operates Florida-based chain of stores in Southeast with sales of some $330 million in 1973 - success from 50% self-service, discount prices, prescriptions to elderly at almost cost)... After Norway is invaded by German forces, Thomas Olsen (owns 60-vessel fleet started in 1880s) and family, including son and engineer Joakim Lehmkuhl, escape Nazis (reaches U.S. in 1941, starts fuse factory in Connecticut plant of almost defunk Waterbury Clock, changes plant operation after war to mass produce watches, using alloy bearings instead of jewels, with Lehmkuhl in charge while Olsen returns to Norway, sells first Timex watches in 1949 through variety of retail outlets instead of traditional jewelers who refuse low mark-ups, starts intensive advertising in 1956 with theme of "torture tests" to sell some 7 million watches/year by 1960, invades international market in 1962, achieves sales of some $200 million in 1970 - 1/3 of all watches sold in 1969 are Timex, makes electronic watches in 1972 - promoted 1975, with retirement of physically incapacitated Lehmkuhl in 1973 names son Fritz new president in 1981, after financial losses sells business to Sinclair Computers in 1982)...

Minnesota Mining & Manufacturing diversifies to lessen dependency on traditional products (develops some 1,000 new products by 1955)... With loan of $50,000 from family friend, Robert O. Anderson buys small run-down oil refinery in Artesia, NM, becomes Atlantic Refining in 1963 (forms Atlantic Richfield in 1966 with merger to acquire reserves in California and Texas, finds oil in Alaska in 1968, acquires Sinclair oil business in 1969, acquires Anaconda's mining and metal-processing operations in 1977 for resources to start oil shale venture - abandoned)... First U.S.-built helicopter, designed by Russian-born Igor Sikorsky for United Aircraft (builds some 5,000 by death in 1972), is successfully flown (gets first Army Air Corps contract in 1943, is used for Burma rescue mission in 1944, first medical evacuation in 1950 during Korean War, vertical deployment by Marines in 1951 and for formation of special Army unit in 1956)...

Winter Park, Colorado's oldest ski area, opens... Benjamin Graham, David Dodd: Security Analysis (pioneers mathematical study of value of common stocks and field of security analysis)... James B. Beam Distilling Co. produces first limited-edition decanters (evolves with "cult following" over years)... British shipbuilders visit U.S. with plans for new freighter (results in Todd Shipyards, Henry J. Kaiser head of consortium, to build Liberty ships - 1,490 at 7 yards, only 18-20 of 96,000 workers experienced ship builders, of total 2,708, most of any type produced, at 18 yards, in opening of San Francisco's Richmond yard to build vessels with standardization, arc welding, and prefabrication to lower costs 25% less than other builders and to cut production time for 1 ship from 27 days to around 4, and in building Robert E. Peary in 1942 in record 63 hours after keel laid)...

Edward J. Noble, head of Life Savers, buys NYC radio station, sold 1943 (buys Blue Network, 146 affiliated stations, from RCA for $8 million in 1943, grows to 200 stations as American Broadcasting Co. in 1946, merges with United Paramount in 1953, is succeeded by Leonard H. Goldenson of Paramount - 2nd to CBS by 1979).

1941

General Events

President Roosevelt submits (January 8) budget of $17,485,529,000, $10,811,000,000 for defense, to Congress... U.S. Supreme Court: United States v. Darby Lumber Company (upholds constitutionality of 1938 Fair Labor Standards Act)... Congress passes (March 11) Land Lease Act to supply war materials to any country vital to U.S. interests... Office of Price Administration is created (April 11)... U.S. military meet with British and Dutch officers to prepare strategic plan for possible operations against Japan... President Roosevelt declares (May 27) state of unlimited national emergency... President Roosevelt freezes (June 14) U.S. assets of Germany, Italy... Fair Employment Practices Committee is formed (June 25) to prevent discrimination due to race, creed or color in defense industries...

President Roosevelt freezes (July 25) all U.S. assets of Japan... Congress passes (September 20) Revenue Act of 1941 to raise taxes to pay for defense... Rejecting FDR's mediation, John L. Lewis calls (October 27) for workers in "captive mines" to strike (is supported by 5 million members of CIO, ends strike on November 22 for arbitration)... Congress declares (December 8) war on Japan for December 7th attack on Pearl Harbor (declares war on Germany, Italy on December 11)...

U.S. Supreme Court rules Negroes are entitled to all first-class services on railroad trains... Army tank production is crippled in Michigan when CIO members refuse to handle parts made by AFL... Nearly 2.5 million workers are involved during year in 4,288 strikes, most since 1919 (grows by 1945 to nearly 7 million workers in 14,471 strikes)...

U.S. troops take over North American Aviation plant at Ingleside, CA, when striking workers cripple defense production... To avoid anti-trust suit ASCAP is required by government to share licensing privileges (ends Society's ban on radio music)... U.S. Army Air Corp forms all-black 99th Pursuit Squadron... President and vice president of Air Associates, private business, are discharged by U.S. Government because of labor dispute, a violation of defense contract... National Labor Policy Board is proposed by conference of leaders from National Association of Manufacturers, U.S. Chamber of Commerce, CIO and AFL to establish process for settling strikes, formulating national wage policy, and eradicating racketeers and communists in unions...

Some 300 businessmen work for government on $1-a-year contracts... AMA is convicted of violating Sherman Anti-Trust Act in opposing public health insurance... George Brown, AFL vice president for union of stagehands, and Willie Bioff, union's West Coast representative, are convicted for extorting money from 4 major movie studios... Financier Robert A. Lovett becomes Assistant Secretary of War for Air Force (-1945, reorganizes Army Air Corps, appoints Charles "Tex" Thornton to head new statistical control unit - headquarters at Harvard with cadre of 9 officers, including Robert S. McNamara and Arjay Miller, to oversee some 2,800 officers worldwide)...

President Roosevelt is pressured to desegregate defense effort when A. Philip Randolph, president of Brotherhood of Sleeping Car Porters, threatens to lead march on Washington... Wassily W. Leontif: The Structure of the American Economy, 1919-1939... Unions pledge no-strikes to support war effort... RCA establishes central research laboratory... U.S. places bans, most removed by 1988, on home production in garment industry to combat exploitation of immigrants and other low-wage workers.

Business Events

General Motors, producing some 50% of car market, plans no changes in passenger-car models... National Industrial Recreation Assn. is started by 11 firms, increases to over 900 members by 1957... Travel Industry Association of America is formed (evolves by 1987 as U.S.' 2nd largest employer and 3rd largest retail business)... Congress, press attack Standard Oil for maintaining agreement with Germany's I.G. Farben to exchange patents, research... After fleeing Poland in 1939, Olga, Jan Erteszek start business making garter belts for women in Los Angeles with $10 (achieve first success with sales to Bullocks Wilshire, invent panty slip in 1961, is cited in 1984 as one of 100 best U.S. companies, operate Olga Co. as $67 million business with some 1,800 employees at 13 plants before acquisition by Warnaco in 1985)...

After strike at River Rouge plant and government pressure, Ford Motor Co. recognizes United Automobile Workers Union... Revere Copper and Brass advertises architect Paul Nelson's concept to use assembly line to build better houses in future... Pizzeria Uno develops deep-dish pizza in Chicago (becomes popular menu item after W.W. II)... Charles E. Wilson becomes president of General Motors to replace William S. Knudsen who resigns for governmental service (-1953, proposes cost-of-living wage increase for workers in 1948, increases to come from higher productivity, and company-wide pension plan in 1950 in return for use of automation or technological innovations)...

Steel man Tom Girdler becomes head of San Diego's Consolidated Aircraft (designs first mass-production assembly line for bombers)... Carl Karcher, grade school drop-out, opens hot dog stand in Los Angeles with $326 (expands business to operate 316 stores and achieve yearly volume over $200 million by 1981)... Procter & Gamble hires expert in consumer services (experiments with consumer phone line in 1971, pioneers 800-number system in 1979)... Ford Motor Co. makes first plastic car-body...

P.E. Holden, others: Top Management Organization and Control, first major empirical study of organizational practices... Moorehead Patterson becomes president of father's American Machine and Foundry business of 1897 (-1962, diversifies business making tobacco and bakery machines with automatic pin-spotter for bowling in 1946, perfected 1952, and then acquires interests in bicycles, toys, athletic gear, exercise equipment, water skiis and scuba gear - by 1962 with 45 plants, 19 research laboratories, sales of some $415 million and 16,670 employees)...

Honeywell Heating Specialties of Wabash, IN, later Minneapolis, develops first successful electronic autopilot (starts Belgian subsidiary in 1946 and Scotland plant in 1950, acquires Raytheon's interests in Datamatic, 1957 and General Electric's computer division in 1970 to enter computer technology field, operates by 1982 with worldwide sales of $5.59 billion and employs some 100,000 people)... James Burnham: The Managerial Revolution (predicts managers will be elite ruling class in "managerial society")... Tom Hull, operator of El Rancho hotels in Fresno and Sacramento, opens El Rancho Vegas, first sumptuous hotel-casino in community of some 8,000 (books top shows to attract gamblers from Los Angeles, is followed in 1941 by El Cortez, acquired in 1944 by mobster Bugsy Siegel who opens gaudy Flamingo in 1946-47, Last Frontier in 1945, and Golden Nugget in 1946 to promote Las Vegas, population of some 20,000 in 1944, as El Dorado for gamblers)... Bernard Kilgore is managing editor of Wall Street Journal (-1967, transforms paper into national daily from circulation of 32,000 to 1,132,000).

<h2 style="text-align:center">1942</h2>

General Events

President Roosevelt submits (January 7) budget of $58,927,902,000, over $52 billion for war, to Congress... Office of Production Management is replaced (January 16) by War Production Board, Donald M. Nelson of Sears as chairman (-1944, starts conversion to war production by limiting non-essential manufacturing and banning use of scarce materials, starts reconversion planning in mid-1943 to avoid post-war industrial dislocations and massive unemployment - opposed by military as against war effort)...

Emergency Price Control Act authorizes (January 30) Office of Price Administration to set ceilings on prices and rents... Congress obtains (March 26) labor's agreement to ban all strikes during war... American-British joint chiefs of staff forms to coordinate war efforts in planning "strategic conduct of the war"... War Production Board halts (April 8) all construction not needed for war effort... Gas rationing is started (May 15) on East Coast to conserve rubber, within 1 year tires not available in black market (covers all states by December 1)... U.S. contracts (September 18) for entire rubber supply of Mexico for 4 years... Revenue Act regulates (October 21) excess profits from defense contracts...

Coffee is rationed (November 28)... Daylight Savings Time is adopted for duration of war... FDR asks governors to set highway speed limits at 40 mph to conserve tires... For first time U.S. Navy accepts Negro recruits... OPA refuses oil to plants, apartments and businesses that can but don't convert to coal... Vannevar Bush develops analog calculator to prepare artillery firing tables for U.S. Army... Social scientist Beardsley Ruml, treasurer of R.H. Macy Department Store 1935-45, proposes withholding method for income tax collection, enacted 1943... James Farmer, others form Congress of Racial Equality... Lanham Act provides funds for day care centers... War Manpower Commission is created... Architect George Nelson proposes downtown pedestrian malls...

"Little Steel" formula for wartime adjustments in wages of certain steel workers permits rises in wages with increases in living costs... U.S. Army Air Force creates pioneering Psychological Research Unit... Stabilization Act grants President power to regulate wages, salaries (freezes direct pay for duration of war)... Magnetic recording tape is invented... OPA rations sugar (freezes rents and rations coffee)...

Radio Directors' Guild organizes as union... War Production Board sponsors formation of labor-management committees to improve productivity, adopted by over 800 plants... Eliel Saarinen: The City (discusses urban planning)... U.S. seizes some 50,000 patents owned by firms of enemy countries... War Labor Board is formed to settle labor disputes, warns employers to avoid sex discrimination... Jose Sert: Can Our Cities Survive? (discusses need for urban planning)...

Secret Manhattan project is created as joint activity of government and business, Lt. General Leslie R. Groves in charge, to develop atomic bomb (-1947)... In following British experience, Eighth Bomber Command creates first U.S. operations research team (is used by Anti-Submarine Warfare Operations Group of U.S. Navy - first successful U.S. effort in operations research)... Committee for Economic Development is created by Paul G. Hoffman of Studebaker, William Benton from advertising, and Marion B. Folsum of Eastman Kodak to sponsor research on national, international economic policy... U.S. Army reorganizes (creates separate commands for Air Force, Ground Forces and Service of Supply with War Plans Division in headquarters general staff to assist Chief of Staff in planning, supervising and directing operations of Executive Group, a secretariat activity, Strategy and Policy Group for strategic planning, Theater Group for monitoring operations of areas and providing general staff for various theater commands, and Logistics Group)... U.S. Navy commissions first Negro officer (commissions first black admiral in 1972).

Business Events

Ford Motor Co. stops producing civilian cars to do defense contracts... Juan E. Metzger, father and partner start Dannon's Yogurt, NYC (stays as president when acquired by Beatrice food conglomerate in 1959, continues as consultant when acquired by BSN Groupe of France in 1981)... Texas oil man Clint Murchison drills first producing well for natural gas in Barker Dome Discovery, sells to El Paso Natural Gas in 1950 for $3 million plus royalties (acquires Dallas bus line in 1944 to develop Transcontinental Bus with 1,000 buses in 1955, acquires Henry Holt Publishing in 1951 - merged later with other properties to form Holt, Rinehart, Winston Publishing, buys Chicago building materials firm in 1951 - consolidated with other interests to form Union Chemical and Materials in 1954, creates Management Corp. in 1952 to oversee holdings in candy, glass, safes, banks, ranches, and fishing tackle business - empire of some $600 million by 1955)...

National Association of Suggestion Systems is formed... Henry J. Kaiser creates Permanente Foundation to provide health maintenance plan for all employees (opens plan to public in 1945, becomes Kaiser Foundation Health Plan in 1952 to operate chain of 19 hospitals)... Macy's presents Latin-American fiesta to promote products from region... Henry J. Kaiser builds integrated steel plant at Fontana, CA, largest steel producer west of Mississippi by 1959 (acquires Fleetwing Aircraft in 1943 - renamed Kaiser Metal Products after war, starts Kaiser Gypsum in 1944, forms partnership in 1945 with Joseph W. Frazer to build cars, forms Kaiser Aluminum and Chemical in 1949)...

All assembly lines making automobiles are stopped for duration of war... Pan Am's Pacific Clipper makes first round-the-world flight in some 200 hours... Former art critic Walter K. Gutman is hired by New York brokerage house of Goodbody & Co. as junior security analyst on no-pay trial basis (receives first salary in one month, is assigned in 1949 to write house's weekly market letter, becomes financial oracle to predict, contrary to opinion of financial seers, bull market in bonds in 1957 and record high for Dow-Jones Industrial Average in 1958, fails to identify May market crash in 1962, joins Shields & Co., private underwriter founded 1923, in 1958 to publish entertaining market newsletters)... Advertising Council is formed by corporate interests to promote cause of U.S. business...

With $500 borrowed on mother's furniture, John Johnson publishes Negro Digest (launches Ebony magazine in 1945, starts Fashion Fair cosmetics in 1973 - by 1980 enterprises include radio station and Supreme Life Insurance Co.)... Arthur D. Little consulting business designs "Operation Bootstrap" for economic development of Puerto Rico... Bell Aircraft tests first U.S. jet plane... Alex Osborn at New York advertising agency of Batten, Barton, Durstin and Osborn develops brainstorming as creativity technique (introduces technique to clients in 1953, receives national recognition for innovation with Time article in 1957)... General Electric develops all-electronic tracer control system for machinery... Inventor, over 300 patents, and designer Peter Schlumbohm develops Chemex Coffee Maker with filter and no moving parts.

1943

General Events

President Roosevelt submits (January 11) budget of $108,903,047,923, some $100 billion for war effort, to Congress... Shoes are rationed (February 7)... Coupon books are issued (March 1) for rationing of processed foods, meats, fats and cheese... To halt inflation President Roosevelt freezes (April 8) prices, wages and salaries... John L. Lewis orders United Mine Workers to strike to protest wage freeze (on threat of Federal take-over of mines calls off strike)... President Roosevelt orders (May 27) end to racial discrimination on defense contracts...

Current Tax Payment Act introduces (June 9) withholding of Federal income taxes to finance war effort... Threatened by shut-down of railroads by striking workers, U.S. siezes lines (-1944)... Some 40,000 Akron rubber workers strike 5 days to protest WLB's wage award (return to work after ultimatum by President Roosevelt)... Postal Zoning System divides country into 124 major offices (forms metro system with 85 sectional centers, eventually 552, in 1963 to serve nearby post offices)... Scottish-born Douglas A. Fraser becomes president of United Automobile Workers' local, union president for 1977-83...

CIO creates Political Action Committee with Sidney Hillman as head... LSD hallucinogenic drug is discovered by accident when chemist swallows dose... Portal-to-portal wages are won by strike of John L. Lewis' United Mine Workers... Federal troops are needed in Detroit to put down riot of Whites protesting employment of Negroes, seen in several other major cities... American Society of Civil Engineers recommends local branches form collective bargaining committees... Military uses insecticide bombs for spraying bugs, fumigation (pioneers development of aerosol products)... University of Chicago forms Committee on Human Relations in Industry with members from business, sociology and anthropology to do research in industrial sociology... A.H. Maslow: "A Theory of Human Motivation," Psychological Review (proposes hierarchy of needs to explain reasons for behavior)...

President creates Committee on Fair Employment Practices... Office of War Mobilization is formed (May 27) to coordinate activities of War Department, Navy Department, Munitions, Office of Economic Stabilization, War and Labor Board, Price Control Office, Transportation Board, Manpower Board and War Production Board... As result of strikes by United Mine Workers, Smith-Connally Anti-Strike Bill is passed, June 25 (provides jail terms for strike leaders and 30-day cooling-off period, bans union donations to political parties, establishes work week of 48 hours)... California Food Research Institute develops powdered fruit juice... Ernest Crocker, Arthur D. Little chemist, develops synthetic spices for nutmeg, cinnamon and white pepper...

U.S. Post Office takes Esquire to court on charges of distributing obscene materials... California State Nurse's Association becomes bargaining agent for professional members in negotiating labor contracts with various hospitals... By Presidential order work week of 48 hours is established for all defense workers (grants time-and-a-half for work over 40 hours)... Office of Strategic Services establishes first U.S. assessment center to evaluate capabilities of candidates as secret agents (follows development in early 1900s by German psychologists, in 1930s by German military high command to select officers – model for British War Office for evaluating officers).

Business Events

When Edsel Ford dies, Henry Ford re-assumes post as president of Ford Motor Co., losing money for 15 years, when his recommendation of security chief Harry Bennett fails (names Henry Ford II, newly-released from military service, as vice president to battle Bennett for control of business with support of mother and grandmother, surrenders reins to Henry II in 1945 – Bennett and cohorts ousted)... Andre Meyer, French-born financier (formed France's first consumer finance company in 1920s, revived Citroen car business with sale to Michelin tire firm), becomes senior partner of Lazard Freres' New York office (amasses personal fortune of some $250-500 million by death in 1979 from creative financial engineering and personal contacts with European investors in arranging acquisitions, forming conglomerates)...

Robert S. McNamara, after advising Air Force on designing statistical control system, is granted leave of absence by Harvard (helps RAF to establish statistical control system, joins "Tex" Thornton at Ford Motor Co. in 1946 as one of "Whiz Kids," after serving as manager of planning and financial analysis becomes comptroller in 1949 – president of Ford in 1960)... David Sullivan starts pioneering black ad agency in NYC, limited to selling black products in black media (-1949, is followed by Detroit's Fusche, Young & Powell in 1943, Chicago's Vince Cullers in 1956)...

American Enterprise Institute is formed by businessmen as conservative counterpart to 1916 Brookings Institution... Albert Lea business of Minnesota prepares detailed plan for post-war growth... Federal Communications Commission requires NBC to divest itself of one of its 2 radio networks (retains Red as NBC, drops Blue which becomes American

Broadcasting Co.)...   Edward C. Johnson, II, pioneer of mutual fund industry, takes over Fidelity Fund (retires in 1974 after building business from $3 million in assets to group of 14 firms with almost $3 billion in assets)... First woman is allowed to work on floor of New York Stock Exchange... Harvard Advanced Management program for executives is started... Branch Rickey, pioneering baseball administrator, becomes president of Brooklyn Dodgers baseball franchise... In biggest industrial merger to date Consolidated Vultee Aircraft is formed by Vultee Aircraft and Consolidated Aircraft.

1944

General Events

U.S. Air Force announces (January 7) production of first jet fighter, Bell P-59 Airacomet... Washington reports (March 7) women comprise 42% of workers in West Coast aircraft plants... President Roosevelt submits (January 10) budget of $70 billion, practically all for war effort, to Congress... Congress approves (March 29) $1.350 billion for United Nations Relief and Rehabilitation Agency for post-war assistance... Most meat rationing ends (May 3)... Servicemen's Readjustment Act, GI Bill of Rights, provides (June 22) financial assistance to veterans after war...

International Monetary Fund and International Bank for Reconstruction and Development are created (July 1-22) by conference of 44 nations at Bretton Woods, NH... Philadelphia is paralyzed (August 1) by transportation strike... Production of some home appliances is approved (August 14)... Congress passes (October 3) Surplus War Property Act... 6th War Loan Drive is launched (November 19) to raise some $14 billion from sales of war bonds... Sidney Hillman, president of Amalgamated Clothing Workers since 1914 and co-founder of CIO in 1935, organizes American Labor Party (co-founds World Federation of Trade Unions in 1945)... Government spends some $700 million on research, up from $70 million in 1938...

Lloyd B. Sponaugle of Ohio applies for patent on machine tool automatically controlled by programming manually directed machine motions (is developed in 1945 by Leif Eric de Neergaard of New York, by GE in 1947 and Gisholt Machine Tool after 1950)... Cost-of-living rises by almost 30% (results in thriving "black market" of some $1.3 billion)... War Production Board authorizes manufacturers to make commercial trucks...

Pioneering field of group behavior, Turkish-born Muzafer Sherif receives 2-year State Department fellowship to study group conflict (becomes Yale research fellow in 1947-49 to do experiments in group conflict and cooperation, becomes director of University of Oklahoma's Institute of Group Relations in 1949-66 to study causes, cures for intergroup conflict)... After defying order by National Labor Relations Board to extend labor contract, U.S. Army seizes Montgomery Ward under wartime powers, physically removes chairman Sewall Avery from office... Rensis Likert, Douglas McGregor, and Kurt Lewin discuss feasibility of group dynamics center at MIT (pioneer movement)...

James Young: A Technique for Producing Ideas (pioneers study of creative thinking)... Total union membership is some 30% of non-agricultural labor force... After 2 years to design and 4 years to build, Harvard graduate student Howard Aiken builds Mark I computer with financing and technical support from IBM... AT&T rejects union proposal to put member on board of directors...

Racketeer Louis, "Lepke," Buchalter dies after serving as middleman between unions, industry... Air Force commissions Dr. Theodore von Karman, colleagues to forecast next 20 years of air power (issue <u>Toward</u> <u>New</u> <u>Horizons</u> as planning document for Air Force thinking)...

Fashion Institute of Technology opens, NYC (graduates many leading U.S. designers, such as Calvin Klein)... Some 16 million women work in labor force... U.S. Public Health Service warns dangers of DDT... Philadelphia Transit System is disrupted by strike on racial issues (takes U.S. Army 3 days to maintain order)... U.S. Navy tests helicopter for sea-air rescue... John von Neumann, Oskar Morgenstern: <u>Theory</u> <u>of</u> <u>Games</u> <u>and</u> <u>Economic</u> <u>Behavior</u> (pioneers development of game theory and linear programming, describes strategy as series of actions by firm that are determined by particular situation)...

Henry Bergson: <u>Creative</u> <u>Evolution</u> (pioneers study of creativity)... Director of War Mobilization & Reconversion bans (December 1) horse racing to save critical materials (-May 9, 1945).

Business Events

Paul Hoffman, head of Studebaker car business, eliminates distributors to increase profits for dealers... Financier Robert R. Young of Allegheny Corp., holding company of Van Swearingen empire of railroads, fails to take over Pullman Car Co. (consolidates C&O, Pere Marquette, Nickle Plate and Wheeling & Lake Erie railroads in 1945 - genesis of Chessie system)... Lawyer Walter O'Malley forms syndicate to acquire Brooklyn Dodgers baseball franchise (becomes president in 1950, moves franchise to Los Angeles in 1957 to average over 2 million customers/season and over 3 million after 1978)... Ray Dunlap, chemist for J.R. Simplot Co. of Idaho, develops process to freeze french fried potatoes (evolves from business started by Jack Simplot during early 1920s as 8th grader to buy interest-earning script used to pay teachers - basis for bank loan to buy, sell hogs to earn $7,800 on graduation from high school in late 1920s, uses funds to acquire over 30 potato drying and packing sheds in 1930s, by accident acquires process to make onion powder in late 1930s, by end of W.W.II. supplies 30% of dried potatoes and onions used by military, opens first phosphate mine in 1946 to enter fertilizer business - basis for 100 Soilbuilder Service Centers, acquires interests in Dominican gold mine, lumber business in Colombia, potatoes in Turkey and Idaho ski resort, is fined $80,000 in 1977 by Federal Court for failing to report income, is fined $1.4 million in 1978 by Federal Court for attempting to manipulate future's market and is banned from trading for 6 years by Commodities Futures Trading Commission, operates by 1985 one of world's largest privately held enterprises with sales of some $1.5 billion)...

Monsanto Chemical announces process for non-shrinking, non-wrinkling wool clothes... Plans to create Trans-America Football League and All-American Football Conference in 1945 are announced... Boeing tests post-war "Stratocruiser" (produces 55 by 1950)... Ex-ad man William Benton petitions FCC for subscription radio network... Londonderry of San

Francisco launches national advertising campaign to sell quick-mix ice cream powder... Joe Frazer, associates acquire control of Graham-Paige Motors... Libbey-Owens-Ford announces prefabricated glass kitchen (contains electric garbage disposal, hydraulic dishwasher, electric clothes dryer, ceramic electric range in color, plastic dishes, cordless electric iron and refrigerator with revolving shelves, freezing compartment and mechanisms for ice-water and ice-cubes)...

Lockheed Aircraft employee some 93,000 workers, around 2,500 prior to war... After graduation from high school (organized small Chinese-style mutual fund for other students) and working as successful stock salesman for Honolulu office of Dean Witter, Chinn Ho, son of clerk at Pacific Club and grandson of emigrant rice farmer, creates Capital Investment Co. (develops business to become one of wealthiest on islands with interests in hotels, tourist developments, minor-league baseball team, Honolulu Stadium and _Star-Bulletin_ paper)...

Walter H. Annenberg, publisher of father's _Daily Racing Form_, issues _Seventeen_ magazine (acquires 5 radio stations, publishes _TV Guide_ in 1953, acquires _Philadelphia Daily News_ in 1957, becomes ambassador to Great Britain in 1969)... Juan Trippe, president of Pan American Airways, starts chain of Inter-Continental hotels, 92 in 49 countries before selling in 1980s (gets idea during lunch with President Roosevelt who wanted to assist South American countries in economic growth)... Boston textile business of Special Yarns, started in 1923 by Royal Little, becomes Textron (changes charter in 1952 to diversify outside textiles, builds pioneering conglomerate of some 70 firms outside textile industry in mid-1960s)...

Justin W. Dart, formerly with Walgreen drug store chain 1932-41 as manager of store operations and CEO, follows Louis K. Liggett, founder in 1903, as head of United Drug (evolves as Dart Industries in 1950s with Tupperware, West Bend kitchenware and Duracell batteries).

1945

General Events

U.S. adopts (February 26) midnight curfew... Germany surrenders (May 7) to Allies... War Manpower Commission removes all controls... War ends (August 14) in Orient... President Truman orders (September 28) federal control of natural resources beyond continental shelf... President Truman seizes (October 4) 26 oil companies... Nationwide shoe rationing ends (October 30)... Tire rationing ends (December 20)... Teamsters Union asks repeal of Wagner Act and end of NLRB... WLB sets minimum wage of 55 cents/hour for textile workers... 10 Chrysler and Briggs plants in Detroit are closed by strikes... President Truman orders Navy to take over strike-bound Goodyear plants in Akron... 19,000 workers in coal, utility and dairy industries strike employers... 100,000 employees are laid-off in New York as war contracts end...

35 mph speed limit is lifted... John L. Lewis ends coal strike... Nationwide strike of 180,000 workers close GM plants (ends after 4 months with pay raise of 18.5 cents)... President Truman asks Congress for law to end strikes... McCarran-Ferguson Act exempts insurance industry from federal anti-trust laws...

In period to 1955 some 27 million workers are idled by over 43,000 strikes... War Stabilization Board is created to replace War Labor Board in planning for conversion to peacetime economy... 13 airlines petition Civil Aeronautics Board for Pacific routes... Federal Reserve Board eases credit controls to permit installment buying... Unions pressure 9 of largest airlines to grant employees 40-hour week... Silicone polymers are developed in this time... Vannevar Bush: <u>Science:</u> <u>The</u> <u>Endless</u> <u>Frontier</u> (results in creation of National Science Foundation for basic research)... Elton Mayo: <u>The</u> <u>Social</u> <u>Problems</u> <u>of</u> <u>an</u> <u>Industrial</u> <u>Civilization</u>...

University of Chicago creates Industrial Relations Center as consulting group to do research studies and educational programs for business in industrial relations, organization and management development, followed by Cornell's Industrial and Labor Relations Center and others at Yale, University of Illinois... Second Circuit Court of Appeals: <u>United</u> <u>States</u> <u>v.</u> <u>Aluminum</u> <u>Company</u> <u>of</u> <u>America</u> (rules Alcoa monopoly for market position and potential powers even though firm did not abuse its dominance of industry)...

New York passes first state Fair Employment Practices Act... U.S. Supreme Court: <u>Allen</u> <u>Bradley</u> <u>Company</u> <u>v.</u> <u>Local</u> <u>Union</u> <u>No.</u> <u>3,</u> <u>IBEW</u> (prohibits collusion of union and firm to form monopoly)... U.S. Army Personnel Research Section develops board interview to determine which officers will be retained in post-war army... Kurt Lewin forms MIT's Research Center for Group Dynamics to conduct experiments in group dynamics (after death in 1947 is transferred to University of Michigan in 1948 as part of its Institute for Social Research)... Union membership reaches some 14 million... Computer pioneer Vannevar Bush proposes revolutionary device Memex, condensed library of information for house (appears in 1980s with compact audio disk).

Business Events

With $3,000 L.S. Shoen starts U-Haul national chain of rental trucks, trailers in Oregon (rents 20 trailers by end of 1946 - 200 in 1948, builds peak network of 14,000 gas stations in 1970, diversifies in late 1970s by renting such items as chainsaws, lawn mowers, canoes, exercise bikes, and mobile homes, incurs long-term debt of $452 million in 1980s, after losing money and market battle with rival Ryder's, each with about 45% share of rental market in 1987, is ousted from board in 1986 by children taking over business)... Ford finishes war production after making 8,600 bombers, 278,000 jeeps and 57,000 aircraft engines (halts production and lays off 50,000 workers after unauthorized strikes)... GM, Ford and Chrysler reject union demands for 30% increase in wages... First U.S. refrigerator plane crosses country with full cargo of perishables...

William J. Levitt starts building 1,600 small houses at Norfolk, VA... Patrick E. Haggerty becomes general manager of laboratory and manufacturing division of Geophysical Service, president in 1951 and chairman 1966-76 (reorganizes as Texas Instruments in 1951)... Supported by mother and grandmother in handling Henry Ford, Henry Ford II becomes president of Ford Motor Co., business losing some $9 million/month (-1980 with retirement, ousts Harry Bennett, fires over 1,000 executives, and sells many properties, including Brazilian plantations and soy bean farms, hires Ernest R. Beech, president of GM's Bendix Corp., in 1946 to

establish audit system, decentralize operations and increase production
with automation, hires "Tex" Thornton and Air Force statistical group,
dubbed "Whiz Kids" with future presidents Robert McNamara and Arjay
Miller, to do organizational planning and introduce military management
techniques, raises wages for workers in 1946 with union guarantee of no
illegal strikes, introduces industry's first pension plan in 1949 and
first all-new post-war car in 1949 - Thunderbird in 1954, Edsel in 1957,
and Mustang in 1964)... McCann-Erickson ad agency pioneers motivational
research in industry (rejects previous statistical studies of consumers
as rational beings)...

Sam Walton, brother open five-and-dime variety store, AR (by 1962 operate
9 stores franchised by Ben Franklin stores of Chicago, when prevented in
opening discount store starts independent Wal-Mart business in 1962)...
Railway dome observation car is appears... W.W. II fighter pilots, ground
crewman serving in Pacific theater start Flying Tigers air-cargo carrier
(after losing some $95 million after 1983 in price wars with Japan's
Nippon Cargo Airlines, struggles for survival in 1986 with bloated costs,
loose operating controls and fuzzy strategy, is acquired in 1988-89 by
Federal Express for $880 million)...

J. Peter Grace becomes head of 1854 W.R. Grace International trading
business (starts development of chemical business in early 1950s, drops
existing operations, including 23-ship fleet of Grace line and Latin
American interests, in late 1950s, grows as conglomerate in 1960s with
150 acquisitions, including auto parts, office supplies, breweries,
restaurants, motor homes, cattle breeding, retail chains, and shrimp
production to achieve sales of $7.3 billion in 1985 - $200 million in
1950, is attacked in 1986 for weak earnings)... Industrialist Henry J.
Kaiser and Joseph W. Frazer, president of Graham-Paige Motor Co., create
Kaiser-Frazer Corp. with $53 million to build cars for post-war market
(acquire 5% of new-car market in 1948, acquire Willys-Overland with Jeep
business and Brazil plant in 1953, abandon passenger car-market in 1955
to sell only Jeeps, last produced in 1986, and commercial vehicles)...

Federated Department Stores, Abraham & Straus in Brooklyn, Filene's of
Boston, Lazarus in Columbus and Bloomingdale's of NYC, starts expansion
program (in period 1947-77 grows from 4 to 20 stores)... Macy's of NYC
acquires San Francisco retail business (forms California division in
1947 and Kansas division in 1949, reorganizes business to operate 32
stores by 1956)...

General Motors plans to make small, economical car, the Cadet, to sell
for under $1,000 (abandons project in 1947 due to problems in converting
to post-war market)... Raytheon engineer pops corn from curiosity to see
if microwave energy cooks food (results in first microwave ovens in 1947
for restaurants and hotels - first for consumers in 1955 by Tappan which
imports small Japanese models in 1985, is followed by GE's Hotpoint
microwave in 1956 - phased out in 1984, Raytheon's Amana unit in 1967,
Litton in 1970, South Korean units in 1978, and ovens by Japan's Sanyo,
U.S. market leader in 1983, and Matsushita in 1979)... First pre-cooked
frozen meals are prepared for U.S. airline passengers... In this time
(-1949) 1899 Pressed Steel Car Co. is transformed by diversification into
conglomerate U.S. Industries (after consolidating in 1965 from over-
expansion, operates 125 divisions in 1973 to achieve revenues of some
$1.6 billion from mostly unknown products - sales of $126 million in

1965)...

After operating various hotels since first in 1918 and opening Long Beach Hilton in 1939, Conrad Hilton acquires Chicago's 3,000-room Stevens Hotel, world's largest (forms Hilton Hotel Corp. in 1946, opens Puerto Rico hotel in 1947, starts Hilton International in 1948 - 250 hotels by 1970, acquires famed NYC's Waldorf-Astoria in 1949 to operate 13 hotels, acquires Statler chain in 1950s, approves with reluctance son's trade of Hilton International stock for TWA shares in 1967, operates 175 hotels and 136 franchised inns by 1970s - 2nd largest U.S. chain to ITT's Sheraton)... Herbert Simon: <u>Administrative</u> <u>Behavior</u> (studies decision making and organization)...

Catepillar Tractor, IL, starts pioneering counseling program to improve mental health of employees... Douglas Aircraft develops project RAND to study space vehicles for Air Force (becomes RAND Corp. in 1948 as private nonprofit think-tank to contract for independent research projects)... B.B. Gardiner: <u>Human</u> <u>Relations</u> <u>in</u> <u>Industry</u>... Henry J. Kaiser starts Kaiser Community Homes to build low-cost housing in Los Angeles, San Francisco, Portland (completes some 16,000 units)... Pioneering National Executive Search business provides unemployed executives with career counseling, marketing services... Irvine Robbins, Burton Baskin start ice cream store business, grows to some 2,500 stores by 1982 (suffers slow-down in growth in 1970s from competition of fancy ice cream brands, such as 1962 Haagen-Dazs - 169 stores by 1982)... First postnuptial resort in Pocono Mountains opens, PA (pioneers growth of area as self-proclaimed "Honeymoon Capital of the World" to compete in market with Niagara Falls)... Some 3,500 fast-food outlets operate in U.S., some 440,000 by 1975...

During period (-1949) Batesville Casket Co., IN, makes metal caskets by mass production (introduces assembly line process to industry)... Marshall Fields' Merchandise Mart is purchased for almost $13 million, $12.5 million borrowed from insurance company, by Joseph P. Kennedy (over next 20 years increases in value to $75 million and generates annual rentals of some $13 million)...

American Society of Training Directors forms... TWA starts commercial flights to Europe to compete with Pan American, American Export Airlines (results in rate war)... After canning bean sprouts and chop suey during World War II Luigino Paulucci borrows $2,500 to start Chun King Chinese foods in Minnesota (-1949, sells in 1966 to R.J. Reynolds business for some $63 million, uses proceeds in 1967 to start Jeno's pizza products in Duluth, sells business to rival Pillsbury in 1981, uses profits to develop small businesses in area to provide employment idled by decline of Mesabi Mines, after abandoning Pizza Kwik in 1987 launches China Kwik as nationwide Chineese-food home-delivery business)...

Anthony De Angelis starts meat packing business (acquires well-known packer Adolph Gobel, Inc., in 1949 to land contract for federal school-lunch program, is forced to pay $100,000 by Agricultural Department in 1952 for over-charges and short-weights on contract, declares bankruptcy of Adolph Gobel, Inc. in 1953 and is required to settle income tax lien of $1.2 million by Internal Revenue Service, forms Allied Crude Vegetable Oil & Refining to store surplus vegetable oils for export market, starts subleasing oil tanks in 1958 to American Express Warehousing)...

E.S. Tupper, former DuPont chemist, starts business to make unbreakable, flexible, air-tight plastic food containers (influenced by marketing approach of Stanley Home Products sells products directly to women with first neighborhood "Tupperware Party" in 1951, disenchanted with complexities managing huge company sells to Rexall Drug and Chemical Co. of Dart Industries in 1958 - merger with Kraft in 1980, after falling sales in 1980s launches new marketing program to sell products by lunch-hour and "rush-hour" parties at home and work, introduces mail-order catalog in 1988)... American Management Association launches executive seminar program (goes from revenues less than $1 million to some $22 million in 1968 with 800 full-time employees after training some 59,000 managers from 20,000 firms).

1946

General Events

Some 7,700 Western Electric telephone mechanics strike (January 9) for higher wages... United Electrical, Radio and Machine Workers strikes (January 15) in 16 states... Steel mills are closed (January 21) by United Steel Workers Union demanding higher wages... Employment Act is passed, February 20 (creates Council of Economic Advisors, provides for annual national economic report, commits government to "maximum employment, production, and purchasing power")... Office of Economic Stabilization is created (February 21) to plan conversion to peacetime economy... After 113-day walk-out against General Motors, United Automobile Workers return to work with higher wages... After government takes over to avert strike, railroads are halted (May 23) by strike of Trainmen and Locomotive Engineers Brotherhood...

Reorganization Act restructures (June 20) executive branch... Wartime price controls are extended (July 15) for year... Federal Reserve reports (July 22) half of workers receive incomes under $2,000... Atomic Energy Commission is created (August 1)... Price controls on meats are lifted (October 16)...

200,000 workers strike Chicago packing plants... 800,000 steel workers strike in Pittsburgh... U.S. rocket reaches altitude of 50 miles... After striking GE for 2 months, workers return to work with wage increase just over 18 cents/hour... U.S. farm prices reach highest level since 1920... James Petrillo, president of American Federation of Musicians, temporarily bans members from working on TV... AT&T announces plans for car-phone service... New York docks are paralyzed by strike of 200,000 workers... President Truman vetoes bill for federal mediation in labor disputes as being unable to end strikes... Philadelphia bakeries are closed by AFL strike... Worse U.S. maritime strike closes docks on all coasts... A&P food chain is convicted for monopolistic practices...

New Yorkers dine on horse meat as prices of standard meats soar... OPA freezes prices of all foods, except sugar, and beverages... First Women's Golf Championship is played at Spokane County Club, WA, sponsored by United States Golf Assn. in 1953 (after near bankruptcy in 1975 becomes profitable in 1980s with corporate sponsors)... Personal pager, size of small radio, is introduced (evolves by 1980s as pen-size electronic instrument)... Generation of baby boomers is launched, some 76 million births by 1964... _Life_: "A Major U.S. Problem: Labor"...

Inter-Group Relations workshop on improving use of discussion groups meets at State Teacher's College at New Britain, CT, sponsored by Connecticut Interracial Commission and MIT Research Center for Group Dynamics (leads to 1947 formation of National Training Laboratories at Bethel, MA)... Chester Gould draws wrist radio for Dick Tracy cartoon strip, reality in 1982... American Institute for Foreign Trade opens, AZ (becomes Thunderbird Graduate School of International Management in 1968)... Carl Rogers starts "personal growth" program using encounter groups for returning servicemen...

In defiance of Government John L. Lewis, some 400,000 United Mine Workers strike for health, welfare and retirement benefits (results in seizure of mines, after 2nd strike is indicted for contempt and fined $10,000 and UMW fined $3.5 million - upheld by Supreme Court in 1947, and passage of 1947 Taft-Hartley Act)...

U.S. Supreme Court: <u>Morgan</u> <u>v.</u> <u>Commonwealth</u> (rules buses in interstate commerce must allow seating without discrimination)... Simon Kuznets formulates Gross National Product concept... Rensis Likert starts Survey Research Center at University of Michigan (pioneers survey research and feedback)... American Sociological Society forms industrial sociology section... Texan Jose Silva develops Mind Control, packaged personal growth program of meditation, self-hypnosis, and guided fancy...

ENIAC, world's first all-electronic digital computer (with price of $487,000 consists of 30 tons of equipment and 18,000 vacuum tubes) is operated at University of Pennsylvania by designers John Presper Eckert, John Mauchly (-1955 when decommissioned after performing military and scientific calculations - displayed at Smithsonian Institution in 1956, start business, Electric Control as first U.S. computer manufacturer, in 1946 after refusing to turn over patent to University, is sold to Remington-Rand in 1949 - drop market 1963, design first commercial computer UNIVAC in 1951 for Bureau of Census, lose patent rights for electronic computer in 1973 as original idea of John D. Atanasoff in 1935)...

Hobbs Anti-Racketeering Act is passed to curb undesirable activities of Teamsters Union... Stanford Research Institute is founded at Menlo Park, CA, as "think tank" in cooperation with Stanford University (-1949, receives independence from Stanford University in 1970 to become SRI International)... Some 23 million man days are lost during year due to strikes, 5% of total... Lea Act is passed to stop featherbetting practices of AFL Musicians' Union.

Business Events

Edward C. Johnson II acquires moribund Fidelity Fund in Boston (after accumulating assets of some $3 million by 1962 amasses $4.3 billion by mid-1960s and $5.4 billion in 1978 after slumping market - $56 billion in 1986 as 2nd only to Merrill Lynch's $72 billion, operates 104 different funds in 1986 along with holdings in Boston cab company, real estate, 2 executive recruitment firms, venture capital partnership, bimonthly newsletter with over 100,000 readers, and off-shore investment business)... After military service, Robert Irsay is hired by Acord Ventilating Co., father's prosperous sheetmetal business in Chicago (with ill feelings resigns in 1951 to start own sheetmetal company - City's largest by 1971 after forcing father's firm out of business in 1953, sells company in 1971 for $8.5 million, acquires winning Baltimore Colts' NFL football franchise in 1972 in strange deal - 6 coaches and 12 losing seasons by 1986, moves franchise in hush operation to Indianapolis in 1984)...

Tekrad, later Tektronix, is incorporated in Portland, OR, by Howard Vollum (devises first oscilloscope in 1934 as physics student at local Reed College), Jack Murdock (operates radio and home appliance store in 1930s) and associates to make and repair electronic instruments and equipment with 6 employees - 77 in 1949, 501 in 1954, 4,910 in 1964 and 12,693 in 1974 (makes first successful oscilloscope to test electronic signals in 1947, contracts with first foreign distributor in Sweden in 1948 - Belgium 1954, West Germany 1955, and Austria in 1958, forms sales force in 1950, opens NYC field office in 1951 and first foreign office in Canada in 1957, starts first foreign plant on Island of Guernsey in 1958 - Holland plant in 1961, signs contract with Japan's Sony in 1965, starts formal operational planning in 1972, evolves by 1980s as $1.5 billion business making over 800 products with some 20,000 employees, State's largest employer, at 8 industrial parks and facilities around world)...

Steven D. Bechtel, Jr., head 1961, reorganizes father's construction business as Bechtel Corp. to consolidate engineering and building activities, employs 25,000 with 9,500 engineers, 600 technical professionals, over 2,000 procurement specialists and some 35,000 temporary workers by 1975 on global projects of $40 billion (builds oil pipeline across Canadian Rockies in 1950s and one of world's largest refineries at Aden in 1952 in evolving as worldwide business before suffering downturn with contract cancellations in 1984, lets 22,000 employees go 1982-86 before revival in 1987)...

Scientist Simon Ramo, after working for General Electric in research, is hired by Hughes Aircraft to head electronics department (resigns in 1953 with colleague Dr. Dean E. Wooldridge to start Ramo-Wooldridge Electronic business in Los Angeles with funds from Thompson Products of Cleveland, diversifies in 1954 with Pacific Semi-Conductors, merges with Thompson in 1958 to form TRW to provide overall direction for Air Force's ballistic missile program)...

After operating Florida Pipe & Supply business in discarded materials with father and brother, Louis E. Wolfson acquires surplus shipyard (acquires control of North American, electric power combine, in 1947 - awards himself and associates substantial salaries and dividends on firm's cash and reserves, sells pipe business in 1949 for $2.5 million, starts stock raid on Merritt-Chapman & Scott, construction and ship-building business, in 1949 - with control in 1950 pays himself high salary and issues dividends of 40% in 1950 and 25% in 1954, is investigated in 1952 by Congressional committee, Comptroller General's office and Washington grand jury for having inside information on 1946 shipyard deal, acquires Washington's Capital Transit, divesture of North American, in 1954 with profits from shipyard deal, raids Montgomery Ward in 1954 for control of reserves of some $300 million - loses battle in 1955, sells North American in 1955 after collecting 150% in dividends on investment, raids American Motors in 1956 - abandons battle in 1958 with investigation by SEC, sells Capital Transit in 1957 after siphoning off profits before franchise canceled by public outrage, serves prison term for misdeeds)...

Monarch Airlines is started in Denver with 3 DC-3s (becomes Frontier Airlines in 1950 to serve 40 cities and 7 states with 12 DC-3s, is acquired by subsidiary of RKO Enterprises in 1964, serves 89 cities in 27 states, Canada and Mexico before nose-dive in 1982 with fare wars, launches non-union, discount Frontier Horizon Airline in 1983 - sold to Skybus in 1984, is acquired in 1985 by People Express to beat offer of Texas Air, declares bankruptcy in 1986 before acquisition of People Express by Texas Air)... 6 commercial TV stations are licensed, 442 in 1956...

Blount, Inc., billion-dollar worldwide construction and engineering service in 1980s, is formed in Alabama to construct fish ponds in rural South... For first time in GE history all plants are closed by union of electrical workers (results in "Boulwarism," proposed by Lemuel Boulwere, to negotiate with unions on tough take-it-or-leave-it approach instead of traditional haggling, drops 1915 profit-sharing plan unilaterally in 1947)...

Mobile Industrial Luncheon Service for factory workers is started by William Rosenberg, MA (evolves to operate 100 trucks, with threat of vending machines starts Dunkin' doughnut business in 1950)... Fortune: "Automatic Factory" (introduces proposal of Canadian J.J. Brown, E.W. Leaver for new industrial system with equipment to process information and regulate controls in operating machinery without men)... Laurence Tisch, brother Preston acquire New Jersey hotel, operate 12 by 1955 (acquire 118 run-down movie houses of Loews theater business in 1959 for real estate sites)...

General Electric develops computer method to guide machine tools (-1953)... Pilot Paul Butler starts Butler Aviation to provide fuel and service for private aircraft at U.S. airports... American Society for Quality Control forms... John Emery starts Emery Air Freight (changes from freight forwarding business in 1981 to cargo airline, buys troubled overnight express Purolator Courier in 1987 for $313 million to face bankruptcy in 1988)... American Research & Development is formed in Boston to provide venture capital for new research-based enterprises using wartime technology for peacetime purposes... William Norris, others start Engineering Research Associates, pioneering computer firm, in Minneapolis (after firm is acquired by Sperry Rand starts Controlled Data in 1957 - $1 of original stock worth at $324 by 1982)... Cleveland Rams franchise in National Football League moves to Los Angeles... Hooper Rating Service, measures size of radio audience with random phone calls, is adopted by advertising's Cooperative Analysis of Broadcasting to replace Crossley recall method of rechecking listening habits (is acquired by A.C. Nielsen in 1950 for $600,000 to dominate market)...

German-born David T. Chase, survivor of Nazi death camp, starts new life in Hartford, CT (begins career waxing cars, working in tree nursery and peddling goods door-to-door before going into construction business, leases rental space in 1956 to discount merchandise business called Topps - value of rental properties increases with purchase of Topps by larger company in 1960, starts real estate venture in 1970s to build huge office tower amid recession, evolves as $2 billion empire by 1985 with interests in real estate, cellular communications, insurance and broadcasting)...

After discharge from U.S. Navy as electrician's mate, school drop-out James Ling starts electrical contracting business with $3,000 (achieves sales of $1.5 million before forming public corporation in 1955)... Catherine P. Clark starts Brownberry Ovens to make distinctive bakery goods free of preservatives or artificial ingredients (sells in 1972 to Peavy Corp. for $12 million)... Lew Wasserman becomes president of Hollywood talent agency of Julius Stein's Music Corporation of America (dominates industry as matchmaker of packaged TV programs and movies)...

German-born Herber Bayer is hired as director of corporate design (pioneered by Germany's AEG before World War I and Peter Behrens, mentor of Walter Gropius founder of Bauhaus in 1919) by Container Corporation of America, followed by IBM's use of graphic design, corporate logo in 1955... Some 230 U.S. firms comprise major household appliance industry (falls to 25 by 1980 with GM, Ford, Westinghouse, United Technologies as dropouts)... Carroll M. Shanks becomes president of Prudential Insurance (-1962, uses finders for tips to make stock purchases and loans, is forced to resign with pension of $100,000/year for life on charges of conflicts in interests, results in company's formulation of ethical guidelines for gratuities, stock purchases, loans)...

Machine vending industry's sales volume is some $600 million, around $2.5 billion by 1960... General Foods decentralizes operations (-1949, organizes into 16 operating divisions, each with staff activities in law, finance, manufacturing and engineering services, public relations, advertising, purchasing, and traffic, reorganizes in 1972 as 5 strategic business units: coffee, desserts, main-meal dishes, breakfast foods, beverages and pet foods)... Despite providing accurate predictions to some 200 subscribers, financial guru Frederick N. Goldsmith is forced by court order to stop publishing market letter for insiders (starts letter 1916 to provide investors with tips derived from daily comic strip "Bringing Up Father" and psychic holding seances with James R. Keene Wall Sreet's number-one market manipulator in 1890s - early 1900s, develops publication to earn some $39,000/year from "Bible" of several Stock Exchange members)...

Warren E. Avis starts first car-rental business to serve airports with loan of $10,000, grows to 3,900 locations in 135 countries by 1987 (is acquired in 1954 by owner of Hertz franchise in Boston for $8,000, is acquired in 1956 by group of Boston investors, in 1962 by Lazard Freres investment bank, in 1965 by ITT - spun-off as public company in 1973, in 1977 by Norton Simon, in 1983 by Esmark in buying Norton Simon's business, in 1984 by Beatrice's purchase of Esmark, in 1986 by Kohlberg Kravis Robert & Co. with purchase of Beatrice in 1986 by Wesray Capital , and in 1987 by employees with $1.75 billion stock ownership plan, largest of kind in history)...

Estee Lauder forms partnership with husband to market skin preparations devised by Vienna-born cosmetic chemist (when major advertising agencies reject $50,000 account as under minimum of $1 million, uses money in 1946 to provide free samples at fashion shows and promote products by mailers with coupons, wins first major account from Saks Fifth Avenue in 1948, achieves success with Youth-Dew, perfumed bath-oil, in 1953, enters Canadian market in 1958 to achieve yearly sales of $850,000 with 5 employees, introduces products in England at Harrods of London in 1959, achieves first million dollars in sales in 1960 - $85 million and over

1,000 employees in 1973, introduces pioneering Aramis line of men's cosmetics in 1965 to beat Revlon's Braggi in 1966, introduces Clinique line, beating rival Revlon, in 1968 with products for younger women who wanted "pure," fragrance-free cosmetics - profitable 1972)...

Russell Kelly opens temporary office employee service in Detroit, becomes Kelly Girl Service in 1959 and Kelly Services in 1966 as industry's largest (achieves sales of $1.5 million in 1954 - $85-90 million in early 1970s from some 300 offices in U.S., Canada and Europe, starts Kelly Marketing services in 1962 - Labor and Technical services in 1964, opens first Canadian office in 1968- first European office at Paris iin 1972, starts Encore program in 1987 to utilize workers over 55, is world's largest in 1988 with 550,000 temporary and 3,800 full-time employees, enters Australia market in 1988 to operate branches in Canada, Puerto Rico, Ireland, United Kingdom and France)...

First automatic coffee dispenser is introduced at professional football game in Philadelphia, business grows to gross some $14 million in 1955 (evolves as industry with hiring of Schrafft's restaurant catering service in 1950 by Mutual Life Insurance of New York for coffee breaks)...

Basketball Association of America is formed by owners with arenas in big cities to compete with stars of small-city, Midwest-based National Basketball League, founded 1937 (appoints Maurice Podoloff as commissioner - retires 1963, persuades 4 NBL teams to join BAA in forcing NBL to join BAA in forming National Basketball Assn. in 1949 with 17 teams, introduces 24-second clock to speed up game for fans in 1954, negotiates first TV contract in 1962)... Frederick Mellinger opens small shop in Hollywood to sell racy lingerie (expands with mail-order business and 160 satellite stores before recording first losses of $148,000 in 1985 and $518,000 in 1986)...

Weather Services Corp. is formed, MA, to sell forecasts... After military duty Gene Klein sells used cars with zany promotions near L.A. (introduces Volvo car in 1957, sells U.S. distribution rights in 1959 for $2.6 million, becomes head of struggling National Theatres and Television with 230 movie houses - by 1972 National General worth over $1 billion, joins investors in 1966 to buy San Diego Charger's football team for $410 million - out in 1984 with over $50 million, by chance in 1982 meets horse trainer D. Wayne Lukas - No. 1 U.S. owner by 1988 by buying on yearlings and weanlings at auctions, spends some $39 million by 1988, instead of breeding, wins 41 races and over $5 million in 1987 - both records, after winning 300 races and some $19 million wins Kentucky Derby in 1988)...

German-born John W. Kluge buys first radio station (after building Metromedia into broadcasting giant, sells 7 TV stations to Rupert Murdock in 1986 for $2 billion, with cellular telephone business, Ponderosa restaurant chain and film production company looks for leveraged buyouts in 1988).

1947

General Events

350,000 striking telephone workers win (April 7) higher wages after first nationwide strike... American Helicopter Society demonstrates flying device attached to body... Iowa is 13th State to outlaw closed shop... Air Force Captain Charles Yeager is first to fly supersonic speed in Bell Aircraft's X-1 research plane... World Bank opens for business with $250 million reconstruction loan to France... Manhattan retires last trolley to use diesel buses... Washington predicts record surplus of $4.7 billion... President Truman asks Congress for wage and price controls...

State Department Secretary George C. Marshall creates policy-planning staff... By 1957 number of clerical workers in labor force increases by 23%, employment of factory workers falls 4%... Logger Joe Cox invents chain saw (results in formation of Oregon Saw Chain - by 1980s with over 4,000 employees in 4 countries, is acquired in 1984 by Blount, Inc. of Alabama, worldwide construction and engineering business)... Dave Tobin, president of Teamsters Union since 1907, is forced to appoint Dave Beck as executive vice president, new president in 1952-57... After some 5 years, sugar rationing ends (June 11)... Taft-Hartley Act is passed (June 23) over Presidential veto (bans closed shop, jurisdictional strike and secondary boycott, allows employers to sue unions on broken contracts or for strike damages, outlaws refusal to bargain, establishes legality for "right-to-work" laws, creates Federal Mediation and Conciliation Service)...

Bipartisan Hoover Commission is created to study operations of executive branch (issues 1949 report to recommend Postal Department be removed from political patronage, recommends adoption of planning and budgeting system)... House Un-American Activities Committee investigates communist influences in movie industry... Some 57,000 scientists are employed in industrial research laboratories, another 30,000 by government and 50,000 by universities... Portal-to-Portal Act clarifies issue of payments for travel and clean-up time... National Labor Relations Board rules in "Time Publishing Company" case employer is not required to negotiate with union refusing to bargain in good faith... Talcott Parsons: The Theory of Social and Economic Behavior (urges use of systems concept)... First fully-automatic transatlantic flight is made by U.S. Army Douglas C-54 Skymaster from Newfoundland to England (is followed in 1948 by commercial Convair of Consolidated Vultee and in 1949 by British B. De Haviland Comet)... Laura Z. Hobson: Gentleman's Agreement (attacks discrimination of Jews in business)...

W.F. Ogborn: Social Effects of Aviation (pioneers sociological forecasting)... Kurt Lewin: "Frontiers in Group Dynamics," Human Relations... Buckminster Fuller discovers concept of geodesic dome (is used by U.S. Air Force in 1952 to house Artic radar units and to build Honolulu auditorium in 1957 - up in 22 hours)... T.C. Koopmans: "Optimum Utilization of the Transportation System," Proceedings of the International Statistical Conference (pioneers development of linear programming, is followed by Air Force's comptroller George B. Dantzig with "Programming in Linear Structure" in 1948)... Scientists at AT&T's Bell Laboratories invent transistor (sell license to Japan's Sony in 1952 for $25,000 to produce first transistor radio in 1954 and television set in 1959)...

Small group of psychotherapists, non-directive counselors, social psychologists and educators, led by Lee Bradford, create National Training Laboratories at Bethel, MA (develops program to train discussion groups with sponsorship of Office of Naval Research, National Education Association and MIT Research Center for Group Dynamics, pioneers development of sensitivity training, T-group training, group dynamics and organizational development)... Federal Government wins conspiracy case, taking over various city transit lines to replace trolleys with buses, against General Motors (abandons market in 1955), Firestone Tire & Rubber, Standard Oil of California and other firms (results in fines of $1,000/executive and $5,000/company)...

Industrial Relations Research Assn. forms to study personnel and industrial relations, labor economics, etc... Arthur Miller: "All My Sons" (attacks business in play for lacking social responsibility).

Business Events

Branch Rickey of Brooklyn Dodgers signs Jackie Robinson, first black major league baseball player... U.S. Steel demands open shop in 1947 labor contract... Chicago station televises pro-football games of Chicago Bears... Roy L. Ash is hired by Bank of America as chief statistical control analyst (is hired by "Tex" Thornton, operating head of Hughes Aircraft, in 1949 as controller, starts Electro-Dynamics in 1953 with Thornton, becomes Litton in 1954)... United Fruit launches Chiquita brand bananas, first introduced as novelty item at 1876 Philadelphia Centennial Exposition... After research since 1931, Procter & Gamble introduces Tide laundry detergent, first to remove tough dirt without leaving deposits...

Eighth-grade drop-out Kirk Kerkorian, after serving during World War II as flight instructor, ferrying planes to Britain for RAF, and selling surplus war planes in South America, starts first nonscheduled airline service for gamblers between Los Angeles and Las Vegas, becomes Trans-International Airline in 1959 (sells airline business to TransAmerica in 1962 for $107 million in cash and stock when unable to finance more jet planes, buys Las Vegas' Flamingo Hotel - Casino for $12.5 million to train staff and builds pioneering International Hotel, City's first largest, in 1964, re-acquires T.I.A., in 1964, acquires Western Airlines in 1968 with unsecured loan from Bank of America for $73 million, acquires control of MGM in 1968 after stock battle, builds huge MGM Grand Hotel-Casino in 1969, acquires United Artists in 1981 from TransAmerica for film library and cable network to form MGM/UA, sells MGM Grand Hotels in Las Vegas and Reno in 1985 to buy 2 Las Vegas hotel-casinos - sold to Bally Mfg. in 1986 for $440 million, sells parts of MGM/UA to Ted Turner in 1986 - some repurchased, plans takeover of Pan American World Airways in 1987, starts MGM Grand Air in 1987 as all-frills service Los Angeles-to-NYC, splits MGM/UA in 1988)...

Flamboyant Liberace, professional pianist since starting in 1934 at Milwaukee ice cream parlor, is main attraction at Persian Room of New York's Plaza Hotel (-1987, opens in Las Vegas at Last Frontier Hotel in 1948 to introduce "glitz" to show business)... Herb Abramson, Ahmet Ertegun start Atlantic Records to promote black music and artists (record Ray Charles, Aretha Franklin, The Rolling Stones, Phil Collins, Led

Zeppelin)... J. Walter Thompson ad agency is first in industry to achieve billings over $100 billion (is followed by BBDO and Young & Rubicam in 1951, McCann-Erickson in 1954 - all pass $200 million mark in 1957)...

Moses Asch starts Folkways Records... Ford Automation Department, term automation coined by Ford engineering executive Del Harder, is created with automatic handling equipment and sequence-control mechanisms to mass produce engine blocks... Nancy, Rudolph Talbot open store catering to "country club" woman in Hingham, MA (is acquired in 1973 by General Mills to operate 119-store chain in 1988 when put up for sale)... Gordon B. McLendon acquires radio station KNET in Palestine, TX, (develops 458-station Liberty Broadcasting, U.S.' 2nd largest network, with "format" programming by 1953 before demise)... Pan American is first airline to offer round-the-world service, costs some $1,700... Industry sales of prepared cake mixes are some $79 million, rises to over $165 million by 1953...

B.F. Goodrich introduces first tubeless automobile tire (when rejected by consumers promotes product in 1948 as able to seal itself with visual test, sues Firestone in 1953 for patent infringements and U.S. Rubber in 1954 - rejected by court in 1956 as public domain, is used on all new cars in 1955)... Contractor William Levitt starts building community of Levittown on Long Island (-1951, after spending over $50,000 on research designs Cape Cod House in 1949 to sell for $7,990 - $90 down and $58/month for veterans only, builds 17,447 houses using just-in-time materials, mass production techniques and building crews going from house to house, follows with 2nd Levittown of some 16,000 houses in Bucks County, PA, in 1951)...

14 manufacturers make television sets, 80 firms in 1950 and 9 major brands left in 1966... Bloomingdale's, NYC, of Federated Department Stores pioneers postwar ranch store expansion (opens first suburban store in 1949)... Standard Oil of California and Texaco admit Exxon and Mobil as partners of ARAMCO... Tulsa's Sunray Mid-Continent Oil starts pioneering industrial chaplin program (is adopted by Reynolds Tobacco in 1949)... Robert B. Miller starts temporary-help service (becomes Employers Overload by 1960s)... Pension fund is established for big league baseball players... Lippincott & Margulies provides designing services for products, packages and office interiors (advises on corporate images in late 1950s, acquires Chrysler account in 1962 to receive national recognition for "corporate identification program")...

Wurlitzer produces Model 1015, Cadillac of juke boxes... After various jobs, Sicilian-born Anthony T. Rossi starts Tropicana Products, FL, to sell gift boxes of oranges and grapefruit (markets fruit juices in 1949, becomes as largest customer of Florida oranges by 1980s to achieve sales of some $120 million throughout U.S., 12 countries, is sold to Seagram Co. for $1.2 billion in 1988)... Willard Rockwell creates Rockwell Mfg. to combine interests in power tools, valves, machinery with 1925 meter business (acquires firms making cash registers, taxi meters, fare registers and parking meters to operate with 15 plants, almost 5,000 employees and sales over $62 million, is absorbed in 1967 merger with North American Aviation to become U.S.' 7th largest defense contractor as Rockwell International)...

Winchell's doughnut house chain in Western States is started (sells later

to Denny's 24-hour nationwide restaurant chain, operates 835 shops by
1985)... Edwin Land introduces Polaroid Land Camera for instant
photography (conceives idea in 1943 when 3-year-old daughter asked how
long it would take to see pictures, introduces color film in 1963,
pocket-sized instant camera in 1970s and Polaroid movie camera in 1978,
after acquiring 524 patents retires in 1982 after market failure of
Polavision, wins patent suit with Eastman Kodak in 1986)...

Gene Autry Productions is formed by entertainer (uses movie and music
profits to acquire chain of Texas movie theaters, flying school, 3
western radio stations, 5 ranches, 2 western music publishing houses and
California Angels baseball team in 1961)... J. Willard Marriott starts
10-year expansion program to develop eating business with 6 new "Hot
Shoppes"/year (opens Pantry House as first restaurant and first hotel
cafeteria in 1948 - operates 45 eating places in 1952 in 9 states and DC
and in-flight meal service for dozen airlines, opens first hotel in
1957)...

Preston Tucker proclaims Torpedo "The car of tomorrow - today!" with air-
cooled rear-engine, disk brakes, padded dashboard and other innovations
for $2,450 (-1949 when forced out of business by financial problems,
avoids stockholder fraud by having built 51 cars - 46 roadworthy in 1988
to sell for up to $100,000)... Former model, stylist, copywriter and
fashion reporter, Eileen Ford, husband start modeling agency, "one you
could trust" (uses 7 trips/year to Europe, 4/year to West Coast by 1980s
to find right girls from some 100,000 applicants)... NBC starts
televising baseball (loses contract in 1990 to CBS' bid of $1.08 billion
for 4 years)...

Charles Wilson's Haloid Co., founded 1906 to make sensitized photographic
paper, acquires Chester Carlson's xerographic patents (introduces first
commercial copier in 1959, becomes Xerox in 1961 - sales of $2.4 billion
in 1972, loses over $100 million in computer market in 1969-74 - IBM
enters copier market, enters high-tech office work-stations in 1980s,
diversifies in financial services in 1983 after losing market share to
Japanese copiers, re-focuses on "smart" copiers in mid-1980s).

1948

General Events

Over 200,000 coal miners strike (March 15) for more liberal pension
plan... Federal judge fines John L. Lewis $20,000 for contempt of court
during March strike (requires union to pay fine of $1.25 million)...
President Truman orders (May 10) Army to take over strike-bound
railroads... New York, last U.S. City with 5-cent fare for public
transportation, doubles subway fare to 10 cents... President Truman asks
Congress for price controls to curb inflation... U.S. Consumer Price
Index reaches (August 24) high of 173 on 1935-39 base... Census Bureau
reports California leading in population growth since 1940 with 9.8
million new residents... After 85 years of service New York's Hudson
River Day Line closes with increasing use of cars...

Designer Charles Eames, created "potato" chip chair in 1946, creates
prefabricated house (designs modern lounge chair in 1956)... With
President William Green ill, former plumber George Meany takes over

operations of AFL (becomes president for 1952-80)... Marshall Plan is established to assist in economic recovery of Europe, rejected by Communist nations in East Europe (ends 1951 after distributing some $12.5 billion in foreign aid)...

Francis M. Rogallo devises hang-glider, followed in 1970-74 by Homer Kolb's ultra-light, motorized flyer... Norbert Wiener: <u>Cybernetics: On Controlled</u> <u>and</u> <u>Communications</u> <u>on</u> <u>Animal</u> <u>and</u> <u>Machine</u> (creates new science, introduces concept of feedback)... Office of Strategic Services, OSS Assessment Staff: <u>Assessment</u> <u>of</u> <u>Men</u> (discusses use of assessment center during W.W. II in screening candidates with simulated situations and exercises, based on research on human characteristics and potential by Harvard's Henry A. Murray during 1930s)... MIT offers first course on non-military applications of operations research... Mississippi is last State to pass workman's compensation law, Maryland first in 1902... Government sponsors first national conference on industrial safety...

Federal Trade Commission uses word "conglomerate" in report to describe acquisition of unrelated businesses (warns public on phenomenon)... U.S. Agriculture Department uses empty limestone caverns near Kansas city for storage purposes (by 1980s are used by variety of businesses with underground operations)... T.H. Fielding: <u>Travel</u> <u>Guide</u> <u>to</u> <u>Europe</u> (promotes tourism business with some 3 million copies by 1980s)... Steel mill town of Dondora, PA, declares major air pollution crisis with 19 deaths (is followed by London's "killer smog" in 1952 with some 4,000 deaths, NYC's smog in 1953 with some 200 deaths)...

In return for more health, welfare and retirement benefits, John L. Lewis, United Mine Workers, signs contract with coal operators to modernize mining operations with machinery... Congress passes Federal rent control bill... Peter Goldmark, Columbia Records, invents long-playing record (evolves from technique used by British Coastal Command for training records during W.W. II)... U.S. Supreme Court: <u>Sipeul</u> <u>v.</u> <u>Board</u> <u>of</u> <u>Regents</u> <u>of</u> <u>University</u> <u>of</u> <u>Oklahoma</u> (rules no state can discriminate against law applicant because of race)... By executive order President bans segregation in armed forces (calls for end to racial discrimination in Federal employment)...

Equitable Building, designed by Pietro Belluschi, is built in Portland, OR, to pioneer aluminum and glass curtain wall building in U.S. architecture... U.S. Supreme Court: <u>United</u> <u>States</u> <u>v.</u> <u>Paramount</u> <u>Pictures,</u> <u>Incorporated,</u> <u>et</u> <u>al</u> (rules business, and other movie companies, must sell chain of theaters - merger with ABC in 1953, results in rise of movies by independent producers and talent agencies)... Some 15,000 machinists strike Boeing to win union shop and seniority, ruled illegal strike by U.S. Court of Appeals... MIT starts program to give firms access to university's research for a fee (evolves with 300 affiliates by 1987)...

Business Events

After operating 7 pipe shops and nightclub in Portland, OR, Norm Thompson puts ad in <u>Time</u> to sell hand-tied fishing flies (results in creation of Norm Thompson Outfitters as mail-order house by son-in-law Peter Alport in 1949 - 1983 sales of $25 million in one of U.S.' fastest growing industries with items to "Escape from Ordinary," is acquired in 1973 by Parker Pen, is acquired in 1981 by leveraged buy-out, introduces Norm

Thompson Solutions, Inc., catalog of practical products, in 1986)...
Samuel J. Lefrak becomes president of father's Lefrak business building
and managing apartment houses (acquires 29 pieces of Manhattan property
in 1951 with bid of $5 million and $50,000 down payment, when banks
refuse to lend funds to complete transaction sells property at loss to
generate tax reduction and uses cash flow from rental properties to
finish deal - by 1957 with 2,000 new apartments and 4,600 by 1959, builds
8 major developments in 1960 for $48.5 million, achieves billionaire
status in 1987 Fortune by holding down costs, by purchasing materials
early, often at distress sales and stockpiling for use later, and by
holding land acquisitions until needed)... After only 9 years as
employee, started as $14-a-week mail boy, Marion Harper becomes president
of McCann-Erickson advertising agency (in largest switch of agencies
captures Coca-Cola account in 1955, creates Interpublic group in 1961 as
holding company for advertising agencies)...

Edward Orkney starts G.I. Joe's business in Portland, OR, to peddle W.W.
II goods (evolves by 1980s as $85 million operation in Pacific Northwest
with 9 G.I. Joe's, 3 Action Outfitters, and 15 Jean Machines)... General
Electric is convicted for conspiring with German firm of Krupp during War
to restrict trade and fix prices on tungston carbide tools... Former
heavyweight boxing champion Jack Dempsey opens Manhattan restaurant,
pioneers growth of celebrity restaurants (-1978)... Dow Chemical
introduces first latex paint, followed by first acrylic latex paint of
Rohm and Haas in 1953...

Harry Axene leaves Dairy Queen chain of eateries to start Tastee Freeze
franchise business... John Walson starts first U.S. cable network in
Mahonoy City, PA, to improve reception of TV stations in nearby
Philadelphia (becomes Community Antenna Television)...

Bloomingdale's, Manhattan department store, opens gourmet food department
(develops trendy image for "Bloomies" with new home furnishings in 1950,
Place Elegance' as first boutique in 1956, new men's store in 1961, and
new departments in women's apparel in 1965)... Best Western International
lodging business is started in California (evolves as affiliation of
independent hotels and motels to operate some 500 properties by 1960,
creates in-house advertising agency in 1976, handles some 2,700
operations by 1980 in U.S., 18 countries)... Personnel Psychology is
published... American Society for Personnel Administration forms (starts
project to formulate ethical code for administrators in 1957)...

Joy Mfg. of Pittsburgh builds and tests first models of continuous mining
machines... Two Milwaukee lawyers start Manpower as temporary employment
agency for blue-collar and white-collar workers (starts franchising in
1954, opens London office in 1956, evolves as industry's largest with
1,337 offices in 33 countries before 1987 acquisition by London-based
Blue Arrow for $1.34 billion in cash)... Eugene Ferkauf, dubbed "Duke of
Discounting," starts Korvette chain of discount stores, follows Two Guys
discount business of 1947 in New Jersey, with tiny NYC luggage shop
(achieves sales of some $622 million in 1964 as fastest growing retailer
with 52 stores, after 2 mergers is sold in 1979 to French retailing and
manufacturing business, is liquidated in 1981)... Earl Planty, others:
Training Employees and Managers for Production and Teamwork... Public
Relations Society of America organizes... Saga, one of U.S.' largest food
services in 1980s, is started when 3 college students take over

operations of Hobart College's money-losing cafeteria (evolves to operate 421 college units and restaurant chains of Black Angus steakhouses, Straw Hat Pizza, Refectory and Velvet Turtle, is acquired and revived with management controls by W.R. Grace in 1978, adds Grandy's for fast food chicken and Spoons for fancy hamburgers to achieve revenues of some $733 million in 1980 with 3 restaurant chains and food services at 373 colleges, 293 corporations and 122 hospitals)...

General Motors signs labor contract with UAW (includes industry's first provision to adjust wages with changes in cost-of-living index, is dropped in 1985 by GM for some 110,000 salaried employees)... After opening in 1939 McDonald brothers, close drive-in restaurant in San Bernardino, CA, to install Speedy System to make hamburgers, french fries and milk shakes on high-volume basis with self-service, mass-production techniques (grant franchise in 1953 to Phoenix place, sell right to franchise operations to Ray Kroc in 1954, sell out to Kroc in 1961 - 10-billionth hamburger sold in 1972 and 50-billionth with 8,000 places in 1984)...

After resigning from Glenn L. Martin Aircraft, engineer Howard Head starts business to develop aluminum skis with $6,000 won playing poker (perfects ski in 1950, installs new management team in 1967 after realizing ineptness as manager, sells business to AMF in 1969 for $16 million to play tennis, after dissatisfaction with engineering of tennis ball machine advises Prince business on improvements - 25% of stock by 1971, acquires patent in 1976 for innovative Prince racket with oversize surface to improve his tennis game)... CBS raids NBC radio for leading programs (captures Jack Benny Show, others to become No. 1 in ratings by 1949)...

Gillette razor business diversifies product line with Toni home permanents (acquires Paper Mate ballpoint pens in 1955, Braun AG of West Germany, makers of electric razors, in 1967, and adds toiletries division in 1968)... Liquinet is introduced to U.S. market as first hair-spray product...

After working for Berlin investment house in 1930, leaving Germany in 1933 and traveling world to gain entry to U.S., corporate raider Leopold D. Silberstein arrives in to U.S. as stateless person with $75-100,000 made in pre-War ventures on U.S. stock market (buys old Pennsylvania Coal & Coke in 1951 to build $126 million enterprise with 15 companies, raids Fairbanks Morse in 1956 - abandons battle after court suit, is ousted in 1958 from Pennsylvania business after proxy battle over firm's precarious financial position after meeting commitments to buy stock in Fairbanks Morris)... IBM demonstrates Selective Sequence Electric Calculator...

After certification of new helicopter, University of California drop-out Stanley Hiller starts business making helicopters for commercial and military customers (with success pioneers corporate turnaround field of 1970s-1980s to make some $100 million by investing and reviving 6 firms, including Reed Tool, Bekins, and York International)... True Value national hardware chain is started... By accident Ed Lowe, operator of father's coal, ice, and sawdust business, provides customer with sawdust for cat litter when previous sand freezes (develops Indiana-based Lowe Industries with Tidy Cat 3 and Kitty Litter brands, 1987 sales of $110 million to dominate industry of $350 million).

1949

General Events

Justice Department files (January 14) suit to sever Bell Laboratories, Western Electric from AT&T (settles in 1956 after concessions by AT&T to make existing patents available to others without charge and provide future patents on reasonable terms, sues again in 1974 under Sherman Anti-Trust Act, forces dismemberment in 1982)... Some 500,000 striking steel workers win retirement benefits... Fair Labor Standards Act is amended (October 26), increases minimum hourly wage from 40 to 75 cents in 1950... U.S. Supreme Court upholds Taft-Hartley Act in allowing states to ban closed shop... MIT professor Claude Shannon designs first computer to play chess... BINC, U.S.' first stored-program computer, is tested...

U.S. Signal Corps makes transistors on small scale, pioneers use for communications equipment... First round-the-world non-stop flight is made in Boeing B-50A Superfortress after 4 aerial refuelings in 94 hours, one minute... Arthur Miller: "Death of a Salesman"... Averaging 607.2 mph, U.S. Air Force jet flies across U.S. in 3 hours, 46 minutes... 11 communists are convicted in conspiracy to overthrow government...

After research since 1947, John T. Parsons, president of firm making helicopter rotar blades in Traverse City, MI, obtains Air Force contract to build "automatic contour cutting machine" operated by punch-cards or tape (subcontracts work to MIT Servomechanism Laboratory to develop controls for automatically programmed tools)...

RAND Corp. makes weapons systems analysis (provides methodology for programmed budgeting, used in this time by Bureau of Reclamation, military, U.S. Coast Guard and several other agencies)... U.S. Supreme Court: Inland Steel Company v. United Steel Workers of America (requires employers to bargain on pension plans)... Walter Paepcke, head of Container Corporation of America, sponsors first Bicentennial Goethe Festival at Aspen, CO, resort (becomes Aspen Institute for Humanistic Studies to bring business people and educators together)... Per capita income of U.S. is some $1,453, only New Zealand, Canada and Switzerland above $800... Claude Shannon, Warren Weaver: The Mathematical Theory of Communications (pioneers field of information theory)... Pittsburgh's Golden Triangle development is started, sponsored by Richard King Mellon, to revitalize City's downtown area... CIO, Walter Reuther president, expells 2 unions in anti-Communist drive, 19 others in 1950... CIO and free democratic trade unions of various countries withdraw from Communist-dominated World Federation of Trade Unions (leads to International Confederation of Free Trade Unions in London)... University of Chicago scientists coin term "Behavioral Sciences"... Housing Act provides funds for large-scale slum clearance and low-rent public housing.

Business Events

General Motors cuts car prices, industry's first since end of W.W. II... Northwest Airlines is first in U.S. to serve alcoholic beverages in flight... General Motors pays over $190 million in dividends, biggest in history... J. Paul Getty contracts with Saudi Arabia for 60-year concession (guarantees minimum payment of $1 million/year, finds large oil reserves in 1953 on apparent barren tract, obtains control of father's George F. Getty oil business from mother and acquires Mission Corp., holdings in Tidewater Oil and Skelly Oil, in 1953, consolidates all interests in 1967 to form $3 billion enterprise)... After graduating from college Vienna-born Charles G. Bluhdorn starts commodity import-export business (acquires small Michigan Bumper in 1957 to build Gulf and Western conglomerate)...

Annual Pillsbury Bakeoff, classic promotional contest for amateur cooks, is launched by flour business, $126,000 in prizes in 1988 ... Wilson Sporting Goods introduces Jack Kramer tennis racket (sells over 10 million rackets, 2nd biggest seller to Ted Williams glove, before ending production in 1981)... IBM creates World Trade Corp. as independent company for overseas markets, expands to sell products in 79 countries with manufacturing facilities in 15 (operates in France, Holland, West Germany and Scotland by 1960 to gross over $1 billion by 1965 and $3 billion in 1970)...

Ned Doyle, Maxwell Dane and William Berndach start advertising agency (realize success using soft-sell approach with Volkswagen account in 1959 and Avis car-rental business in 1962)... NBC forms first television network with 25 stations... National Records Management Council is created by academic, business and community members to encourage business to maintain archives for research... Ford Motor Co. is industry's first to fund pension plan for blue-collar workers... Town and Country Shopping Center, first after war, opens in Columbus, OH (is transformed as functional mall with 1985 opening of $140-million Horton Plaza in San Diego, designed by Jon Jerde as stage for shopping excitement)... E.H. Sutherland: White Collar Crime...

First annual Southern "500" event for stock cars is held at Darlington, SC (pioneers post-war car-race market)... John Van Arsdale starts Provincetown-Boston Airline to carry passengers to Cape Cod resort community (starts Florida operation in 1952 to keep planes busy during winter, retires in 1980 to leave business to 2 sons who expand to 113 planes in serving major East Coast cities and resorts after airline deregulation in 1982 - grounded 1984 for safety violations)...

W. Given: Bottom-up Management (urges participation of workers in business decisions)... Dry-cleaning business, "One Hour Martinizing," is started, NYC (is used by some 2,500 shops by 1969)... Milwaukee's Schlitz brewery business, founded in 1849 by German-born August Krug, buys Brooklyn brewery, adds 7 more regional breweries by 1971... After Paramount's 1946 anti-trust suit, movie business of MGM is reconstituted with MGM to make movies (is rescued from financial troubles in 1968 by self-made millionaire Kirk Kerkorian) and Loews to operate theaters (is acquired in 1960 by resort operators Laurence, Preston Tisch)...

Commercial production of epoxy resins is started... After resigning from Ford Motor Co., "Tex" Thornton becomes vice president, general manager of Hughes Aircraft (hires Roy Ash as controller, resigns in 1953 after differences with Howard Hughes who wanted business to focus on government contracts, starts Electro-Dynamics in 1953 with Ash - becomes Litton in 1954 to evolve as conglomerate)...

Joe Di Maggio, New York Yankees, is first baseball player to receive yearly contract over $100,000... After consent decree, Adolph Zukor's Paramount movie business reforms as Paramount Pictures to produce films (enters television market 1953, is acquired by Gulf & Western 1966) and United Paramount Theaters to handle movie houses (is acquired 1953 by American Broadcasting)... First Volkswagen cars appear in U.S., over 9.5 million by 1989 as best-selling European import... Jockey Bill Shoemaker makes first ride, over 8,000 winners by 1988 as leading jockey of all time (is first to win over $100 million in purses in 1985, wins 250 races by 1988 with prizes over $100,000).

1950s

General Events

Aaron Director, University of Chicago law professor, advocates law-and-economics jurisprudence with cost-efficient justice... Mass production of poultry evolves...

Business Events

McDonnell aircraft business starts space research (creates space research center in 1960).

1950

General Events

President Truman authorizes (April 19) economic rehabilitation of Navajo, Hopi tribes... President Truman sends (June 30) military forces to Korea to repell invasion of North Korean troops (-1953)... Special Committee to Investigate Crime in Interstate Commerce reports (August 18) organized crime is taking over legitimate businesses...

With threat of railroad strike, President Truman orders (August 25) U.S. Army to take over operations... Defense Production Act establishes (September 8) wage and price controls... Celler-Kefauver Act amends (December 29) Clayton Anti-Trust Act (prevents corporations in acquiring property to lessen competition)...

Soft-coal strike expands to 400,000 miners in 6 states (when 370,000 refuse to obey court order to return to work, indicts John L. Lewis for contempt - not guilty)... 1895 American Bowling Congress removes 34-year-old ban limiting membership to white males...

Bureau of Mines designs first practical production of oil from coal... U.S. has 2,200 drive-in theaters, double number of 1949... First computer simulation of "war games" is devised... Senate committee investigates Reconstruction Finance Corporation for financial misdeeds... Researchers at California Institute of Technology prove automobile exhaust emissions and smog in Los Angeles are linked...

U.S. Census reports population of 151.3 million, 96.8 urban and 54.5 rural... John McDonald: Strategy in Poker, Business and War... In this time dejected veterans of W.W. II form Hell's Angels as outlaw motocycle gang, CA (evolves by 1982 with 4,000 hard-core U.S. members, largest and most dangerous of some 600 such gangs, with activities in drugs, extortion, prostitution, and pornography)...

Some 20 "think tanks" operate in Washington, DC, Atlantic Research firm first in 1944 to produce rocket for U.S. Navy (grows to 123 by 1957, 232 by 1965)... Federal Records Act, as recommended by 1948 Hoover commission, is passed to schedule retirement of federal records, to establish record centers (creates Records Managerial Division in office of General Services, claims savings over $34 million for 1952-53 fiscal year)... E.H. S. Chase, others: <u>The Social Responsibility of Business</u>... United Auto Workers, General Motors sign 5-year contract with no reopening provisions (provides for pensions, automatic cost-of-living raises, modified union shop and guaranteed annual wage increases)... U.S. holds 68% of world's, non-Comunnist, gold reserves, 27% in 1973... U.S. produces 52% of world's goods and services, some 22% by 1988.

Business Events

Ladies' Professional Golf Association is formed by 11 players, Babe Zaharis leading money-winner on golf tour with $14,800... A.C. Nielsen, inventor of Audimeter to record radio stations turned on, devises simular device for TV to provide popularity ratings of programs (tests new device for actual viewing habits in 1987-88)... James Brunot, philanthropic social worker, submits crossword game, Scrabble, invented by unemployed friend Alfred Butts in 1933, to Selchow & Righter (after rejection and successful home business licenses game to Selchow in 1952, is sold to Coleco in 1986 after introducing popular Trivial Pursuits game - bankruptcy by 1989)... General Motors reports earnings of $654,434,232, largest recorded by U.S. corporation... Columbia Broadcasting System is authorized (October 11) to give television broadcasts in color (starts November 2)... RCA demonstrates all-electronic color television tube...

To obtain funds needed to complete data projects for Census Bureau, Eckert-Mauchly's Electric Control Computer Corp., is sold to Remington-Rand (becomes UNIVAC division with acquisition, delivers first UNIVAC computer to Census Bureau in 1951, programs UNIVAC to predict correct results of 1952 election, sells first business computers to CBS in 1953 and General Electric in 1954, merges with Sperry gyroscope business in 1955 to form Sperry-Rand, uses punched cards and FORTRAN program in 1956)... Some 1.5 million TV sets are used, about 10 million in 1951...

House of Morgan shows financial resources of some $667 million, GM's working capital with $1.6 billion... Allied Stores opens Northgate in Seattle as U.S.' first regional shopping center... California Perfume business, started 1886 by door-to-door book salesman David H. McConnell, becomes Avon Products (starts international expansion in 1954 with Latin-American market, is listed by New York Stock Exchange in 1964, introduces false eyelashes to product line and uses blacks for first time in advertising in 1970 - hair coloring in 1971, is forced to recall contaminated night cream and baby powder products in 1971, with 2 women executives appoints first woman to Board of Directors in 1972, signs covenant with Reverend Jesse Jackson's Operation PUSH to spend $59 million to hire more blacks and help minority businesses, with some 500 products achieves 85% of cosmetics' door-to-door market in 1974 with some 450,000 Avon ladies in U.S., 15 countries)...

Boston Celtics draft Chuck Cooper, first black basketball player in NBA (names Bill Russell first black NBA coach in 1966)... U.S. business invests some $12 billion overseas, mostly with petroleum and mineral ventures in Canada, Latin-America and Middle East (expands to around $65 billion by 1968)... In this time, General Electric starts pioneering research activity to study personnel problems (is followed by IBM, Equitable Life Assurance, DuPont, B.F. Goodrich, Chrysler, General Motors, Maytag, Exxon, Sears, AT&T)... Monsanto registers trade name of Acrilan for artificial fiber... Boehm Studios opens in Trenton, NJ, to make fine porcelain (after almost closing twice evolves by 1985 to employ some 400 employees at studios in England, South Wales to produce objects for 115 museums worldwide)...

Restauranteur Eddy Mays, Portland, OR, gets idea for restaurant credit card after running low on cash on trip to National Restaurant Association meeting in NYC (leads to National Credit Card Co. in Oregon within 1 year, nationally in 2 years and internationally in 3rd year)... Ralph Cordiner becomes chief officer of General Electric (-1963, decentralizes operations with profit centers - model for other firms)... Manufacturing's share of all non-farm jobs is 33.7%, drops to 21.4% by 1982... Pittsburgh Pirates sign pitcher Paul Pettit for $100,000, baseball's first bonus baby (after 1950 injury 1950 goes to minors in 1954)... On death of father L.S. Skaggs takes over 1939 Skaggs Drug Centers in Salt Lake City (acquires American Stores in 1979 to operate 1,000 outlets and Chicago's Jewel Co. in 1984 to do business with 1,700 stores in 40 states with sales of $15 billion as first U.S. coast-to-coast drug store chain)... After intense competition NFL absorbs best teams of All-American Football Conference... Herman Miller office furniture business, founded 1923, adopts participative management system with work teams in using Scanlon plan to cut costs, successful through 1986 market slump...

Arma, founded 1918 to make instruments and control devices for Navy, demonstrates numerically controlled lathe (abandons project in 1951 after no orders)... After selling sandwiches, coffee and donuts to factory workers since 1946, William Rosenberg starts Dunkin' Donuts business in Quincy, MA (expands chain with franchising in 1955 - some 1,400 shops with Dunkin' Donuts University in 1968, starts national advertising in 1978)... After running out of cash in restaurant, Francis X. McNamara designs Diners Club credit card for travel and entertainment, followed by first plastic card in 1955, American Express card in 1958, BankAmericard in 1959, Sears' Discover card in 1985, and HomeBuyer Express Card in 1988)... National Association of Investment Clubs forms to aid small investors in pooling funds for stock portfolio, average of $90,000 in 1988 (evolves as field of some 14,000 clubs by 1970 before almost disappearing in 1973-74 recession, climbs to around 6,500 by 1988)...

Gilbert Weston starts Lamb-Weston in Portland, OR, acquired by Amfac in 1978 (becomes U.S.' largest producer of frozen processed potatoes with sales of $400 million, 7 plants and 4,300 workers in 1987, is sold to venture of Golden Valley Microwave Foods, MN, and ConAgra food conglomerate, NE, in 1988 for $276 million in cash)... Strum Ruger begins to make small arms, earnings of $9.6 million on sales of $94 million in 1985 from replacing most manual machinery with controlled technology as industry's leader in using automation... Cleveland Browns, created by coach Paul Brown (revolutionizes the game with meticulous organization and statistical studies) and absorbed in 1949 with All-American

Conference, edges L.A. Rams to win title of National Football League...

Aspen, impoverished little mining-town-just-turned-ski-resort, CO, hosts World Alpine Ski Championships to gain worldwide renown, followed by Vail ski-resort complex, CO, in 1962 to host World Alpine Ski Championships in 1989 as U.S.' largest ski resort.

1951

General Events

President Truman freezes (January 1) prices... After 12-day strike, railroad workers return to work with higher wages... Office of Price Stabilization sets (April 28) beef prices... U.S. Supreme Court: <u>Garner</u> <u>v.</u> <u>Los</u> <u>Angeles</u> (upholds right of State to require job applicants to sign non-Communist affidavits)... President Truman cancels (August 1) tariff concessions to Soviet-bloc nations... First major pilot strike grounds all flights of United Airlines... Washington cites average income of $1,436, up $116 over 1949... Stanford University sponsors pioneering Stanford Research Park, catalyst for growth of high-tech firms in Silicon Valley (after development provides $2.1 million annually to university, is followed by some 12 others by 1983 and 80 by 1987)... Rachel Carson: <u>The</u> <u>Sea</u> <u>Around</u> <u>Us</u> (launches modern environmental movement)... Electric power is produced from atomic energy at Arcon, ID... Delbert Miller, William Form: <u>Industrial</u> <u>Sociology</u>... Controlled annual importation of Mexican farm workers is renewed (-1961 when terminated)...

Work building Route 128 around Boston is completed (provides site for high-tech firms with Wang Laboratories in 1951 and Digital Equipment in 1957 - 40 by 1955, 600 by 1965 and some 900 by 1980s)... George Katona: <u>Psychological</u> <u>Analysis</u> <u>of</u> <u>Economic</u> <u>Behavior</u>... Physicist Charles Townes discovers amplification of microwaves by stimulated emission (shares Nobel Prize in 1964 for MASER)... U.S. Supreme Court rules retailers not signing minimum-priced agreements are not bound to follow minimum prices of manufacturers (leads to growth of discount operations until 1988 ruling that manufacturers can stop selling to discounters to protect full-priced retailers)... AT&T starts first transcontinental direct dialing with microwave relay facilities... Arthur Freed, Cleveland disk-jockey, coins term "Rock'n'Roll"... Walter Byers is hired by National Collegiate Athletic Association, becomes first executive director to enforce regulations (-1988, prepares NCAA for post-war mass market of sports by televising games, tournaments).

Business Events

AT&T is first U.S. corporation to record over one million stockholders... Pennsylvania Railroad is indicted for manslaughter for actions in train wreck... <u>Computers</u> <u>and</u> <u>Automation</u> is first magazine in field... After operating 1941 shipyard near Norfolk, VA, during W.W. II and developing welding process to replace riveting in building tankers, Daniel Ludwig signs 10-year lease for modern ship-building facilities in Kure, Japan (builds first of supertanker fleet in 1956, operates 6 in 1968 to best Greek rivals while refining oil in Panama and Scotland, producing coal in West Virginia and Australia, operating world's largest solar salt-water plant in Mexico, and overseeing Princess luxury hotel chain)... William S. Paley organizes Columbia Broadcasting as 7 divisions: CBS Radio, CBS

TV, CBS Laboratories, Columbia Records - sold to Sony in 1987, CBS-Columbia to make radio and television sets, and Hytron Radio and Electronics (acquires New York Yankees baseball franchise in 1964 - sold 1973, after problems in succession retires as chairman in 1983, buys Ziff-Davis' 21 publications for $362.5 million in 1985 - sold for $650 million to focus on broadcasting, returns in 1986 as acting chairman to assist in reviving business burdened with debt after fighting take-over by Ted Turner)...

After training as TWA mechanic, serving in Army Air Corps, and working as TWA flight engineer, Allen Paulson starts company to convert passenger airliners into cargo planes (forms American Jet Industries in 1970 to convert piston-powered small planes as propjets - revenues of some $35 million in 1978, purchases unprofitable corporate-jet subsidiary of Grumman in 1978 with American Jet as collateral, acquires general aviation business of Rockwell International in 1980 to form Gulfstream Aerospace - sales of $196 million in 1978 and $582 million in 1981 with Cadillac of corporate jets)... David Ogilvy creates advertising campaign for shirts to convey image of class and quality with Hathaway Man in ads with debonair eye patch... Fortune: U.S.A., The Permanent Revolution (reports on deluge of new products in marketplace)... Donald C. Power develops General Telephone and Electronics by acquiring independent phone companies (by 1980 operates 19 companies servicing 18 million telephones, AT&T with 140 million in 31 states, Latin America and Canada)... CBS starts broadcasting color television, only 25 sets of some 10 million capable of receiving in color... Joel Dean: Managerial Economics...

Toronto lawyer-promoter Samuel Ciglen buys Great Sweet Grass business, yearly deficits since 1943 for $150,000 (sells over 2 million new shares on promises of oil and gas discoveries, promotes sales with "boiler shops," is charged by SEC in 1956 for failing to justify oil and gas reserves - trading suspended, is barred from listed transactions in 1957 by American Stock Exchange after gullible public loses at least $12 million)... 1930 Geophysical Service of Dallas becomes Texas Instruments (acquires manufacturing license for transistors from Bell Laboratories in 1952, produces first silicon transistor in 1954, invents integrated circuit in 1958, during 60s develops Objectives, Strategies, Tactics System to institutionalize planning for innovation, starts behavioral science project in 1961 to test motivational theory of Frederick Herzberg, adopts managerial grid technique in 1968 as basis for programs in job enrichment and job simplification, after using matrix organizational structure since 1968 adopts decentralized profit centers in 1980s to improve competitive ability)... Joseph F. Lincoln: Incentive Management: A New Approach to Human Relationships in Industry and Business (discusses business philosophy of "intelligent selfishness")...

General Motors funds Michigan Institute to study industrial health problems... William Douglas starts Careers, Inc., NYC, to recruit personnel for large corporations (pioneers trend in recruiting British scientists to start "Brain Drain" of 1950s)... National Vocational Guidance Association, other groups form Personnel and Guidance Assn. of America... After inventing magnetic core for computers in 1945, Chinese-born An Wang starts Wang Laboratories in Boston (operates business as one-man rule with blend of Confucian philosophy and American entrepreneurship, in 1964 introduces one of first desk-top electronic calculators, enters word-processor market in 1972 - 35% of world market by 1980)... Albert Gallatin Thomas starts Industrial Controls Corp. in Chattanooga as patent-holding company to exploit his developments in automated machine tools (designs basic analog computer to simulate machine tool motions in generating digital tape to control other machine-tool machines, fails for lack of capital)... Chrysler introduces Concord compact car...

George von Rosen publishes Modern Man magazine, features Jane Russell as first cover girl, with semi-nude pin-ups, nude art models, previously seen since 30s only in Classic Photography and Sunshine & Health (provides articles for action-oriented male readers interested in outdoor activities)... After working for Oregon's Bend Bulletin Paper, O.K. Rubber Welders retread business in Prineville is acquired by Les Schwab, then 34, with $14,000 - $11,000 borrowed (grosses $155,000, 5 times previous ownership, in 1952, opens 2nd tire store in 1953 in partnership with manager, uses ownership format to expand business to achieve annual sales of $4 million in mid-1980s with 171 tire centers in 5 western states)... Merv Adelson, UCLA drop-out, starts first 24-hour supermarket in Las Vegas with $10,000 loan from father (invests in real estate, starts Lorimar in 1969 to produce TV shows, such as Dallas and Knots Landing, with partner, leaves 1986, and $450,000, merges Lorimar and Telepictures Corp., TV-show syndicator, in 1986 to create $800-million entertainment business, sells assets in 1987 to offset heavy losses in video division and syndicated programming, agrees to friendly takeover of Warner Communications for $630 million and assumption of $550-million debt - challenged by bid of Denver oilman, Marvin Davis, for some $690 million)...

After acquiring La Choy Foods during W.W. II, 1894 Beatrice dairy food business plans expansion program (achieves 175 acquisitions by 1961 to operate creameries in 42 states, starts diversification in 1964 to sell 9,000 products, 100 brands by 1980, acquires Esmark food conglomerate in 1984 to become U.S.' 36th largest industrial corporation with 8,000 product lines using over 200 known brand names, accepts leveraged buy-out bid from Kohlberg Kravis Roberts in 1985)... Elroy McCaw, WA, buys NYC station WINS for $500,000 (converts troubled business into U.S.' first rock 'n' roll station in mid-1950s, sells to Westinghouse in 1962 for $10 million, dies in 1969 - most loose empire of radio and TV stations with cable systems sold to pay debts, is succeeded by son Craig in 1973 who takes over last remaining business - cable system a $38 million operation by 1984, forms partnership in 1981 with Associated Publications eager to diversify into radio and videotex, after FCC opens bidding on cellular licenses in 1982 forms McCaw Cellular Communications, gets financing from E.W. Scripps Co. in 1984 and AT&T in 1985 for cellular equipment, pays $122 million for cellular and radio paging business of MCI in 1986, evolves as 1988 market leader with services in 127 cities, sells 22% of stock to British Telecommunications in 1989 for $1.5 billion to enter world market).

1952

General Events

To avoid steel strike President Truman orders federal take-over of steel mills in Youngstown, OH, ruled unconstitutional by Supreme Court on June 2... Congress ends (June 28) wage and price controls... Price controls are lifted on almost all fresh and processed vegetables and meats... U.S. Supreme Court bars (November 10) segregation on interstate railroads... U.S. signs 5-year pact with India (grants $50 million for economic development)... Screen Guild approves first TV actor-producer contract... For first time in 68 years U.S. oceanliner, United States, records fastest crossing of Atlantic in 3 days, 10 hours and 40 minutes, to average 35.95 knots - Great Britain's City of Berlin with first record of 15.2 knots in 1875... AFL starts drive to ban gangsters from unions...

NYC starts helicopter mail, parcel post service... MIT establishes Sloan School of Management... Justice Department Anti-Trust Division acts against IBM for marketing practices (wins consent decree in 1956)... John S. Ellsworth, Jr.: Factory Folkways: A Study of Institutional Structure and Change... McGuire Act permits firms to enforce fair-trade agreements against non-signers... Buildings, designed by Mies van der Rohe, at 860-880 Lake Shore Drive, Chicago, IL, are built, hallmark for international style of architecture... John Kenneth Galbraith: American Capitalism: The Concept of Counterveiling Power (suggests economy transformed by growth of large-scale organizations)... Charles R. Walker, Robert H. Guest: The Man on the Assembly Line (reports dissatisfaction of workers in mass production)... Paul Buchanan trains managers in interpersonal relations at Naval Test Station at China Lake, CA... Alex Osborn: Applied Imagination (promotes interest in creativity, starts Creative Education Foundation at University of Buffalo in 1954)... Frederick Allen: The Big Change (discusses loss of Horatio Alger myth with craving of youth for security)... Government returns railroads back to owners (1950-)... Former plumber George Meany becomes AFL president on death of William Green (-1979)...

Walter Reuther becomes head of CIO... Dave Beck of Seattle becomes president of International Brotherhood of Teamsters (-1957 when convicted for filing false income tax returns, increases membership from some 180,000 to over 500,000 until replaced by Jimmy Hoffa - around 2 million members in 1980s, serves jail sentence 1962-65)... Air Force contracts Bureau of Labor Statistics to study problem of shortages in skilled tool and die makers (reports pool of craftsmen drying up and predicts inability of market to fill some 20,000 openings)... Kurt Vonnegut: Player Piano (describes world divided after automation with engineers and managers pitted against displaced workers)... After lobbying efforts by United Mine Workers Congress passes first Federal Mine Safety Act... Lever House, designed by Gordon Bunshaft, opens, NYC, as model elegant office building.

Business Events

Walt Disney assembles group, called Imagineers, of artists, writers, designers, engineers, architects, technicians, and craftsmen to plan and build Disneyland (opens 1955)... After devising first microwave relay system, Bill Daniels sets up pioneering cable system in Casper, WY (as broker helps build many of U.S.' largest cable firms in late 1950s, persuades Cox Broadcasting in 1965 to enter field, forms American Television & Communications in 1968 - 2nd largest system, owned by Time, Inc., in 1989, starts Prime Ticket Network in 1985 as regional sports channel - merger in 1988 with Home Sports Entertainment to form largest regional sports network, opens Young Americans Bank, Denver, in 1987 to teach children how to handle money)... Gibson Company, founded 1870s, produces Les Paul's rock 'n roll classic electric guitar...

Shanghai-born dealmaker Jerry Tsai joins Fidelity Fund to become leader in investment community with pioneering ultra-aggressive style of money management and success as stockpicker (resigns in 1965 with path to top blocked to start Manhattan Fund in 1966, sells to CNA Financial in 1968 for $30 million and CNA stock before market drops, resigns from CNA in 1973 to acquire small brokerage house, acquires small Associated Madison as base to buy other insurance companies, expands Associated with mail-order Beneficial National in 1980 to increase earnings from $800,000 to over $5 million, merges with American Can in 1982 to push old-line company into financial services, after $1 billion in acquisitions by 1986 becomes CEO of financial giant, sells traditional can business in 1986 for $570 million to create Primerica, acquires Smith Barney brokerage business in 1987 for $750 million in cash)...

Goodyear is first in rubber industry to exceed $1 billion in annual sales... TWA launches first "tourist class" service with flight to Ireland... General Motors offers air conditioning for 1953 cars... Salt Lake City restaurant owner Pete Harman persuades Colonel Harland Sanders to sell rights to his Kentucky fried-chicken secret recipe of 11 herbs and spices for royalties...

Henry Crown, head of Chicago's Material Services supplying building materials to contractors, and associates buy NYC's Empire State Building for $51 million (sell building to New York syndicate in 1964 for $64 million - Crown makes $50 million on investment of some $6 million)...

Engineer Peter L. Scott resigns from Texas Instruments to start Hermetic Seal Transformer in garage (sells business of $8 million to Dresser Industries in 1957, retires from Dresser in 1963 at age of 35 to live on Florida yacht, starts Scott Electronics in 1964 - sold to NCR, resigns from NCR for presidency of Norden Systems, division of United Technologies, in 1975, revises business of some $50 million in cockpit displays and computer printers as $3.5 billion electronics enterprise, resigns in 1984 when Harry J. Gray, chairman of UT, refuses to plan for successor, is hired in 1986 to run $1.8 billion Emhart business, maker of garden tools, locks, shoe machinery, and circuit-board-assembly machinery, with plan to acceletate use of modern technology and improve sales in Asian market)...

Boeing authorizes $15 million, 25% of net worth, to develop 707 jet plane for commercial traffic (tests plane 1954, receives Pan American order in 1955 - operational 1958)... New York's Consolidated Edison starts alcoholic consultation clinic (follows pioneering effort by Allis-Chalmers in 1946)... Publisher Generoso Pope acquires National Enquirer, circulation of 17,000, for $75,000 (transforms paper into national tabloid as U.S.' leading scandal sheet - circulation of 4.5 million in 1988)... Shepherd Mead: How to Succeed in Business Without Really Trying... Non-Linear Systems is started at Del Mar, CA (launches participative management program in 1960-61 - ineffective by 1965)...

Marriott Corp., business with some 5,000 employees operating 45 eating establishments, 13 Pantry Houses, in-flight meal service for 12 airlines, and food services for government agencies and industrial cafeterias, sells stock to public to raise capital for expansion (opens first hotel in 1957 - 4 by 1964, 20 by 1972 and 51 by 1980s with only one unionized, operates 1,000 eateries in 1972, 300 franchised, in 7 different lines - also 2 luxury restaurants, acquires American Resorts Group, operator of time-share vacation condominiums in 1984 to operate 143 hotels and resorts)... Clarence B. Randall, president of Inland Steel: <u>A Creed for Free Enterprise</u>... Jack La Lanne televises health and exercise program in San Francisco (-1977, operates 110 health and fitness centers by 1982 - plans for health food restaurants and nutrition centers)...

John Diedold, George Terbough: <u>AUTOMATION - The Advance of the Automatic Factory</u> (pioneers new industry)... 110 commercial TV stations operate throughout U.S., 450 in 1956... After introducing Sailfish boat in 1947, Alexander Bryan, Courtland Heyniger design Sunfish sailboat, world's most popular by 1982 with over 200,000 sold (produce fiberglass boats in 1959, sell to American Machine and Foundry in 1969)...

William J.J. Gordon joins Arthur D. Little consulting business of Boston to form "invention design group" (develops synectics program for creativity, creates Synectics consulting business in 1960)... Thompson Products holds annual meetings of top executives for organizational planning (continues after formation of TRW in 1958)...

First U.S. professional sports car race after W.W. II is held on Sebring track, FL... Dr. Painless Parker, first U.S. retail dentist dies, millionaire from 28-office chain (despite 1977 failure of Sears' chain, leads to franchise dentistry in 1980s)... Texas Instruments starts job enrichment program (fails to achieve goal of 16% involvement by 1968)... General Dynamics is created by merger of Electric Boat, Electric Launch, Electro-Dynamics (merges with Material Services of Henry Crown in 1959 to become major defense contractor)...

IBM creates Ergonomics Department... Operations Research Society of America forms... Henry S. Dennison, idealistic manufacturer of stationery supplies, dies (1877-, results in abandonment of many pioneering employee programs by 1971 with unionization)...

Off-Broadway theater opens as anti-Broadway movement with Circle-in-the-Square's production of "Summer and Smoke" (gives 398 of 442 shows in 1977-78)... Ernest Dale: <u>Planning and Developing the Company Organization Structure</u> (studies hundreds of organizational charts)... CBS opens Television City in Hollywood as complex of production facilities... Sonotone introduces hearing-aid with transistor to replace 3 vacuum tubes, used in nearly 75% of all hearing-aids by 1954...

Barney Rosset starts Grove Press to publish uncommercial, unconventional or shocking works of talented writers... Jim Collins opens Hamburger Handout self-service drive-in business in Culver City, CA (acquires Kentucky Fried Chicken franchise in 1960, evolves by 1981 as one of U.S.' largest fast-food franchise businesses with 231 outlets of Kentucky Fried Chicken, largest in chain, and with Sizzler Family Steak Houses - 137 outlets and 341 franchises)...

Braniff acquires Mid-Continental Airline to become U.S.' 6th largest, 12th in world (declares bankruptcy in 1982)... A.L. Tunick starts Chicken Delight fast-food franchise business (sells to Consolidated Foods in 1965)... Mary Wells, Macy's fashion manager in 1951, is hired as copy group head of McCann Erickson advertising agency (moves to Doyle Dane Bernbach in 1957 - copy chief and vice president by 1963 to earn $40,000, starts agency with John Tinker and Partners in 1964 to develop imaginative promotional campaigns for such clients as Alka Seltzer and Braniff, opens ad agency with partners in 1966 with Braniff as first client - billings in 6 months of some $30 million and 45 employees)...

After failing to find decent lodgings on trip to Washington, DC, in 1951, Kemmons K. Wilson and contractor Wallace E. Johnson, inventor of production system for assembling houses with standardized parts, open first Holiday Inn in Memphis, TN (start franchise system in 1953 with building contractors - 21 inns by 1956 and 1,750 by 1982 in all 50 states and continents but Antarctica, employ administrator in 1955 to supervise operations, open Holiday Inn University in 1959 to train managers, start buying back franchises in 1962 - 125 by 1973, open first European inn in Holland in 1968 - Japan in 1973 and South America in 1974 to operate 212 lodgings overseas in 58 countries by 1981, acquire holding company of Continental Trailways with its travel agency and Delta Steamship lines in 1969 for $200 million, start chain of Trav-L-Parks in 1970 - 45 by 1973, operate 1,549 inns in 1973 - 3 times more than nearest rival ITT-Sheraton chain, open hotel/casino in Atlantic City and start gaming joint-venture with Harrah's of Nevada, acquire Perkins steak restaurant chain in 1979)...

Thomas Watson, Jr., becomes president of father's IBM with sales of some $266 million - $1.2 billion in 1958 (-1971, continues unbiased hiring and recruits minorities, prepares IBM's first formal organizational chart in 1952, introduces 701 computer for scientific users in 1952 and 702 model for business users in 1955 - 85% of market by 1956, becomes chairman in 1956)... Carrier introduces first central air-conditioning system for homes, first portable by Fedders in 1954...

With permission of Screen Actor's Guild, Jules Stein's Music Corporation of America creates Revue Productions to produce TV shows... Oregon's Hoyt family ranch enters purebred cattle business (evolves by 1988 to operate on 1.2 million areas, public and private, with computer monitoring 5 corporations, 35 profit centers and 60 partnerships and keeping data on every cow and bull in herds, with 120 employees, annual advertising budget of $300,000, and exports of $1 million)...

Jacob Epstein, Doubleday publishing, starts series of inexpensive quality paperbacks (launches $6 million venture in 1988 with mail-order catalog as ideal bookstore)...

Pay 'n Pak home improvement store chain, 106 centers in 17 states with revenues of $390 million in mid-1980s, is started in Longview, WA... After introducing first U.S. magnetic tape recorder in 1947 with funds from Bing Crosby Enterprises, Alex Poniatoff's Ampex demonstrates first practical means to record TV on tape, work of Ray Dolby with 3M tape (introduces first recorder in 1956, leads to Sony's BetaMax recorder in 1964 - goes to VCR in 1988, Holland's Philips with first video cassette recorder in 1970, U.S.' Carti-Vision recorder for home use in 1971, Sony's prototype camcorder in 1980 - Hitachi in 1980 and Matsushita in 1981, and all 13.2 million VCRs sold in U.S. from Japan or Korea in 1987)... Franklin National Bank of New York is first to issue bank credit card...

Former pharmacist Herbert Haft starts Dart drugstore chain (after building 74-store firm with annual revenues of $283 million sells to operating managers in 1984 for $160 million, launches first of 6 unsuccessful takeovers to make some $200 million by 1988, fails to acquire 2,257-store Kroger grocery chain in 1988).

1953

General Events

President Truman establishes (January 16) offshore oil reserves as Federal property... Office of Price Stabilization lifts (February 6) controls on wages and salaries (removes controls on eggs, poultry, tires and gasoline on February 12 and all controls on March 17)... Congress establishes (April 1) Department of Health, Education and Welfare...

President Eisenhower uses (October 1) Taft-Hartley Act to prevent strike of dock workers... Washington reports largest peacetime deficit of $9.4 billion... H.E. Gilbert becomes president of Brotherhood of Locomotive Firemen and Enginemen (defies President Kennedy in 1963 in dispute with railroads over feather-bedding)... U.S. Supreme Court confirms 1922 ruling that major league baseball is not subject to Federal anti-trust laws...

Charles E. Wilson, former president of General Motors at Senate confirmation hearing for Secretary of Defense: "For years I thought what was good for our country was good for General Motors, and vice versa" (is attacked for putting GM above U.S.)... Irwin Bross: Design for Decision (promotes use of statistics in making decisions)... David Novick: Efficiency and Economy Through New Budgeting and Accounting Procedures (recommends in Rand report that first program budgeting system be adopted by Air Force and extended later to other services)...

Small experimental atom-powered motor is built... Earl Warren, former governor of California, becomes Chief Justice of Supreme Court (-1969)... Small Business Administration is created as federal agency... Frank Harary, Robert Z. Norman: Graph Theory: As a Mathematical Model in Social Science (follows 1878 work of British mathematician J.J. Sylvester)... Howard B. Bowen: Social Responsibilities of the Businessman...

Major League Player's Association is formed as a union by baseball players, followed by NFL Player's Association for football in 1957... In this time former pilot George A. Doole, 1909-85, joins Central Intelligence Agency (creates Pacific Corp., CIA holding company for Air America, Civil Air Transport, Southern Air Transport, Air Asia, and other small lines, to operate one of world's largest airlines during 1960s, "retires" in 1971)... New Jersey court approves company's unrestricted gift of $1,500 to Princeton University.

Business Events

Paul Sills co-founds Chicago's Playwrights Theater (spawns City's theatrical renaissance with development of other companies, such as Second City, Steppenwolf, Wisdom Bridge)... James E. Stewart takes over father's Minneapolis lumberyard, builds $70 million do-it-yourself home-building centers (sells to Lone Star Industries, U.S.' largest cement business, in 1971 for $33 million in stock - Lone Star CEO in 1973)... Desilu, producer of TV's "I Love Lucy" show, acquires RKO movie facilities to produce TV programs... General Motors enters earth-moving field with purchase of Euclid road machinery business...

Truck manufacturer White Motor Co. acquires 1898 Autocar truck business (acquires Reo in 1957 and Diamond T in 1958 to become largest in industry, enters farm machinery field with purchase of Oliver in 1961, expands with Motec Industries in 1963)...

Charles S. Roberts designs Tactics to pioneer commercial war games, sells 2,000 (forms Avalon Hill Co. in 1958 to achieve success with Gettysburg, first commercial wargame on historical events, to open war game market, is joined in field by Simulations Publications in 1969)... Reynolds announces production of Jamaica bauxite...

Kaiser Jeep acquires 1903 Overland automotive business making military trucks, sold to American Motors in 1970 and resold to LTV Corporation in 1983 and Chrysler in 1987... IBM delivers first 701 computer to Los Alamos research facility (installs 31 more in year with 164 on order - Sperry-Rand sells 33 with 24 on order)...

Carl H. Pohlad becomes president of Bank Shares, MN, empire of 40 banks by 1980s with over $4 billion in assets (after salvaging scandal-ridden transit system of Twin Cities develops chain of bottling operations throughout midwest to become Pepsi Cola's 3rd-largest independent bottler, joins take-over artist Irwin L. Jacobs in 1975 in number of profitable deals, acquires Minnesota Twins franchise in 1984 - world champion in 1987)...

1923 Hertz truck rental business, acquired in 1925 by General Motors, is purchased by Omnibus, holding company of bus operations (starts car leasing division - later Hertz International for car and truck rentals in over 100 countries, start Hertz Equipment Rental to serve building industrial firms in 1965 and United Exposition Service to serve trade shows, conventions, and expositions in 1967, is acquired by RCA in 1967 - United Airlines in 1985, opens first Skycenter at Huntsville, AL, airport to serve travelers in transit, creates Hertz' Number One Club in 1972, is sold to Ford-financed group in 1987)...

Triangle Publications produces TV Guide, evolves with largest circulation of any U.S. magazine - 14 million readers in 1968 (is sold with Triangle in 1988 to media magnate Rupert Murdock for $3 billion)... Ziff-Davis Publishing, started in 1927 by noted lecturer and author William B. Ziff, is inherited by William B. Ziff, Jr. (revives business losing money on gross of some $4 million to develop empire by 1980s with revenues of $500 million from 30 consumer, trade and computer magazines, several electronic information and software services, 6 television stations and other businesses, with threat of cancer starts divesting in 1980 to acquire some $1 billion in cash by 1986 - cancer in remission)...

Hyatt von Dehn, financial operator and real estate developer, opens first major inn near Los Angeles International Airport (sells property to Pritzker family of Chicago in 1957 when needing cash for deals)... Standard Steel Springs and Timken-Detroit Axle are merged by William

Rockwell, president of both concerns (renames business Rockwell-Standard in 1958 to become one of U.S.' largest suppliers of automotive parts, merges with North American Aviation, giant aircraft and aerospace enterprise, to form North American-Rockwell in 1967 - Rockwell International in 1973)...

Threatened with condemnation proceedings, Hooker Electrochemical is forced to deed property (used as site for chemical waste in 1942-52, along Love Canal of Niagara Falls, NY, to local board of education (sells acreage to housing developers in 1957 despite warnings from Hooker land should only be used for surface activity, results in hundreds of families being evicted in 1978-80 from toxic contamination)...

George Bush, U.S. President in 1989, and Hugh, Bill Liedtkes start Zapata Petroleum (borrow $1 million and repay in one year, acquire Bush's interest in 1955, acquire South Penn Oil in 1962 with backing of J. Paul Getty - merger in 1965 to form Pennzoil, acquire United Gas, 10 times its size, in 1965, start POGO in 1970 to finance aggressive exploration, divest United Gas Pipe Line in 1974, are forced by SEC in 1975 to pay $100,000 to former stockholders on charges of insider trading and to return $100 million in dividends received from United Gas, discover oil with Texaco in 1982 off California, acquire 20% of Getty Oil in 1923, sue Texaco in 1984 for acquiring Getty - awarded damages of $11.1 billion in 1985 - court challenges and bankruptcy by Texaco in 1986, settle suit for some $3 billion in 1987-88)...

Wallace Laboratories markets Miltown tranquilizer... Electro-Dynamics of Charles B. Thornton, Roy L. Ash and Hugh Jamieson acquires Litton, small manufacturer of microwave ovens with sales of some $3 million (with key acquisition of larger Monroe Calculation in 1985 to enter nonmilitary field, build Litton Industries as leading conglomerate with mergers - 25 by 1961 with sales of $3 million in 1953, $83.2 million in 1958 and over $1 billion by 1966 from some 5,000 diversified products)...

After producing over 300,000 cars since 1948 to become 4th largest in U.S. industry, Kaiser-Frazer Corp. abandons unprofitable venture (continues operation of Willys Motor making "Jeep" commercial vehicles - sales of $136 million in 1958)...

David Lilienthal: _Big Business:_ _A New Era_ (advocates mergers and new combinations)... Swanson Frozen Foods introduces first TV dinners... Experimental Aircraft Association forms to encourage development of canard, ultralight planes... Sam Cummings starts Interarms Corp. to sell weapons, equipment (evolves as largest private dealer of military equipment by 1981)...

The Institute of Management Science forms... Boston Braves baseball franchise moves to Milwaukee, WI (moves later to Atlanta, GA)... CBS obtains TV rights for football games from 11 of 12 NFL teams... After working for Houston's Stanley Home Products selling household specialties at parties in homes, Mary Kay Ash is hired by Gifts of Dallas to sell decorative accessories - earns $25,000/year and works 60-hour weeks in 10 years (resigns in 1963 to start Mary Kay Cosmetics with $5,500 and 9 beauty consultants, independent contractors, to sell skin cream products at home parties - sales of $198,514 in first year, $800,00 next and $235 million in 1981, opens Los Angeles branch in 1970s, Atlanta in 1972,

Chicago in 1975 and Toronto in 1978, is ranked 12th fastest growing business in 1981 by Business Week - 1,400 employees and 150,000 beauty consultants, some earning as much as $32,000/month)...

DuPont invents U.S. Dacron Polyester, first used in clothing by Hart, Schaffner and Marx (is heralded at first as "miracle fiber" before viewed as sleaze in double-knit suits, after 1970s tops cotton as most-used fiber in U.S., is used by fashion designers in 1980s)... American Broadcasting Co., formed 1940 by Edward J. Noble, and Paramount Theaters merge, lawyer Leonard Goldenson of Paramount is president (persuades Warner Brothers to produce movies for TV in 1955, pirates Fred Silverman from CBS in 1974 to head ABC programming, achieves No. 1 in ratings in 1976, is acquired by Capital Cities Communications in 1985 for $3.5 billion - last in ratings)...

After doing expensive hair styling on New York's Fifth Avenue, Karl Stanley opens first Cut & Curl beauty shop on Long Island for middle-class clientele (operates chain of Edie Adams' Cut & Curl shops in 40 states by 1980, introduces Great Expectations in 1980s as unisex salon business, operates 473 franchised beauty salons by 1983 with sales of $89 million)...

Advertising Research Foundation is formed as consulting business for agencies and clients... Chicago's Carson Pirie Scott is first department store to sell insurance...

After leaving sociology graduate program at Northwestern in 1950 and working in variety of jobs, including stints in promotion department of Esquire and as promotion manager in 1951 for George von Rosen's Modern Man magazine, Playboy is published by Hugh Hefner, age 27, raises $600 from bank loans on furniture to buy Marilyn Monroe's photograph for centerfold with $500 and $10,000 from stock to friends, relatives (after orders of nearly 70,000 copies of first issue publishes 400,000 copies/month in 2 years, starts Trump, satire magazine on radio and TV programs, in 1956 - abandoned 1957, starts TV show "Playboy Penthouse" in 1957 - carried by only 20 of 580 U.S. stations in 1961, starts International Playboy Clubs in 1959 - Chicago first in 1960, sponsors Chicago Playboy Jazz Festival in 1959, forms Playboy Tours in 1960 - only 25% of planned volume in 1961, introduces Show Business Illustrated in 1961 - discontinued, records membership of some 51,000 in 1961 with Playboy Key Clubs, airs Playboy Philosophy in 1962-63, is forced to sell stock in 1971 to raise cash - top value of $30.25 in 1978 to around $7 in 1986, exhibits pubic hair of Playmate in 1972 to compete with Penthouse, is investigated for drugs in 1972 - aide convicted in 1974, achieves circulation high of 7.2 million readers in 1972 - some 5.5 million in 1979 and around 4 million by 1984, launches Oui in 1972 as raunchy, youth oriented magazine to challenge Penthouse - sold 1981, reports profits of $1.1 million in 1975 on sales of $197.7 from 5 hotels, 4 casinos, 17 clubs, 2 modeling agencies, motion picture and TV production company, book club, mail-order business with licensed products, and book publishing business - nets $2 million on revenues of $198 million in 1976 and loses $14.4 million in 1982 on sales of $210 million, in 1981 is forced to sell gambling licenses for 4 profitable British casinos, names 29-year-old-daughter Christie president in 1982 - CEO in 1988, is rejected in 1983 for casino license by Atlantic City, introduces first male Rabbits at New York Playboy Club in 1985, sells Playmate video cassettes in 1985, closes clubs in 1986 and faces loss of some 10,000 magazine outlets in 1986 when Playboy is removed from shelves of several national convenience store chains).

1954

General Events

After month-long strike International Longshoremen's Association returns (April 2) to work after NLRB ultimatum... Congress establishes (May 3) St. Lawrence Seaway Development Corp. to build channel with Canada between Montreal, Lake Erie (-1959)... U.S. Supreme Court: Brown v. Board of Education of Topeka (rules "separate but equal" doctrine does not offer equal protection)... CIO and U.S. Steel agree on 2-year pact with wage increases and expanded welfare benefits... Gross national product of $365 billion is reported for 1953...

President Eisenhower signs (August 2) Housing Act to ease housing shortages... U.S. supplies electricity to 50 million customers, 98% of population... 360 TV stations operate in U.S., 231 open in 1953... Milford, CT, inventor patents device to make artificial snow... New York Thruway opens... U.S. Civil Service fires 2,600 people under Communist Control Act...

California'a governor closes L.A. oil refineries on 16th day of heavy smog... U.S. Post Office stops junk mail to "householders"... New Jersy is first State to legalize Bingo games, 44 more by 1987... Workers at paternalistic Kohler plumbing business in Wisconsin strike for union recognition (-1960 when NLRB forces firm to bargain and sign contract in 1962 - Kohler judged guilty of unfair labor practices by U.S. Supreme Court and ordered to pay $4.5 million in back pay and benefits to striking workers and to re-hire most fired workers)...

U.S. submarine Nautilus is converted to nuclear power, world's first (-1980)... Rigid farm price supports are replaced by "parity" program which allows Department of Agriculture to barter surplus crops to other countries for strategic goods...

Atomic Energy Bill permits (August 30) private ownership of atomic reactors in producing electrical power (results in construction of first commercial atomic power plant at Pittsburgh)... Adolph A. Berle, Jr.: The Twentieth-Century Capitalist Revolution... Jacques Ellul: The Technological Society...

J.D. Glover: The Attack on Big Business... WQED in Pittsburgh is first television station to be owned, licensed as community-operated enterprise - country's first educational channel at University of Houston in 1953 (evolves as part of Public Broadcasting System)... David M. Potter: People of Plenty: Economic Abundance and the American Character (maintains traditional abundance resulted in expectations of never-ending cheap energy)... Bell Laboratories develops solar battery...

Menninger Foundation, Topeka, KS, psychiatric treatment facility, forms Division of Industrial Mental Health... B.F. Skinner devises first device for programmed instruction (uses succession of easy-to-difficult learning steps with instant reinforcement for each correct response)... Science-fiction writer L. Ron Hubbard founds Church of Scientology (evolves with claims of some 6 million members and assets over $200 million in 1980s, sponsors management development programs in mid-1980s)... Methodology for Planning-Programming-Budgeting System is published (is recommended for Defense Department in 1958 by Rockefeller report as based on strategic doctrine with missions, is extended by President Johnson's executive order in 1965 to all Federal departments and agencies)... U.S. Air Force agrees to underwrite manufacturing projects using automated machine tools (receives proposals from aircraft industry but not machine tool industry).

Business Events

Ex-FBI man George Wackenhut starts security firm, largest publicly traded in U.S. in 1988 with sales of $428 million... Former jockey valet, groom, trainer and farm manager H.E. "Tex" Sutton starts forwarding business to transport horses by railcar, uses planes in 1969 (evolves to gross some $6 million yearly by 1988 in handling nearly 3,000 horses)... Leonard J. Savage: Foundations of Statistics (develops decision tree technique for managerial decision making)...

Corporate pirate Louis E. Wolfson launches raids on Montgomery Ward, mail-order business and 575 retail stores with annual sales of some $700 million, to plunder reserves of some $300 million amassed by Sewall Avery in belief post-war depression would occur as after W.W. I (loses battle in 1955, results in forced retirement of Avery and replacement of autocratic leadership with decentralized structure of Sears, is sold to Mobil petroleum in 1976 for $1 billion)...

1902 Dayton retail department store in Minneapolis expands outside City with new stores (launches Target as upscale discount chain - 226 outlets by 1980, merges in 1969 with Detroit's 1881 J.L. Hudson department store business, acquires Mervyn's, West Coast chain of some 50 stores selling apparel and housewares in 1978 - 147 places by 1980s, in 1985 acquires Lechmere, 10-store discount business in consumer electronics and small appliances, and starts RG Branden's chain to sell household goods, announces 5-year strategic plan in 1985 to spend $4 billion on expansion)...

General Motors plans to spend $1 billion to expand production... 573,374,622 shares are traded on NYSE in 1953, highest since 1933... Metropolitan Life Insurance tops AT&T as world's largest private corporation with $12 billion in assets... Frozen food industry reports sales over $1 billion in 1953... RCA starts mass-producing color TV sets... IBM plans electronic computer, costing $25,000/month, for business use in 1955... Boeing tests 707 jet transport plane, designed to carry 109 passengers across Atlantic in just over 6 hours at speeds up to 600 mph (-1983, stops production after selling 957 to 100 airlines)...

General Motors produces its 50-millionth car... IBM displays all-transistor calculator... Economist Alan Greenspan, chairman of Federal Reserve in 1987, starts economic consulting business... First Annual International Fancy Food and Confection Show opens, NYC... Gimbel's department store business, NYC, starts branch program (operates 22 stores, 27 Saks Fifth Avenue, and 4 Saks-34th Street in 1965, operates 68 units, sales of $900 million, in 1977, Macy with 76 stores and sales of

$1.6 billion, before acquisition by British-American Tobacco, closes 39 stores in 1986)... Philadelphia Athletics baseball franchise moves to Kansas City... Time, Inc. issues <u>Sports Illustrated</u>... Joseph F. McCloskey, Florence N. Trefethen (eds): <u>Operation Research for Management</u>... Reyers, Sharon, PA, shoe store since 1885, is purchased by Jubelirers, father and son (develops business as shoe mart with constant promotion and personal service to record yearly sales of $6-8 million - $350,000 average)... James McLamore and David Edgerton open franchised Insta/Burger King in Miami (after franchise troubles start Burger King chain with patented broiler in 1956, sell to Pillsbury in 1967 - 274 places to nearly 4,000 by 1984)... First El Torito restaurant with Mexican food opens in Southern California, evolves as chain of 22 eateries (is acquired by W.R. Grace Company in 1976 - over 100 units by 1983)...

With assistance of Texas oil men Clint R. Murchison and Sid W. Richardson, Robert R. Young, Allegheny Corp., wrests control of New York Central Railroad from Eastern financiers (revives line with drastic cuts in labor force, modernization of equipment before recession in 1957 and suicide in 1958)... H.B. Neill: <u>The Art of Contrary Thinking</u> (proposes stock market philosophy that "when everyone thinks alike, everyone is likely to be wrong")... William J. Baroudy, Sr., becomes head of American Enterprise Institute (increases budget from $80,000 to $8 million by 1978 to present views of business on public policy)... U.S. with 6% of world's population runs 60% of world's cars (uses 58% of all phones, 45% of all radios, and 34% of all railroads)... Carnation devises method to make instant dry milk that dissolves quickly in water (results in Coffee-Mate and other instant breakfast products)...

Peter Drucker: <u>The Practice of Management</u> (introduces expression "Management by Objectives" which had been used in crude form by General Motors in 1922 and Standard Oil of New Jersey in 1933, is adopted by General Mills in 1955, describes strategy as analyzing present situation and resources in order to change them if necessary)... J.G. Glover: <u>Fundamentals of Professional Management</u>... James Bright: <u>Automation and Management</u>... Frank J. Andress: "The Learning Curve as a Production Tool," <u>Harvard Business Review</u>... 1876 Eli Lilly, Indianapolis pharmaceutical business enters agricultural market to utilize research resources (acquires 1909 Elizabeth Arden cosmetic business in 1971-72, shifts focus to age-combatting products, sells to Faberge in 1987 for $700 million)... First Shakey's Pizza Parlor opens in Sacramento (expands to Portland, OR, in 1956, operates 377 outlets by 1988)... Rod Serling: "Patterns" (portrays in television show power conflict in top management)...

Steve Ross and daughter of owner of NYC Riverside Chapel and chain of funeral parlors are married (while working for father-in-law starts Abbey Rent-A-Car and Abbey Limousine in 1959 with 5 partners, reaches agreement with Kinney, City's largest parking lot business, to obtain free parking for rentals, merges with parking lot business in 1961 to form Kinney Service Corp., issues stock with market value of $13 million in 1962 to obtain capital of $17 million, merges with National Cleaning in 1966, in 1968 acquires National Periodical Publications, operator of newsstands at airports, and Ashley Famous Agency with clients in entertainment field - sold 1969 to avoid conflict of interest, sells Kinney Rent-A-Car in 1968 for $11 million, buys Warner Brothers-Seven Arts in 1969 for $400 million, acquires Garden National Bank of New Jersey in 1969 when long-range planning committee identified money management as promising field - divested in 1980 with change of 1970 Federal Banking law, acquires Electra Records in 1970 and Asylum Records in 1972, sells funeral business in 1971 for $30 million and establishes National Kinney with $43.5 million as separate company with real estate business of Kinney Service, with revenues of some $378.8 million establishes Warner Communications, records, magazines, and movies, as 294th on Fortune 500 list in 1971, acquires Cypress Communications, cable business, for $73 million in stock in 1972 - later another cable television business for $32 million in stock, opens Warner Brothers Jungle Habitat, wildlife amusement park in New Jersey, in 1974, buys Atari video game business for $2 million in 1974 - sold 1984 for $240 million, sells foreign publishing business in 1974 for loss of $15.3 million, gets top salary of $22.5 million in 1981)...

Studebaker-Packard Corp. is formed by merger (discontinues making Packards in 1958 and Studebakers in 1964 to become financial holding company)... Henry J. Kaiser develops Hawaiian Village resort in Honolulu to pioneer island's post-war tourist business (-1959, sells in 1961 to Hilton Hotels for $21.5 million)... Thomas Murphy, Harvard MBA, is hired to save near-bankrupt Albany television station (with rescue starts development of Capital Cities Communications to operate 7 TV stations, 54 cable-TV systems, 12 radio stations, 27 weekly newspapers, 10 dailies, and 45 other publications by the 1980s - revenues of $940 million in 1984, acquires ABC in 1985 for $3.5 billion)...

American Motors is formed by merger of Hudson Motor with Nash-Kelvinator (produces Metropolitan compact car of Nash in 1954-62, bases future strategy in 1956 on compact, practical Rambler car - first introduced in 1950, achieves sales of 90,000 cars in 1957 - 180,000 cars, 4.6% of industry, in 1958 and 435,000 cars in 1960 to lead new car market with highest sales of U.S. independents, sells Kelvinator to White Consolidated in 1968, buys Kaiser Jeep business in 1970 - acquired by Chrysler in 1987 with dissolution of AMC, sells part ownership to State-owned French Renault in 1978 - abandons venture in 1987)... Ray Kroc, successful malted-milk machine salesman, buys franchise rights for systematized hamburger business of Maurice, Richard McDonald in San Bernardino, CA, (opens first McDonald's in Des Plaines, IL, in 1955)...

Regency, first all-transistor radio, appears for Christmas market... Howard Hughes turns over ownership of Hughes Aircraft to Hughes Medical Institute (is acquired in 1985 by General Motors for $5 billion to make Institute richest of U.S. charitable organizations)... Dan Hanna opens first car wash in Milwaukie, OR (operates 27 Portland franchises by 1969 - 6,700 worldwide by 1980, forms Hanna Acceptance as financing arm in 1969, evolves as Hanna Industries with sales of some $60 million to supply car-wash machines to 65-70% of world market by 1980s, obtains GM contract in 1984 to supply dealers with car-wash equipment - later Toyota, American Motors, Chrysler and BMW, sells equipment for places in Australia, U.S.S.R. and China 1987-88)... George Johnson, sharecropper's grandson, starts pioneering Johnson Products with Afro Sheen for black hair care (evolves as $38 million business in 1960s with Afro hair styles, falters when International Playtex develops curl market for blacks in late 1970s)... Hearth Craft is started in Portland, OR, to make fireplace equipment, one of world's largest in 1980 with sales of $15 million (is acquired in 1980 by Mobex and General Fireplace in 1983 to move production to Indiana)... Arthur Andersen & Co., Chicago-based accounting firm founded 1913, installs first commercial computer at General Electric, sales of $160 million in 1986 from systems integration work (opens Systems Integration Center in 1988 to tie together products of 35 firms as leader in field with staff of 8,500 computer experts, faces conflict in 1988 between traditional auditing and growing consulting business)... Campbell Soup goes public, Dorrance family with majority control (grows by 1985 with 44,000 employees, 80 plants and over 1,000 products, including Pepperidge Farm, Vlastic Foods, and Mrs. Paul's Kitchens)... Morrison Cafeterias incorporates, started 1928, LA (grows by 1988 as U.S.' largest chain with sales of $275 million from 164 places - chased by Furr's/Bishop's Cafeterias with 155 places, sales of $250 million, before trying 1988 takeover Wyatt chain of 120 outlets, sales of some $200 million)... After 1929 idea Marion W. Isbell opens Phoenix motel, first of Ramada Inns' worldwide chain of 800 hotels, motels by 1988 (buys Marie Callender Pie Shops in 1986 - problems with cutthroat competition in coffee-shop-style restaurants, attracts raiders in 1988 with troubles in betting on $200 million Tropicana hotel-casino at Atlantic City).

1955

General Events

Atomic Energy Commission states (January 9) plans for private industry to operate atomic power plants (offers financial assistance)... Federal Trade Commission reports tripling of business mergers since 1950... UAW and Ford agree on contract (provides first supplemental unemployment benefits)... U.S. plans (July 29) to launch earth-orbiting satellites... President Eisenhower signs (August 12) bill to increase minimum wage to $1/hour in 1956... Interstate Commerce Commission bans segregation on interstate trains, buses... Con Ed of New York builds first private nuclear plant... U.S. Air Force unveils self-guided missile... Bell Telephone uses sun to power first telephone call, GA... Charles J. Hitch: An Appreciation of Systems Analysis (leads to R.N. McKean's Efficiency in Government Through Systems Analysis in 1958)... Ford Foundation awards funds to Harvard, Carnegie Institute of Technology to study uses of behavioral sciences in business administration...

In this time spa at Big Sur Hot Springs, CA, is transformed into pioneering Esalen Institute by founder Mike Murphy and Richard Price to extend human potential with group therapy, psychodrama, massage, sensitory awareness, and Oriental philosophy (is established as outlaw university in 1962 to launch human counter-culture human consciousness movement by training some 700 psychotherapists, starts popular San Francisco center in 1967, spawns several Esalen-type communities in U.S., Canada and variety of commercial ventures, after failing in 1970s to realize new humanity is acquired by Association for Humanistic Psychology, umbrella organization for programs in personal growth, release and/or liberation)... Screen Actors Guild strikes movie studios of California, also in 1960 and 1980 (is followed by strikes of Writers Guild of America in 1960, 1973, 1981)... Herbert Simon, Harold J. Leavitt and Robert Schlaifer at Carnegie Institute of Technology study human behavior in decision making... National Air Polution Control Act is passed (starts research on environmental problems)... Professional basketball players form union of Players Association... Male-only National Press Club of Washington, DC admits women as observers (admits women as members in 1971, merges in 1985 with women-dominated Washington Press Club of 1919)... Texas court extends workmen's compensation law to cover psychological illness in Bailey v. American General (is expanded with 1960 case of Carter v. General Motors to cover psychological illness as disabling injury, to cover environmental-induced stress with 1970 case of Alcorn v. Arbo Engineering)... In this time Rand Corp. designs "Monopologs" as logistics game for U.S. Air Force, followed in 1957 by American Management Assn.'s "Top Management Stimulation"... Some 16 million workers, over 85% of union membership, are united with merger of AFL and CIO, George Meany president...

Despite Congressional investigations in 1953-54 for corruption, James Hoffa becomes vice president of International Brotherhood of Teamsters (is indicted by Federal Grand Jury in 1957 for bribing Senate employee to obtain confidential information - acquitted, becomes union president in 1957 when Dave Beck is convicted in filing fraudulent income tax returns - Teamsters forced out of AFL-CIO, is acquitted in 1958 on wire-tapping charges, revises union constitution in 1961 to replace local and regional bargaining with national contract, is indicted 1962 for accepting payments from employer - hung jury, is indicted 1963 for jury tampering in 1962 case - convicted, is convicted in 1964 for fraudulent use of union pension funds, selects Frank Fitzsimmons as acting president while in prison, is forced to resign as union president in 1971, is released from prison in 1971 on condition not to engage in union activity until 1980, fails to regain union presidency in 1974, disappears in 1975 on way to meeting, is declared legally disappeared in 1982 and legally dead in 1985)...

Federal Reserve System ups requirements for stock market margins to squelch speculations... New tax code allows deductions for travel to conventions... Yale's tuition goes from $800 yearly to $1,000, reaches some $18,000 in 1987... Government reports those earning over $100,000 receive most of income from dividends and capital gains on assets rather than from business profits or salaries... For first time Bureau of Labor Statistics includes beer in Cost-Price Index... For first time, not counting military recruiting, Government job recruiters visit colleges to fill some 10,000 Federal jobs... Railroads are allowed to ship "Piggy-back" trailers by rail without being required to have ICC certification as motor carrier... Colleges graduate only 60% of needed engineers... FTC rules cigarette manufacturers cannot make health claims in advertising...

Sloan Wilson: The Man in the Grey Flannel Suit (attacks organizational regimentation)... Federal Trade Commission reveals business mergers have tripled since 1950... William F. Whyte: Money and Motivation (reports uses of employee participation in organizational change)... FDA rules that aspirin bottles must be labeled "Unsafe for Children"... U.S. Air Force sponsors first use of large-scale analog computers to study chemical distillation, followed in late 1950s by similar study of Navy on mechanization of dockwork... Black seamstress Mrs. Rosa Parks rejects order of Montgomery City bus driver to give her seat to white rider (results in 311-day bus boycott led by Reverend Martin Luther King, Jr., other black leaders of Montgomery Improvement Association, results in Supreme Court ruling that Alabama's laws requiring segregated buses are unconstitutional)... CIO sponsors National Conference on Automation (launches decade of debate and controversy on issue)... U.S. Air Force changes specifications on $100 million worth of orders for machine tools to require numerical controls for computer programming (pioneers computer graphics in early 1960s with computer design systems)... When offended by "girlie" magazines and porno paperbacks, Charles H. Keening, "Mr. Clean," starts moral crusade Citizens for Decent Literature in Cincinnati to rid newsstands of pornography (pressures politicians to close theaters showing sex films)... Western Reserve University's library school is first in field to offer a computer course.

Business Events

NYSE records (September 26) greatest single-day dollar loss of $44 billion... No-iron Dacron fiber is introduced... Bell Aircraft displays fixed-wing vertical takeoff plane... Beech Aircraft introduces first executive jet plane... RKO sells film library for TV distribution... RCA labs build first musical synthesizer to produce first computer-generated sounds... Borroughs enters computer market by merging with Electro-Data Corp... RCA introduces large-scale computing system of BIZMAC (abandons computer market 1971)... Dorrance family's Campbell Soup business acquires Swanson frozen foods of Omaha (acquires Pepperidge Farms in 1961 and businesses in dog food, restaurants, garden, chocolate and pickle businesses in 1970s to record 1979 sales of $2.2 billion)... Meier & Frank department store in Portland, OR, opens its first branch in Salem, 7 by 1980 (is acquired by May Co. in 1965)...

Ted Jones opens first branch of father's brokerage business, founded in 1922, in St. Louis, MO (evolves by 1988 with corps of 1,358 brokers in small towns of 37 states to net $32 million in 1987)... IBM grants first stock options to employees... Leonard Goldenson, president of American Broadcasting-Paramount Theaters convinces Warner Brothers movie business to produce television shows... Revlon sponsors $64,000 Question show for TV, first quiz program presented on prime time (-1958 when dropped as result of quiz show cheating scandals in 1958-59)... Tappan Stove Co. introduces first electronic range, priced at $1,200... In this time Matson Navigation uses containers to ship goods between West Coast ports and Hawaii (pioneers containerization industry)...

William F. Buckley founds National Review as national magazine for conservative philosophy (publishes first issue in 1956)... Volkswagen of America is founded as subsidiary, 3 employees and sales under 33,000 cars, of West German firm (by 1980 operates with nearly 10,000 employees and sales over 200,000 cars before decline in mid-1980s)... General Electric Research Laboratory converts graphite into industrial diamonds (starts commercial production in 1957)... Edward Schleh: Successful Executive Action (presents first full discussion of management by objectives, leads to first MBO seminar at University of Michigan in 1959 and in George S. Odiorne's Management by Objectives as first book with title in 1965)... David Lilienthal forms Development and Resource Corp. as private firm to provide managerial and technical assistance to underdeveloped nations...

Newmyer Associates, started during World War II by ex-journalist as public policy consulting business to gather and analyze information on selected topics, is acquired by 2 sons after death (is followed by competitor Government Research in 1970 to collect information for foreign and U.S. companies - 65 U.S. and 125 foreign clients by 1985)... Arnold Palmer joins pro golf tour (promotes golf as spectator's sport)... Chase National Bank of New York and Bank of Manhattan, nation's 15th largest with 67 branches, merge to become City's largest (although passed by Citibank in 1970s becomes U.S.' 3rd largest with 226 branches in New York, 105 offices and 34 subsidiaries around world)... Zenith sells remote-control device for television sets, followed in 1985 by General Electric's universal remote-control unit for home equipment... Rand Corp. designs Delphi technique to do long-range forecasting in this time... Four partners start home-building business (evolves as Prime Motor Inns to acquire Howard Johnnson's 125 Howard Johnson hotels and motor lodges, 375 franchised lodges and 199 franchised restaurants for $235 million in 1985 to become nation's 4th largest lodging business)...

Ellis Johnson: The Application of Operations Research to Industry... Leonard H. Lavin acquires Alberto-Culver hairdressing business, sales under $500,000, for $488,000 on receiving tip ill owner needs to sell (with extensive advertising budget of $2.5 million, emphasizing TV, generates yearly sales of some $80 million by 1963)... After creating window displays for Chicago's Carson Pirie Scott's department store and designing hats in spare time, Indiana-born Halston is hired by Lilly Dache to design hats (joins New York's Bergdorf Goodman, largest retail outlet in City for European couture with 250 dressmakers and 150 tailors, in 1959 as hat designer, opens first ready-to-wear collection with backing of Texas socialite in 1968 - success as snob designer with recognition by Mrs. William Paley, sells label rights in 1973 to Norton Simon's conglomerate for some $12 million, achieves sales of $90 million in 1975 with 12 franchising contracts)...

First Fortune 500 list of biggest U.S. corporations shows General Motors as No. 1, dethroned by Exxon in 1975 (regains title in 1978, drops to 2nd in 1980, 3rd in 1981 and 1982 behind Exxon and Mobil, 2nd in 1983 and 1984 before reaching No. 1 again in 1985)... Ford Motor Co. introduces low, sleek Thunderbird car... Air traffic since W.W. II is estimated to have tripled in number of flights... Packard compares its cars with those of brand "X" in advertisements... U.S. foreign investments are some $25 billion, double 1946 total... American Automobile Assn. urges car makers to focus on safety rather than "hazardous unwarranted horsepower"... About 3.8 million golfers play on some 5,000 golf courses... Atomic power station opens at Schenectady, NY...

Singer Elvis Presley hires "Colonel" Tom Parker, Dutch "emigrant" to U.S. in 1927, former ex-carny and previous agent for Eddie Arnold and Hank Snow, as personal manager (-1977)... James Ling sells stock in electrical business, yearly sales of some $1.7 million (acquires California aerospace electronics firm in 1956 and another electronics firm in 1958 to create Ling Electronics - sales of $6.9 million by 1959, acquires Altrec's sound equipment business in 1955 to form Ling-Altec - then University Loudspeaker and Continental Electronics, purchases Timco, defense contractor, in 1960, acquires Chance-Vought aircraft business in 1961 to create Ling-Timco-Vought, buys Okonite Co. in 1965 from Kennecott Copper, restructures L-T-V to obtain capital to buy Wilson & Co., Great American Corp., includes National Car Rental and Braniff Airways, in 1967, restructures Wilson & Co. into 3 new firms to raise $44 million in 3 new stock issues, acquires Jones & Laughlin steel business in 1969, after anti-trust actions block organizational plans and financial difficulties is forced to resign as chairman in 1970)... Malcomb McLean, previously operator of trucking line, acquires Pan Atlantic Steamship (starts Sea-Land's ship container business in 1956, sells to R.J. Reynolds in 1969 for profit of $157 million, is re-acquired by McLean's U.S. Lines in 1978 for $111 million, files for bankruptcy on 27-ship fleet in 1986 with debts of $1.3 billion)... In planning since 1952 Disneyland theme park opens, July 17, in Anaheim, CA (is financed by ABC with $4.5 million in return for Disney television show in 1954, records one-millionth customer by Labor Day, 3.8 million visitors after one year and 250 million by 1985 (opens Walt Disney World, FL, in 1971 - EPCOT in 1982 and MGM studio in 1989, licenses Japanese park in 1983, develops $2 billion French theme park to open 1992)... California's Mammouth Mountain operates its first chair lift (operates 23 chair lifts by 1980s to handle some 14,000-17,000 skiers/weekend)...

Following lead of Young & Rubicam Advertising, McCann-Erickson agency creates public relations unit, followed by 2 more ad agencies by 1957... William Hamling publishes Rogue magazine for men, sells some 300,000/month by 1956 (expands into publishing sex-oriented paperbacks in 1959 to earn $4 million in 1960-63)... Revlon goes public at $12/share - $420 17 years later (introduces Charlie fragrance for younger women in 1973, is acquired by Pantry Pride in 1985 after stock battle)... On verge of abandoning tax preparation business to focus on providing bookkeeping and management assistance to small businesses, H&R Block advertises for tax work, obtains some $25,000 in fees to stay in field (opens 7 offices in NYC in 1955 to record sales of $56,000 in first year, starts franchising in 1956 to oversee 39 offices in 1958 - 8,190 U.S. offices and 1,160 overseas by 1982, starts national TV advertising in 1961)...

After obtaining license to franchise McDonald's fast-food concept, Ray Kroc opens first new McDonald's restaurant in Des Plaines, IL (by 1957 operates 37 places - 100 in 1959, 228 in 1960, 1,000 in 1969, 1,500 in 1970, 6,200 in 1980, 7,259 in 1982 with sales of $7.8 billion and 10,000 in 50 countries in 1988 with sales of $14.3 billion on advertising budget of some $900 million, employs public relations firm in 1957, opens Hamburger University in 1961, starts research facility in 1962 to invent computer-controlled frying equipment in 1962 and develop Filet O Fish in early 1960s, issues stock in 1965 for $22.50/share - $30 at day's end and $50 at month's closing, opens first place outside U.S. in Canada in 1967 - some 2,000 worldwide by 1986 as world's No. 1 with Kentucky Fried Chicken next with 1,773 locations overseas, opens in Japan - 575 as largest chain, West Germany and Australia in 1971, introduces Egg McMuffin for breakfast trade in 1973, opens new place in Stockholm in 1975 - bombed in protest against U.S. imperialism, pioneers new locations with new place in Chicago's fancy Water Tower Place in 1976, introduces industry's first full breakfast menu in 1977 - 15% of sales of some $1 billion, in 1981, introduces first chicken products in 1981, opens 8,000th eatery in 1984 and operates 9,530 worldwide - one opening every 17 hours, opens first East European fast-food eatery at Belgrade in 1988)...

After buying and managing commercial land foreclosed during 1930s in 1940s, Harry Helmsley starts Helmsley-Spear real estate business, one of largest by 1980s to become billionaire (names wife Leona head of Helmsley Hotels in 1980, acquires Standard Oil's nationwide Hospitality Inns in 1980s to create Harley chain, is indicted with wife in 1988 for evading

$4 million in income taxes)... Great Northern Railroad runs its last passenger train with steam engine.

1956

General Events

AFL film union asks unions to boycott "Daniel Boone" movie filmed in Mexico with non-union workers... Labor columnist Victor Riesel, outspoken foe of labor racketeering, is blinded in both eyes by acid thrown by attackers (leads to indictment of labor racketeer John Dio and 5 others)... Some 650,000 steel workers strike, railroads forced to lay off 30,000 employees... Congress authorizes (June 29) over $33.4 billion to build 41,000-mile nationwide network of highways linking most major cities (predicts 150,000 new construction jobs)... Two U.S. collegiate schools of business use computerized business games, some 64 by 1962... Bank Holding Company Act limits out-of-state acquisitions of banks...

Sylvia, Benjamin Selekman: Power and Morality in Business... John McCarthy of Dartmouth College coins term "artificial intelligence" for computer field (leads to research activity at MIT in 1957, first center 1967, and Stanford in 1963, with first systems by Stanford and Xerox in 1970s)... Toll road system from NYC to Chicago is completed... Herbert Simon and Allen Newell design "Logical Theorist" as "thinking" computer program... First transatlantic telephone cable is laid, service in 1959 (leads to fiber-optic cable in 1988)... 156-day strike is settled by Westinghouse Electric and union of electrical workers, who had advertised "You can't be sure if it is Westinghouse"... For first time blue-collar workers are outnumbered in labor force by white-collar employees in clerical, technical and managerial positions...

Interstate Commerce Commission ends racial segregation on buses and trains, extended to stations in 1961... Commissioner of Labor Statistics predicts one-third of 1965 labor force will be women... Gallup poll shows most Americans feel rich actually pay too much in taxes.

Business Events

Mechanics and Farmers Savings Bank in Bridgeport, CT, opens first drive-in service... Du Mont television network, pioneered medium in 1930s and largest in 1954, stops broadcasting... Naples' Sbarro family opens Italian gourmet deli in Brooklyn (develops business to operate 220 cafeteria-style Italian fast-food restaurants throughout U.S., Puerto Rico and Canada by 1980s)... Coca-Cola introduces "family-sized" bottle (acquires Minute Maid frozen orange juice in 1960, acquires Duncan Foods, maker of coffee and tea products, in 1964, launches line of nutritional beverages in 1968 and introduces branded line of mixers in 1969, acquires Milwaukee firm, makers of equipment for pollution control and desalting seawater, in 1970, achieves sales of $1.87 billion from 250 products and 750 bottlers in U.S. and 850 overseas)... Hungarian-born George Soros, after graduating from London School of Economics, moves to U.S. to work as broker, stock analyst (starts Quantum firm in 1969 with $250,000 - Rothschilds and other rich Europeans provide $6 million, amasses $1.5 billion in profits by 1987 as Wall Street's canniest investor - nets $150 million in 1985 in switching dollar investments into Japanese yen)... Johnson Wax business starts diversifying with "Raid" bug killer (introduces "Off!" first aerosol insect repellant, in 1957, "Pledge" first aerosol furniture polish, in 1958, "Glade," first aerosol air freshener, in 1961, and "Glory," first home carpet cleaner, in 1968, operates Johnson Diversified in 1979 with 15 firms in recreational equipment)... Thomas J. Watson, Jr., named capitalist of century by <u>Fortune</u>, becomes head of father's IBM (-1971, decentralize centralized management structure with check-and-balance system to practice contention management, sells traditional time clock business to Simplex Time in 1958 to focus on computers, drops electronic tubes for transistorized circuits in 1958, puts all employees on salaries in 1958 to eliminate differences between factory and office work, introduces "quality circles" around 1963, uses hybrid ceramic and metal circuits while rivals use silicon chips, introduces System 360 in 1964 - adopted by most major customers as standard computer, gains 65% of U.S. computer market in 1965 - Sperry Rand 2nd with 12%, fights U.S. charges of monopolistic practices in 1969 - suit dropped 1982, retires in achieving success by selling service not just machines)...

Douglas McGregor, Lee Bradford and Rensis Likert give first National Training Laboratories' program for managers... Ford Foundation sells $690 million in stock of Ford Motor Co. to public, $28,000 original investment of Henry Ford... Douglas Aircraft introduces DC-7C planes for regular non-stop transatlantic service... Crowell-Collier publishing business declares bankruptcy, caused by loss of advertising revenues going to TV... John Backus designs FORTRAN in this time as first standard computer language, introduced in 1957 by IBM (is followed in 1959 by COBOL written by Grace Hopper and others, by the BASIC program in 1965)...

Federated Department Stores buys Burdine chain of 4 stores (expands to 17 stores by 1980 to provide customers with drama in shopping)... 8 major steel companies form industry bargaining group (after enduring 116-day strike in 1959 maintain 23 years of industrial peace)... First annual 10-day Kentucky Derby Festival of parades, boat races and parties is started in Louisville for 82nd running of famed horse race... Basic oxygen furnace for making steel, first developed in Austria, is used first in U.S. in this time by McClouth Steel... Warren Buffett starts investment partnership, Omaha (after compounding funds at annual rate of 29.5% dissolves business in 1969 to form Berkshire Hathaway, becomes $2.8 billion portfolio and affiliated firms, the Sainted Seven, in 1988 with following rule: "The time to get interested is when no one else is. You can't buy what is popular and do well")...

R. Hansberger becomes president of Boise Payette (transforms 1913 firm of 3 sawmills with sales of some $35 million into Boise Cascade's conglomerate of $1.8 billion in 13 years, is ousted in 1972 from losses in land development business)... James Vicary, New Jersey market researcher, develops subliminal advertising... Henry J. Kaiser creates Kaiser Industries as holding company for interests in aluminum, chemicals, steel, cement, cars and engineering services... After co-inventing transistor and teaching at Stanford, William Shockley starts Shockley Transistor Corp. in California's Silicon Valley (spawns microchip industry when 8 former employees start Fairchild Camera and Instruments in 1957 - 53 former employees of Fairchild start semiconductor firms later)...

William F. Whyte, Alan R. Holmberg: "Human Problems of U.S. Enterprises in Latin-America," Human Organization (pioneers study of U.S. activities in international business)... CBS pays NFL some $1 million for annual rights to televise professional football games, increases fees for rights to $14 million by 1964 (forces ABC, in order to break into market, to subsidize new American Football League in 1964 with $42 million contract for 5 years)... Annual Master's Golf Tournament at Augusta National golf course, started in 1934 by Bobbie Jones with Clifford Roberts as director, is first televised by CBS... After operating small juvenile-furniture store since 1948, Charles Lazarus starts toy supermarket business, Toys 'R' Us, to create year-round market for toys (sells to Interstate Stores in 1966, buys business back in 1978 with bankruptcy of Interstate, shows sales over $3 billion as world's largest toy retailer in 1987 - growth rate of 19% since 1983, expands to 350 places by 1988 in U.S., Canada, Britain - 18 stores with 9% of market in 3 years, West Germany, Hong Kong and Singapore, including 24 megastores overseas since 1984, and plans for 200 foreign operations)...

Ben W. Heineman becomes head of Chicago & North Western Railway (starts diversifying in other businesses in 1965 to create Northwest Industries with products from underwear to whiskey, sells financially-troubled railroad to employees in 1972)... W.H. Whyte: The Organizational Man (studies corporate regimentation)... After becoming a physician, taking field hospital to Russia to aid famine-stricken peasants in 1920s, bartering surplus U.S. wheat for Soviet products, and representing 38 U.S. firms in U.S.S.R., Armand Hammer retires (lends failing Occidental Petroleum, operator of 8 nearly played-out wells, $100,000, takes over in 1957 to protect tax shelter investment, develops business as billion-dollar corporation in 1960s with new oil finds in North Sea and Libya, negotiates 20-year fertilizer contract with Soviet Union in 1973, thwarts takeover of Standard of Indiana in 1974, pleads guilty to illegal political contributions in 1976, negotiates with China in 1979 to develop world's largest open-pit coal mines, acquires Cities Service for $4.2 billion in 1982, signs accord with U.S.S.R. to build giant petrochemical plant, buys Cain Chemical for $1.2 billion and plans personal art museum 1988)...

Glidden paint business develops fiberglass strong enough to make pleasure boats... Store owners in 2 Southern states are required by unions to put up signs indicating they are selling Japanese textiles... Procter & Gamble markets Crest, pioneering fluoride toothpaste... Bank of America is forced by law to spin off First Interstate as independent banking operation (after becoming 12-state regional bank, 9th largest in U.S., with assets of $50 billion, proposes merger in 1986 to financially-troubled BankAmerica with assets of $117 billion)... After rejecting offer of $164,000 in early 1950s to sell gas station and chicken restaurant, Colonel Harlan Sanders, former farmhand, buggy painter, railroad fireman, streetcar conductor, insurance salesman, soldier and lawyer, is forced to auction business when bypassed by location of Interstate 75 7 miles away (lacking sufficient Social Security income for retirement and remembering success of 1952 franchise, travels country to license special method of preparing chicken with pressure cooker and 11 herbs and spices to restaurants for royalty on each chicken sold, 200 franchises with sales of some $100,000 in 1960 - 600 places in 1963 with revenues over $2.3 million, starts training center in 1964, sells in 1964 to John Y. Brown and venture capitalist Jack Massey for $2 million plus lifetime salary)... For first time Dow Jones industrial average closes over 500... World's first "two-story, enclosed shopping experience" opens in Edina, affluent suburb of Minneapolis... F.P. Caruthers designs programmable numerical control for machine tools, first Automatrol then Specialmatic later (unveils innovation in 1960 at Chicago's Machine Tool Show)... Year's largest budgets for advertising are spent by Chevrolet, $30.4 million, and Ford, $25 million... Resources for the Future hires German-born economic forecaster Otto Eckstein as a consultant (-1959, starts Data Resources in 1966 to provide businesses with economic forecasts, sells in 1979 to McGraw-Hill for $103 million)... Greek-born Leo Stefanos, operator of Dove Candies in Chicago, creates DoveBar, huge stick of top-quality ice cream dipped in premium chocolate to sell for $1.45-$2.00/bar, to stop sons chasing ice-cream trucks (is developed by son, partners as DoveBar International in 1983, is sold to Mars candy in 1986)...

General Electric creates TEMPO, Technical Management Planning Organization, as independent profit center (uses some 200 physical scientists, sociologists, economists, and engineers in think-tank to provide consulting services and study the future)... Nate Sherman and son, pipe manufacturers, start chain of Midas Muffler auto repair shops (are forced to recognize pioneering association of franchisees in 1970 to handle disputes, operate some 1,300 U.S. and 1,400 foreign outlets by 1983)... Adolph and Joel Krisch, struggling pawn shop operators in Roanoak, VA, buy 17th franchise of Holiday Inns for $3,000 IOU (open 2nd motel in 1960, by 1981 operate American Motor Inns , 50 places from Maine to U.S. Virgin Islands as firm's largest franchisee, with subsidiaries of Universal Communications Systems and American Motel Schools)...

Bernard Cornfeld starts Investors Overseas Services in Paris to sell mutual funds on installment plan to U.S. expatriates and military servicemen (moves headquarters of successful business to Geneva in 1958 and enjoys "swinging" lifestyle, incorporates IOS as Panamian business in 1960, registers with SEC in 1960 as dealer in order to sell to U.S. military bases in other lands, develops business to sell $74 million in 1962 - goal to achieve "Worldwide People Capitalism," starts British subsidiary in 1963 to invest funds in other countries - opposed by Bank of England as funds must stay in Britain, starts selling in U.S. with acquisition of Investors Planning in 1965, hires James Roosevelt, son of former President, in 1966 to promote business with contacts - uses other dignitaries at times to impress clients and overcome governmental problems, is forced to stop U.S. operations in 1967 by SEC - action used to promote business elsewhere as not under SEC's jurisdiction, registers aliens as "students" in order to obtain Swiss work permits for sales force, is forced by Swiss to disban selling organization, sell funds through 2 Swiss banks and to stop using Switzerland in promotional literature to obtain reputation for soundness, operates business in 1969 with some 14,000 employees as world's largest financial sales organization, with middle-class clients in over 100 countries including Communist nations, with some $2 billion of assets in funds - $1 billion in life insurance policies, $260 million in real estate assets, $200 million in banks and financial institutions, and with $3 billion in sales/year, goes public in 1969 with shares selling up to $19 - 6 months later at $1.50 to wipe out sales representatives mortgaging assets to buy at $15, joins mutual-fund joint ventures in 1969 with bank Banque Rothschild, Credit Suisse and Bank of New York to regain credibility, announces plans in 1970 to start "Peoples Fund" for investments as low as

50 cents, is ousted in 1970 after losing $12 million during bear market, is replaced by Sir Eric Wyndham White after crisis from inept management, loss of confidence from some bad investments, exploding costs in insider loans)... Vince Cullers starts pioneering black advertising agency, oldest in continuous operation, followed in 1971 by Chicago ad agency of Thomas Burrell... To avoid threatened breakup AT&T signs consent decree not to operate in any field outside telecommunications and to share discoveries of Bell Labs... Agricultural equipment business, J.I. Case, founded 1842 (builds first tractor in 1869) buys crawler business of American Tractor Corp. (after failing to survive industry's restructuring in 1960s-1970s is acquired by Houston's Tenneco, buyer of International Harvester in 1984, in 1985)... Garden State Plaza shopping center opens in Bergen County, NJ, some 30,600 more by 1988 with 1,846 under construction... Charles E. Williams starts catalog and retail kitchenware business, Williams-Sonoma (sells to W. Howard Lester in 1978, goes public in 1983, operates 5 catalog operations and 5 retail chains in 1989 - sales of $172 million in 1988).

1957

General Events

Gordon Gould invents the laser (loses patent race to Charles Townes, inventor of maser in 1951, and Arthur Schawlow in 1958, after approval by Patent Office on prior rights wins first infringement claim in 1987)... Senate committee starts (February 26) hearings on corruption in International Brotherhood of Teamsters... President Eisenhower signs (August 29) Civil Rights Act (creates Civil Rights Commission to investigate infringements of rights)... After launching of Sputnik (October 4), President Eisenhower names James R. Killian, Jr., as aide for space technology... AFL-CIO expells Bakery Workers, Laundry Workers and Teamsters (returns to fold in 1987 to avoid government trusteeship for corruption) for corruption... U.S. Supreme Court puts pro football under anti-trust laws... Alan Freed hosts "Rock 'n' Roll Show," first prime-time network special on rock music... Carnegie Institute of Technology designs business game so students can learn management from simulated problems... In this time UCLA uses computerized business game, other schools use IBM Management Decision-Making Laboratory game... With funds from Air Force and Carnegie Corp., Northwestern University research team designs simulation game for decision-makers of make-believe nations... D.G. Malcolm (ed.): Report of System Simulation Symposium (discusses new Monte Carlo Technique in which simulated sampling replaces regular sampling used in real world)...

Ayn Rand: Atlas Shrugged (advocates philosophy of reason, individualism, rational selfishness, capitalism)... Institute for Social Research, University of Michigan, surveys Americans on how they feel about themselves, 2nd in 1976 to detect trends... Vance Packard: Hidden Persuaders (attacks advertising)... Harvard's B.F. Skinner introduces programmed instruction with teaching machines, first devised at Ohio State University in 1915 but not used (leads to computerized education at University of Illinois in 1960)... Single parents form Parents Without Partners as self-help group, some 25.7% of families with children under 18 in 1984 are headed by single parents... Housing Act liberalizes mortgage benefits and provides public housing for elderly... Synthetic amino acids are produced, leads to synthetic penicillan in 1959... PERT,

Program Evaluation Review Technique, is devised in this time as work-flow network by U.S. Navy for Polaris missile project... Basic patent, first filed in 1952, on numerical control of machine tools, is granted to John T. Parson (obtains 2nd basic patent in 1962)... Douglas McGregor explains motivational Theories X and Y in Adventures in Thoughts and Actions... Millard Fuller enters University of Alabama law school (by graduation clears $50,000/year with Morris Dees by investing profits from campus in real estate, by 1964 runs successful mail-order business with 150 employees to become wealthy, starts Partnership Housing in 1968 to help poor get homes - 27 houses by 1972 after resigning from business, calls new venture Habitat for Humanity in 1976 - by 1981 projects in 64 U.S. cities and 11 overseas and by 1987 241 in North America and 50 in 25 countries, plans projects for 2,000 U.S. cities and 60 countries by 1996)... Meredith Wilson: "Music Man" (stars super salesman Harold Hill in musical play).

Business Events

In November 60 crime leaders meet in Appalachian, NY, to determine market jurisdictions for various operations... Collier's stops publishing 85-year-old Woman's Home Companion... Italy's Fiat enters U.S. automobile market... Philco builds Philco 2000, first commercial solid state transistorized computer, followed by Sperry-Rand in 1958 and IBM in 1959... J. Irwin Miller, Cummins Engine Foundation start program to improve architecture of Columbus, IN (sponsor 50 works of modern architectural designers by 1987)... Pittsburgh Steelers' professional football team hires Lowell Perry, first black assistant coach in NFL... Group of investors save Strasburg Railroad, U.S.' 2nd oldest founded in 1832, from wrecker (handles some 30,000 tourists in 1986 for 4 1/2-mile trip through countryside to village of Paradise, PA)...

Henry Scott, lube man for Consolidated Freightways, and partner acquire small janitorial service in Portland, OR, for about $500 (develops business by 1987 with 300 employees in 5 states to achieve annual sales of some $5 million - honored as minority businessman by U.S. Small Business Administration)... Ralph W. Ketner and 2 associates, former employees of Winn-Dixie Stores, start Food Lion no-frills low-priced grocery chain of 430 stores in southeast as Food Town (after bitter price battle with Winn-Dixie close 9 of 16 stores, rebound in 1968 by slashing prices 10%, sell in 1974 to Belgian grocer Delhaize - stake of $16 million worth $1.6 billion in 1987, grows to 522 stores by 1988 over 8 southwestern states with plans for 1,000 by 1992 - 1988 work stoppages by Belgian employees to demand better wages, benefits for U.S. workers)...

Schlitz Brewery of Milwaukee loses industry's top spot to Anheuser-Busch of St. Louis... Clothing industry launches multi-million-dollar advertising campaign to make men more style conscious, sales in 1960 of some $9.7 billion jump to nearly $18.6 billion by 1969... Employee Relations Department of Esso Standard Oil hires behavioral scientist Herbert Shepard to study organizational behavior (conducts pioneering experiments in organization development with Robert Blake, others in 1958-59)... Mysterious Pritzker family of Chicago, evolves from 1902 law practice of Kiev-born Nicholas J. Pritzker to acquire wealth in various real estate transactions and business deals, acquires Hyatt Hotel near Los Angeles International Airport (opens 2nd at Burlingame in 1959 - 6 more at West Coast airports in 1962-66 and 135 hotels and resorts worldwide by 1988, creates Marmon-Herrington business in 1960 to gross $265 million/year from 21 profit centers for 60 different firms making variety of commonplace products from auto parts to machinery and building equipment, establishes Hyatt Corp. of America in 1962 - Hyatt International in 1969, opens Atlanta's Hyatt Regency, designed by John Portman with innovative atrium, in 1967 to pioneer U.S.' "Grand Hotel," acquires Northridge Industries, operator of lodges, motels and coffee shops, and Elster's, interior design and furnishing service for hotels, in 1968, acquires small chain of acute care general hospitals in 1972 - later pioneers U.S. time-sharing resort business with Innisfree, acquires Las Vegas Four Queens Hotel and Casino to enter gambling business, acquires bankrupt Braniff Airlines in 1983 - sold 1988, opens 62-acre Hyatt Regency Waikoloa, world's most expensive resort at $360 million, on Hawaii's Big Island in 1988-89 - first of 25 fantasy resorts)...

Union Carbide hires behavioral scientist Douglas McGregor of MIT to assist line managers, subordinates in working together more effectively as groups, pioneers use of behavioral science techniques in business... Lawyer Robert Dedman starts Club Corporaton of America, TX (operates first club in 1959, manages 153 private clubs, plus 4 foreign, in 1984 for income of $340 million)... Boston University researchers start Itek Corp. with financing by Rockefellers... U.S. railroads carry 249,065 piggyback carloads, some 1.9 million in 1982... Howard Morgens becomes head of Procter & Gamble (expands business with television advertising)... First commercial pipeline for transportation of coal slurry opens, OH (-1963)...

Financing for starting Fairchild Camera and Instrument, later Fairchild Semiconductor (is acquired by Schlumberger giant oil-field service company in 1979 for $425 million, is sold to National Semiconductor in 1987 for $122 million instead of Japan's Fujitsu after protests of protectionists), in California's Silicon Valley is arranged in part by venture capitalist Arthur Rock, founder of Davis & Rock venture capital business in 1961 (funds Teledyne in 1960, Scientific Data Systems in 1961, Intel in 1968, Apple Computer in 1978, and Diasonics in 1978)...

U.S. commercial atomic power is launched with submarine reactor at Shippingport, PA, (becomes industry of 84 reactors in 1984 after 107 canceled orders... Brooklyn Dodgers baseball team plans to move franchise to Los Angeles in 1958... Sambo's restaurant chain opens in Santa Barbara, CA (operates 526 eateries by 1975 with earnings growing 46%/per year since 1965 - 750 units in 1976, after changing managerial compensation package of 20% ownership to higher salaries and benefits is forced to replace some 250 managers in 1977, is attacked for name as racial slur against blacks, closes in 1980s due to ineffective restaurant managers)... Philip Morris tobacco business starts diversification program with Milprint, supplier of packaging material (acquires Polymer Industries, chemical firm specializing in packaging adhesives, in 1958, creates American Safety Razor division in 1961, acquires Miller Brewery in 1970 to become industry's No. 2, and California land development business in 1972)... Austrian-born commodities trader Charles G. Bluhdorn acquires Michigan Bumper (acquires auto replacement parts distributing firm in 1958 to become Gulf & Western Industries in 1960, expands 1960-65 with acquisitions of firms manufacturing and distributing auto parts, starts building conglomerate in 1965 with purchase of New Jersey Zinc)... Wham-O in San Gabriel, CA, markets plastic disc, called "Frisbee" after old American pie-plate business (starts fad)... Ford Motor Co. introduces Edsel car (-1959, stops after losing $200-$350 million)... For first time in its history, IBM grosses over $1 billion, sales of some $30 million in 1937 (achieves sales of $7.5 billion in 1970 and $29 billion in 1981, spends $3.6 billion in 1982 on research and development)... Aircraft industry adopts Automatically Programmed Tools system... San Antonio's Kaspar Wire Works, founded 1898 to make corn shuck baskets from smooth wire discarded by farmers switching to barbed wire, makes first coin-operated newspaper dispenser for San Antonio Light (evolves to dominate mechanical rack industry)... Warner & Swasey Machine Tool Company exhibits "Servofeed" turret lathe, self-programmed with electronic memory and magnetic core recorder, at Chicago's Machine Tool Exposition...

Digital Equipment, U.S. first only computer business, is started in old woolen mill near Boston by MIT engineer Kenneth Olson, partner with funds from Rockefeller family to make transistorized circuit boards and small, rugged, inexpensive computers for engineers (introduces revolutionary minicomputer in 1965, evolves with decentralized organization to realize revenues of $7.6 billion in 1985 and challenge IBM with super minicomputers in low-end of main frame market - former employees create Datapoint and Data General in 1968, after sales double and earnings quadruple with one minicomputer design and single set of software between 1984-88 is forced to expand product line and form joint ventures, alliances to compete in market)...

Businessman Robert Nourse founds TEC in Milwaukee, OR, as think tank of CEOs, becomes subsidiary of Vedax Sciences of San Diego by 1988 with 1,500 members worldwide from firms with sales of $2 million - $1 billion... Macy, NYC, is first department store to record $2 million in sales on one day, 12/16... 17 Washington State utilities form Washington Power Supply System as construction consortium to build nuclear plants (issues $2.9 billion in bonds for 88 Northwest utilities in 1977 for projects 4 and 5, after rising costs to $5 billion in 1979 and $12 billion in 1981 cancels projects in 1982, defaults on bonds in 1983, settles with underwriters in 1987 for $92 million and investors, no money, in 1988 as trial begins to sort out biggest municipal default in history)... By chance high school dropout Michael Bond gets idea for first Paddington Bear story while visiting London, spawns business to license clothes, china, marmalade, television programs, home videos and theatrical productions... Eli Broad starts Kaufman & Broad Homes, largest homebuilder in California and builds 4,800 units worldwide in 1988 (spins off homebuilding in 1988 to focus on financial services, insurance).

1958

General Events

American Association for Retired Persons forms to provide insurance to retirees (evolves by 1987 as U.S.' largest special-interest group of some 27 million members, is attacked in 1988 for $32 million in tax-free earnings from insurance, travel services, mutual funds and discount drugs)... U.S. launches (January 31) its first satellite, Explorer I... President Eisenhower signs (April 1) Emergency Housing Act to stimulate economy... National Aeronautics and Space Administration is created (July 29) with mandate to search for industrial uses of aerospace technology... Labor Pension Reporting Act requires (August 28) reports to Secretary of

Labor on employee welfare and pension plans... Washington establishes Advanced Research Projects Agency as U.S. space body... U.S. employment reaches (March 11) highest mark since 1941... Washington reports U.S. with 47 million TV sets, 2/3 of world's total... National Defense Education Act (September 2) provides (September 2) student loans and aid for technical education... President Eisenhower uses Taft-Hartley Act to end dock and steel strikes... FTC starts drive to ban misrepresentative TV ads... Herbert A. Simon, Allen Newell: "Heuristic Problem Solving: The Next Advance in Operations Research": Operations Research...

Frederick G. Lesieur (ed.): The Scanlon Plan: A Frontier of Labor-Management Cooperation... Walter Reuther, president of UAW, proposes profit-sharing plan to automobile industry, rejected as "radical scheme"... Bureaucratic lenient Civil Aeronautics Administration is replaced by Federal Aviation Agency... First National Conference on Air Pollution meets... U.S. Supreme Court rules professional football part of interstate commerce... Work on slim and elegant, bronze-and-glass Seagram Building, designed by Mies van der Rohe and Philip Johnson as epitomy of international architecture, is finished, NYC (1954- , is viewed at first as perfect building then reviled as severe and inhumane, is followed in 1982 by antithesis in funky Portland Services Building, OR, designed by Michael Graves)...

Conservative John Birch Society is formed in Indianapolis by candy company executive Robert H.W. Welch, Jr., 11 others to oppose big government, high taxes and communism (records some 100,000 members and 4,000 chapters by 1968 - about 50,000 members by 1984)... Frederick Herzberg, associates study motivational drives of Pittsburgh engineers, accountants (results in motivation-hygiene concept of job attitudes)... Arthur Schawlow of Bell Laboratories and scientist Charles Townes develop first practical laser with intense beams of coherent light (share 1964 Nobel Prize for Physics, are sued in 1982 by Gordon Gould, former student, with charges his ideas were basis for invention)... First international communications satellite is launched, used by private enterprise in 1972... John Kenneth Galbraith: The Affluent Society... Alaska lands in Kenai range are opened for oil exploration... U.S. Supreme Court rules non-union workers can sue union for punitive damages when kept from work because of strikes, picket lines... Professor Edward Wenk, Jr., is first science and technology adviser to Congress.

Business Events

Rolodex business, founded 1938, introduces Rotary Card File for desk-top storage of information... Paramount sells TV rights to pre-1948 movies for $50 million... United Press and International News Services merge to form UPI... Paul Krassner pioneers underground press with The Realist satire magazine... Jack Stanley, age 19, leases first gas station (in 1971, after branching into fuel barging and storage, acquires small Louisiana oil refinery, while wildcatting for oil discovers gas in 1972, builds ammonia plant in Texas for fertilizer in 1975 - bankruptcy when market collapses, emerges from Chapter 11 in 1979 as GHR Energy - bankruptcy in 1983 with debt of $1 billion, tries takeover of new Transamerican Natural Gas in 1987 - blocked by creditor)... Jean Hoerni of Fairchild Semiconductor devises planar technique to make transistors... Code-A-Phone is first commercial telephone answering device... WHAM-O Manufacturing, CA, launches plastic hoola-hoop fad (sells some 20 million in 6 months)... Harold J. Leavitt, Thomas L. Whister: "Management in the 1980s," Harvard Business Review (predicts new information technology will reverse trend toward decentralized, "participative" management)... General Mills, after earlier effort by Joseph E. Seagram & Sons, starts corporate art collection, followed by Ciba-Geigy in 1966 and Rapid-American Corp. in 1969... Kobayashi family starts Maui potato chip business, HI, with $500 investment to make perfect chips (achieves over $1 million in sales by 1980s from market limited to Islands and some West Coast cities)...

American Express issues first credit cards (replaces paperboard form with plastic card in 1959 - named "money card" in 1969, serves some 14 million holders by 1982 - 2 million for Diners' Club and 70 million each for Visa and MasterCard)... Academy of Management Journal is issued... Engineer Jack Kilby of Texas Instruments develops first true integrated circuit, first marketed in 1962 (is followed in 1971 by Intel's first microprocessor)... Ramo-Wooldridge, formed by 2 veterans of Hughes Aircraft (technical director, system engineer for intercontinental ballistics missile project) and Thompson Products (maker of parts, valves, aircraft engines) form TRW (becomes leading aerospace firm, some 40,000 employees, over 100 plants and sales of $533 million in 1964)... Standards for coding checks are established, used by all banks within 10 years...

Crosby family takes over struggling Mary Carter Paint Co. (with James Morris Crosby in charge, parlays business into multi-billion-dollar gambling-based empire Resorts International with casinos in Bahamas, Paradise Island in 1960s, and Atlantic City with private security company of Intertel, leads to power struggle after death in 1986 between family seeking control and 8 former girl- friends wanting cash)... NBC employs William Rubens to do TV market research, industry's first... San Francisco lawyer Louis O. Kelson helps employees of West Coast newspaper to buy company (leads to some 10 million workers buying out over 9,800 firms by 1989 after 1974 Employee Stock Ownership Plan Act)...

Harundale Mall, U.S.' first all-enclosed shopping center, opens outside Baltimore... Western Union introduces Telex messages (creates Mailgram service in 1970, operates first domestic satellite communications in 1974, introduces Easylink electronic mail service in 1984, 40% of 1988 market, to incur deficit of $58.4 million on sales of $1.1 billion, operates 11,000 agents in 1988 to handle money transfers and telegrams - $300 million business)... With 2 Boeing 707s, National Airlines starts first domestic jet passenger service between New York, Miami...

Dwight E. Robinson: "Fashion Theory and Product Design," Harvard Business Review (shows reflection of fashion trends in product design)... Michigan Bell Telephone starts pioneering U.S. assessment center to determine potential of managers... Fashion designer Claire McCardell, pioneers sportswear, dies (1905-)... IBM uses surveys to determine employee morale... Polish-born Jack Tramiel acquires interest in Toronto typewriter business with loan of $400,000 (develops first integrated home computer business, Commodore International with personal management and mass merchandising instead of specialty retailers - sales over $1 billion in 1983, "resigns" in 1984 when replaced by management team, acquires, money-losing Atari computer business)... Malcolm Bricklin, 19-year-old University of Florida drop-out, buys building supply business (expands

Handyman chain to 149 units nationwide by 1960, starts making cars in 1971 - bankruptcy in 1975)... Bill Tanner becomes manager, later owner, of Pep Records in Memphis (develops company as major bartering business with sales of some $100 million by 1981)... Douglas Aircraft introduces DC-8 to compete in jet passenger market (despite some success fails to capture market dominated by Boeing 707, is forced to merge with McDonnell Aircraft of St. Louis in 1966 to become 2nd largest defense contractor, introduces DC-10 to compete with Boeing's 747 - failure after series of crashes including worst U.S. air crash at Chicago's O'Hare airport in 1979)... David Ewing (ed.): Long-Range Planning for Management... Esso refineries at Baton Rouge, Bayonne, and Bayway use T-groups for organizational development... James Abegglen: The Japanese Factory (pioneers study of Japanese management)... General Electric converts heat energy into electrical energy, starts solar energy age... IBM is 44th member of the Billion-Dollar Club... For first time U.S. airlines carry more passengers than buses, railroads...

First Coca-Cola plant inside Iron Curtain opens in Poland... Space Journal is published... For first time margarine sales top those of butter... General Foods sells frozen baby foods... TWA hires first black flight attendant... DuPont introduces new liquid gas (leads to avalanche of aerosol products)... Hawaiian Brewery uses first aluminum beer cans... U.S. manufacture of Hamilton Watches is transferred to Switzerland to take advantage of low wages... Montgomery Ward opens first shopping center retail store in Denver... Cheating scandal is uncovered on TV game show "Dotto" (leads to investigations of cheating on other quiz shows)... Garment industry uses Velcro fasteners... Sears starts selling accident and health insurance...

First major Russian trade show in U.S. opens in NYC... American Airlines makes record commercial flight from L.A. to NYC in 4 hours, 43 minutes to average 630 mph... Philco Transac introduces first all-transistor computer, rents for $28,000 - $48,000... After developing nose-cones for guided missiles, Corning Glass Works, NY, introduces new cookware that can be heated then frozen without cracking... To settle anti-trust case, RCA is forced to disclose some 100 patents for color TV and share any new products over next 10 years for reasonable royalties... Five New England railroads merge, forms 5th largest line with 5,300 miles of track and $900 million in assets... Traditional tool and die making process of automobile industry is changed from machining to electrical discharge method (results in shorter lead times, greater accuracy to millionths of an inch)... New York Giants baseball franchise moves to San Francisco...

Frank and Dan Carney, 2 students at Wichita State University, start Pizza Hut fast-food business with $600 (after acquisition by Pepsico becomes world's largest pizza chain in 1987 with over 5,400 units in U.S. and 6,200 worldwide - Domino's 2nd with 4,375 units, Little Caesars with 1,950, Pizza Inn with 719, Godfather's with 586, and Round Table Pizza with 550, opens first Moscow pizza parlor in 1988)... As head of Allied Crude Vegetable Oil & Refining Anthony De Angelis, "salad oil king," subleases vegetable oil tanks to American Express Warehousing (is sued in 1960 for civil fraud by Justice Department on shipment of soybean oil to Spain - settles out of court for $1.5 million, declares bankruptcy in 1963 after swindling over $100 million on non-existent oil from speculators, traders, bankers, brokers and shippers, receives 20 years in prison and fine of $20,000)... After Consolidated Controls, maker of controls for aircraft and nuclear submarines, had been purchased by Condee manufacturing group, Joe Engleberger develops Unimation in Danbury, CT, to pioneer development of industrial hydraulic robots (unable to afford Japanese patent loses market to their mass-production, becomes separate company in 1962 to introduce prototype robot, is contracted in 1970s by General Motors, first major customer, to make over 50 automatic welders, evolves as largest U.S. producer, 45% of U.S. robot market in 1981, of some 3,000 robots used by U.S. manufacturing firms - 10,000 in Japan, 850 in West Germany, 600 in Sweden, 500 in Italy, 360 in Poland, 200 each in France and Norway, 185 in Britain and 25 in Soviet Union, is acquired by Westinghouse in 1983 for $107 million, after losing money is sold in 1987 to small Michigan firm making industrial robots and conveyor machines)...

When California recreational vehicle factory in Forest City, IA, closes, John K. Hansen, owner of farm equipment dealership, furniture store and funeral home, personally persuades investors to reopen plant to make Winnebago travel homes (retires as president in 1971 with sales of $45 million in 1970 - $212 million in 1973 as industry's No. 1 producer, loses $6.7 million in 1974 after oil embargo, replaces son and son-in-law to install systems of cost and quality controls, customer service and material handling, returns to direct leadership in 1979 to repay debt of $18 million in 18 months and amass $18 million in cash, introduces pioneering fuel-efficient motor home in 1983 to recapture top place in market, appoints firm's 5th president in decade in 1983)...

Following lead of British Overseas Airways, Pan American World Airways starts regular transatlantic jet service (crosses in 7 hours)... Rockefeller interests finance Caneel Bay Plantation resort, St. John in Virgin Islands... After studying at Ecole de la Chambre Syndicale de la Couture Parisienne, Texan-born Victor Costa starts fashion business to copy style of fashion designers at lower prices (sells $30 million of high-fashion refinements in 1987)... Professional Bowlers Assn. forms (goes on national TV in 1961, for first time lists 10 bowlers in 1988 making over $100,000 in one year - record high of $225,485 to top first $100,000 mark in 1975)... Preston L. Smith opens ski resort, VT, at Killington, offers lifetime ski passes to investors of 4 shares for $1,000 - worth $400,000 by 1988 with operations at Mt. Snow, VT, and Bear Mountain, California's largest... Sarah Caldwell founds Opera Company of Boston, City centerpiece with authentic performances and U.S. premiers by 1980s with international reputation... National Education Corp. of Irvine, CA, world's leading for-profit educator in 1988 with sales of $450 million, starts with one home study course, adds vocational schools - 53 by 1988, textbook publishing, and self-development training later (acquires U.S.' two largest industrial training firms in 1986 and 1987).

1959

General Events

Alaska is 49th State (Hawaii 50th)... St. Lawrence Seaway opens (April 25) to permit ocean shipping in Great Lakes... Federal debt ceiling is raised (June 30) to $295 billion... Labor Reform Act restricts (September 4) union power... Secretary of Agriculture is authorized to distribute surplus food with food stamps to needy... Landrum-Griffin Act curbs

(September 14) racketeering and blackmail in unions... U.S. launches first weather satellite Vanguard II... Florida's land boom sells lots by mail... Manhattan is blacked out with massive power failure... Model all-electric American kitchen opens at U.S. exhibition in Moscow... Investment banker Clarence Dillon, Under Secretary of State, helps establish Inter-American Development Bank to promote economic development in Latin-America... Savannah, first U.S. nuclear-powered merchant ship, is launched... President Eisenhower uses Taft-Hartley Act to halt 116-day strike, longest in industry's history, of some 500,000 steel workers at 28 companies producing 95% of U.S.' steel (is used to stop strike of longshoremen)... Air Force Brigadier General Benjamin O. Davis, Jr., is first black to become Major General...

In statement to special House committee investigation of quiz shows, Charles Van Doren, son of scholar Mark Van Doren, admits 1956 role in "$64 Thousand Question" show had been fixed (leads to arrests in 1960 of 13 contestants on TV quiz shows for perjury)... Stafford Beer: Cybernetics in Management... Benjamin Selekman: A Moral Philosophy for Management... Chicago's Second City comedy troupe pioneers improvisational theater in U.S... San Francisco Mime Troupe pioneers "Gorilla Theater" to initiate social change with agitation, education, entertainment)... William A. Williams: The Tragedy of American Diplomacy (argues U.S. imperialistic international relations are motivated by economics)... Theodore Maiman, Hughes Aircraft, devises first ruby laser, followed by free electron laser in 1980s... R.A. Gordon, J.E. Howell (funded by Ford Foundation): Higher Education in Business (criticizes business school curricula as too vocational)...

Graphic Studio is founded at University of Florida in Tampa, FL (develops art form)... Frederick Harbison, Charles Myers: Management in the Industrial World... Crawford H. Greenwald, president of DuPont: The Uncommon Man: The Individual in the Organization... Federal Government adopts cost-based budgeting, accrual accounting systems... F.C. Pierson (sponsored by Carnegie Foundation): The Education of American Businessmen: A Study of University-College Programs in Business Administration (recommends greater study of social sciences)... FTC charges 15 tube and tire manufacturers with price fixing... U.S. Post Office announces use of vending machines to sell envelopes, stamps (introduces automated postal services in 1984 and robot clerks in 1988)...

FTC investigates phony TV advertising... San Francisco doctor tells American Heart Association heart trouble can be linked with stressful occupations... After 30 years federal judge rescinds ban by Postmaster General against D.H. Lawrence's Lady Chatterley's Lover... Edwin F. Shelly of U.S. Industries applies for patent on "automatic handling and assembly servosystem" (becomes Transferobot)... U.S., 11 nations sign treaty to ban military activity, nuclear materials in Antarctica, new treaty in 1988 to protect land's economic development... California appeals court rules in Peterman v. International Brotherhood of Teamsters that an employer can't fire an employee in refusing to commit perjury (starts evolution in establishing employee rights in termination of employment).

Business Events

Paul N. "Red" Adair, after capping first blow-out in Oklahoma oil fields in 1938 and working for Myron Kinley, dean of oil well fire fighters, starts business... 1919 Pitney-Bowes postage meter business is forced by consent decree on anti-trust suit to give technical information and royalty-free use of patents to competitors (starts diversification in 1961 with acquisition of West German firm making addressing equipment, acquires license in 1965 to make electrostatic office copiers, purchases business in 1966 with collating equipment, firm in 1968 making retail price tags, and maker of plastic credit and identification cards in 1968, starts 1970 venture with Alpex computers to make point-of-sale register systems)... NYSE reports nearly 13 million Americans own stocks...

American Airlines starts first transcontinental jet service with Boeing 707s... Catherine Graham, husband Philip take over father's _Washington Post_ (after acquiring _Newsweek_ in 1961 and death of Philip in 1963, publishes paper to become recognized in 1980s as leading woman business executive)... General Electric introduces GE210 computer (abandons market in 1970)... To avoid company transfer to Los Angeles, Ron Fraedrick mortgages house to open Mexican take-out stand in Eugene, OR (after expanding to 240 Taco Time units in 15 states, Canada and Venezuela, some 24/year in 1980s, opens first Japanese place in 1987 with plans for 100 by 1992)... After graduating from college in chemistry to work in aerospace industry, Jerry Buss invests savings with partner in small apartment building (expands with California real estate boom to operate properties over $500 million in shopping centers, hotels and apartment buildings by 1979 - estimated wealth of $90 million in 1987, with partners acquires Los Angeles Lakers, Los Angeles Kings hockey club, and Forum Arena for $67.5 million - $70 million-a-year sports empire with regional cable channel by 1987)...

Henry Crown merges his 1919 Material Services Corp. with General Dynamics to form giant defense enterprise (-1960, is forced out of General Dynamics after power struggle in 1965-66 with $100 million, returns to rescue failing business in 1970-71 to build family empire of some $1.5 billion by mid-1980s despite fraud investigations by Pentagon after 1983 - no personal charges of wrongdoing, loses Navy contract for continuing business misconduct in 1985)... After working as screenwriter and publicity man, Bart Lytton starts Los Angeles savings and loan empire of some $750 million (merchandising money like girlie shows to scandalize conservative bankers makes Lytton Financial Corporation 5th largest in U.S., is forced to sell Beverly Hills Savings & Loan in 1965 by Federal Home Loan Bank due to improper purchase, starts expansion in 1966 during declining real estate and tight-money market, after losses from 1965 is forced by creditors to sell interests in 1968)... Corn oil margarine appears in stores...

American Football League is formed (opens in 1960, obtains TV exposure with ABC in 1964, drafts Joe Namath in 1965 to achieve public recognition, merges in 1966 with NFL after bitter competition)... Foreign cars constitute 12% of U.S. automobile market, Volkswagen leader with some 6%... General Electric hires Lawrence L. Ferguson to head Behavioral Research Service... Mattel toy business introduces Barbie "fashion doll," modeled on German pin-up doll (evolves to sell nearly over 500 million dolls worldwide by 1989 - Barbie fashions one of world's largest markets in women's clothing)... American Express provides overseas banking services to individuals, banks, corporations (becomes firm's major business by 1968 with formation of American Express International Banking Corp., acquires Fireman's Fund American Insurance Companies in 1968)...

Charley Sifford is first black to play regularly on professional golf tour... Richard Farson, others form Western Behavioral Sciences Institute as think-tank to study leadership for U.S. Navy (sells in 1982 to start School of Management and Strategic Studies - students nationwide communnicate with faculty via closed-circuit computer network)... High-performance Daytona Speedway opens, FL, to commercialize stock car races... After dropping out of high school during 30s to help father in operating small dairy and starting retail chain of milk and ice cream stores, Carl Lindner starts American Finance in Cincinnati as savings and loan association with $18 million in assets, financial holding company of $2.6 billion by 1984... Sid Richardson, Texas gambler and wildcatter (acquires and loses 3 fortunes), dies (1891-, leaving estate of some $105 million in oil wells, real estate and 30 public companies to foundation and $2.8 million in cash to each of 4 sons of nephew Perry Bass who form Bass Brothers Enterprises - by 1984 worth $2-4 billion)...

New York brokerage house of Donaldson Lufkin Jenrette is started by 3 graduates of Harvard Business School (enter field as only U.S. area not having new idea for 100 years, issue stock in 1970 as first exchange member to go public)... Electronic display terminals for stock transactions are first used (follows stock market ticker in 1867 and screening of ticker tape in 1925)... Neiman Marcus produce first Christmas catalog, started in late 1920s, with extravagant his, her gifts (shows store-labeled trash bags in 1987)... Peter Ueberroth, age 22, becomes manager of small nonscheduled airline (develops profitable business with Hawaiian market - part ownership in 1960, starts air service - loses some $100,000, starts Transportation Consultants to provide reservation services to small airlines without offices, uses profits in 1965 to acquire small travel agencies and hotels, forms First Travel in 1963, purchases Ask Mr. Foster travel business in 1972 for $1 million to evolve as 2nd largest in field with 200 offices worldwide, some 1,500 employees and sales of $300 million by 1984 Olympics)...

Dominic Tampone, former stock boy, becomes president of New York's Hammacher Schlemmer (transforms old-line hardware and houseware store into place known for elegant gadgets)... High-school drop-out Anthony A. Martino starts AAMCO automatic transmission repair business in Philadelphia (sells business of 550 outlets with sales over $100 million in 1967, starts MAACO Enterprises, paint-and-body-shop business, in 1972 - by 1984 with 375 units nationwide)... DuPont introduces "Lycra" spandex as stretch fabric... After scraping together some $70,000, Stuart G. Moldaw starts chain of preppy clothing stores for women (sells 17 stores in 1970 for profit of $4 million, after 2 other retailing ventures starts USVP in 1981 with 2 partners, $38 million to capitalize ventures in specialty retailing, consumer products, and high-tech projects - fund of some $140 million by 1986)...

Elegant Four Seasons Restaurant opens in NYC to feature American, French cuisine (is followed in changing trend of food habits by New York's De Pay Canal House in 1969 to feature native American dishes with ethnic influences and by Alice Waters' Chez Panisse, CA, with innovative

American cookery)... Pepsi-Cola is first in U.S. soft drink industry to contract with Soviet Union to open bottling plants - 25 by 1988 with limited competition from Coca-Cola... Barry Gordy, Jr., starts Motown Records in Detroit, $700 borrowed from family, to record black artists (evolves with sales of some $50 million in early 1970s to become U.S.' largest black-owned company with revenues of some $104 million in 1982, sells to MCA Records and Boston Ventures in 1988 for $61 million)... After distributing food supplements for Nutrilite Products, Richard De Vos and Jay Van Andel start Amway in Ada, MI, to sell household products (use pyramiding distributorships to provide economic opportunities for those desiring to improve their lives, achieve sales of some $1.5 billion in 1981 with about 1 million distributors, mostly part-time, are indicted for fraud by Canada in 1982 - settle out of court)... Westinghouse rents home appliances... A&P grocery chain offers free food coupons to compete with trading stamps given by other chain stores... Sonatone hearing-aid business introduces rechargeable batteries... Bullova Watch makes electronic watches... BankAmericard is first comprehensive credit card (evolves as Visa - first Soviet Union credit cards in 1988)... Montgomery Ward sells artificial Christmas trees...

IBM designs electronic reservation system for airlines... William Nichersen: How I Turned $1,000 Into a Million in Real Estate - In My Spare Time (becomes best seller with sales of some 10,000/week)... Standard Packaging invents freezer bag that can be heated in boiling water... After leaving Raytheon as president when not given absolute authority, Harold Geneen becomes president of International Telephone and Telegraph, stagnating business with sales of $765 million (-1980, when Latin American countries nationalize telephone systems in 1960s starts to acquire U.S. companies, such as Sheraton hotel chain, Hartford Fire Insurance, Levitt & Sons construction business and Bobbs-Merrill Publishing, so long as they add to ITT's earnings, with aggressive leadership manages U.S.' 13th largest corporation in 1970s with 250 companies in 60 countries to achieve revenues over $8.5 billion - annual growth rate of 10%/year in 1970s, is succeeded by Rand Araskog to divest holdings worth $1.7 billion to regain organizational focus)...

First Thunderbird Motor Inn opens in Portland, OR (grows by 1983 to operate 53 Red Lion/Thunderbird Inns in 8 western states to gross some $225 million as largest privately-owned U.S. hotel business, is valued about $620 million in 1985 when sold)... Russian-born Serge Semenenko becomes vice chairman of Boston's First National Bank (extends numerous loans to enterprises in communications, entertainment to rescue, revive, movie industry)... Russ Meyer films "The Immoral Mr. Teas" (exhibits bare bodies in art theaters to earn some $1 million on investment of $24,000, pioneers market of "skin flick" movies)...

Texaco's Port Arthur refinery production is operated by TRW digital computer, used by Monsanto's Louisiana ammonia plant in 1960... IBM launches Speak-Up Program to improve communications with employees... Sears creates Homart Development Corp. for expansion into shopping centers... Oil and Gas Journal: "Digital Computers - Key to Tomorrow's Pushbutton Refinery"... NFL Commissioner Bert Bell starts pioneering pension plan for professional football players... Shoney's Big Boy fast-food business, started in West Virginia by Alex Schoenbaum in 1953, is acquired by Ray Danner, former apprentice tool-and-die maker, grocer, bowling alley and movie operator, vending machine salesman, produce wholesaler and professional musician (operates nearly 1,300 outlets in 31 states by 1986 as U.S.' 17th largest, is cited as best-managed operation in food service industry)...

Laurence Tisch with brother Robert, resort operators since 1946, acquires Loews theater business of 118 seedy movie houses for real estate (acquires Lorillard Tobacco with friendly take-over in 1968, acquires Equity Funding in 1973 just before it collapses, acquires CNA Insurance after 9-month battle during industry slump in 1974, acquires Bulova watch in 1979 as worldwide glut of watches develops - money loser until 1984, buys super tankers in 1983 at distress-sale prices - 7 by 1986, operates $6.7 billion conglomerate in 1986, becomes acting CBS president in 1986)... With savings of $10,000 Rocky Aoki opens first Benihana Japanese restaurant with table-top cooking in NYC, pioneers growth of theme restaurants (after almost going bankrupt twice expands by 1986 to operate 47 restaurants in U.S. and 25 in Japan, plans to invade Europe)...

By accident new lawyer Mark McCormack meets golfer Arnold Palmer (signs golfer for appearances and product endorsements, develops International Management Group with TV subsidiary and 20 offices worldwide by 1987 to handle business, merchandising and managing events, and legal affairs for over 350 athletes... Billy Sullivan buys Boston franchise in American Football League for $25,000, uses life savings of $8,300 and loans (obtains 9 partners at $25,000 each for working capital, builds stadium in 1971 - sole ownership in 1981 with loan of $15 million, with loan acquires control of franchise in 1976 with son, reaches Super Bowl XX in 1986, with debts of some $126 million sells to Victor Kiam, Remington electric shavers, for some $90 million in 1988 to avoid bankruptcy).... Henry L. Hillman inherits $150 million steel, coal, and chemical fortune (leaves coal and steel industries to become one of U.S.' most active venture capitalists - billionaire by 1988)... First annual National Finals Rodeo is held by Professional Rodeo Cowboys Assn., prize money over $2 million in 1988.

1960s

Business Events

General Motors creates administrative board to handle dealer conflicts... Teledyne plans acquisition strategy to become a conglomerate (uses earnings of acquired firms in 1970s to develop stock portfolio)... IBM signs agreement with Japan to exchange basic patents for right to manufacture in Japan (signs 5-year agreement in 1985 to buy Japanese computer technology resulting from country's massive research efforts generating 430 patents by 1985)... Chuck Rolles starts pioneering theme restaurant business in Hawaii, California... Swing, perhaps first bar of kind in U.S., opens in Studio City, Los Angeles as gathering place for males, females to work out sexual arrangements... Procter & Gamble uses work teams, studied by scientists led by Erick Trist in late 1940s at London's Tavistock Institute of Human Relations, to run plants at 18 sites by 1986... IBM starts building global telecommunications network to link 400,000 employees in 145 countries by 1988, followed by Texas Instruments, American Airlines, and Wang Laboratories.

1960

General Events

President Eisenhower submits (January 7) budget to Congress, shows $200 million surplus... Blacks demonstrate (January 8) in Durham, NC, against only stand-up service at lunch counters... California is (April 6) first state to pass smog-control bill... After 10-day strike (closes 22 Broadway shows), longest since 30-day walkout in 1919, Actor's Equity signs (June 13) labor contract with New York Theater League... U.S. cuts (July 6) imports of sugar from Cuba by 95% in retaliation for Cuba's takeover of U.S. interests... Solar cells are used to recharge car battery... AFL-CIO supports Negro boycotts... Tiros I, first weather satellite, is launched (starts evolution of remote-sensing satellites for digital cartography to show everything from mineral deposits to household income)... House sub-committee investigates payola in record industry...

District attorney indicts disc jockey Alan Freed, 8 others in taking over $100,000 in bribes from record companies to plug songs... Nashville, TN, is South's first city to integrate lunch counters... U.S. launches first telecommunications satellite, Courier I-B... U.S. embargos goods to Cuba... After development in mid-1950s North Carolina Governor Luther Hodges opens Triangle Research Park in center of Duke, North Carolina and North Carolina State Universities (attracts IBM in 1966 to achieve recognition, evolves by 1980s as largest research complex with 6,300 acres, work force of 27,000 and annual payroll over $1 billion)...

President Eisenhower states "Four Commandments" for governmental fiscal responsibility: Shall not use taxing power to weaken or tyrannize the private economy; Shall not resort to borrowing power to escape sacrifices that go with responsibility; Shall not delude people into taking the 'deceptively' easy road of deficit spending, unbalanced budgets or inflationary fiscal policies; Shall not use the power of appropriation falsely to offer the people something for nothing... Census reports population of 179.3 million, 125.3 urban and 54.0 rural... Contractor Del E. Webb opens Sun City, AZ, as planned retirement community to pioneer industry... Harvard Students Agencies: Let's Go: Europe (pioneers student travel)... Over 4,800 college students get MBA degrees, some 23,000 in 1970, 46,000 in 1980, 71,000 in 1986 and 62,000 in 1983...

Socialists form League for Industrial Democracy (creates division of Students for Democratic Society, becomes new organization by rebellious college students in 1962 to attack U.S. for "racism, militarism, and imperialism," leads to some 300 active chapters with 35,000 members by 1968)... "Sit-in" demonstration is held in Woolworth lunch counter in Greensboro, NC, to protest racial segregation (starts wave of sit-ins)... Albert Shanker, others form NYC's United Federation of Teachers (becomes president in 1964)... Robert S. McNamara, former president of Ford Motor Co., becomes U.S. Secretary of Defense (-1968 when made president of World Bank for 1968-81, appoints Charles J. Hitch of Rand Corp. as Comptroller in 1961 to realign budget by missions instead of services, develops Planning-Programming-Budgeting System in 1961 with strategic planning by Joint Chiefs of Staff and systems analysis with cost-benefit studies of missions, creates Systems Analysis staff in 1965-69)...

By serendipity in programming computer to solve 13 equations on earth's atmosphere, meteorologist Edward Lorenz discovers 2 prime features of disorder and chaos to challenge determinism of 18th-Century philosopher/mathematician Pierre Simon de Laplace (in 1963 pioneers study of chaos in finding weather predictions and reality usually diverge after 10 days as weather is inherently chaotic)... Kenneth E. Boulding, W. Allen Spivey: Linear Programming and the Theory of the Firm... Enovid, Norlutin birth control pills of Dr. John Rock, work since 1938, and Dr. Gregory Pincus are approved for sale in U.S. by FDA, used by some 1.2 million women by 1962 and around 10 million by 1973... Herbert Simon: The New Science of Management Decision... Newsweek: "Machines Are This Smart" (reports on advances in computers, robots, automatically programmed tools, bionics)... Charles J. Hitch, Roland N. McKean: The Economics of Defense in the Nuclear Age (is issued by Rand Corp. to advocate systematic treatment, analysis of military activities)...

Douglas McGregor: The Human Side of Enterprise... Case Institute of Technology establishes first doctoral program in organization development... Spring break of collegians at Fort Lauderdale, FL, is institutionalized by film "Where the Boys Are"... World's first working laser, based on work of Charles H. Townes in 1955, is devised by Theodore H. Maiman, Hughes Research Laboratories (follows prediction by Albert Einstein in 1916, is named "laser" in 1957 by Gordon Gould, is used in 1973 by U.S. Air Force to down winged drone)... A. Mitchell, Stanford Research Institute, starts research on "lifestyle" analysis of U.S. living patterns... W.W. Rostow: The Stages of Economic Growth: A Non-Communist Manifesto... Less than 184,000 of 5 million public employees are union members, only 200,000 of 8.5 million office workers and only 12,000 of 600,000 engineers, draftsmen and technicians... Harry Bridges, International Longshoremen's and Warehouse Union, signs pioneering labor contract with Pacific Maritime Association to mechanize waterfronts in return for pensions, guarantee of no layoffs (jacks up production over 140%, increases top wages to nearly $50,000/year and reduces jobs from 16,400 to 9,600 with no layoffs by 1980s)... Oregon Museum of Science and Industry, Washington Park Zoo are first to use public auctions to raise funds... By 1986 U.S.' garbage grows 80% from 87.5 million tons to 157.7 - 192.7 in 2000... U.S. produces 56% of total global output, 26% in 1987 to Japan's 9%, European Community's 22%, Soviet Union's 14%... U.S. Senate holds hearings, chaired by Estes Kefauver, on pharmaceutical industry (reveal excessive prices, unlawful collusive price-fixing, illegally rigged bids for government contracts, misleading advertising to doctors, and inappropriate influences on FDA).

Business Events

Control Data, 2nd computer-only business, introduces 1604 model... NCR, Honeywell use transistor systems to replace vacuum tubes in computers... Jack A. Laughery opens fast-food drive-in in Greenville, NC (becomes Hardee's Food Systems with 2,800 units in 1986, 1 franchisee with 266 places, by focusing on small, blue-collar towns, requires each of top 60 executives to spend one week/year to serving customers)... Institutions hold 17% of all stock listed on New York Stock Exchange (increases by 1987 to over 50% in 200 largest U.S. corporations)... After emigrating to U.S. in 1956 as refugee with 2 suitcases and $20, Serbian-born Milan Panic starts International Chemical & Nuclear with $200 to produce exotic chemical compounds for pharmaceutical researchers, sells some $8,000 worth in 1961 (shows first net in 1963 on low profit margin, acquires

U.S. Nuclear Corp., sales of some $1.5 million in radioactive material twice those of ICN, for $10,000 in cash and $100,000 in convertible note in 1966 - fires top 40 people and cuts prices to make money first year with financing from Eastman Dillon acquires 1833 Strong Cobb custo manufacturer of pharmaceuticals in 1967 with sales of $10 million - abou triple those of ICN, acquires 12 more companies by 1971 to increase sale from $3.6 million to some $110 million)... Cameron Hawley: "Needed More Tough-Minded Leaders in Business," Personnel... Adolph Berl observes free enterprise manager of large corporation and commissar i charge of government-owned Soviet industrial combine are essentially sam type of person... 3M launches research project to develop all-weather all-purpose surface for horse racing (installs first at Meadows harnes track in Washingon, PA, in 1962 - fails to catch on, develops Tarta track surface in 1965 and Tartan Turf in 1967 - used for football field in 1968, drops business in 1974 with petroleum shortage and insignifican revenues of $9 million in corporate total of some $3.6 billion)...

With $6,000 Leone Levin, worth some $140 million in 1985, starts Famil Dollar Discount business for low-income shoppers (evolves by 1987 t operate 1,272 compact no-frill stores in southeast and midwest state from headquarters in Charlotte, NC, ousts son and cousin when earning skid in 1987)... General Motors introduces rear-engine, air-coole Corvair car, produces some 1.7 million by 1969 (is denounced in 1965 a dangerously unstable by consumer advocate Ralph Nader, after productio ends in 1969 results in 1971 business of Corvair Parts by Cal, Jone Clark to serve some 100,000 cars still on road)... David Lilientha coins term "Multinational Corporation" to describe new form of busines enterprise... F.W. Woolworth variety business starts Woolco discoun chain (-1983 to close 336 stores)...

After graduating from Columbia University Allen G. Rosenshin is offered jobs, selects advertising over publishing as it pays about $10/week mor (joins Batten, Barton, Durstine and Osborn advertising agency in 1963 t write copy, becomes creative head in 1975 - successful with Peps account, engineers merger in 1986 with Doyle Dane Dernbach Group an Needham Harper Worldwide to form world's largest ad agency with billing of some $5 billion and around 10,000 employees)... Merrill Lyncl establishes long-range planning section, conceived and advocated b Donald Regan, to transform brokerage office chain into financia supermarket with activities in insurance, real estate and some bankin services (pioneers broker as merchant banker in 1985)... After acquirin first department store in 1948, William T. Dillard, started retai business with dry goods store in Nashville, AR, starts expansion pla (purchases department stores in Tulsa, Little Rock and Austin in 1960 before focusing on locations in suburban malls and small-town markets acquires 12-store chain of St. Louis-based Stix Baer & Fuller in 1984, 1 stores of Dayton-Hudson in Arizona and Las Vegas in 1985 and marginall profitable R.H. Macy stores in Kansas in 1986)...

NFL receives some $3.8 million for yearly television rights, contracts for $23.7 million in 1965, $46 million in 1970, $162 million in 1978, an some $400 million in 1982 contracts... Reuben Mattus starts selling fanc Haagen-Dazs ice cream, pioneers trendy market (operates 101 ice crea parlors by 1981)... After operating magazine's Paris bureau since 195 John Fairchild becomes publisher of father's Women's Wear Daily (develop journal of manners, trends and scandal as most influential in fashio

industry)... Thomas G. Spates: Human Values Where People Work (traces
evolution of personnel administration)... After borrowing $500 College
drop-out Thomas S. Monaghan, brother open Dominick's Pizza in Ypsilanti
near Eastern Michigan University (acquires brother's share and starts new
partnership in 1961 to open 3 outlets, dissolves partnership in 1965 to
start Domino's Pizza to feature consistent home delivery in 30 minutes -
over 60 stores by 1973, 820 in 1982, some 1,000 in 1983 and around 4,280
in 1987 with sales over $1.9 billion to challenge Pizza Hut's 4,800
places, opens first Canadian pizza parlor in 1983 - later to Australia,
England, West Germany, Philippines and Japan, acquires Detroit Tigers
baseball franchise in 1983 for $50 million)... Edward E. Carlson becomes
president of Westin Hotels to oversee 19 operations (expands business to
60 hotels in 13 countries before acquisition by United Airlines in
1970)... Theme park Freedomland U.S.A. opens in Bronx, NY (closes 1964
after losing some $20 million)... William Newberg becomes president of
Chrysler (is fired within 2 months for having stock in firm's
suppliers)...

Marion Harper forms advertising conglomerate of Interpublic as holding
company with four divisions: McCann-Erickson to serve domestic accounts,
McCann-Marshalk to handle "traditional" accounts, international group
with nearly 50 offices overseas, and Communications Affiliates to provide
services in research, public relations and sales promotions (adds later
Long Island dude ranch as retreat and air taxi service to Manhattan,
acquires ad agencies in 1962-64 to become world's largest in advertising
with 141 branches in 37 countries, 1,350 corporate clients with billings
of some $711 million, and with some 8,300 employees in 24 divisions,
after failing to make profit in 1966 and violating bank loans is forced
to resign after near bankruptcy in 1967 - nears bankruptcy again in
1979)... First Playboy Club opens in Chicago, last U.S. club closes 1988
(opens clubs in   New Orleans and Miami in 1961 - 22 during heydays of
1970s, generates 40% of Playboy's 1965 revenues of $47.8 million and 5%
of 1984's revenues of $192 million, after losing British casino licenses
for 4 clubs in 1981 for illegalities closes remaining clubs in 1986 to
continue with franchises in Des Moines, Lansing, Omaha, 4 in Japan and 1
in Philippines)...

Pro golfer Jack Nicklaus co-designs first golf course, 80 in 24 states
and 11 countries by 1988 (by 1985 operates grab bag of enterprises, radio
station, educational sales program, investments, condominiums, car
leasing, restaurant, land development, optical products and oil
developments, with debt of $175 million, revamps strategy to generate
profits by 1988 from golf course designs, product licenses and golf
videos)... NFL Cardinals move from Chicago to St. Louis, followed by
Oakland Raiders leaving capacity crowds to bigger stadium in Los Angeles
- $213 million in damages when blocked by NFL, by Baltimore Colts to
Indianapolis in 1984 and St. Louis Cardinals to Phoenix in 1988... After
selling records in father's Sacramento drugstore in 1952 and going broke
distributing records to discount outlets, Russell Solomon borrows money
to form Tower Records (opens first out-of-town outlet in San Francisco -
at time U.S.' largest, evolves by 1988 with 53 stores, 2nd in world to
Musicland, and over 47 in books, videotapes, and art)... First Taco Time,
Mexican restaurant chain of 232 outlets by 1985, opens in Portland, OR...
Jack Loizeaux starts Controlled Demolition, MD, to pioneer use of
explosions to raze structures - over 5,000 by 1988 with 32-story high-
rise in Sao Paulo, Brazil, tallest... Pete Rozelle, General Manager of

Los Angeles Rams, is NFL Commissioner (starts pioneering NFL Properties in 1963 to license products to firms)... With under $1,000 Delford M. Smith, partner, sells out 1962, start Evergreen Helicopters, OR, to handle contracts for U.S. Forest Service, sales of $26 million in 1988 from major oil companies and timber work (forms international airline in 1974 for express mail services for U.S., U.S. Postal Service, Department of Defense and 3 foreign carriers - 1988 sales of $151 million in phasing out contract for UPS, forms holding company in 1978 - 1988 sales of $233 million, after buying air base, AZ, from CIA proprietary arm in 1975 forms air center in 1979 - 1988 sales of $28 million, forms aircraft sales and leasing in 1983 - 1988 sales of $14 million, forms losigtics arm in 1984 to serve Evergreen, other airlines - 1988 sales of $13 million handling cargo at 36 major U.S. airports, gets contested contract from U.S. Postal Service for bid of $136.8 million in 1987 over at least 5 lower bids - costs balloon to $194.6 million)... Matt Reese, dean of political consultants in 1980s, earns reputation during Kennedy campaign (switches from political clients to corporate work in 1982, sells out in 1987 for $35 million)... After Cuba takeover by Fidel Castro, Jorge Mas flees to Miami (after working as stevedore, joining Bay of Pigs invasion, and working as shoe salesman and milkman, is hired in 1970 by construction firm, with bank loan buys firm in 1971 - by 1988 doing $20 million/year with some 400 employees)... Bernard Nussdorf starts Quality King Distributors, leading gray-market business in 1987 with sales of $350 million in selling all kinds of goods to retailers for up to 30% below regular wholesale prices, is started in Queens, NY.

1961

General Events

President Eisenhower warns (January 17) public of rising power of "military-industrial complex" in Farewell Address... Fair Labor Standards Act raises (May 5) minimum wage to $1.15 in 1961 and $1.25 in 1963... Congress makes (September 5) airplane highjacking a federal crime... Agency for International Development is created (September 5)... Congress establishes (September 22) Peace Corps, created in March by Presidential order... U.S. Supreme Court orders DuPont to sell its 25%, $3 billion, of stock in General Motors... MIT develops first computer time-sharing system... Clarence Dillon, Secretary of Treasury, launches Alliance for Progress at Punta del Este, Uruguay, to stimulate economic growth of Latin-America... Chicago is first city to use computer for law enforcement... Government extends FHA mortgages to condos, long popular in Europe (by 1979 results in more condos built than rental units)...

National Institutes Health Clinic Center, MD, institutes first computerized system to monitor patients... Outward Bound Program for wilderness survival is started, CO... Walter Reuther, former president of UAW, proposes to auto industry that all hourly workers be salaried, rejected... FDA requires cosmetic makers to have safety clearances before selling products... Sports Broadcasting Act provides legal basis for network contracts with major sports leagues... David C. McClelland: The Achieving Society... Food Stamp Program is started to combat poverty, boost farm income (by 1982 evolves as $11 billion program serving some 22 million clients amid charges of fraud)... Clarence Randall: The Folklore of Management... Amitai Etzioni: A Comparative Analysis of Complex Organizations... J. Cawey, Chief Justice of U.S. District Court, rules

29 electrical equipment firms conspired in fixing prices, rigging bids and sharing market (jails 7 executives)... President Kennedy signs Executive Order 10925 to eliminate employment discrimination and establish President's Committee on Equal Employment Opportunity... Roy Master starts Foundation of Human Understanding in Los Angeles to save souls from corruption... American Federation of Teachers becomes bargaining agent for faculties of NYC public schools...

Pennsylvania Surface Reclamation Act is passed... Jane Jacobs: <u>The Death and Life of Great American Cities</u> (advocates urban renaissance)... Agency for International Development is created... U.S. Supreme Court upholds state and local censorship of motion pictures... Federal budget of $80.9 billion is record amount for peace time... Interstate Commerce Commission formulates specific rules on forbidding racial discrimination in interstate bus transportation...

Antulio Ramirez Ortiz hijacks first U.S. plane to Cuba... Herman Kahn, former analyst for Rand Corp., and others start Hudson Institute "think tank" (develops reputation for forecasts of future)... Amalgamated Clothing Workers drops second boycott of Japanese textiles... Civil Aeronautics Board rules operations of exclusive or semi-exclusive clubs by airlines with charges are illegal... First public education TV station opens, NYC... Army uses new mobile printer for instant maps, replaces old pre-printed maps... All trucks and cars are required by 1963 to be equipped with "positive crankcase ventilation"...

Kollsman Instrument Corp. invents first laser gun... Veljko Milenkovic files patent application for "Single Channel Tap Motor Control for Machine Tools" (contributes to development of robotics)... United Electrical, Radio and Machine Union: <u>Guide to Automation</u> (attacks new technology)... General Electric is No. 1 in obtaining U.S. patents (holds first until 1986 to place 4th after Canon, Hitachi, Toshiba).

Business Events

Two New York crime families start Gallo-Profaci War in struggle for market dominance (leads to new war in 1971 between 2 gangs and minorities)... Ford Motor Co. acquires Philco, maker of television, radio and electronic equipment (consolidates with Aeronautronics division in 1963)... Merrill Lynch opens office in Japan (obtains securities license in 1971 and seat on Tokyo Stock Exchange in 1986)... William A. Patterson's United Airlines acquires financially-troubled Capital Airlines to become U.S.' top carrier... Diebold introduces push-button file cabinet, priced at $2,175, to retail market, operates like Ferris Wheel... After New York Stock Exchange records greatest daily volume of $118,034,886, largest since 1933, May 28 sees greatest one-day drop in prices since 1929...

To stimulate sales Sears drops down-payments on credit purchases... Rich's Department Store in Atlanta operates first robot vending machine... AT&T develops light beam for transmitting phone calls... TWA shows first-run movies to first-class passengers on coast-to-coast flights... Revlon introduces Eterna 27 face-cream collection (pioneers in advertising "scientific" skin-care treatments)... Charles Thornton, Roy Ash purchase Nevada ranch (discover gold in mid-1960s - Gold Quarry possibly 2nd biggest find since Homestake Mine in late 1800s)... Iowa Beef Processors is started in Denison, IA, with loan from Small Business Administration (evolves as largest meatpacker by 1981 to butcher at slaughterhouse in selling boxed beef, after winning 9 strikes escapes master contract, copied later by Excel, Armour and Wilson - union membership down to 65% of employment in 1988 from 90% in 1970s, to reduce labor costs, is acquired by Occidental Petroleum in 1981, locks union out 1986 when contract ends, is fined $2.6 million by OSHA in 1987 for safety violations on complaints of union - plus $3 million, agency's largest total, in 1988, recognizes Food & Commercial Workers Union in 1988)...

Lockheed is one of first corporations to promote minority employment... Rensis Likert: New Patterns of Management... After leaving law school Leslie Wexner, 2nd biggest loser at $1.451 billion in 1987 October Crash, joins family's clothing store in Columbus, OH (resigns in 1963, disagrees with parents on which line of merchandise to sell, to start Limited retail business to sell just sportswear with $5,000 borrowed from aunt - parents close business to join his, acquires 222-store Lane Bryant chain in 1982, acquires 800 Lerner stores in 1985 to operate some 2,500 outlets, including 161 stores of Limited Express for teenagers, young women and 65 outlets of Victoria's Secret with sexy lingerie, achieves sales over $3 billion in 1987 to become No. 1 in women's apparel with 2,857 stores, plans 1,000 more by 1989, in sensing changes in trends before competitors, identifying submarkets and merchandising with flair)...

Giorgio's, exclusive store for customers by appointment only, opens on Rodeo Drive, Los Angeles, sold to Avon in 1987 (starts development of street with fancy stores to attract wealthy, gawking tourists)... ABC airs pioneering TV program "Wide World of Sports" as 20-week summer replacement (follows with "Monday Night Football" program in 1970 and "The Superstars" in 1973)... Former accountant Lynn Townsend, first hired as controller in 1957, becomes president of Chrysler (acquires contracts in space program in 1961, revives auto business by hiring designer and accountant from Ford, expanding dealer network, instituting tight controls and by reducing staff, offers drivers 5-year, 50,000 mile warranty on drive-train repairs in 1962, introduces Barracuda car in 1964 to compete with Ford's Mustang, nets $112 million in 1968 during most profitable quarter in firm's history, records $4.4 million deficit in last quarter of 1969 - first since 1961)...

Harold Koontz: "The Management Theory Jungle," Journal of the Academy of Management... San Francisco Tape Music Center is first U.S. multimedia workshop... George Propstra of Vancouver, WA, starts Burgerville USA fast-food restaurant chain (by 1984 runs 23 units in Oregon, Washington)... American Motors adopt industry's first profit-sharing plan... Greyhound Transportation starts diversification plan (evolves by 1980s with financial services and general services with insurance, car leasing, travel, airport ground activities, food businesses, such as Armour, consumer products, and pharmaceuticals, spins off original bus business in 1986)... Reader's Digest starts annual sweepstakes contest to boost circulation (gives away some $26.5 million by 1984, followed by Publisher's Clearing House in 1967)... In period to 1968, 11 firms acquire some 500 companies... Philip Crosby at Martin Marietta develops Zero Defects Program for quality control (as former director of quality for ITT, starts consulting firm in 1979 to promote cause of quality control)... Richard Sommer starts Hillcrest Vineyard, pioneers Oregon's wine industry... After attempts in 1958 to measure symptoms and causes of motivation, Texas Instruments starts research program in job enrichment... Chicago Cubs baseball team adopts managerial system, College of Coaches, with rotating field leaders (-1965)... Frito corn chips, founded in 1932 by Elmer Doolin with $100, and Lay potato chips, started during early 1932 by Herman W. Lay, merge to form Frito-Lay (with sales of some $200 million is acquired by Pepsi-Cola in 1965 to create Pepsico, buys 1914 Grandma's Foods, OR, to enter soft-cookie market in 1980, achieves sales of some $2.4 billion in 1984 to earn profits of $377 million in snack food market)... Smith-Corona introduces small computer and printer... Celanese Corp. invents new plastic tougher than cast metal...

United Nuclear Corp. is started as reprocessing business... General Motors is indicted on charges of monopoly in locomotive market... Stouffer Corp. introduces line of frozen foods for churches, schools, etc... For first time Japan's Sony sells stock to U.S. public... To reduce costs, Ford Motor forms subsidiaries overseas for tooling work... IBM introduces Selectric, typewriter with no moving carriage or typebars... Harley-Davidson is first U.S. motorcycle manufacturer to manufacture overseas... Hughes Aircraft tests ion engine for space exploration... Chicago's WFMT is first profitable FM stereo radio station... Western Union develops push-button telephone... Franchise of Burger Queen, local chain of 12 outlets in Louisville, KY, is granted to George Clark, partners for $5,000 and 3% of gross (opens first place in Shelbyville outside Louisville to gross $500,000 in 1965, changes name of 160-unit chain in 1981 to Druther's)...

After working for Dallas bank, Harold Simmons acquires local drug store (buys Houston drug store chain in 1967 with first hostile takeover, trades 100-store chain in 1973 for $50 million in stock of Jack Eckerd Corp., uses funds to specialize in hostile deals, acquires NL Industries in 1986 in raid of $257 million, after buying firms at bargain prices becomes billionaire by 1988)...   With gift of $25,000 from father 22-year-old Saul Steinberg starts computer-leasing business in Brooklyn law office (acquires Reliance Insurance of Philadelphia in 1968, goes private in 1981 with $550 million leveraged buy-out to become leading financial dealer in 1980s, after earning 25% on holdings in first 6 months of 1986 plans to issue stock so public can participate in ventures)...

Eastern Airlines pioneers hourly no-frill shuttle service between Boston, New York and Washington, joined in market by New York Air in 1981 and Pan Am with frills in 1986 (is sold to Donald J. Trump in 1989 for some $360 million)... Charles J. Bradshaw, partner acquire franchise in Hardee's Food Systems (expand business as Spartan Food Systems to operate 250-restaurant chain of Hardee's and Quincy Family Steak Houses, is acquired in 1979 by Transworld, airline holding company with 90 Hilton International hotels seeking diversification, for $80 million, becomes president of Transworld in 1984, resigns from $2.6 billion food and lodging business in 1986 after showdown with firm's chairman on acquiring nursing home business proposed by rival for top slot)... First public copy machine, 50 cents/document, is operated in Boston... Pioneering trade show to promote, sell franchises is held in NYC... American Express publishes upscale Travel & Leisure magazine, joins field dominated by Travel-Holiday first issued around 1900 (is followed in market by

European Travel & Life to cover lifestyles of rich and shameless in 1985)... American Assn. of Equipment Lessors is formed, over 1,000 members by 1988 in leasing equipment to 8 of 10 U.S.' businesses...

George Gillett gets college degree in liberal arts (after being salesman for Crown Zellerbach and associate with McKinney & Co. management-consulting firm, uses savings to acquire 22% of Miami Dolphins pro football team with partner in January, 1967, after being president and general manager of Harlem Globetrotters, sells stake in Dolphins to buy Globetrotters with partner in August, 1967 for over $3 million - by 1970s team nets $3 million/year before selling in 1975 for twice purchase price, by 1989, builds empire of 12 TV stations, 4th largest network, and buys Vail ski-complex in 1985 for $130 million as ski resorts decline from 1,000 in 1979 to 650).

1962

General Events

President Kennedy denounces (April 10) hike in steel prices as "totally unjustified and irresponsible" (forces industry to cancel increases)... Telstar communications satellite transmits first worldwide TV... Because of birth defects from tranquilizer Thalidomide, President signs (October 10) bill to protect public against harmful drugs... Trade Expansion Act promotes (October 11) foreign trade by reducing tariffs... By executive order (November 20), all Federal agencies are required to eliminate discrimination based on race or religion in any Federally-funded housing... U.S. Supreme Court rules airports must compensate neighbors for noises and vibrations...

U.S. Air Force announces first TV broadcast by satellite... For first time U.S. national debt exceeds $300 billion... U.S. creates Communications Satellite Corp. with monopoly for international market (starts venture in 1984 with Holiday Inns to provide entertainment programs)... Daniel Bell introduces concept of post-industrial society at Boston forum... Manpower Development and Training Act is passed... President Kennedy sends Committee for Economic Development to France to study centralized industrial planning (fails to formulate U.S. industrial policy on return, is emulated in 1975 by Advisory Committee on National Growth Policy Processes)...

Time: "The City" (reports on transformation of St. Louis, started in early 1950s, in developing new atmospheric Gaslight Square with 50 taverns, cabarets, restaurants and antique shops in former slum area)...

Helen Gurley Brown: Sex and the Single Girl... Ivan E. Sutherland describes possibilities of computer graphics in doctoral thesis, basis for Computer-Aided Design/Computer-Aided Manufacturing program... Two researchers at University of Michigan devise laser technique for holography, based on theory for three-dimensional images by Dennis Gabor, Hungarian-born scientist, in late 1940s... U.S. operates 200 atomic reactors, Britain and U.S.S.R. each with 39... Astronaut John Glenn is first American to orbit Earth... Manhattan's Local 3, International Brotherhood of Electrical Workers, demands reduction of work week of 9,000 master construction electricians from 30 hours to 20... Seattle's Century 21 Exposition opens, first World's Fair in U.S. in over 20 years... Pop-top can appears... Charles R. Walker, Robert H. Guest: The Man on the Assembly Line... U.S. Post Office devises Zip Code to speed mail delivery in 1963 (extends 5 numbers to 9 digits in 1983)... Chris Argyris: Interpersonal Confidence and Organizational Effectiveness... Clerks, other employees of Jacksonville-to-Miami railroad walkout, longest in U.S. history (-1974)... Alfred D. Chandler, Jr.: Strategy and Structure: Chapters in the History of American Industrial Enterprise (describes strategy as determining long-term goals, adopting courses of action, and allocating resources, shows convergence of several U.S. firms, DuPont, General Motors, Sears and Standard Oil of New Jersey, in adopting organizational structures with centralized headquarters to control decentralized operations with accounting and statistical information systems)...

By executive order government workers are granted right to join unions (requires federal agencies to bargain with unions)... MIT students develop non-commercial computer game called Spacewars, followed in 1972 by Nolan Bushnell's Pong as first coin-operated video game... Anthony Boyle becomes acting president of United Mine Workers, president in 1963 (is defeated in 1972 election by insurgent group of Arnold Miller, is convicted in 1972 for using union funds to make illegal political contributions, is convicted in 1974 in arranging murder of Joseph Yablonski, opponent in 1969 election)... Cesar Chavez, migrant laborers organize National Farm Workers Assn. in California fields (despite competition from Teamsters signs contracts with minor grape growers in 1966 and major growers in 1967 after strikes and boycotts)... International Association of Machinists, U.S. Industries launch project to study effects of automation on workers...

Warren Schmidt, colleagues at American Machine & Foundry submit patent application for "automatic apparatus" (advances development of robotics)... Trade Expansion Act lets U.S. bargain with European Common Market... Pop artist Andy Warhol gives his first one-man show, NYC (cites "Good business is the best art.").

Business Events

Phil Anschutz takes over father's small Denver-based oil drilling business, 75,000-acre ranch in Utah (becomes oil baron in 1978 after discovering one of biggest oil and gas fields under ranch, sensing bust in petroleum market sells $1 billion in energy-related properties in 1980-82 at top of market, speculates in stock market in 1982 to net $60 million, restructures Ideal Basic Industries in 1983 to earn $40 million, becomes billionaire by 1987 as one of largest owners of Denver real estate to propose building of controversial $127 million convention center)... After arranging with Onitsuka Tiger, one of Japan's best makers of athletic shoes, for U.S. distributorship, Phil Knight and Bill Bowerman, former University of Oregon track and field coach, start Blue Ribbon Sports (when Tiger stops shipments in 1972 obtains new Japanese supplier to make their Nike shoes, promotes shoes with first endorsement by athletes in 1971, designs revolutionary waffle-sole shoe in 1975, starts Athletics West in 1977 to sponsor athletes, sells athletic wear in 1979, reaches $1 billion in sales in 1985-86 with success of Michael Jordan basketball shoes - 2nd largest in U.S. market after Reebok)... Low-budget lodging industry is pioneered with opening of Motel 6 in Santa Barbara, CA, with rooms for $6/night (expands to 401 properties in 3

states by 1986 - undercut in prices by rival Quality International with
333 Comfort Inns, is challenged in low-price market by 13 other budget
chains - Marriott's Fairfield Inns and Ramada's Roadway Inns join
industry in 1987)... S.S. Kresge variety chain, 1987 sales of $24
billion, opens first K mart discount store, operates nearly 4,000 places
in U.S., Canada, and Puerto Rico by 1987 as U.S.' largest retailer after
Sears (becomes K mart Corp. in 1976, pases J.C. Penney to become No. 2
retailer in 1977, starts Waldenbooks - 1,100 stores as No. 1 book chain
by 1986, sells 68 Kresge and 18 Jupiter variety stores to McCrory Corp.,
subsidiary of Meshulam Riklis' privately-held Rapid American -largest in
variety market with some 1,240 stores and sales of $1.8 billion, launches
line of women's clothing in 1984 and hires Martha Stewart, famed caterer
and hostess, in 1987 to plug kitchen, bedroom and bath products)...

Boeing tests 131-passenger 727 Trijet (sells over 1,800 as most popular
commercial airliner ever)... IBM designs first disk storage for
computers... Vail ski resort, U.S.' largest by 1987, opens, CO... 1914
Noxell skin treatment business with Noxema launches Cover Girl
reasonably-priced cosmetic line - market leader in 1986 over Revlon and
Maybelline (after 5 years of research introduces Clarion make-up products
in 1986 for women over 30 - merchandised with computer for personalized
color selections)... After being "Driver of the Year" Roger Penske quits
racing to start Penske Racing, by 1988 most successfyl Indy car owner
with 7 wins in 20 starts, and open Chevy dealership (forms holding
company in 1975 with 500 employees and sales of $18 million - over 9,000
employees and sales over $2 billion from 8 dealerships, 2 major
racetracks, tire distributorships, industrial engines - joint venture
with GM, and Penske Truck Leasing after acquiring Hertz and Leaseway
truck rental businesses)...

Richard Green starts Compliance Data Center to protect clients against
stock fraud by deadbeats, stock manipulators, money launderers and
crooked brokers on Wall Street... After serving in U.S. Navy and becoming
top salesman for IBM (acquires job after chance meeting on aircraft
carrier with company executive), H. Ross Perot starts Electronic Data
Systems with $1,000 in Dallas to design, install and operate computers
(achieves first success with state contract to administer Medicare and
Medicade programs, goes public in 1968 - some $300 million in paper
profits, starts giving money to charity in 1969 - over $100 million to
various causes by 1986, loses some $450 million in 1970 when stock
plunges from $150 to $85 in weak market - greatest individual loss on
stock market in single day, drops some $60 million in 1974 when his 2
Wall Street firms fail, in 1979 dispatches team to Iran to rescue 2
employees imprisoned in Tehran, sells EDS to General Motors in 1984 for
$2.5 billion - $1 billion in cash, is ousted from GM in 1986 with $700
million buyout after conflict over firm's direction, invests in Steve
Jobs' new NeXT computer venture in 1987, forms Perot Systems in 1988 to
battle GM's EDS)...

Boeing tests prototype hydrofoil vessel for U.S. Navy... After selling
$100 million electronics business, William Lear, designer of Motorola's
first practical car radio in 1932 and inventor of autopilot, etc., with
8th-grade education, starts new enterprise to popularize Learjets for
executive travel (after inadequate marketing sells business in 1967 to
Gates Corp. after investing $15 million in 1970s fails to develop
efficient steam-propulsion system for buses and cars, starts LearAvia in

1976 to develop revolutionary ultra-light passenger plane)...

Arnold Palmer is leading money-winner on pro golf tour with total prizes of $81,448.33 (is first player to earn career prize money of $1 million in 1968)... After bilking E.L. Bruce Co. of some $2 million Eddie Gilbert flees to Brazil to avoid imprisonment... Aaron Rents starts with folding chairs and tables (evolves as largest furniture rental company, 146 stores, by 1985 with sales of some $91.2 million - 500-store Rent-a-Center largest in 1987 rental market)... Airline industry is stunned when Continental introduces economy fare for Chicago-Los Angeles route... Ford Motor Co. uses Telemarketing to promote sales, pioneers new industry...

Sports Unlimited is started in Detroit to sell coupon books with discount tickets for games (is used by major companies, such as General Motors, Litton, and Xerox, as bonuses for employees, achieves sales of about $15 million in 1982)...

After series of odd jobs Australian-born Robert Stigwood starts small talent agency to cast actors for TV commercials (uses business to become independent record producer for groups like Cream and Bee Gees, acquires British rights for productions of "Hair" and "Calcutta," acquires U.S. rights for British TV shows of "Sanford and Son" and "All in the Family," acquires all performance rights to rock opera "Jesus Christ Super Star," evolves by 1980s as rock tycoon with 150 permanent employees worldwide to produce movies of "Saturday Night Fever," "Grease" and "Sgt. Pepper's Lonely Heart's Club Band")...

Polish-born Henry de Kwiatkowski, former organizer of Pakistan Airline, Buddhist monk, movie actor, Cambridge student, and sculptor, starts Kwiatkowski Aircraft with $3,000 to sell used planes (grosses some $2 billion in sales by 1982)... Engineer Ken Iverson is hired as division manager by Nuclear Corporation of America, becomes Nucor later (advances to command in 1965 when business flirts with bankruptcy, after selling or closing divisions and reducing staff, shows pre-tax profit of $1.3 billion in 1966, starts firm's mini-mill operation to make carbon-steel in 1969, earns $44.5 million on steel sales of $600.3 million in 1984 with modernization, productivity and bonuses, with corporate staff of 17 and over 14 decentalized divisions runs $800 million business in 1987)...

Dave Drum starts Kampgrounds of America (-1975 when sold as nationwide franchise business)... New Balance introduces Trackster, first modern running shoe... Curtis Publishing hires Matthew Culligan to revive failing business, mostly result of losses by once popular 1821 Saturday Evening Post, (dismisses 2,200 of firm's 9,000 employees to cut costs, rejects offers from CBS and NBC to sell, reduces issues to 45/year, loses libel suit for some $3 million in 1963 - by end of 1963 some $25 million in libel suits from hard-hitting journalism, changes magazine to biweekly in 1965, drops unwanted subscribers in 1968 to focus on "class" market, declares bankruptcy in 1964 after losing some $62 million since 1961)...

With loan of $1,000 Louisville lawyers David Jones, Wendell Cherry start Heritage House of America to manage nursing homes, oversee 10 homes by 1968 (change name of business to Humana in 1968 and issue stock to enter field of hospital management, divest 41 nursing homes in 1972 to concentrate on hospitals - 91 by 1984 in 22 states, England, Switzerland and Mexico, start MedFirst to operate neighborhood clinics in 1981 - 120 by 1984, achieve revenues over $4 billion in 1984, hire Dr. William De Vries in 1984 from Utah Medical Center to develop artificial heart implant program)... David Thomas is assigned to rescue 4 struggling Kentucky Fried Chicken places in Columbus, OH, by Hobby Horse restaurant business (with $1.7 million on sale of profitable operation in 1968, opens first Wendy's fast-food hamburger restaurant - 9 by 1972 with sales of $1.8 million, opens 100th place in 1975, 500th in 1976, 1,000th in 1978 and 2,000th in 1982 with sales of $1.6 billion, serves breakfasts in 1979 -opens first outlet in Europe, acquires Sister's International, quality restaurant chain specializing in chicken, in 1981, operates 3,500 units worldwide with volume of $2.7 billion by 1986)... American Society for Industrial Security has 2,490 members with chapters in 48 states...

Robert L. Waltrip starts Service Corp. International as chain of funeral homes (operates 316 funeral homes and 18 cemeteries nationwide plus 2nd largest U.S. casket-maker, in 1986, starts co-op in 1986 to provide products, group insurance, auto leasing to small independent mortuaries)... Ad agency of Fred Papert, Julian Koenig and George Lois is first in industry to go public, 5 public of top 10 agencies by 1969...

After resigning from Safeway grocery business to avoid out-of-state promotion in 1960 to open John's One Stop in Portland, OR, John Piacentini starts Plaid Pantry small convenience store chain (is challenged by industry's first union and strike in 1985, operates 161-store chain, 1986 sales of $100 million, before sale to Pacific Crest with 1,316 convenience stores in U.S., Canada and Southeast Asia and sales of $820 million, for $21.2 million)... ABC hires Malvin Goode as correspondent, first black in television news... When denied entry into discount store field by Benjamin Franklin store chain, former franchisee Sam Walton starts independent off-price Wal-Mart business in Rogers, AK, 51 discount stores with sales of $78 million by 1972 (employs staff of 46,000 in 1982 - almost 150,000 by 1988, is- ranked by _Forbes_ in 1985 as U.S.' richest man with holdings of $3.6 billion, operates 1,031 outlets and 52 Sam's Wholesale Club warehouse-stores in 1986 with sales of $11.9 billion - $16 billion in 1987 to rank No. 3 retailer behind Sears and K mart, as market's biggest loser drops some $1.751 billion in 1987 Crash of October 19th, opens 3 Hypermart USA stores, each 220,000 sq. ft. to sell everything under one roof, in 1987-88)...

J.C. Penney retailer opens nationwide catalog service (buys drug store chains and insurance firms, one of U.S.' largest in mid-1960s, buys 87-store Sarma chain, Belgium, in 1968, runs over 2,000 stores by 1979 as U.S.' 3rd largest retailer, hires award-winning high-fashion designer Mary McFadden in 1985 to create signature collection for young, middle-class women)... Studebaker starts making Avanti cars, designed by Raymond Loewy (becomes independent after Studebaker's bankruptcy in 1966, is rescued from 1986 bankruptcy by Michael E. Kelly, CEO of New Avanti Corp., by 1988.

1963

General Events

U.S. Postal Service raises (January 7) rate of postage on first-class mail to 5 cents/ounce... Dr. Martin Luther King, Jr., delivers "I Have a Dream" speech to some 200,000 civil rights leaders and marchers in

Washington... Former French champion Rene Lacoste patents metal tennis racket... After strike of 114 days New York newspaper unions return to work at 8 papers, records estimated losses of $190 million in circulation and $250 million in advertising while employees lose over $50 million in wages and benefits (leads to failure of New York Mirror)... MIT labs devises first Computer Aided design program (allows users to create and change structures on computer screen)... Stewart M. Lee teaches pioneering college course on consumerism... Equal Pay Act prohibits pay differences between men and women doing work of equal skill, effort and responsibility... New Hampshire approves state lottery, first since ban on interstate lotteries by Congress in 1895, in order to balance its budget, adopted by 14 more states by 1979 and 29 others with District of Columbia by 1988...

Vocational Education Act assists states to start vocational schools... Friction welding is developed... New York's Guggenheim Museum exhibits pop art... Jessica Mitford: The American Way of Death (attacks funeral industry for shoddy and gawdy practices, results in FTC regulations for undertakers in 1984)... Betty Friedan: The Feminine Mystique (inspires women's movement)... Clean Air Act is passed... Fred Keller devises Personalized System of Instruction...

Amalgamated Clothing & Textile Workers starts campaign to organize workers of J.P. Stevens & Co., U.S.' 2nd largest textile operation with some 34,000 millworkers at 80 plants (-1980 when settled after bitter boycott and pressure on banks)... Congress passes law to require compulsory arbitration of disputes between railroads and operating brotherhoods on abolishment of certain jobs... University of Pennsylvania creates Wharton Econometrics to do economic forecasting (is acquired by Ziff Corp. in 1980, is almost acquired in 1983 by France with support of Research and Industry Ministry but opposed by Finance Ministry)... Joseph McGuire: Business and Society, pioneers environmental study of business...

Ohio court of appeals rules former Goodrich employee can work for International Latex so long as he refrains from revealing Goodrich's industrial secrets (follows first ruling on issue in 1905 by Judge Oliver Wendell Holmes, Jr., in stating firm had right to retain trade secrets)... Harold Barnett, Chandler Morse: Scarcity and Growth... Michael Harrington: The Other America (reports on poverty level of 40-50 million Americans, triggers President Johnson's war on poverty)... Developer James Rouse designs model community of Columbia, MD, without urban sprawl on 14,000 acres (evolves by 1985 as racially and socially diverse community of some 60,000, 1,500-odd businesses in 8 villages)...

Tariff schedule is reformed to reclassify thousands of items in 8 categories to simplify duties with one rate/product, commodity... In this time Provanzano family of mobsters acquires control of Teamsters Local 560, some 9,000 members, in Union City, NJ (after charges of corruption results in first federal trusteeship in 1986)... National Federation of Independent Unions is formed... U.S. Supreme Court rules agency shop legal, NLRB v. General Motors, and states can ban agency shops, Retail Clerks, Local 1625 v. Schermerhorn... Family Motor Coach Assn. holds first convention, some 60,000 members in 1988, to celebrate joys of traveling.

Business Events

Guthrie Theater, Minneapolis, pioneers U.S. regional houses (by 1988 gets 54% of $8.5 million annual budget from box office and 13% from corporations)... Pioneering Original Improvisation Theater opens, NYC, to help young performers polish skills and materials... GM reports record income of $1.4 billion for 1962... Texas real estate financier Billie Sol Estes is convicted for swindling dozen major finance companies of $24 million in mortgages on non-existent fertilizer tanks, sentenced to jail for 15 years... National Football League suspends Paul Horning of Green Bay Packers and Alex Karras of Detroit Lions for betting on games and associating with gamblers or "known hoodlums"... Stocks rise (November 26) $15 billion in biggest one-day rally on NYSE... Digital Equipment introduces first minicomputer to market...

American Airlines installs industry's first computerized airline reservation system (uses 62,026 terminals to link travel agencies and airports worldwide in 1988 - United with 40,688, Texas Air with 20,000, TWA and Northwest with 13,814 and Delta with 9,300)... Norton Simon, head of conglomerate Hunt Foods, starts raid on slipping Wheeling Steel - 35% investment by 1965 (retreats from take-over in 1967 after corporate in-fighting and failure to revive business)... Horse trainer Jim Fitzsimmons hires woman "exercise boy" (is followed in 1967, after court suit, by first woman jockey licensed by Maryland)... Ronald F. Gordon starts Multi-National Corp. to find overseas customers for U.S. electronic companies (-1970s, becomes president of Atari in 1974 until sold to Warner Communications in 1976, starts Friends Amis, Inc., in 1977 to make portable computers - sold in 1979 to Japan's Matsushita Electric for $10 million, starts TeleLearning in 1982 as communications network to handle correspondence courses of various universities)...

In this time SRI International pioneers vision-controlled robots, used by some 250 companies by 1984 to design robotic-vision systems for quality control... Hoffman-La Roche introduces Valium tranquilizer... DuPont introduces Corfam artificial leather (abandons product in 1971 after losing some $80-100 million)... General Tire starts program to diversify into chemicals, plastics, space ventures, etc., one of first in industry to build a conglomerate... Richard Johnson, others: The Theory and Management of Systems (becomes popular textbook)... Only 1.5% of tomatoes grown in California are harvested by machine, nearly 95% by 1968... Charles Tandy, Ft. Worth businessman, acquires 9 Radio Shack stores, founded 1921 (builds empire of some 7,500 franchises to sell computers and electronic products by 1988, contracts in 1988 to supply personal computers to Japan's Matsushita for resale as under Panasonic brand)...

Business Week: "Multinational Companies: How U.S. Business Goes Worldwide"... Norman Dalkey: Olaf Helmer: "An Experimental Application of the DELPHI Method to the Use Experts" (discusses planning technique developed by Rand Corp.)... Abe Schuchman: Scientific Decision-Making in Business... William A. Douglas, Careers, Inc., recruits European scientists and technicians for positions in U.S. firms... Robert E. Farrell, partner with $5,000 open old-fashioned ice cream parlor in Portland, OR (expands to 140-unit chain when acquired by Marriott Corp. in 1972 for $8.8 million - annual revenues of some $50 million by 1980, with profits from sale starts Engine House Pizza Parlors in 1976, sells to Quaker Oats in 1978 for 6-figure profit)... Los Angeles Times, Palm

Beach Post Times use RCA 301 computers to automate typesetting process...
After father's suicide, Ted, "Captain Outrageous," Turner at age of 24
inherits financially-ailing Atlanta billboard business (revives business
as Turner Communications to become millionaire while in 20s, buys 2
financially-troubled independent TV stations in 1970, acquires Atlanta
Braves baseball team in 1976 for $1 million in cash and $1 million for
next 9 years, starts satellite transmission for cable TV in 1976 to gain
national exposure with super station, defends America's Cup sailing race
in 1977 and acquires Atlanta Hawks baseball franchise for $500,000 and
assumption of $1 million note, fails with music-video cable network in
1984, goes into debt to acquire MGM in 1985 for $1.5 billion - spins off
assets for cash to retain library of 3,300 films for cable network,
sponsors Goodwill Games in 1986 with U.S.S.R., after losing expensive
battle for control of CBS in 1985-86 cedes control of Turner Broadcasting
in 1987 to group of industry investors after bail-out of $562.5 million,
starts new cable venture in 1988 with improving market)...

Bates Advertising hires Thomas Richardson as full-time copywriter, one of
first blacks in industry... After arriving in U.S. from Turkey in 1960
with $16, Erol Onarian starts business in Virginia suburb of Washington
to repair television sets (evolves by 1986 as video-tape-rental operation
with sales of $120 million from 101 stores)... Designer Kenneth Jay Lane
starts business selling imitation jewels (expands from 4 branches in 1983
to 11 by 1986 with popularity of gawdy jewelry)...

Nelson Teltz, age 22, joins family's $2.5 million New Jersey
Institutional Food-Supply business, renamed Flagstaff later (is joined by
accountant Peter May, age 31, in 1972 to handle $50 million business,
acquires 51% of Coffee-Mat, renamed Trafalgar, and starts consulting
firm, acquires 9.5% of New York bank holding company and 6.5% of Faberge
in 1980 - sold in 1981, acquires Avery Coal to create energy company,
acquires control of Triangle Industries in 1983 and uses junk bonds of
Drexel Burnham Lambert to finance expansion, sells Trafalger in 1984 and
spins-off Avery to shareholders, acquires National Can in 1985 to achieve
sales of $1.6 billion and American Can packaging in 1986 to create empire
with $3 billion in sales)...

National Football League forms NFL Charities, donates some $9 million by
1988... Don Tyson, owner of Arkansas chicken processing business, buys
small Northeastern poultry firm to enter new market, 32 plants by 1988 as
U.S.' largest chicken processor with sales of $1.9 billion (buys Prospect
Farms, holds contract to supply Sambo's restaurant chain, in 1969 - later
supplies McDonald's, Burger King and Wendy's, bids $941 million for Holly
Farms Foods in 1988 to enlarge capacity for supplying restaurants,
institutions and overseas markets - challenged by ConAgra bid of $995
million)...

Trader Lewis L. Glucksman joins Lehman Brothers' investment house to
oversee specialized financing of commercial paper (after Robert Lehman
dies in 1969, becomes managerial director with house reorganization in
1973 - Peter Peterson chairman, after power struggle forces Peterson out
in 1983, resigns after takeover by American Express' Shearson brokerage
firm in 1984)... When RCA refuses to make house brand TV sets, Sears
contracts with Sanyo, later Toshiba (sells 6.5 million sets by 197)...
Sheraton chain opens pioneering hotel on Hawaii's Maui, lures tourists
from Oahu... Tom Moyer opens drive-in theater in Oregon, 11th largest by

1988 with 335 screens at 90 sites as Luxury Theatres (is target in 1988 for acquisition by United Artists theater circuit with 2,048 screens, U.S.' largest, at 485 locations in 34 states, Puerto Rico and Hong Kong)... Fred Borch becomes CEO of General Electric (-1972, creates strategic business units, forms headquarters staff services of finance, strategic planning, technology, and legal and government with separate staff services for operating units, is followed in 1972-80 by Reginald Jones to implement Borch's strategic planning system and to create a sector organizational structure, each a macro-business or industry area, for strategic business units)... Mellow Truck Express starts business near Portland, OR (as a result of 1980 truck deregulation closes 1988)... Jean Nidetchs hold first Weight Watchers seminar (sells business to H.J. Heinz in 1978).

1964

General Events

President Johnson in State-of-the-Union message to Congress declares (January 8) national "war on poverty"... Federal Trade Commission gives (January 11) proof that cigarette smoking causes lung disease (requires warning of hazards on all cigarette packages in 1965, forces cigarette firms to stop advertising on TV and radio in 1971)... President Johnson signs (February 26) tax bill with $11.5 billion in cuts... Anti-Poverty Bill provides (July 23) $947 million to combat illiteracy, unemployment and other conditions of needy... Congress passes (August 7) Gulf of Tonkin Resolution, gives President Johnson power to repel armed attacks against U.S. forces in Viet-Nam... England's Beatles invade U.S., followed by Rolling Stones... U.S., Japan are linked by underwater communications cable...

Federal Small Business Administration forms SCORE, Service Corps of Retired Executives, to advise entrepreneurs on starting and operating new businesses... Civil Rights Act forbids sex discrimination in workplace (grants enforcement powers to Equal Opportunity Commission in 1972, hears 24,300 complaints in 1973-74 fiscal year)... Verrazano Narrows Bridge, world's longest suspension span, opens for traffic in New York Harbor... Some 72,970,000 people work in civilian labor force, unemployment over 4 million... Avant-garde designer Rudi Gernreich, popularized mini-skirt, introduces monokini swimsuit for women (outrages Kremlin, Vatican)...

Roger Hermanson: <u>Accounting</u> <u>for</u> <u>Human</u> <u>Assets</u> (follows 1961 article of Theodore Schultz on "Investment in Human Capital" to pioneer human resource accounting)... <u>Fortune</u>: "The Nationalization of U.S. Science" (reports government funds 2/3 of U.S. research and development)... Ad Hoc Committee: <u>The</u> <u>Triple</u> <u>Revolution</u> (warns President Johnson on dangers in evolutions of cybernetics, weapons, human rights)... American University of Washington, DC creates Center for Technology Administration to improve operations of "think tanks"... Some .9% of U.S. Army personnel are women, 2.4% in 1973, 6.7% in 1977, and some 10% in early 1980s... Union of Air Line Pilots Assn. forms (operates by airline locals until 1984 when various airlines start winning contract concessions)... Lotfi Zadeh, NYC, conceives Fuzzy Logic (replaces Aristolelian thought of distinct categories of clear and sharp boundaries with degrees in sets of information, helps form North American Fuzzy Information Processing Society in 1982)... Jerry Wurf becomes president of American Federation of State, County and Municipal Employees (expands membership five-fold to some million members as largest union of public employees)... Economic Opportunity Act is passed to help "permanent poor" with education, job training and nutrition (provides Federal funds for such community action groups as Job Corps and Vista - a domestic Peace Corps, funds Food Stamp Program - 22 million users in 1984 for $12.4 billion)... President Johnson signs bill to authorize study of peacetime uses of nuclear explosives (in period 1965-83 tests over 70 atomic explosive devices to escavate underground cavities, generate seizmic waves, etc.)... After 20 years "Bracero" program, legally permits Mexican workers to enter U.S. for temporary employment, ends...

Albert Shanker becomes president of United Federation of Teachers (after launching pioneering 2-week strike by NYC teachers in 1967 is jailed 15 days for violating state law on strikes by public employees, is jailed 15 days in 1968 with another strike to oppose City's proposed school decentralization)... E. Digby Baltzell: Protestant Establishment: Aristocracy and Caste in America (coins WASP for White Anglo-Saxon Protestant)... California Governor Pat Brown asks State's aerospace firms to use new method of systems analysis in resolving such problems as transportation, waste management, poverty, crime and unemployment.

Business Events

Fairchild Semiconductor drops prices to stimulate commercial use of integrated circuits... Whiskey-a-Go-Go, U.S.' "first" disco, opens in Los Angeles on Sunset Strip (uses go-go girls to set frenzied tempo for dancing Watusi, Frug, Monkey, Funky Chicken, and other Twist variations)... Sarah Lee bakery is first to operate fully automated factory, uses computer to process pastries from baking to freezing and packaging... In first computer crime, Texas programmer steals $5 million of computer software from employer... San Francisco's Condor Club pioneers topless entertainment with bare-breasted dancer Carol Doda...

U.S.' machine-tool industry exports 23% of world market, about 4% in 1986 while Japanese imports go from 4% to 47%)... By chance Boston lawyer Bob Woolf represents Red Sox pitcher involved in car accident (by 1987 becomes agent to negotiate over 2,000 contracts for top athletes)... With borrowed funds Robert T. Shaw starts American Securities Corp., KY, to sell life insurance (merges with others to form American Pyramid Companies, acquires ICH as holding company in 1975 build business with leveraged buyouts -assets of $800 million in 1987)... Arby's roast beef chain, 182 places by 1987 with sales over $1 billion - 200 new franchises in 1987 including Japan and Canada, opens in Youngstown, OH...

Charles King starts King World to syndicate TV reruns (discovers new market with Merv Griffin's "Wheel of Fortune" and "Jeopardy" shows in 1975, pioneers first-run syndicated shows, such as "Oprah Winfrey Show," in mid-1980s)... Universal movies pioneers new tourist business by allowing visitors, some 30,000/day, to see studio's 500 sets, facilities and elaborate exhibits (starts $120 million expansion of Universal Studio tour in 1987 and builds new attraction near Florida's Disney World)... Ford sells sporty Mustang car for $2,368, sells record 418,000 in first year (allows Lee Iacocca to become unofficial president until designated 1970)... Lockheed Aircraft develops jet capable of flying 2,000 mph... U.S. Golf Association and ABC sign TV contract... Freedom National Bank opens in Harlem, NY, to make loans to minorities unable to borrow money from major banks (after surviving near bankruptcy in 1974 evolves to become City's most profitable by 1981 in achieving business goals before social goals)... Mustang Ranch opens outside Reno as brothel, legalized by 1971 Nevada law (evolves as U.S.' largest such business before acquisition in 1985 by California real estate firm for $18 million, seeks approval in 1988 for stock issue)... John F. Mee: "Ideational Item: Matrix Organization," Business Horizons (pioneers description of new organizational structure)...

With funds from such companies as IBM and AT&T, Bob Schwartz, former journalist with Time, starts School for Entrepreneurs (is established in 1977 to provide students with "a model of an entrepreneur whose goals are more related to the love-image of this generation than to the mechanical, money-oriented goals of the older generation")... Diner's Club credit card business starts vacation savings club (evolves with membership of some 25,000 by 1980s)... Newsweek: "The American Invasion of Australia" (reports on U.S. investments of some $4 million/week)... Hasboro introduces G.I. Joe toy soldier, total sales of $1.2 billion by 1989 ("furloughes" toy in 1978 after opposition to war toys)... Eastman Kodak designs Industrial Relations Information Systems, pioneering computer program for personnel administration (follows U.S. Army's computer program for military occupational specialties and programs in 1950s by Ford, IBM, Exxon and General Electric for personnel data files)...

Robert Blake, others: "Breakthrough in Organizational Development," Harvard Business Review (describes managerial grid approach to change organizational behavior)... First movie specifically made for TV is produced... Peter Drucker: Managing for Results: Economic Tasks and Risk-Taking Decisions... AT&T demonstrates Picturephone at New York World's Fair (proves too expensive for general public - idea used by businesses for video conferences in 1980s)... Coachman Industries is started, IN, to make recreational vehicles (evolves as industry's 2nd largest by 1984)... Swiss-born Fred J. Hayman, former food and beverage manager at Beverly Hilton hotel, is hired to run Giorgio's on Rodeo Drive in Beverly Hills (transforms retail business into exclusive boutique for rich and famous, introduces special fragrance for $150/ounce in 1981, ups sales from $30 million in 1983 to over $100 million in 1985)...

Harry Patten, partner start business selling rural land to big-city folks in Vermont (open first regional office in Maine in 1982 to operate in 15 states by 1956 as largest gainer on NYSE)... IBM introduces Magnetic Tape Selectric Typewriter, pioneers concept of word processor in office automation... Chris Argyris: Integrating the Individual and the Organization... West German firm of Robert Bosch introduces portable TV camera to U.S. market, followed in 1972 by electronic camera... The Journal of Marketing Research is issued... Aramis introduces pioneering male fragrance, line of male cosmetics by Roy, Linda Silver in 1983... Studebaker-Packard stops building cars in U.S... Chemist Robert S. Aries is ordered by federal judge to pay damages to R&H chemical business after stealing their oil additive formula and fleeing to Europe (is viewed as dean of trade-secret thieves for piracy from Merck & Co., Sprague Electric and illegal use of trademarks of British, French firms)... After starting in business as independent oil man in 1955 with $1,300 T. Boone Pickens forms Mesa Petroleum to consolidate operations (becomes best-paid U.S. executive in 1980 with salary and stock options of $7.86 million, starts raiding petroleum companies with inept management and undervalued assets by attacking Cities Services in 1982 - pockets $31.5 million in skirmish after City Services is acquired by Occidental Petroleum, after spending $1 billion and failing to find oil and gas in Gulf of Mexico changes strategy in 1983 to wildcat on Wall Street, battles for control of Gulf Oil in 1983 with $1.3 billion in credits - nets $760 million when Gulf is purchased by Chevron in biggest U.S. merger of $13.2 billion, attacks Phillips Petroleum in 1984 - aborts raid after buy-out by Phillips for profit of $89 million after forcing arbitragers to lose millions on lower price, fails in raid on Unocal, U.S.' 14th largest oil enterprise, in 1985, is attacked in 1986 for saddling oil firms with higher debts as major oil firms convert some $36.6 billion in equity to debt after 1981)... Col. Harlan Sanders sells Kentucky Fried Chicken business to Jack Massey, venture capitalist, and John Y. Brown for $2 million and life-time salary (expand outlets from 600 to around 3,570 by 1971, sales of some $700 million, when acquired by Heublein for some $250 million to open first Western fast-food restaurant in China in 1988)...

General Foods introduces freeze-dried instant coffee Maxim, pioneered in West Germany by Nestle before invading U.S. market later with Taster's Choice... Former door-to-door salesman, William Penn Patrick starts Holiday Magic, pioneering pyramid marketing venture, to sell perfume distributorships for line of fruit-scented cosmetics (becomes multi-millionaire with complex web of franchises, 400 subsidiaries and Leadership Dynamics Institute, pyramid promoter Glenn Turner a student, before being killed in 1973 plane crash)... At urging of Ford Foundation, Monsanto installs first artificial grass surface for sports at Providence's Moses Brown School, RI (installs Astroturf in Houston Astrodome in 1965-66, supplies by 1985 some 60% of world's synthetic turf fields with some 250 installations in U.S., 550 others in world)...

NBA establishes pension plan for players... High-school graduate and machinist Stanford R. Ovshinsky, self-educated scientist and son of Lithuanian-born scrap dealer, starts Energy Conversion Devices in Troy, MI, to transform amorphous silicon materials into oronic devices to store information or energy and convert light and heat into electricity (is funded by United Nuclear in 1976-77, Atlantic Richfield 1979-83, Standard Oil 1981-83, and American Natural Resources 1982-85 to operate with 11 plants and 400 employees in 1984, although acquiring 226 U.S. patents, including key one for erasable optical memories, records losses for 20 years by 1986, accepts financing in 1987 from entrepreneur William Manning who institutes financial discipline with control of business)...

IBM introduces System/360 family of main frame computers, quickly wins 70% of market... While Doug Tompkins starts North Face mountaineering store in San Francisco (sells in 1969 for $50,000 - $40 million business by 1988), wife Susie starts home dress business with 4 lines for young women, evolves as Espirit by 1988, sales of $1.6 billion in 25 countries from sloppy clothes lifestyle, as couple quarrel over control and direction (start Espirit Kids, 16 stores by 1987, to sell funky clothes for children)... David Packard, co-founder of Hewlett-Packard electronics with $595, starts foundation, assets of $145 million in 1987, to support scientific and health research and social programs... After leaving father's candy business in 1932 to build British candy enterprise, Forrest Mars, Sr., takes over father's U.S. firm, 2nd largest in U.S. market, 37%, with sales of $7,360 million by 1988 from candy, pet food,

food and electronics to battle Hershey, 44% share with buy of Cadbury Schweppes' U.S. division in 1988, Nestle and Rountree, each with some 25%.

1965

General Events

President Johnson launches (January 4) crusade for "Great Society" in State-of-Union Message to Congress... U.S. Marines land (March 8) in Vietnam... NASA launches Early Bird, first commercial satellite in space (transmits first live trans-oceanic telecasts of Communications Satellite Corp.)... Race riot erupts (August 11-16) in Watts district of Los Angeles (results in 34 killed, thousands arrested and damages of some $40 million)... Department of Housing and Urban Development is created (September 9), headed by Robert C. Weaver as first black Cabinet Member... Anti-pollution bill requires (October 1) emision standards for new cars, trucks... Indonesia seizes rubber plantations of U.S. firms...

Syria nationalizes 2 U.S. oil companies... U.S. Supreme Court rules a business can close to avoid unionism... U.S. ends economic aid to Taiwan (drops special trading privileges, along with Singapore, Hong Kong, and South Korea, in 1988 as Four Tigers have net trade balance with U.S.)... U.S. bans (December) oil sales to Rhodesia... California is most populated state... Of U.S., Britain, West Germany, France and Japan, U.S.' share of research and development is 69%, drops to 55% by 1985... Dartmouth Professor John Kemeny designs BASIC computer program for non-computer professionals... Some 30 million people in Northeast are caught in electrical brown-out when simple relay device malfunctions... Edward Schein, Warren Bennis: Personal and Organizational Change Through Group Methods: The Laboratory Approach...

Monsanto subsidiary's Nutrasweet discovers artificial sweetener Aspartame by accident, approved for use in carbonated beverages in 1983 (introduces Simplesse in 1988 as pioneering fat-substitute)... Moses Rischim: The American Gospel of Success... U.S. employment is some 75 million, 65 million in 1957 (while overall union membership drops in same period, shows rise of James Hoffa's Teamsters from 1.6 million to 1.76 million with credo of "If it breathes, organize it")... Ghirardelli Square is renovated in San Francisco (pioneers growth of charming urban shopping-and-eating malls or markets)... Commerce Department reports average price of new house is about $20,000, $42,600 in 1975 and $101,000 in 1984...

National Outdoor Leadership School opens to develop personal skills for surviving in wilderness (evolves to use approach in management development programs)... Philadelphia Board of Education and teachers' union sign labor contract... Journal of Applied Behavioral Science is issued... Congress passes Medicare and Medicaid programs for elderly and poor... George Stigler, president of American Economic Association, declares economists had developed all of major theories and concepts needed to ensure stable prices and full employment... Water Quality Act is passed... Federal Reserve System tightens credits to counter inflationary effects of rising federal deficit created by wars on domestic poverty and communism in Vietnam... Highway Beautification Act mandates removal of all billboards within 650 feet of federal highways (results in growth of billboard sales from $150 million in 1966 to 1983 mark over $1 billion)... Ralph Nader: Unsafe at Any Speed (criticizes automobile industry for stressing style, horsepower and comfort over safety, attacks General Motors for unsafe Corvair car, receives recognition in 1966 after revelation of GM's surveillance and harrassment - apology to Senate Sub-Committee by GM's president, inspires passage of 1966 National Traffic and Motor Vehicles Safety Act)... In this time Air Force produces film "Modern Manufacturing: A Command Performance" (promotes use of numerically controlled machine tools)... Defense Department's Planning-Programming-Budgeting System is adopted throughout Federal Government by Presidential order... A.W. Marshall: Costs/Benefit Analysis in Health... President Johnson asks businesses to limit direct investments abroad, rejected by most... U.S. Supreme Court rules employers can use lockouts as bargaining pressure... Justice Department indicts 7 oil companies for price fixing... U.S. Supreme Court rules unions are subject to anti-trust laws when conspiring with company to force rival out of business... Some unions encourage members to retire at 62 or before so younger workers can have jobs...

Government's 9-year-old anti-trust suit against General Motors for monopolizing bus manufacturing business is settled out of court (allows GM to retain bus business)... U.S. unions send contract negotiators to help labor organizations overseas... Executive Order 11246, amended by Executive Order 11375 later, bans discrimination on race, color, religion, sex or national origin in government contracts (requires affirmative action plans)... International Executive Service Corps is formed, CT, as non-profit group to send volunteers, most retired business executives, to Third World, 84 countries by 1989, to help middle class improve their business practices.

Business Events

La Costa, plush hotel and spa for wealthy dieters, opens, CA... IBM's share of computer market is 65.3% - 74.5% in 1959, with Sperry-Rand at 12.1% - 17.8% in 1959, Control Data 5.4%, Honeywell 3.8% - 4.2% in 1959, Burroughs 3.5% - 4.2% in 1959, General Electric 3.4%, RCA 2.9% - 1.4% in 1959... International King's Table business organizes in Eugene, OR (operates 89 self-service buffet restaurants in 9 Western states by 1988, volume of some $90 million when sold to Horn & Hardart Co.)... Electronic data interchange to link firms, customers and suppliers is developed (-1969)... Lew Wasserman, head of Music Corporation of America, is required by Government to sever movie production and talent agency interests (drops agency business to diversify into publishing, foreign distribution of movies, and audio-visual home entertainment)... Fred Segal opens "first" U.S. jeans-only store to demonstrate utilitarian item can be fashionable (later starts trendy stores with unusual stylish wares in Los Angeles with slogan "Look, See, Feel, Be, Love, All" and opens Santa Monica shopping mall in 1985 as warren of sophisticated specialty boutique stores and restaurants with spacious children's playground)...

French-born Socialist Jean Riboud becomes chairman of Schlumberger, world's premier oil-services company, TX (increases revenues 19-fold to $6.4 billion and profits 44-fold to some $1.2 billion in 1980s, builds world's largest oil-field service business by 1980s, devotion to technology and strict management controls, acquires Fairchild Camera and Instrument in 1979 to lose millions, acquires oil-driller SEDCO in 1984 for $1 billion - loses with drop in crude oil prices, retires with cancer in 1985, is replaced by designated successor Michel Vailaud, in 1986, after bitter family fight, is replaced by American D.E. Baird, first non-French CEO, as French family re-asserts control, sells Fairchild in 1987 to stem losses)... Quick Shop MiniMart chain opens, 52 franchises by 1985... H.I. Ansoff: Corporate Strategy: An Analysis Approach to Growth and Expansion (describes strategy as determined by product/market scope, growth factor, competitive advantage and synergy)... After developing portable pump for home hydrotherapy in late 1950s to provide relief for family member suffering arthritis, Roy Jacussi invents first totally self-contained whirlpool bath in this time for family business, known for agricultural pumps, founded in 1915 (sells first in 1968 to herald elegant bathrooms of 1980s, is sold in 1979 to Kidde, Inc., for $70 million)... Max Scherr publishes Berkeley Barb as underground newspaper (proselytizes for revolution, drugs and "free" sex, reaches circulation high of 90,000 in 1969 before closing in 1980, achieves profits by paying low wages and selling sexually explicit ads by massage parlors and those seeking sexual adventures)... Helen Gurley Brown is editor of staid Cosmopolitan (transforms magazine for the new woman, increases circulation from 800,000 to nearly 3 million)... Stephanie Kwolek, junior DuPont research scientist, develops solvent to make Kevlar, perhaps most important fiber since nylon, to combine lightness and strength... Most NYC major newspapers are hit by 3-week strike...

Henry J. Kaiser is first industrialist to receive AFL-CIO Murray Green Award... Robert N. Anthony: Planning and Control Systems: A Framework for Analysis (views strategic planning as complex activity in identifying direction, monitoring progress, allocating resources and developing inter-institutional relationships)... George Odiorne: Management by Objectives... Rockefeller's Mauna Kea beach resort opens on Big Island (heralds growth of Hawaii's tourist industry)... Howard M. Garfinkle starts nationally known Five-Star Basketball Summer Camp for budding players, first competitor in 1977... The Christian Science Monitor: "Automation Goes to Sea"... Space General Corp. makes systems study on prevention of crimes for State of California... Bonwit Teller opens boutique shop to feature clothing designed for men by Pierre Cardin...

AT&T starts field experiments in job enrichment, 19 by 1968... Boeing starts development of 747 plane with investment of $500 million from Pan Am (-1970)... As outgrowth of hobby, Gene Milstein starts business selling wild flower seeds, CO (introduces seeds for houseplants and herbs in 1971, kits for edible sprouts in 1978 and plastic bags in 1980 with seeds and growing mixtures, operates by 1980s as international business of Apple Seed Co. with 15 full-time and 15 part-time employees)... Dow Jones Industrial Average passes 900 mark... First permanent-press shirts appear... Fisher-Price pre-tests toys for youngsters... New York Stock Exchange plans to use computer service in handling bookkeeping chores for member firms... Sears markets battery-powered vacuum cleaner... Pick-up camper is newest recreational vehicle... Corning introduces self-darkening sunglasses, first commercial use of photochromic glass... Flea market for bargain hunters opens, NYC... B.F. Goodrich introduces new vinyl siding for buildings... Olivetti Underwood introduces world's first desk-top computer, priced at $3,200...

State Mutual of America offers non-smokers lower life insurance rates... Keydata Corp. introduces computer time sharing, first U.S. business information utility to operate via private telephone lines... Borden

Foods sells disposable diapers in supermarkets... Martin Lerner starts Institute of Computer Technology to train computer operators (is forced by fierce competition to sell to Sylvania in 1970, with lists of high school seniors acquired as prospects for institute starts American Corp. to provide businesses with lists of high-school students, eventually 2.5 million names, and college students, eventually 3.5 million, to net $1.3 million on sales of $4.3 million in fiscal 1986)... General Electric experiments in this time with participative management (tries work teams at 12 plants with mixed results)... After 3 years of construction Judge Roy Hofheinz opens Houston's Astrodome, world's largest air-conditioned arena (installs Astroturf when grass dies, is acquired in 1979 by Houston Sports Association to remodel for $46 million - $14.4 million more than original cost, generates up to $1 billion for local economy by 1985)...

Charles G. Bluhdorn, after creating Gulf & Western in 1958 to build auto parts distribution network in Southeast U.S., starts diversification strategy with acquisition of New Jersey Zinc (adds other firms, such as Paramount Pictures, South Puerto Rico Sugar, Simon & Schuster, Madison Square Garden, Consolidated Cigar, Desilu Productions, and Armour Packing, to conglomerate, 61st largest industrial corporation in 1982 with sales of $5.3 billion from industrial products group, systems group, precision engineering group, metal forming group, auto parts group, leisure activity group with Paramount Pictures, natural resources group, and food products group)... With loan of $1,000, Fred De Luca, age 17, opens first Subway Sandwiches & Salads near Milford, CT (with 1988 sales of some $480 million plans 2,900 outlets for 1989)... To keep firm private after death, Sam Johnson, head of 1886 $2 billion wax business, begins planning to transfer estate to heirs by forming free-standing firms that could be sold off to avoid dissolving original business (on advise of Booz Allen & Hamilton consultants in 1969 buys 15 recreational equipment makers in mid-1970s, divests Johnson Diversified in 1985 and Johnson Worldwide Associates in 1987).

1966

General Events

Black activist Maulana Karenga launches Kwanzaa, based on African traditional harvest festival, as 7-day event on December 26th as alternative to commercialization of Christianity... NYC's bus and transit system is crippled (January 1-13) by strike of Transport Workers Union (leads to jailing of union leader Michael Quill and 15% hike in wages)... Clean Water Restoration Act is signed (February 23)... ICC approves (April 27) merger of rival Pennsylvania, New York Central railroads to form one of 10 largest nonfinancial corporations with assets of $4 billion (declares bankruptcy in 1970 after battle by lines for top spot, gets government subsidy in 1971 to keep running, becomes part of government's Conrail system in 1976)... U.S. Treasury stops (August 10) printing $2 bills... L.B.J. signs (September 9) car safety bill (creates National Traffic Safety Agency)... Love Pagent Rally is held (October 6) near Golden Gate Park, San Francisco... Department of Transportation is created (October 15)...

Congress passes (October 20) legislation to rebuild urban areas with $925 million... Truth-in-Packaging bill is signed (November 3), requires food labeling to identify contents...

U.S. reports Viet Nam War costs $2 billion/month... First Federal case on computers indicts computer programmer for using bank computer to ignore his overdrafts... Postal Services terminates Postal Savings program... California is first State to make LSD drug illegal... _Time_: "The Futurists: Looking Toward A.D. 2000"... Richard Greenblatt, MIT student, designs pioneering computer chess program (evolves to where super computers in 1985 can hold their own against all but international grand masters)... Daniel Katz, Robert L. Kahn: _The Social Psychology of Organizations_ (studies organization as a system)... _Newsweek_: "The Story of Pop" (reports new art movement of Andy Warhol, Roy Lichtenstein and others whose work of 1960 increases in value from $150-500 to $500-8,000 in 1966)... Betty Friedan, others with support of United Auto Workers and Communications Union form National Organization for Women... All California cars are required by State law to have exhaust control devices... Marvin Miller is first executive director of Major League Players Association, average salary rises from $19,000 in 1967 to $29,303 in 1970, to $44,676 in 1975, $143,756 in 1980, $371,571 in 1985 and $485,000 in 1989...

Walter A. Weisskopf, others: _Looking Forward: The Abundant Society_... U.S. Supreme Court rules Government cannot suppress a book as obscene if it has merit as literature... Motor Vehicles Safety Act regulates emission controls, etc... Uniform Time Act prevents communities in setting their own local hours (establishes regular daylight-savings time period)... _Business Week_: "Brain Drain Starts to Hurt" (reports on impact of U.S. recruiting scientists in Britain, Europe)... Cold War GI Bill of Rights grants veterans special benefits in education, housing, health and jobs... Nationwide protests against War in Vietnam appear in San Francisco, Chicago, Boston, Philadelphia and Washington... Blacks riot in Chicago, Baltimore, San Francisco, Cleveland, Omaha, Brooklyn, Jacksonville, Atlanta... Congress passes legislation to finance urban redevelopment... Minimum wage is raised from $1.25/hour to $1.40 by 1967 and $1.60 by 1968... U.S. Supreme Court rules employer can sue a union for libel in organizing drive... Senate committee investigates industrial espionage... Women appear in mini-skirts and dresses (fails to catch on in 1987-88 revival), hip-huggers and bellbottom pants... Massachusetts passes law to require full disclosure of interest charges on all installment credit agreements... U.S. prime interest rate rises to 6%... Airline strike, stopping service on 60% of airlines, is settled after 5 weeks... Housewives in various cities boycott many supermarkets to protest high prices of food.

Business Events

NYC's _Herald Tribune_, founded 1841 by Horace Greely, _Journal American_ and _World Telegram_ merge... General Motors recalls 1.5 million Chevrolets to correct throttle defects.. Boston Celtics name Bill Russell coach of basketball team, first black in position in professional sports... Texas Instruments introduces first hand-held calculator (instead of visual display prints results)... Walt Disney dies (results in stagnation of Walt Disney Co., in 1984, after 3 years of declining profits and stock battles by raiders, is revived by Michael D. Eisner in 1987 with strategy to reduce dependence on theme parks, hotels and real estate by reviving movie and TV business, developing new income from resources, such as catalog and Disney Store chain in 1987 and searching for new assets, licenses 14,000 products to some 3,000 firms for $97.3 million by

1988)... Marriott business, in-flight food services, restaurants, and hotels, acquires Big Boy restaurants with 23 outlets in Southern California and 500 franchises nationwide (operates some 1,000 eateries by 1972)... National Commission on Technology, Automation and Economic Progress praises machine tool automation as "probably the most significant development in manufacturing since the introduction of the moving assembly line"... American Express issues Gold Card as premium credit card, copied by Visa and MasterCard in 1982 (introduces American Express Platinum Card in 1984 with annual fee of $250 - some 60,000 users by 1985)... 47 St. Photo opens as camera discount business - by 1980s perhaps NYC's most successful gray-market retailer (is upheld as legal by U.S. Supreme Court in 1988)... Leaving family wine business Robert Mondavi starts own winery, CA (pioneers making quality wine in U.S)...

Caesar's Palace opens in Las Vegas (starts program of live sporting events in 1969 to promote casino)... Warren G. Bennis: "Organizational Revitalization," California Management Review (predicts new management structure to replace traditional bureaucratic organization)... Andy Warhol: "The Chelsea Girls" (promotes underground film movement)... R.G. Barry Corp., assisted by University of Michigan's Institute for Social Research, prepares pioneering human resource accounting system to record firm's investment in human resources on current cost basis (-1968 when operational)... C.C. Furnas: "The Next Hundred Years - 30 Years Later," (reviews failures to American Petroleum Institute on forecasts made in his 1935 publication)... At meeting of American Society for Quality Control, quality guru Dr. Joseph M. Juran attacks new trend of Zero Defects, used by 7,500-12,000 firms since 1964... Stephan Vazzano of Connecticut's Savoy Laundry is first employer jailed for failing to bargain "in good faith" with union... National Science Foundation reports steel firms spend $ .60/$100 of sales on research and development...

Keith Davis, Robert Blomstrom: Business and Its Environment, becomes leading text in new field... For first time Dow Jones Industrial Average tops 1000 mark (closes over 1,000 for first time in 1972)... After working as analyst at TWA and Eastern Airlines, Frank Lorenzo, born to Spanish emigrants in 1940, and Robert Carney start airline financial advisory business (evolves as Jet Capital by 1969 to lease airplanes, acquires failing airline, known later as Texas International, in 1972 to revise business with restructured debt and low fares)...

Law graduate Ivan F. Boesky joins New York brokerage firm (by 1972 operates arbitrage department of Wall Street's Edwards & Hanly, starts pioneering independent brokerage firm devoted exclusively to art of arbitrage with $700,000 in 1975 to compete with investment banks, nets some $7 million in 1977 in first big coup with takeover of Babcock & Wilcox - worth $94 million in 1979, after losing some $10.5 million in 1983 earns estimated $50 million in 1984 Texaco takeover of Getty Oil and $55 million on Chevron's purchase of Gulf while dropping $40 million when Phillips Petroleum fends off raider T. Boone Pickens, startles financial world in 1986 by raising pool of some $900 million to play arbitrage game, is banned from trading and fined $100 million in 1986 by SEC in largest insider trading settlement, receives 3-year jail sentence)... CBS, National Football League sign 2-year $18.8 million contract to put games on first prime-time TV... U.S. Steel raises prices with Government approval... Snack foods are 11th most profitable items carried by supermarkets... After producing 2 successful movies for TV, Universal

Studios enters new market on full-time basis... American Machine and Foundry creates robot food handler (tests device at Minneapolis fast-food drive-in)... LaBanque Continentale opens, NYC, for depositors with minimum balance of $25,000... Alaskan supermarket owner builds first commercial greenhouse to grow vegetables by artificial light, used in 1980s by clandestine marijuana growers... Maxwell's Plum, flamboyant restaurant and singles bar, opens, NYC (closes 1988)... After spotting site by chance, pilot Dan Laughlin buys rundown motel and saloon with gambling equipment on Cclorado River, NV, for $225,000, named Laughlin in 1968 (is site of Circus Circus hotel-casino of Las Vegas, Reno in 1987 - 9 resorts with 4,118 rooms by 1989 as new mecca for gamblers from Southern California)... Montgomery Ward Insurance Co. sells life insurance by direct mail, IL...

Bank of America extends credit-card business nationwide... Ford plans to develop electric car for testing in 1967 and manufacturing in 1971... Cheetah, mass-entertainment nightclub for 18-25 group, opens in Chicago to provide continuous music, movies and color TV... RCA acquires Hertz rental-car business (is acquired by United Airlines in 1985 and sold 1987)... DuPont enters prescription market with drug to prevent Asian flu... Revlon introduces Braggi Collection of grooming aids for men... Virgil Conrad obtains Pizza Hut franchise for Corpus Christi, TX, (develops chain of 56 in 1970s with 5 Orange Julius outlets, 1 TraveLodge and 25 Church's Fried Chicken restaurants)... NFL, American Football League merge to end market battle in professional football...

B. Dalton Bookseller, U.S.' first major national bookstore chain of 777 outlets, is started (is sold by Dayton-Hudson retailers to Barnes & Noble Bookstores in 1986 to pass Waldenbooks, K mart subsidiary with 1,100 stores, as U.S.' largest retailer of books)... After founding Regal drugstore chain in 1947, Bernard Shulman retires as CEO (is succeeded by Sidney Dworkin - by 1983 Revco U.S.' largest drugstore chain with nearly 1,700 stores and sales shy of $2 billion, loses on vitamin scandal in 1983, goes private in leveraged buyout in 1986, after alleged nepotism and mismangement of 2,000 stores is reorganized under Bankruptcy Code in 1988).

1967

General Events

In most extensive rail strike in U.S. history, some 600,000 railroad employees, 95% of industry, are idled by strike of International Association of Machinists... Racial rioting breaks out (July 23-30) in Detroit, causing damages of $250-400 million in worst violence of year... Thurgood Marshall is (August 30) first black Justice on Supreme Court... Air Quality Act allots (November 14) $428 million to curb pollution... President Johnson creates (November 20) National Commission on Product Safety... FCC orders TV, radio stations to air health warnings when advertising cigarettes... UAW, Ford sign contract after 46-day strike... Violence by blacks is seen in 67 major cities... Youthful crowds in Haight-Ashbury area of San Francisco celebrate Summer of Love... Life: "The Other Culture" (reports on worldwide underground art movement with orgiastic happenings, brutalities, and vandalism)... Sport of sailboarding is started when Cole Schweitzer, surfer and computer engineer, and Jim Drake, sailor and aeronautical engineer, put a sail on a surf board, CA... American Academy of Arts and Sciences: Toward the Year 2000... Age Discrimination in Employment Act prohibits discrimination in employment for ages between 40-65... Corporation for Public Broadcasting is created as non-profit organization to supervise non-commercial radio and television stations (starts programming in 1969)... Yankelovich, Skelly and White interview 600 representative Americans to identify 35 social trends... Dutch-born Wilem J. Kolff, inventor of first successful kidney-dialysis machine in 1945, is hired by University of Utah to develop center for biomedical engineering (-1986, spawns biomedical startups of Motion Control in 1974 to make "Utah Arm" prosthesis, Symbion formed with Robert K. Jarvik in 1976 to develop artificial heart and ear, Bunnel in 1980 to make respirators for infants, Deseret Research in 1983 for biomedical engineering and testing, Life Extenders, developers of artificial bladder and sphinchter, in 1983, and Vascular International in 1983 to make synthetic blood vessels)... David Rockefeller, 150 business leaders create Business Committee for the Arts as non-profit organization to support arts...

Saturday Review: "Can We Stay Prosperous?" (warns roots of affluence may weaken)... Time: "Violence in America"... NHL Players' Association forms as first hockey union... Newsweek: "Anything Goes: Taboos in Twilight" (reports explosion of sexual permissiveness in arts and society to outrage thousands of readers)... John Kenneth Galbraith: The New Industrial State... Some 50,000 demonstrators storm the Pentagon to protest Vietnam War... Blacks, Carl Stokes and Richard Hatcher, become mayors of Cleveland, Gary... Stanford University biochemists produce first synthetic DNA... Herman Kahn, Anthony J. Wiener: The Year 2000...

Federal Women's Program is started to improve status of women in Federal employment... Lewis Mumford: The Myth of the Machine, Volume II in 1970... AFL-CIO creates Council of Professional, Scientific and Cultural Employees to organize white-collar workers... James D. Thompson: Organizations in Action... National Training Laboratories gives first non-degree training program in Organization Development... Chicago Board of Education, American Federation of Teachers sign contract to cover some 23,000 teachers.

Business Events

With $300 million from sale of TWA Howard Hughes starts buying Las Vegas gambling properties, 6 plus Harolds Club in Reno before secret flight in 1970 (although blocked by monopoly charges in buying more hotels during stay acquires TV station, airport, real estate on strip, mining claims, and some 30,000 acres of desert near Las Vegas)... Universal Products, CA, starts mail-order business to sell sex materials... Ford Motor Co. recalls 217,000 cars to check brakes, steering... General Electric recalls 90,000 TV sets for possible radiation leaks... General Motors recalls 1.1 million Chevrolets for faulty steering... Ford recalls all 1967 Mustangs... El Paso Natural Gas, NM, detonates world's first commercial nuclear blast... Computer World is new field's first publication... AT&T introduces "800" toll-free number for consumer services (produces revenues of $4.5 billion in 1968 - fastest growing sector of long-distance market)... Irvin Feld, concert promoter and owner of record-store chain, and several partners buys Ringling Brothers and Barnum & Bailey Circus from Ringling heirs for $8 million (sells to toy maker Mattel for $50 million in 1971 - continues management, buys business back in 1982 for $22.8 million, is followed by son Kenneth in 1984 who doubles revenues to $250 million by 1987 from circus, Las Vegas illusionists Siegfried and Roy, "Disney on Ice "shows," home video cassettes, "food and taste" festivals, and real estate ventures, plans world tour for circus in 1989)... McDonald's fast-food restaurant chain expands to Canada, Puerto Rico (forms international division in 1969, opens in Japan, West Germany and Australia in 1971, Spain, Denmark and Philippines in 1981 - 31 countries by 1983, Andorra, Finland and Taiwan in 1984 - 41 countries by 1985, opens in Argentina, Aruba, Cuba and Turkey in 1986, and in Belgrade in 1988 - first fast-food outlet in East Europe)... Robert Moog devises electronic music synthesizer, forced to sell business in 1969 after management, marketing problems...

James M. Roche, CEO of General Motors, is highest paid executive in U.S. industry with salary of $200,000... A diamond per D-flawless carat sells for $1,250, $7,000 in 1976, $62,000 in 1980, $15,000 in 1982 and $17,000 in 1988... Publisher's Clearing House starts annual sweepstakes contest (awards prizes of $10 million in 1986 and $20 million in 1987)... First Consumer-Electronics Show is held... Blacks are seen in 5% of all TV ads, 13% in 1976... World Future Society issues The Futurist magazine... George Champion: "Creative Competition," Harvard Business Review (reports on use of private business to provide governmental services)... Gates Corp. acquires troubled William Lear's executive jet plane business (dominates market to 1978 when challenged by General Dynamics, Gulfstream Aerospace, Beech Aircraft)... Burger Chef Systems, fast-food franchising business with 700 outlets, is acquired by General Foods for $16 million (after 4-year pre-tax loss of $83 million sells in 1982 to Hardee's, a Canadian fast-food operation)... American Basketball Association is created (merges with NBA in 1970 after market war for players and locations)...

In this time Emery Air Freight starts training program using B.F. Skinner's Behavioral Modification with Positive Reinforcement (- 1976, increases sales of $62.4 million to $79.8 million in 1968 and reports savings of some $2 million by 1971, is followed by B.F. Goodrich in 1972-76 and General Electric in 1973-76)... Newsweek: "America's Huge Catered Affair" (reports on rise of personal services from 45% of total U.S. labor force in 1948 to 55%)... Psychology Today magazine is issued to inform public on social sciences... Russell W. Peterson, "New Venture Management in a Large Company," Harvard Business Review (is used by DuPont in developing new markets)... Ralph A. Rotnem, Wall Street historian, theorizes hem lines and stock prices move together in same direction... Muriel Siebert is first woman to buy seat on New York Stock Exchange... Fred Fiedler: A Theory of Leadership Effectiveness (uses contingency concept in study)... McDonnell Douglas Aircraft is formed by merger of 2 firms... Jann Wenner publishes Rolling Stone magazine (achieves circulation of one million/month in 1985, introduces US in 1985 to compete with People in celebrity journalism)...

Pioneering theme restaurant chain of Victoria Station opens in San Francisco with old railroad box cars and imported memorabilia of British railways (operates 46 units before starting 2nd theme restaurant operation of Quinn's Mill in 1976 to revitalize business, closes 40 restaurants in 1985 to continue with 50, with liabilities of $38 million and assets of $6.5 million files for bankruptcy in 1986)... Electrical engineer Charles E. Sporck, 3 others from Fairchild Electronics business start National Semiconductor in California's "Silicon Valley"... Og Mandino: <u>The</u> <u>Greatest</u> <u>Salesman</u> <u>in</u> <u>the</u> <u>World</u> (sells 8 million copies in 17 languages)... Ling-Temco-Vought acquires packing house and sporting goods business of Wilson and Co. (is followed in market by acquisitions of Armour in 1970 by Greyhound, Cudahy in 1971 by General Host, Swift by Esmark in 1972, Oscar Meyer in 1981 by General Foods, Iowa Beef Processors by Occidental Petroleum in 1981)... With $5,000 loan from uncle, Glenn W. Turner starts Kostoc Interplanetary business in Orlando, FL, to sell cosmetics with pyramiding distributorships (promotes business in 1970 with "Dare to be Great" program to acquire multimillion-dollar fortune, is forced to sell business and declare bankruptcy after 1973 when 1,000 civil suits for over $900 million are combined into single class-action suit – no contest, is indicted in 1985 by Phoenix grand jury on charges in operating pyramid scheme to bilk investors of $1.5 million in 1979-80)...

After working as salesman for Boston necktie manufacturer and tie designer for Beau Brummel men's furnishings, fashion designer Ralph Lauren starts business to sell some $500,000 of narrow Polo ties with backing of Manhattan clothing manufacturer (starts Polo line of menswear, sporty but restrained, in 1968, designs first high-fashion casual wear in 1971, introduces tailored shirts for women in 1971 and first collection of womenswear in 1972, avoids bankruptcy by hiring operations manager in 1972 and using savings of $100,000, acquires factory in 1978 to make tailored menswear, introduces cologne and boyswear in 1978 – Western Wear collection flops, opens London shop in 1981 – by mid-1980s 32 Polo boutiques worldwide, styles girlswear line in 1981 and luggage, eye glasses in 1982, designs home-furnishing line of products for J.P. Stevens textile business in 1983 – after initial problems sales of $50 million in 1986, markets women's handbags in 1985, plans sales of some $1.3 billion, 4 times that of 1981, for 1986 with children's wear at $75 million, fragrances at $250 million, Polo menswear at $420 million, foreign sales at $190 million, womenswear at $210 million and Chaps Western line at $80 million from 48 francised Polo shops, 132 department store boutiques, 16 discount outlets and world's largest one-designer store, Manhattan Polo emporium in 1986, as showcase and testing laboratory, runs 68 stores nationwide by 1988)...

Pillsbury acquires Burger King fast-food franchise business for $14 million (rejects offer of $100 million in 1972 to sell, launches "Have It Your Way" ad campaign to differentiate product, opens first of 26 Greyhound Burger Kings in 1975 to replace their Post House places, expands menu in 1977 with new products from test kitchens, hires Behavioral Science Research in 1980 for consumer research, uses hard-hitting ads in 1980 to show customers prefer Burger King over rivals (opposes union of Detroit workers in 1981, operates mobile restaurants in 1985, acquires fast-food market share of 9% in 1986's $50.5 billion industry, popularizes croissant trend in 1987 with breakfast sandwich, accepts $5.7 billion takeover by Britain's Grand Metropolitan in 1988)... Rensis Likert: <u>The</u> <u>Human</u> <u>Organization:</u> <u>Its</u> <u>Management</u> <u>and</u> <u>Value</u> (discusses human resource accounting)... To meet competition Boeing introduces 737 short-range jet to carry 107 passengers (after initial orders from foreign carriers produces 930 of small, twin-engine planes by 1981 airline deregulation and over 1,000 more by 1988 as best-selling commercial airliner)... With purchase of 3 Seattle Rhodes department stores and Bells of Burien, Lamonts retail chain is born, sells moderately priced brand-name merchandise for family (runs 43 Northwest stores by 1988 with plans for 50 by 1990)... Dick Lord, colleagues start Lord Geller ad agency (sells to J. Walter Thompson advertising in 1974 for $325,000 - operates as independent, is acquired with JWT Group in 1987 hostile takeover by Britain's Martin Sorrell, after months of warfare quits in 1988 to start new agency with previous associates, clients)... After evolving in 1920s as carney game on outskirts of county fairs, 34 dog tracks operate in 7 states, 51 in 15 states by 1989 as horse-racing attendance stagnates.

1968

General Events

During year, 221 major demonstrations protest Vietnam War at 101 colleges, universities... Some 50,000 march (June 19) in Washington to support Poor People Campaign...   Yale accepts first women students... Co-op City in Bronx, NY, is largest U.S. housing cooperative... First-class mail rises to 6 cents/ounce, 8 cents in 1971 and 10 cents in 1974... First Special Olympics for handicapped children is held in Chicago... Computer programmer Doug Engelbart, Stanford Research Institute, demonstrates Augment system in San Francisco (heralds word-processing, teleconferencing, work stations, computer graphics)... Artist Andy Warhol: "In the future everyone will be world-famous for 15 minutes"... Riots are seen at Chicago Democratic Convention (August 26-29)... North American Electric Reliability Council forms to prevent blackouts by balancing demand, supply of electricity on interconnected grid, formed in 1960s by U.S., Canada... Union membership is some 25.2% of labor force, drops to 20.9% in 1980...

Otto Klima, Jr., Gibson M. Wolf: "The Oceans: Unexpected Opportunities," Harvard Business Review... Alliance for Labor Action is formed by United Auto Workers, after withdrawing from AFL-CIO on differences in policy and politics (rejoins 1981), and International Brotherhood of Teamsters... Bureau of Narcotics and Dangerous Drugs is created... U.S. abandons effort to maintain price of gold at $35/ounce... Labor Department reports (December 11) unemployment rate of 3.3%, lowest in 15 years... Air Force commissions first black general... Federal Trade Commission reports 16,601 mergers since 1945 (from 1967 records 83% of all large acquisitions in manufacturing and mining by conglomerates, records record number of 2,407 manufacturing and mining firms acquired by mergers)... Dwight E. Robinson: "U.S. Style of Life Invades Europe," Harvard Business Review...

U.S. Supreme Court allows Bell customers to attach non-AT&T equipment to telephone systems... Faced with rising deficits Harvey Leichtenstein becomes general manager of 1859 Brooklyn Academy of Music (reduces deficits with innovative programming, budgets, financial controls, fund raising and modern marketing methods)... Oregon's Warm Springs Indian Reservation obtains pioneering $400,000 Federal grant to start high-tech assembly plant (opens Kah-Nee-Tah resort and hotel in 1972 for economic development)... Brandt Allen: "Danger Ahead! Safeguard Your Computer," Harvard Business Review... Fortune: "Good Living Begins at $25,000 a Year" (reports on reasonably comfortable, secure life of upper 2%)... Consumer advocate Ralph Nader,   volunteers investigate Federal Trade

Commission (starts studying other government agencies with Nader Raiders in 1969)... <u>Fortune</u>: "Systems Engineering Invades the City" (reports use of aerospace technology to resolve urban complexities)... Interracial council is created in NYC with support from major banks to guarantee loans to fledgling businesses of blacks... Justice Department issues guidelines on horizontal, vertical and diversified mergers... Federal Truth in Lending Act is passed... Museum of Appalachia opens in Norris, TN, to give authentic experience of yesteryear's mountain life, some 800 tourists first year and 80,000 in 1985... Don Canham becomes University of Michigan's athletic director (-1988, with revolutionary sports marketing program grosses $16.1 million in 1985, $20 million in 1987)... SEC accuses Merill Lynch of insider trading... SEC finds certain officials of Texas Gulf Sulphur guilty in using insider information to profit on stock market upheld by U.S. Court of Appeals... Vassar College, founded 1865 as one of U.S.' oldest and most prestigious women's school, accepts first male students... Pentagon contracts with some 22,000 prime contractors and 100,000 subcontractors, some 5,300 communities with at least 1 defense plant.

Business Events

Joseph Papp stages "Hair," rock musical with nudity to protest Vietnam War and echo attitudes of alienated youth... Carl, Barbara Swett start 24-hour Printright/Laserquick printing business in Portland, OR, an industry of 1,100 shops in 1969 and 24,000 by 1988 (evolves as industry's 12th largest by 1987 with 30 shops in Portland and Seattle - Kinko's Graphics, CA, No. 1 with 300 units nationwide and 1986 sales of $64.8 million)... Ringling Bros. and Barnum & Bailey Circus opens tuition-free clown college (franchises clown school to Japan's Naturally Yours, a health food firm, in 1988 to help Japanese in service fields to learn how to relate to foreigners)... Sons T. Cullen and Ken take over Davis Texas oil business on death of father, started in 1937 from savings as clerk and built into empire of nearly 80 privately-held companies with leaders in contract oil drilling, oil-field supply and armored-truck production (operate conglomerate in 1981 with sales over $2 billion, after scandalous living by T. Cullen are forced in 2-year court battle by creditors to declare bankruptcy in 1987 with debt of $575 million - stripped of ownership by Texas bankruptcy court)...

For first time since October of 1929, New York Stock Exchange records (April 15) highest trading over 16.4 million shares... Pan Am pioneers helicopter service from JFK Airport to Newark, NJ... Red Lobster chain of restaurants opens, FL (sells in 1970 to General Mills Restaurants to operate 400 places in 35 states, 40 in Canada and 20 in Japan in 1987)... 1884 Bath Iron Works, ME, merges with Congoleum-Nairn (pioneers modular ship construction with pre-outfitting in late 1970s)... Finley, Kumble law firm, operates by 1988 with some 700 of hottest lawyers in 13 cities and London, is formed in NYC by 8 lawyers, 70 by 1978 (grows by aggressive strategy in hiring stars from rivals and merging with smaller firms to compete in market with Chicago-based Baker & McKenzie, largest with 1,000 lawyers in 1987, after internal warfare dissolves in 1988 with debt of $83 million)... Time, Inc., after creating Selling Areas-Marketing in 1966, acquires Little, Brown publishing (moves into cable television with Home Box Office, buys Book-of-the-Month Club in 1977, and operates Washington's <u>Star</u> paper in 1978-81)... William G. McGowan, John D. Geoken form Microwave Communications to provide microwave-radio transmissions between St. Louis and Chicago (leads to 1972 strategy meeting of Bell executives to crush interloper, battles AT&T with FCC to win in 1975 in Federal court, obtains damages of $113 million in 1985 – in appeal, forges alliance with IBM in 1985)... Enzymes are added to laundry detergents (starts new battle of soap makers for market share)... Boston Consulting Group, pioneer of strategic concept for planning: Perspectives on Experience (discusses use of Learning Curve concept for business)... Pioneering U.S. dinner-theater, Chanhassen, opens, MN...

Dress designer Norman Norell introduces first made-in-America perfume (grosses $1 million in first year, is followed by Revlon's Charlie fragrance for young, active women in 1973)... Forentco pioneers furniture rental business, followed by GranTree Corp. in 1971... Tax-shelter architect Craig Hall acquires $4,000 share of rooming house in Ann Arbor, MI (parlays investment by 1980s into empire of 60,000 rental apartments, 4 million square feet of office space and savings and loan association – 100 real estate partnerships by 1985, after lending ailing partnerships some $56.7 million from private fortune to avoid bankruptcy drops several tax shelter projects as general operating partner in 1986 to cut losses in falling real estate market)... After making pianos for over 85 years, Baldwin starts diversification program (-1982, files for bankruptcy in 1983)... Control Data locates key plant in run-down section of Minneapolis (in 1978 joins local consortium of corporations and church groups to form City Ventures Corp. to develop business activity in City's blighted areas)... The Whole Earth catalog is published (issues some 2.5 million copies on anti-technological living)...

Blacks form Group for Advertising Progress to seek greater role in field... Inventors Robert N. Noyce, co-inventor of integrated circuit, and Jack Kilby, formerly of Texas Instruments, start Intel in Santa Clara, CA, with $2.5 million in venture capital (invent first microprocessor in 1971, by 1982 Japanese with 40% of market, to spawn PC age, achieve sales of $850 million by 1980, develop industry's most modern plant in 1983 to run 24-hours/day, 7 days/week to maximize production and lower costs, introduce next-generation mainframe superchip in 1988)... U.S. Open Tennis Championship offers first direct cash prizes to tennis players – $14,000 first prize for men... Motorola drops use of time clocks for production workers... Terry Emmert starts heavy-structure moving business in Oregon with 2 old trucks, some cribbing and credit – no cash (evolves by 1980s as Emmert International to re-locate such structures as train depot, oil rig, yacht and nuclear reactor, despite advice of all experts re-locates 1,600 ton hotel, largest structure ever moved, in San Antonio in 1985)...

Malcom Bricklin, wealthy owner of chain of hardware stores, introduces Japan's Subaru car to U.S. market (starts own automobile company in 1972 to make sport coupes – ends 1975 in bankruptcy, starts distributing Fiat sports cars in 1984, introduces Yugoslavia's Yugo car with price of $3,990 in 1985 – bankruptcy in 1989)... George Goodman as Adam Smith: The Money Game... Women's Wear Daily promotes "midi" skirt fashion (fails to replace "mini")... Sears drops military toys from catalog (reinstates items in 1982)... Waste Management business is started in Chicago to handle industrial garbage (evolves as world's largest in industry by 1987 with sales of $2.8 billion, some 424,000 customers including Winter Olympics, 31,000 employees and anti-trust suits in 1987-88)... After running out of financing for real estate development, Vincent G. Marotta looks for new venture (hires local inventor to build better coffee machine, introduces Mr. Coffee in 1972)... Renee C. McPherson becomes president of Dana Corp., chairman in 1972 (adopts Scanlon Plan to transform stodgy auto parts manufacturer into productive enterprise, urges managers to abolish time clocks, establishes "Dana University" to train managers for promotion, retires in 1979 to become Dean of Stanford Business School)... Hobart Alter, largest maker of polyurethane-foam surf boards by 1960, introduces first Hobie cat sailboat... Unisex fashions appear in trendy Manhattan department stores... After resigning from General Motors when passed over for presidency, Semon E. Knudsen becomes president of Ford Motor Co. (-1969 when fired by Henry Ford II as "things did not work out as I hoped" and replaced by Lee Iacocca, developer of popular Mustang car)...

At 22 years of age Donald J. Trump, Midas dealmaker of 1980s, joins father's $40 million real estate business in apartment complexes (starts building $3 billion empire with $80 million renovation of New York's dilapidated Commodore Hotel with $120 million tax abatement during City's financial crisis in 1976 - opening in 1980 as Grand Hyatt Hotel during demand boom to generate yearly profits of $30 million, acquires 5 more hotels and builds elegant Trump Tower, buys New Jersey Generals of U.S. Football League in 1983, acquires Hilton's Atlanta City hotel in 1985 to open Trump's Castle, battles entertainer Merv Griffin for control of Resorts International, casino properties in Bahamas and Atlantic City, in 1988 - split property)... Alejandro Zaffaroni starts Alzo business to develop skin patches as controlled release devices for drugs (finally acquires contracts in 1980s from drug companies after spending some $100 million in 16 years of research)... Ted Forstman, 2 partners start buyout business with $400,000 (by 1980s assists 4 major firms, including Dr Pepper, to go private)...

Fred Turner becomes president of McDonald's fast-food business (continues motto of "quality, service, cleanliness, and value," (replaces founder Ray Kroc as chairman in 1977 to expand with eateries on 300 Navy bases and Connecticut turnpike, breakfast service, Chicken McNuggett - McRib a failure, McSnack as scaled-down unit for shopping malls, and McStop for truck centers, achieves sales of $8.7 billion in 1983 - $3.1 billion for Burger King and $1.9 billion for Wendy's, opens 500 new units, one-third outside U.S., in 1984)... W.R. Grace chemical business acquires some coffee shops to start restaurant group (acquires El Torito chain of Mexican food places in 1976, evolves by 1985 to operate 863 eating, dining places in 6 distinct categories to achieve sales of some $748 million)... U.S. auto makers are required to add safety and omissions equipment (results in gray market of European cars not modified - perhaps 1,500 cars in 1980 and some 60,000 worth $1 billion in 1985)...

Philip Morris introduces Virginia Slims cigarette for modern women... Atlantic Richfield discovers oil at Alaska's Prudhoe Bay (leads to government's auction of oil leases for $900 million in 1969)... Arnold Palmer is first professional player on golf tour to earn $1 million... General Foods plans radically innovative plant for Gaines dry dog food at Topeka, KS (starts operations in 1971 with self-managing teams responsible for production to eliminate layers of management and supervisory personnel, with promising start achieves higher productivity and improves quality of work life, deteriorates after 1973 with resistance and hostility of managers replaced and by-passed with new organizational structure)... <u>Newsweek</u>: "Male Plumage '68" (reports newspapers covering menswear go from 100 in 1955 to over 800 by 1965)... American Institute for Decision Science is formed... While coaching Davis Cup team lawyer Donald Dell, former Davis Cup tennis player, forms ProServ to handle racquet and clothing endorsements for players (forms agency in 1972 to represent professional tennis players and develop game as mega-bucks sport, acquires first non-tennis athletes as clients in 1972, starts Professional Services in 1976 as marketing company for clients - 8 offices worldwide and revenues of $25 million by 1985)... Four radio networks operate in U.S., 9 in 1974 and at least 23 by 1985...

<u>Fortune</u>: "Look Who's Rushing Into Real Estate" (reports on land acquisitions by Chrysler, Westinghouse, ITT, Alcoa, Penn Central, Boise Cascade, Hallmark)... Colorado's Outward Bound School starts 10-day wilderness-orientation course for managers, used by such major corporations as Eastman Kodak, IBM and Coors to screen perspective employees or prepare managers for promotions... After offered 50% interest from Bary Schwartz in father's grocery store, fashion designer Calvin Klein borrows $10,000 to start women's ready-to-wear business (achieves success with $50,000 order after chance visit by Bonwit Teller president, operates $100-million business by 1978)... General Electric starts pilot program using automated machine tools and job enrichment (replaces piece rate pay of workers with day-rates, ends program 1975 when management refuses to cede traditional authority)...

Dr. T. Frist, son with venture capitalist Jack Massey launch Hospital Corporation of America (operates 422 health care facilities when merges with American Hospital Supply in 1985 to form $7.6 billion enterprise, world's largest)... Charles Brelsford McCoy is first non-member of DuPont family to become head of world's largest chemical business... Ford starts to develop steam-powered car... Black artist Annuel McBurrows is hired by Remco to design line of black dolls... A video war game appears, stopped by demonstrators as too violent... Lockheed lets women employees wear mini-skirts to work... For first time in 75-year history, Abercrombie & Fitch, purveyor to upper class, holds warehouse sale... Wall Street's Shearson Hammill investment house opens branch in Harlem...

In replacing Jack I. Straus, Ernest L. Molloy is first family outsider in 80 years to head R.H. Macy & Co... General Motors plans small subcompact car... Candy maker Hershey, founded 1886, launches its first advertising campaign ... 3-M introduces world's first full-color copying machine... President of New York metals company is found guilty in conspiring to blow up Zambia bridge to slow down copper exports and drive prices up... Steel industry launches campaign for protective quotas against imports, joining similar lobbying efforts of textile, glass and oil industries...

Albina Corp. is started in Portland, OR, to provide minority employment with grant of $550,000 for working capital by Office of Economic Opportunity (-1970, closes when unable to control costs and defaults on $400,000 loan)... John J. Hooker, former Governor of Tennessee, starts selling franchises for new Minnie Pearl Fried Chicken chain (issues stock in 1968 to open at $20/share and peak at $68 - 50 cents in 1970, operates 263 outlets in 1969, collapses in 1970 when Hooker resigns to run for Governor)... Former crop-duster William C. Britt starts one plane commuter airline in Terre Haute, IN (evolves as Britt Air by 1984 to operate 46 planes and carry over one million passengers to 34 cities before acquisition in 1985 by People Express)... After drifting in and out of jobs, Alvin Goldstein, partner start publishing <u>Screw</u> with $350 (flaunts society with nudes in untouched realism, scathing and scatological editorials, lists of bars, places for swinging couples, and tests of "marital aid" sexual devices, prints nearly 100,000 copies after 10 issues - sales of 4,000 on first printing).... Diverse Industries enters adult entertainment field to sell sexual wares by mail-order... Cox Enterprises, Atlanta-based publishing business, acquires Manheim Auctions (by 1988 becomes first nationwide network with 21 outlets selling used cars - Anglo American Auto Auctions with 20 and General Electric Capital, discovers market of leased cars, with 17)... Dealmaker Karl Eller buys small billboard firm, builds giant Combined Communications with U.S.' largest outdoor-advertising business, 7 TV stations, 14 radio stations, and 2 newspapers, sold to Gannett in 1979 for $367 million (after serving as head of Columbia Pictures becomes head of Phoenix-based Circle K convenience chain in 1983, triples Sunbelt stores to 4,600 by 1987, sales from $747.8 million to $2.3 billion, after buying 473 7-Eleven stores from Southland in 1988 acquires 538 stores of Charter Co. in Northeast - 2nd largest in field)...

La Quinta Inns, over 200 coast-to-coast by 1988, is born... Chris-Craft Industries switches from wood to fiberglass in building boats... Hirschel Thornton opens world's first drive-in mortuary, Atlanta... After college graduation, Michael Ovitz lands job in mail room of William Morris talent agency, an agent by 1969 (quits in 1974 to start Creative Artists Agency with loan of $21,000 and 4 partners, handles 675 famous clients in 1989 to dominate Hollywood as matchmaker, project-maker)... After appearance of American Soccer League in 1933 (-1970s), National Professional League and United Soccer Assn. merge to form North American Soccer League (after high of 24 teams fades away in 1983 as Major Indoor Soccer League appears in 1978, only 1 team of 11 profitable in 1987, and new American Soccer League opens in 1988 with 10 teams).

1969

General Events

U.S. sues (January 17) IBM for monopolizing computer market, dropped 1982... Santa Barbara's harbor, CA, is closed (February 5) by oil spill from Union Oil's well A-21... Department of Agriculture suspends (July 9) use of DDT... Neil Armstrong is (July 20) first to walk on moon... Woodstock Music Festival is held (August 18-20) in Bethel, NY, for 300,000 - 400,000 counter-culture youth 16-34, world's biggest happening... FDA bans (October 18) cyclamates as sugar substitute... Some 250,000 hold (November 15) anti-war protest in Washington, largest in U.S. history... Tax reform law is signed (December 30) to reduce individual tax rates by 5%, removes some 9 million low-income people from paying taxes... MIT bans government research projects... 12 unions shut down General Electric with acrimonius strike... M.M. Yoshino, <u>Japan's Managerial System</u>... Oregon creates pioneering Department of Environmental Quality... Friends of the Earth forms in San Francisco to preserve environment... Ralph Nader, funded by Carnegie and other foundations, forms Non-Profit Center for Study of Responsive Law (forms study groups to investigate government agencies)... Frank Defore: "Your Time, Not Your Dollar," <u>Sports Illustrated</u> (reports on transformation of U.S. life in building some 355 arenas with capacity of 5,000 spectators

or more, 105 with 10,000 or more - 2 out of 3 built since 1949)...
<u>Newsweek</u>: "The Troubled American" (reports on difficulties of white
middle-class majority)... FCC permits MCI to hook its long-distance
network with local phone systems... Members of National Organization for
Women invade all-male Oak Room of Manhattan's Plaza Hotel during lunch
period... United Transportation Union is formed by unions of trainmen,
conductors, brakemen, switchmen, firemen and enginemen... <u>Life</u>: "The
Commune Comes to America"... Council of Engineering and Scientific
Organizations is formed to represent some 50,000 engineers in 9
associations...

Maximum tax on long-term capital gains goes from 25% to 49%, drops to 28%
in 1978... Chicago's black Coalition for United Community demands 25,346
skilled-trade jobs and 30% membership in 19 building craft unions...

Gay rights movement is started when New York Police try to close gay bar,
Stonewall & Inn, in Greenwich Village, NYC... Women wear pants suits for
everyday wear... Several hundred well-born, well-fed and well-educated
revolutionaries, Bernadine Dohrn and others, gather in Chicago to hold
"The Days of Rage" in protesting Vietnam War (plan secretly to inspire
working class to revolt against society)... After violent mine explosion
kills 78 miners in West Virginia, Coal Mine Health and Safety Act is
passed.

Business Events

Donald Fisher opens The Gap specialty-store business in California to
sell blue jeans, after phasing out jeans in 1983 operates 666 places in
1987 to sell prepackaged, moderately-priced sporty clothing (acquires
Banana Republic Travel & Safari Clothing business with 2 stores, 83 by
1987 and plans for 100 by 1988, in 1983, starts GapKids in 1986, 35
places in 1987, to compete in market with Sears' 750 boutiques with
McKids Clothes licensed by McDonald's, F.W. Woolworth's Kids-mart with
293 off-priced outlets, and Benetton's 80 shops, Italian chain with 4,500
stores worldwide, opens tony Hemisphere shops for upscale market in
1987)...

General Motors recalls 4.9 million cars to check for defects in February
(in March recalls 1.1 million for brake checks)... 1873 Kohler family
plumbing business in Wisconsin and other major plumbing manufacturers are
charged with price fixing in Federal anti-trust suit (are found
guilty)... U.S. tuna boats fishing 260 miles off of Peru are attacked by
Peruvian torpedo boats, one captured for invading fishing area...

Avon Products door-to-door cosmetic business starts business in Japan -
by 1987 with 370,000 Avon ladies to equal U.S. force (sells 40% of
subsidiary to Japanese public in 1987 for $280 million)... Ford Motor Car
Co. contracts with Japan's Mazda to become affiliate and supplier...

Black lawyer, Bruce Llewellyn, acquires Fedco Foods, small Bronx
supermarket chain, after mortgaging house and assets to Prudential
Insurance for $3 million loan (rescues Harlem's Freedom National Bank of
New York in 1971, expands 10 stores to 27 by 1983 to gross $85 million,
joins Julius Erving and Bill Cosby in 1983 to acquire share in Coca-Cola
Bottling of New York, sells Fedco in 1984 for $20 million and starts UHF
station with partners in San Diego, acquires affiliated station in 1985

to head 5th largest black-owned U.S. firm, acquires Philadelphia Coca-Cola bottler in 1985 with Erving - increases sales by 20%)... After teaching jazz dance classes, Judi Sheppard Misset develops Jazzercise in Chicago area (evolves to operate some 3,000 franchises and serve some 350,000 body-conditioning students by 1980s, realizes sales of $42 million in 1983)... Mack Hanan: "Corporate Growth Through Venture Management,"   Harvard Business Review (reports on use by Dow, Westinghouse, Monsanto, Celanese, Union Carbide, 3-M)... Gus Dussin opens first Old Spaghetti Factory in Portland, OR (expands to 22 places by 1985 - 16 owned and 6 franchised with units in Japan, West Germany)... Erich Jantsch (ed.):   Perspectives of Planning (presents comprehensive environmental concept for long-range planning)... Creem, "America's Only Rock'n'Roll Magazine," is published (suspends operation in 1985)...

William Millard starts Systems Dynamics to sell custom-tailored software to businesses using certain IBM computers (develops early personal computer in 1975 - bankruptcy in 1979 after manufacturing problems with debt of $1.9 million and $250,000 promissory note to venture capital group, starts Computer Shack in 1976 with $10,000 to develop franchised chain computer stores, operates 800 Computerland outlets worldwide by 1984 to realize sales of $1.4 billion, is forced by 1985 court ruling to give 20% interest to venture capital group holding promissory note and to pay punitive damages of $150 million)... Fortune: "The Merger Movement Rides High"... Learning Tree Day Care center chain business is started...

After moving from New Jersey to mountain retreat in Colorado, Susan and Stephan Schutz start greeting card business, Blue Mountain Art (sell over 200 million cards by 1986 with Susan's poetry using personal-growth jargon from human potential movement, sue Hallmark card business in 1986 for $50 million for developing similar cards - win undisclosed sum in 1988 with Hallmark dropping Personal Touch line)... Harry Stern starts Technical Equities in San Jose, CA, as small real estate investment and sports promotion business (evolves by 1985 as diversified operation of 22 companies with sales of $134.4 million, files for bankruptcy in 1986 after attracting some 700 investors, at least 70 sports figures, to use variety of high-tech firms and real estate deals as supposed tax shelters)... American Tobacco becomes American Brands after acquiring Sunshine Biscuits, James Beam, Andrew Jergens, Master Lock, Franklin Life Insurance...

Dayton-Hudson Corp. is created by merger of department stores of Minnesota's Dayton and Detroit's Hudson (operates 339 stores to achieve sales over $2.1 billion in 1979)... Life insurance industry launches $2 billion Urban Investment Program to revive blighted cities... Saturday Review: "The Rise of World Corporations"... Financially ailing Anchor Brewery of San Francisco is rescued by Fritz Maytag, pioneers market of micro-breweries... Geiger Burger Associates is formed in NYC to design pioneering air-dome structure for U.S. Pavillion at Japan's 1970 World's Fair in Osaka (serves as model for Silverdome, world's largest fabric-covered stadium, in Pontiac, MI)... Ford Dealer's Alliance is formed to protect interests of individual dealers with Ford Motor Co... J. Meadlock starts Intergraph with $39,000 as computer-aided design business (by 1983 increases equity to some $80 million)... Three lawyers start courier service for quick delivery of documents from California to Hawaii (form DHL Worldwide Courier Express network, largest international system by 1980s, in 1972 with Po Chung, Hong Kong entrepreneur, start developing

U.S. market in 1980s)... Dana Corp. starts quality-of-worklife program, model for Procter & Gamble and General Motors in 1971... To improve employee relations American Airlines starts industry's first full-scale program in transactional analysis... Norma Kamali introduces fashion of pants (transforms sweat clothes as fashion apparel in 1981)... For-profit National Medical Enterprises is formed to operate chain of hospitals... Instinet is started as computer stock-trading system to let institutional investors trade big board stocks without paying brokerage and exchange fees, rejected for use by NYSE (acquires 20% of over-the-counter business in 1980s)... International Association for Financial Planning forms, some 4,900 members by 1979 and 14,500 in 1983... New York's leading Wall Street firm of Cravath, Swaine & Moore hires beginning lawyers for $15,000 (seeks new lawyers in 1986 at starting salaries of $53,000-65,000)...

Prudential Insurance adopts compressed work week for computer center, followed by adoption of flextime by Hewlett-Packard in 1972 and alternative work schedule program by Government in 1979... John Smith becomes head of Indiana-based Mayflower moving business (acquires ADI Appliances, midwestern wholesaler, in 1981, R.W. Harmon & Sons, 2nd largest school bus operation, in 1984, to increase revenues by 27% to $481 million in 1984)... Dwight D. Carlson starts Xycom, MI, to make car emission analyzers (-1973, starts Perception in 1980 with patents from Environmental Research Institute of Michigan to develop machine vision for robotic devices, joins Stanley R. Sternberg, formerly of ERI, to start Machine Vision International in 1981)... In first 7 months nearly 100 new advertising agencies open in NYC... Stephen Chefan sells chain of 15 men's clothing stores in Detroit to retire to Florida (when bored, starts real estate venture in 1970 to sell some 1,000 fully furnished, expensive turnkey-houses by 1985)...

AMF acquires Wisconsin's motorcycle maker Harley-Davidson... Morris Siegal starts Celestial Seasoning in Boulder, CO, pioneers herbal tea market (grosses some $12 million in 1980, sells to Kraft foods in 1984)... Thomas A., Amy Harris: I'm OK - You're OK (popularizes transactional analysis personal development movement)... Perry Mendel starts child-care business, Kinder-Care, in Alabama as commercial venture (evolves as industry's Goliath to operate 1,100 places in 1987 with McDonald's approach to standardize, rationalize and centralize)... General Mills acquires Izod shirtmaker (divests in mid-1980s to focus on food products)... Stephen M. Huse acquires failing carry-out Little Caesar's Pizza Treat in Bloomington, IN, (opens first Noble Roman franchise in 1973 to develop chain of some 255 places, mostly in Midwest, by 1981)...

Oil tanker Manhattan sails Northwest passage to check practicality in shipping Alaskan oil to East Coast... By 1980 only 12 mergers over $1 billion are formed, over 30 such transactions in 1980-85... Saturday Evening Post, founded 1821, suspends publication (re-starts in 1971 as quarterly, is followed by closures of Look in 1971 and Life in 1972)... General Motors recalls nearly 5 million cars for adjustments in mechanical defects... Jay Richard Kennedy: "The Chairman" (presents story first as film, then in paperback and last as hard cover edition)... After publishing in Britain, Brooklyn-born Bob Guccione introduces Penthouse magazine to compete with Playboy... When traded by St. Louis Cardinals to another baseball team, veteran Curt Flood files suit against baseball's "reserve clause" (is rejected in 1972 - eventually wins)...

General Motors halts production of rear-engine Corvair, criticized by Ralph Nader as unsafe... Joanne Wallis, former Mrs. Oregon, starts pioneering Image Improvements in Oregon to advise business people on how to present themselves to others (evolves by 1980 to operate branches in 19 states and Canada)... First Skipper's fast-food seafood restaurant opens in Bellevue, WA, 205 outlets by 1986... After receiving Harvard law degree in 1960 and joining Wall Street law firm for contacts, John Samuels starts business during spare time to trade Appalachian coal of small operators to Ruhr Valley (forms International Carbon and Minerals in 1971 with retired metals trader Leonard Cohen, to develop financing with European connections, and Pierre Schneider, to locate customers, with first office in Luxembourg - New York headquarters in 1973, acquires West Virginia mines in 1973 to provide reliable supply of coal just before price of metallurgical coal soars 50% in 6 months, operates business at age 42 with sales of some $500 million in 1975 to earn about $50 million)...

Neil S. Hirsch starts Telerate, electronic information business, with $30,000 to sell financial information to traders (after 6 years and $2.4 million to show profits, realizes 60% of U.S. market in 1985 with sales of some $140 million)... Treasure hunter Mel Fisher, financed by 700 investors of Treasure Salvors in first of 35 investment schemes, starts high-tech search for Nuestra Senora de Atocha and her sister ship, sunk by 1622 hurricane near Key West (discovers 3 silver bars in 1973, locates ship in 1985 to find treasure trove over $400 million, is sued 1987 over distribution of find)... Boeing introduces 747 jet plane, largest commercial liner with space for up to 500 passengers and range up to 6,500 miles...

IBM forms General Products to sell computers to small businesses (while successful leads to incompatible computer lines and U.S. antitrust and private suits)... First Boston Corp., created in 1935 when Chase Manhattan and First National of Boston (is fined $500,000 in 1985 for possibly laundering money for international drug dealers) divest investment banking activities, represents Bangor Punta in battle with Chris-Craft Industries for control of Piper Aircraft (appoints aggressive dealmakers Joe Perella and Bruce Wasserstein, leave 1988 after losing in power struggle to Mergers & Acquisitions department in 1976, forms joint venture in 1978 with Credit Suisse - doubtful in 1988 with troublesome international bond market, in 1980s handles many takeovers, such as DuPont's $7.4 billion acquisition of Conoco in 1981, to become leader in field, is taken over in 1988 merger by Credit Suisse for $1.1 billion)...

Stew Leonard, wife open small dairy store in Norwalk, CT, by 1988 "world's largest dairy store" with volume nearing $100 million, some 100,000 customers/week... Smoke Enders is started to help those quit the habit, joined in rising 1988 corporate market by 1977 Smoke Stoppers and Smokeless, each with 1987 sales of $3-4 million... Lionel Corp., 1901 toy train business, acquires 15 specialty toy retailers, Philadelphia, to enter new field, 78 retail toy supermarkets in 16 states by 1988 (in mid-1980s moves production to Tijuana, Mexico, to cut costs, after disaster is revived in 1986 by Detroit investor Richard P. Kughn after buying business for $25 million, by 1988 achieves sales of $50 million/year, up 150%, and 60% market share by emphasizing quality at original plant,

MI)... Walter Wiggins opens first resort hotel of Divi chain on Aruba, Dutch Antilles (by 1988 expands to 10 hotels, time share lodgings and condominiums on Caribbean Islands).

1970s

General Events

U.S. contracts with Ivan Southerland, David Evans of University of Utah to build flight stimulator to show realistic unfolding landscape for pilot training (pioneers techniques of computer graphics)... As conventional training programs were not effective in preparing recruits to handle sophisiticated weapons, U.S. Army develops new training methods with computer instruction.

Business Events

TGI Friday's obtains reputation as one of NYC's most successful singles bars (becomes chain of 111 family-oriented restaurants by 1985).

1970

General Events

U.S. Post Office is created (August 12) as independent government corporation (achieves $1.5 billion surplus in 1982, drops direct-operation subsidy in 1983)... Over 340,000 members of UAW take walk-out against General Motors, industry's largest strike in 20 years, September 15-November 15... In 3rd national rail strike in 50 years 500,000 members of 4 unions strike (December 11) railroads for higher wages (postpone strike for 80 days with bill by Congress raising wages 13.5%)... Baseball suspends Detroit Tigers pitcher Denny McLain for gambling ties... U.S. Army promotes first women as Generals... Hars G. Khorana, University of Wisconsin, is first to synthesize artificial gene... Cesar Chavez, United Farm Workers, gets 10-day jail term for organizing illegal nationwide boycott of lettuce (signs contract with 26 California grape growers after successful boycott)...

FDA recalls over 1 million cans of tuna because of mercury contamination... Environmentalists hold Earth Day to convince public of ecological crisis... Gwinnet County, 18 miles from Atlanta, has population of 72,300, almost quadruples by 1987 to 250,000 as U.S.' fastest growing megacounty since 1984 (highlights evolution of megacounties, such as Fairfax, VA, adjacent to Washington, and Orange County between Los Angeles and San Diego)... U.S. Navy starts pilot program in human relations (evolves as organization development program)... Economic Stabilization Act gives President Nixon authority to impose wage and price controls, (established 1971)... Environmental Protection Agency is created...

Federal Pay Comparability Act requires Federal employees be paid on level comparable to that of private sector... Pioneering training program in organization development, designed by Gordon Lippitt and Dick Beckhard, is used to improve Red Cross' organizational effectiveness (-1977)... Postal workers in New York start wildcat strike in demanding higher wages (spreads nationwide to some 200,000 of 750,000 Postal workers in first mail strike of 1900s, are replaced until settlement by military troops)... 19th population census shows population of 203.2 million, 149.3 urban and 53.9 rural (reveals declining birth rate from delayed marriages, more divorces and smaller families)... 448 universities and colleges are either closed or disrupted by student protest, violence... Alvin Toffler: Future Shock... Occupational Safety and Health Act mandates safe and healthful working conditions for employees... Time: "The American Family: Future Uncertain"... Racketeer Influence and Corrupt Organization Act attacks leaders of organized crime, applied to business with 1,095 cases in 1986 with approval of Supreme Court in 1985 (is used in 1986 to put Teamsters Local 560 of Union City, NJ, and Cement Workers Local CA, NYC, under trusteeship - Teamsters Local 814, NYC, in 1987 with plans in 1988 for Seafood Workers Local 359, NYC, and Roofers Union Locals 30, 30B, Philadelphia)...

Anthony G. Athos: "Is the Corporation Next to Fall?" Harvard Business Review (discusses impact on business of youth with radical perceptions of world)... Newspaper Preservation Act is passed (with anti-trust exceptions allows 22 big-city competitors to combine operations to survive by 1986)... Federal Reserve Board deregulates interest rates on bank deposits over $100,000 with maturities under 6 months... Edward C. Banfield: The Unheavenly City... The Fox dumps gallon of raw sewage on plush carpet of U.S. Steel's Chicago office to protest firm's pollution of Lake Michigan, 30 more such incidents by 1984... Architects J. Wines, A. Sky create SITE, "sculpture in the environment" (design Best Products showroom in 1971 with frivolous facade to start trend in new architecture)... Office of Management and Budget replaces Bureau of the Budget...

Joan Garrity: The Sensuous Woman... By law all banks are required to report all cash transactions of $10,000 or more to IRS... After 2 years of development, scientist Charles Rosen, project team at MIT create Shakey, first electronic-moveable robot... Letty Cottin Pogrebin: How To Make It In A Man's World... Newsweek: "The Spirit of '70'" (reports on current social turmoil)... Saturday Review: "Who Owns the Environment?"... Takilman Commune forms in remote valley, OR (starts Green Side Up, tree-planting cooperative, in 1975 to provide employment and cash flow, starts co-op buying club in 1977)... Interstate Commerce Commission approves merger of 4 railroads as Burlington Northern (as labor contract gives employment protection to railroad clerks, results in "rubber rooms" for idled workers to sit out 8-hour shifts)... Maggie Kuhn starts Gray Panthers as advocacy group for elderly... El Paso Job Corps Center, David Carrasco director, opens to train unemployed barrio youths for work, by 1988 processes 8,000 with 96% employment rate as No. 1 center of 107 during 1978-88.

Business Events

Allen H. Neuharth takes charge of Gannett chain of small-town newspapers (transforms business into media empire by 1980s to operate 86 daily papers, 6 television stations and 40 radio stations, launches USA Today in 1982 for nationwide distribution - profitable by 1987, buys Detroit's Evening News Association in 1985 to acquire U.S.' 6th largest daily, 9 smaller papers, 2 radio and 5 TV stations, syndicates TV show USA Today in 1988 via 118 stations covering 84% of country)... Using idea of ITT scientist Charles K. Kao in mid-1950s, Corning Glass Works develops process to make gossamer strands of glass for conducting light... Pan Am flies first Boeing 727, 330 passengers, from NYC to London... NYSE falls (May 25) 20 points to 7-year low... General Motors pays consumer advocate Ralph Nader $425,000 to settle invasion of privacy suit, investigated by GM for attacks on Corvair car... 116-year-old McSorley's bar, NYC, admits first women customers... Pension funds hold some $85 billion in stock (exceeds $325 billion in 1983 and may hit $1 trillion by 1990)... Norm Winningstad starts Floating Point System to pioneer Oregon's Silicon Forest (after questionable management practices and weak product line reorganizes under bankruptcy in 1987)... Travelers Companies start using office technology to improve office performance (by 1987 reduces clerical staff from some 66% of work force to 33%, increases use of "knowledge workers" with savings to boost sales and profits)...

Robert F. Mager, Peter Pipe: <u>Analyzing</u> <u>Performance</u> <u>Problems</u> (pioneers use of flow charting to resolve management problems)... U.S. television manufacturing industry is composed of 17 major producers (drops to 13 by 1973 with 1 from Japan, 9 by 1976 – 3 from Japan and 1 from Taiwan, South Korea and Holland, 6 by 1979 – 7 from Japan and 1 elsewhere, 5 by 1982 – 8 from Japan and 4 elsewhere, 3 by 1985 – 8 from Japan and 5 elsewhere, 2 by 1986 and 1 by 1987)... Honda introduces All-Terrain vehicle to U.S. market to do farm chores, etc. (promotes product in 1981 for family recreation – public opposition in mid-1980s after increasing injuries, deaths)... Institutions own 17.5% of all corporate stock, over 30% by 1987... GE sells its computer activity to Honeywell, followed by RCA's sale of computer business to Sperry Rand in 1971... First home computer game is developed, uses joysticks to send signals through TV set...

Classic pitchman Zig Ziglar, former instructor at Dale Carnegie Institute, starts motivational training business, TX (by 1980s gives some 100 programs/year for usual fee of $10,000/hour, puts on 3-day seminars in Dallas, sells books and tapes, does programs for business clients, such as IBM and J.C. Penney, to operate profitable business with "Zigmanship" – bookings to 1989)... Travel industry has some 6,700 agencies, 10,260 in 1974, 14,804 in 1978, 19,203 in 1981 and 27,193 in 1985... Some 25 million new jobs appear in service sector by 1986... Designer Bill Blass starts fashion business (after success, franchises name to accessories, automobiles, home furnishings, chocolates)... Hartford Fire Insurance Co. is acquired, engineered by Felix Rohatyn of Wall Street's Lazard Freres (is named "Felix the Fixer" for arranging megadollar deals), by Harold Geneen's International Telephone & Telegraph for massive cash flow – ITT's biggest acquisition in becoming conglomerate (after anti-trust suit by Justice Department settles in 1971 to retain insurance business while divesting other subsidiaries)...

With Government money of $22,000 paid children of soldiers killed in war, twins Dee, Lee Bangerter buy nursing home (develop Care Enterprises as 4th largest nursing home chain – revenues of $151.6 million in 1984, parlay 1983 Winn Enterprises with step-brother Ted Nelson into $1.2 billion food and financial service company with Knudsen dairy business in 1983, Mountainwest Savings & Loan in 1983 and Foremost Dairies in 1985)... Frito-Lay, Pepsico subsidiary, pleads no contest to charges in fixing prices of snack foods... Some 1,200 firms handle 500,000 franchises... Two marketing specialists from Procter & Gamble obtain patent rights for cross-country waxless skis (start Trak, Inc., become market leader with 30% share in selling 800,000 pairs/year in 1980s –

total market of some 50,000 pairs in 1970s)... After trend started in late 1950s - early 1960s on West Coast, Pink Orchid is one of first massage parlors in NYC to advertise services for males (operates some 12 parlors in 1971 and over 40 by late 1972)... Major commercial banks establish prime interest rate of 8%... Bell Laboratories develops pocket-size laser capable of carrying hundreds of thousands of telephone calls, TV signals, etc... Werner Erhard starts Erhard Seminars Training in this time to transform personal lives by dislodging trainees from traditional beliefs (grosses some $9.5 million in 1975, graduates some 83,000 est students by 1976 and 500,000 by 1980s before decline in 1982, is sued for half of everything with divorce in 1983, is sued by IRS for $2 million in back taxes, starts Forum in 1985 to help people make things happen by being excellent)... In expecting Americans to spend more money eating out, John F. Baugh expands Sysco frozen-food business (becomes food-service industry's largest by 1980s, some 3,500 rivals in supplying restaurants, hospitals and other institutions)...

George A. Steiner: "Rise of the Corporate Planner," Harvard Business Review... U.S. shipowners operate some 20 cargo lines, 7 by 1985... Fortune: "Franchising's Troubled Dream World" (reports some 95% of growing industry only in business since 1954)... Time: "Change and Turmoil on Wall Street" (reports on failures or mergers of 139 brokerage houses)... Fortune: "The Year of the Executive Axing"... IBM patents chip-bearing memory card (leads to first memory credit card marketed by French journalist R.C. Moreno in 1974 and first U.S. smart card of Minneapolis bank in 1982)... Gordon Macklin becomes president of National Association of Securities Dealers (starts automating quotations of over-the-counter stocks in 1971 to challenge role of NYSE by 1980s with computer trading between 5,200 members of electronic stock market)... Car rental business of Rent-A-Wreck opens, Los Angeles (operates 340 franchised outlets across U.S. by 1985)...

Reading Game starts for-profit learning center business for children (franchises 70 centers in 6 states by 1986, is followed by Huntington Learning Centers in 1977 - 50 franchises in 11 states by 1986, by Sylvan Learning in 1979 - 220 centers in 39 states by 1986)... Time: "The Rising Problem of Drugs on the Job"... Gloria Morgan Vanderbilt joins Riegel Textile as fashion director (acquires fame with designer blue jeans for young women)... John Riccardo becomes president of Chrysler (unable with debt to fund development of small cars, loses $52 million in 1974 and $259 million in 1975, shows profit of $423 million from large cars in 1976 with end of oil embargo)... General Motors plant at Lordstown, OH, is converted into highly efficient production system, known as "super plant" for latest engineering innovations and control techniques, to make Vega cars (closes in 1972 after absenteeism, grievances and defective work results in losses of some $45 million and strike of UAW against intolerable conditions)... Atlanta millionaire apartment developer Cecil D. Day starts budget-chain of lodgings for travelers (sells business in 1984 to Reliance Capital Group for some $275 million - 617 Days hotels and motels by 1987)... Airlines carry 97% of passenger traffic across North Atlantic, 48% in 1957 and 75% in 1963...

High school drop-out Arthur Jones sells first Nautilus body-building machine (develops business with 37 models to achieve 1984 sales of some $300 million)... Princess Diane Furstenberg scandalizes jet set by starting fashion business, NYC (opens Seventh Avenue showroom in 1972 with loan of $30,000 from father - in few months grossing some $1.2 million and $64 million by 1976, is emulated in 1981 by wealthy Venezuela-born Carolina Herrera)... R.J. Reynolds tobacco business becomes Reynolds Industries after acquiring Sea Land container ships, American Independent Oil, Burmah Oil in U.S., Patio Foods, Chun King, Morton Foods and Del Monte canning... 1866 A.H. Robins Co., VA, acquires rights to Dalkon Shield birth control device (starts marketing in 1971, suspends sales in 1974 on urging of FDA after evidence linking device to 4 deaths, after law suits campaigns to urge women to remove device in 1984, places $615 million in reserve fund in 1985 to pay claimants for future damages, declares bankruptcy in 1985 after settling 9,230 cases, some 15,100 pending, for nearly $500 million, after bids by Rorer Group, PA, and French pharmaceutical giant Sanofi takes $3.2 billion buy-out of U.S.-based American Home Products, $4.5 billion health care firm with $700 million in cash and little debt, in 1988)...

J.C. Penney retailing business starts acquiring leased jewelry departments (by 1983 is 4th largest U.S. retail jeweler with promotions, discounts)... Edward E. Carlson's Westin International hotel business is acquired by United Airlines' holding company (5 months later becomes head of United Airlines with losses of some $46 million, largest in United's history, revitalizes business to show operating profit of $3 million for 1971 by reorganizing top executives to stress team management, emphasizing concern for people, decentralizing for visible management, forming profit centers, slashing payroll by 7%, reducing flights from 1,800 to 1,490, and by touring operations to meet employees for suggestions, retires 1983)... GM's operation at Tarrytown plant, NY, with production and labor problems is revived with Quality of Working Life program in cooperation with United Auto Workers...

Dealmaker James Ling, creator of LTV, is ousted in "Palace Revolt" as head of conglomerate (launches Omega-Alpha as holding company to acquire Okonite, LTV's cable and wire business, and then Transcontinental Investment with interests in real estate, finance and phonograph records, files for bankruptcy in 1973, is accused of fraud in 1974 by SEC - settled out of court, is diagnosed in 1981 as having Guillain-Barie syndrome, operates Hill Investors as private investment in 1980s)...

General Foods acquires Viviane Wood's franchised door-to-door skin care business, divested in 1975... New York Stock Exchange undergoes financial crisis (hires financier Felix Rohatyn to rescue institution)... Joel Terranova starts pioneering high-school football scouting service, becomes $40,000 business by 1986...

Financier Robert Vesco gains control of financially-troubled Investors Overseas Services, created by Bernard Cornfeld in 1956 (after indictment in 1973 for fraud, accused by SEC for embezzling some $224 million and making illegal political contribution of $200,000 to Richard Nixon's re-election campaign, flees to Costa Rica, to Bahamas, leaving just ahead of deportation and CIA abduction, and finally to Cuba, house arrest by Castro after cheating on contraband)... By 1984 manufacturing output rises 53%, services by 62%... H. Doyle Owen, son of general store owner, starts Owen's Unclaimed Baggage at Scottsboro, AL, to salvage lost luggage and property of airlines... After dropping out of business classes at Arlington State College, TX, and peddling clothes, Kenny Bernstein quits racing cars to start towing business in Dallas, 9 trucks by 1972 (quits towing in 1973 to open first Chelsea Street Pub - 17 by 1978, returns to racing in 1978 with no sponsor - wins International Hot Rod Association's Funny Car championship in 1979, by 1988 operates 5 corporations: King Entertainment for drag racing team, King Racing for NASCAR events, King Protofab Racing for Indy 500 races, King Racing Components to sell on-board computers for race cars, and King Sports for public relations and marketing)... La Petite babysitting business starts in Kansas City, MO (grows as U.S.' 2nd largest by 1988 with 625 centers to net $10.1 million in sales of $130 million in 1987)... Circus Vargas is formed, one of few in 1988 still performing in tent... Grant Tinker, wife Mary Tyler Moore form MTM Entertainment to produce successful television shows (leaves 1981 to be CEO of NBC - 3rd in ratings, with NBC No. 1 leaves 1986 to start new TV production company, bankrolled by Gannett publishing giant)...

Philip Morris tobacco giant, genesis 1847, buys Miller Brewing, 7th in market with Anheuser-Busch, Schlitz and Pabst first 3, from W.R. Grace Co. for $130 million, industry's 2nd largest in 1988 with 20% share to Busch's 40% by using modern marketing techniques (opens new market in 1974 with Lite low-calorie beer, buys 7-Up in 1978 for $520 million - sold 1986, buys General Foods, restaurants of Burger King, Steak & Ale, Bennigan's, and Distron and package foods of baking mixes, frozen pizza, frozen fish, Jell-O, Post cereals, Maxwell House Coffee, etc., in 1985 for $5.6 billion, introduces Matilda Bay wine cooler in 1987 to battle Seagram's coolers and Gallo's Bartles & Jaymes, operates in 1988 with tobacco 53% of sales, food 36% and beer 11%, bids $3 billion, U.S.' largest acquisition, for Kraft in 1988 to reduce non-tobacco earnings to 35%)... With grubstake of $1,600 Richard Dennis builds fortune of some $200 million by 1987 in speculating on Chicago commodities markets (after losing some $100 million in 1987 October Crash leaves business in 1988 for political causes)...

Xerox starts PARC, Palo Alto Research Center, to conduct basic research in physics, digital technologies, and computer sciences (completes Alto experimental computer in 1973 but fails to exploit technology with political infighting, bureaucratic inertia and aversion to risk)... College dropout and former agent for William Morris talent agency, David Geffen starts Asylum record business (as leading purveyor of California Sound sells to Warner Bros. in 1972, after working for Warner starts Geffen Co. in 1981 with 3 employees to produce records for Warner Communications, by 1988 nets $26 million from producing records, movies and Broadway shows)... Arizona businessmen petition NCAA for permission to stage Fiesta Bowl for post-season football game, rejected but accepted in 1971 after threat of monopoly charges (with competition for more sports programming lands TV contract with CBS in 1974 and NBC in 1978, despite opposition of Rose, Orange, Sugar and Cotton Bowls switches game to New Year's Day in 1982, despite scorn of other bowls is first with national sponsor, Sunkist Growers, later Mobil Cotton Bowl, USF&G Sugar Bowl, Florida Citrus Bowl, Mazda Gator Bowl, and Sea World Holiday Bowl, with $7 million contract in 1985 - leading bowl event in 1989 with top-ranked teams).

1971

General Events

Postal Service signs first Federal labor contract... After political battle Senate chops (March 23) funds for supersonic plane to carry 300 passengers at speeds up to 1,800 mph... Eleven mayors warn (April 21) U.S. on collapse of cities... National Railroad Passenger Corp., Amtrak, is formed (May 1) as semi-public corporation with government subsidies to handle intercity passenger traffic (covers above-rail operating costs in 1987 by carrying 21 million passengers)... Congress votes (May 19) to kill nationwide rail strike... President Nixon removes (June 10) 21-year embargo of trade to mainland China... President Nixon signs (July 12) first public employment legislation since 1930s (orders 90-day wage and price freeze August 25)... Flexible guidelines for wage and price rises go (November 14) into effect to slow annual inflation to 2.5%... With $5 billion trade deficit, U.S. dollar is (December 18) devalued...

Berkeley chemists announced first synthetic production of growth hormone... NYC police strike for 6 days... U.S., Ecuador settle fishing dispute... FDA recalls contaminated Bon Vivant canned foods... Some 400,000 phone workers strike... Campbell Soup recalls contaminated cans... AFL-CIO leader George Meany urges Congress to take control of economy from President Nixon... U.S. pays Turkey's farmers $35 million not to grow opium poppies... NY starts legalized offtrack betting... President Nixon declares U.S. will not redeem foreign-held dollars for gold... For first time GNP reaches trillion-dollar mark... B.F. Skinner: Beyond Freedom and Dignity (as behavior is determined by its consequences, proposes operant conditioning, positive reinforcement for behavior modification)... Harvard enrolls first women...

Charles A. Reich: The Greening of America: How the Youth Revolution is Trying to Make America Liveable (reports progression of consciousness as hallmark of period)... Ralph Nader forms Public Citizen as consumer lobbying group... Columbia University School of Social Work creates Industrial Social Welfare Center (provides 100 social workers in 1978 to such firms as Polaroid, International Paper and Equitable Life)... J. Sterling Livingston: "Myth of the Well-Educated Manager," Harvard Business Review... In uanimous ruling U.S. Supreme Court declares arbitrary discrimination against women as unconstitutional... National Institute on Alcohol Abuse and Alcoholism develops employee assistance programs to help employees with drinking problems (adds other programs later on physical, psychological problems)...

Newsweek: "The Black Movie Boom"... Plant closure act, WI, requires firms with 100 or more employees to give 60-day notice of merger, relocation, liquidation and shut-down (is followed by ME in 1981)... Union Women Alliance forms in San Francisco to gain equality in wages with men... In this time New York Convention and Visitors Bureau promotes City as "Big Apple"... Newsweek: "The Artist and the Computer"... Alaska Native Claims Settlement Act creates 13 native-owned regional corporations and some 200 village corporations to improve lot of natives with economic growth (funds programs with nearly $1 billion and 44 million acres)... Oregon is first state to pass "bottle bill," requires deposits on all beer, soft drink containers... The Farm is started, TN, as spiritually-oriented agricultural commune by some 300 West Coast hippies (evolves by 1981 with some 1,500 members to operate school, health clinic, recording studio, flour mill, cannery, construction firm, health-food market, and publishing company)... U.S. Supreme Court: <u>Griggs</u> <u>v.</u> <u>Duke</u> <u>Power</u> <u>Company</u> (rules employment test having effect of barring blacks from jobs as unconstitutional)... U.S. Army studies use of organization development (adopts program of Organization Effectiveness later)... Postal Service supervisors are given transactional analysis training by University of Oklahoma... U.S. Department of Commerce reports some 156 franchise firms operate some 3,300 outlets in other lands, 279 in 1980 with over 226,000 franchises overseas - 3,400 in Japan, 2,000 in Britain, 450 in Africa and 90 in Mexico... From Operation Breadbasket Reverend Jesse Jackson forms Operation PUSH in Chicago to provide inner-city students with pride, discipline, and work ethic, builds network of chapters in 32 cities by 1988 (shows in 1980 audit by Commerce Department the lack of accounting system and financial safeguards)...

Dave Meggyesy, former player for St. Louis Cardinals football team: <u>Out</u> <u>of</u> <u>Their</u> <u>League</u> (attacks NFL as an industry)... President Richard Nixon identifies 5 clusters of economic power: Western Europe, Japan, China, U.S.S.R. and U.S... Nevada permits counties to license bordellos, 37 approved 1988... "Dr." Clifford Noe, declared international swindler on highest level by British judge in 1972, is convicted of forgery (is convicted of mail fraud in 1977 and interstate transportation of forged securities in 1978, leaves jail in 1982 to retire from white-collar crime, buys Integrity insurance firm, NJ, with over $100 million in fake securities and bonds, is caught with nephew in 1988 Federal sting operation for handling false securities).

Business Events

Stephen Sondheim: "Follies" (heralds end of traditional musical with show-stopping production numbers)... After obtaining MBA degree, working for Standard Oil of New Jersey, Lamb-Weston and as financial consultant, Frank Lamb rents land to try farming, OR (acquires 12,000 acres of undeveloped desert land near Columbia River, uses technology, irrigation and employee incentive program to make farm productive, uses computer model in 1981 to meter irrigation and conserve energy to save some $1.4 million)... Russell G. Cleary becomes head of 1847 G. Heileman brewery, WI, with sales of $104 million (after 19 acquisitions by 1986 melds 9 ailing regional breweries as industry's 4th largest with sales of $1.33 billion)... Quinton I. Smith, Jr., becomes head of Towers, Forster & Crosby, traditional management consulting business specializing in executive compensation with sales of $12 million from such clients as Union Carbide since 1917 and Monsanto since 1939 (-1987, diversifies in market with acquisition of Cresap, McCormick & Paget in 1983, 300 consultants worldwide by 1986, to become industry's 2nd largest by 1986 with sales of $380 million to $635 million for Arthur Andersen & Co.)...

Ford recalls all Pinto cars to correct engine defects... Mack Truck contracts to build U.S.S.R. plant... Due to rising postal rates and declining advertising revenues from TV competition, <u>Look</u> stops publication after 34 years... Alexander's, NYC, promotes "hot pants" with fashion show... Intel invents micro-processor... Faced with anti-smoking messages under FCC "Fairness Doctrine," cigarette makers pull ads from TV and radio (starts media decline in ad revenues)... Water-bed industry, sex symbol of 1960s, produces sales of $13 million, $2 billion business by mid-1980s... Sanford Ziff starts Sunglass Huts with loan of $6,000, FL (operates 124 shopping-center kiosks by mid-1980s with sales of some $24 million/year, world's most efficient with sales of $5,200/square foot)... Britannia launches Seattle's apparel industry (becomes nation's largest privately-owned jeans maker with annual sales of $300 million by 1980 before declaring bankruptcy in 1983 - acquired by Levi in 1986 spawns City's Shah Safari in 1975, Generra, acquired 1985 by Farah Mfg., in 1980, Seattle Pacific Industries, City's largest by 1987, in 1981, International News in 1983, and Code Bleu in 1984 to join cooperative retailing center Zebra Club)... Tennis star Billy Jean King is first woman athlete to win $100,000 in single year... Xerox tests zero-base budgeting...

Arden-Mayfair, Carnation plead no contest to charges of fixing prices on dairy products... General Motors recalls some 6.7 million cars to replace faulty engine mounts... Wall Streeters Bruce Bent, Henry Brown create pioneering money-market mutual fund, followed by Merrill Lynch's Cash Management Account in 1977... Rich Mellon, 28-year-old son of retired deli owner, partner raise some $47,000 to open counter-culture restaurant R.J. Grunts in Chicago (develop business of Lettuce Entertain You Enterprises by 1984 to operate 18 individually unique Chicago eateries with sales of some $40 million, open first Ed Debevic's diner in 1980s to revive classic eatery)... After attending weekend religious retreats and self-growth workshops in early 1960s and giving such seminars in late 1960s, Lou Tice starts Pacific Foundation in Seattle with $1,000 to peddle inspirational motivational programs (evolves as multi-million-dollar business by 1980s with weekend seminars attended by tens of thousands of individuals and up to 500 business programs - success from market penetration with name recognition from corporations recognizing increasing value of human resources)...

Fortune: "High Style Disrupts the Men's Wear Industry"... To promote use of recycled paper Sandra Boynton designs Sentimental Greeting Cards (forms pioneering business in 1974 to achieve sales of some $20 million from cards, $10 million from other products in 1985)... General Motors adopts centralized strategic planning concept (switches to decentralized operations when implementation fails)... Merrill Lynch hire Ogilvy & Mather advertising business to design slick TV commercials (promotes "Bullish on America" theme with herd of thundering bulls)... Cessna aircraft introduces executive jet plane... Ross C. Alderson, William C. Sproull: "Requirement/Analysis Need Forecasting and Technological Planning Using the Honeywell PATTERN Technique," Industrial Applications of Technological Forecasting...

Docutel of Dallas develops automatic teller machines for banks (acquires Olivetti's U.S. subsidiary in 1982)... National Cash Register is forced to write off some $139 million on losses from computer business... Professional baseball league office starts drug education program... Stride Rite starts pioneering childcare service for employees, followed by some 2,500 firms by 1986 to help employees with child care... Cetus is first U.S. firm formed to use genetic engineering in modifying micro-organisms and producing industrial chemicals (is followed in biotechnology industry by Genentech, first to splice gene, to produce useful gene and go public in 1980, in 1976, Genex in 1977, Biogen in 1978, Molecular Genetics in 1979, Genetic Systems in 1980, Immunex and

Chiron in 1981, and T Cell Sciences in 1984)... Gerald L. Friedman starts American Municipal Bond Assurance to pioneer field of financial guaranty... Engineers at Bell Laboratories plan cellular radio system for cars, tested in Chicago in 1978 and commercialized in 1980s - status symbol in 1985... Horchow mail-order business to sell lavish merchandise is started in Dallas... Spectradyne invents system to allow hotel guests to dial TV programs on hotel networks (attains virtual monopoly on hotel business, provides motels with R-rated movies - racy foreign films in 1984, tests TV set computerized check-out system for hotels in 1984)...

After 121 years of family ownership Levi-Strauss & Co. becomes public corporation... After working in Fairchild's semiconductor division on photodiode arrays in late 1960s, physicist Edward Snow, electronics engineer Gene Weckler form Reticon with John Rado to develop image chips, 80 times more efficient in collecting light than photographic film...

Westec Security is started with $150,000 to make electronic-alarms for home security, acquired in 1982 for $14 million... Japanese car makers capture some 6% of U.S. small car market, 21% by 1980 (establish voluntary quotas in 1981)... Mary Ayres is first woman board member of American Association of Advertising Agencies... After joining Merrill Lynch brokerage house as management trainee in 1946, Donald Regan, former Marine Lt. Col., becomes chairman (-1980 when appointed U.S. Secretary of Treasury and then Chief of White House Staff in 1985, pioneers one of Wall Street's first planning departments, diversifies operations with broad range of services to create financial supermarket)...

Mattie Simons acquires rights to Harvard's National Lampoon (uses magazine's logo for paperbacks, theater productions, comedy albums and nationally syndicated radio programs, sells stock in 1975, produces movie "National Lampoon's Animal House" in 1978, grosses $210 million, to start movie business, plans in 1985 for television, video cassettes and line of sportswear, reports loss of $760,000 in first 6 months of 1985 with drop in magazine circulation)... National Advertising Review Board is created to handle complaints on taste, social responsibility and honesty of ads... When prime engine maker Rolls Royce collapses, financially-troubled Lockheed is saved from bankruptcy after extensive public debate by federal loan package from Congress for $750 million... Thomas Burrell opens black advertising agency in Chicago to design ads for both black, white firms (evolves as largest owned by black in 1984 with billings of $150 million)... Dow Jones starts News/Retrieval electronics service to provide clients with information on securities, general business (evolves as 8th largest in 1985 market with revenues of $100 million - rivals Dun & Bradstreet with 1985 sales of $325 million and TRW with 1985 sales of $160 million)...

After 4 attempts by unions to organize workers, GE's Appliance Park East plant in Columbia, MD, creates worker-management committee to handle grievances of employees (results in dwindling of union activity)... Mini-conglomerate Republic Corp. is saved from insolvency by Sanford C. Sigoloff, former nuclear physicist in business world since 1957, to pioneer corporate turn-around field with Stanley Hiller, Jr. (repeats turn-around success with failing retailer Daylin in 1974, is hired in 1982 to rescue building business of Santa Monica-based Wickes Co. from bankruptcy, revives business by 1985 to operate 245 lumber centers, 138 home improvement stores and 15 furniture showrooms, acquires Gulf &

Western conglomerate's consumer-and-industrial-products group in 1985 of $1 billion in cash, after failing to acquire National Gypsun, net $3 million on stock fight, and Owens-Corning Fiberglass, nets $30 million on stock battle during buyer frenzy on Wall Street, acquires Homecrafters Warehouse chain in 1986 and continues to seek other acquisitions with $1.5 billion in cash)... National Association of Security Dealers Automated Quotation is created (lists 4,444 corporations on 2,100 terminals nationwide in 1986 as world's 3rd largest stock exchange)... Travers J. Bell, Jr., partner pool $175,000 to underwrite minority-owned business, first black-owned member of NYSE (becomes business over $15 million by 1987)... GranTree, founded as consumer finance business in 1919, branches into rental furniture, 74 showrooms in 9 Western and Southwestern states by 1988 to follow industry leader, Aaron Rents, with 182 showrooms and Cort Furniture with 87 outlets in industry of some 500 showrooms (after entering retail market drops consumer finance in 1975, phases out retail stores in 1986, is acquired in 1987 via leveraged buyout by Spectrum of Los Angeles to go national and focus on rental office furniture)...

Bill Harrah, pioneering Reno gambler, is first in industry to sell stock in casino business to public... After some 6-7 years as apprentice in France, studying with European violin makers, and attending Violin-Making School of America, Salt Lake City, for 3 years, Paul Schuback opens shop in Portland, OR (becomes $500,000 business with branch in Houston by 1988)... GE teams up with France's SNECMA to design and make new jet engine, captures 63% of 1987 market to 27% for Pratt & Whitney and 10% for Rolls-Royce... Grateful Dead, rock-and-roll group of San Rafael, CA, incorporates (becomes $35 million business by 1988 to dispense funds to homeless and other causes via Rex Foundation, over $500,000 since 1985)... Former attorney Herb Kelleher starts Southwest Airlines at Dallas' Love Field, closer to downtown than international airport, for flights to Houston (grows as U.S.' 10th largest with routes from Texas to Illinois and California and no-frills service, buys TransStar Airlines for $60 million to compete with Continental - loses, starts Detroit flights in 1988 at City Airport - more convenient than Metro Airport hub)...

Needing money to support family Sandra Kurtzig starts ASK Computer Systems, CA, as part-time business in spare bedroom (evolves by 1987 with sales of $125 million in software for minicomputers)... Dr. Wesley Aplanalp buys Binyon Optical store, Portland, OR, with bank loans of $80,000 (sells 13 optical stores and 7 Eyeworld "superstores" in Northwest in 1988 to Sears' Eye Care Centers, chain of 50 stores in 5 states).

1972

General Events

NASA space shuttle project of $5.5 billion is approved, January 5... Projected budget for fiscal 1973 shows deficit of $25.5 billion, largest in peace time... President Nixon visits (February 21) China... Environmental Protection Agency bans (June 14) use of chemical pesticide DDT... Cesar Chavez signs Florida's first contract to protect migrant farm workers... After 2 weeks mass strike by major league baseball players ends... U.S. pilots stop overseas flights to demand stronger actions against hijacking... U.S., U.S.S.R. agree to cooperate in science, technology... Census Bureau reports (July 17) medium income of $10,285... Government requires foreign airlines in U.S. to adopt anti-hijacking procedures... Harvard receives $1 million from Mitsubishi to establish chair in Japanese studies... FTC indicts Xerox for monopoly on office copiers... Census Bureau reports population near no-growth rate from poor economy, more single and working women, birth pills, and legalized abortion... President Nixon launches "New Federalism" program to share federal revenues with city, county, and state governments (-1986)... California legislature passes law to permit informal marriages (launches State's commercial wedding chapel industry by transforming informal 1,075 of 178,000 marriages to 48,000 of total 210,000 in 1980)... Equal Rights Amendment is introduced, abandoned 1982 as 3 states short of ratification... During Presidential campaign candidate George McGovern's speech is booed by Akron rubber workers after promising to increase inheritance taxes for rich... First union of tennis players is formed with assistance of lawyer-agent Donald Dell...

Department of Health Education and Welfare issues special report on work (reports millions of workers economically trapped, socially scorned and bored with jobs)... American Frank Shorter wins Olympic marathon (with 4th and 9th places launches U.S. boom in running)... Office of Economic Opportunity provides funds to Indians to harvest jojoba seed, neglected by farmers for some 30 years... Steven Jay Gould, Niles Eldredge proposed "Punctuated Equilibrium" as new theory of evolution (view evolution process of abrupt fits and starts, interspersed with long periods of no change)... Time: "The Nomadic American"... To end jurisdictional strikes, featherbedding, and unnecessary work practices halting construction work in St. Louis, PRIDE, program for Productivity and Responsibility Increase Development and Employment, is instituted by building contractors and unions to establish cooperative labor-management relationships (is followed by Denver's Union Jack program and MOST program of Columbus, OH, in 1976 - others later at Indianapolis, Beaumont, TX)...

Boston's street singer Steve Baird is harassed by police (results in action to make street entertainment, started in 1960s by numerous jesters and troubadours, legal)... Office of Technology Assessment is created... Operation of San Francisco's Bay Area Rapid Transit, BART, is started, followed by new rail systems in 6 cities by 1984 with plans by 13 others... Connecticut forms pioneering Product Development Corp. to encourage industrial growth (begins operations in 1975 - 27 other states by 1980s)... Coastal Zone Management Act assists states to protect shores... Noise Control Act is passed... James Beard's American Cookery is published (promotes glories of U.S. cuisine)... Marine Mammal Protection Act is passed to save dolphins from being killed by commercial tuna fishermen... Democratic presidential nominee George S. McGovern is not endorsed by AFL-CIO... Bureau of Labor Statistics reports 31 million new jobs by 1988... Condos, new fad, are 40.3% of new housing... Osage Municipal Utilities, IA, starts conservation program, reduces use of natural gas by 45% and cuts growth in electricity demand to under 3% by 1989... Metropolitan Museum of Art hires Diana Vreeland, former editor of Harper's Bazaar and Vogue, as consultant for its Costume Institute, pioneers trend of fashion as art.

Business Events

Ronald Fenton and trial lawyer F. Lee Bailey (drops out later) publish risque <u>Gallery</u> adult magazine... LTD Corp. divests E-Systems, Dallas electronics business (becomes $4 billion business by 1982 with defensive electronic warfare systems)... Chicago's Jovan introduces Musk Oil fragrance for men (promotes Andron in 1981 as ultimate cologne for men with claims of "animal arousal" from phedromone Alpha androstenol)... Monsanto, Emerson Electric form pioneering InnoVem Capital as joint capital business... Some 4.6% of all women in work force are executives - 7.8% in 1982 and 9.2% in 1985...

One of U.S.' earliest and largest Quality-of-Worklife programs is started at Bolivar, TN, plant of Harmon International Industries (-1976)... Floundering airline, becomes Texas International later, is acquired by Frank Lorenzo's Jet Capital Aircraft leasing business (realizes profits of $40 million in 1978 after losing stock battle with Pan Am for control of National Airlines, creates non-union New York Air in 1980 to compete in East Coast shuttle market, acquires ailing Continental Airlines in 1982 to revive business after bankruptcy in 1983 as low-fare carrier)... After developing first successful coin-operated game of Pong, Nolan Bushnell starts Atari with $500, grosses $3 million first year (after selling business to Warner Communications in 1976 starts Pizza Time Theater, chain of restaurants with video game arcades and singing robots, declares bankruptcy 1984)...

Xerox holds 95% share of market for copiers, 65% in 1977 (shifts in laser printers in mid-1980s for new billion-dollar business in 1988)... Israeli-born Ted Arison, after helping to start Miami-based Norwegian Cruise Line, launches Miami's Carnival Cruise Lines with <u>Mardi</u> <u>Gras</u>, earns $153 million on sales of $564 million in 1987 (along with casino and resort hotel in Bahamas evolves as industry's largest by appealing to middle-income families with 7 "Fun Ships" with casinos to capture 20% of cruise market of 32 major lines with 100 ships by 1988, acquires Holland America's Seattle operations, 4 ships, 18 hotels and Westours travel agency, in 1988 for $625 million to boost share to 26%, plans 3 superliners, starting 1989, to carry 700 passengers each for total $600 million)...

Triad Systems is started, CA (pioneers industry's vertical marketing by selling computer systems tailored for particular industries)... Magnavox introduces video game of Odyssey... Beringer's winery, CA, is acquired by Switzerland's Nestle, followed by winery acquisition of Spain's Freixenet... The Limited chain opens Victoria's Secret to merchandise romantic intimate apparel (evolves 1982-87 as chain over 100 shops, plans 300 more by 1989)... Tom Golisano starts Paychex to process payrolls for small, medium-size firms (evolves by 1985 as industry's No. 2 with sales of $51 million)...

Michael L. Dever acquires co-ownership of Toyota Motor franchise for $15,000 (develops pioneering super-dealer business by 1986 as $360 million enterprise with 13 auto dealerships, motorcycle store, car-leasing operation and real estate business, plans $35 million hotel/retail complex in 1987 with space for 8 car dealerships)... Intel develops microprocessor silicone chip... Financial-consulting firm of Bruce Bent, Harry Brown makes CDs, only sold in amounts of $100,000, available to small investors... For first time since 1900 more bicycles are sold than cars... Xerox appoints ombudsman to handle employee grievances... World Hockey Association starts first season... Heisman trophy winner Johnny Rodgers is first client of football agent Mike Trope (by 1982 negotiates some $100 million in contracts for 150 football players)... Theodore Levitt: "Production-Line Approach to Service," Harvard Business Review (discusses innovations of McDonald's fast-food business)... Pornographic movie "Deep Throat" is filmed, earns some $50 million by 1982 (provides funds to Joseph, Anthony and Louis Peraino to build Florida-based crime empire with investments in New York garment companies, investment firms, pornographic theaters, drug smuggling and record publishing firms)... American Bakeries, General Host and Ward Food plead no contest to charges in fixing prices of bread... Northern Natural Gas pleads no contest in mail fraud for bribery of local elected officials... Texas Instruments develops first electronic calculator...

Fred Borch institutes strategic planning system at General Electric (organizes structure with president's office, corporate executive office, corporate administrative staff, corporate executive staff, executive boards, strategic business units)... Academy of Management Journal devotes one issue to general systems theory... Congress investigates ITT for tampering in federal anti-trust case by illegally suggesting political contributions for out-of-court settlement... After starting doughnut shop in 1962 at age of 16, 10th-grade drop-out Alvin Copeland starts super-spicy fried-chicken business, New Orleans (evolves as fast-food 725-unit chain, Popeye's Famous-Fried Chicken, and Copeland's Cajun-American Cafes with sales of some $500 million in 1974, tries takeover of Church's Fried Chicken chain in 1988 to become U.S.' No. 2)... With small fortune from machine tool business Earl Owensby starts movie business, NC (produces 33 features, all profitable, by 1987 with two-fisted Americana for foreign, south and midwest markets)...

Teledyne pioneers buyback movement in repurchasing stock... Home Box Office cable TV network starts in Wilkes-Barre, PA, with 365 subscribers... Viede France is started, VA, by 4 friends to produce "perfect" French bread (receive funds and technical advice from Grands Louins de Paris as France's largest miller, operate bakeries in 5 metropolitan areas by 1975 - 18 by 1984 to supply some 4,000 supermarkets and retail outlets, start retail cafe and bakery business in 1979 - 31 units by 1984 in addition to operating 13 full-service restaurants, realizes sales of some $55 million in 1984 - 28% increase over 1983)... Control Data starts work to develop Playdough as computer teaching system (after spending some $90 million on research gets first profits in 1983)... Christopher F. Reckmeyer, varsity football player, and brother Robert start business selling marijuana to high school students, VA (acquires $1.7 million estate in 1981 - brother with $435,000 layout, is arrested in 1985 for nationwide marijuana and hashish operation reaping some $100 million in profits - property in 15 companies used in laundering money seized by officials, pleads guilty to reduce charges)...

Life stops publication after advertisers go to TV (becomes monthly later)... Secretive Howard Hughes creates $2 billion Summa Corp. as holding company for interests in Airwest, Hughes Aviation Services, Hughes Television, NV operations with 6 casinos and TV station, Southern CA real estate and other miscellaneous enterprises... Ms., founded by Gloria Steinem, is published (goes mainstream as general-interest

magazine in 1988)... Century 21 real estate business is started in Orange
County, CA (operates 7,400 franchised offices nationwide by 1980)...
After ending-up with half-finished bankrupt apartment complex, Robert
Wooley starts Embassy Suites in Phoenix, AZ, to pioneer hotel business
for upper-middle-class clientele (with acquisition by Holiday Corp.
operates chain of 83 by 1987 with 70 in planning - joined in market by
Ramada and Hilton in 1987)... U.S. airlines starts screening luggage to
prevent hijacking... CBS acquires Steinway piano-making business... 1891
Keuffel & Esser, oldest U.S. maker of slide rules, drops out of slide
rule market with appearance of pocket calculators... Tennis pro Howdy
Letzriny starts Wild World of Sports, FL, to offer tennis package program
of lessons and video taping to corporation conventioneers (with success
of videos becomes $400-600,000 business by 1987)... After neglecting
grocery stores in suburbs, A&P, world's largest retailer in 1965,
launches "WEO" campaign to fight Safeway, Kroger chains with "Where
Economy Originates" (by 1973 loses top spot to Safeway - 3rd in 1978
before acquisition in 1980 by West German retailing conglomerate)...

General Mills acquires Eddie Bauer mail-order and retail business, WA
(after selling Wallpapers To Go and Izod Lacoste puts profitable Talbots,
119 stores for women, up for sale in 1988 to focus on food lines, sells
Bauer's 58 stores and mail-order to Spiegel catalog business in 1988 for
$260 million in cash)... Harry J. Gray becomes head of United Aircraft
Products, stodgy $2 billion aerospace defense contractor (builds United
Technologies as $16.7 billion conglomerate with canny acquisitions, after
losing touch balks at leaving helm in 1984 by undermining potential
successors, after board pressure accepts retirement for 1989 to groom
replacement)... After co-founding Control Data, Seymour Cray starts Cray
Research with partners in Minneapolis to build supercomputers, 60% of
market by 1988 with Control Data, closest rival, with 12.7% and Japanese
firms 23% (produces fastest Cray-1 in 1976, leaves chairmanship in 1981
to become consultant, develops innovative Cray-2 in 1985 to outdistance
competition, plans Cray-3 for 1987-88, loses key designer Steve Chen,
researchers in 1987 to build parallel-processing computer with backing of
IBM - joined in race by AT&T and Scandia National Laboratories)....

Chicago financial markets, Board of Trade, Mercantile Exchange and Board
of Options, start trading futures contracts based on Treasury bills and
currencies to pioneer stock-index futures to give portfolio managers a
hedge for cash investments (are blamed for stock market debacle on
October 19, 1987, are investigated for irregularities in 1988-89)...
Olympic runner Marty Liquori, partner open first Athletic Attic store
with wares for joggers in Gainesville, FL, chain of 100 in U.S., New
Zealand, and Japan by 1988 with sales of $40 million.

1973

General Events

After 17 months mandatory wage and price controls are lifted, except for
food, health and housing (January 11)... Peace treaty with North Viet Nam
is signed (January 27) to end war... Administration impounds $8.7 billion
appropriated by Congress for federal programs... Dollar is devalued 10%
(February 12) to improve balance of trade... President Nixon reimposes
(March 6) price controls on oil, gas... President Nixon freezes (June 13)
prices of all retail goods for 60 days... Vice President Spiro Agnew

resigns (October 10) after pleading "no contest" to charge of tax evasion... To pressure Israel to withdraw from occupied Arab lands, Arab oil-producing nations embargo oil exports to U.S. and European allies (results in long lines at gas stations, eases March, 1974)... Alaska Pipeline Bill is signed (November 16) to build 789-mile pipeline across state in delivering oil to lower U.S... All 531 U.S. airports screen boarding passengers... President Nixon asks (November 27) gas stations to close on Sundays (orders cut-backs in home heating oil, 15% reduction in gas production, and speed limit of 50 mph)... Senate Committee hears testimony about apparent conspiracy of CIA and ITT to disrupt Chile's election of Marxist Salvador Allende in 1970 (finds both at fault)... FDA recalls all diet drugs with amphetamine... Government report says Pentagon spends millions yearly to aid failing firms...

Alcatraz prison in San Francisco Bay opens for tourists... NJ tollway reduces speed limit to 50 mph to save use of gasoline... President Nixon signs Emergency Petroleum Allocation Act... First annual Truck-in is held by owners of customized vans, tricked-out with fancy extras... Arizona is first state to limit smoking in public places... Insurance industry analyst, Ramond Dirks, is investigated for passing tips from former executives of Equity Funding Corporation of America on possible downfall to 5 institutional clients (is censured by SEC for insider trading to permit clients to sell stock before scandal revealed, is absolved by U.S. Supreme Court in 1983)... COYOTE is formed as union of prostitutes in San Francisco... Conservative Heritage Foundation is established in Washington as pioneering advocacy think-tank with grant of $250,000 from brewer Joseph Coors, CO (raises $11.2 million for operating capital in 1985 to compete with rivals Brooking Institution with budget of $12.4 million and American Enterprise Institute with $12.8 million budget)...

U.S. economy is hit by recession, worst since 1930s (-1974)... Pregnancy Discriminatin Act amends Title VII of Civil Rights Act... U.S. share of global trade in special business services, such as engineering, consulting, brokerage, and licensing activities, is some 15% (declines to 8% by 1983 with rise in discriminatory rules by other countries to fall behind France, West Germany, Britain)... Postal service with China is resumed after being suspended for 25 years... Interstate sale of sperm whale oil is banned... Grand jury investigates rumors of payola in cash and drugs in record industry... After resigning as President Nixon's wage-and-price czar, C. Jackson Grayson starts $8 million fundraising campaign to found American Productivity Center (opens in Houston, TX, in 1977)... Drug Enforcement Agency is created... Commerce Department reports foreigners have invested some $16.5 billion in U.S., over $95 billion in 1983... Tanning device is invented so sun worshipers can get artificial tans...

Robert Tannenbaum, Warren H. Schmidt: "How To Choose A Leadership Pattern," Harvard Business Review (uses contingency method in classic article)... UAW, 9 international unions sue National Right to Work Legal Defense and Education Foundation to reveal its membership, rejected by U.S. District Court in 1984... John P. Cambell, others: "The Development and Evaluation of Behaviorally Based Rating Scales," Journal of Applied Psychology (introduces new performance appraisal technique)... Philip Meyer: Precision Journalism (in pioneering work encourages reporters to improve investigative journalism with computers)... One of U.S.' first fabric structures is "tent" erected as campus center for La Verne College near Los Angeles... David C. McClelland writes pioneering article on determining on-the-job competencies in American Psychologist... Daniel Bell: The Coming of Post-Industrial Society... Oregon is first state to adopt 55-mph speed limit for roads... Paul Chance: "Parapsychology is an Idea Whose Time has Come," Psychology Today... University of Minnesota, State Department of Education and State Educational System form Minnesota Educational Computing Consortium to develop computer learning programs, services for sale to educational users in U.S., world... B.T. Whatley, Tuskegee Institute, starts Farm Club (permits members to pick produce on farm for annual fee)... Newsweek: "The Broken Family: Divorce U.S. Style"...

For 2nd time in 2 years dollar is devalued... Vocational Rehabilitation Act requires federal contractors to have affirmative action plans for physically handicapped... Health Maintenance Act establishes health maintenance organizations... Consumer Product Safety Commission is created... Scientists at Sanford University, University of California at San Francisco develop techniques in gene-splicing or "recombinant DNA"... National Academy of Science starts project to discover "superplants"... Equity Funding pleads guilty to charges of SEC for issuing $2 billion in fictitious insurance policies.

Business Events

Des Moines Register sponsors first Annual Great Bicycle Ride Across Iowa for 800 bicyclists, some 9,000 in 1987 (by 1987 evolves as great moving party to distribute some $100,000 to communities from registration fees and licensed products)... Executives of Gulf and Ashland oil companies plead guilty in making illegal contributions to President Nixon's re-election campaign... Occidental Petroleum, U.S.S.R. sign largest private contract in U.S.-U.S.S.R. trade... IBM is found guilty in anti-trust suit, ordered to pay Telex $325.5 million... McDonald's opens first college facility at University of Cincinnati (opens first zoo outlet in 1974 at Toronto)... Banks use 2,000 electronic bank teller machines, over 65,000 by 1987... Pioneering children's Palace Book Store opens in Portland, OR, 353 competitors throughout U.S. market in 1987...

Beacon Hotel starts chain of Guest Quarters Suite Hotels for business travelers in Alexandria, VA, in 7 states by 1987... When Georgia Pacific is required by FTC to sell 20% of assets, Harry Merlo forms Louisiana-Pacific to operate 45 plants in West, South (expands by 1986 to 126 plants nationwide with sales of $1.5 billion)... Moet-Hennessy, founded 1743 as France's oldest champagne producer, acquires vineyards in Napa Valley, CA, 25 more foreign buyers, including Mumm, Piper-Heidsieck, and Taitinger, by 1988... Group of investors and Harvard business professors, headed by Walter Forbes, start venture to sell merchandise to home-computer users via electronic catalog (after losing some $4 million when home computers aren't readily available, switches to telephone orders with 800-number, expand to nationwide electronic shopping mall in 1981, as Comp-U-Cards International in 1984 becomes market's largest in 1987 with sales of $142 million)...

John Malone becomes president of TCI, near-bankrupt group of local TV cable systems (develops business to dominate cable market with 7.7 million subscribers while increasing U.S. value of operation 2,500%, bails out financially-troubled Turner Broadcasting Systems in 1987 to expand business)... Chicago Board Options Exchange lists first stock options... August West Systems is started in Portland, OR, as chimney-sweep business... Anthony J.F. O'Reilly becomes head of H.J. Heinze canning business (sponsors Profitability Improvement Program with teams of managers from different disciplines, functions to identify projects for cutting costs)... Nyad is started, FL, to publish lesbian materials... Burnham & Co. acquires Philadelphia's Drexel Firestone & Co. and its junk-bond dealer Mike Milken (starts trading new junk-bond issues in 1978 - market of $1.5 billion in 1978 to some $40 billion in 1986, is used in 1983 by Milken to pioneer financing of hostile takeovers - unsuccessful in 1984 raid of T. Boone Pickens on Gulf Oil, is investigated in 1988 by Congress, is target of SEC civil fraud charges in 1988 - Drexel Burnham Lambert pleads guilty in 1988 to 6 felony counts and record fine of $650 million and fires Milken in 1989 as part of record plea bargain)...

Some 20 sex clubs do business in Southern CA, 8 by 1974... Interior decorator Angel Donghia endorses line of bed linen (licenses decorator fabrics, furniture, china, glassware later)... Of industrial firms in world employing over 20,000 employees U.S. has 52.6%, Britain 12.5%, West Germany 7.2%, Japan 7% and France 6%... Woodside Management Systems forms in Boston as consortium of 6 local travel agencies to compete with national travel agencies (evolves with 65 members and some 2,500 offices worldwide by 1985)... Henry Mintzberg: "A New Look at the Chief Executive," Organizational Dynamics (uses empirical research to classify activities of manager by roles instead of traditional functions)...

Campbell Soup acquires Pietro's pizza chain of 5 units, operates 62 by 1984... American Machinist reports less than 1% of U.S. machine tools are numerically controlled... Students, Spanish teacher at Coronado High School, CA, form "Coronado Company" as illegal drug business (-1981 when ended by authorities)... GM's Packard Electric Division at Warren, OH, plans to stop hiring, building new plants (leads to 1977 agreement by union, management to cooperate in developing new relationships, Jobs Committee in 1978 to increase employment, problem-solving committees and work teams later to compete with low-wage competition, and new agreement in 1983 with two-tier wage structure for new workers and regular employees)...

Anti-Monopoly game appears during Christmas shopping season, wins 1982 court ruling on trademark infringement by Parker Bros... Frederick Smith, son of millionaire Memphis businessman, starts Federal Express as special package-delivery, next-day service with $4 million, followed by Postal Service's Express Mail in 1978, United Airlines in 1981 with package-express division, and United Parcel Service with air-freight business in 1982 (after early losses achieves sales of $800 million by 1982, dominates overnight market with sales over $220 million in 1987 to fight off UPS, buys Tiger International in 1988 for $880 million to go global in 1989)... Leone Ackerly starts home cleaning service of Mini Maids of America, Atlanta (operates 96 franchises in 24 states with sales over $9 million in 1987 - Jani-King in office cleaning with 1,200 in 1988)... Promoter-lawyer G. Davidson creates World Football League (-1975)... Gardner Kent, former Haight-Ashbury flower child in 1960s, starts Green Tortoise Bus Line without approval of ICC to provide counter-culture followers with inexpensive cross-country travel, legalized in 1981... Gary Gigax, shoe repairman, designs Dungeons & Dragons as fantasy role-

playing game, attacked in mid-1980s for harmful influence on teenagers...
Chef Gene Banchet opens pioneering Le Francais restaurant in Wheeling,
IL, community of 23,089 (evolves by 1982 as one of U.S.' best with
reservations up to year in advance)... Four factory-outlet stores operate
in Reading, PA, almost 100 by 1982... Braniff International emloys
sculptor Alexander Calder to paint planes with contemporary designs...
Steel industry employs some 509,000 workers, around 200,000 by end of
1985... After working for global metal trading business of Philipp Bros.,
operated by German-born Ludwig Jesselson (resigns when Jesselson puts him
on tight leash after daring oil raids), Belgium-born Marc Rich starts
commodity trading business with $700,000 (hires Philipp employees and
outbids former employer for contracts despite losses, rewards traders
with enormous incentives and free rein as long as they generate money in
building world's biggest trading operation in 1980s with revenues of $15
billion, agrees to order of NY judge in 1982 to submit Swiss documents
for tax investigation with $50,000/day fine - impounded by Swiss
authorities for violation of sovereignty, is indicted, denounced by
Izvestiya, in 1983 for tax evasion of $48 million - U.S.' largest, avoids
charges of U.S. tax evasion, fraud and racketeering by fleeing to
Switzerland in 1983 to continue business, settles tax charges in 1984
against U.S. subsidiary by paying record fine of $172 million, by 1988
becomes world's 2nd largest trader after U.S.' Cargill with sales of $13
billion/year)...

International Personnel Management Association is created by merger of
Public Personnel Association, Society of Personnel Administration...
Peter Phyrr: Zero-Base Budgeting... Georgia textile mill adopts 3-day,
36-hour work week... Playgirl displays male frontal nudity (files
bankruptcy in 1986, is rescued to focus on market of career-minded women
in mid-20s)... Nathaniel Wyeth invents first plastic container capable of
holding carbonated beverages... Mead Corp. starts Lexis electronic data
system to provide lawyers with legal, general business information by
accident after purchasing small printing plant with computer-based
technology in 1968, 75% of computerized legal research market in 1988...

Just before recession hits Britain, financier Gordon White opens branch
of Hanson Trust in NYC with $3,000 in cash, all Britain allowed out of
country (uses leveraged buy-outs in hostile takeovers of mismanaged low-
tech firms to build empire by 1987 of $10.9 billion with 8 enterprises
employing over 35,000, including Endicott Johnson shoes, Smith Corona
typewriters - buys 22-firm conglomerate SCM in 1968 for $930 million and
sells pulp and paper business for $960 million to operate in 1988 with
its assets over $4 billion, Jacuzzi baths, Ground Round restaurants,
Hygrade frankfurters, Kaiser Cement and Kidde, 108-company conglomerate,
in 1987, avoids 1987 October stock market crash to continue expansion
with $6 billion war chest for acquisitions in limited takeover market)...

Ebony publisher John Johnson launches Fashion Fair Cosmetics for
blacks... Fred Wasserman, Pamela Anderson start Maxicare Health Plans as
health maintenance organization, CA (by 1982 operate with membership of
140,000 before going nationwide with acquisitions and joint ventures,
acquire HealthAmerica and HealthCare in 1986 to become U.S.' largest HMO
with 1986 revenues of $1.6 billion, operations in 25 states, 20,000
physicians and over 1,600 hospitals and pharmacies to serve some 2
million members)... After years of talks General Motors, UAW sign first
nationwide Quality-of-Worklife Agreement... IBM introduces new disk drive

to revolutionize storage of computer data... Campbell food business puts
Spanish labels on cans... After Helena Rubinstein dies 1965, Colgate-
Palmolive acquires her cosmetic business... Texas Instruments with ITT
creates worldwide electronic network, Wang designs own in 1984... Sea
World opens in San Diego, its 3 parks acquired by Harcourt Brace
Jovanovich publishing and insurance conglomerate in 1976 (takes over
rival Marineland in Rancho Palos Verdes, CA, in 1987, acquires debt of
$2.7 billion fighting takeover of British publisher Robert Maxwell in
1987)... Steven Udvar-Hazy, Louis Gonda start International Lease Finance
in Beverly Hills, CA (earns $51 million on revenues of $180 million in
1987, makes largest plane order in history, 1988, to buy 100 Boeing jets
and 30 Airbus planes for $5 billion for lease to airlines)...

NYC's Chase Manhattan Bank opens in Moscow, first U.S. facility in
U.S.S.R. in 50 years... Seeking to support 3 children Ninfa Maria
Rodriquez Laurenzo, a widow, opens a Mexican restaurant in Houston, by
1988 10 places gross $20 million... William Hamilton, partner start
Inslaw to design computer software for law-enforcement agencies (obtain
$9.9 million from Justice Dept. in 1982 – suspends payments in 1983 for
inadequate performance, file for reorganization under Chapter 11 of
bankruptcy laws in 1985, sue Justice for $30 million in 1986 for
appropriating software and forcing bankruptcy – win in 1987)... Alice H.
Waters opens Chez Panisse in Berkeley with $10,000 loan to pioneer
California cuisine (opens 2nd restaurant in 1984, opens $20 million
Central Market to house some 90 vendors in Oakland in 1988)...

Australian-born Rupert Murdoch expands media empire with first U.S.
acquisition of San Antonio Express and News for $20 million, adds Star in
1974 for $12 million, New York Post in 1976 for $30 million – sold 1988
for $37 million, New York magazine, The Village Voice – sold 1985 for $55
million, and New West, sold for $3.5 million in 1980, for $17 million,
Boston Herald American in 1982 for $8 million, Chicago Sun-Times in 1984
for $100 million – sold 1986 for $145 million, New Women in 1984 for $23
million – spends $6 million in overhaul, Twentieth Century-Fox in 1985
for $575 million, Elle in 1985, Ziff-Davis trade publications in 1985 for
$350 million, European Travel & Life in 1986 for $5 million plus,
Automobile in 1986, Metromedia TV stations in 1986 for $2 billion to
build Fox network, Harper & Row in 1987 for $300 million – sells half
interest, Premiere in 1987, In Fashion in 1988, and Triangle
Publications, TV Guide, Seventeen and Daily Racing Form, in 1988 for $3
billion (gets U.S. citizenship in 1985)... Financial Accounting Standards
Board replaces Accounting Principles Board to determine new professional
guidelines.

1974

General Events

President Nixon signs (January 1) bill to set highway speed limit of 55
mph... OPEC ends (March 13) oil embargo (refuses to reduce crude oil
prices)... 110,000 clothing workers start nationwide strike... Gallup
poll reports (July 14) inflation chief concern of public... Gas stations
threaten to close to protest federal fuel policies... New Jersey adopts
mandatory plan to limit gasoline sales to cars with odd-numbered, even-
numbered license plates on alternate days, adopted on voluntary basis by
NY, MA, others... Scientists in Science report Freon gas from aerosol

spray cans destroys air's ozone layer... President Nixon resigns (August 9) from office as result of Watergate break-in... President Ford creates (August 24) special agency to monitor wages, prices... Consumer Price Index sets (September 20) record 1.3% rise in August... U.S. files anti-trust suit to break up AT&T (leads to divestment of Bell System in 1982)... President Ford asks (October 8) public to reduce driving 5% and use cold water to conserve energy... Mayor Beame, NYC, freezes hiring, cuts 1,510 jobs to save $100 million... President Ford signs (November 26) bill to grant $11.8 billion over 6 years to improve mass transit systems... Department of Labor reports (December 6) jobless rate of 6.5%, highest since 1961... FDA approves food coloring... Radio-Electronics shows how to build a personal minicomputer... In period to 1984 U.S. economy generates 18 million more jobs over losses, while Western Europe sees 3 million jobs disappear...

Bankrupt Parsons College in Fairfield, IA, is acquired by Beatles guru Maharishi Mahesh Yogi as center for Transcendental Meditation (creates meditation community in 1979 to spawn businesses by disciples, many with MBA degrees, such as Great Midwestern Ice Cream Co., sales of $3 million in 1986, Corporate Education Resources, sales of $3.5 million as leading maker of microcomputer software, and First Age of Enlightenment Credit Union - receivership in 1985, and to promote economic growth of Fairfield by attracting non-Sidha capitalists, such as Magnetics Research International with sales of $2.1 million)... National Football League players stay out of training camps during summer for 6 weeks before strike collapses (strike 57 days in 1982, canceling 7 games, to win higher salaries and benefits, strike 24 days in 1987 on issue of free agency only to lose, file anti-trust suit to challenge monolopy of NFL's reserve system, college draft and contracts)...

Trade Act gives relief to domestic producers if they are injured by imports (grants extended unemployment benefits to qualified laid-off workers, provides financial assistance to train workers for new jobs)... Taxpayers not belonging to a company pension plan are permitted by law to start individual retirement accounts, extended to virtually all in 1982 with total of $240 billion in such accounts by 1986... Congress passes act to establish Employee Stock Ownership Plans... Rouse Co., MD, starts development of Boston's seedy Faneuil Hall Marketplace (opens Quincy Market in 1976, South Market in 1977 and North Market in 1978 to complete $30 million project, revitalizes area to attract some 30,000 visitors daily to enjoy street entertainers, international bazaar of stalls, boutiques, unique eateries)... Equal Credit Opportunities Act eliminates discrimination by sex, marital status...

Dr. Raymond Damadian patents magnetic resonance imaging (devises first machine in 1977 - copied by GE, Toshiba, Siemens and others in copying machines, is upheld on patent rights in 1985 on infringement suit)... Regional Rail Reorganization Act authorizes formation of Consolidation Rail from 7 bankrupt railroads and Penn Central in 1976 (shows first profits in 1981, after public opposition to sale to Norfolk Southern in 1985 sells Conrail to public in 1987 for $1.6 billion in largest initial offering in U.S. history)... Financier Anthony Bliss becomes General Manager of Metropolitan Opera (facing deficit of $500,000 uses business methods to save opera - $100,000 surplus in 1982 budget of $63 million)... Hispanic groups boycott Adolph Coors brewery, CO, to end alleged employment discrimination and demand support for Hispanic community (-1984)... Universal Product Code is designed for supermarket industry... For first time since 1933 gold is sold legally in U.S... Housing and Community Development Act eliminates sex discrimination... Work is started in building 798-mile Alaska Pipeline from North Slope to Valdez Terminal on South Coast (-1977, requires construction crew of some 14,000)... Budget Reform Act requires consideration of appropriations, revenues as entity... U.S. Army funds research on ceramic engines, followed in 1981 by Japan's Ministry of International Trade and Industry with 10-year program to develop ceramics as next-generation industry... Harvard University Medical School, Monsanto sign 12-year contract for joint cancer research... First U.S. gay Chamber of Commerce is secretly formed in San Francisco, 45 more nationwide by 1984, evolves to represent savings and loan associations, car insurance agency, funeral parlors, newspapers, hotels, travel agencies, bath houses, etc... Construction of Sears Tower in Chicago, world's tallest building with over 110 stories, is finished at cost of $200 million (is put up for sale in 1988)...

Year-long daylight savings time is adopted to save fuel, repealed later... All remaining price and wage controls from 1971 are dropped... Taft-Hartley Act is amended to specify certain internal union activities as illegal... Major league baseball players, teams adopt arbitration process to settle salary disputes... Norman Kurt Barnes: "City Center Gets Down to Business," _Fortune_ (reports on use of new management techniques to operate 7 companies in opera, ballet and theater)... Air Force jet sets record flight, reaching speeds of 2,000 mph, from NY to London in 1 hour, 44 minutes, 42 seconds... Employee Retirement Income Security Act starts first systematic regulation of private pension plans (establishes Pension Benefit Guaranty Corp. as federal insurance company to protect workers, retirees)... Ten cents is needed for first-class mail, 11 cents in 1975, 13 in 1976, 15 in 1978, 20 in 1981, 22 in 1985 and 25 cents in 1988...

Boston forms Combat Zone, first designated urban porn district (by 1988 loses business with buyouts by land developers for building sites and use of VCRs)... Executives of U.S.' 7 largest oil firms try to convince Senate investigators energy crisis is real and not contrived by them... United Mine Workers President Arnold Miller wins 3-year, 52% pay-and-benefit hike for members (although far exceeding inflation is forced by miners to renegotiate agreement)... Health Care Act puts nonprofit hospitals, nursing homes under NLRB jurisdiction... Privacy Act gives federal employees right to examine their personnel files... Federal Deposit Insurance Corp. rescues Franklin National Bank, assets of $3.7 billion, from bankruptcy (saves New York Bank for Savings, assets of $3.4 billion, in 1982, Continental Illinois, assets of some $40 billion, in 1984, Bowery Savings Bank, assets of $5.3 billion, in 1985, First City Bancorp. of Texas, assets of some $12 billion, in 1988, and First Republic Bank of Texas, assets of $32.5 billion, in 1988 - largest bailout of $4 billion).

Business Events

Blue Cross and Blue Shield health plans merge... Cleveland Indians name Frank Robinson as first black manager in major league baseball... Interbrand is started to develop names for products, such as Polaroid's Spectra and analgesic Nuprin, to compete in new industry... Spencer Silver, after trying 1968-73 to determine what to do with weak adhesive, develops Post-it products for 3M to stick paper to paper... Marsh Supermarket in Troy, OH, uses first scanner at check-out counter to read Universal Product Codes... Merck scientists start research for cholesterol inhibitors (after investment of $125 million wins approval of FDA for Mevacor in 1987 to beat Japanese to marketplace)... After fashion designer Anne Klein dies, 26-year-old Donna Karan is given job (with Japanese backing starts own fashion house in 1985 to become newest fashion success in 1987)... Actmedia is formed to put ads on grocery shopping carts (is challenged in 1985 by Cooperative Marketing with flag-shaped ads on store shelves - by 1987 contracts with 7,300 stores)...

Gary Fisher puts together pioneering mountain bicycle as "mongrelized ballooner" (becomes millionaire in mountain-bike business)... Pickle family circus of 25 members forms in San Francisco... Ingersoll Milling Machine, founded 1887, installs industry's first computers (designs world's first electric transfer production line in 1982, drops membership in National Machine Tool Builder's Assn. in 1984 to protest its lobbying for governmental restrictions on machine tool imports)... J.C. Penney Co. repositions itself in market as "modestly-priced, fashion-oriented, national department store" (moves headquarters from Manhattan to Dallas in mid-1980s)... Black George Smith with 3rd grade education starts Smith Testing & Service Co. (starts Continental Inspection in 1975 and Smith Pipe & Supply in 1976, grosses some $24 million in 1978)...

Home-Stake oil-drilling firm is declared a tax fraud (results in losses by numerous celebrities in tax shelter)... By chance Julianne Street, widowed 1971, starts business, PA, to provide fresh herbs for area's haute cuisine (as Apple Pie Farm supplies products to quality restaurants, hotels, gourmet markets and other purveyors of fine foods on East Coast during 1980s)... Journal of Consumer Research is issued... Oscar de La Renta incorporates fashion business, started in mid-1960s after working for Balenciaga... Motorola's television plants are acquired by Japan's Matsushita electrical business... Golfer Deane R. Beman is commissioner of PGA Tour (promotes sport with marketing and merchandising, real estate development, golf-course operations - stadium golf course, TV productions and corporate sponsorships of tournaments, increases assets of $730,000 and income of $3.9 million to $41.6 million and $48.3 million in 1985)...

ITT's Harold Geneen is year's highest paid executive with total compensation of $791,000 (is topped in 1975 by John Harbin of Halliburton with $1,593,000, in 1980 by T. Boone Pickens of Mesa Petroleum with $7,866,000, in 1982 by Frederick Smith of Federal Express with $51,544,000, and in 1984 by Pickens with $22,956,000)... While American Motors increases sales 18.1% with small cars, Ford's sales decline by 20.5%, Chrysler by 18.5% and General Motors by 35.7%, loses place as most profitable U.S. corporation to Exxon with 65,000 workers laid-off and some 57,000 more furloughed... Gary Dahl sells some 1.3 million Pet Rocks, $4 each, during Christmas season (pioneers fad merchandising)... Lifespring is started, CA, to provide self-improvement training (evolves as cult movement)... Lockheed is first U.S. corporation of note to adopt Japanese quality control circle concept... After issuing newsletters since 1972 to regular patrons of his 35-40 bars and restaurants, OH, Larry Flynt publishes Hustler magazine for adults to provide blue-collar audience with sexually explicit photos, cartoons and other (with circulation over 1.5 million in 1979 - under 1 million in 1984)... U.S.

Windpower is started in New England as research, development business (erects largest farm of windmills, CA, in 1981)... Milton Glaser starts graphic design business (gets from sales of $868,000 to $2.3 million in 1983)... After leaving William Morris talent agency, Wally Amos starts homemade chocolate chip business of Famous Amos with $25,000 from singers Marvin Gaye, Helen Reddy (opens first store in Hollywood in 1975 - 36 worldwide franchises by 1987)... Ashram, pioneer chain of health spas, is started, CA (operates over 60 places by 1984)... Great Chefs of France Cooking School is started, CA, financed later by winemaker Robert Mondavi... Dow Jones Industrial Average records 663, lowest since 1970 recession... AT&T, U.S.' largest employer, bans discrimination against homosexuals...

Four years out of MIT, boy wonder Raymond Kurzweil borrows $150,000 to start Applied Intelligence business (develops first computer in 1982 with capability to recognize spoken words and transcribe them as printed text, unveils Voice Writer later with capability to recognize up to 10,000 words and print them as fast as spoken)... Occidental Petroleum, Associated Milk Products, Northrop, and Diamond International are found guilty of making illegal political contributions... With spiraling labor costs, dwindling ad volume, and shrinking circulation, New York Times, acquired 1896 by Adolph S. Ochs, nears bankruptcy (is revived with new labor contract to cut costs and automate, redesigns paper for affluent readers who fled city for suburbs, prints national edition in 1980, buys 5 small dailies and 2 TV stations in 1985 to operate 53 firms in 1986)...

After 58 straight quarters of straight profit gains of at least 10%, ITT shows 13% decline... After failures in making sportscars and all-aluminum homes, TV celebrity "Mad Man" Muntz starts new venture to make giant-screen television sets (peddles cars, sales of $12 million in one year, in 1940s, TV sets, sales of $55 million in one year, in 1950s, and car stereos in 1960s with eccentric commercials)... Allied Chemical, American Cyanamid and DuPont plead no contest to charges in fixing prices of dyes... Professional International Track Association is formed (-1976)...

Time, Inc. issues People magazine, pioneers celebrity journalism... IBM opens pioneering job training center for handicapped... Mildred Auksel, husband Joel start C.I. International in Tempe, AZ, with loan of $20,000 on house to sell oil paintings by neighborhood in-home parties (gross $125,000 first year and some $3.4 million in 1985, start selling franchises in 1986 for $60,000 each)...

Franklin National Bank of NY, 19th largest in U.S., declares bankruptcy in biggest U.S. bank failure (after mysteriously jumping bail of $3 million in 1979 with fake kidnapping by underworld, convicts international financier Michele Sindona, advisor to Vatican since 1969, in 1980 for defrauding bank of some $45 million - 25-year sentence, extradites Sindona to Italy in 1984 to receive 15-year term in 1986 for 1974 failure of Banca Privata Italiana and life sentence for 1979 murder of bank liquidator Giorgio Ambrosoli investigating fraudulant activities - death in 1986 by suicide or murder)... First specialty off-price Closetime store opens in CA (operates 235-store sunbelt chain by 1986)...

Robert E. Brennan starts First Jersey Securities (expands business in 1980s to operate 36 offices with some 1,000 agents handling around 100,000 accounts, after continuous investigations by SEC and other authorities for violations of law resigns in 1986 to devote time to International Thoroughbred Breeders and Due Process Stables, is sued in 1986 for fraud in selling investors stock in small firms with no or litle returns)... Pendleton Woolen Mills pioneers custom-size line of garments for big women, OR... Fishing International is formed in Santa Rosa, CA, to provide anglers with dream fishing trips throughout world, some 4,000 clients in 1986... James G. Treydig starts Tandem Computers (develops first fail-safe computer system and personal computer in 1977, in 1982 expands $300-million-a-year business with some 3,000 employees into $1 billion operation with 11,000 employees in 1985 by hiring experienced personnel, managing with loose supervision and giving ready access to top management, eliminating timeclocks, providing recreational facilities, social activities, generous stock options, sabaticals, and other benefits)...

Thomas J. Neff joins Booz, Allen & Hamilton as executive headhunter (joins Spencer Stuart in 1976 - president 1979, increases sales to $81.7 million, 137 consulants, by 1989 - 3rd in field behind Korn/Ferry International, $91.5 million and 258, and Russell Reynolds, $91.0 million and 181 consultants)... When fired from sales job at KCOP-TV, Los Angeles, Norman J. Paltiz forms Westwood One with savings of $10,000, by 1988 runs U.S.' No. 2 radio network with some 6,000 affiliated stations to follow ABC (starts business by syndicating 24-hour Motown music to 200 radio stations with 3 major national advertisers as sponsors, acquires Mutual Broadcasting in 1985 for $30 million to hit big time and NBC radio network in 1987 for $50 million to control one-third of market)...

Pacific Power of Portland, OR, starts employee volunteer project to do community work (leads to Oregon firms forming council in 1981 to promote voluntary employee involvement in civic programs)... American Hospital Supply installs order-taking computer terminals in hospitals... Deacon Maccubbin opens Lambda Rising in Washington, DC, as specialty gay bookstore...

Tinkerer Ed Anderson builds first automatic minidonut machine in Minneapolis garage (enters export market in 1984 as Lil' orbits to attract 100 responses for franchises)... Nine legal sports-gambling books, NY, handle $4.6 million/year in bets, 62 legal books in 1984, handle wagers of $808 million... John Broussard starts pioneering matchmaking business of Cherry Blossoms, $500,000/year by 1988, for Asian women and U.S. men, followed in 1979 by American Asian Worldwide Services - some $350,000 in 1988...

Grain trader Cargill buys North Star Steel, Minneapolis, for $84 million (becomes industry's 9th largest in 1988 with success as minimill using new technology to make steel from scrap)... Edward Gaylord inherits father's Oklahoma Publishing (builds country-western empire, including Grand Ole Opry and cable's Nashville Network, to become billionaire by 1988)... Walgreen is first drug chain with sales over $1 billion - 650 stores in 1979 in 32 states plus Puerto Rico and nearly 300 restaurants.

1975

General Events

Bureau of Labor reports (January 15) unemployment at 7.1%, highest in 13

years (climbs to 9.2% in June, 33-year high)... President Ford calls
(January 15) for attack on energy dependence, inflation and recession in
State of Union address... Six unions in AFL-CIO boycott loading of grain
for U.S.S.R... With FCC order, National Association of Broadcasters sets
7-9 p.m. as "family time" for TV viewers... 10,000 auto workers hold
(February 5) rally in Capitol to demand jobs, end to recession...
Northern Marianas Island becomes (February 14) U.S. Commonwealth, first
new territory since Danish West Indies in 1917... Congress approves
(February 26) $22.8 billion tax cut... Ernest Callenbach: _Ecotopia_
(writes fable about a country in western U.S. that sacrifices consumption
in order to ensure survival, unable to find a publisher borrows $3,500
from friends to print some 2,500 copies, sells rights to Bantam Books in
1976, by 1988 sells some 500,000 worldwide in 8 languages and 11
printings)... Congress halts strip mining in Death Valley...

Bill extending unemployment benefits to maximum of 65 weeks is signed,
June 30... U.S. exchanges 6 million tons of grain with U.S.S.R. for 10
million tons of oil... U.S. lifts (August 21) 12-year ban on exports to
Cuba... Government sues 6 cigarette firms for inadequate health
warnings... Supreme Court rules professionals not exempt from antitrust
laws (begins series of rulings to establish rights of doctors, other
professionals to advertise services in market, spawns field of
consultants advising clients on hard-sell pitches, leads to 1988 Justice
Department investigation of price fixing by doctors in 3 cities)...

Minnesota is first state to require businesses, restaurants and
institutions to establish no-smoking areas... U.S. shows trade surplus of
$3 billion, trade deficit of $156 billion in 1986... Bob Hall is first
wheelchair athlete to compete in Boston marathon... For first time
suburban office construction exceeds office construction in central
cities, ratio of 60% surburban and 40% city in 1987... New York
Legislature passes (November 25) $200 million tax bill to finance debt-
ridden NYC... NYC averts bankruptcy with Federal loans up to $2.3
billion... Two medical researchers discover that hybrid cell can be
cloned to produce antibodies, followed in 1979 by Hybritech's production
of monoclonal antibodies for commercial market to achieve 40% share by
1984...

Securities Acts Amendment encourages nationwide competition in trading
securities (abolishes minimum fixed brokerage fees, central reporting of
transactions, central order routing system, and national protection limit
on orders, spawns rise of discount brokers - 20% of transactions by
1986)... U.S.' population grows by some 4.8% since 1970, towns of 2,500-
25,000 increase by 7.5%... Federal Appeals Court rules on action by
Wilson Foods in 1972 (allows breaching of union contract only if
bankruptcy is at stake)... Metric Conversion Act is passed... In period
to 1986 consumption of beef drops by 9%, chicken rises nearly 35%... In
this time (-1979) Soviet Union secretly attempts to acquire 3 banks,
Northern CA, as means for access to advanced technology... U.S.
Commission on Transnational Corporations is formed to draft code of
conduct for multi-national enterprises... National Conservative Political
Action Committee is created (launches New Right)... 5 states pass
"memorials" for balanced federal budget, 25 others by 1979... Energy
Conservation Act sets standards for fuel-efficient cars... California is
first to pass state law to govern organizing, bargaining of agricultural

workers... Soviet Union forms Belarus Machinery Co. in Milwaukee to sell Russian-built tractors... California enacts bill to limit malpractice claims against doctors, 30 states by 1985... First annual National Passive Solar Energy Conference meets... RCA SATCOM I is launched into space (provides TV programming via satellite for Time's Home Box Office cable network)... E.O. Wilson, Jr.: <u>Sociobiology:</u> <u>The</u> <u>New</u> <u>Synthesis</u> (proposes societies evolve to suit environment)... Robert Alberti, Michael Emmons: <u>Stand</u> <u>Up,</u> <u>Speak</u> <u>Out</u> <u>and</u> <u>Talk</u> <u>Back</u> (pioneers field of assertiveness training for women)... Congress bans price agreements between manufacturers and retailers that would prevent discounting...

Betty Rundback: <u>Bed</u> <u>&</u> <u>Breakfast</u> <u>USA</u> (pioneers, first of kind since 1930s, new field of lodging in best-selling book for travelers)... 18-hour strike by doctors at Chicago's Cook County Hospital ends by agreement with Cook County Health and Hospital Governing Commission... Biologists hold conference, CA, to discuss concerns on proposed gene-splicing experiments... In this time Stanford's Edward Shortliffe designs Mycin computer program to help doctors diagnose infectious diseases and choose remedies, becomes more accurate than humans... Seattle Children's Theatre opens in small theater outside city's zoo (evolves by mid-1980s with attendance of 100,000, 6,850 subscribers and budget of $932,000, achieves success weaving funding sources of schools and government with corporate and foundation sponsors)...

Forbes & Wallace, last department store in Springfield, MA, closes its doors (leads to revival of worn-out factory center with service sector, such as Mass Mutual and Monarch Capital insurance firms in 1980, and small-scale manufacturing to provide some 65% of city's employment in 1988)... U.S. Supreme Court rules federal government has exclusive rights to any oil and gas resources on Atlantic outer continental shelf beyond 3-mile limit.

Business Events

<u>Time</u>: "The TM Craze: 40 Minutes to Bliss" (reports movement of some 600,000, 30,000 enlisting each month, with national headquarters in Los Angeles, 370 TM centers and some 6,000 instructors - 2,000 in other countries for some 300,000 meditators)... <u>New</u> <u>York</u> <u>Times</u> reports (August) on T-shirt fad, started early 1960s when Budweiser sold emblazoned shirts with personal and political statements printed by T-shirt shops while-u-wait... Soviet-born Lev N. Landa, director of Moscow's Programmed Instruction Institute at Academy of Pedagogical Science, migrates to U.S. (forms Lanamatic Systems to develop training programs, using flow charts based on logical thoughts and actions of experts in particular field, to prepare novices for work, results in development of expert programs for computers)... Big 3 auto makers offer (January) rebates to customers to spur flagging sales... First software for personal computers is a game program... McDonald's opens first drive-thru outlet in Oklahoma City, converts 2,800 units to new operation by 1979... International Volleyball Association forms professional league (-1980)...

Black Muslim businesses, restaurants, fish markets and bakeries, go under with death of Nation of Islam leader Elijah Muhammad... Burrelle's Information Services, founded 1888 as clipping service for clients, is transformed by Robert C. Waggoner with industry's first computers to cover television and radio (starts NewsExpress in 1984, monitors some

16,000 publications, to provide daily service to clients for
$18,000/year)... Intel introduces personal computer Altair 8800 as build-
it-yourself kit for electronic hobbyists and hackers, followed in market
by models of Japan's MITS and Imsai, Tandy and Apple in 1977, and IBM in
1981... Fearing FDA will order listing of beer ingredients on labels,
didn't happen, Schlitz of Milwaukee, founded 1849 to become No. 1 in beer
industry, starts brewing beer in this time with corn syrup instead of
barley malt (results in financial disaster from flat beer, is sold to
Detroit's Stroh in 1982)... Fred Meyer, chain of 91 multi-department and
8 specialty stores in Northwest, pioneers with outlets in stores for
savings and loan association, Safeway grocery chain installs automatic
teller machines in 1985...

1896 Olympia brewery business, WA, acquires 1884 Theodore Hamm brewery of
St. Paul (merges with 1883 Lone Star brewery of San Antonio in 1976)...
W.T. Grant variety store chain declares bankruptcy, largest U.S.
retailing failure... Producer Merv Griffin, former band singer and talk-
show host worth some $600 million in 1988, syndicates "Wheel of Fortune"
and "Jeopardy" TV game shows via King World to independent TV stations
for some $100 million/year, sells to Coca-Cola in 1986 for $250 million,
buys Beverly Hilton for $100.2 million in 1988, fights tycoon Donald
Trump in 1988 for control of Resorts International - spoils divided)...
Steve Wozinak, electronic expert, and Steve Jobs, handles fund-raising,
product design and marketing, start Apple Computer business in garage, CA
(accept venture capitalist A.C. Markkula as partner in 1977, introduce
successful Apple II computer in 1977, incorporate in 1980 to sell stock
at $22/share with Jobs as chairman, hire John Sculley of Pepsi-Cola as
president for yearly salary of $1 million and signing bonus of $1
million, launch Macintosh computer in 1984 to sell record 70,000 in 100
days)... For first time New York Commodity Exchange trades gold...

Robert K. Brown, former Green Beret, publishes <u>Soldier</u> <u>of</u> <u>Fortune</u>
<u>Magazine</u> (evolves with circulation of some 166,000, is found guilty in
1988 for ad by mercenary hired for murder)... Bethlehem Steel employs
high of some 115,000 workers, 48,500 by 1983 (becomes first major U.S.
firm with comprehensive program for permanent layoffs)... For first time
1919 General Motors Institute, only U.S. college operated by industrial
firm, grants degrees in engineering and industrial administration (as 1
of 18 business-supported degree granting schools becomes independent
college in 1982 - 140 U.S. firms give academics courses by 1983)... In
this time (-1979) luxury stores open on Rodeo Drive in Beverly Hills to
establish area as shopping playground for wealthy (leads to closings of
Lanvin Paris, Fendi, Ungaro and Celine boutiques and openings of
moderate-priced shops and discount clothing business in 1985-86)... Top
Fruehauf executives are convicted of criminal tax evasion...

In these years (-1979) Edward Dunbar opens discount gas station in Castro
Valley, CA (expands into chain of 34 stations around San Francisco to
earn $33 million/year, is sentenced to 5 years in prison in 1985 for tax
fraud of $32 million - highest recorded)... Northrop sells F-5 fighter
planes to Switzerland in barter deal (trades some $209 million of Swiss
exports to other countries)... Colombia-born Carlos Leheer Rivas is
deported to Colombia for selling marijuana (within few years becomes
billionaire drug lord, is extradited to U.S. in 1987 for trial and
convicted in 1988 - property confiscated and draws life plus 135
years)... Xerox launches Printing Systems as separate venture to do

electronic publishing... Rock Island is first Class I railroad liquidated... In this time Bed & Breakfast International organizes to provide national reservation service, by 1980s with some 200 national or regional agencies... Pan American, TWA plead no contest to charges of illegal fare-cutting... Gulf Oil, Phillips Petroleum agree to consent degree for using slush funds for political contributions... 70 U.S. resorts provide vacation real estate time-sharing, imported from Europe in early 1970s (evolves from some 10,000 users to around 500,000 by 1985)... Strategic Planning Institute forms... During this time (-1979) Lane Nemeth starts Discovery Toys business (evolves with some 10,000 in-home demonstrators in 1984 and sales of $34 million)... 10-team women's professional softball league organizes (-1979, is abandoned after poor promotion, weak financing, internal conflict, inexperienced management)...

Together Development business is started in Rochester, NY, as matchmaking agency (evolves to operate 55 outlets, some franchised, in 14 states by 1985 to achieve sales of some $5 million/year)... Hyatt chain introduces French concierge concept to U.S. hotels in Regency Clubs, some 1,000 in luxury hotels by 1987... First Team Auction business, GA, shows sales of $54,000 (grows to some $90 million with over 100 auctions nationwide in 1986)... Chicago's law firm of Baker & McKenzie employs 326 lawyers (expands to some 1,808 in 1986 to become No. 1 legal megafirm – 27 others with 300 lawyers or more)... White Consolidated acquires Westinghouse's appliance business... United Brands agrees to consent degree with charges by SEC for bribing Honduran official... Women's Bank, U.S.' first, opens, NYC, to give special attention to women depositors, borrowers (after substituting sound business practices for political ideals shows profitability in 1979)... Record 120,000 Americans declare personal bankruptcy... Floundering South Bend Lathe is saved from closing by 500 employees using Employee Stock Ownership Plan to purchase firm's stock (pioneers movement)...

Bill Gates, 19-year-old Harvard drop-out with Paul Allen and venture capitalist David F. Marquardt, starts Microsoft, Albuquerque, to design software programs (converts BASIC language for mainframe computers to personal computers to achieve success, sales of $16 million in 1981 to $172.5 million in 1986 as industry's 2nd largest to Lotus Development, moves business to Seattle area in 1979 to achieve success with programs for IBM computers, at age of 30 sells stock in 1986 to realize $1.6 million in cash and $350 million on 45% share of stock)... 3 major real estate chains operate in U.S. (evolve with 7 nationwide, including Century 21 with 7,400 offices, Electronic Realty with 3,500, and Red Carpet with 1,250 in 1981, and 48 regional operations)... Holiday Inn starts consumer research activity... Houston-based Kwik Kopy operates regional chain of 150 copy centers, each franchised for $8,000 (expands by 1980 to 470 stores, each franchised for $29,500 – Postal Instant Press with 1,222 places in 1988)...

Baseball arbitrator sets a precedent in sports by ruling option clauses in contracts of pitchers Dave McNally, Andy Messersmith only bind them to their clubs for one extra year (negates baseball's reserve clause, results in rise of average salary from $52,300 in 1976 to $143,756 in 1980s with many free agents acquiring 7-figure, multi-year contracts)... When money management business flounders Leslie C. Quick, Jr., forms Quick & Reilly Group as discount brokerage house (caters to other discounters in 1975 to handle 60 firms with some 660,000 accounts in 1988, evolves by 1988 as 3rd largest discounter with 59 branches, 600 employees and 1987 sales of $28.2 million)... George R. Heublein, after investing $600,000 in Washington horticultural supply business, acquires Oregon's Melridge, originated in 1961 by Dutch horticulturalist Jan de Graff who developed first virus free lily bulbs in 1968 to pioneer market, for $600,000 (raises millions in 1983 from stock issue to become world leader with businesses in Holland, Austria, England and Burundi by 1987 and enjoy lavish lifestyle, files for bankruptcy reorganization in 1987 with accusations of insider trading and false financial reports in suits by new management and stockholders)... In this time Hayne Leland and Mark Rubinstein, Berkeley professors, devise portfolio insurance to give investors a hedge against future downturns in stock market, covers hundreds of millions in assets by 1984 (as a result of buying and selling stocks in large quantities are accused, including partner John O'Brien with marketing skills, in being primary cause of stock market crash on October 19, 1987)...

Ross Johnson, former head of Canadian subsidiary, becomes president of Standard Brands, chief executive in 1976 after boardroom fight (merges with Nabisco in 1981, sells Nabisco to R.J. Reynolds for $4.9 billion in 1985 and becomes president of new organization, is CEO of RJR Nabisco in 1986 to reorganize core businesses in cigarettes and packaged foods by sheding loose-leaf tobacco operations, Heublein's liquor, and Kentucky Fried Chicken, tries $17.6 billion leveraged buyout with top managers, Shearson Lehman Hutton in 1988, charged by board in using stake to net $200 million on break-up of conglomerate in acquiring assets over $2 billion by 1993, only to attract other offers up to $25 billion in bidding frenzy - U.S.' largest takeover by Kohlberg Kravis Roberts with RJR Nabisco being sued by bondholders for losses up to $16 billion)...

Saturday Market, 35 vendors, opens on weekends from April - December in Portland, OR (by 1988 operates with budget of $450,000, staff of 13, and at least 300 stalls/weekend)... Nestor business is formed to pioneer design of neutral networks to let computers learn like humans, joined in market by hundreds of rivals in 1985-89... Philadelphia wholesaler Donald T. Marshall's Sun Distributors pioneers market consolidation by 1989, field of 320,000 independent firms, mostly Mom-and-Pop operations, drops to 285,000 in $1.6 trillion industry, in buying 20 firms in glass, 5 in hardware and 15 general wholesalers while Super Valu, $10 billion food distributor by 1989, grows to supply 2,800 stores... In this time (-1979) Robert Van Tuyle starts to form efficient, low-cost network of nationwide nursing homes, 1,000 homes in 40 states by 1988.

1976

General Events

Congress overrides (January 27) Presidential veto to provide $45 billion for health, welfare and manpower programs... Tax Reform Act reduces tax shelters and raises taxes on wealthy by requiring minimum payments... National Airlines is hit by 127-day strike... Census Bureau reports (February 7) metropolitan areas of South, Southwest only ones with substantial growth since 1970... U.S. Supreme Court rules states may ban employment of illegal aliens... National Health Science Foundation reports U.S. lead in science to be declining... After protests by environmentalists first Anglo-French Concorde SST is allowed to land in U.S... Congress passes (July 22) bill over Presidential veto to provide $3.950 billion for jobs... After 9 years MIT scientists synthesize first complete functioning gene... Appeals Court voids NY's Blue Laws... 165,000 members of UAW shut down Ford with strike... Record $3.25 million is paid for Rembrandt oil... Over Presidential veto Congress provides (September 30) $56 billion for social services... FDA bans red dye No. 4... $68 million football stadium opens at Meadowlands, NJ, becomes base for NY Jets and NY Giants pro football teams... U.S., Romania sign 10-year trade pact... Milton Friedman, laissez-faire economist, wins Nobel Prize... First "Rocky" film is produced (revives Horatio Alger theme of "Road to Glory")... U.S. Army hires Simulations Publications to design tactical wargame for training... Baltimore Colt end John Mackey wins anti-trust suit against NFL for restrictions on free agency...

California Conservation Corps is formed to employ youth in public service work... First complete computer game, Colossus Cave, is designed at Princeton... University of Chicago Graduate School of Business establishes Center for Decision Research... Reformed golfer Jack Osborne founds United States Croquet Assn. to revive sport (holds 1st annual championship in 1977, goes from 60 clubs in 1981 to 300 by 1988 with 3,500 members)... When union workers of Coors Brewery, CO, strike to protest lie-detector tests, firm hires non-union workers (ousts union with employee election in 1976, settles controversial AFL-CIO boycott in 1987, one of longest in modern times - unravels 1988 as Teamsters step in)... Copyright Act grants purchasers of copyrighted work right to use or resell material (creates Copyright Royalty Tribunal to require users of copyrights, such as cable industry and broadcasters, to pay fees into fund for allocation to copyright owners)... "The Environment" is formed as urban commune by 85 friends, members living together in Los Angeles apartment house, as professionals and artists believe they can grow spiritually and be financially rich in atmosphere of love, friendship and good feelings (besides individual activities acquire shares in 3 businesses by 1981 to gross some $35 million)...

Governor Michael Dukakis creates Massachusetts Industrial Finance Agency to stimulate economic growth (by 1986 provides some $3 billion for industrial development and loan guarantees for 1,700 projects to create over half-million new jobs)... First International Joint Conference in Artificial Intelligence meets in U.S... 3,420 registered lobbyists do business in Washington, DC (grows to some 8,800 by 1985 with non-registered estimated at 10,000-20,000 - over 30 for every member of Congress)... Debtors Anonymous, modeled on Alcoholics Anonymous, is formed by truly compulsive spenders... Toxic Substance Control Act is passed... New Jersey voters approve legalized gambling for Atlantic City... Penobscots open pioneering Indian bingo-game parlor, ME... Public Buildings Cooperative Use Act encourages use of commercial activities in government building...

National Institutes of Health formulate federal guidelines for regulating laboratory research on gene-splicing... John T. Molloy: <u>Dress for Success</u>... Alaska Natural Gas Transportation Act is passed to build gas pipeline from Alaska to U.S., never started... Some 2,000 visitors see wares of 13 firms at Chicago's Robot I Exhibition, 1986 show with some 200 firms and 20,000 attendees... Foreign Corrupt Practices Act makes bribes, commissions overseas illegal... 1966 skateboarding fad heats up with introduction of polyurethane wheels and fiberglass boards (leads to California Amateur Skateboard League in 1980 and National Skateboard Association for professionals in 1983)... First Night, pioneering day-long festival of arts as substitute for usual New Year's drunken revelry, is held in Boston (with success sells consulting services to other U.S. cities - 13 by 1986)... Robert Heilbrunner: Business Civilization in Decline... U.S. Supreme Court upholds Detroit zoning ordinance to require "adult theaters" be at least 1,000 feet from any two other such places... U.S. Supreme Court grants advertising protection of First Amendment...

Time: "Let the Costume Ball Begin" (reports on current theatrical fashions)... Reverend Wildmon forms National Federation for Decency (with Coalition for Better Television advocates consumer boycotts in 1980 of firms advertising unacceptable programs)... After research on embedded drugs in 1960s Judah Folkman devises method for humans to absorb drugs with continuous relief... Newsweek: "Getting your heads together" (describes popular consciousness movement of Yogi classes, "growth" courses, "awareness" cruises, Esalen, Transcendental Meditation, Mind Control, Arica)... Event Concepts sponsors annual professional volleyball championship in Southern CA (-1984, ends with strike of players for more money)... Quincy Market, part of Boston Faneuil Hall renewal project, opens as festival complex of 165 shops, boutiques, markets, stalls, restaurants, taverns, museum and offices (generates sales of some $480 million in 1982 with 18 million visitors)... After 10 years United Transportation Union, Florida East Coast Railway settle longest strike in railroad history...

Congress passes law to admit women to military academies... Bill Koch wins silver medal at Innsbruck in cross-country skiing, first such medal ever won by U.S. in Winter Olympics (starts U.S. boom in Nordic skiing)... Jimmy Carter wins Iowa presidential primary (becomes $20 million winter tourist industry by 1988)... Maynard Jackson is first black mayor of Atlanta (requires underwriters of $305 million bond issue to employ blacks, on retiring in 1985 helps establish National Association of Securities Professionals to advance cause on Wall Street)... When unable to buy personal computer for school, Jonathan Rotenberg, age 15, starts Boston Computer Society with adult Richard Gardner (becomes largest group of enthusiasts in U.S. by 1987 with 23,000 members each paying $35/year in dues, introduces personal computer in 1987)... Scottish-born Douglas A. Fraser, metal finisher and welder for Chrysler in 1936, becomes president of United Automobile Workers (-1983, is named to Chrysler's Board of Directors in 1980 in return for union cooperation in rescuing business)... Yale opens its graduate School of Organization and Management to prepare students for administrative positions in business, government and nonprofit organizations (after conflicts, including student protest, between functional areas and new organizational experiential program, reorganizes in 1988 to focus on traditional MBA courses).

Business Events

Left-wing investigative Mother Jones magazine is published, San Francisco (exposes perils of Ford Pinto car, is remade for general market in 1988)... Pan Am is first airline indicted for criminal negligence in crash... Tom Duck, retired insurance agent, moves to Tucson (starts Ugly Duckling Rent-A-Car business in 1979 with leased cars, by mid-1980s becomes industry's 5th largest with sales of $64 million from over 550 franchises in 41 states and licenses of Ugly Duckling logo to everything from license plates to golf shirts)... Lockheed Aircraft admits to paying $1.1 million to Dutch Prince Bernhard, $2 million to Japanese officials (loses Canadian contract in scandal)... Pan Am starts Boeing 747 non-stop service between NYC-Tokyo... ABC offers industry's first $1 million-per-year contract to Barbara Walters of NBC... NBA, ABA basketball leagues merge... Charles Revson, creator and head of Revlon's No. 1 cosmetic business, dies (declines to No. 3 before acquisition by financier Ronald Perelman, after working for father's $350 million conglomerate Bellmont Industries acquires small conglomerate McAndrews & Forbes for $47.7 million to build empire with Technicolor in 1983 for $100 million, Consolidated Cigar in 1984, and Pantry Pride's convenience-store chain in 1985 for $60 million, in 1985-86 for $1.8 billion to operate assets over $2.99 billion)... New York Times converts to computer word-processing...

Abercrombie & Fitch with 19 stores, opened 1892 to outfit outdoor endeavors of wealthy gentlemen, declares bankruptcy, NYC (is liquidated 1977, sells name to 1892 Oshman's Sporting Goods of Houston - opens first store in Dallas in 1982 and sells 27 Abercrombie & Fitch stores to Bidermann, NY wholesaler of apparel, in 1985 for $30 million in cash and $20 million in notes, plans 100 stores in 1990s)... Volkswagen starts first foreign car production in U.S. at New Stanton, PA (sells 162,005 vehicles in 1981 - 73,920 in 1986, produces one-millionth car in 1985 before closing in 1987-88 due to competition)... After first business folds Robert Moog, inventor of music synthesizer, joins computer scientist Raymond Kurzweil to pioneer electronic music (introduce innovative digital synthesizer to reproduce sounds of traditional instruments)... By chance Gary Rogers, owner of failing theme restaurant, acquires Dreyer's Grand Ice Cream of Oakland when owner fails to get bank loan for expansion (becomes one of most dynamic small businesses in U.S. in 1980s)...

Patrick L. McConathy starts McConathy Oil & Gas, Shreveport, LA, with partners to pioneer new generation of wildcatters (after testing some 100 wells operates 20 commercial wells to achieve revenues of $18-24 million in 1987)... Robert Mondavi Winery is first in Napa Valley to attract tourists with concerts, art exhibits and cooking classes... Sophia Collier, Connie Best start Natural Beverage, Brooklyn, to market Soho Soda, fruity fizz drink (sells 12 flavors in 33 states with sales of $30 million in 1987)... 100 firms sponsor some 76% of network TV ads... Business making inflatable advertisements is started, San Diego (becomes multi-million-dollar activity by 1985)... Saul, Robert Price open first Price Club, pioneers price discounting in San Diego as warehouse business to sell goods to members with low mark-ups, prices 20-40% under supermarkets and discount stores, no credit, no service (expands to 20 clubs to achieve sales of some $1.4 billion as industry's leader in 1985 - $3.323 billion in 1987 with 2 million members, is followed by Sam's Wholesale Club with 11 outlets, Costco Wholesale Club with 12 places, Pace Membership Warehouse with 6 branches, CUB Foods of Super Valu stores with 44 units, and 37 Bi-Marts - sold with 147 Pay 'n Save drug stores in 1988 for $232 million to Thrifty, Los Angeles, with 640 drug stores and discount stores and 3 sporting goods chains with 194 stores)...

McDonald's introduces Egg McMuffin breakfast sandwich, pioneers breakfast meals in fast-food industry (expands to complete breakfast menu in 1977,

serves 1 of every 4 eaten outside home in U.S. in 1986)... Entrepreneur
William F. Farley, age 33, acquires Anaheim Citrus Products, asking price
of $1.7 million, with $50,000, borrows rest from banks on assets
(develops business by 1985 as one of largest privately-owned industrial
corporations with leveraged approach, acquires 3 more firms with
leveraged buyouts by 1985 before acquiring $1.4 billion Northwest
Industries with funds from banks, preferred stock to operate $2 billion
empire)...

Three men from Bear Stearns investment firm form Kohlberg (leaves 1987
because of aggressive strategy) Kravis Roberts & Co. to specialize in
leveraged buyouts, financing via high-yield junk bonds from Drexel
Burnham Lambert, with special limited partnerships (between 1976-82
raises 3 pools of funds for 35 different LBOs - $5.6 billion buyout fund
in 1988 with capability to borrow up to $56 billion from banks, handles
1st $1 billion LBO in 1984, starts hostile takeovers in mid-1980s,
pioneers managerial role in buyouts in 1985 - by 1988 with huge
conglomerate, U.S.' 7th largest behind GE with sales of $38 billion, with
23 firms producing everything from French colonial furniture to dairy
products, engineers $6.2 billion LBO of Beatrice food and consumer-
products conglomerate in 1985 - makes $7 billion by selling off parts,
$4.2 billion LBO of Safeway Stores in 1986 to sell or close 1,174 of
2,336 stores - drops from No. 1 to No. 3 in field, $3.8 billion LBO of
Owen-Illinois, glass containers and health care, and $2.4 billion LBO of
Jim Walter construction in 1987, and $1.8 billion LBO of Duracell
batteries in 1988, wins bidding war with $24.5 billion for RJR Nabisco,
U.S.' 19th largest with 1987 sales of $15.8 billion, in 1988, U.S.
largest takeover to top Chevron's 1984 buy of Gulf for $13.4 billion)...

Eastman Kodak introduces instant camera (after selling some $16.5 million
halts production in 1986 by order of U.S. Court of Appeals on patent
infringement suit by Polaroid, drops business in 1988)... United
Technologies acquires Otis Elevator for $398 million, U.S.' largest
acquisition until topped by McDermott International's acquisition of
Babcock & Wilcox in 1977 for $748 million, UT's takeover of Carrier in
1979 for $1 billion, France's Elf Aquitaine's takeover of Texas Gulf in
1988 for $2.3 billion, DuPont's takeover of Conoco for $7.8 billion in
1981, Texaco's takeover of Getty Oil for $10.1 billion in 1984, and
Socal's takeover of Gulf for $13.4 billion in 1984 (acquires Carrier air
conditioning in 1979 and Mostek microprocessor technology in 1980 - sold
1985 with $546 million write-off, forms Building Systems in 1982 to
design "intelligent" buildings, builds City Place in 1982 in Hartford,
CT)...

John Donald MacArthur, billionaire insurance entrepreneur and real estate
tycoon, dies (leaves foundation with $862 million to make grants, no
strings attached, to "exceptionally" talented individuals)... Metromedia
acquires Harlem Globetrotters basketball team for $11 million (is
acquired with Ice Capades skating show and Ice Chalet, ice skating rink
chain, in 1986 for $30 million by International Broadcasting)... E.S.M.
Group is formed, E.S.M. Government Securities a subsidiary (acquires
losses to point of insolvency in 1978 - not shown on books, is forced
into receivership in 1985 with losses of $320 million, triggers run of
depositors on Cincinnati's Home State Savings Bank with funds in E.S.M.
Securities, forces Ohio to close 71 state-chartered thrifts to avoid
panic, results in State indictment of Home State Savings' head and

Federal indictments of E.S.M. officials)... Fort Lauderdale accounting office of Alexander Grant & Co. is hired to audit books of E.S.M. Government Securities (in largest settlement made by major public accounting firm pays $50 million to 17 municipal governments losing money in collapse of E.S.M. and seizure by Federal authorities in 1985)... After working on cars since 1972 Steve Marchese, 2 partners start pioneering car detailing business in Costa Mesa, CA, some 4,000 such shops in U.S. by 1986 (sells franchises in 1986 for $45,000 each, closes over 90 deals in some 5 months)... William Millard borrows $250,000 from venture-capital firm to start Computerland Corp. (becomes world's largest computer retailer with 245 stores in U.S. and 14 countries by 1982)...

Using science of ergonomics Bill Stumpf, MN, designs handsome, elegant, comfortable Eron chair, sells nearly 2 million by 1986 (designs Equa chair with Don Chadwick in 1984 to sell some 350,000 by 1986)... Edmond Scientific (is started in 1942 as bedroom business by disabled Norman Edmonds to sell camera lenses by newspaper ads, develops Edmond Salvage with surplus optical equipment from U.S. armed forces after W.W. II, grinds own lenses in 1974) introduces Astroscan inexpensive telescope, sells nearly 4,500 during course of Halley's Comet in 1985-86... Archer-Daniels-Midland and Cook Industries plead no contest to charges in defrauding customers by short-weighting... Venture capitalist Robert A. Swanson, scientist Herbert W. Boyer start Genetech, first commercial venture in bio-tech field to produce interferon, human insulin with gene-splicing (produce first genetically engineered human protein in 1977, clone human growth hormone in 1979, sell stock, first in industry, in 1980 - in first 20 minutes from price of $35 to $89 and close at $71.25, produce first vacine by gene-splicing in 1980, clone interferon in 1981, license human insulin to Eli Lilly in 1982 - first gene-splicing drug on market, test tissue activator in 1984 - tentative approval in 1986, receive FDA approval for human growth hormone in 1985, develop commercial process to make vitamin C in 1985, introduces t-PA wonder drug in 1988 to become top pharmaceutical firm)...

Liz Claiborne, husband open clothing business to dress women executives (sell stock in 1981, reach Fortune 500 list of largest industrial companies in 1986 as one of fashion's hottest labels, shows growth rate of 36% for 1983-87, plans 13 First Issue stores by 1989, retires in 1989)... International Diamond is started to sell investment diamonds, bankruptcy in 1982... Wickham Skinner: "Manufacturing - Missing Link in Corporate Strategy," Harvard Business Review (reports production function de-emphasized by firms favoring marketing, finance in planning)...

General Tire & Rubber accepts consent decree in charges by SEC in using illegal slush fund for political contributions... Cadillac makes last mass-produced U.S. convertible, revived in 1982 by Chrysler... After 23-year career at BankAmerica, Joseph J. Pinola becomes chairman of United California Bank with network of 21 banks in 11 western states (launches expansion program in 1978 to develop First Interstate Bankcorp as U.S.' 9th largest by 1986 with 23 banks, 950 branches in 12 western states, assets of $49.7 billion and 38 bank franchises with assets of $4.6 billion, proposes merger with troubled BankAmerica in 1986 - rejected)... Borg-Warner adopts strategy to reduce vulnerability to swings in traditional manufacturing by moving into service sector (evolves from 12% of total sales to about 33% in 1982)... Barter Systems opens in this time in Oklahoma City to arrange exchanges of goods and/or services between clients (handles some $200 million in transactions during 1980)... I. Magnin of Federated Department Stores pleads no contest to charges with fixing prices of women's clothing... First Great Expectations Center opens, Los Angeles, as oldest private membership club for singles (becomes industry's largest with 6 centers, 5 franchised, and some 9,000 members in 1980s)... Canada's Four Seasons Hotels invades high-class U.S. hotel market (operates 11 and manages 19 by 1980s, is joined later by Meridien chain of Air France, Novotel's L' Hotel Sofitel, Dunfey Hotels of Aer Lingus and by upgrading of Holiday Inns, Ramada Inns and Hyatt Regency chain)... Casa Gallardo restaurant with Mexican menu opens St. Louis (is acquired in 1979 by General Mills to develop chain of some 21 outlets by 1983, is followed by Chi-Chi's Mexican food chain, MN, in 1977 with 73 places in U.S., Canada by 1982)... Joan Barnes, former dance and recreation teacher, starts preschool exercise program for children, San Francisco (with local popularity sells Gymboree franchises in 1979 - by 1986 250 with sales of $8 million, after licensing name to manufacturers of childen's products opens first retail stores for line of playwear in 1986)... Federal Paper Board, Mead, Fibreboard, Container Corporation, American Potlatch, and 6 others in industry plead no contest to charges in fixing prices of folding cartons...

Henry Mintzberg: "Planning on the Left Side and Managing on the Right," Harvard Business Review... Howard R. Hughes, eccentric entrepreneur with holdings in major aircraft company, helicopter business, casinos and hotels, ranches and mines, magazine, television station, and real estate, dies leaving no heirs... American Society for Personnel Administration starts accreditation program for personnel managers... After 7-year rise through ranks, William H. Bricker becomes head of Diamond Shamrock oil business (acquires coal producer Falcon Seaboard for $250 million in 1978, acquires Amherst Coal in 1981 for $220 million, during recession acquires drilling rights in Alaska's Beaufort Sea in 1982 for $160 million - dry hole in 1983 to lose $60 million, purchases ailing Natomas oil in 1983 for $1.5 billion, loses $605 million for 1985 while providing executives with lavish perks, after refusing 3 offers to sell business is forced to resign by Board in 1987)... Chrysler adopts Quality of Worklife Program...

Brigade Quartermaster mail-order catalog is issued to provide action-oriented males with choice military clothing, equipment... To promote business Heinold hog market of Kouts, IN, sponsors team of racing pigs on Midwest fair circuit (attracts some 3 million fans in 1986)... Former model Martha Stewart starts catering business in Westport, CT, home (publishes first cookbook in 1982 to develop culinary empire in art of showing off in entertaining, becomes lifestyle consultant for K mart's home fashion division in 1987)... Warner Communications acquires Nolan Bushnell's Atari video game business (develops Video Computer System, despite competition by Mattel's Intellivision in 1980 and later by Coleco, Milton Bradley, Emerson Radio and Fisher-Price Toys of Quaker Oats to acquire nearly 75% of electronics home-game market by 1982, after losing $539 million in 1983 with crash of market in video games sells Atari in 1984 to Jack Tramiel, former head of Commodore International, for $240 million)... After Digital Equipment opens minicomputer market in 1960, IBM brings out Series/1 line... After retiring as head of Georgia-Pacific Corp., Robert Pamplin, 65, acquires small sand-and-gravel firm in Portland, OR (after 2 acquisitions runs business in 1988 with sales of $420 million)... 67 Spanish radio stations operate in U.S., 182 by

1988... Mobil petroleum buys Montgomery Ward for $1 billion, U.S.' 6th largest retailer with 419 stores and sales of $5.251 billion in 1979 (after 113 years drops mail-order catalogs in 1985) to Sears' 864 with sales of $17.514 billion, and Container Corp. for $1.7 billion (after disappointing results sells Container in 1986 for $1.2 billion and Ward's revitalized 315-store chain in 1988 to management investor group for $3.8 billion leveraged buyout)... Membership in American Society for Industrial Security increases 133% by 1980... Baseball owners, players sign pact to permit partial free agency... Designer Willi Smith, dies 1987, and Laurie Mallet start Willi-Wear, Ltd., a $22 million sportswear firm by 1988 (opens first U.S. Willi-Wear surreal boutique for men and women in 1988 to join 2 in London and 1 in Paris)... Carolee Friedlander starts jewelry business, sales of $16 million in 1987, to design fashionable fake pieces... After working as financial analyst and building mobile homes, Salvatore H. Alfiero builds Mark IV Industries by 1988 as one of hottest little takeover conglomerates, assets of $19 million in 1983 to $612 million in 1987 with $200 million in cash for raids...

Sugar Ferris, editor of <u>Bass 'n Gal</u> magazine, forms women's fishing circuit (schedules 5 big tournaments in 1988 with $257,000 in prize money - men's 1968 Bass Anglers Sportsman Society with over $2 million)... David Draper starts business, C&C with $120 million in sales by 1988, installing sunroofs in cars (evolves to modify Ford Mustangs as convertibles and Chrysler minivans for export to Europe, sells in 1987 to Masco Industries for expansion funds)... Independent Educational Consultants Assn. forms as industry trade group of those advising high school students on admittance to college, grows from 15 to 120 members by 1988... Former astronaut Frank Borman is new head of Eastern Air Lines with high costs and huge debt (-1986, cuts labor costs in 1977 with innovative profit-sharing plan to compete in fare wars - resentment of workers by 1983, takes unilateral wage concessions in 1983, loses battle with union in 1983 when machinists win strike for 32% pay raise over 3 years, gets $367 million in concessions from machinists in 1984 in return for managerial role, in 1986 gives unions ultimatum: 20% pay cuts or bankruptcy, is forced out in sale to Texas Air in 1986).

1977

General Events

U.S., Switzerland sign treaty to give U.S. special help in cases with money laundering by organized crime (sign 1982 accord to cooperate in investigating stock-swindle cases - 1983 Swiss Parliament makes insider trading a crime)... After jurisdictional battles, Cesar Chavez's United Farm Workers signs agreement with Teamsters Union to end conflict in organizing migrant farm workers... U.S., Canada sign $10 billion pact to build gas pipeline from Alaska to Midwest... President Carter urges citizens to keep home temperatures at 65% to conserve energy... 6 windmills are tested at Rocky Flats, CO, for generating power... HEW bans discrimination against 35 million disabled Americans... U.S., Cuba agree on fishing rights... Members of Clam Shell Alliance hold first Seabrook protest at atomic plant to oppose building of power operation, NH... 799-mile Trans-Alaskan oil pipeline opens to deliver oil to Valdez for shipments to lower states... <u>New York Times</u> reports trend of early retirement... Government backs (September 23) landings of Anglo-French

Concorde planes in 13 cities... President Carter attacks (October 13) oil industry for opposing energy plan... U.S. quits (November 1) International Labor Organization because of U.S.S.R. influence and violations of procedures (returns in 1980 after reforms)... Civil Aeronautics Board bans cigar and pipe smoking on U.S. planes (leads to elimination of all smoking on flights under 200 miles in U.S. in 1988 and formation of Great American Smoker's Club to charter flights for smokers between Dallas and Houston)... Washington traffic is snarled by farmers protesting economic conditions, seen at 30 state capitols... U.S. Postal Service drops airmail and railroad post offices (institutes Express Mail Service to realize break-even point in 1985 on revenues of $543 million)... General Telephone and Electronics accepts consent decree on charges by SEC in making illegal political contributions... James F. Fixx: The Complete Book of Running (inspires jogging movement)...

Movie documentary "Pumping Iron" glorifies world of body-builders (promotes widespread interest in sport, is followed in 1985 by "Pumping Iron II: The Women")... President Carter announces National Energy Plan as energy problem is "the moral equivalent of war" (states goals to reduce consumption, build reserves, develop alternative sources)... SRI International's Edith Weiner and Arnold Brown, pioneer consultants in field of trend-spotting, devise methodology to identify social trends in business intelligence project... U.S. Lines accepts consent decree on SEC charges in giving illegal rebates... Department of Labor reports some 1.9 million women operate businesses, 2.9 million in 1982... Occidental Petroleum, as does Uniroyal and Zale jewelers on similar charges, accepts concent decree on SEC charges for using slush fund to make illegal political contributions here, abroad... Federal Maritime Commission fines Sea-Land Services $4 million in making illegal payments to customers...

Reverend Leon H. Sullivan, former board member of General Motors, formulates ethical code for U.S. firms doing business in South Africa (is signed by 153 of some 300 U.S. firms with operations in South Africa, introduces Phase II in 1984 to urge U.S. firms to be active in social, economic, and political liberation of blacks in country, leads to GM, other firms leaving country in 1988)... U.S. Supreme Court strikes down ban on advertising by lawyers (allows lawyers in 1982 ruling to advertise specific services)... Elvis Presley, "King of Rock 'n' Roll," dies in Memphis (leads to opening of Graceland estate in 1982, becomes mecca for tourists - 640,000 visitors in 1988 to spend some $10 million on tickets, food, souvenirs)... Group of MIT computer devotees create Infocom as interactive computer game so players can become personally involved in fictional action (introduce "Zork I" in 1979, evolve as industry's leader by 1985)...

North Dakota grants legal gambling rights to charitable organizations... Renaissance Center, built by consortium led by Henry Ford II, opens to revitalize downtown Detroit (defaults on mortgage in 1983)... Singer Anita Bryant, followers start anti-gay-rights crusade (results in loss of advertising work by singer after boycotts of endorsed products)... On insistence of U.S., trustees of Teamsters Central States Pension Fund are replaced by independent managers... First statewide electronic funds transfer system is established, IA... William Ophulf: Ecology and the Politics of Scarcity... California requires public schools to offer courses in personal economics... Wisconsin passes no-fault divorce law to provide compensation to wife after contributing financial support to family while partner obtains professional degree (is upheld by State Supreme Court in 1982)... First annual Personal Computer Forum is held... Anheuser-Busch Brewery accepts consent decree on FCC charges in making illegal payments to customers... First corporate challenge race for running teams of businesses is sponsored by Manufacturers Hanover Trust, NYC (expands to 9 cities in 1983)... Officials of Chemical Bank of New York plead guilty to charges of violating bank secrecy act in laundering money for alleged narcotics dealers... Michael Korda: Success (stresses appearance more important than intelligence, leadership, shrewdness, creativity, technical skills or motivation for successful career)... Space shuttle Enterprise is tested for flight... Foreign Corrupt Practices Act prohibits U.S. firms from making payments to government officials of other countries... Iconocolastic house with shocking-pink, red facade is built in Miami, designed by Arquitectonica team of architects with goal to enliven drab functional structures of modern buildings...

Pacific Northwest Labor College is formed in Portland, OR, with funds from major unions (-1984)... Gossamer Condor, designed by Paul MacCready, is first man-powered plane to fly over 3-mile course... NFL, National Football League Player's Association sign their first collective bargaining agreement... Foreigners obtain 34% U.S. patents, 47% in 1987... Film "Saturday Night Fever" captures disco decade... Stanford researchers devise Emycin computer expert system... U.S. consumer groups boycott Switzerland's Nestle for distribution of baby-food formula in Third World, legal in countries but not U.S. (-1984 when Nestle drops product)... Richard Caliguiri becomes mayor of economically depressed Pittsburgh (-1988, transforms old steel town into gleaming corporate center with new bridges, roads and upgrading older neighborhoods)... Scouting/USA is new name for Boy Scouts.

Business Events

New York Times reports supermarkets with declining volume due to rising trend in eating out... 17-year-old jockey Steve Cauthen is first to win $5 million in yearly prize money... Bethlehem Steel reports $477 million loss in 3rd quarter, largest in U.S. history... New York Times reports (October 31) on trend in weekend marriages by couples living apart... In one of U.S.' biggest sex discrimination suits, Reader's Digest agrees to pay 2,600 female employees $1.5 million... Carmen Koch Jones, age 61, opens Kids Korner Fresh Pizza in Wausau, WI (operates 40 locations n 8 states by 1987 to highlight elderly starting own businesses)... Tandy introduces TRS-80 computer for distribution through its Radio Shack stores, 6,700 in all states by 1987 and 386 computer centers (achieves $3.3 billion in 1986 sales as king of retail market)...

Commodore International introduces Pet personal computer for mass market (presents innovative AMIGA multi-tasking computer in 1986)... Some 8,000 Hispanic-owned businesses are operated in Dade County, FL (jumps to around 16,000 by 1985 as Miami becomes center for Latin Americans)... Timberline Reclamation is started as business, MT, to rehabilitate streams (evolves as $500,000 operation in 1984, is joined in market by Environmental Concern business to revive ecology of damaged marshes, prairies and forests - $4 million in project in 1985)... Some 20,000 shopping malls generate $300 million in sales, 50% of total retail sales... After frustration in not finding suitable apparel, Nancye Radmin starts Forgotten Woman retail business, NYC, to sell clothes for overweight women (becomes chain of 16 upper-end specialty stores catering to large-size women)... Dal Carter acquires grocery store in suburb of Portland, OR (invents automatic credit system to replace cash dividend stamps with encoded plastic cards, store's computer)... Raymond Mueller, president of chemical-equipment company, and 2 investors start Comair as regional airline in Cincinnati as side-line venture with $60,000 (in 1984 cooperate with Delta Airlines in joint marketing program to do $46.8 million business with service to 22 cities)... Lehman Brothers, Goldman Sachs underwrite first rated bond conceived as junk for LTV, used in market of early 1970's in trading of below-investment-grade bonds of Penn Central and real estate investment trusts)... Alfred D. Chandler, Jr.: The Visible Hand: The Managerial Revolution in American Business...

Tradewell business is started to find new markets for inventory products of other firms (grosses some $100 million in 1984)... After farming 15,000 acres of conventional crops with difficulty, Agrifuture grows jojoba and kenaf in San Joaquin Valley, CA (earns some $114,000 on revenues of $2.4 million from exotic crops)... Coco-Cola acquires Taylor Wine business (after failing to challenge Gallo winery with massive advertising and low prices sells to Joseph E. Seagram & Sons in 1983)... After selling profitable businesses in axles and electronic products which comprised two-thirds of sales, Napco Industries develops first national distribution network in supplying non-food products to supermarkets... Eastern Airlines reserves sections in planes for smokers, Northwest bans smoking on all domestic flights in 1988... Sanyo of Japan acquires Warwick Electronics, Whirlpool plant making TVs for Sears in Forest City, AR (leads to violent strike in 1985 after bitterness and mistrust)...

Brandt Legg, VA, at age of 10 makes 25-cent investment in stamp, resells item moments later for $85 (after dropping out of high school as too busy making money, starts career as philatelic entrepreneur to acquire $12.4 million, runs 22 corporations by 1986)... Communications Control is started, NYC, to sell "high tech" security devices (achieves sales of some $30 million in 1981)... Dr Pepper sponsors summer-long rock festival, NYC... GM's Chevrolet plant in Adrian, MI, forms Quality Control Circles (after 2nd try in 1979 becomes successful in 1981)... New ultralight aircraft is created when John Moody puts go-kart engine on back of hang glider for demonstration at Oshkosh flying meet... Pioneering Management Analysis Center is created as consulting agency to advise businesses on integrating strategy with firm's culture... Ralston Purina acquires NHL St. Louis Blues hockey team (after losing some $19 million sells franchise in 1983)... For first time sales of Coca-Cola are topped by those of Pepsi...

Joel Hyatt starts Legal Services in Kansas City to pioneer no-frills, low-cost clinics (with advice of H & R Block expands with advertising to 175 franchised offices by 1985 as largest in nation with some 20,000 clients/month)... Jewel Tea Co., Chicago supermarket chain, pioneers generic labeling of packaged products... Merrill Lynch provides Cash Management Account for middle-income investors as one-stop financial service, amasses some $125 billion in deposits by 1986 (patents account in 1982, is imitated by banks and savings and loan associations in 1982, launches Working Capital Management Account in 1986 to provide financial services for small, medium-sized businesses)... 1977-78 season's share of prime-time television audience for 3 major networks is some 91%, 73% for 1984-85... George Lucas: "Star Wars" (in 3 years achieves total income of $524 million, by 1983 grosses some $365 million on investment of $30 million in 1980 sequel, "The Empire Strikes Back," releases "Return of the Jedi" in 1983)... After working as football coach and selling insurance door-to-door for ITT Financial Services, super-salesman, A.L. Williams, starts private agency to sell insurance underwritten by Massachusetts Indemnity & Life (sells $65.5 billion worth of coverage in 1985 with gospel of "no-frills," inexpensive term-life insurance as best deal for customers as they can invest money saved for higher returns, despite critics sells $81 billion in term insurance in 1987 with 183,000 working-class agents)...

After embezzeling some $61,000, including forging signature of actor Cliff Robertson, at Columbia Pictures, David Begelman is ousted as production chief after battle among board members and outsiders (is rehired as consultant with higher salary - later head of MGM and United Artists, leads to firing of president Alan Hirschfield in 1978 for discharge, later head of Twentieth Century Fox, and in black listing of Robertson for several years in pressing charges)... Commodity-style trading in bonds is developed at Chicago Mercantile Exchange, Chicago Board of Trade (promotes futures and options markets for stocks in 1982 to become world capital for new trading)... Merrill Lynch acquires Ticor Relocation Management (acquires United First Mortgage in 1978 and Paula Stringer Realtors in 1979, puts up real estate division for sale in 1986 to focus on securities business)...

With Harvard MBA Ken Hakuta starts Tradex to export U.S. goods to Japan (with tip from Japanese parents imports Wallwalker toy to U.S. in 1982, sells some 30 million before fad dies and 120 million after craze by unorthodox marketing to earn some $20 million on total sales of $57 million by 1986, topping sales of Pet Rock and Rubik's Cube, to acquire name of Dr. Fad)... After losing some $2.3 million Radio City Music Hall, opened 1932, plans to close in 1978 (is denounced by public outcry, after $2.5 million renovation reopens in 1979 and hires Richard Evans, president of Atlanta-based Leisure Business specializing in rescuing ailing recreational enterprises, as chairman, revives operation with contemporary fare, such as rock concerts, comedy acts and stage spectaculars, to replace traditional family entertainment, creates Concert Division in 1979 to stage 120 events/year in hall and elsewhere - 97% sold-out, markets corporate sponsorships, expands activities with Theatrical Production Division and Production Service/Events Division to stage trade shows and business meetings, shows first profits since 1955 of $2.5 million in 1985 - 40% of income from new activities)...

Merle Harman opens pioneering Fan Fair store at Milwaukee mall to sell sports memorabila to fans, 90 stores by 1988 (is followed in market by Kevin Olson's Pro Image in 1985 - 90 stores in 33 states with sales of some $34 million by 1988, Gary Adler's SpectAthlete in 1986 - 65 stores in 1987)... Thomas I. Unterberg and A. Robert Towbin merge 1899 L.F. Rothschild & Co. with 1932 C.E. Unterberg Towbin Co., becomes L.F. Rothschild Holdings as Wall Street leader in promoting stock of new high-tech firms (after struggle with young turks on strategy, leave in 1986 to head worldwide technology group of Shearson Lehman Group while new management diversifies)... Peter Lynch takes over Boston's Fideltiy Magellan, becomes No. 1 money manager of U.S.' biggest mutual fund by mid-1980s (sees value of fund's shares grow over 2000% before crash of 1987 when assets plunge 28% from $10.7 billion to $7.7 billion)... James Robinson becomes CEO of American Express, first service business to top $1 billion in sales, 1986, and U.S.' largest investment manager in 1988 in handling $298 billion (loses takeover by McGraw-Hill in 1979 in trying to diversify, acquires brokerage house of Shearson Loeb Rhoades in 1981, acquires Trade Development Bank of Switzerland from Edmond Safra, reclusive Lebanese billionaire, and Investors Diversified Services, MN, in 1983, acquires Lehman Brothers investment house in 1984, sells 50% of Warner Am Ex, struggling cable TV business, and spins off Fireman's Fund for $1.3 billion in 1985, sells 13% Shearson to Japan's Nippon Life, introduces Optima credit card and acquires E.F. Hutton in 1987 to top Merrill Lynch as U.S.' largest retail brokerage)... Michael Spinks turns professional boxer (retires 1988 after earning some $25 million)...

To fight marketing attack of Miller Brewing, Anheuser-Bush reorganizes marketing department (focuses on network TV sports programs - sole beer advertiser on ESPN sports cable network, uses 2/3 of $344 million ad budget in 1987 in sports to increase 1977 market share of 22% to 40% - Miller 2nd with 20.7%)... Studio 54 opens as NYC's hottest disco, closes after conviction of owners on tax evasion... Wells Fargo offers employees a sabbatical program for personal growth... After struggling to find right career, Don Wirfs starts semi-monthly, Sunday flea market at Portland's local coliseum (-1984, rents tables to vendors for $8, launches two-day sales at City's Expo Center in 1981 - 400 booths and attendance of 7,700, adds Seattle show in 1986 - Sacramento, Tacoma, Reno, San Francisco in 1987, runs 3 Portland shows/year to evolve by 1988 as "America's Largest Antique & Collectible Sales" with 1,300 booths).

1978

General Events

U.S., Japan sign (January 13) accord to ease trade tensions... President Carter invokes (March 6) Taft-Hartley to force miners back to work, leads to UMW signing contract on March 24 after longest strike of 109 days... Washington reports machinery and manufactured goods are No. 1 imports over oil... After trading in 1977 for 270, U.S. dollar drops (November 1) to postwar low exchange rate of 175 yen (after high of 362 hovers in 120s in early 1988)... CBS premiers soap opera "Dallas" on night TV... Congress appropriates $40 million, under national Historical Parks Program, to transform core of Lowell, pioneering MA textile mill town of 1821, into 137-acre preservation district (increases employment, 13% unemployment in 1975 to 4% in mid-1980s, and revives economy with Wang Laboratories in 1979 to attract other firms)... Wordstar is first true word-processing program for microcomputers... President Carter signs loan guarantee of $1.6 billion to help NYC avoid bankruptcy... Cleveland, OH, is first city since Depression to default on loans (pays off debts in 1987)... B.F. Goodrich pleads no contest to charges of tax evasion in political slush fund... Comprehensive Employment & Training Act funds public, private training programs for unemployed... Federal Trade Commission warns it will go after celebrities who make false claims in product endorsements... Congress creates National Consumer Cooperation Bank to lend credit to worthy cooperatives and place loans with co-ops owned by people with low incomes (is privatized by Federal Government in 1981, operates with assets of $258 million in 1985)... William J. Wilson, black University of Chicago sociologist: <u>The</u> <u>Declining</u> <u>Significance</u> <u>of</u> <u>Race</u> (concludes "economic class is clearly more important than race in predetermining job place and occupational mobility")... Phoenix opens garbage collection to bids from private contractors (pioneers privatization movement by submitting 43 major contracts for public services to bidding by 1985)... First annual Ironman Triathlon event to swim 2.5 miles, cycle 112 miles and run 26.2 miles is held, HI, over 1,000 super-endurance contests by 1983... Pregnancy Discrimination Act requires condition be treated as any other disability... Team of scientists from Harvard, Joslin Diabetes Foundation announce success in programming bacteria to produce pro-insulin... Civil Service Reform Act is passed (reorganizes Civil Service Commission, creates Office of Personnel Management and Merit Systems Protection Board, establishes federal labor relations authority to monitor government's labor-management relations, introduces merit pay system for high-level managers, prohibits federal agencies in discriminating in job appointments, removals, suspensions, and performance evaluations, gives federal employees right to join unions and bargain collectively on all employment issues but pay, forbids strikes)...

James B. Beam, Schenley and Seagram distilleries file guilty pleas in bribing state liquor officials...... In reverse discrimination suit Allan Bakke's claim in being denied admission to medical school for being white is upheld by U.S. Supreme Court (approves affirmative action, rejects rigid quotas)... Boise Cascade, Inland Container, International Container and 2 other firms plead no contest in fixing prices of corrugated containers... Daniel Boorstin: <u>The</u> <u>Republic</u> <u>of</u> <u>Technology</u> (argues each technical innovation creates conditions for next)... Top rate on capital-gains taxes goes from 49% to 28%, stimulates boom in venture capital market... <u>U.S.S.</u> <u>Saratoga</u> aircraft carrier tests fast-food menu, adopted by all aircraft carriers later... U.S. is 6th in world with per capita income of $9,700, 9th in 1979 with $10,610... G.L. Lippitt, R.E. Stivers: <u>The</u> <u>Multocular</u> <u>Process</u> (presents interdisciplinary macroproblem-solving methodology for handling value conflicts)... Congress approves Federal tax credits for investments in alternative energy sources (stimulates interest in windmills, solar power, etc.)...

Sea Train Lines pleads guilty to charges in making illegal rebates, violating currency regulations... After unsuccessful strike by migrant tomato pickers, MI and OH, against Campbell Soup Co., workers start boycott (-1985 when settled with recognition of Farm Labor Organizing Committee)... Department of Energy announces plans to finance $2.1 billion commercial synthetic-fuels project, ND (results in creation of Synthetic Fuels Corp. in 1980 with initial budget of $15 billion, opens Great Plains Gasification Project in 1984, is threatened with closure by Congress in 1985)... Natural Gas Policy Act is passed to de-control gas prices by 1985... National Energy Conservation Policy Act is passed... NASA grants funds to Lehigh University to work on first commercial space project (develops first manufacture of "microspheres" in 1983 as standards to calibrate delicate scientific instruments, to make precise measurements)... John T. Molloy: <u>The</u> <u>Woman's</u> <u>Dress</u> <u>for</u> <u>Success</u> <u>Book</u>... Airline Deregulation Act eliminates Federal controls on fares, routes (results in 30 airlines becoming 200 by early 1980s, 5 biggest control 70% of market in 1988, and in industry losing some $500 million by 1986, is followed by Western Europe in 1987)... Tenneco pleads guilty to charges of mail fraud in bribing local official... California voters adopt Proposition 13, designed to reduce property taxes by industrial Harold Jarvis (ignites U.S. tax-reduction movement, leads to 1986 passage of slow-growth proposition U by Los Angeles voters, 15 slow-growth measures on local ballots in 1987, and limits on car insurance premiums in 1988)... Thomas J.C. Raymond, Stephen A. Greyser: "The Business of Managing the Arts," Harvard Business Review... Federal Bankruptcy Reform Act provides more generous benefits to those declaring financial disaster... Ralph Nader's Health Research Group urges government to ban pain killer Darvon... As result of toxic waste contamination in 1942-52 by Hooker Chemical (deeded land to local school district with warning on future use), health emergency is declared for Love Canal neighborhood of Niagara Falls (forces evacuation of hundreds of families by 1980, results in law suits against Hooker and involved governments for some $15 billion and use of Love Canal as symbol of toxic-waste problem)...

Most rail freight, commuter service nationwide is paralyzed by strike of clerks' union... Gold sells for $245/ounce, goes over $400 in 1979... Ford Motor Co. is indicted by Indiana Grand Jury for wrecklessness, negligence in deaths of 3 women killed in crash of Pinto... FBI agents seize some $100 million worth of sound-recording equipment in nationwide raids to wipe out half of illicit U.S. recording industry... Grete Waitz, Norway, wins 1st of 8 NYC marathons (receives $20 for cab fare to airport, gets $40,000 in appearance money for 1986 race and wins $25,000 and $30,000 Mercedes-Benz for 1st place finish)... Tax code, 401(K), allows individuals to start tax-deductible savings plans (becomes popular in 1988 when IRAs lose tax shelter status)... Congress declares USOC as principal Olympic group (organizes with 105-member governing board and moves headquarters to Colorado Springs, with record profits from 1984 Summer Games grants each federation some $41.2 million and puts remaining $85 million into special fund for "long-term needs" of athletes, nearing bankruptcy in 1985 evolves with management woes and bickering with federations controlling 60% of board)... Amendments to Age Discrimination in Employment Act extend coverage for most workers to age 70.

Business Events

Center for Creative Leadership, NC, designs Looking Glass Inc. as intensive simulation to prepare managers to run a business (trains some 4,000 executives of major corporations by mid-1980s, is followed by games of Financial Services Industry, designed by faculty of NY University, and Simmons Simulator, Inc., developed by Columbia University in 1978 for IBM)... Dean Singleton, trouble-shooter for fellow Texan Joe Albritton, becomes head of Albritton's newspaper division to acquire 6 papers and revive them with budget surgery (joins Richard Scudder, NJ newspaper owner, in 1983 to buy their first paper with capital from Scudder and Media General, VA-based communications conglomerate, builds chain of Media News Group by 1987 to operate U.S.' 11th largest newspaper business, 56 papers worth $1.2 billion, with major newspapers in Denver, Houston, and Dallas)... During worst week in history of Wall Street Dow-Jones Industrial Average closes at 838.01 (October 20), down 59.08 from prior week due to escalating interest rates... Reggie Jackson of NY Yankees endorses Reggie candy bar...

Chrysler sells its European subsidiaries to Peugeot-Citroen... Pan Am acquires National Airlines for $350 million... Charles A., "boy wonder of tax shelters," Atkins becomes managing partner of Securities Group, umbrella organization of several investment partnerships (-1983 when ended with law suits, after promising $4 in paper losses for every $1 invested is convicted in 1987 in largest tax fraud case for illegal scheme to produce millions in fraudulent tax deductions for celebrities and wealthy)... Hearst publishing issues <u>Country Living</u>, magazine of Americana (records fastest growth in Hearst's history to achieve circulation of $1.5 million by 1987)... Corporate raider Natalie I. Koether, husband form investment business of Shamrock Associates (develop business from $1.2 million to some $20 million in 1987 with over 40 acquisitions of undervalued firms - 12 targets pay greenmail)... Meredith Brokaw, wife of NBC anchor man, and partner open first Penny Whistle Toys on Manhattan's Upper East Side to sell top-of-the-line products with $25,000 (open 3 more outlets by 1987 to achieve sales of $1.9 million)...

Top 8 U.S. airlines control 81% of domestic market, 91% in 1987... Sports agent Richard Sorkin, former sports writer representing over 50 NHL and NBA players in early 1970s, is jailed after pleading guilty to grand larceny in squandering some $1.2 million of clients' money... Philippine-born Eminiano Reodica opens Grand Chevrolet dealership in Glendora, CA (builds sales of $120 million in 1987 by catering to emigrant market - Asians 60% of revenues)... Pentecostal evangelist Jimmy Bakker of PTL, People That Love or Praise The Lord, opens $175 million Heritage USA theme park (becomes 3rd-largest attraction in U.S. with some 5 million tourists/year visiting 2,300 acres with Bakker's Assemblies of God Church, 500-room luxury hotel, mall with 25 boutiques and amphitheater for staging passion plays, nativity spectacles - receipts of $29 million in 1986, is put up for auction in 1988 during bankruptcy, no takers at $100 million minimum, and sold to Canadian developer)...

Judy Moody, using bank of sun lamps, opens first tanning parlor of Tantrific Sun in Searcy, AR (opens first franchise in Memphis in 1979, sells 10 more at $25,000 each in 3 days - 100 by 1980, faces bankruptcy in 1980)... VisiCala, first all-purpose electronic computer program designed by Dan Bricklin, is marketed by San Jose firm, later VisiCorp (is followed by Lotus in 1981 with 1- 2 -3 program and 1984 Symphony program)... Magnavox introduces laser-vision disk for television... Mel Zuckerman opens Canyon Ranch, "America's total vacation/fitness resort," in Tucson... Contract Staffing of America is formed to lease personnel to doctors, dentists (evolves with some 1,500 employees in 1983 to realize sales of some $26 million in market of 100 firms, leases 4,000 employees to some 300 companies in 1987)... AT&T shifts strategy from service-oriented telephone business to market-oriented communications business...

Growth Opportunity Alliance of Greater Lawrence, MA, is created as non-profit coalition of small firms to improve efforts in quality control... National Education Corporation of California starts forming national network of technical vocational schools (operates 49 schools with some 35,000 students by 1983 in addition to providing correspondence courses to some 55,000 students in U.S., 20,000 overseas)... Software Arts is started to provide operating program, languages and applications for personal computers... 179, 112 personal bankruptcies are declared during year, 523,825 in 1981 and 341,189 in 1985... Some 100 corporations sponsor day-care centers for children of employees, about 2,580 by 1985... Charles L. Bird acquires tiny popcorn store, Dallas (starts Corn Popper business to sell 32 flavors, starts franchising in 1981 - 113 places by 1985)... Richard Grot, Eric L. Harvey start Performance

Systems, Dallas, as consulting business to merchandise programs in positive discipline, developed in early 1970s by Canadian industrial psychologist John Huberman (is used successfully by GE in 1979)... First Oil Can Henry's₇ quick-stop auto-service center, opens in Portland, OR (operates 6 units in 1984 to achieve sales of $2.2 million, plans 6 more units for 1986, sells 14 centers to Jiffy Lube, world's largest with 862 units, in 1988)... Texas Instruments introduces Speak & Tell, electronic device with speech synthesizer, as learning aid for children (pioneers technology for electronic speech)... Marine Resources is incorporated by U.S. entrepreneur, Soviet Union to fish in Pacific with U.S. trawlers, U.S.S.R. factorship... Firestone Tire & Rubber issues largest tire recall in history (spins-off worldwide tire business to Tokyo-based Bridgestone in 1988, continues with sales of auto parts and services via 1,500 company-owned stores)...

After borrowing $2,000 from mother, lawyer Robert M. Parker, Jr., publishes The Wine Advocate as bimonthly newsletter to educate consumers on wine (resigns from law practice in 1984 to develop publication, some 21,000 subscribers worldwide by 1987 to become one of world's most influential figures in wine industry)... After inventor Bill Lear (car radio, 8-track stereo, automatic pilot, Learjet) dies, innovative Lear Fan jet project, plane of epoxy and graphite composite, is continued by widow Moya over strong objections of children (meets terms of British investors with first successful flight on December 32, 1980, before 1981 deadline, goes broke in 1985)... GM's Packard Electric Division, International Union of Electrical Workers start joint program to increase productivity, save jobs and encourage worker participation (after 1983 rejection of dual-wage plan for new and old workers, sign 1984 contract to lower wages gradually in return for lifetime work)... Directory of Personal Image Consultants lists 37 entries, 150 in 1980 edition, 206 in 1982 and 256 in 1985...

26 teams of major league baseball show average profit of $4,526 (shows total loss of $45 million in 1983 - $1.7 million/club)... Mel, Patricia Ziegler invest $1,500 in old Spanish paratrooper shirts for resale (start Banana Republic Travel & Safari Clothing business in San Francisco with imported anti-fashion khaki clothes for sale by mail-order and store (sell 3 stores to The Gap, retail chain of 600 places, in 1983 to develop chain of 65 outlets as retailing "theaters")... After resigning from academia, cultural anthropologist Steve Barnett is hired by Planmetrics, Chicago-based consulting firm, to head cultural analysis group (uses skills to advise such clients as Kimberly Clark, Campbell Soup)...

Pepsico acquires Mexican fast-food Taco Bell chain (operates industry's largest chain in Mexican food, nearest competitor Taco John's with nearly 400 outlets, in 1986 with some 2,300 units to achieve sales of nearly $1.4 billion - plans 4,000 places and sales of $4 billion by 1990)...

American Can designs computerized system to rank investment risks in some 70 countries... With profits from "Star Wars" trilogy and other mega-hits, George Lucas starts Lucasfilm to provide clients with technical, theatrical and merchandising services (evolves to operate multi-million-dollar business on 3,000-acre Skywalker Ranch in Marin County with 280 employees in such activities as Industrial Light and Magic Studio, Computer Development Division, pioneers development of Hyermedia by 1988 as blend of computers, video, photography and sound)... After peddling homemade cakes, confections at markets and to small retailers, Dean Kolstad with Jeff and Gary Peisach, food wholesalers catering to restaurants, starts Ms. Desserts (evolves by 1986 as $6.2 million business to supply some 2,500 customers, hotels, gourmet and deli shops, and restaurants, with fancy treats)... Sunshine State Bank of South Miami is secretly acquired with illegal drug profits to operate as banking front for drug business, indicted in 1984... Charter line World Airways sues CAB for permission to schedule regular flights (after 6 years of losses in new service, returns to handling military and commercial charters)... Surimi, Japanese staple of blended seafood for some 900 years, is introduced to U.S. market (is used for imitation crab by JAC Creative Foods of Los Angeles in 1981 to pioneer mass market, 13 processors by 1986... Ford employs some 506,000 workers to make 6.5 million cars and trucks (employs around 370,000 in 1986 to make nearly same output in changing culture to stress product quality, employee participation)...

Carl Icahn starts career as corporate raider by acquiring Baird & Warner (after 16 deals by 1986, including ACF Industries, leading producer and lessor of rail cars, and TWA, battles Frank Lorenzo for Texas Air in 1985 to acquire over $400 million in profits - mostly greenmail, fails in $10.5 billion takeover of steel and oil business of USX, formerly U.S. Steel, in 1986, manages profitable ACF and TWA in 1988 while "participating" in Texaco's settlement with Pennzoil, with estimated personal net worth of $700 million bids $14.8 billion for Texaco in 1988, plans public company for takeovers in 1988)... After 32 years of employment with Ford Motor Co., Lee Iacocca is fired as president by Henry Ford II as "I just don't like you" (within few months becomes head of financially-hemorrhaging Chrysler with losses of $8 million in 1970, $52 million in 1974, $260 million in 1975, and $205 million in 1978, immediately cuts salary to $1/year, establishes general pay freeze and cuts salaries of middle and senior managers, in 1979 reduces costs by cutting work force from some 131,000 to around 68,000 by 1983 to lower firm's break-even point by 50%, divests South American operations in 1979 - 1980 to GM and Volkswagen, appears in 1979 TV ads to promote cars, obtains Congressional loan guarantee for $1.5 billion in 1979 after intense public debate, posts loss of $536.1 million in 1979 - highest ever for firm, gets concessions from UAW in 1980 - union president Douglas Fraser on board, introduces small K-car in 1980, posts loss of $1.7 billion for 1980, offers anyone $50 just to test-drive new car in 1981, gets more UAW concessions in 1981 for total of $660 million, to avoid bankruptcy with reserves of only $1 million obtains more time from suppliers to pay bills, gets new government loan in 1981 for $300 million, shows loss of $475.6 million in 1981, sells Detroit Tank plant to General Dynamics in 1982 for $348.5 million, offers workers wage increases tied to future profits in 1982 - rejected, ends Canadian strike of 38 days in 1982 with higher wages, shows profit of $170.1 million in 1982 - first in 5 years, grants U.S. workers first pay increase since 1981 in 1983 - restores all concessions by 1984, pays $1.2 billion in 1983 to government for loans, posts profits of $700.9 million, highest in its history, in 1983, pays first dividends in nearly 5 years in 1984, reorganizes in 1985 in 4 parts, autos, finance, technology and aerospace, with umbrella organization to oversee all operations)... Chung Forest opens cut-rate fashion business Susanna Beverly Hills, CA, with $90 (in growing industry achieves sales of $2 million in 1987)... Some 350 vegetarian restaurants operate in U.S., over 1,000 by 1988 in U.S. and

Canada... Neoconservative Paul H. Weaver, former Harvard professor and Fortune writer, is hired by Ford Motor Co. in public relations (-1980, quits when disillusioned by managers not believing in capitalism, not relating to workers and having little feeling for wants of customers)... Digital Equipment, MA, joins AI theoretician John McDermott, Carnegie-Mellon University, to develop X Con computer expert system (becomes only commercial expert system in 1981 to evaluate worth of technology)... Flamboyant speed racer and manufacturer of custom auto-parts, Mickey Thompson, first in U.S. to travel over 400 mph in 1960, branches in partnership with Mike Goodwin into sports promotion field (becomes leading sponsor of motor-sports at arenas like Los Angeles Coliseum and Rose Bowl, sues Goodwin in 1984 for control of "stadium off-road racing," after bitter lawsuits wins judgment in 1986 for $500,000 to force Goodwin into bankruptcy, wins judgment against Goodwin for $800,000 in 1988, is slain in 1988 "contract" killing)... Texas pawnshop operator J.R. Daugherty starts wildcatting during oil boom with life savings of some $300,000 (after one dry hole after another returns to pawnshop in 1983 to parlay one store into intrastate chain of 35 as Cash America Investments, opens "estate jewelry store" in Ft. Worth in 1986, is first U.S. pawn-loan business to go public in 1987 to raise $15.5 million for expansion and use corporate organization to dominate scattered mom-and-pop industry)...

After flying for Northwest Airlines and serving as executive for Hughes' Air West, David R. Hinson invests in Chicago's shaky Midway Airlines, chief executive in 1985 after previous management failed to court business travelers (acquires bankrupt Air Florida for 3 economical Boeing 737s, operates as no-frills carrier in 1979, switches to all-business class in 1982 to lose $44 million, revives operation as small, all-coach carrier with practical monopoly of downtown location to offer fares, 20% below those of rivals - $3.9 million profit in first 9 months of 1986)... Edward R. Telling is CEO of Sears (-1986, defying tradition recasts retail business with president Edward A. Brennan, CEO in 1986, as consumer services conglomerate to earn $1.35 billion on sales of $44 billion after settling internal war between buyers, closing 50 unproductive stores, and adding Dean Witter brokerage and Coldwell Banker's real estate network to Allstate insurance business in 1982, starts Sears World Trade in 1982, introduces "Store of the Future" strategy in 1983, launches Discover credit card in 1985, drops World Trade in 1986, launches specialty merchandising in 1986 to fight new competitors, sells Savings Bank and buys Eye Care Center of America in 1987, buys Pinstripes Petites and Western Auto Supply in 1988 and puts catalog business in separate division, opens "Brand Central" appliances and electronics departments, puts up Sears Tower and Coldwell Banker for sale, and commits Sears to new strategy of "everyday low prices" to replace constant promotions by 825 outlets to compete with smaller, more efficient retailers and avoid takeover, slashes prices of some 50,000 items in March, 1989 to fight K mart and Wal-Mart)...

Keith Gollust, Paul Tierney, Jr., and Augustus Oliver form investment business of Coniston Partners (by 1987 manage with 10 employees group of 5 investment partnerships worth over $600 million by strategic-block investing in undervalued firms before takeovers or breakups)... First Annual International Erotic Video Festival opens, NYC... CART, Championship Auto Racing Teams, is formed by owners to win bigger role in promoting races (holds 15-race season in 1988 with $15.5 million in prize money - 105 firms pay some $75 million to sponsor teams or whole races with Philip Morris biggest in spending $15 million)... Bankers Trust New York Corp. is plagued with bad real estate loans (after selling off retail banking and credit-card operation and stopping unprofitable loans to blue-chip corporations, becomes thriving merchant banker financing acquisitions and leveraged buyouts with $56 billion in assets by 1988)... Black, Marie A. Jackson-Randolph, opens first Sleepy Hollow Educational Center in Detroit, grows as day-care chain of 14 and elementary school by 1988... After getting Master's degree in psychology, Mitch Kapor sells stereo to buy Apple II computer (as free-lance programmer designs Tiny Troll, statistics and graphics computer program, in 1979, after $500,000 in royalties sells rights in 1981 for $1.2 million, writes first 1-2-3 spreadsheet program for business in 1982 with Jonathan Sachs, with financing from venture capitalist Benjamin Rosen forms Lotus in 1982 with Sachs to write computer software programs - first-year sales of $53 million, becomes industry's largest in 1984 with 700 employees and sales of $157 million, resigns in 1986 with shares worth $54 million - sales of $256 million and 1,200 employees, starts On Technology with Peter B. Miller in 1987)...

Smith & Hawken, purveyor of quality English garden tools, opens in a warehouse, CA (grows as $30 million business by 1988 in capitalizing on gardening trend)... After borrowing $420,000 to buy 2,000-year-old greek coin - resold for some $1 million, Bruce McNall, owner of Numisatic Fine Arts - coin sales of $19.1 million in 1987 by mostly mail-order, buys racehorse for $50,000, evolves as Summa Stables by 1988 with sales of $8 million/year (co-founds Dallas Mavericks basketball team in 1979 - sells out 1982 to run film company with Nelson Bunker Hunt, forms Gladden Entertainment with David Begelman, formerly with Columbia pictures, to produce hits grossing over $100 million, becomes sole owner of losing Los Angeles Kings hockey team in 1987, engineers shocking 1988 Wayne Gretzky trade for some $15 million)... Major TV networks reach 92% of prime-time viewers, 70% by 1988... Max Robinson joins ABC Evening News, first Black to anchor network news program...

Struggling NYC broker, Meyer Blinder, moves to Denver, worth some $200 million by 1988 as "King of Penny Stocks" (builds Blinder & Robinson as market leader by buying blocks of stocks of new firms, promoting issues with hype, investigated by SEC for false claims, and reselling stocks to buyers via U.S. network fo some 1,300 agents)... In San Francisco avid runner Richard Thalheimer gambles $1,000 on ad for runner's digital watch (with success launches Sharper Image catalog with glitzy upscale gadgets for "Yuppies," becomes $66 million firm in 1987 before first losses in 1988 from rising competition)... John Lasker, Jeffrey Stein start selling sweatsuits and Army-Navy surplus clothes around the corner from Hollywood's Rodeo Drive, sales over $200 million from 23 Camp Beverly Hills stores (plans to go nationwide with 75 new stores in 1990s)... Super salesman, Sonny Vaccaro leads Nike's attack on Converse' dominance of high-school, college market for basketballs shoes (with innumerable contacts signs contracts with coaches, from $5,000 to $200,000 for rights to supply their teams - sales of $7 million rise to some $300 million by 1987, signs Michael Jordan in 1984 for $1 million contract plus royalties to sponsor line of shoes, rules market by 1988).

1979

General Events

Some 3,000 farmers, supporters clog streets of Capitol to demand higher price supports... U.S., China formally resume (January 1) relations... U.S. sues (January 5) 9 of largest oil companies for overpricing in past 5 years... President Carter asks (February 26) Congress for authorization to impose gas rationing and other emergency measures to reduce U.S.' consumption of oil... China agrees (March 1) to pay 41 cents/dollar for U.S. assets seized 1949... Seminole Indians, FL, open their first bingo parlor, by 1988 operate 4 giant parlors for some $10 million/year... President Carter orders (April 25) gradual reduction of controls on domestic oil prices... President Carter orders (May 5) gradual end to controls in oil prices... President Carter denounces (June 1) Mobil's opposition to decontrol of oil prices... OPEC raises (June 28) oil prices 16%, 50% in last year... After Iran seizes U.S. Embassy and holds hostages (November 4), President Carter freezes Iranian assets in U.S...

Chicago dedicates State Street Mall... Betty L. Harragan: <u>Games</u> <u>Mother</u> <u>Never</u> <u>Taught</u> <u>You</u>: <u>Corporate</u> <u>Gamesmanship</u> <u>for</u> <u>Women</u>... U.S. Supreme Court upholds paying of state unemployment benefits to striking workers... Victor Zue, Chinese-born MIT scientist, is invited by Carnegie-Mellon to demonstrate unique ability to read computer voice spectograms (starts development of machines able to respond to oral commands)... San Francisco Renaissance is started as non-profit community-development group (starts profit project in 1982 to train unemployed)... General Accounting Office opens 24-hour toll-free line to handle tips from public on government fraud, over 87,000 leads by 1987... Pamela McCorduck: <u>Machines</u> <u>Who</u> <u>Think</u>... Joint union-management effort is undertaken at GM Chevrolet Gear & Axle plant, Detroit, to cut costs, improve quality...

Since 1967 Small Business Administration has granted some 18,000 loans for $1.3 billion to franchise operations... Opera singer Beverly Sills becomes general director of New York City Opera (-1989, retires to board after putting opera in black and forming $3 million endowment fund)... Bell System sponsors American Orchestras on Tour... An Wang, Wang Laboratories, creates Wang Institute of Graduate Studies to grant degrees in software engineering... After Boy Scout membership drops from 6 million to 4 million in 6 years, program is revived with Explorer Scouts, Tiger Clubs for pre-Cub Scouts, special activities for handicapped, and relevant programs for urban scouts... R.J. Reynolds Industries pleads no contest to charges in fixing prices of ocean shipping... With inflation rate hitting 15%, highest in 33 years (peaks at 20.5% in 1981), Paul Volcker becomes chairman of Federal Reserve Board (initiates tight money policy to reduce inflation rate to less than 4% by 1983, under 5% by 1985, is re-appointed for 1983-87)...

Department of Energy launches $160-million project to develop infastructure for sustaining electric vehicle manufacturing industry... Howard J. Ruff: <u>How</u> <u>To</u> <u>Prosper</u> <u>During</u> <u>the</u> <u>Coming</u> <u>Bad</u> <u>Years</u>... U.S. Labor Department, backed by unions, sues ski maker, VT, for employing women in homes to knit ski clothes (rescinds ban after public outcry)... Firestone Tire & Rubber pleads guilty to charges filing false tax returns... Independent truckers start wildcat strike to protest rising fuel prices... Warner Woodworth, Reed Nelson: "Witch Doctors, Messinacs, Sorcerers, and OD Consultants: Parallels and Paradigms," <u>Organizational Dynamics</u>... TV evangelist, Baptist minister Jerry Falwell (resigns in 1987), supporters form Moral Majority to create Religious Right Movement... Allied Chemical pleads no contest to charges of tax fraud in paying kickbacks... <u>John F. Leavitt</u>, built to revive wooden cargo ships, is abandoned off Long Island Coast during storm on maiden voyage... U.S. severs diplomatic relations with Taiwan to recognize People's Republic as legitimate Government of China... Three Mile Island reactor near Harrisburg, PA, shuts down after accident to avoid nuclear melt-down...

Lockheed successfully tests small ocean thermal energy conversion unit, HI (bases device on concept of French physicist in late 1800s and tried unsuccessfully by Cuba in 1929, fails with larger plant in 1981)... Federal ruling allows physicians to advertise services... Lane Kirkland succeeds George Meany as president of AFL-CIO... FCC permits AT&T to sell non-regulated services, such as data processing... FTC issues first federal regulations to govern franchise industry... Joseph Patrick Kennedy II, others start non-profit Citizen's Energy, MA, to provide low-cost heating oil to elderly, poor (evolves by 1984 as $366 million operation by buying crude from oil countries at official prices, contracting with refinery to process crude, and retaining heating oil for distribution while selling other petroleum products for profit - 25% for development in poor nations and 75% to reduce price of heating oil for needy)...

U.S. Supreme Court: <u>Steelworkers v. Weber</u> (allows employers, unions to jointly adopt quotas to eliminate racial imbalances)... 3 women employees sue State Farm for sex discrimination (covers 1,113 women in 1988 settlement for payments up to $420,000)... California voters approve Proposition 4 to restrict government spending... After working for international agencies, Mildred and Glen Leet start Trickle Up program with own funds to help poor, by 1988 over 7,000 projects in 99 countries, with seed money to start businesses... Jack Joyce is president of International Union of Bricklayers (to reverse falling membership proposes in 1985 to start joint union-employer marketing program, develop new products, start new training centers, launch organizing drive in Sunbelt)...Of 189 U.S. bank failures by 1987 Comptroller of the Currency finds 35% from fraud or insider abuse "a significant factor."

Business Events

Lawyers Eugene and Nina Zagat prepare guide for Manhattan restaurants (by 1997 evolves as New York City Restaurant Survey, multi-million-dollar publishing business)... After leaving law school in 1970 and working as carpenter, Stephen Israel, former organic farmer, forms Great American Salvage business to save, sell historic items of value from buildings slated for demolition, VT (by 1987 operates profitable business with 2 Manhattan showrooms and 4 East Coast franchises)... In NYC 11 banks are robbed (August 30) in 1 day, brings month's total to 137... With losses around $400 million, U.S. Steel closes 15 plants and mills in 8 states to idle 13,000 workers... Superior Livestock Auction, CO and TX, uses video tapes to sell cattle to assembled buyers (uses satellite television in 1987 to reach buyers throughout country)... Frozfruit of Gardenia, CA, introduces first frozen fruit bar (pioneers market expanded nationwide by Dole Food's bars in 1984)... Monsanto fails to warn Sturgeo, MO, on risks of spill containing toxic chemical dioxin, ordered in 1987 to pay $16.2 million after longest jury trial in U.S. history of 44 months... 1856 Blitz Weinhard brewery of Portland, OR, is acquired by Pabst brewery of Milwaukee for $6⁻million to become industry's 6th largest (is acquired in 1982 $214.4 million takeover of Pabst by G. Heileman brewery, 4th largest of La Crosse, WI, is acquired in turn by Australian financier Alan Bond, acquired fortune in mining and real estate ventures to own Perth's Swan and Castlemaine brands, in 1987 for $1.26 billion to create 4th largest brewery operation in international market)...

First Jiffy-Lube fast-oil-change automotive service chain opens (grows by 1988 to operate over 862 centers in U.S., Canada and France with plans for Australia, Great Britain and Holland, faces financial problems in 1989)... 1837 Tiffany & Co., selling exclusive jewelry and luxury items to wealthy (operates corporate division to sell gifts to firms for clients, employees) is acquired by Avon Products (-1984 when acquired by executives in leveraged buyout, launches signature line of sport watches, handbags, scarves, and fragrances to celebrate 100th anniversary with 8 U.S. stores, 1 in London and 15 boutiques in Japan)...

TransWorld Corp. is formed as holding company for TransWorld Airlines, Canteen Corp. and Hilton International (acquires Century 21 real estate business and Spartan Food System which operates 400 Hardee's fast-food franchises in 1979, spins-off airline to shareholders in 1984, sells Century 21 and buys Interstate United food service company in 1985, acquires American Medical Services, nursing-home chain, and changes name to TW Services in 1986, sells Hilton Hotels to Allegis in 1987 and buys Denny's, founded 1953, $1.3 billion chain with over 1,200 family restaurants and 87 El Pollo Loco places for $840 million to complement Canteen catering and contract dining business)... 133 drug wholesalers do business, 86 by 1989 - similar consolidation in food wholesaling...

Abby Hirsch opens Godmothers as matchmaking business, NYC (grows by 1988 with offices in Washington, NYC, to serve some 1,000 clients)... Ford Motor Co. acquires 25% of Japan's Mazda Motor Corp., affiliate and supplier since 1969... Some $6.5 billion is spent on licensed goods in retail marketplace, around $40 billion in 1984... David R. Leggett starts Automotive Import Recycling, NJ, to turn old cars into new (becomes leading business in car remanufacturing industry, started in 1932 by Arrow Automotive Industries of Massachusetts, by 1985)...

Plastic shopping bags are used by supermarkets to replace paper bags of 1883 (garners 5% of market in 1982 and 20% in mid-1980s)... Former charter jet pilot Jerry Wilson starts Soloflex, NM, moves to OR in 1980 to make compact exercise machines for homes (after losing some $80,000 first year evolves with 1984 sales of some $17 million with slick advertising)... Seeburg, jukebox king of 1948-78, is reorganized under bankruptcy laws...

Entertainment Sports Programming Network airs first 24-hour televised schedule of sports... Monsanto employs some 64,000 people, about 51,000 by 1984 as reorganization shifts business from traditional chemicals to biological sciences in preparing for 1990s... Flight simulator program is designed for computers to train pilots on landing, taking off (evolves as Flight Simulator II to become most popular software game in 1984)... Ford Motor Co. starts employee involvement program to reduce production costs, absenteeism and improve product quality... <u>Fortune</u>: "The Prospects for Productivity" (gives rates of 3.2% for 1947-66, 2.1% for 1966-73, 0.8% for 1973-79, and 2.1% for 1979-89)... Intel starts program to cut bureaucracy (employs 50% of 10,000 U.S. employees in administration and 64% in engineering, selling and non-production activities)... Ira Bachrach starts NameLab in San Francisco to create new names for products and companies, such as Compaq computer, Zap Mail, Sentra and Honda's Acura... Crain Communications publishes <u>Chicago Business</u>, pioneers rise in local, regional business publications - some 100 by 1985... After U.S. is unable to win release of 2 executives of Electronic Data Systems from Iranian prison, H. Ross Perot, company president, rescues them with special team... Since 1970 franchise owners form over 40 associations to protect their rights with franchisers...

Whirlpool Corp. launches quality assurance program, followed by B.F. Goodrich's chemical group with quality institute in 1982... Arthur Treacher's chain of fast-food restaurants specializing in fish and chips is acquired by Mrs. Paul's seafood business from Orange Company, FL (after dropping from 700 outlets to some 400, is saved from bankruptcy with acquisition by Lumara Foods)... Westinghouse Electric forms committee with $20 million to explore methods to increase productivity (adopts program to use Japanese approach of participative management)... Gray market in discounted cameras (results from excessive inventories and foreign exchange rates) is some 2% of total camera sales, some 10% in 1980 and 20% in 1981... Hartford Insurance Group underwrites some 200 computer insurance policies (increases to 5,000 in 1982 with such special features as information damage, computer crime)...

Chicago's Illinois National Bank and Trust starts formal quality control program to improve services... American Robot is started, Pittsburgh, with funds from Rockefeller Venture Fund (signs 7-year agreement in 1984 to supply designs, parts to Daikin Industries of Osaka, accepts minority interest of Ford Motor Co. in 1985 to fund research and development in order to compete with 1981 joint venture in robotic development of GM, Japan's Fanuc Ltd.)... Sherry Lansing becomes president of 20th Century Fox, first woman to head major movie studio (-1982)... National Restaurant Association estimates some 38% of industry's business is handled by fast-food places, 32% in 1975 and 24% in 1970... Bill Agee, chief executive of Bendix Corp., hires Mary Cunningham with Harvard MBA as executive assistant (after promotion to executive vice president for strategic planning is forced to resign her position in 1980 after negative reactions by employees, stockholders, public)...

Facing bankruptcy 1892 Rath Packing of Waterloo, IA, is purchased by employees, declares bankruptcy in 1984... County Mutual Insurance, IL, creates information center to collect needed data from records... Lousiana-Pacific buys Portland franchise for Timbers soccer team as means to raise money for local charities (-1982 after losses)... Association of Road Racing Athletes is formed, Boston, to promote open racing with prize money... Dave Parker of Pittsburgh Pirates is first baseball player to sign contract for over $1 million/year... Jack Breen becomes head of Sherwin-Williams, disorganized and directionless paint business with executive deadwood and debt from funding expansion of 1,400 retail stores operated as inventory outlets (imports financial experts, institutes strict controls, reduces long-term debt, decentralizes decision making and terminates hundreds of executives to revive business with sales up 34% in stagnant industry of 1983-86, acquires Dutch Boy Paints in 1980 and Gray Drug Fair's chain in 1981, opens 200 new decorating centers by 1986)... Simmons Airline is started, Chicago, to serve small cities in North Central states (joins Republic Airline in 1985 in pioneering marketing venture to shuttle passengers on short flights to Republic's "hub" for longer flights)... BehaviorScan, new market research system for tracking consumer actions in grocery stores and on television sets instead of measuring intentions and memories, is launched by Chicago's Information Research... James L. Dutt becomes head of Beatrice, $12.6 billion multinational food and consumer goods business (-1985 when ousted by board after consolidating operations with autocratic leadership, promoting former executive secretary as assistant vice president over senior managers, acquiring Esmark in 1984 for $2.7 billion to increase long-term debt to some $3.7 billion, and losing one of firm's most respected senior managers)... Crown American buys Hess's Department Stores of 1898 (becomes successful chain, PA, of 37 stores serving medium-sized market with glitzy style of "retailing is theater")...

For first time, shares in Thousand Trails, Seattle-based campground business, are sold to public (evolves by end of 1985 as industry's leader with 43 preserves, membership of some 86,000)... After working for Merrill Lynch since 1975 as junior technical analyst Robert R. Prechter publishes financial newsletter (is recognized for accurate predictions based on neglected "Elliott Waves," proposed in 1939 by accountant R.N. Elliott to emphasize primary role of investor psychology swinging from pessimism to optimism in rhythmic cycles, uses theory to predict every major ebb and flow of stock market 1982 on)... Home receiving antennas to receive television programs via satellites appear in market (forces HBO, Cinemax cable networks in 1986 to scramble signals for non-payers of services and require decoders for users - by-passed by new devices in 1988)... After experimenting with special consumer phone line in 1971 Procter & Gamble pioneers use of 800-number phone system for customers...

Albert Lowry, former Canadian butcher from Thunder Bay: <u>How To Successfully Manage Real Estate in Your Spare Time</u> (is followed in real estate pitchman market in 1980 by Robert G. Allen's <u>Nothing Down</u> to pioneer get-rich seminars, after estimated net worth of $30 million in 1981 declares bankruptcy in 1987)... Agri Electronics designs computer program for handling cattle... Honda motorcycle factory opens in Marysville, OH (starts automobile plant in 1982 to become U.S.' 4th largest auto maker in 1985 introduces Acura car in 1986 to complete in luxury market, ships first U.S.-built cars to Japan in 1988)... Some $636 million is expended in changing public corporations into private enterprises (rises to record $10.8 billion in 1984)... Stuart A. Rose acquires 4 retail stores of Rex TV & Appliance in Dayton (pushes expansion of business of Audio/Video Affiliates to $250 million chain of 110 stores in 7 years by leveraged takeovers, proposes buyout of $1.4 billion Cyclops in 1987 to acquire specialty retailer Silo with sales of some $550 million from over 100 stores nationwide in appliances, consumer electronics)... After starting as telephone answering service in 1967, Headquarters Companies is started to sell franchises in executive centers for business clients, some 45 by 1981... General Telephone and Electronics acquires Telnet Communications for some $55 million (launches electronic mail system for businesses in 1980s)... Jerry Dominelli, "The Genius," starts J. David & Co. business as investment pool to speculate in foreign currency markets (declares involuntary bankruptcy in 1984 after losing over $100 million from 330 investors, is convicted for fraud and income tax evasion, leads to investors' suit against accounting firms representing investment business for fraud, negligence and malpractice)... Paul Fireman acquires North American distribution rights for English Reebok track shoe, founded 1895 (achieves success with aerobics exercise shoe for women in 1983 to realize sales of $12.8 million - $66 million in 1984 and $306.9 million in 1985, acquires England's Reebok in 1984 for $700,000, after acquiring walking shoe business of Rockport in 1986 and Avia in 1987 to expand product line becomes No. 1 in market with some $1 billion to top Nike, Converse and Adidas sells sportswear in 1986, shows growth rate of 155% for 1983-87)...

Cousins Menchem Golan, Yoram Globus, formerly operators of Noah Films to dominate Israel's film industry since 1963, acquire Cannon, minor Hollywood schlock studio in financial trouble, for $350,000 (develop profitable business to produce 25-30 low-cost movies/year with happy endings, acquire major theater chains in Holland, Italy, U.S. and Britain, purchase distribution, producing companies in West Germany, Britain's Elstree Studio, and Showtime Cable of U.S.' Viacom Enterprises, despite sales of $353 million sells assets in 1986 - 1987 in attempt to resolve financial difficulties from expansion to avoid bankruptcy)... David M. Roderick becomes head of U.S. Steel, created 1901 by J.P. Morgan from steel empires of Andrew Carnegie, Judge Elbert Gary, and William H. Moore (transforms business by shutting down over 150 plants and facilities to cut capacity by 30% and reduce labor force, some 108,000 in 1973, to 31,000 in 1984, acquires Marathon Oil in 1981 to become energy enterprise with steel only 32% of revenues, changes name to USX in 1986 with steel as only one group)...

W. Berry Fowler starts after-school tutorial parlor in Portland, OR (develops Sylvan Learning Corp. in 1981 to provide remedial enrichment learning programs for children missing out in public school system, operates $4.7 million business in 1985 with 105 franchises nationally to compete with American Learning Corp. of CA, Huntington Learning Center of NJ)... Just for Play business incorporates to sell risque, naughty lingerie (uses home parties to sell merchandise)... Space buff entrepreneur Gary Hudson and wealthy real estate developer David Hannah, Jr., launch Space Services of America as private business in Houston, TX, to put telecommunications and earth-scanning satellites into orbit for clients (tests Conestoga I successfully as first privately financed space vehicle in 1982)... 42 mergers are recorded for savings and loan institutions, 142 in 1980... Rand Arnskog becomes head of ITT (after previous flurry of acquisitions by Harold Geneen in building conglomerate, eliminates money-losing and unpromising operations, such as Canadian timber lands and food processing activities, to build telecommunications and financial-services empire by 1986)...

With $500,000 self-styled supersalesman Victor Kiam acquires failing Remington electric shaver business, lost over $30 million in past 4 years, from Sperry Rand in $25 million leveraged buyout (turns company around by trimming $2 million from payroll in firing 70 executives, eliminating $300,000 in executive perks, starting bonus plan for higher productivity, and initiating aggressive marketing program with personal appearances on TV commercials to increase sales by $7 million, repays borrowed $24 million within one year, with $375 million business buys New England Patriots football team in 1988 for $80-$90 million)... First Interstate Bancorp starts bank franchising in granting First National Bank of Golden, CO, and American Security Bank in Honolulu use of name, services... After 6 years of research Xerox develops Ethernet, community network computer system... Pionering pact to protect top management from termination by company takeover is designed with "Golden Parachutes" by Reliance Electric when threatened by Exxon... Following pioneering efforts of W. Edward Deming and Joseph M. Juran in 1950s, Philip Crosby Associates is formed to advise clients on quality control with zero defects (graduates some 35,000 executives from Quality College by 1986)... Nelson Bunker Hunt, brother W. Herman with 4 associates launch scheme to corner silver market (abandon effort in 1980 after losing over $1 billion with collapse of market)...

Gary Waldron, IBM International financial planner, obtains one-year leave-of-absence to develop youth gardening program for Bronx's Group Live-In-Experience, non-profit agency for abandoned and run-away childen operating government-funded gardening program (returns after resigning IBM position to transform project after loss of goverment funds as community-oriented business growing exotic herbs in vacant lots and plastic greenhouses, prospers in 1983 as South-Bronx Greenhouse to supply 50 of City's finest restaurants - over 3,300 restaurants and markets in 1985 to gross $1.2 million in sales and provide employment to area's youth)... Reynolds Industries, Winston-Salem tobacco conglomerate, acquires Del Monte, world's largest canner of fruits and vegetables, for $600 million (acquires Heublein in 1982 for $1.3 billion to obtain Kentucky Fried Chicken business, sells to Pepsico in 1986 for $850 million, and Smirnoff vodka, spins off Sea Land in 1983 and sells 2 subsidiaries to Phillips Petroleum for $1.7 billion, acquires Sunkist soft drinks in 1984 for $57 million to complement line of Canadian Dry and Hawaiian Punch drinks - Sunkist and Canadian Dry to Cadbury Schweppes in 1986, acquires Nabisco's, U.S.' No. 4 food business in 1985, for $4.9 billion to achieve total sales of $16.6 billion)...

Sydney Biddle Barrows, descendent of Pilgrims and holder of management degree, starts Cachet escort service, evolves as $1-million-a-year prostitution ring to serve some 2,300 wealthy clients willing to spend up to $1,000 for evening of pleasure (-1984 when busted after using modern business methods, being named female executive of year, and providing employees with group medical coverage, is fined $5,000 in 1985, publishes Mayflower Madam in 1986 to become celebrity)... Ron Barr opens Armchair Sailor Bookstore in Newport, RI (expands with 5 franchises by 1986 with plans for some 25 more)... First Boston's Real Estate & Development subsidiary hires developer G. Ware Travelstead, requires he must invest in projects (after 12 projects by 1986, designs $4-billion scheme for London, called Canary Wharf, as financial center on Thames with 33 office buildings)... In this time chef Prudhomme opens K-Paul's Louisiana Kitchen outside New Orleans to promote Cajun cookery...

Gentle Dental chain is started... After massive heart attack and negative vote by board on major acquisition, Kemmons Wilson, creator of Holiday Inns, retires (after dabbling in some 90 ventures starts budget-priced Wilson Inns in 1988 with plans for some 100 located near expensive hotels)... Virginia Rulon-Miller, one week after 13.3% raise, is fired by IBM for dating fellow employees (wins case in 1984 for

$300,000)... Reynolds Metal discovers gold reserves near Perth, Australia (diversifies from aluminum into gold, precious metals as price of gold soars from $300/ounce to $875 - $480 in 1988)... Colin T. Walker starts 60-Minute Tune–Up in Bellevue, WA, opens 1st outlet in 1980 (with 64 franchised and 5 company-owned outlets in 5 states, 1987 sales of some $12 million, goes national in 1988)... Home Depot of Bernard Marcus and Arthur Blank pioneers concept of warehouse retailing for "do-it-yourself" home improvements market, evolves as industry's fastest growing with 86 hanger-size outlets, sales near $2 billion, throughout South and West in 1988 - K mart's Builders Square with 118 places and sales of some $500 million in trying to balance service and discounting... Minneapolis' Tennant Co. receives news of defects on factory floor sweepers exported to Japan and Toyota's entry into market (with 40% of North American market starts quality improvement program, advised by Philip Crosby, to achieve 60% of North American market and 40% of world market in 1987 with employee involvement... By 1981 some 50 franchised chain restaurants open in Allentown, PA...

Robert E. Williams, desktop computer salesman, starts Management Information Source in Portland, OR, to help beginners in using computers (produces 80 instructional books to explain software programs by 1988 for sale through 10,000 retail outlets and foreign countries)... After Las Vegas marriage, U.S. engineer Lou Forence and Essie, mail-order bride from Philippines, start American Asian Worldwide Services as matchmaking business (grows as one of largest in industry of some 100 to gross nearly $250,000 in 1986)... Edward J. DeBartolo hires H.J. Wilson Co. to build shopping mall in Tampa, FL, in turn hires H.J. High Construction as contractor (leads to union boycotting mall's 85 stores to protest substandard wages - Supreme Court upholds union's right to secondary boycotts in 1988)... Businessman Miles Wolff buys inept Durham's Class A baseball club for $2,500, NC, worth some $1 million after turn-around...

Meat packer Oscar Mayer buys turkey-processor Louis Rich Co. (is bought in turn by General Foods in 1981 which is bought by Philip Morris tobacco giant in 1985)... Kathleen F. Jensen, Angela Franklin start Professional Nursing Service in Modesto, CA, with only car and silver tea set for collateral (with $9,000 loan build profitable business by 1988)... After hustling at this and that unsuccessfully, Alan Rosen, Mr. Mint or Duke of Dough, stumbles into trading baseball cards, by 1981 makes $1,000/week to become leading merchant by 1988 in new high-stakes field (starts advertising in 1982 to make deals for up to $100,000)... Leaving father's real estate business Steven, Mitchell Rales enter takeover game (after building manufacturing conglomerate with several acquisitions become big-time raiders in 1988 in bidding for Interco, $3.3 billion giant in furniture, apparel and shoes)... Oliver, John Grace launch proxy fight for small real estate trust, by 1988 with interests in variety of firms ranging from geothermal energy to chain of day-care centers.

1980

General Events

With inflation at highest level in 33 years, price of gold goes (January 18) to high of $802 on NY market, soars $159 in week's time (reaches $875 before dropping to $300 in 1982, hovers around $450 in 1988)... Scientists produce interferon, viral-fighting substance, by genetic

engineering... FBI indicts 55 for pornography and film piracy...
President Carter plans (March 14) to cut federal spending by $13 billion
to fight inflation... 33,000 NYC transit workers strike... U.S. Supreme
Court rules faculties at private universities are not covered by union
laws in being managerial employees... Price of silver drops (March 27) $5
to $10.80, ruins efforts of Hunt brothers to corner market, wipes out
$4 billion profit and hands them $1.5 billion debt to 23 banks (to escape
contracts to buy at $35/ounce sell vast silver holdings and Canadian oil
properties worth $500 million, after losing another billion or so from
falling oil prices sue banks in 1986 for fraudulent conduct in handling
family's assets, seek bankruptcy protection for Placid Oil in 1986, are
ordered by court in 1988 to pay $130 million to Peruvian firm)... Banking
industry is deregulated, March 31 (results in higher interest rates for
small investors and interest payments on checking accounts)... AT&T is
fined $1.8 billion in anti-trust conviction... U.S. Supreme Court rules
new life forms created in lab can be patented (leads to animal patents in
1988)... With controls on oil prices lifted in 1979 and profits soaring,
President Carter signs (April 2) Crude Oil Windfall Profits Tax Act...

Alaska ends (April 16) state income tax... Washington reports (May 21)
jobless rate of 7%, largest in 3 years... Motor Carrier Act derelegates
(June 20) trucking industry (leads to dissolution of some 4,500 carriers,
spawns about 11,500 new low-cost non-union carriers)... In this time fire
management specialists of U.S. Forest Service develop computer models to
predict how fires will spread and how various fire-fighting methods will
work (is used to quell 1985 Idaho blaze for less than $400,000 vs.
estimated $3.7 million under old system)...

U.S. Postal Service introduces INTELPOST, high-speed international
electronic message service... World's first multi-megawatt wind farm is
built at Goldendale, WA (after some $60 million is dismantled 1987)...
United Steel Workers, big steel makers agree to form "labor-management
participation teams" to revitalize industry (with piecemeal results
institute program top-down in 1986)... For first time in U.S. history,
U.S. is visited by more tourists, over 20 million foreigners, than
Americans touring other countries... Corporate Democracy Act is submitted
to Congress to make businesses more accountable to their
constituencies... Baseball players strike 8 days during exhibition play
in salary dispute with owners... Railroad Deregulation Act establishes
flexible freight rates...

Lutheran minister D. Douglas Roth, other ministers propose Pittsburgh
corporations should provide assistance to laid-off steel workers (after
confrontations, disrupting church services of executives and refusing to
leave church, is defrocked in 1985)... Over 1,000 Blue Shield employees
walk out to protest use of non-adjustable chairs, glaring lights at
video-display terminals... New Allen Center for Kellogg Graduate School
of Management opens Northwestern University (evolves with tailor-made
graduate study programs for over 1,500 executives of some 24
corporations, is ranked U.S.' No. 1 MBA program in 1988 by Business
Week)... Year's inflation rate hits 13.5% (drops to 10.4% in 1981, 6.1%
in 1982, 3.2% in 1983, 4.3% in 1984, and 3.6% in 1985)... Carnegie-Mellon
University creates CMU Robotics Institute (under direction of Raj Reddy
becomes world's largest industry-financed center researching robotics,
manufacturing technologies)... Merit-pay experiment is tested at China
Lake Naval Weapons Center, CA, to replace traditional civil service pay

system, proposed for all federal workers in 1986... Charlotte Wruck: Jewels for Their Ears (describes historical role of males wearing earrings, suggests current fad may have started in Boston with gay men around 1970)... Some 245,000 college students study business administration, around 134,000 in 1971... FCC approves AT&T's plan to build Washington-Boston telephone network with fiber-optics technology... Monetary Control Act requires all banks to report all cash transactions over $10,000 with overseas banks (puts savings and loan, credit unions and non-member banks under reserve fund requirements for national banks)... For first time public consumes more wine than liquor...

Department of Education, National Science Foundation issue report to conclude most Americans illiterate in science, technology... One-earner households compose 22.4% of labor force, 49.6% in 1960... Chicago police force elects Fraternal Order of Police as bargaining agent... Rev. Jesse Jackson's Operation PUSH starts drive to use purchasing power of blacks to increase employment of blacks... First Gay and Lesbian Awareness Day is held on April 13... For first time since 1920 U.S. census data shows rural areas, small towns growing faster than metropolitan areas...

Harborplace, designed by Rouse Co., opens in Baltimore to revitalize waterfront area... U.S. embargoes grain to U.S.S.R. after invasion of Afghanistan... Paperwork Reduction Act forces governmental agencies to be accountable for informational management... Some 53% of San Francisco residents live as singles... First official trade exhibit of China in U.S. is held, San Francisco... Scientists at Yale, UCLA conduct experiments to design genes for specific purposes... Lester C. Thurow: The Zero-Sum Society (proposes national investment committee to determine which industries merit funds)... Douglas R. Casey: Crisis Investing: Opportunities and Profits in the Coming Great Depression... Massachusetts holds first state lottery to raise funds for art projects... California is first state to pass computer-fraud law... Solar One, world's largest generator of electriciy with power from sun, is built, CA (-1981)...

Nation's Business: "Minerals: The Resource Gap"... Union members are 21% of labor force, 25% in 1970... Equal Employment Opportunity Commission issues guidelines on sexual harrassment (results in rise of grievances from 4,272 in 1981 to over 6,300 in 1984)... Lisa Birnbach (ed.): The Official Preppy Handbook... International Resource Development of Norwalk, CT, predicts computers will operate with verbal instructions by 1983... Congress authorizes Commerce Department to issue licenses for seabed mining in 1981 (prohibits commercial mining until 1988 to allow Law of Sea Treaty time for ratification)... South Dakota is one of first states to abolish limit on bank interest rates (in 2nd law establishes State as new center for credit operations, such as Citibank of NY, in 1982 law lets banks buy insurance companies)...

To implement Henry George's idea in 1879, Pittsburgh's tax rate on land is increased to 13.3% with 3.2% levy on buildings... U.S. Anti-Trust Division starts campaign against illegal bid-rigging by road-building contractors, some 400 criminal convictions by 1983... According to census, Americans of Asian, Pacific Island origin have increased 120% from 1970 , population of whites rises 6.4%, blacks 17.4% and Hispanics 60.8%... National Aquaculture Act encourages development of fish farming... General Meyer becomes Army's Chief of Staff (institutes Airland Battle Doctrine to increase fire power, mobility of light divisions with high technology)... Robert Hayes, William Abernathy: "Managing Our Way to Economic Decline," Harvard Business Review (argues U.S. managers know more about redeploying assets than running business, suggests U.S. managers largely to blame for dwindling industrial competitiveness, for emphasizing short-term gains, for being too cautious and overly analytical, and for failing to invest in technology)... Strike of 17 years is settled by agreement of Amalgamated Clothing & Textile Workers, used public pressure on firm's lenders, directors and stockholders to win recognition, J.P. Stevens textile business (leads to similar battles with Hormel in 1985-86 and International Paper in 1988)... Alvin Toffler: The Third Wave (discusses computer revolution)... F. Spinney: Defense Facts of Life (raises questions on military value of complex technology)... Federal Reserve Board lets U.S. banks open international banking facilities to compete with offshore branches in Caribbean, elsewhere...

U.S. Census shows population over 226 million and migration of people from Frost Belt states of Northeast, Mideast to Sun Belt states from FL to WA... U.S. Supreme Court rules workers have right to refuse to work if there is risk of serious injury or death... U.S. shows trade surplus of $27 billion in high-technology goods, $4 billion in 1985... To generate new jobs Masters and Mates union buys mothballed Monterey for $3 million as cruise ship for Hawaiian Islands, no foreign competitors allowed by Jones Act (leads to near bankruptcy of union by 1985 until excused by 1986 Tax Reform Act)... New York-based Local Initiatives Support Corp. raises $140 million by 1988 from 500 companies and foundations to finance low-income housing... After selling his Technicon Corp., a medical instruments firm, for $400 million to Revlon, Edwin C. Whitehead founds Whitehead Institute for Biomedical Research at Cambridge, MA, premier world center by 1988... For first time Census Bureau studies centenarians, 15,000 to 45,000 in 1988...

Congress passes act to create cleanup fund for handling hazardous wastes (leads to 1983 contract to Portland's Riedel, founded 1929, to handle spills in all states west of Mississippi, forms Riedel Environmental Technologies in 1986 as separate venture - 1987 sales of $55.5 million, and 10 offices and workforce of 509)... Congress lifts restrictions on interest rates paid by S&Ls, permits loans for a raft of new businesses in 1982.

Business Events

Exxon shows record profit of $ .3 billion for 1979... Gulf & Western introduces new battery for electric cars... Two foundations acquire Harper's Magazine to block bankruptcy... Procter & Gamble recalls tampons to avoid risk of Toxic Shock Syndrome... Cartwright is pioneering microbrewery in Portland, OR (although failing in 18 months inspires successful Widmer Brewing, Columbia River Brewing)... After offering time messages in 1928, weather reports in 1937, Dial-A-Joke in 1974 and Santa Claus messages in 1975, AT&T starts Dial-It 900 service, callers pay 50 cents for first minute (is used at first for mostly public opinion polls and then sexually-oriented messages in 1983 - local dial-up services after Bell break-up in 1984)... Average car costs $7,574, $13,520 in 1987... Marc, Kiki Ellenby acquire small farm in subtropical Dade County, FL (pioneer State's agribusiness of exotic tropical fruit to become one of largest by 1987)... C. Phillip Elliott starts Elliott Enterprises, FL, to manage investments for affluent, elderly clients (sells "conditional sales agreement," backed by municipal bonds with 3rd party - usually Elliott, to guarantee tax-free yield of 9% - 15% for up to 5 years - monthly investments of $600,000 by 1986, is charged in 1987 by SEC for selling unregistered securities and misrepresenting investment activities - assets only cover about 50% of $50 million "invested" since 1980)... Japan's Genichi Taguchi shows Bell Labs new approach to quality control, developed by Japan's Electrical Communications Laboratories, for designing product with sufficient capability to achieve quality despite variations in production lines (is used by AT&T in 1983, saves $60 million by 1985, ITT and Ford)...

After quitting $300,000 job with mutual fund giant Putnam, Norton H. Reamer starts business to build investment empire by mergers, acquisitions in cottage industry with borrowed $200,000 (acquires United Asset Management in 1983 - 15 firms with $18 billion in assets by 1987)... After spending 15 years building Atlanta-based Fuqua Industries as $2 billion holding company of hodgepodge of firms, J.B. Fuqua focuses on consumer products and services... National Telemarketing estimates 1,650 firms employ 4,500 people in telemarketing, 142,000 firms use over 2 million employees to make telephone sales in 1986... After developing Henri Bendel since 1960s as trendy NY store, using concept of Street of Shops as collection of boutiques, Geraldine Stutz, formerly with _Glamour_ magazine and Genesco's I. Miller shoe chain, purchases business from Genesco... _Newsweek_: "The Productivity Crisis"... _Time_: "Sears Searches for Success" (reports struggle of merchandising giant to find winning concept after slipping with stylish items during 1970s)...

1925 Howard Johnson restaurant and lodging business is acquired for some $630 million by Imperial Group of Britain, conglomerate with interests in tobacco, food and breweries (after retaining 210 Ground Round Restaurants, sells 500 hotels and motels, 617 restaurants to Marriott in 1985 for $438 million to keep 418 company-owned restaurants and 4 upscale plaza-hotels and sell 199 franchised restaurants, 500 hotels and motor lodges to Prime Motor Inns for $373 million)... After working with Texas International Airlines since 1973, chief operating officer in 1974, Donald Barr, colleagues start low-fare People Express Airline to provide "no-frills" service from Newark, NJ, to Columbus, Buffalo and Norfolk - by 1985 expands to 49 cities (develops organizational structure with 11 managing officers over 29 general managers over some 1,000 team leaders, views every employee as owner to participate in profit-sharing and as manager to share work in customer service, maintenance and flight activities, fires organizational architect Lori Dubose in 1984 after losses of $14.2 million, acquires Denver-based Frontier Airlines for national service and Britt Airways, regional commuter line for 29 Midwestern cities, to serve 133 airports in 1985, declares bankruptcy for Frontier in 1986 after pilots' union blocks sale to United Airlines, is acquired in 1986 by Texas International to avoid financial collapse)...

In this time Influential Focus is formed to detect environmental trends, some 50 major clients by 1985... With $5,000 saved from Bar Mitzvah, Bill Zanker launches Learning Annex, NY, to provide public with how-to-do, personal improvement courses (becomes "largest" non-credited adult education center in U.S., 50 competitors by mid-1980s, with branches in Chicago, Atlanta and plans for Washington, Philadelphia, Boston and West Coast by 1987 - first of kind to go public, opens first overseas branch in London in 1987)... Faced with mounting financial problems Pan Am Airlines sells headquarters building, NY, to acquire cash... After failing to survive price discounting war it started in 1972-73, 51% of Great Atlantic & Pacific Tea Co., founded 1859 to pioneer mass retailing, is acquired by Tengelman Group, West Germany's 2nd largest chain of supermarkets with some 2,000 stores in Germany and Austria, from Hartford Foundation, owner after heirs die in 1950s (after 4 years of losses and selling 600 unprofitable stores operates 1,016 stores in 1981, 3,468 in 1974, to achieve first profits since 1977 in 1982)... Manufacturer's Bank of Los Angeles is acquired by Japan's Mitsui Group... GTE's Strategic Systems Division obtains $325 million contract to prepare MX missile specifications for Defense Department (pioneers use of electronic publishing)...

Fortune publishes annual list of 500 largest industrial firms (shows only 282 still remain from first list in 1955, 185 absorbed by mergers, 29 dropped as too small, and 4 out of business)... 10 federally insured banks are declared in fault, 10 in 1981, 42 in 1982, 48 in 1983, 79 in 1984, 120 in 1985... Dutch-born Tony Bosboom starts Fabric Wholesalers in Portland, OR, as specialty retailing business (evolves by 1985 with sales of $38.7 million from 54 stores in 5 West Coast states, some 1,500 employees)... Kroeger grocery chain pioneers trend of supermarkets selling plants and flowers, in 730 of 1,100 outlets by 1985 (allows Cincinnati customers in 1988 to make donations for homeless by rounding bills at checkstand)... With loan from venture-capital group, David Houck acquires closed steel works, OH, from U.S. Steel (revives business by selling specialty steel - no losing quarters from 1982-85, starts resurgence of other low-tech ventures in depressed area)...

General Motors creates task force to develop computer network for manufacturing automation, demonstrated 1985... Joe Kelly, Kamran Khuzan: "Participative Management: Can It Work?" Business Horizons (questions if European approach of worker representatives on board of directors will work in U.S.)... John J. Stollenwerk, partners acquire Allen-Edmonds shoe business in WI, losing some $100,000/week (revitalizes operations by limiting sales to upscale stores, increasing advertising budget to focus on high quality and increasing exports)... Merger of Kraft, Dart creates $9.9 billion food and consumer products empire (sever mismatch in 1986 - Kraft accepts $13 billion takeover, U.S.' largest ever, in 1988 by Philip Morris)...

With retirement of Henry Ford II, president Philip Caldwell becomes chairman of Ford Motor Co. with engineer Donald E. Petersen president, chairman 1985 (launches Taurus-Sable new car project, discards traditional organizational structure to create team Taurus to integrate planning, design, engineering and manufacturing with ideas from workers, suppliers and customers, after spending some $3 billion introduces new cars in 1985-86 season to rave reviews, selling some 130,000 midsize sedans with backlog of orders for over 100,000 cars, acquires First Nationwide Financial, U.S.' 9th largest savings and loan in 1985 - later GM, Chrysler with financial services, earns $3.3 billion on sales of $62.7 billion in 1986 to top GM's $2.9 billion on $102.8 billion in sales, after failing to work out deals with Fiat, Austin Rover and Alfa Romeo acquires Britain's Austin Martin Lagonda Group to implement globalization strategy starts customer satisfaction surveys in 1986)... Venture capital business of Goulder, Thoma & Cressey is started, Chicago, with assets of $60 million, $160 million by 1986... Job-placement or counseling services are provided to departing employees by 16% of 1,000 largest industrial companies, 51% by 1987... Lisp Machine, CA, and Symbolics, MA, are started to exploit growing interest in development of artificial intelligence systems (are followed in 1981 by Japan's Fifth Generation Project to develop AI-based computers, by creation of U.S. consortium, Microelectronics and Computer Corp., in 1982 to challenge Japanese, by development of AI work station of Pegasus in 1984, and by introduction of 3 AI software products by IBM in 1985)... Investment guru Joseph Grandville advises clients to buy (results in 30-point surge on Wall Street market)...

Computer Camp, CA, opens so children, ages 10 to 18, can learn computer languages, devise electronic games... CSX railroad system is created by merger of Chessie System, Seaboard Coast Line... Since 1972 some 14,000 NY franchise operators lose about $40 million to parent companies... Public spends some $1.7 billion on athletic footwear, $2.5 billion in 1985... Union Planters National Bank of Memphis designs pioneering variable-rate consumer installment loan... According to International Association of Tanning Manufacturers, 22 chains of franchised tanning salons do business in U.S... Sun-Diamond is created, CA, to design overall marketing program for cooperatives of growers of hazelnuts, raisins, walnuts, prunes, and figs, sales of some $500 million by mid-1980s to be ranked 454th in Fortune's list of nation's largest business enterprises... IBM establishes management development centers...

Some 225 U.S. manufacturing firms are operated by Japanese interests... Mark Hughes, 24-year-old, starts Herbalife International, grows to sell 23 products to promote weight loss, better health and reduce stress by cleansing body system to promote mental alertness (gives customers discounts in selling products to others, is investigated by FDA in 1982-85 for distributing unsafe products, shows sales of $500 million in 1985, is targeted by CA in 1985 with consumer protection law suit for product misrepresentation, marketing pyramid scheme)... Racing horse Spectacular Bid is syndicated for $22 million... National Distillers is fined $750,000 for making illegal payments to customers... Ted Turner creates Cable News Network, 300 employees, to televise throughout U.S. with world's first 24-hour-a-day programming of news (after achieving first pre-tax profits in 1985 operates with 1,500 employees and budget of $100 million to serve 38.5 million subscribers)...

Frank Lorenzo's Texas International Airline starts non-union New York Air to compete in lucrative East Coast shuttle market between Boston, NY, and Washington... After buying a regular bank Gulf & Western devises first U.S. "nonbank" with no checking accounts or commercial loans, followed by almost 100 more by 1984 to skirt laws on interstate banking... Bethlehem Steel pleads guilty to charges of mail fraud on bribes for ship-repair business... Columbus Dispatch, OH, is first newspaper to distribute news by computer network to some 3,000 homes... Prime interest rate for banks reaches high of 21.5%... Eli Lilly & Co., IN, plans to make synthetic insulin... Ford assembly plant of 4,500 employees in Mahwah, NJ, closes after producing some 4.6 million cars since 1955 (represents 1 of 13 such plants permanently closed to idle some 184,000 workers)... Communications Satellite Corp. announces plans to develop nation's first satellite home television system... Dow Jones Industrial Average again reaches 1000 level... Union Oil opens first U.S. commercial geothermal plant to generate electricity in Imperial Valley, CA... Channel 2000, an experiment at home banking and electronic information, is started in Columbus, OH, with 200 households... Atlantic-Richfield is found guilty for unjustly firing an employee... Color Me a Season's business, provides color-consulting seminars in homes so women can determine appropriate colors for apparel and cosmetics, is copyrighted (grows with pyramiding marketing approach to sell distributorships, cosmetics)... AT&T creates independent subsidiary, "Baby Bell", to compete in computer communications market...

Time, Inc. launches <u>Discover</u> as news magazine for science (-1983)... Atlantic-Richfield develops teleconference network so key employees can confer with each other by satellite (-1982)... For some $90 million French auto maker Renault acquires 22.5% of American Motors... Safeway's Canoga Park Store in Los Angeles opens as discount food barn... Westinghouse Electric creates intra-communications network...

Buffy Bus is started, Seattle, to provide shopping tours for bargain hunters (starts Portland bus in 1982)... Bordeaux is started, IA, to market apparel made by 100-150 seamstresses at homes (with sales of some $300 million, is investigated in 1986 for violating 1943 ban on home manufacture of clothing, jewelry)... Designer-jeans craze is ignited with Calvin Klein's sexual sell, features model Brooke Shields in provocative ads (introduces Obsession perfume in 1985 with risque ads)...

GM's share of automobile market is some 46%, drops to 42% by 1985... Some 7 million Americans are self-employed, 5.2 million in 1970... Ross C. Ahntholz joins Olin chemical giant as pioneering director of informations services, followed by adoption of chief information officers by Wells Fargo Bank, Pillsbury in 1983... 142 savings and loan associations merge, 42 in 1979...

Computer genius Dennis Greenman starts brokerage business, FL (concocts get-rich-quick-scheme, "The Short-Term Trading Program," with computer to spot profitable arbitrage deals, collapses by 1981 with investors losing upward of $50 million from Ponzi scam)... IBM Credit Corp. is created, evolves with assets of $5 billion by 1986 to earn $100 million on revenues of $500 million...

Jantzen, OR maker of sports and swimwear founded 1910, is acquired by clothing manufacturer Blue Bell for $51 million (is acquired with Blue Bell in 1986 by VF Corp. for $800 million)... TV Real Estate airs in Spokane, WA, so house buyers can view homes... Frederick Lenz, doctorate in English literature and former disciple of Hindu guru Sri Chinmoy, moves to California with guru's instructions to open laundromat and learn humility (as Zen Master Ramal starts medication group for psychic development, promotes Rama Seminars with 1987 budget of some $500,000 before 1988 problems in public relations)...

After first business deal in 1946 to borrow $50,00 to buy radio station, former governor John Connally returns to Texas after failing to win Republican presidential nomination, uses accumulated assets of $6-10 million to build $300 million empire by 1983 with borrowed money (after oil market slump declares bankruptcy in 1987 and auctions property in 1988)... Bennetton of Treviso, Italy, enters U.S. market (opens 700 mid-priced boutiques by 1988 - 4,500 worldwide, plans to open 300 more by

1990)... Thomas E. Feil starts V Brand Corp. to design advanced phone systems for banks and brokerage houses, shows earnings of $22.5 million on 1986-87 sales of $54 million (signs $20 million contract in 1988 with AT&T to distribute V Brand products)... Keith Code, former pro Superbike racer, opens California Superbike School, handles over 16,000 students by 1988... Basketball coach Jim Valvano is hired by N.C. State, rejects U.C.L.A. offer in 1988 for 5-year, $2.5 million contract... Houston's Astroworld is first theme park with rapids ride, idea from artificial kayak course at 1972 Munich Olympic Games - 19 more by 1988...

Spurred by stockmarket success of Genetech, Blech brothers, one in advertising and other a stockbroker, start Genetic Systems with scientists from University of Washington, sell in 1986 to Bristol-Myers to earn $60 million on $200,000 investment (start Nova Pharmaceutical in 1982 to fashion new drugs out of altered molecules - $200 stake worth $7 million by 1983, start Vista Organization in 1983 to make movies - lose $2 million by 1987, after starting Cambridge BioScience with $275, selling holdings for some $20 million, start Celgene in 1986 to develop a microbe to eliminate hazardous waste - worth $51 million in 1988, sell share of Nova to SmithKline Beckman for $100 million)... Some 1,500 limousine firms generate sales of $800 million, 4,500 in 1988, Carey International largest in 300 cities, do $1.5 billion...

Financial News Network is new cable network (makes first profit from business-news-and-sports in 1986 before NBC launches Consumer News & Business Channel in 1988)... By 1988 over 200 new U.S. semiconductor firms appear in market while U.S.' market share slips from 57.2% to 39.4% and Japan grows from 27.4% to 48%... Westinghouse begins to form E-mail office system (links 10,700 managers, employees in U.S. and 37 countries with 6,000 PCs by 1988)... Movie star Sophia Loren is first with celebrity perfume, followed by Linda Evans in 1984, Elizabeth Taylor in 1987, Cher and Herb Alpert in 1988 and Mikhail Baryshnikov in 1989 (leads to copycat fragrances by Debra International in 1985, $40 million in sales by 1988, to "duplicate" scents for mass-market)... To replace traditional dingy novelty shops Ken Fletcher opens first Magic Masters outlet, 5 shops for upscale patrons in 1988 with plans for 3 more in 1989... In this time, Fred Schwartz, aka Fred the Furrier, imports inexpensive pelts for working women (in creating a mass market for furs with TV advertising operates 23 Fur Vault stores by 1987 before first losses in 1988, retires as sucessor tries for upscale image)... By 1988 ski resorts decline by 35% to 650.

1981

General Events

President Reagan plans (March 6) to cut federal employment by 37,000 jobs... Washington announces (March 10) plan to link welfare benefits with work requirements... U.S. Supreme Court protects benefits for people quitting work for religious beliefs... Senate prevents (May 20) President Reagan in making cuts in Social Security pensions... Census Bureau reports more blacks now live in suburbs of major cities... After 7 weeks major league baseball stike ends (July 31) when players, owners agree on issue of free-agency compensation... Some 300,000 Americans undergo cosmetic surgery, 500,000 in 1986... U.S. Census reports number of unmarried couples living together nearly triples from 1970 to 1.56

million households in 1980... National Security Agency makes secret rule that a homosexual can retain job, security clearance... After 13 years absence UAW reaffiliates with AFL-CIO... FDA approves use of collagen shots to smooth out wrinkles, used by over 300,000 to improve looks by 1986)... In this time "Crack," cheap form of cocaine for mass market, appears in Los Angeles (evolves with youth earning $100/day as lookouts, $300/day as runners and up to $3,000/day as dealers in major cities by 1988)... Over 9 million workers are unemployed as inflation rate drops to some 7%... Ruth Yannatta Goldway is elected by New Left activitists as Mayor of Santa Monica, CA (forms "populace" consumer-oriented government)... Cascade Run Off at Portland, OR, is first road race to advertise prize money for runners... After dropping from $13 billion in 1978 to $300 million by October, 1981, Commerce Department warns U.S. auto makers could run out of working capital by 1982... First hydro-electric power plant in area in over 50 years is dedicated at Lawrence, MA...

FTC dismisses 8-year-old anti-trust suit against Exxon, Texaco, Gulf, Standard Oil of IN, Mobil, Standard Oil of CA, Shell and Atlantic-Richfield... For first time 1904 Explorer's Club accepts women as members... Daniel Yankelovich: New Rules: Search for Self-Fulfillment in a World Turned Upside Down (reports on sexual revolution of 1965-75, "Me" decade of 1970s, and new "ethic of commitment" for 1980s)... On taking office President Reagan issues executive order to require 150 government agencies to do cost-benefit analyses, benefits must outweigh costs, before proposing new rules of significance... Bill is passed to grant Individual Retirement Accounts tax deductibility (results in rise of accounts from $26 billion to some $250 billion by 1986)... Deans of graduate schools of business at Stanford, Harvard declare informal truce in publicity battle as to which is No. 1...

First detected U.S. cases of AIDS, Acquired Immune Deficiency Syndrome, are seen in NY, San Francisco, Los Angeles... Air Force launches $3 million Manufacturing Science Program to encourage greater study of production processes in colleges... President Reagan signs legislation to provide 3-year tax cut, to index of taxes with inflation, and to cut $130.5 billion from budget... Inmates at Arizona Center for Women are employed by Best Western motel chain to handle telephone reservations, followed by other prisons handling projects for TWA, NY State Department of Motor Vehicles in 1985... U.S. District Judge, NY, issues pioneering ruling against theater requiring woman lobby attendant to wear "revealing and sexually provocative uniform"...

North Dakota permits charitable and non-profit organizations to operate gambling games if proceeds go to charity... Timothy Hall, John Kemp for first time successfully insert gene from one plant in chromosone of another, an unrelated species, and made to express itself... Paul Tsongas: The Road from Here (issues Neo-liberal manifesto on economic policy with governmental support of industrial development, high-tech growth with training programs, tax reforms)... Carnegie-Mellon University prepares pioneering strategic plan to seek excellence in areas of competitive advantage, copied by Stanford and University of Miami... Some 14,500 women, 25,9% of total, register in college MBA programs, 758, 3.5%, in 1971... George Gilver: Wealth and Poverty (provides manifesto for supply-side economics)... For first time national debt tops $1 trillion mark (reaches $2 trillion in 1986 - $6,737/capita versus

$3,613 in 1975)... North Carolina Supreme Court rules shopping center liable for mugging in parking area as is Long Island motel for 1974 rape of singer Connie Francis... Harris Poll reports 78% of U.S. workers felt less pride in work than 10 years previously and 73% indicated less motivation... Single Mothers by Choice organizes, over 1,000 members by 1985... National Organization for Changing Men forms to help new man achieve identity other than "macho" or "wimp"... National Center for Health Statistics reports some 647,000 divorced men are remarried, 334,000 in 1971, and some 616,000 divorced women are remarrying, 423,000 in 1971...

Library of Congress finishes computerizing its card catalog... At Cornell University technical meeting electrical engineering professor Lester F. Eastman is "hooted" when suggesting "ballistic" transistor (pioneers ultratiny high electron-mobility transistor, "super chip," with Bell Labs in 1984)... Allied Industrial Workers, formed 1935 by AFL for auto workers, plans to merge with stronger unions... Atlantic: "The Education of David Stockman" (cites head of Office Management and Budget saying, "None of us really understands what's going on with all the numbers")... Louisiana is first State to create local enterprise zones to encourage economic development in depressed rural, urban areas with tax breaks...

U.S. Customs Service starts Operation Exodus to stem illicit export of defense-related technology (seizes 2,851 shipments by 1984)... San Jose, CA, is forced by striking municipal workers to provide pay-equity adjustments for sex discrimination, followed in 1983 with ruling by federal court judge that State of Washington must provide equal pay for jobs of comparable worth... Beech Aircraft asks Burt Rutan to design new executive airplane (although tried unsuccessfully by U.S. and German military in 1944, creates Starship I, canard plane with curved wings)...

Economic Recovery Act allows employers to deduct cost of child-care benefits for employees... JANUS, $2.45 million computer program to simulate combat, is designed and tested for reality by scientists at Lawrence Livermore National Laboratory, adopted in 1983 by Army War College as video-war game... Columbia, world's first operational space shuttle, is launched to provide "routine access" to space... Delaware passes Financial Center Development Act (removes ceiling on interest rates, reduces back taxes, and allows non-state banks to operate in state, passes laws in 1988 to deter hostile takeovers)... Gallup Poll gives $227 as minimum weekly budget for family of 4, up from $199 in 1977, $101 in 1967, $60 in 1954, $30 in 1937... Crosbyton, TX, is first U.S. City to generate solar energy for commercial purposes... Sandra Day O'Connor is first woman member of U.S. Supreme Court... Tax Foundation states for first time in post War history employment of states and local governments lags behind U.S. population growth...

Cost of living shows increase of 138% since 1970 while Federal spending on entitlement programs rises $20 billion to $297 billion... Americans save 4.7%, 8% in 1970 - West Germans at 13.5% and Japanese at 19.5%... Almost 50% of Minnesota workers strike... When Professional Air Traffic Controller Organization participates in illegal strike after rejecting government contract terms, first official nationwide walk-out by public service employees, President Reagan fires some 12,000 workers to break strike with replacements (followed by ruling of Federal Labor Relations Authority that PATCO is no longer labor organization (declares bankruptcy in 1982)... U.S. agricultural exports realize all-time high of $43.8 billion, some $26.5 billion in 1986... Caspar W. Weinberger becomes Defense Secretary (-1987, downgrades Pentagon's 1961 Program Analysis & Evaluation Office of Robert S. McNamara from position of Assistant Defense Secretary to Office Director)... U.S. closes consulate in Medellin, Colombia's cocaine center for cartel processing leaves from Bolivia and Peru since late 1970s, for security reasons... U.S. halts trade and technology to U.S.S.R. to protest Poland's martial law... During first 5 months Federal Home Loan Bank Board approves 71 voluntary mergers of thrift institutions, 29 for same period in 1980... Women's Committee of Directors Guild of America signs agreement with major movie studios to hire women, minorities... Writers Guild, some 200,000 members, strike television, movie industry for over 12 weeks, 2 weeks in 1985 debacle and some 15 weeks in 1988...

Loret M. Ruppe is new Peace Corps Director (while helping Third World nations with health, education and agriculture projects, launches program to help poor to start tiny businesses - pioneered by Mahatma Gandhi's cottage industry movement in India)... Baltimore opens $30 million aquarium (records 1.45 million visitors in 1987 to pump $5 into local economy for every invested dollar - representative of other cities)... Charlie Bryan is new head of Eastern's machinists union (loses nomination for seat on board of airline, demands huge pay hike in 1983 - wins with strike after challenge by Eastern president Frank Borman, parlays Borman's demands for huge concessions in 1984 to get 25% of Eastern stock, board seats and management role, in campaign to improve productivity in 1985 saves $30 million, forces Borman out in 1986 with Texas Air takeover, with law suit blocks Texas Air's attempt to spin off lucrative Eastern Shuttle in 1988 and prevents Eastern hiring outside mechanics and pilots, strikes in 1989 - Eastern goes into bankruptcy).

Business Events

Chrysler reports 1980 losses of $1.710 billion, largest in U.S. business, GM with $763 million, most since 1921, Ford with $1.5 billion, American Motors with $198 million and Volkswagen with $30 million loss... U.S. Steel acquires Marathon Oil for $6.3 billion... Commodore introduces 2 low-price computers, VIC20, first home computer to sell over 1 million units, and Commodore 64 for under $500 (are joined in market by Radio Shack's Model 1 and Timex's Sinclair 100, first priced under $100)... Gene Call opens marketing business, Los Angeles, to train therapists on how to improve their promotional techniques (by 1987 handles 2,000-3,000 clients)... Lee Chilton turns hobby of resuscitating ailing baseball gloves into regular business, worldwide operation by 1987... Playorena opens on East Coast to provide children with exercise centers (operates 70, 7,500 pupils, by 1987 - 1980 Gymboree with 252 places and some 50,000 clients)... Completion Bond is started, Los Angeles, to insure production of films for movie producers, mostly independents who need funds from outside investors... Robert K. Gray, former White House official, starts one-stop firm in Capitol to provide clients with services in public relations, lobbying, political campaigning, advertising, planning events... 1927 Double-Cola business, Chattanooga, woos India's government to bottle its drinks in India (beats out Coca-Cola and Pepsi in 1987 after promising to use India's raw materials and reinvest profits)... Sports fan F. Ross Johnson becomes president of Nabisco Brands (pumps some $58 million into sports events, mostly golf, tennis, and auto racing, to promote corporation - 10 corporations with events-marketing departments in 1982 and at least 400, such as Anheuser-Busch, AT&T, Beatrice, Philip Morris, Adolph Coors and Coca-Cola, by 1987 to bankroll practically every sport)... First Interstate Bancorp is created by Western Bancorporation with 21 affiliates in 11 states, first such financial institution to offer de facto interstate banking... White Motors is acquired by Sweden's Volvo for some $100 million... Consolidated Freightways' money-losing Freightliner manufacturing business is acquired by West Germany's Daimler-Benz for over $260 million... After selling oil properties (becomes partner in father's Davis Oil in 1960 to drill with money of other people to acquire wealth with oil crisis of 1973) to Hiram Walker for $630 million, Denver wildcatter Marvin Davis, partner Marc Rich acquire control of 20th Century-Fox movie business (sells 4 Denver office buildings for $500 million in 1982, acquires Rich's stake in Fox for $116 million, sells half of Fox to publisher Rupert Murdoch in 1985 for $250 million - rest to Murdoch later in year for $325 million, sells oil properties in 1985 to Apache for $180 million, fails on bid of $3.75 billion to take over CBS in 1985)... Time: "In Search of Stable Market" (reports use of risk analysts by firms to reduce danger in investing overseas)...

Newsweek: "The New Urge to Merge" (reports cash-rich corporations, chiefly in energy field, battling each other for acquisitions - 1,184 mergers for $35.7 billion in first 6 months versus 1,889 mergers in all of 1980 worth $44.3 billion)... With 35 franchised offices in U.S. and Canada, Dentcare is largest dental chain in North America (collapses by 1983 with over-ambitious plans and high overhead in executive salaries)... After operating 18 Wendy's restaurants and owning part of health club, Doug Shelley starts D'Lites chain of fast-food restaurants for slender set, Atlanta (operates some 100 places in 19 states before floundering in 1986 from overheated expansion, locations in blue-collar areas)... Auto sales are lowest in 20 years... 24-pound Osborne I computer, world's first complete portable, is introduced to market, bankruptcy in 1983 despite 1982 sales of $70 million... Norfolk Southern Railroad holding company acquires 19% of Piedmont Airlines...

American Airlines shakes up industry with program, ADVANTAGE, for frequent flyers (is followed by United Airlines with "Mileage Plus" program to reward frequent flyers with free tickets, spawns industry by 1986 of some 40 airline coupon brokers, with Agco oldest and Fuller Coupon Bank of La Jolla, CA, as one of largest with 70 people at headquarters and 7 satellite offices, to barter, trade and/or re-sell bonus tickets, by 1988 results in wild competition and attacks on use of coupons by firms employing frequent flyers and IRS)... Santa Fe International oil business is purchased by Kuwait Petroleum, largest U.S. investment by OPEC government until Saudi Arabia's proposed payment of $1.2 billion in 1988 for 50% of Texaco...

Calgene is created, CA, to do research in agricultural genetics, joins some 50 other small firms in field... Kansas City Star reports foreign subsidiaries of U.S. corporations traded with Iran during hostage crisis despite 1980 trade embargo... Boston-based VR Business Brokers makes pitch to prospective franchisees, NYC, to sell franchises for $22,500 in business to sell businesses... 1910 Salomon Bros., world's largest trader in government securities, is acquired by 1914 Philipp Bros., world's largest commodity trader, to form Philbro-Salomon in $550 million transaction (is investigated in 1987 on charges of cheating customers in coca-futures market)... After informal partnership in 1980, Wesray is formed as leveraged buyout business by William E. Simon, former Treasury Secretary (provides contacts with companies seeking buyers and financial institutions for debt financing, prepares overall strategy) and former accountant Ray Chambers to handle operations (achieve first success in 1982 with acquisition of Gibson Greeting Card business to realize some $200 million by 1986 and another $137 million from 5 other transactions)... Charles Schwab & Co. of San Francisco, formed 1971 to become largest U.S. discount broker after elimination of fixed-rate system in 1975, is first brokerage house acquired by bank with purchase by Bank of America for $57 million, resold to Schwab in 1987 for $230 million to avoid financial difficulties... Newman Communications pioneers market of tape cassette publishing (increases sales under $200,000 to over $7 million by 1984 - total 1986 market of some $250 million)...

Over 300 businesses, trade associations form Product Liability Alliance urge reform of nation's product liability laws... Public Storage opens first ministorage warehouse in Portland, OR (expands to 14 other city locations and operates 550 facilities in 33 states by 1986)... 1,448 rotary drill-rigs operate, TX, to pump oil, down 50% by 1982 with collapsing oil prices... After Las Vegas accident and unable to practice orthopedic surgery, Dr. Ivan Mindlin starts Computer Group (becomes U.S.' biggest known-sports betting ring, reputed to have won 60-65% of bets before FBI raid in 1985)... Agreements to provide greater opportunities to minorities are signed by Coca-Cola and 7-Up with Rev. Jesse Jackson's Operation PUSH (results in 7-up's first black-owned bottling plant in 1985 and Coca-Cola's first black franchise in 1985 to basketball star Julius Irving, others)... Fashion designer Norma Kamali styles male sweatshirts for young women...

Entrepreneur State-A-Business is started to sell how-to-do manuals to small businesses (expands with franchises to 26 major cities in 17 states by 1986)... P.S. 121 graduate Eugene M. Lang, founder of Refac Technology Development, promises 59 6th graders of P.S. 121 in East Harlem, NYC, to pay tuition for all those attending college, emulated by other business leaders... Some 587,000 firms incorporate during year, 53,000 more than 1980 and 80% more than in 1975 (leads to 17,000 failures, 45% over 1980)... AT&T, CBS start joint venture to equip 200 households in Ridgewood, NJ, with video-tech system to permit two-way communications between users and computer data bank with information on news, weather, sports, education, and entertainment... $70,000 is medium price for new home, $20,000 in 1965...

Smith Kline Beckman forms representative joint venture with Fujisawa Pharmaceutical to market its drugs in U.S... The Washington Star, founded 1853, closes... Chicago's Economy Savings & Loan Association declares bankruptcy, caught in profit squeeze between new high interest rates and old low mortgage rates... Some 66 transactions with price tags of $50 million or more are made by firms to divest themselves of unwanted operations, 39 in 1980... Chris Di Petta and partners start Punch Line, Atlanta, as club to showcase new comics (open 9 more by 1986 to pioneer trend, start agency, Snikkers, later to book comics with clubs)... Cable MTV offers youth market round-the-clock rock music videos (evolves from 300 cable outlets to some 2,000 by 1985 before losing audience in

1986)... United American Bank of Knoxsville starts banking-at-home plan
with personal computers... Computer Camp International start pioneering
computer camp for youngsters, CT... Tandy sues firms, CA and Hong Kong,
for allegedly copying part of firm's software for personal computers...
GM asks staff political-risk feasibility on reopening assembly plant in
Buenos Aires (although few banks and oil firms with formal risk-analysis
departments prior to Iranian Revolution is adopted by many large
corporations afterward)... Atlas Savings & Loan, first U.S. gay-owned
bank, opens in San Francisco (evolves from $2 million in assets to over
$100 million by 1984)... Fortune: "The Next Industrial Revolution"
(reports developments in CAD/CAM with estimated industry sales of $750
million, minimal in 1976 and possibly $8 billion by 1990)... In trying to
shift from traditional electro-mechanical assembly lines to electronic
production, AM International loses some $245 million... Chicago Cubs
baseball franchise is acquired from Wrigley family by Tribune Co. for
$20.5 million as resource for WGN radio station, pay-TV sports channel...

With 3rd place finish in Women's Open, golfer Kathy Whitworth is first
woman athlete to achieve career winnings over $1 million - 31 male
golfers over mark... IBM enters personal computer market, developed by
project team outside regular bureaucracy (as market standard sells some 3
million, despite many clones, by 1986, introduces PS/2 line of personal
computers in 1987 - clones by 1988, after 3 years of disappointing
profits reorganizes in 1988)... After experimenting since 1972 to find
alternative to "insipid-tasting desserts," David Mintz, former kosher
caterer, introduces "Tofutti," frozen dessert from mashed soybeans
(becomes $17 million business by 1985, exports tofu creation in 1986 to
Japan)... New Court Securities becomes Rothschild, Inc. with Robert S.
Pirie, descendant of Chicago department store family, as chief
executive... Digital Equipment, Hewlett-Packard, Data General
minicomputer companies introduce new office-automation systems...

Stewardship Bank of Oregon opens in Portland, OR, to use "Christian
principles" in business operations (tithes 10% of profits to Christian
educational organizations)... VideoJournal, cassette magazine, is issued
for industrial market... Video-game addicts spend estimated $5 billion in
playing arcade games, about twice take of all Nevada casinos or U.S.
movies and 3 times more than combined TV revenues and gate receipts of
major league baseball, basketball, football... After averaging some
180,000 new businesses in 1960s, almost 600,000 new enterprises appear
during year... Automobile Industry Action Group is started by Chrysler,
Ford, GM, American Motors and some 400 large suppliers of automotive
parts to develop electronic communications network, followed by
Organization for Data Exchange by Teletransmission in Europe by 9 major
automotive firms in 1984 to communicate with suppliers, customs
authorities, shipping agents...

IBM creates quality institute (adopts flexible work schedules)... MGM/UA
offers investors limited partnerships in movie ventures... Financially-
troubled Hyatt Clark bearing business, NJ, is purchased from GM by
Employee Stock Ownership Plan (declares bankruptcy in 1985 with declining
demand, bickering between union and managers)... Some 50% of U.S. movies
are filmed in CA, 30% in 1983 and 21% in 1984... Shaklee, San Francisco
maker of vitamins, sponsors U.S. ski team (develops new diet program for
racers in 1984)... After operating since 1974 as part-time, freelance
venture, Fallon Elligott Rice Advertising Agency is formed, MN, to out-

smart competition rather than out-spend them (acquires <u>Wall</u> <u>Street</u> <u>Journal</u> account in 1985 from Madison Avenue agencies by selling imagination with wit, irreverence, shock)... Richard LaMolta of Brooklyn devises Chipwich, ice cream sandwich between 2 chocolate-chip cookies, quickly sells some 25,000/day... After starting Atari video-game business and Pizza Time Theaters with automatoms, Nolan Bushnell creates Catalyst Technologies to supply venture capital to new technology companies, such as electronic machines for travel arrangements (starts Axlon in 1985 to sell computerized stuffed animals, with little success joins Steve Wozniak, co-founder of Apple Computer in 1975, in 1986 business to make TechForce robot toys)... In pioneering move American Can acquires insurance company, 3 more by 1983 (is emulated in acquisition of financial service enterprises by Ashland Oil, BAT Industries, Crown Central, Ethel, General Electric, National Steel, RCA, St. Regis, Sears, Xerox)... GM, UAW agree to system of flexible work assignments at Cadillac Livona plant (pay workers according to skill levels and 4 wage grades)... Jeremy Sage, 18-year veteran in arranging birthday parties for children, opens Jeremy's Place, NYC, to provide special facilities for children's parties...

RCA, after 15 years of research costing some $150 million, introduces SelectaVision VideoDisc player (-1984 after losing over $500 million in battle with video cassettes)... National Video, franchiser of video tape stores, opens in Portland, OR (claims U.S.' largest with 648 places in 47 states and Canada by 1986)... <u>Fortune</u>: "Westinghouse's Cultural Revolution" (reports transformation of business in adopting Japanese style of management)... Robert C. Goizueta, Cuban refugee in 1959 with $20, becomes head of Coca-Cola (sells steam boiler manufacturer in 1981 for $95 million, acquires Columbia Pictures in 1982 for $750 million, acquires pasta maker Ronco in 1982 for $10 million - sold 1984 for $20 million, launches Caffeine Free Coke and Tab in 1983, sells Wine Spectrum and its Taylor brand in 1983 for $230 million, introduces New Coke and Cherry Coke in 1985, is forced to bring back old Coke as Coca-Cola Classic in 1985, acquires TV production business in 1985, is involved in 1985 suit with Pepsi Cola by 4 independent bottlers, NC, for violating anti-trust regulations with Calendar Marketing Agreements to pay high-volume retailers for exclusive promotions and displays on certain days - loses while Pepsi settles only to face more suits in 1987)... General Electric creates Biological Energy as product development venture...

<u>Newsweek</u>: "The Silicon Valley Style" (reports new corporate world de-emphasizing offices, titles and formality, making decisions by encounter sessions, and providing extensive benefits, social activities to hold employees from raids by competitors)... Knight-Ridder newspaper business, AT&T successfully test Viewtron, videotex network with TV information... Michael Crete, R. Stuart Bewley of Lodi, CA, introduce California Cooler, carbonated white wine with fruit juice (sell 700 cases in 1981 and 80,000 in 1982, become market leader over 75 imitators when acquired by Louisville's Brown-Forman, maker of Jack Daniels bourbon, in 1985 for $146 million, lose No. 1 spot in field over 100 to Gallo's Bartles & Jaymes in 1986)... Former Disney employee Abraham Lincoln starts Alchemy II to make animated figures for Disney's TV shows (sells marketing rights to Donald D. Kingsborough in 1984, acquires over $68 million in orders from large retailers, such as Sears and Toys 'R' Us, in 1985 for high-tech teddy bears, other dolls)... National Basketball Association retains

Control Data's Life Extension Institute to assist players with personal problems... Sears acquires Dean Witter, 5th-largest security business, for $600 million (adds Coldwell Banker, U.S.' largest real estate brokerage business, later for some $175 million to create giant financial services operation with Allstate Insurance)... Prudential Insurance acquires Bache brokerage business for $385 million...

American Express, 1980 sales of $5.5 billion, and brokerage firm of Shearson Loeb Rhoades, 1980 sales of $653 million, merge (acquires part of Geneva's Trade Development Bank in 1983, mutual fund of Investors Diversified Services and investment banking business of Lehman Bros. in 1984, and financially-troubled E.F. Hutton in 1987, charged for money laundering scheme in 1988, to create investment business with $4 billion in assets to handle over $100 billion for clients, is first foreign investment firm to get French banking license in 1988, restricted since 1807, introduces new, unbundled stock units in 1988 for investors)...

John F. Welch, Jr., chemist by training, becomes head of General Electric, youngest ever at 45 (strips echelons from hierarchy to decentralize to 20 operating divisions, uses Management Development Insititute as agent in changing corporate culture, sells $5.6 billion of unwanted businesses to shift resources from manufacturing to services, eliminates some 100,000 employees, over 25% of work force, as "Neutron Jack" starts 50-year, $1 billion automation program in 1982 - Louisville dishwasher factory first automated in 1983, pleads guilty in 1985 to overcharging government on 1980 contract, acquires Employer's Reinsurance, No. 2 in field, for $1.1 billion in 1985, creates Corporate Executive Council in 1986 to promote corporate teamwork, acquires RCA in 1986 for $6.5 million to increase GE's revenues from $28 billion to $40 billion, acquires brokerage firm of Kidder Peabody in 1986, becomes disaster by 1988, for $600 million to join General Electric Credit, U.S.' largest diversified finance company with assets of $22 billion, in 1987 sells RCA's NBC radio network and consumer electronics business of $3.8 billion to French-owned Thomson for medical-equipment division and $700-800 million in cash, invests $580 million in Britain's General Electric in 1989 to prepare for 1992 when Europe lowers its internal trade barriers)...

Boeing introduces 767 jet liner, based with others from basic design of 707 in mid-1950s, to pioneer generation of fuel-efficient, commercial aircraft... After 5 weeks of financial maneuvering, court room battles, public name-calling and political infighting, Conoco, 9th largest oil firm and 2nd largest coal company, is acquired for some $7.6 billion in cash and stock by DuPont, largest U.S. chemical business, after fighting off Texaco, 3rd-ranking oil firm, Canada's Seagram, world's largest liquor distiller, and Mobil, 2nd-largest oil company (results in Seagram becoming largest single owner of DuPont with 20% share after acquiring Mobil's accumulated stock)...

Roger B. Smith, hired as accounting clerk in 1949 and served as head of corporate directions group in 1971, becomes chairman of General Motors with market share of 45% - 36% by 1989, reporting first loss since 1921 (forms joint ventures with Suzuki Motor in 1981, Japan's robot-maker Fanuc in 1981-82, Toyota Motor in 1983 to operate CA plant, and Korean carmaker in 1984 to make subcompact cars, acquires Texnowledge and Electronic Data Systems of H. Ross Perot for $2.5 billion in 1984, reorganizes in 1984 to replace 7 previous car divisions with 2 super groups for small and large cars, acquires Hughes Aircraft in 1985 for $5 billion to join previous acquisitions of 3 mortgage financing businesses and 5 firms in machine vision, sees decline in market share, largest in U.S. auto industry, in 1986 after spending some $33 billion on new products and factories since 1980, reports 9 month earnings of 1987 as $2.7 billion - Ford with $3.7 billion, gives splashy $20 million show in 1988, year of reckoning, to show confidence in future)... To avoid insolvency Pan American World Airways sells chain of Intercontinental Hotels, from first hostelry in Belem in 1946 to 83 luxury hotels in 48 countries, to London's Grand Metropolitan hotel and food business for $500 million...

After seeing ad in _Farm Magazine_ with cattle-marking paint pistol, Charles Gains, author of _Pumping Iron_, Hays Noel, NY stock broker, and Robert Gurnsey, owner of New London ski shop, create National Survival Game, NH (design game to provide players, using paint pistols and protective head gear, with simulated guerrilla warfare, becomes worldwide business by 1986 of $2 million with some 30,000 participants/weekend in North America)... Shares in pioneering International Thoroughbred Breeders are sold to public (acquires some 300 breeding horses, is followed in 1983 by public stock issue of Kentucky's Spendthrift Farm)...

Linda Harrington opens Harrington's Executive Clothiers for women in Portland, OR (after seeing computerized tailoring process of Bill Tighe's Custom Art Technologies in 1984 buys rights for automated-tailoring process, prices of custom-tailored suits to compete with expensive "off-the-rack" clothes, for 10 Western states, files for bankruptcy in 1988)... At age of 15 Barry Minkow starts ZZZZ Best, Los Angeles, to clean carpets in family garage with savings of $6,200 from cleaning carpets and 3 employees, 80 employees and 3 offices on 1984 high school graduation (borrows money in 1985 from loan shark for expansion - settles out of court, reporting sales of $2 million, implied by insurance contracts for restoration work, sells stock in 1986, one of many to score big going public, to reap $13 million at age of 20, in 1987 plans to buy, April 16, KeyServ Group, $80 million business with 21 offices cleaning carpets for Sears, with $2 million loan, June 26, from Prudential-Bache Financial to build "General Motors of Carpet Cleaning," declares, July 8, bankruptcy, is indicted in 1988 on 54 counts of racketeering, fraud, money laundering)...

Hayne Leland, John O'Brien and Mark Rubenstein devise portfolio insurance as stock market hedging technique (form business, LOR for short, to market method, sell coverage for $60 billion of assets to fund managers, lose customers, some $30 billion, after 1987's October market crash)... Jerome J. LiCari, Beech-Nut's director of research, warns supervisors apple-juice products adulterated (results in firm's 1986 470-count indictment and fine of $2 million in 1987 for 215 felony counts)... California millionaire William M. Lansdale with political connections charters La Isla Virgen in Delaware (as chief stockholder opens office in Virgin Islands as tax shelter, gets 63% return on investment in 1984, is investigated in 1986 by IRS and local authorities for owing at least $4.5 million in unpaid taxes, is exempted by Tax Reform Act of 1986)...

Vegetable and strawberry grower Garth Conlan borrows $3 million from Wells Fargo branch at Castroville, CA (when farm losses exceed limit in loan contract is forced into bankruptcy in 1983 by Wells Fargo, sues for damages from bank's heavy-handed tactics, recovers $35 million in 1987 in pioneering suit)... Bob Page, certified public accountant, state auditor for NC and buyer of china, glassware at area's flea markets, quits job to start Replacements, Ltd., world's largest in field by 1987, to supply customers, some 360,000 with out-of-date patterns, to gross $6 million with staff of 70 - $10 million likely in 1988... After working for Citibank and Latin American Investment, suave Roberto Castro Polo starts Private Asset Management Group to advise clients investing minimum of $1 million, $110 million fund by 1987 (after extravagant living is sued, Europe and NYC, in 1988 for fraud, waits extradition in Italy on Swiss warrant)...

Flat broke, Patrick Kelly, black designer from Deep South, accepts one-way ticket from NYC to Paris (after selling hand-sewn coats on sidewalks, gets popular Paris boutique as first steady customer in 1985, with 17 employees and sales over $7 million in 1988 wins membership in prestigious 44-member Chambre Syndicale of French designers)... Nabisco acquires Standard Brands to run 50 businesses (is sold in 1985 to R.J. Reynolds in 1985 for $4.9 billion, sells Kentucky Fried Chicken to PepsiCo, owner of Pizza Hut and Taco Bell food chains, and Canada Dry, after buying Almaden Vineyards in 1987 sells Heublein to Britain's Grand Metropolitan spirits, food, and hotel conglomerate)... Donald R. Dixon acquires Vernon Savings & Loan Assn., TX (after lavish living and risky loans in Texas real estate market declares personal bankruptcy in 1987 - Federal Savings and Loan Insurance Corp. takes over and files its largest civil suit for $540 million)...

After heading BankAmerica for 10 years, gambles with fixed home mortgage sales that interest rates will fall in 1979-80, A.W. Clausen selects Sam Armacost as new CEO (-1985 when fired for return of Clausen after losses of $1.8 billion over 3 years)... After putting Shearson Loeb Rhoades together as profitable brokerage (builds Carter Berlind & Weill to $0.9 million in assets in 1961, CBWL-Hayden Stone to $119 million in 1970, and Shearson Hayden Stone to $358 million in 1974), Sandy Weill sells business, $2.3 billion in assets, to American Express (resigns as president of American Express in 1985, joins ailing Commercial Credit in 1986 to build profitable firm of $4.9 billion by 1986, takes over Jerry Tsai's Primerica giant of $17.5 billion, in trouble with 1987 buyout of Smith Barney, in 1988 to create financial colossus with resources in insurance, securities, asset management, mortgage banking, specialty retailing and consumer finance, credit)...

Stouffer food business, owned by Nestle since 1970s, introduces Lean Cuisine low-calorie frozen dinners (enters European market in mid-1980s)... France's Elf Aquitaine petroleum giant acquires Texasgulf in natural resources for $2.7 billion... U.S. hosts 26 factory outlet shopping centers, 194 by 1989... Chris-Craft Industries spins off original boating business founded 1865 - bankruptcy in 1989.

1982

General Events

United Auto Workers, Detroit's Big Three car makers join to create comprehensive education and training program to develop literate, skilled workers... Settlement is reached (January 8) by AT&T, Justice Department on break-up of communications giant (allows AT&T to retain Western Electric, Bell Laboratories, long-distance operations and interests in telecommunications while staying out of electronic publishing for 7 years, is required to divest $80 billion in 22 local Bell Telephone companies in 7 regional groups - form Bellcore as lab to develop superconductor with silicon in 1988, results in $3.2 billion reorganization by 1986 - 27,400 jobs eliminated)... U.S. asks (January 10) allies to embargo materials for Soviet natural gas pipeline, rejected... Gasoline prices drop with world oil collapse... President Reagan, January 26: "State of the Union" (proposes New Federalism whereby certain government programs, funds would be administered by states, and creation of "urban enterprise zones")... Teamsters ratify (February 16) new contract with wage freeze...

U.S. bans (March 10) Libya's oil imports for its support of terrorism... For first time in nearly 17 years consumer prices fall .3% (April 23)... Census Bureau reports (July 19) poverty rate of 14%, highest since 1967 and 7.4% increase from 1980... U.S. offers (August 20) multi-billion-dollar package to help Mexico through financial crisis... NFL Players Association strikes (September 20), first in sport's 63-year history (settles after 57 days, longest in sports history, with 5-year contract for $1.28 billion)... FDA approves (October 29) human insulin made by gene splicing...

ICC approves (September 13) merger of Union Pacific, Missouri Pacific and Western Pacific to create system with 22,000 miles of track in 21 states... Federal Reserve Board reports (December 16) U.S. factories operating at 67.8% of capacity, lowest since first compiled in 1948... FTC drops limits on frequency, duration of TV ads... Congress passes emergency legislation to force striking locomotive engineers back to work... U.S., Switzerland sign special accord whereby Swiss agree to cooperate in investigations of stock-swindle cases... U.S. Postal Service uses employee involvement groups so management and employees can settle their differences... Federal Reserve permits CitiCorp banking to sell certain computer services in data processing market... Communications Workers of America prepares long-range plan for coping with technology of information age (proposes retraining, transferring of benefits with workers to provide employment security)...

Anti-Trust Division of Justice Department issues new guidelines on mergers (stresses measurement of market concentration as biggest change in opposing increases on concentrations)... U.S. Supreme Court in American Tobacco case upholds seniority systems even if they favor white males... Time: "Computer Generation" (reports rising involvement of youth with new technology)...

American Law Institute specifies management responsibilities in report on corporate governance... NLRB rules firm cannot move plant until union contract has expired... Employees of Beverly Enterprises, U.S.' largest nursing home chain, are organized by United Food & Commercial Workers, Service Employees International Union (start drive on Blue Cross with 3 other unions in 1985)... Congressional Office of Technology Assessment studies largest U.S. corporations (reports 23 have tried genetic screening of new employees in previous decade and some 59 with plans to do so)... Semiconductor Research Corp. is formed as non-profit research consortium by 13 U.S. computer-chip manufacturers, followed by Sematech consortium in 1987 to fight Japanese chipmakers... Pentagon's Defense Advanced Research Projects Agency starts project to design and build aerospace plane (approves development in 1984, grants initial contracts in 1986)...

Environmental Protection Agency announces Velsico agrees to pay $38.5 million to clean up 4 toxic waste sites, MI... Some 90,000 foreign emigrants arrive in Los Angeles during year, site for over 2 million Middle Easterners, Asians, Hispanics since 1970... After 18 years Florida Philharmonic Orchestra stops playing, duplicated by 1932 Kansas City Philharmonic... Henry Cisneros is elected Mayor of San Antonio, first Mexican-American to run major U.S. city, followed by F. Pena as Denver's Mayor in 1983... Newsweek: "The Sky's the Limit" (reports new generation of humanistic, stylish skyscrapers)... Boeing Aircraft pleads guilty in making payments to officials in Spain, Lebanon, Honduras, Dominican Republic... Japan's Hitachi, Mitsubishi are caught illegally buying IBM's secrets, CA (while admitting transaction deny materials stolen)...

FTC grants first license for direct broadcasting system to Satellite Television Corp., developed by 1986... Export Trading Act permits commercial banks to form consortium of similar manufacturing firms as export traders (results in international training organizations by General Electric and Sears, phases out Sears World Trade in 1986 after 4 profitless years)... After Japan's computer industry announced joint effort to develop Fifth Generation computers with artificial intelligence, Microelectronics and Computer Technology organizes as $50 million non-profit joint research venture by 21 major computer firms (evolves by 1986 with budget of $65 million and 400 researchers, faces organizational difficulties in 1987)...

U.S., British scientists develop new man-made vaccine from synthetic chemicals... Debt of U.S. farmers is some $194.5 billion, over twice that of 1976... UAW, American Motors sign labor contract whereby workers give up $150 million in pay raises for investments in new product development... United Steel Workers, Wheeling-Pittsburgh Steel agree to reduce labor costs by $35 million over 19 months... Reagan Administration plans to sell some 60,000 acres of U.S. land, 35 million by 1987...

Michael Novak: The Spirit of Democratic Capitalism (discusses complementary values of capitalism and democracy to oppose conflict argued by Max Weber, Daniel Bell)... J. Peter Grace heads task force of business executives, created by President Reagan, to find inefficiencies in government programs (-1985)... Congress deregulates savings and loan industry, by 1988 500 of 3,1500 thrifts are insolvent with 1 in 3 losing money (requires bailout plan in 1989 that could cost $200 billion)... Congress clamps down on one of U.S.' biggest tax dodges: failure to report billions of dollars in tips (leads to many restaurants charging 15% to 18% for service)...

Black Otis Pitts forms non-profit TACOLCY Economic Development Corp. to revive economic well-being of Liberty City, FL, devastated by black violence in 1980 (by 1989 transforms center into $2.1 million thriving shopping center with stores, offices)... U.S. unemployment reaches some 10.3 million, 9.4% highest since 1941... First live cable telecast of Broadway play is made... Herman Kahn: The Coming Boom (provides scenario for prosperity in 2000)... William Tucker: <u>Progress</u> <u>and</u> <u>Privilege</u> (attacks environmentalism)... Marshfield, MA, bans video games for public use... Rotary International drops racial restrictions on membership... Defense Department creates Inspector General's Office to police defense contractors... Tax Equity and Fiscal Responsibility Act allows employers to shift pension plans to employee-leasing firms (leads to creation of some 275 new companies to market of 5 firms in providing about 75,000 workers to thousands of small businesses - Omnistaff, TX, largest in leasing some 10,000 workers to around 1,300 companies, and Uniforce with 69 franchises in 1988)... Congress passes law to encourage states to use work-sharing and/or reduced work weeks to avoid layoffs, used by California in 1978 with idea from West Germany (is adopted by 11 states by 1986)...

Hispanic, Toney Anaya, is elected Governor of New Mexico by landslide, first of background to run state... Garn-St. Germain Depository Insurance Institutions Act is passed (allows Federal Deposit Insurance Corp. to aid troubled banks)... As 3rd union president in 25 years to be convicted of felony, Roy L. Williams, president of Teamsters Union, and 4 others are found guilty in conspiring to bribe U.S. Senator, in defrauding union's pension fund... Despite approval of United Steel Workers, local unions reject new labor contract with pay cuts, concessions to save jobs... Emily Rosenburg: <u>Spreading</u> <u>the</u> <u>American</u> <u>Dream</u> (suggests innovation of technology result of "free-flow of information and culture")... <u>Time</u> selects computer as "Man of the Year"... Justice Department drops 13-year-old anti-trust suit to dismember IBM... U.S. District Court holds NCAA's control of college football violates Sherman Anti-Trust Act...

<u>Newsweek</u>: "The Decaying of America" (reports deterioration of roads, bridges, sewers, etc.)... Court of Appeals is created for Federal Circuit to handle patent litigation (enforces patent rights on suits against infringers)... Federal Government creates South Florida Interagency Task Force to interdict drug smuggling from Central, South America... For first time in 20 years no pension funds of Teamsters Union, largest U.S. multi-employer pension fund, are invested in gambling operations (after loans of some $250 million since 1976, is put under federal oversight in 1982)... Rochester Institute of Technology, NY, is first U.S. school to offer degree in microelectronic engineering...

Boston engineering firm of Camp Dresser & McKee predicts 5.1 million acres of 6 Great Plains states will dry up by 2020... 7 people are killed, IL, from cyanide-laced capsules of Johnson & Johnson's Extra-Strength Tylenol (after recurring in 1986 with one death, abandons over-counter capsules at estimated cost of $150 million)... Webster Production seeks approval from SEC to sell $5 million in limited partnerships to underwrite series of X-rated films for video cassette market... "Hal," talking computer, is used as announcer by Pittsburgh radio station...

Stevens Institute of Technology, NJ, requires all new freshman students to have personal computers... In return for work-rule concessions, Pan Am pilot goes on airline's board of directors to represent employee interests... Hoechst AG, West German pharmaceutical firm, gives 10-year, $70-million grant to Massachusetts General Hospital to create Department of Molecular Biology... Some 140,000 U.S. homes are foreclosed during year's first quarter... U.S. Supreme Court upholds FTC in allowing doctors, dentists to advertise without interference from professional groups... Carnegie-Mellon University, IBM plan to establish "Integrated Computing Environment" by 1985... Bus Regulatory Reform Act deregulates industry (allows for hundreds of new bus lines to enter market)... SEC tests shelf-registration of securities to allow future issues to be registered and sold later by firms as desired... Newsweek: "The Disappearing Land" (reports on loss of top soil for farming and use of low-till cultivation with no plowing)... After 10 years in development and 4 test flights, U.S. space shuttle program becomes operational with launching of Columbia, carries first commercial pay load (is suspended 1986-88 after Challenger explodes on lift-off)... A paralyzed woman walks again with computer-generated electrical impulses...

U.S. Chamber of Commerce plans new closed-circuit television network, used by Roman Catholic Church and AFL-CIO... Massachusetts industry forms venture to build research and education facility for technology... United Auto Workers grants International Harvester wage concessions for job security to fight bankruptcy... Committee of 200 is created by U.S.' top women business leaders to provide forum for members and enhance national visibility of women in business... Presidents, scientists of 5 California universities join business leaders to establish guidelines for commercialization of biology... Clarkson College, Drexel University plan to provide students with computers by 1983... U.S. subsidiary of Japan's Mitsui is indicted for alleged scheme to dump cheap steel on market...

Interior Secretary James Watt opens 1 billion acres of U.S. coast-line for oil, gas drilling... SEC eases regulations for trading foreign stocks and bonds on Wall Street... Ken Auletta: The Underclass (reports alienated, hopeless, powerless in cities making urban life unpleasant, dangerous)... Commerce Department charges foreign steel producers from 7 European nations, South Africa and Brazil in selling in U.S. market at unfairly low prices... Newsweek: "Profiting from the Past" (reports on role of corporate historians at such businesses as Polaroid, AT&T)... Federal, State officials liquidate Fidelity Savings & Loan of Oakland, CA, 21st largest in U.S., to avoid financial crisis...

Oklahoma starts pioneering employment program for welfare recipients with dependent children... UAW, Ford sign labor contract (grants economic concessions to improve firm's market position in return for job and income security, retraining programs for displaced workers, guaranteed income for laid-off workers, and preferential hiring)... Researchers at Texas A&M University discover new technology to produce hydrogen from water as pollution-free, cost-effective fuel... University of Pittsburgh successfully tests computer, Internist I, to diagnose illness... Police in Beverly Hills, CA, apprehend wayward robot... Rev. Donald Wildmon's Coalition for Better Television launches consumer boycott of RCA to reform programs of NBC... Year's unemployment rate, averaging 9.7% with high of 10.1%, is highest since 1941...

UAW, GM sign labor contract (in return for establishment of joint council on operations and system of job security, changes rules to improve productivity, drops annual pay raises, defers 3 cost-of-living increases, cuts holidays, gives new workers lower salaries, and starts joint effort to reduce absenteeism and health-care costs)... Richard L. Trumka becomes head of United Mine Workers, 85,000 active members down from postwar peak of 400,000... Des Moines builds Skywalk System, 32 bridges linking 21 downtown blocks by 1988... Farmer's Home Administration reports delinquency rate of 51% on loans, 26% in 1979.

Business Events

Boston Computer Exchange is formed for buying, selling of used computers, sales of $5 million by 1989... Bored corporate lawyer Bruce Engel buys 2 softwool mills, OR, hardwood mill in 1984 (by 1988 builds WTD Industries with 25 mills and AT Industries in entertainment with 3 bowling lanes, communications with 3 radio stations and 2 publications, and in manufacturing with 4 firms including Seams Right for overnight tailoring services for retail clothing stores)... As a result of 1981 federal tax bill with incentives for historic preservation projects, John Ness starts Heritage Consulting in Portland, OR (with nationwide business opens Washington office in 1986)... After visiting Japan's highly-automated FANUC servomotor plant, GM builds $52 million Vanguard plant at Saginaw, MI, probably world's most futuristic factory by 1988...

By 1988 Mobil slashes white-collar payroll by 17%, DuPont by 15%... "First" cappucino vendor cart appears in Portland, OR, then Central Park and Berkeley's Telegraph Ave. in 1983 (spreads across U.S. at upscale street corners, post modern plazas by 1986)...Playboy's new cable network presents "Everything Goes," first R-rated TV game show... United Technologies builds City Place, $120 million development with electrical-control systems for temperature, fire detection, security, and lighting operated by computers, in Hartford, CT... James Harbour, former director of manufacturing engineering for Chrysler and self-taught expert on Japanese auto manufacture, reports Japanese carmakers build average subcompact car for some $1,700 less than in U.S...

Due to declining demand for gasoline, Exxon closes 850 service stations in Northeast, Midwest... Home video games near (October 3) profitability of film industry... Victor A. Kaufman forms Tri-Star Pictures as 3-way venture with Coca-Cola's Columbia Pictures, Time's Home Box Office and CBS Television, $254.4 million business by 1986 (takes over Columbia from Coca-Cola in 1987 to create Hollywood giant of some $2 billion)... General Motors, Japan's Fanuc form GMF Robotics as joint venture (becomes world's largest robot supplier, nearly triple sales of nearest U.S. competitor Cincinnati's Milacron, before reducing operations in 1986)...

To avoid business transfer, Mike, Laura Hanna start Tender Sender gift wrapping and package mailing service in Portland, OR (expands to 84 outlets nationwide before acquisition in 1986 by National Corp.)... Center for Futures Research reports some 20,000 corporate employees work at home, nearly 600,000 in 1987... With $300,000, Gary E. Hoover starts Bookstop, modeled on Toys 'R' Us chain of toy stores, in Houston to mass market books with discount prices (expands to 12 outlets by 1987 to sell over 1 million books)... 1903 Harley-Davidson motorcycle business petitions U.S. Government for protection against invasion by Japanese models for 5 years (results in 1983 tariff, asks for end of restraints in 1986)... First stadium golf course is designed for Tournament Players' Championship at Sawgrass, FL...

Cathi Stout starts Believercise, TX, to combine worship, physical exercise (grows by 1987 to provide classes in 30 states, overseas)... After developing line of children's bikes, Huffy, started 1887 to make sewing machines, acquires U.S. rights for Britain's Raleigh bicycles (designs innovative bikes for U.S. victories in 1984 Olympics, U.S.' largest bike maker in 1988)... At age 17 Randy Miller resurrects family's seltzer business, dormant for over 30 years, with funds from father, CA (by 1987 sells sugary drinks of Original New York Seltzer in all 50 states and 9 countries to hit sales of $45 million)... Tom Raider launches Tour Alaska business (acquires 46 Southern Pacific double-deck commuter cars for around $1 million in 1986 to plan luxury transcontinental cruise train for tourists in 48 states)... Exxon's $5 billion Colony Oil Shale Fuel Project at Battlement Mesa, CO, shuts down (results in economic revival of area as retirement community in 1987)...

Beecham Products hires market researcher Yankelovich Clancy Shulman to determine if new product Delicare could topple Woolite (sues researcher in 1987 for $24 million in damages resulting from faulty market forecast, raises questions in liability suit on value of market research)... Roger Richmond acquires rights to license image of Marilyn Monroe from beneficiary Anna Freud Center in London (by 1987 signs 51 companies to produce over 100 Monroe products)... Spiegel mail-order house of Chicago, founded 1882 as furniture business, sells operation to West Germany's catalog giant Otto Versand...

Stove Container Corp. starts making paper bags (dominates market of shopping bag ads by 1987)... McDonald's introduces Chicken McNuggets (expands distribution worldwide in 1984 to become world's 2nd largest purveyor of chicken)... Procter & Gamble enters pharmaceutical field (by 1987, after spending nearly $2 billion in acquisitions, becomes U.S.' largest purveyor of over-the-counter remedies)... Bloomingdale's spins off its By Mail catalog operation as separate division (distributes some 4 million catalogs to customers in 50 states in 1987)... After building 2 small firms into $1.5 billion engineering giant Mike Dingman sells Wheelabrator-Frye to Signal Cos. (when Signal merges with Allied Corp. in 1985, forms Henley Group to acquire 35 humdrum firms worth $7 billion in assets, all dumped by Allied-Signal, to revive operations by 1987 in cutting costs and management layers and allowing managers to buy stock)...

TV producer Norman Lear, partner acquire AVCO-Embassy, producer of low-budget exploitation movies, for $25 million (merge operation with profitable TAT Communications, make money with popular TV shows but lose some $30 million on unsuccessful movies)... Despite dire predictions of experts, Canadian Garth H. Drabinsky acquires complex of 14 tiny theaters to show 2nd-run and art films in Los Angeles (as Cineplex acquires Canada's Odeon chain of movie houses in 1984 for $17 million, acquires U.S.' Plitt Theaters in 1985 to operate 1,060 screens, with interests in Universal Studio theme park, FL, is 2nd largest theater chain in 1988 with 1,752 screens to United Artists' 2,275)... Crocker National Bank offers money-market accounts, brokerage services to investors...

American Sports Underwriters forms in Boston to provide athletes with disability coverages... Corporate Ombudsman Associates forms to handle employee problems (by 1986 works for many members of Fortune 500)... W.E. Herrman starts Whole Brain Corp. to teach corporate clients creativity, some 250 clients by 1985 with sales of $1.8 million ... Netair International organizes, Denver (starts nationwide jet taxi service in 1985 with privately-owned jets, paying owners maintenance and hangar costs for access when not in use)... Thomas J. Peters, Robert H.

Waterman, Jr.:   In Search of Excellence (identifies U.S. companies of excellence, is re-studied by Business Week in 1984:   "Who's Excellent Now?")... Right Associates' outplacement business operates 13 offices, 28 by 1985 (results from outplaced activities of businesses in 1960s to aid dismissed, laid-off executives in finding new jobs)... Business Week: "TRW Leads a Revolution in Managing Technology" (reports cross-fertilization of ideas between operating units)... Procter & Gamble files libel suits against individuals for spreading rumors that 1851 trademark represents satanism (abandons logo in 1985 as rumors persist)... Movie Channel Cable Network is acquired by joint venture of Warner Bros., Paramount Pictures, MCA-owned Universal Studios... Enterprise Square USA, $15 million museum-fun park on capitalism, opens, OK (is followed in 1985 by plan of Dallas Cowboys to build 200-acre center with office park, hotel, athletic club, sports-medicine clinic and tourist attractions)...

Hopelessly non-competitive on costs and productivity, Chrysler's Detroit Trim Plant is saved from closure by mutual efforts of employees, local union leaders, factory management (despite boosting productivity over 25% in less than a year, closes 1988)... Actor Paul Newman, partner start salad dressing business (evolves as $25 million operation with spaghetti sauce and popcorn, donates all profits to charity)... Monsanto provides 4-year research grant of $26 million to Washington University, St. Louis to do medical research on proteins, peptides (extends grant in 1986 with another $26 million for work to 1990)... For first time in biotech field, Genetech produces human insulin with gene splicing (leads to human growth hormone in 1985, alpha interferon in 1986 as first genetic vaccine for human use)...

Texas media company is first to provide total market coverage to advertisers with papers, direct mail, radio and TV... AT&T introduces Picturephone Meeting Service... 28 savings and loan associations are authorized to start discount operations in stocks, bonds... Fidelity Savings & Loan Association of San Francisco is acquired by CitiCorp, U.S.' 2nd largest bank... General Electric Credit grants loans to Scott Paper, Eastern Airlines after shifting in 1969 from consumer financing to investment financing... During first 14 weeks Dun & Bradstreet shows 6,205 firms as failures, 56% increase over 1981... For first time Merrill Lynch sells time certificates of deposit...

Some 2,000 customer complaints against brokers are filed with SEC, 15,915 in 1986... After operating pilot projects for employees to do computer work at home, Aetna Life & Casualty, Investors Diversified Services make programs permanent... Drysdale Government Securities is declared in default, causes Wall Street financial crisis (is averted when Chase Manhattan Bank finally agrees, after first denying responsibility, to pay Drysdale accounts)... Grid System introduces Compass Computer, new personal computer innovating in small size, power, design, and time-sharing capabilities...

Scientists of Phillips Petroleum develop single-cell protein as by-product of natural gas (is viewed as possible supplement for diets lacking protein)... Merrill Lynch investment business enters banking field with Capital Resources to lend money... Safeway grocery chain uses Seattle as test market to sell computers... IBM sues 3 fired executives for selling computer secrets to competitors... McDonald's starts job training program for handicapped (handles some 3,000 by 1986)... After accumulating debt of some $1 billion Braniff International declares voluntary bankruptcy, first major airline to shut down operations after deregulation... GM requires steel suppliers to set strict quality standards for products in order to bid for its contracts... Chuck Huggins starts "telephone auction" program on cable TV in San Jose area, CA (develops business of some $250 million by 1986)... Braniff International sues American, United Airlines for unfair competition with computer reservation networks with travel agencies (is followed by 1984 with anti- trust suit against American, United by 11 airlines)... Barry Clifford, divers discover first traces of <u>Whydah</u> <u>Galleon</u>, flagship of pirate Samuel "Black" Belamy carrying perhaps 30,000 pounds of silver, 10,000 pounds of gold and ivory and jewels sunk off Cape Cod by violent storm in 1770 (locate ship's bell in 1985)...

Joe Hunt, age 27, and some 30 rich kids, using freewheeling investment philosophy to support lavish lifestyle, start Billionaire Boys Club in fashionable West Los Angeles as informal business fraternity (after swindles and violence results in scam victim Hunt, others being charged with murder in 1986 - conviction of Hunt 1987 and others in 1988)... After outlay of some $600 million, Xerox introduces 1075 copier, first U.S. product to win prestigious Japanese design award, total sales of some $1 billion by 1985... Claiming thousands of asbestos-related lawsuits could force firm out of business, Manville Corp., largest U.S. producer of asbestos, petitions for reorganization in U.S. Bankruptcy Court, used by A.H. Robins in 1985 to handle thousands of claims by users of Dalkon Shield (emerges from bankruptcy as $2.1 billion firm in 1988 with praise from victims for $2.6 billion trust fund, augmented by up to 20% of annual profits for 30 years, to settle claims)...

Federally insured banks, savings associations are permitted to set competitive interest rates for accounts with minimum holdings of $2,500... Pioneering novel is written, edited, and published electronically by Source Telecomputing... Heath subsidiary of Zenith Radio introduces Hero 1 as household robot, joins household robots of 3 other firms... Phillips Petroleum makes oil strike, potentially greater than Alaskan field, off California coast...

Coca-Cola uses video-game vending machine to dispense soft drinks... Frank Lorenzo's Texas International, after years of legal battles and stock maneuvers, acquires financially-troubled Continental Airlines, U.S.' 8th largest (files for bankruptcy in 1983 with total debt of $1 billion, after canceling labor contracts, reducing salaries and fares, and cutting routes in half operates business as low-cost, low-fare carrier, after losing battle to acquire Frontier Airlines to People Express in 1985 acquires ailing Eastern and People Express in 1986 to become world's largest publicly owned airline fighting unions to reduce costs, after Feds probe management sues unions of pilots and machinists for $1.5 billion in 1988 to claim unions seek to destroy Eastern's reputation, faces Eastern's bankruptcy in 1989 with strike of machinists)...

John Brockman Associates is first U.S. agency to represent writers of personal computer programs... James W. Rouse, retired from business to develop "festival marketplaces," starts Enterprise Development to renovate tenements in urban areas for low-income families (provides urban developments in Norfolk, Toledo, Flint)... After 2 years of tests NY's

Chemical Bank, U.S.' 6th largest, adopts home banking system with computers... Merrill Lynch offers investors first public venture capital fund... Jos. Schlitz Brewery, "The Beer that Made Milwaukee Famous," is acquired by 1850 Stroh Brewery of Detroit after purchasing F. & M. Schaefer Brewery, NY, in 1981... Private pension funds hold over $500 billion... Kansas City Board of Trade lists first stock-index futures... Inventor-entrepreneur Hazard Reeves opens Catologia, first U.S. computer-catalog store, in Montvale, NJ... USA Today is launched as national daily paper with color and snazzy graphics by Gannet Publishing (shows first profits in 1987)... Merger of Norfolk Western, Southern Railroads links North, South... Dreyfus Corp., mutual fund of some $20 billion, applies to operate national bank... Las Vegas hotels show lowest occupancy rate in years... Conquistador Cielo, 3-year colt purchased for $150,000, is syndicated to breeders for record $36.4 million... In shifting from traditional retail banking, 118-year-old Bank of California creates new merchant bank subsidiary, Baron Edmond de Rothschild major stockholder...

Prime interest rate of major banks drops to 14%... Brentano's, NY book store founded 1833, files for protection under federal bankruptcy law... After research since 1975 Intel develops micro-miniaturized mainframe for computers... Walt Disney Production releases movie "Tron" (features computer-generated imagery, developed in 1960s with Defence Department work on computerized flight simulations and use of computer graphics in TV commercials)... After laying off some 9,000 workers in 1974 recession, Motorola adopts reduced work week at Phoenix operation to avoid further layoffs...

GM's auto-assembly plant in Freemont, CA, with absentee rate of some 20% and high number of grievances, closes (reopens as New United Motor Mfg. in 1985 with laid-off GM-UAW workers at prevailing wages, benefits in return for UAW acceptance of no seniority rights, flexible work rules and job classifications, uses Japanese management style, joint venture with Toyota as new United Motor Manufacturing, to produce some 240,000 cars/year with 2,500 employees instead of previous 5,000 or more – absenteeism under 2% and only 2 outstanding grievances)... Farah Mfg. sues State National Bank of El Paso for damages of $18.6 million on charges Bank improperly interfered in business (spawns other suits by borrowers against lenders with victory, is used by Hunt family in 1986 to fight financial ruin)...

EMGO uses bulletproof clothing of Kevlar, invented by DuPont in 1974, in fashion line of jumpsuits, safari jackets... Wickes, U.S.' largest lumber and building supply retailer of $4 billion, declares bankruptcy, saved by Sanford C. Sigoloff... Fed-Mart, $1 billion retailing chain, CA, declares bankruptcy... Tandem Computers, first to make fail-safe computers, is industry's first to link satellite communications service with computer technology for data transmission... Los Angeles stores rent music records... Atlantic Richfield, after canceling credit-card business, requires all transactions by cash in gasoline stations... American Express makes charity donations when credit-card holders make charges...

With pressure from American Newspaper Publishers Association, AT&T drops efforts to put electronic data, such as Yellow-Pages and news, on TV cable systems... Heavens Union is started as business, CA, to deliver messages to deceased via terminally ill patients, handles over 500 requests in first 6 months... Exxon grants cash discounts to gasoline buyers... GM adopts Japanese just-in-time inventory system to deliver parts to assembly plants on daily basis to eliminate costly overhead (requires suppliers to bid for contracts and refund 2% of revenues, slashes inventory costs from $8 billion to $2 billion)... Some 60 of 81 closed stores of A&P supermarket chain in Philadelphia are re-opened by association of employees (obtains wage concessions from unions and funds from A&P for acquisitions, realizes success with bonus program based on costs)... Northeastern International Airways is started, FL, with one plane, one route (evolves as coast-to-coast, 17-city airline with 1,500 employees before bankruptcy in 1985)...

Coca-Cola acquires Columbia Pictures for $750 million (joins CBS and Time's Home Box Office to form Tri-Star Pictures in 1982 as $55 million joint venture in movie and TV productions, purchases Embassy Communications and Tandem Productions in 1985 for some $480 million to acquire TV library, production facilities and syndication, acquires Merv Griffin Enterprises in TV for about $250 million in 1986, acquires Walter Reade organization and 12 movie theaters in 1986 for $25 million to operate 1,500 movie screens, broadcast TV, video cassettes, and pay cable network)... Lucasfilm arranges with Atari to market video games...

Fast-food chain Burger King shows sales of some $2.6 billion from about 3,400 outlets - $7.8 billion for McDonald's with 7,259 places and $1.6 billion for Wendy's with some 2,400 units... Chicago's Commonwealth Edison adopts pioneering employee anti-drug education and rehabilitation program (reduces rates of absenteeism, medical claims and on-the-job accidents by 1985)... After selling out for 12 consecutive seasons in Oakland, Al Davis moves NFL football franchise of Oakland Raiders to Los Angeles despite league opposition (sues NFL in 1982 for unreasonable restraint of trade in blocking move - won, upheld and awarded damages)...

With debts of $245 million A.M. International, once Addressograph-Multigraph founded 58 years ago to make office machinery, files bankruptcy... Sears tests financial service centers in selected stores... 3 networks, National Football League sign 5-year TV contract for $2.1 billion (provides each team with $15 million/year, just over half of average team's revenues)... In order to be more competitive, Texas Instruments replaces matrix organization structure with decentralized profit centers... Merrill Lynch presents live closed-circuit TV show on investing to invited guests at 30 hotels throughout U.S. (results in purchases by 35% of some 30,000 viewers)... After starting year with some 11,000 workers on payroll, Bethlehem Steel's Stefko plant employs around 6,500 by 1983... Robert E. Riordan's small family media business acquires troubled Ladies' Home Journal for some $12 million (revamps magazine to sell in 1986 for $92 million)...

In period to 1986 U.S. Steel eliminates some 27,000 jobs and closes 20 facilities in farming out work to non-union operations... American Nursing Resources is created to lease professionals to hospitals, corporations and individual clients (achieves sales of $11 million in 9 states in 1985)... Zenith decides to sell personal computers to different markets rather than compete with IBM's PC in the consumer market (acquires first government and college contracts in 1983 to dominate these special fields, forms joint high-definition television venture in 1989 with AT&T)... Real estate developer of ministorage warehouses Michael K. Russell and veterinarian William Worley start weekly business paper in Kansas (operate 10 weeklies by 1985, 19 by 1986, and 26 by 1987 to run U.S.' largest chain of business papers with revenues over $75 million, amass debt of $32.5 million, 48% of capital in 1988 with 35 papers)... Oklahoma City's Penn Square Bank with huge package of energy loans closes (triggers failures of 27 other banks)... 134-year-old Philadelphia Bulletin is 4th major daily newspaper to close in 6 months, some 142 since 1970 by closures or mergers... On October 7th NY Stock Exchange trades all-time record of 147 million shares... Dow Jones Industrial Average records high of 1065.49 on 11.3 to start bull market (reaches 1121.81 on 2/24/83, 1209.46 on 4/26/83, 1304.88 on 5/20/85, 1403/44 on 11/6/85, 1500.70 on 12/11/85, 1600.69 on 2/6/86, 1713.99 on 2/27/86 before breaking 1800 and 1900 levels, topping 2000, 2100 and 2200 marks in 1987 to hit 2722 before dropping 508 points, most ever with decline of 22.6%, on October 19 to trigger worldwide decline, to close 1738 on Black Monday to record high of 604.4 million shares traded in loss of some $500 billion, hovers around 2000 in 1988)...

John Naisbitt (after starting Urban Research of Chicago with grant from National Alliance of Business Men to publish training guide for jobless, declares bankruptcy in 1977 - convicted of fraud, after working with research firm of Yankelovich, Skelly & White, resigns in 1981 to start Naisbitt Group to monitor newspapers for trends): Megatrends: Ten New Directions Transforming Our Lives (after selling 6 million copies becomes megastar on lecture circuit with fee of $15,000)... Bendix chairman William Agee plots takeover of Martin Marietta (leads to counter-attack by Martin Marietta to buy Bendix shares in competition with United Technologies - total of both at 44% with Bendix holding 70% of Martin, is resolved when "White Knight" Allied Corp. acquires Bendix, forcing Agee out to marry former aide Mary Cunningham and start Siemper investment business, and divests Martin with heavy debt)...

Celebrity car manufacturer John De Lorean is arrested, CA, on drug charges, supposedly handled to save bankrupt firm in Northern Ireland (graduates in 1948 from Detroit's Lawrence Institute of Technology, is hired in 1948 by Chrysler and by Packard in 1952, becomes GM's head of research and development in 1956 and chief engineer for Pontiac in 1961, becomes Pontiac's general manager in 1965 to revive line with sporty look, heads Chevrolet in 1969 and GM's North American car and truck group in 1974 before resigning in 1973, starts car business in 1974, after lengthy public trial is declared not guilty of drug charges in 1985, is tried in 1986 for swindling investors in bankruptcy - acquitted to face other suits)...

United States Football League organizes to play pro ball during spring, summer months (-1986, starts play with 12 franchises in 1983 - high of 18 at cost of $2-5 million in 1984 before folding in 1986 with 8, approves purchase of New Jersey Generals in 1983 to flamboyant developer Donald Trump, plans shift of schedule in 1984 to fall of 1986 on urging of Trump, starts anti-trust suit against National Football League in 1984 for damages of $1.69 billion - awarded $3 by jury in 1986, cancels fall season in 1986, releases players to continue suit against NFL)... To avoid financial disaster with heavy losses, F.W. Woolworth variety chain business closes all 336 Woolco stores in U.S. (sells 52.6% of British subsidiary for funds by 1986, revitalizes regular variety business by shifting into specialty retailing to operate 22 chains, including Kinney Shoe, Claire's Boutiques in costume jewelry and handbags, Herald Square stationers, Frame Scene stores and Kids Mart - 293 outlets in 1987, starts Face Fantasies as budget cosmetic chain in 1986)... 8 families in Woburn, MA, sue conglomerate W.R. Grace & Co. for causing 6 leukemia deaths by dumping toxic waste near water supplies after 1964 (settle out of court in 1986 for reputed $8 million)... To obtain European flair Cadillac engages Italy's Pininfarina to design elegant car, unveiled in 1986 with price of about $50,000 to compete with Mercedes, Jaguar (is followed by arrangements of Chrysler with Maserati and Ford with Alfa Romeo)... Pioneering Home Shopping Club, live 24-hour TV program, is first aired in Clearwater, FL (to compete with 20 other such programs, starts National Cable Home Shopping Network in 1985 to reach 10 million households)... Chicago lawyer David L. Hoffman moves home to winter resort of Telluride, CO (continues work as firm's tax expert on bonds by telecommunications)...

Rath Packing, IA, is restructured with employee ownership, bankruptcy in 1983... John J. O'Brien, area supervisor for Papa Gino's restaurant chain in New England, is fired after polygraph test (wins damages of $595,000 in 1985)... Some 1.5 million North Americans take cruises, nearly 3 million by 1988... 10 U.S. corporations have budgets to market sports events, some 100 in 1987... McDonald's passes Sears as world's largest owner of real estate (by 1988 sells over 55 billion hamburgers as U.S.' largest beef buyer, purchases 7.5% of U.S. potato crop, and replaces U.S. Army as U.S.' largest job training organization)... United Parcel Service, started in 1908 as Seattle messenger service, starts overnight package service to challenge Federal Express (goes global in 1985 - $2.2 billion in sales in 1988, is $11 billion business by 1989 with 15% of air-express market, Federal with 57%)...

Papa Aldo's opens first pizza take & bake outlet in Portland, OR, suburb (by 1988 runs 84 outlets, 3 company owned, with sales of $12 million, enters Japanese market in 1988)... Edwin T. Cornelius, founder of Pace Group International, produces video cassette English-teaching programs for use worldwide (when state-of-the-art equipment not in use rents studio facilities, technical expertise to clients, 225 advertising agencies, movie and videotape firms, to do "post-production" work, becomes leader on West Coast)... After tinkering in building first bicycles proportioned for women in 1981, Georgena Terry leaves Xerox to work full-time on venture (becomes success with Terry Precision Bicycles for women, 8 models in 7 sizes from $460-$1,500, in 1985)...

By 1988 membership in Union of American Physicians & Dentists jumps fourfold to 43,000... Veterinary Pet Insurance starts in Garden Grove, CA, 50,000 policies in 27 states by 1988... Tracy Gary starts seminars and weekend retreats to help wealthy deal with anxieties being rich... Bridge Housing Corp., funded by local corporations, forms in San Francisco to build moderate-income housing in Bay Area... Sun Microsystems of Silicon Valley, CA, enters computer market (after over $1 billion in sales with work stations joins AT&T in 1988 to challenge IBM, Digital Equipment, Apple and Unisys by creating computer standard for industry)...

David Bloom enters Duke University, graduating 1985 with degree in art history (opens shop in NYC as money manager to take in some $10 million from over 100 investors, after lavish lifestyle surrenders $8 million worth of paintings, real estate and other assets to SEC in 1988 to pay losses of investors - art and property may be worth more than debts, is charged with mail fraud by federal prosecutors, pleads guilty to bilking investors in 1988)... Texas Instruments leads world in semiconductor sales, followed by Motorola, NEC and Hitachi of Japan, and Philips of Holland - 1987 with NEC, Toshiba, Hitachi, Motorola and Texas Instruments...

Scott McNealy, Vinod Khosla start Sun Microsystems, CA (shows growth rate of 127% with sales of $538 million from electronics business in 1987)... Wells Fargo Investment Advisers pioneer use of Tactical Asset Allocation to move funds among stocks, bonds and cash to get highest return...

Former school teacher, Clark McLeod, starts Teleconnect, long-distance phone and telemarketing business, in Cedar Rapids, IA, to do customer surveys for firms and solicit contributions for college endowment funds (grows from 35 employees to 1,280 by 1988)... Quality S Mfg. starts in Phoenix to make trailer hitches, shows 4,295% growth by 1988 in selling directly to 14,000 retailers by telemarketing...

Walter Riley starts G.O.D., Guaranteed Overnight Delivery, as 1-truck business in NYC, 350 trailers by 1988 to cover New England to Virginia with sales of $14 million... Gordon A. Cain starts Houston-based investment firm Sterling Group (handles 15 LBOs by 1988 to show 200% yearly rate of return on common equity, after leveraged buyout of 4 chemical businesses sells Cain Chemical to Occidental Petroleum in 1988 for $2.1 billion - twice what he had paid to net $100 million and to give employees at least $100,000 each for shares)...

EPCOT, conceived by Walt Disney before death in 1966 as Experimental Prototype Community of Tomorrow to demonstrate American know-how ingenuity with such devices as computerized humanoids, opens at Disney World, FL... Japan's Honda starts making cars at Marysville, OH, opens plants in 1987 and 1989 (is followed by Nissan in 1983, Toyota in 1984 - 2 more plants in 1988, Mazda in 1987, Mitsubishi in 1988 and Subaru-Isuzu in 1989, by 1988 shows Japanese investment in U.S. with $5.3 billion in CA, $2.5 billion in NY, $1.9 billion in MI, $1.5 billion in HI, $1.4 billion in IL, $1.2 billion in OH, $1 billion in TX and TN, and $ .7 billion in NJ and WA... Salomon Bros. investment house, NYC, opens office in Tokyo, Japan's 5th largest by 1988 behind Nomura, Nikko, Daiwa, and Yamaichi...

Gus Blythe forms Second Wind, San Luis Obispo, CA, to make conditioners, cleaners and deodorizers for leather athletic shoes (goes for sales of $4 million in 1988 with 5 products carried by 30,000 stores nationwide)... Nabisco negotiates with China to make Ritz crackers (launches $9 million venture in 1988 - Johnson & Johnson negotiates over 4 years before producing Band-Aids in Shanghai in 1987 and Seagram Co. needs 2 years for approval)... M.A. Hanna Co. of Cleveland closes steel and energy plants 3 weeks with nothing to do (by 1988 sheds most of natural resource firms to take write-offs of $400 million and see sales drop from $500 million to $130 million, from 1986-87 buys 5 companies in plastics)... After escaping from Saigon, Do Van Tron arrives in San Jose (as no bank will back him, gets $4,800 in start-up capital from informal ethnic loan club - members contribute monthly amounts and bid for pooled cash by offering various rates of interest with winner paying interest to others, becomes successful by 1988 with plans for building a shopping center)... Long-time employee John R. Betzler warns McDonnell Douglas on improprieties in obtaining Pentagon documents (after transfer and other memos is fired in 1984, receives $260,000 from jury in 1988)... Two Peace Corps volunteers in Dominican Republic help form lending unit for small business, by 1988 loans $1.2 million to start 4,674 microenterprises – nearly 6,000 new jobs... David Norman, Enzo N. Torresi start Businessland, San Jose, to sell computers and services (grows to 117 U.S. outlets, sales of $871.6 million, by 1988 to Computerland's 481 with sales of $930 million, to Entre Computer Centers' 190, sales of $548 million, and to Microage's 166, sales of $231.5 million)...

David H. Murdock, 10th grade dropout, restaurant owner after W.W. II and builder in Phoenix – houses to duplexes, hotels and then factories, takes over Cannon Mills, by 1988 worth $1.3 billion with interests in office buildings, commercial property, leasing, ranch, and food business...

Liberty Village, an 88-store factory outlet complex, opens in Flemington, NJ, a village of 4,000, as a colonial marketplace... Heather Stern starts Personal Profiles, Chicago, as matchmaking business for busy professionals and executives with college degree and making over $30,000/year (handles 1,650 clients in 1988 for $1,450 each)... American Express' Shearson Lehman Hutton works with NYC public schools to start Academy of Finance, 2-year program for juniors and seniors with classwork and on-the-job experience (by 1988 sponsors 30 programs in high schools in 14 cities)... After 50 years of success Caterpillar tractor's business takes nosedive with collapse of global construction market and rise of Japanese competition (after cutting costs by pruning payrolls, workers strike for 7 months, closing plants, and modernizing production methods, reorganizing bloated hierarchy for flexibility and certifying suppliers for quality, recovers by 1989 to break $9.2 billion sales record of 1981).

1983

General Events

Black-dominated City Council of Richmond, VA, approves ordinance setting aside 30% of municipal projects for minority-construction firms, overturned by Supreme Court 1989... San Francisco forms Conservation Corps to help out-of-work youths, mostly minorities, with skills training and high school equivalency classes, followed by NYC in 1984, Kansas City in 1987, and Philadelphia in 1988... Beirut marine barracks is truck-bombed, 241 U.S. servicemen killed (reverses dictum of centuries with military commanders accountable even when not directly responsible - no punishment levied for 1988 Navy downing of Iran plane)... Washington reports (March 18) number of illegal aliens rises to escape Mexico's financial crisis... New Jersey judge allows trial of firms producing Agent Orange (leads to out-of-court settlement in 1984 for $180 million and challenges)... Washington education commission warns (April 26) public on "tide of mediocrity" imperiling U.S...

Presidential panel concludes (June 8) man-made pollution is major cause of acid rain... U.S. sues GM for selling X cars with previous knowledge of defects... Some 200,000 march (August 27) in Washington for social, political changes... President Reagan opposes (December 2) hiring quotas for blacks... Question of liability by investment bankers is first raised in suit between CPC International and McKesson, followed in 1987 with NY's highest court ruling investment bankers liable for fraud if they make deceptive marketing claims to clients... Law professor Henry G. Manne becomes Dean George Mason University's law school (establishes law-and-economic center to expouse cost-efficient justice, developed at University of Chicago in 1950s by Professor Aaron Director)... Employees at Eastern Airlines, facing bankruptcy, grant contract wage concessions of $360 million in return for stock, profit sharing and 4 directorships, followed in 1985 and 1986 when United Steel Workers get stock from Wheeling-Pittsburgh Steel, Kaiser Aluminum, LTV, and Bethlehem Steel for wage concessions (leads to union buyouts, such as attempt of pilots at United Airlines in 1987 to save jobs and control investments)...

University of Arizona creates Optical Circuit Cooperative as industrial consortium, including Boeing, DuPont, IBM and TRW, to develop optical processor for computers... After Phelps Dodge operation, AZ, refuses to accept contract adopted by other copper producers in area, 13 unions start violent strike to protest end of cost-of-living increases, requires police and National Guard to maintain order (-1985 when unions are decertified as bargaining agents by election of old employees, replacements)... In pioneering use of genetic engineering small plot of potatoes, CA, is protected from frost damage by organisms with DNA molecules... Harold Washington is first black mayor of Chicago...

NASA with Netherlands, Britain orbit first infared space telescope... Al Novak files patent application for computer device to blank out unwanted TV, radio programs on continuous basis... U.S.' personal savings rate is 5%, 13% for Canada, 14% for West Germany and 21% for Japan... Sport of snowsurfing starts on slopes of Magic Mountain, VT... Company officers of Film Recovery plant, IL, are indicted for murder of employee, convicted in pioneering case in 1984 for using unsafe working conditions to process film with cyanide... Transport Workers Union signs labor contract with American Airlines (gets pay, benefits for regular workers, agrees to lower starting rates for new employees and restructured jobs, is repeated in 1984 contract of United Airlines, International Association of Machinists)... U.S. Court of Appeals extends copyright laws to cover computer programs...

R.B. Reich: The Next American Frontier (reports need for partnerships of government, business to reduce unemployment and meet challenge of foreign competition, proposes new industrial policy with business training workers and increasing worker ownership)... U.S. Bureau of Standards starts research facility to study uses of automation for small manufacturing plants... Office and Professional Employees Union strikes employer American Federation of Government Employees... Board of Supervisors, San Francisco, adopts pioneering ordinance to govern smoking in workplace, first major city to limit smoking at work...

General John A. Wickham, Jr., becomes Army Chief of Staff (starts developing formations of light divisions of 10,500 men with support units of artillery, engineers, signal units, helicopters, transport units, etc., and armored divisions with 16,500 men and mechanized transport)... 60-acre "Arts District" develops in Dallas with museum, includes auditorium, restaurant and shop, theaters, schools, concert halls and commercial enterprises... Clark Kerr: The Future of Industrial Societies: Convergence or Continuing Diversity?... Hare Krishna temple is opened in Detroit by great grandson of Henry Ford and daughter of Walter Reuther, former UAW president... Scientists at Lawrence Livermore Laboratory, Los Alamos National Laboratory, and SRI form super computer project to coordinate several computers to work on same problem... Stanford University tests robot servants with voice controls for assisting physiclially disabled... AFL-CIO proposes 10% staff reduction to unions of employees, followed by UAW's 7% staff reduction, USW's 17% and UMW's 30%... SEC bans Fox & Co., 13th largest certified accounting firm, in accepting any new publicly held clients until it corrects its procedures... Terrance J. Sejnowski, colleagues at Johns Hopkins University design pioneering neural-network computer... USW, 7 steel companies sign pioneering labor contract with union's first concessions so Big Steel can save estimated $2 billion for modernizing...

Times Beach, MO, is evacuated to avoid dioxin contamination from disposal of industrial waste... Federal judge ends Chicago's traditional patronage system... U.S. Supreme Court upholds right of states to tax multinational on basis of worldwide earnings... University of Pennsylvania creates Joseph H. Lauder Institute of Management and International Studies (follows formal international programs at Harvard, Dartmouth in late 1960s - early 1970s... Syndicated columnist Bob Greene dubbs "super class" of high-living young urban professionals as "Yuppies"... Solar energy is generated from photovoltaic cells (follows development in 1954 by Bell Laboratories, use in 1958 satellite)... Freelance writers create National Writers Union...

After National Steel Company, U.S.' 4th largest producer, stops investments in Wierton mill, some 6,000 employees acquire plant for over $300 million in largest Employee Stock Ownership Plan (take 32% cut in pay to start operations)... Federal Reserve lowers prime lending rate for major banks to 10.5%... Federal Communications Commission requires Bell network to lease 44-Dial-It lines (results in 1987 industry of some $300 million Dial-It pornography with Carlin Communications, NYC, raking in some $130,000/month by 1987 - public utility commission, CA, orders phone blocks for children on customer's request)... U.S. Supreme Court upholds decision by U.S. Court of Appeals that Monopoly is no longer valid trademark...

S. Canby: <u>Military</u> <u>Reform</u> <u>and</u> <u>the</u> <u>Art</u> <u>of</u> <u>War</u> (discusses weapons dictate strategy)... Arizona enacts pioneering competency test program to evaluate public school teachers... Local citizens finance Duluth Growth Co. to buy small businesses elsewhere and move them to area... California issues IOUs to pay bills until deficit of $1.5 billion is resolved... Richard F. Schubert, former steel company executive, becomes president of Red Cross (engineers savings of some $2.9 million/year by reducing bureaucratic overhead, cutting clerical staff by 40%, redefining 60% of all jobs and hiring outsiders to fill remaining positions)... In largest municipal bond failure, Washington Public Power Supply System declares default on $2.25 billion in bonds for construction of 2 nuclear power plants...

Some 700,000 employees strike AT&T (as 90% of all phone calls are handled by automated equipment, settle with AT&T to provide job-displacement training and career development program to prepare employees for work in Bell system, elsewhere)... To halt soaring health costs Congress enacts set of maximum fees for Medicare treatments (fails with continued rise of premiums, including Blue Cross and Blue Shield, in 1988)... Massachusetts starts Employment & Training Choices to provide unemployed with intensive job training and placement services (results in drop of welfare rolls of 8.6% by 1986)... Federal, state and local authorities start CAMP, Campaign Against Marijuana Planting (eradicates some 92% of Northern California's crop, worth more than timber harvest, by 1987)... Video lottery is held in Atlantic City... SEC adopts regulation to make it harder for minority stockholders to start ballot fights on social issues, voided in 1985 by Federal court to let church groups promote views...By 1988 FTC handles 22 telemarketing-fraud cases and obtains $72 million for 6,500 victims...

Succeeding Roy Williams, convicted of conspiring to bribe U.S. senator, Jackie Presser is new head of Teamsters (evades federal charges of racketeering and embezzlement by death in 1988)...

Business Events

John J. Creedon is new CEO of Metropolitan Life Insurance (acquires Century 21 Real Estate, State Street Research & Management, Doubletree hotel-management firm, etc., to manage assets of $114 billion, including $23 billion real estate portfolio, by 1988)... With loan of $252,000 from 32 friends and relatives, James R. Cheek starts assembling troubled inter-city hospitals in developing Atlanta-based Gateway Medical Systems (acquires and revives 10 acute-care centers with aggressive management and tight financial controls before flirting with bankruptcy in 1987)... After operating network of 300 vending machines in Iowa State fraternities and sororities, Phil Akin opens first Duds 'n' Suds tavern-laundry after graduation (at age of 25 operates 73 outlets in 27 states in 1987 as largest U.S. chain of coin-operated laundries, plans 47 more by 1988)...

Bernard P. Tessler opens first The Enchanted Village store for children (operates chain of 15, NY, to compete with Waldenbooks, book retailing subsidiary of K mart with 1,100 book stores, opening 4 Waldenkid stores as "Creative Centers for Children" and planning 40 more by 1988)... After working with IBM, Libyan-born Sadeg M. Faris starts Hypres to pioneer "Third Age of Electronics" with Josephson-junction chips for faster super conduction than given by silicone transistors, 4 contracts from Defense Department by 1987)... Faith Popcorn starts pioneering BrainReserve, NYC, as marketing and trend-analysis consulting business...

NFL Players' Association, representing some 1,550 athletes, certifies high of 1,500 agents to handle contract negotiations for players... Former sculptors Victoria, Richard MacKenzie-Childs start Manhattan business to sell fantasy furniture and ornaments... To fend off raider Carl Icahn, Dan River Fabrics goes private as employee-owned company (while gaining tax advantages fails to improve performance with worker participation, struggles in 1987)... Juan E. Metzger, co-founder of Dannon Yogurt in 1942, creates Tomsun International to peddle Jofu, fruit-flavored tofu snack (achieves sales of $3.1 million in 1986)...

Wall Street lawyer Walter Beebe starts Open Center, NYC, to provide courses in New Age spirituality and superstition (with budget of $1.7 million enrolls some 3,000 students in 1987)... Radio Shack introduces battery-operated computer system... Texas Instruments, Timex and Mattel drop out of home computer market while toy-maker Coleco enters - a disaster... Edward R. Beauvais launches low-fare, non-union America West Airlines with frills and high frequency schedule at Phoenix to serve Southwest (with employees owning 30% and Australia's Ansett Airlines owning 20% of stock, invades NYC, Baltimore and Chicago markets in 1987 to operate U.S.' 11th largest carrier with 80 planes to serve 45 cities)... After Charles G. Bluhdorn, creator of Gulf & Western conglomerate, dies, successor Martin S. Davis sells $2.6 billion in assets and stocks to streamline business into 3 units: entertainment - Paramount Pictures in 1966, publishing - Prentice Hall in 1984, and financial services with Associates First Capital (cuts debt by 1986 from $2.1 billion to under $1.3 billion while increasing operating profits from $503 million to $789 million)... Control Data adopts employee peer review of grievances...

Hanna-Barbera pizzazzy play park for children opens, Houston (closes 1983)... John Sculley, president of Pepsi-Cola USA, is hired as president of Apple Computer by Steve Jobs, co-founder and chairman, to improve firm's marketing capabilities in competitive market (reorganizes business by 1984 into 3 divisions: sales for all products, Apple II family of profitable products, and Macintosh with Jobs for new products, leads to conflicts between Apple II regulars and Macintosh elite, cuts work force by 20% in 1985 with market slowdown, after power struggle with Jobs for final authority assumes full control in 1985 as CEO with support of Board, reorganizes business in 1985 by mostly functions, closes 3 of 6 factories to recover profitability in 1986, sues Microsoft in 1988 of copyright infringements - to cast pall over software industry)...

Reorganization of Braniff Airlines to focus on long-haul, low-fare routes, failed 1982 in trying to be an all-purpose airline, by Hyatt International, controlled by Chicago's Pritzker family, is approved by bankruptcy court (acquires $21.4 million in 1984 from stock offering to resume service as no-frills, low-priced carrier, sells money-losing line in leveraged buyout of $111 million in 1988 with new owners to focus on routes to smaller cities)... GM launches Saturn Project to start new independent automobile corporation (plans to use new methods with cooperation of administration, employees, unions and dealers and to transplant successful techniques to other plants)... Kids 'R' Us is started as discount chain of children's clothing stores by Toys 'R' Us discount business (operates 72 outlets in 1987)... Hudepohl, small Cincinnati brewery, introduces LA as pioneering U.S. low-alcohol beer, acquired by Anheuser-Busch later... Fortune: "Here Come McDentists"...

Piedmont Airlines acquires Henion commuter airline (pioneers trend of acquisition of small lines acquired by majors with 2 in 1984, 2 in 1985, 8 in 1986)... Total output of franchise operations is some $436 billion, 15% share of GNP, 10% in 1973 with sales of $168 billion... Wall Street Journal reports mixed results on uses of automation by manufacturers... Fruit-flavored liquers, low in alcohol, are introduced by apple-flavored De-Kuyper schnapps of National Distillers, founded 1922 (is followed in market by National's popular Original Peachtree Schnapps to pioneer market with over 30 peach cordials)... Wilson Foods declares bankruptcy to seek protection under Chapter 11 from "losses" of $1 million/week from current labor contract (leads to 1984 law to make wage cuts by firms in bankruptcy only possible with court's approval, is upheld in 1986 by Federal Appeals Court in negating Wheeling-Pittsburgh Steel's unilaterial reduction of wages)... San Diego-based Mailboxes, Etc., provides alternative to U.S. Postal Service (evolves as industry's largest with 1985 revenues of $4.6 million from some 400 franchises in 32 states - 600 outlets in 1988)... Market for hardcore video cassettes is some $220 million, $280 million in 1984, $375 million in 1985 and $450 million in 1986... Lezak Group raises some $3 million in blind pool from over 2,000 investors (invests in 6 acquisitions - 4 bankrupt by 1986)... National Basketball Association adopts first anti-drug program in professional sports... Grocery industry develops electronic document transmission system to link major suppliers with supermarkets, other retailers...

After chance meeting on airplane by Japanese-born Kay Nishi, vice president of U.S.' Microsoft, with president of Japanese semiconductor firm, Tandy Corp. markets new battery-powered, 8-pound computer with Microsoft software... Dragon's Lair is first interactive video arcade game with laser-disc technology (allows players to move animated character to avoid dangers on quest, leads to use of interactive employee training programs)... After battling other buyers Standard Oil of California finally acquires Gulf Oil for $13.2 billion (allows T. Boone Pickens, Jr., of Mesa Petroleum to pick up $760 million - $1 billion in greenmail on losing attempt)... Hopland Brewery, U.S.' first brewpub, opens in Mendocino, CA, over 12 others in U.S. by 1987...

Clifford, Stuart Perlman, Las Vegas operators of hotels and casinos, start Regent Air as elegant service for affluent flying between NYC, Los Angeles on one-way ticket for $1,620 (after losing some $17 million sell in 1984 to NY investment banker J. Roger Faherty, after renegotiating leases on planes, cuts staff, lowers price to $785, and drops frills while retaining essential luxuries to compete with first-class service of other carriers, suspends service in 1986 after losing millions)... "Just off the boat" Italian-born Pasquale Gallo is hired by Manhattan Astor Place Barbershop of Enrico, Frank Vezza (as manager attracts younger clientele with shorter, zippier, and eclectic styles, produces happenings on Kamikaze Club stage with 17 cutters designing trendy, personalized styles for clients and audience, receives award, first such for hairstyling salon, from Council of Fashion Designers of America in 1985)...

Dun & Bradstreet Credit Service adopts strategic plan for growth (drops Funk & Wagnalls publishing and makes 23 acquisitions in 1984, including Data Stream, British investment analysis business, U.S. subsidiary of Britain's Thomas Cook travel agency, and A.C. Nielsen TV and radio rating business, opens $40 million computer center in England to serve European customers, completes 10 more acquisitions in 1985)... After discovering frozen Italian treat called Gelato on 1982 trip to San Francisco, Myra Evans, partner with $200,000 from investors opens first Gelato Modo store, Cleveland (capitalizes business for $1 million in 1984, receives some 2,500 inquiries on franchising by 1985)... Angus bull, High Voltage, is purchased for $1.5 million, highest price ever paid for bull... Chef Paul Prudhomme with crew from K-Paul restaurant introduces Cajun cooking of bayou country, LA, to San Francisco (demonstrates cookery to NYC in 1985)... Chicago's Field Museum of Natural History hires Lord & Taylor advertising to increase sales of retail store, later Art Institute of Chicago forms marketing department... Information Professionals, MA, starts to provide retailers with daily weather reports and records of consumer buying habits... Hewlett-Packard introduces first personal computer with touch-screen controls... Air One provides all-business-class service with 9 planes (files for bankruptcy in 1984 after losing over $40 million)... First compact disc record players appear, later those of Holland's Phillips and Japan's Sony to set market standards... Santa Fe Southern Pacific Corp. merger becomes U.S.' 3rd largest railroad system (after rejection by ICC sells Southern Pacific to Rio Grande line for $1.8 billion in 1987)... Japanese firms capture 13% of U.S. semiconductor market, 15% by 1985... Former computer industrialist Gene Amdahl, son start Trilogy Systems to make world's most powerful mainframe computer with wafer superchips (resigns in 1986 after losing market to IBM)... Ralph Lauren's designer collection, over 2,500 high-quality items for homes, is presented at 34 of U.S.' top retailers by J.P. Stevens & Co., $2 billion textile enterprise... USA Network, Cable Health Network show first U.S. nude TV commercials... Business Week: "Business is Turning Data into a Potent Strategic Weapon"...

Hospitals spend less than $50 million on advertising, some $500 million in 1986... U.S.A. Cinemas sells upscale food items, such as Perrier, expresso, fancy chocolates, and premium ice cream in Boston theaters... Apple Computer introduces Lisa personal computer with 2nd generation software (bases work on Xerox's Palo Alto Research Center in 1970s)... After 92 years, J.L. Hudson closes downtown department store in Detroit... First Interstate, 13 banks create nationwide network of automated tellers... During year, 2,533 mergers and acquisitions are either initiated or completed, 9-year record...

Theodore Levitt: "The Marketing Imagination," Harvard Business Review (discusses formation of global markets from mass communications, high-technology, standardization of consumer patterns)... Cummins Engine, IN, forms research and development limited partnership as special venture to develop new engine (if successful, retains option to buy engine in 1987 in exchange for royalties and monetary payments to partners)... Lucky-Goldstar Group is first Korean firm to open U.S. plant, Samsung follows in 1984... Chicago White Sox baseball team uses computer to evaluate players, follows first attempt by Oakland A's... Pioneering Correction Corp. of America starts for-profit business to operate prisons (becomes largest in market with 7 facilities by 1986)... Westinghouse Electric starts prototype plant for future at College Station, TX (employs selected nonunion employees on salaries to produce electronic assemblies in work teams with automated equipment)... Robert H. Field starts High-Tech Parking Systems (devises automated parking garage as warehouse)...

Time, Inc. launches TV-Cable Week with $100 million (abandons project in 6 months after losing $47 million, jettisons Discover science magazine in 1983, drops Picture Week in 1986 after spending $25 million in development, acquires Scott Foresman textbook publisher in 1986 for $520 million, plans merger of $18 billion in 1989 with Warner Communications to become world's largest communication company)... Kenneth Blanchard, Spencer Johnson: The One Minute Manager (provides quick-fixes for management problems in best-seller)... Phone-In Drive-Thru market is tested, Los Angeles... Movie "The Pirates of Penzance" is first released simultaneously in theaters, on cable television... IBM acquires 12% of semiconductor manufacturer Intel... For first time crude-oil futures are traded on Chicago, NY commodity exchanges... After 7 years of research costing some $26 million, Viewtron system is developed, FL, to link banks, home computers... United Dignity starts U.S. chain of funeral homes, FL... All-American Gourmet business in Orange, CA, introduces Budget Gourmet Frozen Entrees, sales of some $100 million in 1986... Pillsbury buys Haagen-Dazs fancy ice cream business with 101 shops for $76 million, sales of $175 million in 1986... Fortune: "The Mass Market is Splitting Apart" (reports division of middle class into high, low income levels)... Oakland Tribune is first general-circulation metropolitan daily owned by a black... Rio Grande Zephyr, last privately operated long-haul passenger service in lower 48, is sold to Amtrak... Executives of United Technologies are required to learn how to operate personal computers... Fortune: "The Corporate Culture Vultures" (reports rise of consultants to mesh company's culture with strategy)... General Host lodging business acquires Midwestern chain of plant stores (purchases Northeast chain in 1984 to operate 124 outlets and develop first national chain of nurseries)...

After obtaining $60 million in grants, tax abatements from Irish government to open new plant, Hyster forklift business pressures states, IL, KY, AL and OR, for grants to modernize plants (closes Oregon's factory after refusal to move local plant to Ireland)... After legal battle with Coca-Cola Procter & Gamble acquires Coca-Cola franchise, KY... Largest U.S. interstate banking combination is formed by merger of BankAmerica and Seafirst, holding company of financially-troubled Seattle-First National Bank with bad loans in energy firms... In avoiding selective high-priced overseas trading approach of Sears and J.C. Penney, K mart forms Trading Services to sell middle-class U.S. consumer products to foreign retailers, wholesalers...

Business Week: "Marketing: The New Priority" (reports role of market research in developing strategy for fragmented market)... IBM contracts with Boston-based Work/Family Directions, for-profit child care consulting group, to establish 16,000 home-based family centers and open 3,000 group day care centers for employees... Dubai sheik buys yearling colt in Keeneland Sales, KY, for $10.2 million, tops previous record of $4.25 million... Western Electric is first U.S. firm, perhaps world, to produce 256K memory chips on commercial basis... Newsweek: "Drugs on the Job"... Medford-based Bear Creek Corp., one of U.S.' largest direct-mail companies since 1930s with fruits from Harry & David's Orchards, is acquired by Nabisco for $74.1 million (sells in 1986 to San Francisco's Shaklee Corp., business marketing nutritional, household and personal care products, for $123 million)...

Locum Tenens opens, Atlanta, as temporary employment agency for professionals, handles some 2,000 doctors in 1986... Forbes Magazine estimates Clint W. Murchison, Jr., Texas oil man, to have net worth of $350 million (declares bankrptcy in 1985, is allowed to retain some $3 million by court in 1986)... Sharon Kleyne, husband with $300,000 start business marketing Nature's Mist, spring water spray for facial care from secret well in Southern Oregon (grosses $1 million by 1986 from sales in 22 states with flashy, stylish promotions)... Over-the-counter broker Joe McGivney promotes Wealth Unlimited to sell middle-class investors, some 22,000 at $750 each by 1988, on how to escape drab lives by investing in young companies (is investigated in 1987-88 for touting firms and suspected of market manipulation)... Former ProServ partners of Donald L. Dell start Advantage International agency to represent athletes...

After winning $81.5 million land-claim settlement against U.S., ME for

Passamaquoddy and Penobscot tribes, Thomas Thureen and Daniel Zilka, former Wall Street investment banker, form Tribal Assets Management to provide Indians with financial advise (assist Chippewas and Cherokees later in economic development - only 40 of 310 tribes with programs by 1988)...

Goodyear Tire & Rubber buys Celeron, oil and gas company, for $800 million in stock (plans to build new pipeline from California to Texas for $1 billion, acquires 20% of world tire market in 1988 - Michelin with 18% and Bridgestone, after acquiring Firestone's tire business in 1987 at 16%)... Otis Elevator builds escalators for U.S. market in West Germany, returns to U.S. production in 1988...

With potential client list from The Atlanta Constitution want ads, Jack Lupas starts business buying used computer paper of data-processing firms, handles 200 tons/month for 150 customers by 1988... Selchow & Righter game business, introduced Scrabble in 1952, sells Trivial Pursuit, sales of some 20 million by 1984 before fad ebbs...

Gary C. Nelson starts J. Higby's Yogurt & Treat Shoppes, 91 stores in 12 states by 1988 and plans for 1,000 (competes in 1988 market with TCBY Enterprises of Little Rock, biggest with 822 stores nationwide and plans for 1,170 by 1989, Heidi's Frozen Yogurt Shoppes with 100 stores and Penguin Place with 113 stores and plans for over 1,000 by 1993)...

Irving Azoff takes over MCA's Music Entertainment Group, goes from $7 million loss to over $40 million in earnings by 1988 with aggressive record distribution, personal management, product merchandising, managing concert halls and new stars...

Compaq Computer in Houston, started by veterans of Texas Instruments as Gateway Technology to make personal computers, sells over $100 million - $1.224 billion in 1987 for growth rate of 62% to get 25% market share after IBM's 30% (challenges IBM in 1988 with market's most powerful personal computer)... Larry Brown becomes basketball coach at University of Kansas (signs multi-year contract worth $400,000/year with basketball camp, shoe contract, and TV show)...

Alenax Corp. sets up, NJ, to introduce Korean-designed bicycle with unique "transbar" system where pedals go up and down, sells some 1,000 in U.S. by 1988 with shipments to Japan and Australia... Mechanical engineer Jerold Zindler starts Design Continuum to style medical and laboratory instruments, wins coveted Milan Compasso D'Oro award in 1987 for product designs...

Marketing analyst Steve Blad takes over bingo parlor for Otoe-Missouri Indians, OK (with experience takes over Big Cypress Seminole Indian's game to generate $15 million in 1987 with showmanship in world's largest bingo parlor seating 5,600 players from U.S., Canada)...

Bill McKay, Harry Williams, vice presidents of Ashland Oil, tell federal investigators of bribes to Middle Eastern government officials to obtain crude supplies, fired (sue Ashland in 1984 for being unfairly dismissed for telling truth, win $69.5 million in 1988 - appealed)... Ford designers create clay model for new sports car (designs car with Mazda engineers in 1984, starts production of Probe in 1988 at Mazda's Michigan plant - ship cars to Japan)... Black, John W. Rogers, Jr., eschewing pro basketball, forms Ariel Capital Management with no clients, manages $430 million in institutional money by 1988 with returns of 25.2%... Dentist Duayne Christensen starts North American Savings and Loan in Costa Mesa, CA (dies 1987 just before regulators seize business for fraudulent investments, is liquidated with American Diversified Savings, seized 1986, in 1988 with record payout of $1.35 billion)... Antonio C. Alvarez II, Bryan P. Marshal form A&M as crisis management business to turn failing firms around after cleaning up Norton Simon (after Timex take on Western Union in 1984 to trim operating expenses and boost cash flow, restructure Gearhart Industries – dumped after success in cutting 25% of work force to lower costs, work for Coleco Industries in 1988 to avoid liquidation)... Access International forms, NYC, as brokerage to sell airline tickets at reduced prices directly to travelers, started in 1950s to fill unsold tickets of ethnic groups visiting homelands (becomes one of fastest growing of consolidators-wholesalers by 1988 with advertising in Europe, U.S. to handle some 120,000 flyers)...

Alan N. Cohen, 2 partners buy Boston Celtics basketball team for $15 million (sell 40% for $48 million in 1986 to 60,000 investors in Boston Celtics Limited Partnership)... Assn. of Volleyball Professionals forms, 28-event pro tour in 1988 with prizes of $1.8 million from corporate sponsorships... After bitter battle Charles, David Koch win control of family firm in oil, gas, coal, real estate and chemicals, billionaires by 1988... Food consultant Carl Wolf starts First World Cheese to sell "nutritional" cheeses in growing market, 40%/year, of $400 million by 1988... Angel Cordero is first jockey to win $10 million in one year...

Major retailers sell 250 different lines of private label clothing, 600 in 1988... Just Desserts, San Francisco bakery, uses 3,000 lbs. of butter/week and 20,000 lbs. of flour in making fancy desserts (uses 7,000 lbs. of butter/week, 40,000 lbs. of flour/week in 1988 in servicing 4 retail shops, 550 restaurants)... Todd Axelrod gives up brokering stocks to turn hobby collecting documents signed by public figures into a business, sales of $2.3 million in 1988 with inventory of 76,000 papers... After pulling all of its programs off regular TV, Disney starts its own cable channel... Leonard Shaykin, partner start business to buy 'em, fix 'em, and sell 'em, amass $500 million by 1989 in handling corporate turnabouts... Texas oilman, Clint Murchison, Jr., facing hard times, sells Dallas Cowboys pro football franchise, bought 1960 from NFL for $600,000, and stadium lease to H.R. Bright, Texas multimillionaire with oil, banking and real estate interests, and partners for $86 million (facing hard times in petroleum industry, sells franchise and lease to Jeral Jones, fortune in insurance, gas and oil, for reported $140 million in 1989 – new high for U.S. sports enterprise).

1984

General Events

U.S. Commission on Civil Rights discontinues (January 17) use of numerical quotas to promote blacks... Washington reports (January 24) lowest inflation rate since 1972... EPA bans (February 3) pesticide EDB for grain products... Department of Housing and Urban Development reports (May 1) 250,000-350,000 are homeless... In largest bail-out of private banks Federal Reserve Board arranges (May 17) $7.5 billion loan to save 1857 Continental Illinois Bank & Trust Company, world's 7th largest, from financial emergency with billions in debt from bad loans... For first time Washington reports (June 29) average price of new home over $100,000... New York passes (July 12) first state mandatory seat-belt law... New York is (August 14) first State to pass law curbing acid rain... U.S. Supreme Court: <u>NCAA</u> <u>v.</u> <u>Board</u> <u>of</u> <u>Regents</u> <u>of</u> <u>University</u> <u>of</u> <u>Oklahoma</u> (rules NCAA restrictions restrain competition, allows colleges to negotiate their own television contracts)... U.S. Supreme Court rules state laws can require Junior Chambers of Commerce to admit women... Congress allows U.S. companies to borrow abroad without paying 30% tax on interest (results in Caribbean tax havens until restrictions in 1987)...

India-born Narendra K. Karmarkar, researcher at Bell Laboratories, develops breakthrough mathematical formula to program problems with thousands of variables for high-speed processing by computers, first AT&T patented program licensed to U.S. Air Force in 1987... Congress passes law to provide for seizure of crime-related assets (allows Government to auction confiscated properties - $550 million in fiscal 1986)... Washington reports (December 11) 76 bank failures, highest since 1937... In contracts with UAW, GM and Ford present educational programs on basic skills, give remedial courses for illiterates... <u>Business</u> <u>Week</u>: "The Death of Mining" (reports losses from shrinking markets, increasing debts, falling prices)...

Innovative 3-hour play "Tamara," devised in 1980 by Toronto's John Krizanc, is staged in lavish Italian villa, Los Angeles (allows limited audience to view simultaneous subplots in various rooms and move through house with actors)... <u>Fortune</u>: "Good News Ahead for Productivity" (after dismal decade reports evidence of higher long-term trends)... <u>Business</u> <u>Week</u>: "Now Unions are Helping to Run the Business"... California law allows spouse on divorce to collect if family income was used to pay education of other spouse... Berkeley Citizens Action, radical left-coalition of students, tenants, minorities, and elderly, acquires control of city council of Berkeley, CA (extends health care welfare benefits to unmarried domestic live-in partners of City employees regardless of sex, bans condo conversions, restricts landlords in removing renters, condemns Isralite settlements on West Bank, withdraws City investments in firms doing business in South Africa)...

<u>Time</u>: "Sex in the '80s: The Revolution is Over"... UAW, Ford sign labor contract, union supports reforms in health care to reduce costs... Committee of Roman Catholic bishops issues pastoral letter (advocates reducing unemployment to 4% with government funding, overhauling welfare system, changing labor laws to help workers form unions and provide remedies for unfair labor practices, shifting emphasis of foreign policy from military programs to those stressing basic human rights, and implementing economic reforms for chronically unemployed, others in poverty)... Where Montreal lost some $1 billion in hosting 1980 Olympic games, Los Angeles Olympics shows surplus of some $215 million by selling TV and licensing rights for $127 million and using volunteers, some 36,000 of total 72,000, to cut costs (results in International Olympic Committee selling worldwide rights to corporate sponsors for $120 million)...

U.S. Court of Appeals rules chairman of Chicago's Libco Corp. violated law by using company pension funds in 3 takeover battles... U.S. Supreme Court rules firm that has filed for bankruptcy can cancel union contract, cut wages, and lay off workers without having to prove pact caused firm to go broke... Top Army, Air Force generals sign agreement to improve cooperation on joint operations, eliminate duplication of missions and weapons... New Orleans World's Fair opens (declares bankruptcy owing over $100 million)... Business Week: "Artificial Intelligence: It's here"...

Time: "America's Upbeat Mood"... Walk-out of 400-member Local 32, International Association of Heat and Frost Insulators and Asbestos Workers, ends when management agrees to lower wages and fringe benefits, union demand to block possible transfer of work to non-union workers... 24 incubator facilities nurture start-up companies during year, some 200-300 by 1986... President Reagan orders NASA to auction rockets developed for earlier space programs (provides basis for development of private-sector launch industry after 1986 decision to take NASA out of commercial flights)... Some 90,000 pleasure boats use Erie Canal, over 100,000 in 1985... Space shuttle Discovery lifts into orbit with pioneering prototype commercial-production facility for private enterprise...

Justice Department issues new guidelines for corporate mergers (approves previously unlawful mergers to allow formations to improve efficiencies in operations, to overcome basic weaknesses)... UAW, Ford start joint venture to train and place workers in new jobs, followed in 1986 by AT&T, Communications Workers of America... Under California's new laws Ronald Austin, UCLA student, is charged with 12 counts of maliciously invading a computer system... Massachusetts is first State to ban almost all drink promotions, known as "happy hours," by bars, restaurants... President's Private Survey on Cost Control concludes Government operations could save some $28.4 billion over 3 years... Union employees at Johnstown plant reject proposed contract concessions of U.S. Steel, forces closure for century-old facility... New play "Dancing in the End Zone," opens on Broadway, first production with cost-cutting concessions from unions (reduces break-even point from $125,000/week to $62,000)...

AMA requests members to voluntarily freeze medical fees for one year... New Bedford, MA, acquires financially-troubled 120-year-old Morse Cutting Tools with right of eminent domain... ICC permits CSX Corp., holding company of 6 railroads, to acquire American Commercial Lines, one of U.S.' largest barge operations (reverses transportation policy of some 70 years)... Revival of aging, seedy Melrose Avenue of Los Angeles evolves (becomes 5-mile parade of nouvelle-cuisine restaurants flavored by punk-rock culture of trendy shops)... MIT is first U.S. university to offer degree in real estate development... California convicts computer hacker Bill Landreth of wire fraud for tapping GTE electronic-mail service (after probation disappears mysteriously in 1985)...

Business Week: "The Shrinking World of U.S. Engineering Contractors" (reports decline in world's largest construction projects, rise of competition by foreign contractors in U.S., overseas)... For first time 49.3% of civilian work force are male, 62.5% in 1950s... Business Week: "Will Money Managers Wreck the Economy?" (reports power of corporate financiers in determining destinies of companies by focusing on tactics to survive present)... Federation of American Clinics is formed by doctors of nation's largest medical groups as national health-maintenance society... Business Week: "The Superdollar"... Congress passes law to arrest computer chip copiers, to prevent shipments of copied chips (becomes model for Japan, other countries)... Business Week: "The Gold

Years are Gone for Farms Co-Ops" (reports cost-cutting, sell-offs, and mergers of cooperative systems developed in 1920s)... Grumman Aerospace shows Air Force's experimental plane X-29A to public (uses forward-swept wings, canards, and 3 computers to adjust wings, needs computers for canards as pilot-plane would self-destruct)... New Jersey requires State's pension funds to divest themselves of all securities in firms with South African ties, followed by NYC in 1985 with law not to purchase from vendors with South African operations and other states - California with largest divesture in 1986... Service Employees International Union, Equitable Life Assurance Society negotiate pioneering labor contract in service sector... Agricultural Workers sue University of California at Davis to prevent use of tax money to develop labor-saving devices for farms...

Milton, Rose Friedman: <u>Tyranny</u> <u>of</u> <u>the</u> <u>Status</u> <u>Quo</u> (proposes 4 constitutional amendments: balanced budget, President to have item veto on budget, flat-rate tax on personal income, requirement of steady money growth by Federal Reserve Board)... Justice Department blocks planned merger of Jones & Laughlin Steel, Republic Steel... Despite opposition of United Steel Workers Union, Cleveland voters approve grant to help build steel minimill... First world conference on 4th dimension is held in U.S... U.S. Supreme Court rules home video taping of television programs for private use is legal... Bureau of Standards' project to make incompatible computers talk with each other is undertaken by IBM, Digital Equipment and Hewlett-Packard at GM Technical Center to develop system of computers, controllers to operate automated factory (leads to Corporation for Open Systems, a consortium of 17 computer firms, in 1985 to design system so different computers can talk with each other)...

<u>Newsweek</u>: "A Marriage of Convenience" (reports on balance of U.S. trade deficit with Japan and Japanese investment in U.S.)... Trademark Counterfeiting Act provides first tough penalties for product imitations (allows customs agents to seize sham goods, to get search warrants to raid pirating firms)... Two 40-kilowatt cells are installed at Racquetball World to test conversion of chemical energy into electricity... Institute of Electrical and Electronic Engineers establishes standards for plant communication networks with automated machinery, leads to guidelines from Bureau of Standards on software, hardware... For first time General Services Administration allows government employees to use credit cards in paying travel expenses...

Reagan administration rejects restrictions on copper imports to protect domestic industry... Congress passes new bankruptcy law (allows unions to dispute bankruptcy reorganization if firm abusing law)... <u>Business</u> <u>Week</u>: "Doctors Are Entering a Brave New World of Competition"... Reagan administration negotiates "voluntary restraining agreements" with steel-exporting countries... Yale University's 1,600 clerical, technical workers strike to protest salaries and benefits and demand equal pay for women, settled in 1985... Oregon court rules Astoria Clinic guilty in 1981 anti-trust suit by Dr. T. Patrick when his hospital privileges were revoked on grounds of alleged incompetence (is awarded over $2 million in damages for conspiracy to eliminate competition, is overturned in 1986 by 9th Circuit Court of Appeals -reversed by Supreme Court in 1988)... Government establishes regulations for funeral industry... Swedish importer is fined $3 million for making illegal shipments of U.S. equipment to U.S.S.R... U.S. signs agreement with China on industrial cooperation (renews accords on science, technology)... Women Economic Development Corp. forms, MN, to loan money to women, including those on welfare, to start businesses (with $1 million fund from local business aids 1500 new firms by 1988, only 50 close)... By 1988 some 400,000 people leave farm life... Competition in Contracting Act decrees whenever possible Pentagon should seek at least 2 bidders for project, prior 57% of private defense contracts with no competitive bidding drops to 14% of 61,000 in 1987-88... NYC passes law to require private clubs of more than 400 members that serve meals and get income from nonmembers must admit women, echoed by Washington, Chicago and San Francisco (is upheld by U.S. Supreme Court in 1988)...

U.S. shows investment credit of $4.4 billion, becomes debtor nation, world's largest, in 1985 with deficit of $107.4 billion - first time since 1914... U.S. Supreme Court strikes down National Collegiate Athletic Assn.'s control over college games on TV (results in rise of regional sports networks by 1988 - ESPN No. 1 in cable market with 97% of viewers)... Presidential commission denies hunger is rampant... Scientific American carries landmark article of A.K. Dewdney on computer viruses, first predicted by John von Neuman in 1949 paper "Theory and Organization of Complicated Automata," heralded by development of Core War program by 3 computer programmers at Bell Labs in late 1950s - early 1960s, and exposed in 1983 by Ken Thompson in speech to Assn. for Computer Machinery... Federal law sets penalties for gaining access to interstate computer network for criminal purposes (leads to first arrest in 1988 of hacker Kevin Mitnick, convicted in 1987 for stealing software via telephone, for gaining illegal entry to computers at Digital Equipment, MA, and University of Leeds, England, to steal computer programs).

Business Events

IBM makes Herbert Schorr head of artificial intelligence work (institutes 50 expert systems by 1988, DuPont uses 200 with plans for 2,000 by 1990)... Campbell Soup acquires Casera, Puerto Rican food company (introduces 50 Hispanic products to U.S. by 1987)... Boston's Camel Hair & Cashmere Institute of America is formed by 9 textile firms as watchdog agency to check mislabeling, counterfeiting... After years of effort Motorola wins $10 million Japanese contract for tone pagers... Consumer groups end (January 26) 7-year-old boycott of Nestle... In overriding previous agreement of Pennzoil, Texaco acquires Getty Oil for $10 billion, allows Bass brothers to reap quick profit of $300 million on rise in value of Texaco's stock (leads to suit by Pennzoil in 1985 for compensatory damages of $7.53 billion and punitive damages of $3 billion - all but $2 billion upheld by Texas Court of Appeals in 1987, forces Texaco to file for protection under bankruptcy in 1987 and settle with Pennzoil in 1987 for $3 billion in cash - approved by bankruptcy court in 1988)...

Over 2,850 people are killed by gas leak at Union Carbide's plant, world's largest plant disaster, in Bhopal, India (is required to pay $270 million in interim relief to victims in 1987 by India court, final settlement by India in 1989 for $470 million)... For European flair and elegance Chrysler acquires part of Italian luxury sports-car maker Maserati (acquires Italy's Lamborghini for $750 million and loss-ridden American Motors in 1987 for Jeep)... Marriott hotel and food business expands with all-suite hotels and medium-priced Courtyard hotels (acquires part of 1925 Howard Johnson hotel, restaurant business in 1985 for 4 plaza-hotels and 418 restaurants)... Israel-born Avi Ruimi, Avi Faltao start Auto-Shade, Los Angeles, to make cardboard window screens to protect car interiors from sun (sell over 12 million at $4.99 in 1986)... Conus is formed as Minnesota-based cooperative by 67 independently-owned television stations to provide members, some with major networks and many non-affiliated, with TV news via satellite for station shows... After interest in his est personal development programs of 1970s wanes, Werner Erhard launches Transformational Technologies to design programs, based on est, to aid businesses in gaining clear vision for changing corporate cultures (by 1987 sells services via 50 franchises to gross $50 million)...

Northwest Nanny Institute, 1 of 7 during year U.S., forms in Portland, OR, joined by 13 more in American Council of Nanny Schools by 1985... Howard Fields builds exotic swimming pools and ponds in Sausalito, CA, revenues over $1 million in 1986... Paul Simon, former linoleum layer, is first TV real estate guru to sell instructional tapes to those desiring to get-rich-quick... After making PBS documentaries, Joe Pytka starts business to produce reality-charged commercials (grosses over $12 million in 1986, receives 12 Clio advertising awards in 1987)... Printer, Jeff Rogovin, starts business publishing baseball cards of minor league players... First Money Management Camp for Kids, sponsored by investment firm Gruntal & Co., opens in Palm Beach, FL (gives each child $100 rebate on $400 camp fee to invest in market)...

Joseph F. Engelberger, founder of Unimation in 1959, starts Transitions Research to enter service-robot business (aided by Sweden's Electrolux designs robot vacuum cleaner for factories, malls, supermarkets and airports and HelpMate as nurse's aide)... With Wal-Mart and K mart chains going upscale, One Price Clothing Stores opens in Southeast (by 1987 operates with nearly 100 outlets and sales of some $40 million from mostly blue-collar customers)... Chemist Stanley Rhodes starts NutriClean as commercial testing laboratory to provide consumers, businesses with contaminant ratings for food products... 1978 Ben & Jerry's Homemade, small VT ice cream business, sues Pillsbury's Haagen-Dazs to break their hold over independent distributors with exclusive contracts (while winning preliminary injunction in 1987 uses offbeat publicity on trial fighting giants to gain almost equal market shares with Pillsbury's Haagen-Dazs and Kraft's Frusen Gladje)...

Bill O'Neill, owner of Los Angeles stock brokerage firm, starts financial newspaper Investor's Daily, with huge computer bank provides statistics, charts and graphs to money managers to challenge The Wall Street Journal (with losses shrinking each quarter gains circulation of 120,000 in 1987 to attract advertisers)... After handling capital ventures and starting TLC Group in 1983, largest black-owned business in 1987, Harvard lawyer Reginald F. Lewis invests $1 million and $24 million loan in leveraged buyout of McCall Pattern (increases profits of 1874 sewing pattern business from some $6.5 million to $14 million in 1986 before selling to Britain's John Crowther Group in 1987 for $95 million in cash and debt, with profits from buyout acquires BCI International Food, Beatrice subsidiary with 64 separate firms in 31 countries, in 1987 for $985 million)... Robert Leventhal inherits helm of 1856 Western Union 10 days before it runs out of cash (avoids Chapter 11 by renegotiating new credit line from 31 banks, chopping 1,600 jobs and cutting pay for remaining 11,000 employees, if shareholders approve plans to rescue business by combining Western Union with ITT's telex operation)... After adding action toys in 1982 and stuffed animals in 1983 to product line Milton Bradley game business is acquired by Hasbro toy business, founded 1923, for $360 million to compete in toy market at each age level (acquires Axlon in 1986 from Nolan Bushnell, founder of Atari, for $3 million to acquire rights for electronic toy and future creations, becomes world's No. 1 toymaker in 1987 with sales of $1.2 billion)...

After Fed-Mart, CA, fails in 1970s, innovative 200,000-square-foot U.S. hypermarket, pioneered in France in 1963 by Carrefour, is opened by Biggs, joint venture of France's Euromarche and Super Valu, outside Cincinnati with 40 check-out lanes to sell everything, generates weekly sales, 10 times the average, of some $2 million, 2nd store in 1988 (leads to 40% of new supermarkets in 1986 being super stores with 55,000-65,000-square-feet of space and in opening of 2 hypermarkets by Carrefour, France's largest grocery chain, in 1987, Wal-Mart's Hypermart USA in 1987-88 with 3 stores - K mart plans to join field in 1988)...

NY Stock Exchange lists 27 firms with non-voting stock to prevent takeovers... After winning 2 stockholder battles, allows financier Saul Steinberg quick profit of $52 million in greenmail, Roy E. Disney, nephew of Walt, with support of Bass family gains control of Walt Disney Productions, last place in industry (with Michael D. Eisner, former head of Paramount Pictures, as chairman develops business as theme park, movies and television, first in industry to integrate media, and real estate activities to become industry's No. 2 by 1988)...

With breakup of AT&T alternative operator services enter market, 40 by 1988 to handle 5% of $563 million of $11.5 billion in operator-assisted calls by leasing lines from carriers to sell phone services at "lower" rates to hotels, airports, hospitals, colleges, etc. (leads to numerous complaints over high fees to FCC)...

NYC's Chemical Bank introduces home-banking system with personal computers as step to checkless and cashless society, canceled 1989 for lack of interest... By 1987 U.S. electronic production rises 8%, Japan by 75%... Portable toolmaker Black and Decker, founded 1910, acquires GE's line of small appliances (after losing leading share of portable tool market to Japan's Makita and West Germany's Bosch, is industry's fastest growing in 1988 by using strategic planning to develop 60 new or redesigned products and close 5 plants)...

Broken Hill Proprietary, Australia, acquires Utah International, natural resources, for $2.4 billion... After college graduation, Jeffrey Silverman joins Nike sports shoe firm as children's product manager (quits in 1985 to start Toddler University with loans of $25,000, after patenting revolutionary shoe with 5 inserts for width reaches sales of $25 million in 1988, goes big time with sales to 134-store Kids 'R' Us in 1989)...

Schlumberger, Netherlands Antilles, buys Sedco oil drilling business for $970 million, is followed by 2 major foreign acquisitions of U.S. firms in 1985, 3 in 1986, 6 in 1987, and 13 in 1988... After severing the Bell system, AT&T adopts individual profit-sharing plans tied to operations, management groups (with success in meeting financial goals expands program in 1988 to all 122,000 managers)... Japan's NEC challenges Intel's copyright for microprocessors, loses in 1989 landmark ruling by Federal Court... David Stern is new NBA commissioner (supports McDonald's first annual international basketball open in 1987, by 1988 arranges TV agreements with 75 countries and peddles merchandise in 40 - some $3.5 million in 1988 revenues from Europe)... Financier Meshulam Riklis buys Faberge perfume business for $180 million, adds Elizabeth Arden cosmetics in 1988 for $700 million (fails to sell both to Anglo-Dutch consumer-goods giant Unilever in 1989 for $1.55 billion)...

Hispanic groups end 10-year boycott of Coors Brewery after agreement by firm to invest some $350 million over 5 years in Hispanic community with jobs, business contracts, and contributions to non-profit organizations (follow $325 million agreement with black community leaders)... After 15 months of work General Motors consolidates 5 car divisions into two groups for large (Buick, Oldsmobile and Cadillac) and small cars (Chevrolet and Pontiac) to become leaner, tougher in competitive market (assigns central staff activities, such as design, engineering, and marketing, to each group)... R.R. Donnelley & Sons, largest U.S. commercial printer in Chicago, forms subsidiary to sell computer-shopping terminals as electronic kiosks in retail stores... McCorp, high-tech Texas banking operation, tests first U.S. automated brokerage machines...

Standard Oil of California acquires Gulf Oil for record $13.2 billion... Ford dealer, MI, installs computer system in automobile showroom to assist sales force (greets customers, compares models, determines operating costs, provides financial terms)... Air Florida, founded 1972 as interstate carrier before shifting to intrastate, international operations after deregulation in 1978, declares bankruptcy... Capital Cities installs pioneering employee drug program, emulated by other major corporations... Influenced by "Star Wars" movies, Photon, designed as world's first live-action game with players pitted against each other in electronic duels, opens, Dallas (opens 4 franchises by 1986 with sales for 94 others)...

K mart discount business acquires San Antonio's 9-store Home Centers of America chain (runs 56 centers in 1986 to provide supplies for home improvement)... Last tuna factory in San Diego closes... General Motors in pioneering effort enlists cooperation of United Auto Workers, Blue Cross and Blue Shield, and Metropolitan Life Insurance to reduce rising medical costs... AT&T introduces personal computer to U.S. market, first phase in developing office automation line... General Motors acquires H. Ross Perot's Electronic Data Systems for $2.5 billion to streamline corporate records, enter computer-service industry, develop high-tech products (ousts Perot from board in 1986 with buyout of $750 million after running battle on what GM needs to do to compete- Perot starts new computer-services firm in 1988 to compete with GM's EDS)...

First McDonald's fast-food restaurant on military facility opens at Navy base, 44 more by 1986 (is followed by Burger King with 54 units on Army, Air Force bases by 1986 to achieve sales of $45 million)... John Kluge acquires Metromedia communications business in leveraged buyout of $1.6 billion (sells 7 TV stations to Rupert Murdoch, 20th Century-Fox for $2 billion and cellular paging business to Southwestern Bell for $1.6 billion)... Lawrence Livermore National Laboratory unveils world's fastest super-computer, $12 million Cray X-MP with capability for up to 2 million calculations/second... Fortune: "America's Most Admired Corporations" (lists IBM, Dow Jones, Hewlett-Packard, Merck, Johnson & Johnson, Time, General Electric, Anheuser-Busch, Coca-Cola, Boeing)... When idea for specialty store catering to working women is rejected by Federated Department Stores, Michael Jeffries and Colleen Brady open first Alcott & Andrews store in Washington (open 5 more by 1986 to top sales of $40 million as one of fastest-growing specialty chains)...

After operating as high-priced fitness center in Houston for 4 years, business acquires 82 health clubs (becomes LivingWell in 1985 and acquires 283 spas, including Elaine Powers Figure Salons, to operate 395 health clubs in 26 states in 1986 - revenues of $129.7 million in 1985)... Manhattan, Inc. is published to glorify money-makers of today... With entry of Thomas J. Lipton in herbal tea market, Morris Siegel sells Celestial Seasons, founded 1969, for $50 million to Kraft food conglomerate (leads to 1988 monopoly suit by Bigelow against sale of Celestial, 50% of herbal tea market, to Unilever's Lipton with 31%)...

Tiny Nalors, Los Angeles' last drive-in eatery, closes... First U.S. area regional interstate banking is approved by all New England states except NH... Visual electronic advertising displays, "Taxigrams," are seen in NY cabs... Charles Band, filmed first feature in 1972 at age of 21, creates Empire Pictures to distribute grade B movies of horror, schlock (produces 11 films in 1985 and 25 in 1986 - more than any major Hollywood studio, signs $50 million contract with Vestron Video, world's largest independent home-video distributor, in 1985 with guarantee for as much as 50% of production costs before filming)... Earnings of big 3 automakers are some $10 billion, tops 1983 record year of $6.5 billion (shows Ford's all-time high of $2.9 billion and GM's record of $4.5 billion)...

Robert Walsh opens Barwash, Yuppie laundromat-delicatessan-cafe, for singles, TX... Manhattan Eyeland opens, NYC, as fashionable eyewear department store... Steve Young, Brigham Young quarterback, signs contract, $40 million for 43 years, with Los Angeles Express of new United States Football League, moves to NFL Tampa Bay franchise in 1985 (joins megabucks club of "Magic" Johnson of LA Lakers with contract of $25 million for 25 years, Dave Winfield of NY Yankees with contract of $21 million for 10 years and Wayne Gretzky of Edmonton's hockey club with contract of $21 million for 21 years)... U.S. Steel acquires National Steel, U.S.' 7th largest...

Attorney Michael Hollis with backing of Equitable Life Assurance starts Air Atlanta, first U.S. minority-owned carrier, to provide customers with two-class luxury service (after $55 million in losses, shows signs of recovery in 1987)... Despite previous failure of Postal Service to transmit computer printouts, Federal Express starts Zap-Mail electronic mail system to transfer duplicated documents door-to-door in 2 hours (abandons project in 1986 after losing nearly $350 million)... Business Week: "Publishers Go Electronic"... IBM, Merrill Lynch start pioneering joint venture to create electronic network of work stations for brokers, followed by E.F. Hutton, Shearson Lehman, and Prudential-Bache...

GibaBit Logic, Harris Microwave Semiconductor introduce first logic circuits of gallium arsenide (launch new era of electronic technology to improve silicon conductors)... Holiday Inns start limited-service Hampton

Inn chain to compete with no-frills, budget motels... New York fashion house of Ann Klein, owned by Japanese textile firm Takihyo, introduces line of apparel for Yuppie class of women managers, non-working women who emulate them... A.C. Nielsen tests new device to monitor television viewing and produce instant demographic data, followed in 1985 by British-based AGB Television Research and Arbitron... Appanoose County Community Railroad, owned by local citizens, operates first train out of Centerville, IA, when rural area is isolated by 1981 bankruptcy of Rock Island line and cancellation of services by Burlington Northern...

During year corporations sell some 900 divisions and subsidiaries, up 40% in 4 years... After chance meeting on Sun Valley ski slopes, Roger L. Miller, economics professor at University of Miami, raises $5 million to start CompuSave business with kiosks in stores, malls as portable catalog showrooms to sell hardgoods at discount prices, appear in Cleveland's Shop-n-Shop supermarkets in 1985... Two visionaries start Vend-A-Bait business, IA, franchises in 9 states by 1985... Matchmaker Breeders' Exchange, KY, is started to sponsor electronic trading in breeding rights (holds public auction of shares in 1985)... McGraw-Hill publishing business restructures to focus on electronic marketing of information to 11 groups of customers...

New York's 47 St. Photo, business of 4 stores and mail-order operation, sells some $100 million worth of cameras, personal computers and other products, leader in gray market of discount retailers by buying from foreign market instead of U.S. authorized distributors... Buffums, Southern California department store chain, starts credit card program for children under 18, issues over 1,400 cards in first 3 months... Chicago Mercantile Exchange, Singapore's futures exchange are linked by computer to provide international trading... Cosmetic-maker Elizabeth Arden installs electronic makeup systems in stores in 15 cities to assist customers with views of different treatments... McTravel, IL, first U.S. discount air-travel agency, advertises (sues American Airlines for banning promotions of discount tickets)...

National Football League forms long-range planning committee (reports 28 teams could lose total of $94 million in 1986, an average of $3.3 million/team)... Zale jewelry-store chain opens employee-child care center at headquarters, TX, joins those of some 1,000 firms - about 500 in 1982 (follows first in-house day care by hospitals)... Time: "Sad Tales of Silicon Valley" (reports growth problems of competitive high-tech industry)... Because of discrimination case Prudential Insurance, Department of Labor agree firm will spend some $3 million to train rejected minority applicants (is required to hire at least 600)...

Clifford Wolfswinkel, Phoenix real estate investor and developer, buys farm land, IA (acquires some 7,000 prime acres by 1986 in gambling prices hit bottom)... Mission Insurance Group, chief provider of liability coverage for day-care centers, quits market... Travelers Corp., insurance underwriter, starts program to eliminate paperwork by linking some 30,000 employees, 10,000 independent agents in communications network (by 1986 operates with 35,000 terminals and personal computers connected to 18 mainframe computers, eliminates some 32 railroad boxcars of paper)... On August 3 NY Stock Exchange trades record high of 236.8 million shares... Caterpillar Tractor, IL, acquires 20% interest in Advanced Robotics, maker of arc-welding robots, to improve productive efficiency... Business Week: "Why the Big Apple Shines in the World Market" (reports Wall Street with 55% of world's total equities market, provides over $2.8 billion for foreign firms in 1983)... GE plans to close plant in Charleston, SC (leads to union proposal with alternative products to keep plant running)... Fortune: "New Ways to Teach Workers What's New" (reports development of computer interactive instructional systems to train employees)... Sears plans video network to link 26 cities by 1985 in largest private teleconferencing system... Hewlett-Packard electronic business changes from engineering firm to focus on markets instead of products...

William S. Anderson, chairman of NCR, is highest paid executive with salary over $13 million... To prevent takeover, Warner Communications pays Australian-born publisher Rupert Murdoch $180.6 million in greenmail, 35% above market price... Sears, Roebuck: Catalog of the Future (shows traditional items, contemporary fashions, lifestyle-oriented merchandise)... After managing successful Summer Olympics in Los Angeles, Peter Ueberoth becomes baseball commissioner (institutes marketing program with national sponsorships for advertisers to promote game of baseball, requiring most to spend at least $5 million on licensing fees, promotional efforts, and necessary charitable contributions)... GE introduces HomeMinder computer to operate household electrical system...

Harold Geneen: Managing (in describing experiences in developing ITT as conglomerate in 1960s-1970s, debunks management concepts)... After being ousted from Commodore International business he developed, Jack Tramiel, sons acquire financially-troubled Atari from Warner Communications for $240 million in notes (completes payment in 1986 after dismantling company, introducing new computers)... Business Week: "The New Breed of Strategic Planners" (reports use of line managers instead of staff experts in planning)... To settle thousands of Agent Orange lawsuits by Viet Nam veterans, 7 chemical companies propose fund of $180 million (is tied up in court to 1986)... "Skunk Works," research division of Lockheed, unveils design for space plane to cruise at 8,000 mph (leads to contracts by Pentagon, NASA for engineering designs in 1986)...

William H. Brine of Milford, MA, 1 of 2 U.S. makers of Lacrosse equipment, receives notice that insurance premium of $8,000/year for product-liability insurance of $25 million will be $200,000 for coverage of $1 million... Sears starts Mature Outlook club for those over 50 (attracts some 400,000 dues-paying members by 1986)... American Association of Advertising Agencies reports 8 mergers in industry during year, 19 in 1985 and 11 in first 4 months of 1986... Business Week: "The Revival of Productivity"... After training flight crews for other airlines, United Airlines forms new subsidiary to develop training programs for U.S. Air Force (acquires Hertz rental car business in 1985 and Hilton International Hotels in 1986, after 2-year, $2.3 billion acquisition spree changes name to Allegis in 1987, to fight corporate raiders ousts chief executive, sells 61 Westin hotels, bought 1970 for $52 million, for $1.35 billion, 1918 Hertz for $1.3 billion, and 92 Hilton hotels for $1.07 billion in 1987 to focus on United Airlines, U.S.' largest with 17% market share, signs marketing agreement with Britain's Caledonian airline in 1987)...

3M plans 10-year program of space experiments on 72 shuttle flights...

Time: "America's Banks: Awash in Trouble"... Florida's citrus industry of $2.5 billion is devastated by citrus canker (loses part of market to Brazil)... IBM acquires Rolm, leading maker of telephone switching equipment, for $1.25 billion (forms joint venture with Germany's Siemens in 1988 to compete in worldwide office switchboard market)... 53 of 200 largest pension funds use stock indexing to make investments, 77 in 1985... Intermark Realty opens, Houston, as clearing house for foreclosed properties with 34 listings, some 1,000 in 1986 with slump in oil prices... Japan's Suntory International acquires Chateau St. Gean Winery, CA, followed by 7 more corporate acquisitions of vineyards in 1987...

Construction is finished on Long Island Lighting's Shoreham nuclear power plant costing $5.3 billion (unable to get operating license for environmental reasons sells facility in 1988 to NY for $1 - dismantled)... Jack A. MacAllister becomes head of U.S. West, AT&T's spinoff in 1983 (transforms Baby Bell into Betawest Properties from Virginia to Hawaii, U.S. West New Vector cellular phone business, Landmark Publishing for yellow page directories, U.S. West Financial Services, and U.S. West Information Systems to market voice and data equipment and services - a 1988 $7.3 billion company)... P&G sues Frito-Lay, Keebler & Nabisco individually for trying to steal patented recipe for soft-chewy cookies...

LTV, created by James Ling, with Jones & Laughlin Steel acquires Republic Steel to become No. 2 in U.S. steel industry and major defense contractor (declares bankruptcy in 1986, with revenues of $8.2 billion is largest failure in U.S. corporate history)... Promoter Howard Schwartz puts on first National Aerobics Championship, nearly 2,500 participants in 1988... Basketball player Michael Jordan signs 7-year contract with Chicago Bulls for $6.2 million, topped by Patrick Ewing's 10-year contract for $30 million in 1985 to become highest paid player in professional sports (signs new 8-year contract in 1988 for reputed $28 million with incentives)...

After operating boiler shops to sell with high pressure Matt Valentine starts Intech in Newport Beach, CA, to sell precious metals by telemarketing (-1987, after losses of $2 million and living extravagantly pleads guilty to mail fraud in 1988)... Fleeing Hungary in 1969 with only $5 and copy of college degree, Maria Ligeti founds Qronos, CA, to develop software system to help manufacturing firms keep track of production and worldwide trends in supply and demand, by 1988 serves 7 major firms... University of Texas drop-out Michael S. Dell, age 19, starts Dell Computer to make clones of IBM's Personal Computer (with sales of $159 million in 1987 goes public in 1988 and fights management problems)... In Oakland, CA, Susan Hemphill starts Alice in Wholesale Land as discounter of children's fashions, by 1988 with 2,500 distributors in 50 states and mail-order business...

Bookkeeper Janet Wells, daughter take over failing Sisterville Tank Works, WV, sales of $3.5 million in 1987... U.S. banks renegotiate terms of $8.6 billion in loans to Argentina to avoid financial crisis... Howard Schultz visits Milan and its many coffee bars (opens 3 expresso joints in Seattle in 1985 - by 1988 with 15 retail stores and 10 bars serving 60,000 customers/week)... William W. Nicholson joins Amway, founded 1955 to distribute home and personal care products via independent distributors, as coordinator of policy and planning (guides Amway into more sophisticated products and services, fails in $2 billion takeover of Avon Products in 1989)... ServiceMaster, Chicago-based cleaning business for mostly hospitals, is No. 1 on Fortune's list of service firms, No. 1 in 1989 for decade return on equity of 63.7%... After transforming Tattler, London-bred Tina Brown takes over Newhouse's Vanity Fair ups circulation from 220,538 to high of 692,537 by 1989 in capturing conflicting trends of '80s... Robert Crandall, CEO of American Airlines in 1980, leads industry in replacement of aging aircraft, takes delivery of one new jet/5 days in 1989 to become second in size, over 500 planes, to Aeroflot (acquires AirCal for $225 million in 1987, runs U.S.' No. 1 in passenger traffic in 1989 to serve 156 airports from Dallas-Ft. Worth with 119 foreign trips/day, one in 1983)...

AEA Investors, created in 1963 as wealthy investment club with many retired corporate leaders to operate with no raids, no junk bonds and no break-ups, acquires Birmingham Steel after flopping in 1973 with Leisure Group, $100,000 share in 1973 worth $26.3 million in 1989... Over pizza Robert B. Haas, Thomal O. Hicks start leveraged buyout firm, Dallas, to do $1 billion in deals in 10 years, pass $4 billion mark by 1989 before parting after clash in styles...

Steven Spielberg directs movie "Indiana Jones and the Temple of Doom," by 1989, age 41 with regular staff of 30, produces or directs 5 of Hollywood's 10 top box-office hits for total gate of $1.256 billion... ClubCorp, started in Dallas by Robert H. Dedman in 1957 with Brookhaven Country Club, acquires legendary Pinehurst Hotel & Country Club, NC (acquires majority interest in Silband Sports, U.S.' second largest operator of public courses with 32, in 1986, acquires troubled Texas thrift with some prize golf courses in 1987, runs 200 private golf clubs, world's largest manager, by 1989 with 18,000 employees, 400,000 club members and revenues of some $750 million...

Martin Davis, CEO of Gulf & Western in 1983 to spin off some 100 subsidiaries, makes FORTUNE annual list of toughest bosses (pays stockholders 240% return on investment from 1983-88, after Time Inc. and Warner Communications seek merger in 1989 fails in $12 billion takeover of Time)... Quarterdeck Office Systems, WA, launches software startup with $14,000 (patents technology for Desqview program in 1989, forces other software makers copying technology to pay millions in royalties)... After opening Southwest Marine as ship-repair facility in Chula Vista, CA, with brother and $100,000 in savings in 1976 and acquiring yards in San Francisco in 1979 and Los Angeles in 1981, Art Engel opens shipyard in America Samoa (although 47 yards were closed on Pacific Coast since 1980, acquires facilities in Portland in 1989 to become area's major shipyard operator)...

South Korea's Daewoo is indicted by Portland grand jury, OR, for dumping steel (after pleading guilty in 1985 to charges of making false, fraudulent statements to Customs Service, is target of civil investigation by Customs Service, $34 million judgment largest ever, in 1989)... Bronx Zoo, pioneered natural habitats for animals in 1941, opens Jungle World with appropriate sounds, some 120 million visit 143 accredited zoos in 1989...

WestAir, $14 million local airline based in Fresno, CA, forms partnership with United Airlines, sales of $185 million in 1989 as largest feeder line... After selling namesake fashion house, stays as designer to add perfume line and 30 licenses, to Norton Simon business, Max Factor cosmetics, Avis rental, and Hunt-Wesson Foods, in 1973, Halston, first in fashion to become celebrity, is removed from business by Esmark, acquired Simon in 1983 (seeks use of own name in 1989)... Assn. of Volleyball Professionals, some 250 members, strikes during World Championships, CA, to protest conditions (wins control of tournaments, 29 with over $2 million in prize money in 1989 - most from Miller Brewing, concessions, TV contracts and endorsements)... Nike sales of athletic-leisure shoes, sports apparel reaches $920 million, $270 million in 1980 (assigns more production to Chinese factories in 1985 - poor quality, claims 26% of $9 billion market in 1989, Reebok with 22% and L.A. Gear with 13%, decentralizes in 1989 to encouage innovation in 24 footwear categories).

1985

General Events

Florida reports (January 22) 90% of orange and grapefruit crops damaged by freeze, leads to rise in imports from Brazil... EPA reveals (January 23) Union Carbide plant, WV, had 28 toxic leaks in past 5 years... U.S. reports (January 25) record trade deficit of $123.3 billion for 1984... U.S. Navy cancels contract with General Dynamics for "business misconduct"... In State of Union message, President Reagan calls (February 6) for "second American Revolution" of tax revision, economic growth and elimination of threat of nuclear war, "Opportunity for all" is the theme...

When E.S.M. Governmental Securities, Florida dealer in U.S. treasury bills and bonds, declares bankruptcy after losses of some $200 million, Ohio closes (March 15) 71 state-chartered thrifts for 3 days to stop run on deposits, resulted from collapse of State's largest, Home State Savings Bank with 33 branches, in loss of $150 million loan to E.S.M... U.S. bans (May 1) all trade with Nicaragua...

For first time Dow Jones Industrial Average goes (May 20) above 1300 points, over 1400 (November 6) and 1500 (December 11)... U.S. Supreme Court rules (June 27) unions cannot penalize members who quit during strike... New Jersey teenage hackers invade Pentagon computer... Pro baseball players start 2nd strike in 5 years... Pentagon plans to test all new recruits for AIDS... Crack, inexpensive form of cocaine, appears in NYC...

UAW signs contract with Exide, maker of car batteries (swaps cutbacks worth $2/hour for profit-sharing plan)... Physician Task Force on Hunger in America reports up to 20 million in need... General Electric pleads guilty to bilking Air Force out of $800,00... Time: "Snapshot of a Changing America" (reveals medium age of 1983 population as 30.9 - oldest ever, single people 23% of U.S. households, families with single heads up by 69% from 1970 to 1983, 20% are over age of 50, some 100,000 will be 100 years or older by 2000, a majority of people are living in South and West, and drop in 18% of college-aged between 1985 and 1995)... President levies sanctions against South Africa (restricts trade of certain items, bans new loans, sale of nuclear-related technology, and sale of gold krugerrands in U.S., and requires all U.S. firms in South Africa to treat black and white workers equally)... Bureau of Labor Statistics reports

2.1 million women, 40% of all working women, holding two jobs or more, 3.8% in 1980 and 2.2% in 1970... Bell Labs announces new superchip capable of storing one million bits of data, 4 times the capacity of the most powerful computer memory chip available (plans production within a year)... Maryland Governor H.R. Hughes limits depositors of 102 privately insured savings and loan institutions to withdrawals of $1,000/month to stem run on deposits started by rumors of fraud... In pioneering action Merit System Protection Board rules Defense Department must fire auditor, two subordinates for retaliating against Pentagon whistleblower...

San Francisco ordinance requires developers of major projects to provide space for day-care centers... Employee sues Commonwealth Edison of Chicago for 6-month unpaid paternity leave... Canadian Lynn Williams is president of United Steel Workers... Congress passes Gramm-Rudman bill, forces reductions in budget deficits to zero in 1991... U.S. Navy, in major policy shift, reserves 40% of future admiral slots for officers specializing in weapons procurement or management... Farm Credit System posts record loss of $2.69 billion on agricultural loans, largest deficit in banking history... Parents Music Resource Center pressures 22 major record firms to put warning labels on sexually explicit records... Duquesne University adopts pioneering prepaid college tuition plan...

Defense Department launches University Research Initiative with $100 million to fund over 80 projects at 70 universities... NASA plans to launch Industrial Space Facility into space in 1989, designed as automated petrolchemical plant... Maryland's highest court rules that makers, sellers of small handguns, Saturday Night Specials, could be liable for injuries inflicted by guns... Al Ries, Jack Trout: <u>Marketing Warfare</u> (describes true nature of marketing as not satisfying human wants but attacking competitors)... <u>Business Week</u>: "Turning an Expert's Skill into Computer Software" (discusses role of "knowledge engineers" to devise expert programs that mimic abilities of skilled professionals)...

University of Michigan forms Industrial Technology Institute to do "research and development for the factory of the future"... <u>Fortune</u>: "Who Needs a Trend-Spotter?" (questions value of business seers predicting trends)... AFL-CIO recommends new cooperative approaches with employers, union mergers to improve clout, new mechanisms to avoid inter-union conflict, new forms of collective bargaining to avoid traditional "adversarial" role, and increasing use of electronic media... <u>Business Week</u>: "Economists Are This Year's Endangered Species"... From 1980 Japanese investment in U.S. nearly triples, operates some 500 manufacturing firms in U.S...

<u>Newsweek</u>: "Water, Water Everywhere" (reports decline of U.S. alcohol consumption)... Los Angeles, largest U.S. city to do so, adopts comparable worth for its municipal pay scale... Martin Weitzman: <u>The Share Economy</u> (urges profit sharing as means for prosperity)... Former Deputy Secretary of Defense Paul Thayer, two associates are required to pay $1 million to settle SEC suit, provided stock tips that resulted in $1.9 million in illegal profits for group of friends... Federal regulators close Beverly Hills Savings & Loan Assn., received no warning from 3 CPA firms used within 90 days before collapse...

Baseball Commissioner Peter Ueberroth requires all officials and employees, not players, to be tested for use of cocaine... Foreigners own some $1 trillion of U.S. assets... U.S., Israel sign trade agreement, U.S.' first, to remove all duties, barriers to commerce by 1995... Wisconsin grants teaching assistants, affiliated with American Federation of Teachers, right to collective bargaining, occurs at University of Michigan and University of Massachusetts at Amherst in 1989... U.S. Supreme Court rules local banks can form regional networks to compete with big banks... New York's Supreme Court rules a person cannot be denied a job simply for obesity...

Promoter Edward A. Markowitz pleads guilty for fraudulent tax shelter scheme that provided $445 million in false income tax deductions to wealthy investors... N.J. Piore, C.F. Sabel: The Second Industrial Divide (describes gradual replacement of mass production by "flexible specialization" of small-scale "craft" output, urges government planning to manage economic changes)... United Steel Workers sign contracts with Bethlehem Steel division, Kaiser Aluminum & Chemical (takes cuts of some 20% in wages and benefits for profit-sharing, stock ownership)... Civil Rights Commission rejects concept of comparable worth, equal pay for different jobs similar in value...

Maryland allows NYC's Citicorp Bank to open branches in State... Business Week: "Part-time Workers: Rising Numbers, Rising Discord"... Since 1981 some 20,000 farms were sold at auctions... New York allows insurance firm to increase its malpractice-policy rates for doctors by 52%... Some 170 Iowa farmers join International Brotherhood of Teamsters... For first time since 1914, owed $3.7 billion more to foreigners than they to us, U.S. is net debtor nation in owing $100 billion... Letitia Baldrige's Complete Guide to Executive Manners provides business leaders with proper etiquette...

Environmental Protection Agency approves "ice-minus" experiment of Advanced Sciences to genetically engineer bacteria to save California's strawberry crop from frost damage... Senator Jesse Helms, others start Fairness in Media as "national crusade" to buy CBS stock to control network... New York Public Library, opened 1911, is fully computerized, world's most heavily used... Fortune: "The New Case for Protectionism" (advocates shielding high-tech industries for special role in research, development)... George Washington University decides to sell or lease its medical school's hospital to a for-profit corporation... Census Bureau reports one of every 15 works for Government, some 15.8 million in all...

U.S. Court of Appeals rules banks cannot use nonbank operations to collect deposits across state lines... Fortune: "When Public Services Go Private" (shows trend since W.W. II in cities using contractors for government services)... Andrew Grove starts advice column for workers in San Jose's Mercury News... MIT starts Media Lab to explore what computers could be doing 10-20 years in the future... Newsweek: "The Monetarists on the Run" (describes decline and fall of such economists from 1979 decision by Federal Reserves to adopt monetarism as its official policy)... Despite opposition of friends and U.S. Patent Office, David Sterner, former imitator of Elvis Presley and ex-bouncer, patents new camera lens to take pictures without film...

Aspen, CO, passes first city law to prohibit smoking in most dining rooms, total ban by Beverly Hills, CA, in 1987 for restaurants and retail stores... Brookings Institution reports U.S. personal saving rate drops

from 9% in mid-1970s to 5.1%, Japan with 15% and West Germany with 13%...
1801 painting of"Reuben Peale with a Geranium," purchased in 1958 for
under $100,000, is sold for $4.07 million, highest price for U.S. work of
art at auction... Montana is first state to pass "unisex" insurance...
Xavier Suarez is Miami's first Cuban-born Mayor... For failing to report
large-scale cash transaction Crocker National Bank, U.S.' 12th largest,
is fined $2.25 million for violating 1980 Bank Secrecy Act... Federal
judge sentences former _Wall_ _Street_ _Journal_ reporter R.F. Winans to 18
months in jail and $5,000 fine for leaking information to stock-trading
ring on impending articles...

Calfornia is first State to require able-bodied welfare recipients to
seek jobs or training to get financial aid, adopted by over 20 states by
1986... U.S., Japan agree to high level talks on opening Japanese markets
to U.S. products... U.S. Supreme Court rules minimum wage and hour
standards covers employees of publicly-owned mass transit, enhances U.S.
regulation of state activties... President Reagan ends curb on imports of
Japanese cars, continued voluntarily... After month-long strike Pan
American World Airways signs three-year contract with transport workers
union, viewed as major defeat by union leaders (creates two-tier salary
schedule for new and old workers, followed by United Air Lines after
brief strike)...

Movie star Rock Hudson dies of AIDS... Former Teamsters' head Roy L.
Williams is sentenced to 55 years for conspiring to bribe a U.S.
Senator... U.S. Supreme Court rules an attorney may use truthful
advertising... After plant closure of Sprague Technologies in 1983,
City's largest employer, North Adams plans economic revival with
development of Massachusetts Museum of Contemporary Art and
Architecture... _Business_ _Week_: "Leaving South Africa" (covers
disinvestments of 18 U.S. corporations of some 300 in country)... Wall
Street's E.F. Hutton, 6,500 brokers, pleads guilty to 2,000 counts of
fraud for operating check-kiting scheme to use up to $1 billion from 400
banks without paying interest, fined $2.7 million (is acquired by
Shearson Lehman in 1987-88)...

Delaware Supreme Court rules former directors of Trans Union Corp. are
financially liable for selling firm too quickly in 1980, followed by
State's 1986 law to exempt directors from financial liability to live up
to "the duty of due care"... UAW, GM sign labor contract for new Saturn
venture (provides for organizational structure of company-union consensus
decision-making)... Despite opposition of parent United Food and
Commercial Workers Union, some 1,400 meatpackers of Local P-9 refuse to
grant contract concessions on wages, benefits to Hormel Packing and start
strike (-1986, results in use of National Guard to quell violence, in
employment of non-union workers to reopen plant, and in rejection by
local of order from national union to end the strike)... California law
gives a celebrity's heirs exclusive licensing rights for 50 years after
star's demise, adopted by 11 more states by 1989.

Business Events

To thwart takeover bid by Turner, CBS goes into debt to buy back 21% of
its own stock for nearly $1 billion... In pioneering action Anheuser-
Busch sues insider traders for forcing up price of 1982 acquisition...
Capital Cities Communications buys ABC, 214 affiliated stations, for $3.5

billion... After extensive research Coca-Cola scraps (April 23) 99-year-old recipe for world's best selling soft drink for new, sweeter cola (after protests by irate customers, brings back, July 10, "Classic Coke")... Montgomery Ward, 319 retail stores and 1,270 independent catalog outlets, closes its 1872 mail-order business.. AT&T lays-off some 24,000 workers, largest in its history... After settling some 9,230 cases for $378.3 million, A.H. Robins Company, still plagued by some 5,100 cases on claims over Dalkon Shield, files bankruptcy (gets approval by federal court in 1989 for reorganization with $2.5 billion reserved for claims)... After bidding war with Ford Motor Co. and Boeing, GM acquires Hughes Aircraft for some $5 billion, its largest acquisition to prepare itself for 21st Century...

Mike Schmidt of Philadelphia is top-paid baseball player, 36 other millionaires, with $2.1 million contract... Eli Ginzberg, George Vojta: Beyond Human Scale: A Large Corporation At Risk... After struggling with 43 different ads throughout the world, Playtex starts global advertising campaign... Business Week: "Mighty Nomura Tries to Muscle in On Wall Street" (reports efforts of world's largest brokerage house, some $3 billion in equity, to enter U.S. security market despite opposition of NYC dealers)... Report shows TV ratings for NFL are down from all-time high in 1981, drops 13% at NBC, 19% at CBS and 24% at ABC... Record 8,674 private pension plans are canceled, double amount in 1980 (with failure of thrifts face regulations in 1990s to protect members)...

Chrysler, last of Big Three, forms joint venture with Misubishi Motors to make small cars... Puma introduces computer running shoe, shows time, calories and distance, to U.S. market... RCA, Japan's Sharp form $200 million joint venture to make computer chips in U.S... Business Week: "The Koreans Are Coming" (describes invasion of U.S. car market by Hyundai's Excel as vanguard of Samsung, Lucky-Goldstar and Daewoo to emulate West Germany's attack in 1950s with Volkswagen and Japan's attack in 1970s with Toyota)... Weston Financial Group, general partner, and 30 investors, limited partners, form syndicate to own, rent 10 houses, MA...

To reduce its bureaucracy DuPont launches one-shot Early Retirement Opportunity for its employees (leads to retirement of some 11,500 workers, emulated by Caterpillar Tractor)... Fortune: "Smart-Power Chips Are the Latest Turn-On" (reports on high-voltage chip by James Plummer, Stanford professor of electrical engineering, to operate household products, electronic gadgets for cars)... Nabisco Brands, R.J. Reynolds Industries form largest U.S.-based consumer products company in $4.9 billion merger, total sales of $19 billion to Procter & Gamble's $12.9 billion... Business Week: "The Sharks Keep Circling Phillips" (reports attempts of raiders T. Boone Pickens, Jr., profits by some $80 million from greenmail, Irwin L. Jacobs, started career in 1950s gathering burlap bags from farmers for cleaning and reselling, Wall Street financier Carl Icahn, and arbitraguer Ivan Boesky to acquire control)...

Fortune: "America's Most Admired Corporation" (lists in order IBM, Coca-Cola, Dow Jones, 3M, Hewlett-Packard, Anheuser-Busch, Boeing, General Electric, Eastman Kodak, and Merck)... After over 6 years in negotiations, McDonnell Douglas signs one-billion-dollar, 12-year contract to build commercial jetliners at state-owned Shanghai Aviation Industrial Corp... E.F. Hutton brokerage offers customers a terminal that can be plugged into a television set to provide up-to-the-minute stock information... <u>Business</u> <u>Week</u>: "The Raiders: They Are Really Breaking the Vise of the Managing Class" (attacks raids on undervalued corporations by acquiring stock or threatening to do so to force managers to defend themselves instead of stockholders and to focus on short-term results instead of growth)... 549,000 barrels of nonalcoholic beer are sold, an increase of 25% while total market of 183 million barrels only rises .3%... Small Luxury Hotels is a nationwide association for cooperative marketing, advertising of their personalized services...

Japan's Sharp introduces Half-Pint microwave oven to U.S. market, sells some 250,000 in 7 months to only 50,000 of its full-size units... "Pretty Boy" Larry Sharpe, ex-champ Buddy Rodgers open Monster Factory, NJ, to train heroes, villains for wrestling craze... Over 3,380 mergers of $1 million or more occur in U.S... 26,200 shopping centers handle 42% of U.S.' retail sales... Videologue Marketing, NYC, offers pioneering multiproduct video catalog, 100,000 subscribers by 1989... Corporate Interviewing Network of Ft. Lauderdale enables clients, some 150 major corporations, to screen job applicants with videotape interviews...

First Skytel opens at Los Angeles International Airport to provide accomodations to travelers on short layovers... CEL Communications: "The Video Encyclopedia of the 20th Century"... Following trend of cosmetic marketers, introduced by Estee Lauder in 1970s, with "purchase-with-purchase," Dayton Hudson Department Stores sells plush teddy bears at discount to customers buying other merchandise, emulated in 1986 by other retailers... Ford tests "interactive" video to train its far-flung auto mechanics...

Franchise chain of Kidpix Theaters is started to offer continuous films for children while parents enjoy shopping malls... Computerized machines dispense discount coupons in many grocery stores in major cities... American Casualty Excess Insurance is created by 34 major U.S. firms, such as IBM and GE, to provide high-risk protection to shareholders, other firms that big casualty insurers are unwilling to handle... Regional merger of two banking holding companies, Sun Banks of Florida and Trust Company of Georgia, is first to cross state line... Marc Rousso's Miami-based International Stamp Exchange lets stamp collectors worldwide trade via telex, also handles trading by personal computers...

<u>Newsweek</u>: "Insurance: Now It's A Risky Business"... John Nielsen: "Management Layoffs Won't Quit," <u>Fortune</u> (reports reductions of middle management by such large firms as Union Carbide, DuPont, AT&T, Ford)... Burger King plans fleet of 20 customized vans in 1986 to serve customers at office buildings, arenas, military bases, etc... First meeting of Electronic Networking Assn. is held by members of electronic information services, i.e., CompuServe with some 240,000 subscribers and Source with about 60,000... DuPont, Philips of Holland form joint venture in optical disks, becomes world's largest supplier... <u>Time</u>: "Buddy System in the Sky" (reports feeder relationships of 25 top regional airlines with major carriers)...

Security Pacific National Bank, Los Angeles, forms subsidiary to provide customers with quantitative reports by Bank's mathematicians... With drop in sales as industry goes from 17,800 planes in 1978 to 1984 low of 2,400, Cessna Aircraft opens Hangar 10 in Dallas Mall as first aviation department store... Baldwin-United, $3.6 billion conglomerate, files for bankruptcy with $9 billion in liabilities (after selling $1.4 billion in assets restructures in 1985 as $400-million-a-year firm with essentially S&H trading stamp business, several small insurance firms)... Cosmetic maker Germaine Monteil starts "40 is Fabulous" ad campaign... Newsweek: "The Advertising Game Tilts Toward the West" (shows rise of California agencies)... Utica National Insurance Group cancels liability policies for 229 local governments (such cancellations by other insurance firms leads to communities forming group insurance plans, i.e., Colorado Intergovernmental Risk Sharing as consortium of 37 cities)...

Fortune: "Merchant's Woe: Too Many Stores"... Annual convention of Society for Commercial Earth Stations attracts some 14,000 participants, 700 exhibits (shows growth of industry with sales of some 60,000 satellite-dish antennas/month)... Yugoslavia exports first Yugo cars, $3,990, to U.S., bankruptcy by 1989... Marketing Science Institute: "Future Trends in Retailing" (predicts stores will have low productivity in 1990s with unused space)... Wall Street's Shearson Lehman sponsors Old Westbury Gardens Invitational Polo Cup, some 200 firms spend $6.5 million on promoting polo events...

United States Basketball League opens with 8 teams to play in spring, summer (plans to add 15 franchises in 1986, only three profitable in 1987 on budgets of $600,000)... Fortune: "Sears, Roebuck's Financially Struggling Empire"... Bloomingdale's chic fashion catalog carries ads...

HBO is first cable channel to use coded signals, forces satellite-dish owners to buy descrambling device... San Francisco-based Pacific Telesis, regional Bell holding company, buys Communications Industries, maker of radio pagers and car phones, for $431 million, most expensive of Baby Bell acquisitions since formed in 1984... Fortune: "Lawyers for Companies in Deep Trouble" (shows rise of new specialists)... Wheeling-Pitsburgh Steel declares bankruptcy, authorized by judge to annul its existing labor pact and set its own wages (is rejected by strike of United Steel Workers to ensure role in possible reorganization)...

Metropolitan Life acquires Century 21 real estate business, followed in 1987 by Prudential Insurance with plans to develop nationwide network of over 1,000 franchised real estate offices... Some 36,000 Canadian cars are sold to U.S. tourists, leads to 1986 actions by Ford and GM to halt gray market... Citicorp reorganization creates investment bank, 2nd largest on Wall Street in 1986 after Salomon Bros... Navistar International, formerly International Harvester, sells original farm-equipment business to Tenneco...

IBM acquires major interest in MCI Communications, long-distance phone business, to strengthen its position in competing with AT&T... After selling milk-based kits to buyers to grow bacteria for sale to cosmetic-makers or sell kits to new dealers, Culture Farms declares bankruptcy, KS, with 27,000 creditors nationwide (is indicted by several states for operating illegal pyramid scheme)... All-day home shopping cable channel of Home Shopping Network goes nationwide (lets customers buy merchandise by phone for delivery by UPS)... West Germany's Klockner-Humboldt-Deutz buys farm equipment unit of Allis-Chalmers (after Ford acquires Sperry's farm business in 1986, leaves Deere as only independent major farm-equipment maker)... General Mills puts up apparel-maker Izod, Parker Bros. toys and Kenner dolls for sale to reinvest in food businesses...

After enduring 274 strikes in 1984, twice 1981 record, and intense politically motivated labor agitation to protest "U.S.-Marcos dictatorship," U.S. Travenol leaves Philippines... Newsweek: "Computers Makes the Sale" (shows use by retailers to help customers make selections, i.e., women shoppers at L.S. Ayres, Indianapolis, can see 10 different outfits on them before acutally wearing them, sales up 700% in one week)... Sam's Town casino, Las Vegas, opens drive-in window for betting on sports... Tandy, electronics retailer with 6,800 U.S. outlets, acquires Tennessee discount chain to revitalize its business in low-price retailing...

U.S.' Clark Equipment, Sweden's Volvo form joint venture to make construction equipment in Holland... New York's Chase Manhattan does not roll over bank loans to South Africa, followed by other U.S. banks (leads to drop in rand's value)... Four independent bottlers, NC, sue local bottlers of Pepsi Cola, Coca-Cola for anti-trust violations with calendar marketing agreements to pay retailers for special promotions, displays and days (settle with Pepsi and win against Coca-Cola, more suits in 1987)... Dow Jones, publisher of The Wall Street Journal and Barron's, acquires Telerate, operator of electronic system to deliver price quotes on government securities (follows links of AT&T and Questron, Merrill Lynch and IBM, Reuters and Instinet, McGraw-Hill and Monchik-Weber)...

Polaroid wins 9-year battle against Eastman Kodak over patents on instant camera, forces Kodak out of market and to pay damages up to $10 billion... After lucrative raids on Cities Service, General American Oil, Gulf and Phillips Petroleum, T. Boone Pickens, Mesa Petroleum, fails to take over Unocal, later bids for Newmont Mining, Homestake Mining and KN Energy fizzle (disturbs Japanese financial market in 1989 with hostile 20% purchase of Koito Mfg., auto parts, for some $770 million)... As part of trend, GM scraps cost-of-living adjustments, COLA started 1948, for some 110,000 salaried employees in 1986...

Milwaukee's Allen-Bradley Co. pioneers automated factory in U.S. by designing assembly-line of 50 general-purpose machines, no operators, to produce 143 product variations, GM opens assembly plant in 1986 to operate all equipment by single computerized network to tie together production, inventory and quality control... Philip Morris, sales of $13.8 billion and 68,000 employees, acquires General Foods, sales of $9.02 billion and 56,000 employees, for some $5.63 billion, largest non-oil acquisition... Raider Carl Icahn acquires control of TWA (gets concessions by unions of pilots and machinists to cut costs, breaks 1986 strike of 6,500 flight attendants in refusing pay cuts and longer hours)...

Boston Marathon, first held in 1897, offers hotel rooms, privileges to attract top competitors, shunned as "professional" marathoners compete for money in other races... Larry S. Flax, Richard L. Rosenfeld quit law practice to open California Pizza Kitchen with trendy toppings, 5 outlets by 1989 with sales of $6 million... Yvonne Rubie and husband, 1970 founders of $14 million food-exporting business, start Golden Ribbon Playthings with Huggy Bean Black line of dolls, sell 100,000 by 1986... Colgate introduces pump toothpaste, invented in West Germany... City and state pension-fund managers, 21 with $100 billion in funds, form Council of Institutional Investors to protect their pension funds in corporate takeovers (oppose greenmail and demand voice in mergers, takeovers)...

Backed by Murjani International with $20 million in arrogant advertising to twit leading designers, Tommy Hilfiger starts line of "noveau prep" sportswear, $16 million business in two years (plans 1,000 stores nationwide by 1990)... R.D. Smith leaves Wall Street's Bear Sterns to create first company devoted to trading distressed securities... Bill Stevenson of Kennedy-Wilson brokers pioneers auctions of luxury homes, sell 15.4% over minimum and 52% over original price... World's of Wonder debuts as toy maker in Freemont, CA (chalks up sales with Teddy Ruxpin talking bear)...

In touring Europe to peddle through-the-skin-drug-delivery system, Michael Sdycher of Thermedics, maker of artificial hearts, stumbles on use of skin patches to release perfume... With $30 million from $112 million divorce settlement from TV producer Norman Lear, Frances Lear publishes Lear's, bimonthly magazine for "The Woman Who Wasn't Born Yesterday" (goes monthly with circulation of 350,000 in 1989)... Jim Koch leaves $250,000 job with Boston Consulting Group to start Boston Beer Co., his Samuel Adams label rated best in 1988 beer-tasting competition of U.S. brewers... After operating million-dollar birdseed business in college, Jerry Machado opens first Wellpet food and supply center in Beaverton, OR (runs 50 stores by 1987)...

Seattle waiter borrows $35,000 to launch Pictionary game, sells 350,000 in first year and 3 million in 1988... Brown-Foreman buys California Cooler winery, 6 more by outside interests by 1987... After building empire of over 20 auto franchises from Rolls-Royce to Toyota, Norman Braman gambles $15 million on importing Sterling luxury cars from Britain's Austin Rover Group, gets 1,000 applications for 153 franchises...

Richard J. Ferris, CEO of United Airlines since 1979, buys Hertz Car Rental for $587.5 million (acquires Pan Am's Trans-Pacific routes in 1986 for $750 million, after failing to acquire Frontier Airlines for $146 million adds 88 Hilton International Hotels in 1986 for $975 million, after spending $7.3 million in research renames business Allegis in 1987)... After participating in family's $300 million Belmont Industries conglomerate and building own conglomerate in 1978 with chain of jewelry stores, producer of licorice extract and Pantry Pride grocery chain with aid of Drexel Burnham Lambert's junk-bond whiz Michael Milken, Ronald Perelman, estimated personal wealth of $5 billion in 1989, adds Revlon to group after messy takeover battle (with $900 million in tax breaks by Federal Government takes over 5 ailing Texas thrifts in 1988 for $350 million)...

Donald McCulloch, 3 partners buy Nutri/System, 1,200 centers and sales of $230 million in 1988 to compete with Diet Center, 2,300 stores and sales of $45 million, Jenny Craig, 318 stores and $200 million in sales, and Weight Watchers, sales of $1.3 billion from 24 countries... With concept from its R&D lab General Mills starts Olive Garden as Italian dinner chain, 144 units by 1989 as one of fastest-growing in U.S. with 250 planned for 1994, to complement its Red Lobster chain... Millard Drexler takes charge of The Gap chain of 550 trendy apparel stores, 900, including 14 in Europe and Canada, in 1989 by selling the wearer and not the ware (launches GapKids in 1986, over 70 stores by 1989, and Hemisphere for higher-priced career clothes with 9 shops)... After co-founders Steve Wozniak, quits, and Steve Jobs, forced out, leave Apple

Computer, CEO John Scully revives ailing business by laying-off 1,200 employees and reorganizing on functional lines to eliminate internal conflicts... William Arlt starts Cooperstown Ball Cap Co. to sew old-fashioned headgear for baseball fans, turns out 500 caps in 1988... Biotrol is founded near Minneapolis to grow bacteria to eat up pentachlorophenol, one of many firms by 1989 using bacteria and fungi to clean aquifers, toxic dumps and oil spills... GM designers, to catch up with Chrysler's minivan launched 1983, start sketching new sleek plastic-bodied passenger van, produce final blueprints in 1986 and introduce GM200 in 1989...

Tramwell Crow's real estate development business with 220 partners and 5,000 employees, founded 1948 to build new warehouse and evolve as one of world's most successful by 1989 with $14 billion empire in 100 U.S. markets over 40 states owning or managing 230 million square feet of commercial space, 78,000 residential units and 7,500 hotel rooms, opens world's first information-processing trade mart, design based on London's 1851 Crystal Palace in Dallas (adds $1.4 billion in new construction in 1988 to amass personal fortune of some $750 million)... Murdoch Magazines, Hachette Publications bring out U.S. version of _Elle_, 44-year-old French fashion magazine (captures women's market of mid-20s to put _Vogue_ in 2nd place, 122-year-old _Harper's Bazaar_ into 3rd)...

After providing NYC hotels with cable services in early 1960s, getting cable franchise for lower NYC to create Home Box Office, sold in 1973 to Time Inc., developing Cablevision, and winning cable franchises for Brooklyn, Bronx in 1979 and Boston in 1982, Charles Dolan loses 47.5% of Sacramento franchise after failing to meet financial commitments (in 1989 pays $549 million for some franchises of Viacom and $18 million for regional sport channel for his SportsChannel America to increase debt to $1.3 billion)...

David Hinson is hired to rescue Chicago's floundering Midway Airlines, founded 1978 (cuts flying staff by 10%, scraps first-class-only service and adds more seats to increase passengers 82% by 1986 -first profits since 1982, buys commuter airline Fisher Bros. Aviation to feed passengers into Midway Airport from 19 U.S. cities, expands system 21% in 1988 to serve 8 new cities, in 1989 plans to buy nearly $900 million in new planes and bids $206.5 million for Eastern's Philadelphia gates, landing rights and Canadian routes for coast-to-coast service)... Plastics industry founds Plastics Recycling Foundation to develop new uses for plastics, new methods for reclaiming used products...

Nancy Olsen opens first Imposters store, San Francisco, to sell fake jewelry, 28 stores and sales of $3 million in 1988... Withey, Andrew Martin with partner launch pre-popped popcorn snack food business, Smartfoods with sales of $35,000 in first year (after selling to Frito-Lay in 1989 for $15 million, start new Annie's All Natural Popcorn & Real Wisconsin Cheddar Cheese to take on former firm in popcorn wars)...

William A. Schreyer is new CEO of Merrill Lynch (adopts strategy to use huge retail network to sell new securities developed by investment group, creates Consumer Markets Group and Capital Markets Group to oversee 18 operating divisions, with cost controls cuts payroll from 47,700 in 1987 to 41,000 in 1989 and relocates in New Jersey to save $100 million/year, by 1989 becomes No. 1 underwriter)... Pete Rose breaks Ty Cobb's batting record (arranges for royalties on T shirts, beer mugs, pennants and plastic figurines of himself, is banned from baseball in 1989 for alleged gambling).... Australian press lord Ruport Murdoch is first major foreign investor in Hollywood with buy of 20th Century Fox, major resource for his Fox TV network and overseas stations, for $575 million, followed by Italian financier Giancarlo Parretti's buy of failing Cannon Group in 1987-89 for $200 million, by Britain's Television South's buy of MTM Enterprises for $320 million in 1988 despite bankruptcy of Dino DeLaurentis after losing some $200 milion in two years, and in 1989 by Australia's Qintex Group paying some $600 million for MGM/UA, by Rank Organization's, operator of Britain's Pinewood Studios, buy of MCA's Universal Studios for $150 million, and by investment of Apricot Entertainment, Japan's first, of $50 million to produce 4 films/year)...

After working for Home Box Office, predicted VCR explosion, in late 1970s and starting Vestron in 1981 with video rights for dozens of films, Austin Furst goes public, sales of $195 million in 1986 (unable to match resources of movie studios faces financial troubles in 1989 after spending spree producing losing movies)... Ogden, miniconglomerate with variety of businesses, loses $21.3 million (by restructuring into pure service company, provides maintenance, housekeeping, security, food and parking for office buildings, stadiums, sports arenas and plants, handles fuel and baggage at 90 airports worldwide, operates waste plants, and provides financial services for waste disposal, hits $1.1 billion in sales, profits of some $94.6 million, in 1989)...

After running Grand Union grocery chain for British financier Sir James Goldsmith for 6 years and taking charge of troubled A & P grocery chain in 1980 for West Germany's Tengelmann Group, James Wood expands with Ontario's Dominion Stores for $116 million (builds A & P as profitable chain of 1,250 stores, 1,600 in 1980 and 15,000 in 1930s, by 1989, sales of $10 billion for market share of 34%-24% in 1983, in cutting costs, closing stores, and strategic acquisitions: Kohl's Food Stores in 1983 for $31 million, NYC's Shopwell and Food Emporium stores for $70 million and NYC's Waldbaum chain for $227 million in 1986, and Borman's stores, Detroit, in 1989 for $76 million)...

1986

General Events

For first time in 7 years price of oil is (January) under $20/barrel... U.S. freezes (January 8) assets of Libya to protest its international terrorism... On January 15, "Black Wednesday," Dow Jones Industrial Average drops 39.10 points, previous record of 38.33 on October 28, 1929 (for first time, February 6, goes over 1600 and, March 20, 1800 mark, and shows, September 11, record single-day loss of 86.6 points)... Space shuttle Challenger explodes (January 28) on lift-off, halts space program (leads to investigation for technical, managerial failures in performance)... U.S. dollar hits (March 17) post-war low against Japanese yen... Maine businessman Dodge Morgan sails around the world in record solo voyage of 150 days...

In largest SEC settlement, 8 foreign investors agree to pay $7.8 million for insider trading on 1981 acquisition of Santa Fe International Petroleum by Kuwaiti government... Business Week: "America's Deflation

Belt" (reports failing commodity prices turning heartland into wasteland)... Teamsters President Jackie Presser is accused of racketeering... Federal grand jury charges (May 28) five on Wall Street with insider trading... <u>Newsweek</u>: "The Drug Crisis: Crack and Crime" (reports new wave of cocaine users spawning epidemic of urban lawlessness)... U.S., Bolivia launch joint raids on cocaine labs in Bolivia... U.S. dollar declines (July 1) against major currencies on Europe's markets... Dow Jones Industrial Average shows (July 7) record drop of 61.87... FDA approves (July 23) production of first genetically-altered vaccine... U.S. reports (August 29) record trade deficit of $18 billion... Senate approves most complete tax reform since W.W. II...

Congress bans (October 17) hiring of aliens... <u>Newsweek</u>: "Burgers: The Heat Is On" (reports impact of declining number of teenagers on fast-food industry)... UAW grants wage concessions to Wallace Barnes Steel, CT (requires payment if plant is sold, closed)... U.S. Army adopts no-smoking policy... In first 6 months wholesale rate drops to 6.5%, lowest in nearly 40 years... President's Commission on Defense Management recomends reforms to clarify lines of authority, require more accountability, and improve communications between services... Veteran's Administration tests robot to help disabled... Rhode Island is first state to require residents separate materials for recycling...

Howard M. Wachtel: <u>The Money Mandarins</u> (reports impact on U.S. economy by ungoverned "supernational" economy of Eurodollar markets, multinational firms)... President Reagan restricts NASA launches to primarily scientific, military pay loads... Purdue University's Food Science Department, funded by U.S. Development Corp. of Indianapolis, uses low-frequency sound waves to preserve food... <u>Newsweek</u>: "A Return to the Suburbs" (reports move of over 5.8 million people to suburbs in 1980-84)... Arthur T. Hadley: <u>The Straw Giant</u> (attacks Pentagon for recruiting from limited sections of society, interservice rivalry, flawed organization, division of resources between support or combat troops and new hardware or maintenance, and personnel mismanagement in assigning people, recommends funding of missions rather than separate services and command responsibilities for Joint Chiefs of Staff)...

Carnegie-Mellon University creates Center for Machine Translation... <u>Newsweek</u>: "The Soho Syndrome" (covers urban revitalization from artists renovating dilapidated neighborhoods)... Informal ad hoc, unregulated trading appears in government certificates giving holder right to purchase wheat, corn or other commodities from government surpluses... AFL-CIO forms office to plan anticorporate campaigns to focus public pressure on firm's lenders, directors, and stockholders, used successfully by Amalgamated Clothing & Textile Workers' Union against J.T. Stevens Co. in 1980... <u>Fortune</u>: "The Worsening Air Travel Mess" (reports deterioration of service with rise in number of passengers)...

<u>Newsweek</u>: "Hearts, Mines and Money" (shows trend in efforts of businessmen to help children stay in high school and go to college)... After 3 years of legal battles, frost-fighting genetically-engineered bacteria are tested on crop of potatoes near Tulelake, CA... <u>Newsweek</u>: "Three's A Crowd" (reports rise of childless married couples, highest since depression)... After 2-1/2 years of construction, Statue of Liberty is restored, supervised by Lehrer-McGovern construction-management firm in coordinating 4 different architectural and engineering firms, dozens

of individual contractors and soem 500 craftsmen and workers... Equitable Life Assurance Society opens new $200 million headquarters in NYC, provides space for annex of Whitney Museum which runs 3 branches in other corporate buildings... Commission on Organized Crime reports Teamsters, International Longshoremen's Assn., Hotel Employees and Restaurant Employees International Union, and Laborers' International Union to be influenced and/or controlled by organized crime... Occupational Safty & Health Administration levies largest fine of $1.4 million on Union Carbide for 130 "willful violations" of safety rules... Oxford Analytica: America in Perspective (predicts U.S. headed for trouble with fading American dream)... Time: "Defecting to the West" (covers flight of British scientists and engineers, over 1,000 in 1985, to U.S.)...

International Olympic Committee grants full participation to all professional hockey, soccer players... San Francisco is first City to issue public assistance credit cards to needy... Time: "Is Middle-Class Shrinking?" (shows possible changes in income distribution)... Congress outlaws mandatory retirement age... Newsweek: "Home, Smart Home" (reports development of "intelligence" house operated by computer)... American Eagle is first U.S. gold coin minted since 1933... Fortune: "The Decline & Fall of Business Ethics"...

Members of Teamsters, United Food and Commercial Workers strike to support Jack H. Brown, president of Stater Bros., when suspended in management battle for control of 94-store California supermarket chain... Since 1980 Big Eight of accounting have paid over $180 million in liability lawsuits... Researchers at University of Wisconsin, Phasex Corp. develop process to extract cholestrol from lard, beef tallow, egg yolks and dairy products... Business Week: "Learning to Shine in the Limelight" (covers training of executives to handle the media)... U.S. Supreme Court rules layoffs of white government workers to preserve ratio balance as unconstitutional...

For first time in its 76-year history, each Boy Scout troop, Cub Scout pack must pay $20 fee to help pay for liability insurance... MIT refines holography to project 3-dimensional picture in air... Newsweek: "Targeting the Tiny Tots" (cites trend in advertising to focus on preschoolers)... First location Expo is held, Los Angeles, as meeting of communities, U.S. and foreign, with TV, movie producers, 115 localities attend 1988... Foreign ownership from real estate to securities rises to $1.33 trillion, U.S. holdings abroad total $1.07 trillion (shows Britain with highest investment of $51.4 billion, $14.1 billion in 1980, Holland with $42.9, $19.1 in 1980, Japan with $23.4, $4.7, Canada with $18.3, $12.1, West Germany with $17.4, $7.6, and Switzerland with $12.1, $5.1 in 1980)...

80 wealthy Americans own yachts over 100 feet, 129 by 1987... Richard Rosecrance: The Rise of the Trading State: Commerce and Conquest in the Modern World (argues military spending of U.S., U.S.S.R. leads to increasing economic power of Japan, China with minimal military expenditures)... Single mid-afternoon accident on San Jose freeway creates (October 29) 8-hour gridlock along connecting freeways and surface streets from Los Angeles to San Fernando Valley...

Teamsters local in New Jersey is placed under Federal Trusteeship... Newsweek: "Gators: Snapping Up Profits" (reports Florida's new cash crop of gator-meat)... Etak of Menlo Park devises Navigator to provide high-tech electronic map for cars... Bell Labs, Alan Huang project head, unveils crude optical computer chip, predicts full-fledged optical computer prototype by 1990... Business Week: "Unions Divided: The Revolt of the Rank and File" (shows trend of locals to buck national leaders)... AFL-CIO introduces discount credit card to boost membership in its 92 unions... Delaware law limits monetary liability of directors in certain circumstances... U.S. Air Force starts 3-year, $9.2 million project to adapt sophisticated technology of flexible manufacturing systems with computers for country's 32,000 machine shops...

Washington University of St. Louis forms 10-year partnership agreement with California venture capital firm to spawn start-up companies from biomedical, biotech research at its school of medicine... Joint Economic Committee of Congress reports "super rich," top 50% of 1% of population, hold 35.1% of U.S.' wealth, 25.4% in 1966... Newsweek: "Is Bingo's Number Up?" (cites trend of Catholic bishops to eliminate game to raise church funds)... California voters approve Proposition 51 on tort reform to limit damages of defendants, limits car insurance rates in 1989...

Fortune: "Swaps Can Shrink Debt - A Little" (reports exchange of troubled loans to Third World countries by creditors for ownership in local firms or property)... Newsweek: "Blowing for the Green" (shows rising trend of "vegetarian chic")... U.S. Army uses Diners Club credit card for those traveling on official business... Self-propelled robot with still, video cameras is used to explore sunken Titanic...

Illinois opens its borders to out-of-state banks from contiguous states... For first time 52-year-old First Boston Corp. is disciplined by SEC on charges of "insider trading" when its equity traders used information from its corporate finance group... Newsweek: "Bringing Up Baby In Style" (shows trend in dressing children in high fashion)... Five Columbia drug lords who control 80% of world's cocaine trade are indicted in Miami... Three Mafia "godfathers" and 5 underlings are convicted in NYC for ruling organized crime... Roger Gamblin of Ohio's Dayton Sinker invents paper with smudgeless ink, tested by Forum of Fargo, ND...

Fortune: "AIDS & Business: Problems of Costs and Compassion"... Peter L. Berger: The Capitalist Revolution... Maryland, Minnesota, Utah and Washington pass general liability laws to limit damages... Newsweek: "Back to the Suburbs" (cites growth of office development in suburban areas, 1980 with 46.4% and 53.6% in central business districts to 1985 with 66% and 34% in downtown sites)... Kansas, Missouri, South Dakota and West Virginia pass laws to limit damages in medical malpractice suits...

Time: "Hitting the Road, Seeing the Sights" (covers rise of vacationeers touring U.S., perhaps some 92 million Americans and 24 million foreigners)... Following 12 other colleges University of Colorado opens federally insured student credit union... Newsweek: "You're So Vain" (shows men spending more time, money in primping, preening)... UAW stops trying to organize Honda's 6-year-old plant in Marysville, OH (fails to organize Nissan plant, TN, in 1989)... National Polo League, 6 teams, plays first season in Palm Beach, FL... U.S. Labor Department reports for first time more women hold professional jobs than men, 6,938,000 to 6,250,000... NYC City Council bans discrimination against homosexuals in employment, housing, and public accomodations... Newsweek: "Computer

Communities" (reports classifying consumers by mailing lists of catalogs)... Fuji entry beats blimps of McDonalds, Citibank and Resorts International to win world's first blimp race, NYC... <u>Newsweek</u>: "The Great Texas Oil Bust" (reports recession leaving many Texans broke)... Despite challenges of NYC's Local 28, Steel Metal Workers International, and Cleveland's Local 23, International Association of Firefighters, U.S. Supreme Court upholds Affirmative Action...

U.S. Supreme Court rules even truthful ads for lawful goods and services may be restricted by state for public welfare... <u>Time</u>: "And Now, Time Out For Tapas" (covers restaurant trend of Spanish-style nibbling pioneered by NYC's Ballroom tavern)... Former Merrill-Lynch trainee Edward A. Marks is arrested, Los Angeles, on suspicion of spiking Contac, other over-the-counter capsules with poison to profit in stock market...

Mail-order catalog, <u>Union Label Shopper</u>, is sent to some 100,000 AFL-CIO members... <u>Newsweek</u>: "Too Late for Prince Charming?" (reports single college-educated women at age of 30 may only have 5% chance in getting married)... <u>Fortune</u>: "Marketers Mine for Gold in the Old" (shows trend in rise of mature consumers)... Illinois-based Dairy Research reports carbonation of milk... Image of Christ is seen on side of soybean-oil storage tank at Fostoria, OH (spawns tourist businesses of photographs, coffee mugs, T-shirts, etc.)... Electronic Communications Privacy Act prevents interception of electronic messages...

Luminescent golf ball, Nitelite, is introduced for evening play (increasing use of courses leads to revival of miniature golf facilities, devised 1929 by John Garnet Carter and franchised worldwide by 1954 Putt-Putt)... Justice Department rules employers may legally fire AIDS victims if required to protect other workers... After forcing Nestle in 7-year boycott to restrict its marketing of potential hazardous baby formula in Third World, Boston-based activist group INFACT starts boycott of GE to drive firm out of nuclear-weapons business...

Pennsylvania State University devises low-pressure, low-temperature process to make diamonds... Cornell University develops COSMOS computer program, lets firms simulate manufacturing operations in testing new lines... <u>Jane's Spaceflight Directory</u> reports Soviet Union with 10-year lead over U.S. in practical use of space... After 17-day strike Communications Workers of America, AT&T sign labor contract (provides wage increases, drops cost-of-living adjustment, grants AT&T more freedom in changing job classifications)... U.S. Supreme Court allows national banks to make widespread use of automatic teller machines owned by other firms without violating branch-banking restrictions...

Federal appeals court rules against Wheeling-Pittsburgh Steel in its decision to cut wages under Chapter 11 of bankruptcy law... National Labor Relations Board rules GM can hire UAW members for new Saturn operation, opposed by National Right to Work Committee... U.S. Navy cracksdown on use of smoking... GE introduces battery-powered cellular phones... U.S., Japan sign accord on semiconductors, U.S. chipmakers call for crackdown on Japanese dumping in 1987... Magnavox, Smith-Corona introduce electronic personal writers... FDA approves Schering-Plough's Interferon for treatment of certain cancers...

U.S. hosts 9,144 newspapers, 11,328 periodicals, 9,824 radio stations,

941 commercial TV stations and 300 public TV stations... San Francisco Ballet issues $1.5 million in bonds, first ever offering by performing arts group, to finance Christmas production of "Nutcracker"... Foundation for American Economic Competitiveness is created to spur initiative in world markets, followed by Congressional Economic Leadership Institute...

FDA approves irradiation to preserve pork, fruit and vegetables, follows approval for wheat and potatoes in 1960s and dried spices in early 1980s... General Services Administration proposes almost total smoking ban for its 6,800 buildings... Boston businesses start $6 million program to guarantee financial aid, jobs on graduation to graduates of City's public schools going to college... Discovery by two IBM physicists, J. George Bednorz and K. Alex Muller, in Swiss laboratory starts race for room temperature superconductivity... Appeals court victory allows Patlex Corp., patent licensing firm, to sue infringers of patents by inventor Gordon Gould for laser technology...

Senate Armed Services Committee agrees, over Pentagon objections, to reorganization of Chiefs of Staff formed 1947 (centralizes authority with chairman to replace his mediator role in interservice disputes, creates deputy to chairman to outrank military services in making decisions)... Business Week: "Down On the 'Boutique Farm': Lychee Nuts, Fallow Deer, Carambolas" (cites growth of specialty farms, primarily Northeast, California and Florida, for sophisticated tastes)... Northern Marianas become U.S. Commonwealth... To encourage universities to sponsor industrial-related research, National Science Foundation sets up 18 Engineering Research Centers on campuses...

With cooperation of Switzerland's Bank Lev, SEC charges Dennis B. Levine, merger specialist and managing partner of Wall Street's Drexel Burnham Lambert, in largest insider trading scheme to earn profits over $12.6 million in 5-year period (after agreeing to tell all pleads guilty to 4 felony charges and surrenders $10.6 million in Bahamian bank and $1 million in other assets to await possibility of paying $2 million in back taxes, leads to conviction of 4 other insiders plus Ivan Boesky, fined $100 million and sent to jail to await possibility of lawsuits by irate investors)... Federal grand jury charges Shearson Lehman brokerage, 7 people with laundering $1.2 million for illegal gambling syndicate in 1982-85.

Business Events

Johnson & Johnson discontinues Tylenol capsules as random deaths reappear due to product tampering... TWA cancels 50% of flights as attendants strike over wages... Business Week: "How Textile Makers Are Dressing for Success" (after 6 years of import competition, overcapacity and diving profits, cites revival of industry with market specialization and lower costs)... After family feud, Binghams sells two Kentucky papers to Gannet Co. for $300 million... GM, Honeywell, Warner Communications, IBM, Coca-Cola, General Electric, Procter & Gamble and 4 others pull out of South Africa, only 131 left in 1989 from 326 in 1982... Seat on New York Stock Exchange goes for $490,000...

Royal Caribbean Cruise Lines plans to launch The Sovereign of the Seas, largest cruise ship with capacity for 26,000 passengers - twice size of most others, in 1988... Business Week: "The PC Wars: IBM vs. The

Clones"... After spending some $50 million Knight Ridder closes its videotex subsidiary to provide consumers with information via home computer terminals, copied by <u>Times-Mirror</u> paper after spending about $30 million... American Motors makes its last-production Jeep... Steven Fink: <u>Crises Management: Planning for the Inevitable</u> (reports detailed preparations required for such unexpected developments as product recalls, industrial accidents and terrorist attacks)... <u>Fortune</u>: "Health Care is Good for Madison Avenue"... Sweden's Electrolux, sells Tappan ranges and Eureka vacuum cleaners in U.S., acquires White Consolidated Industry, 3rd largest U.S. appliance company after GE and Whirlpool, for $773 million...

After sales drop from some $400 million to around $50 million, Selchow & Righter, maker of Trivial Pursuits and Scrabble games, accepts $75 million takeover by Coleco, distributor of Cabbage Patch Dolls... Houston-based Compaq, king of IBM-compatibles, introduces year's most innovative, powerful personal computer to challenge IBM... Ogilvy & Mather advertising agency forms special staff to deal exclusively with rise in health care advertising... Worlds of Wonder introduces Lazer Tag, year's biggest toy fad, expects sales of $40 million by 1987 (lets players shoot infrared-light beam to hit sensors on opponents)... U.S. Holiday Corp. signs agreement with China to manage Tibet's 1985 Lhasa Hotel, a 500-room, $30 million complex run by Tibetan Tourism Co...

<u>Business Week</u>: "Japanese Capital Finds A Home in Middle America" (cites rise of Japanese investments in U.S. to some $200 billion in loans and bonds, about $100 billion in loan guarantees and credit)... With falling circulation Hearst Corp. closes Baltimore's 1773 <u>News-American</u>, acquired 1923... General Motors Acceptance Corp., founded 1919, issues Euromarket commercial paper, becomes U.S.' largest issuer of commercial paper...

Annual Boston Marathon accepts its first sponsorship when John Hancock Mutual Life Ins. rescues troubled event by pledging $10 million over 10 years (allows promoters to offer $250,000 in total prizes to attract elite "professional" runners)... <u>Business Week</u>: "The Difference Japanese Management Makes" (cites success of Japanese operations in U.S. with flexible production teams, just-in-time deliveries, quality control, worker responsibility in production, personal sacrifices by Japanese managers with no or few perks, cooperative labor relations, and steady employment)... IBM introduces 12-pound laptop PC Convertible computer, first made entirely by robotic assembly... Sports Palace, world's first computerized handicapping center with racing data and video racing library, opens at Laurel Race Course, MD...

Skokie Federal Savings, IL, offers Super Bowl CD, one-year certificate with interest rate linked to Chicago Bears performance on Super Sunday, copied by other financial institutions with CDs on sports... Only 721 oil rigs operate in Texas, some 4,500 in 1981... <u>Business Week</u>: "A Policy Only An Insurer Could Love" (reports trend of policies covering customer only against claims filed during life of the policy)... Nynex, NY holding company for Bell operations in Northeast, acquires 81 IBM computer retail outlets for $125-$150 million to expand its 19-branch chain, becomes U.S.' 7th largest computer retailer... Pacific Bell launches Project Victoria to test consumer use of computer-based information system...

<u>Business Week</u>: "'On-Line' Systems Sweeps the Computer World" (covers

rise of transactions processing from $6 billion in 1980 to some $25.4 billion in 1986)... U.S.' Peat Marwick merges with Holland's Klynveld Main Goerdeler to form world's largest accounting firm with revenues of $2.7 billion... Konica Business Machines USA is formed when Japan's 1873 Konishiroku, pioneer in photography products, acquires 1904 Royal Business Machines... After 13 years on LPGA tour Pat Bradley is first woman golfer to post career earnings of $2 million, 11 men top mark...

Bass Anglers Sports Society holds $667,765 MegaBucks tournament for fishermen, pioneers fishing as spectator sport... Business Week: "American Busines has a New Kingpin: The Investment Banker"... FishMaster Computer, attached to fishing rod, tells anglers how to land their catch... Business Week: "Information Thieves Are Now Corporate Enemy No. 1" (cites some 200 court cases on trade-piracy, fourfold increase in past decade)... Two Panda Robot Restaurant uses robots to wait tables, serve food... Some 500 major venture capital firms operate in U.S., invest $2.6 billion in 1985 after high of $3.4 billion in 1983... After once building 15 barges/week Jeffboat launches its last barge on Ohio at Jeffersonville, IN, ends last major shipyard on river...

Time: "The Canadians Come Calling" (covers rising investments by Canadians: Robert Campeau, Reichmann family of Toronto, Vancouver-based Belzberg family, and Montreal's Bronfmans)... Newsweek: "A is for Apple? No, Atemoya" (shows rise of exotic fruits, vegetables in supermarkets)... U.S. Steel's 400-acre Homestead plant, built on Monongahela River in 1892, closes... Nancy Lieberman joins Unites States Basketball League, first woman to play in men's professional basketball league... Since 1984 small investors have formed venture capital clubs in 38 states... Wall Street's Salomon Bros. sells investors first bonds backed by credit-card balances of banks... Newsweek: "Playing Blindman's Bluff" (reports schemes of wheeler-dealers with blind pools)...

Retailing empire of St. Louis-based May Department Stores, U.S.' 4th largest, is composed of 10 department store chains, Midwest discount chain of 62 stores, and self-service shoe chain of 1,867 outlets and has interests in 26 shopping centers, trading stamp business used by over 600 firms... Six Flags amusement chain is acquitted in 1984 death of 8 teenagers at its Great Adventure Park, NJ (retains two business professors, University of Pennsylvania, to testify business had been ethically responsible in designing the park)... Business Week: "Is It Too Late to Save The U.S. Semiconductor Industry?"... Tom Hamilton uses computers and laser printers, introduced 1984, to issue Balloon Life, new technology used by many new, small publishers...

A.C. Nielsen Co. announces it will replace its traditional method of audience ratings by meters and diaries, used for 35 years, with people meters, seen in Europe in 1987... Avon Products acquires Mediplex Group, chain of drug-rehab centers... Fortune: "Business Makes A Run For the Border" (cites some 800 U.S.-owned plants in Mexico to fight low-priced imports)... San Francisco hosts New Vaudeville Festival to exhibit, promote new entertainment by former street performers... Eleven major railroads form Railroad Association Insurance for self-insurance...

Japan's Canon introduces filmless RC-701 camera, priced at $2,600... For first time since 1975 IBM seeks volunteers for early retirement, cuts some 4,000 jobs by 1987... Time: "The Boss That Never Blinks" (covers increasing use of computers by firms to monitor detailed performance of employees and rise of resistance by workers, unions)... Xerox, National Semiconductor form pioneering alliance (lets Xerox see National's secret technology for designing office systems, lets National see Xerox's marketing plans)... Mars candy business acquires ice-cream business of DoveBar International... GM is world's first corporation to top $100 billion in sales... Fortune: "The Puny Payoff From Office Computers" (reveals slow change of white-collar productivity from late 1960s despite investments in billions of dollars)...

Merrill Lynch puts up unprofitable real estate division for sale... Battelle Memorial Institute develops low-cost computer-aided design and manufacturing program of ToolChest... U.S. Club Med of Paris-based resort business launches campaign to sell corporate clients on recreational packages for employees... Business Week: "The End of Corporate Loyalty?" (cites effects of extensive executive cutbacks of troubled and healthy businesses)...

With many users unable to get customer service from manufacturers and dealers, Computer Hand-Holding Co. opens, San Francisco, to guarantee personal assistance in using software... Daniel Hillis, 29-year-old co-founder of Thinking Machine Corp., designs powerful mainframe computer, Connection Machine, with radical new architecture to perform large number of calculations simultaneously... Merrill Lynch, California Angels design program so sports fans can combine baseball and investment counseling during 1987 spring-training period... Newsweek: "Can Corporate America Cope?" (cites attacks on bloated bureaucracies, operations of corporations by managers with little equity in business)...

Drexler Technology licenses LaserCard to Blue Cross of Maryland to record complete medical history of each member on a personal "Life Card," new phase in information storage... To clean out inventory of some one million cars on dealer lots, GM slashes interest rates for financing on most cars to 2.9% for 36 months or gives up to $1,500 in rebates, Ford gives 2.9% for 3 years, Chrysler gives 2.4% for two-year contracts and American Motors gives 0% for two-year deals... Newsweek: "Hollywood's Yukon Trail" (with average cost of films rising 33% in 3 years, cites rising use of Canadian locations by movie producers)...

Federal Express engages Martin Marietta, manufacturer of Titan-class rockets for Air Force, to launch its ExpressStar Communications Satellite in 1989... Dunhill Tailors, NYC, advertises custom-tailored suits starting at $1,925... Nearly 12 self-publishing centers with computers, laser printers appear in San Francisco... Nutmeg apparel business opens in Tampa Bay, FL (within year sells $2.6 million of clothes with collegiate look of certain universities)... Newsweek: "Detroit Runs On Empty" (shows even cut-rate loans can't spur U.S. car sales)...

To continue restructuring of firm in 1980s with brand-name food companies, Quaker Oats acquires Golden Grain Macaroni for $250 million... Turner Broadcasting (after investing some $35 million in games and $15 million in promotions loses some $10-$30 million), Soviet Union sponsor Goodwill Games, $89 million joint venture, in Moscow for 4,000 athletes from 60 countries in 18 sports... Merrill Lynch is first foreign brokerage to trade on Tokyo stock exchange; Salomon Bros., only U.S. firm with permanent seat on Japanese government bond syndicate and lone foreign representative on Tokyo Financial Futures Exchange Committee, is leading foreign broker of 22 firms in 1989 with total 4.5% share of their trading volume... Time: "Working Out in a Personal Gym" (covers boom in home exercise equipment)... Newsweek: "Fishermen Abandon Ship" (shows decline of East Coast industry from urbanization, rising costs, foreign competition, declining resources)... Of over 500 films produced in Hollywood, some 300 are made by independent producers... To lower labor costs, Japan's Victor Co. starts plant, AL, to make videocasette tapes...

Some 40% of supermarkets opened are new super stores... After 4 years Quality Inns International has opened 332 Comfort Inns in "luxury-budget" market... Time: "Have Toque, Will Travel" (covers movement to U.S. of European chefs)... Fortune judges Los Angeles Dodgers, New York Yankees as worth $90-$100 million, highest valued franchises in sports... Following lead of airlines Days Inns of America, Atlanta-based lodging chain of 390 inns with plans for 800 by 1990 in 44 states, offers industry's first "super saver discount"... Newsweek: "Can You Pass the Job Test?" (covers questionable use of honesty tests, polygraph tests, drug tests, personality tests, and genetic tests)...

A McDonald's fast-food restaurant, stylishly designed with indirect lighting, pastel tiles and oak trim, opens in Paramus Park Mall, NJ... After failing in costly battle to acquire CBS, Turner Broadcasting acquires MGM/UA for $1.6 billion, after retaining film library sells most of assets back to Kirk Kerkorian for $300 million and real estate to Lorimar-Telepictures for $190 million... Business Week: "Protectionism Rides Again"... Nell's night club, NYC, opens to raves by members, public... Miami entrepreneur Randy Perini introduces Gregorys cologne, first designer fragrance for boys... Bloomingdale's is first major department store with airport branch...

Newsweek: "A Free Bike with Your Braces" (describes increasing use of promotional techniques by dentists)... Lakewood Industries, MN, is contracted by 3 Japanese restaurant suppliers to ship chopsticks... U.S.' Honeywell, France's Groupe Bull and Japan's NEC form computer consortium... Business Week: "The Disposable Employee Is Becoming A Fact of Corporate Life" (shows rise of temporary workers to make up 25% of labor force)... Old Dominion Systems, MD, uses videotapes to sell stocks... Martin Marietta, 7 regional Baby Bells form joint venture to bid against AT&T for $4.5 billion federal telecommunications contract... Some 15% of TV audience views 3 networks, 20% in 1981...

Business Week: "Water: Where Profits Could Spring Eternal" (cites 15% annual growth of bottled water industry)... IBM and Gerdau Group, Brazil's leading private steel firm, form joint venture, lets IBM to by-pass Brazil's 1984 law restricting business of foreign computer firms... Roger Warner: Invisible Hand, The Marijuana Business... British Petroleum, Europe's largest supplier of animal feed after forming BP Nutrition in 1979, acquires U.S.' Ralston Purina animal feed business..

U.S. Steel changes name to USX, holding company of Marathon Oil, Texas Oil & Gas and U.S. Diversified with interests in steel, chemicals, construction, real estate, transportation and consulting... Fortune: "An Upstart Law Firm Comes of Age" (shows growth of Finley Kumble law firm to 618 lawyers and revenues over $150 million, 3rd largest after Chicago-based Baker & McKenzie with 833 lawyers and New York's Skadden Arps with

650)... Avon introduces bath oil fragrance to reduce stress, pioneers new cosmetics market... By lucky mistake, while looking for method to display ultra-sharp colored images for technical computers, Zenith Electronics discovers technology for new flat video tube, attempted unsuccessfully in early 1980s by several Japanese firms... For first time in 61 years Ford tops earnings of GM, $3.3 billion to $2.95 billion... After acquiring leather-goods business of 1845 Mark Cross, A.T. Cross, 1846 business in elegant fountain pens, acquires nautical timepieces of Chelsea Clocks...

Business Week: "The Hollow Corporation" (cites rise of firms that import components or products from low-wage countries for sale in U.S.)... Business Week: "How IBM is Fighting Back" (details efforts with cost-cutting, new products, stream-lined management, aggressive marketing, and long-term diversification)... From weight of bad energy loans First National Bank & Trust of Oklahoma City, assets of $1.6 billion, closes, 2nd-largest bank failure after 1974 collapse of NY's Franklin Bank...

Karen Greenburg forms Tele-Dymanics as blind pool for investors (merges with Alz Biotech to increase value of investment of $4,500 to $1 million in 8 months)... Ford's subcompact Tracer car, made in Taiwan, is exported to Canada... Business Week: "Power On Wall Street" (covers creation of $100 billion market in low-rated bonds by Michael Milken of Drexel Burnham Lambert)... New York Telephone, other local telephone companies offer customers personalized vanity telephone numbers... Salomon Bros. markets new security, called "Spin," as a note with interest based on performance of Standard & Poor's 500-stock index... NYC's Citicorp, assets of some $176 billion, is replaced as world's largest bank by Japan's Dai-Ichi Kangyo with assets of some $207 billion...

After buying closed Silver Dollar City amusement park, country-singer Dolly Parton opens Dollywood country theme park at Pigeon Forge, TN (attracts 1.3 million visitors first year, starts two-year, $10 million expansion to operate on year-round basis in 1990)... Business Week: "High Tech to the Rescue" (cites hopes for factory automation)... After showing deficit of some $179 million between 1979-82, Singer Co. spins off 135-year old sewing machine business as separate entity to focus on 18-year-old aerospace division, 53% of 1985 revenues and 52% of profits... International Yacht Racing Union allows advertising on hulls, basis for commercial success of 1987 America's Cup Regatta...

Newsweek: "Have I Got A Deal For You" (covers growing business of financial planning, some 24,000 members of International Association for Financial Planning)... Sports Illustrated: "Why TV Sports Are in Big Trouble"... Some 4,500, 7-Eleven stores remove Playboy and Penthouse from shelves for being pornographic... Jeanette W. Loeb is full partner of Goldman, Sachs & Co., first woman in top rank of investment banking...

Proceeded by Tokyo's Showa Co. buy of ARCO Plaza, Mitsui Real Estate buys NYC's Exxon building for $620 million, highest price paid for Manhattan Tower, and ABC Building for $174 million... Plus USA is first microcopier in U.S. market, followed by Silver Reed and Panasonic... Fortune: "Are Japanese Managers Biased Against Americans?" (cites arrival of nearly 50 suppliers since 1979)... Jule's Undersea Lodge at Key Largo, FL, is world's first luxury underwater hotel... Mattel introduces line of dolls with disabilities... Business Week: "Detroit Barrels Down a Back Road to Banking" (covers use of credit subsidiaries by auto makers to become financial institutions with home mortgages, credit cards, etc.)... Living Benefits Insurance is founded by Rob Worleys, father and son, in Albuquerque to provide terminally ill with pay-now life insurance by discounting their regular policies... Zale's jewelry chain, world's largest with some 1,600 stores, accepts all-cash takeover of $640 million by People Jewelers of Toronto, goes private in 1987 (buys U.S.' 1905 Gordon Jewelry Corp., over 600 stores, in 1989 for $310.9 million)...

Paine-Webber R&D Partners helps fund factory-AI program of Romesh Wadhwani's Cimflex Teknowledge with $7 million (gets contract to link together all computerized equipment in Ford Motor's new Landsdale plant, PA, perhaps world's most highly integrated factory)... Newsweek: "Star-Struck Investors Take to Hollywood" (shows producers issuing stock for movie ventures to satisfy rising demand in home-video)... U.S.S.R.-born Mike Smolyansky, Edward Puccosi start Lifeway, Chicago, to produce native kefir, cultured milk product akin to yogurt (after selling in 20 states goes public in 1988 to raise $600,000 for tripling production)...

B.F. Goodrich, Uniroyal merge tire operations in joint venture, troubles in 1987... The Water Bar opens on Beverly Hills' Rodeo Drive, serves 53 varieties from 20 countries including Soviet Union, Romania and China... Time: "Cut-Rate Computers, Get 'Em Here" (cites efforts of IBM, first PC in 1981 to gain 40% of 1985 market, to compete with IBM-compatible computers of rivals)... Sant S. Chatwal, operator of 15 Bombay Palace restaurants in NYC, plans to expand nationwide with 200 Indian fast-food places... After starting Technical Equities in San Jose, CA, in 1969 (builds small real estate investment and sports promotion business into diversified operation of 22 firms with sales of $136.4 million in 1985), Harry Stern declares bankruptcy after attracting some 700 investors, at least 70 sports figures, to participate in variety of high-tech firms and real estate deals as supposed tax shelters... Video cassettes become main source of revenue for movie companies over TV, theaters...

Time: "Putting on the Ritz at the Y" (shows opposition of commercial health clubs to efforts by non-profit YMCA to entering upscale market)... Copie Lilien starts At Last Inc., MA, to sell clothes for obese children, 79 different styles in 1989 catalog... Fox Television Stations acquires 6 TV stations from Metromedia for $1.472 billion to build new network...

National Distillers & Chemicals buys propane retailer Texgas for $187 million and plastics maker Enron Chemical for $572 million (in 1987 sells Almaden Vineyards to Heublein for $128 million and traditional spirits division, Old Grandad bourbon, Gilbey's gin and DeKuyper liquors, to American Brands for $545 million)... Newsweek: "The Era of Wildcatting" (covers speculators hunting bargains in Texas oil fields)... Newsweek: "Studio Commandos" (shows rise of low-budget film makers to generate profits by marketing, home videos)...

Japan's Ginji Yasuda pays $54 million, adds $30 million for renovations, for 1,100-room bankrupt Aladdin Hotel on Vegas strip, first foreigner to acquire Nevada casino (is followed by Katsuki Manabe's purchase of closed Holiday Inn for $32 million, $18 million for remodeling, and Masao Nangaku's buy of bankrupt Dunes for $157.7 million, $300 million for renovations)... Newsweek: "Building Baby Biceps" (cites trend in infant exercise classes, Gymboree with 335 outlets in 31 states and Playorena with 43 outlets in 6 states)... Newsweek: "Hey, Dottie - Diners Are

Back" (covers resurgence in diners of 1950s)... In hostile takeover, Marriott Corp. acquires Saga, No. 1 operator of college dining halls, for $502 million to gain its food service contracts with hospitals, nursing homes (owning some 870 Big Boy restaurants nationwide and 543 Roy Rogers eateries in mid-Atlantic states, sells some 300 Saga restaurants, 117 Black Angus, 21 Velvet Turtles, 147 Grandy's and others in Los Angeles and San Francisco, for $200-$300 million)... After taking charge of ITT, sales of $20 billion in 1985, in 1979 and selling off money-losing and unpromising operations, such as Canadian timberlands and various food processing activities, Rand Araskog spins off most of original telecommunications business, founded 1920 by Virgin Islands' sugar broker Sosthenes Behn, to France for $1.2 billion...

In red for past three years stock of Total Assets Protection, business to foil data thieves, rises from low of $4.50 to nearly $9 as firm expects to become profitable for first time... Fortune: "Having A Hard Time With Just-In-time" (shows difficulties of U.S. firms using Japanese method of inventory control as suppliers are reluctant to pay the costs)...

Doubleday Publishing, not its Mets baseball franchise, is sold by family to West German communications conglomerate of Bertelsman AG for some $500 million... After handling largest leveraged buyout of Beatrice for $6.3 billion, Kohlberg Kravis Roberts engineers $4,284 billion leveraged buyout of Safeway Stores to avoid takeover by Dart Group (leads to grocery union forcing chain to discuss effects on employees)... American Can sells traditional can division to restructure itself into financial services, insurance, mutual funds, and mortgage firms, and specialty retail business with direct-mail, retail chains selling records, sporting goods and home-entertainment equipment...

Newsweek: "The PC Printing Press" (covers boom in publishing by individuals with personal computers, laser printers)... Roy Rowan: The Intuitive Manager (extols such businessmen)... Honda exports Acuras to U.S., first Japanese firm to enter U.S. luxury car market... Directory of Doctors is published, MD, for comparison shoppers... All 80 planes of no-frill People Express are refitted with first-class, business-class sections to increase traffic... Burroughs, computers and electronics, merges with Sperry, computers and electronics, in $4.8 billion deal to form Unisys... GE acquires RCA for $6.4 billion (acquires Kidder, Peabody & Co. for $600 million and GenStar Container, North American Car and Navistar Financial for nearly $1 billion to expand financial services of General Electric Credit)... Fortune: "Pushing Products via Videocassettes"...

Northwest Airlines acquires Republic Airlines to become U.S.' 4th largest with service to 130 cities in 38 states and 17 foreign countries (after bidding war by Pan Am, International Association of Machinists and oil billionaire Marvin Davis, makes $4.3 billion run on United Airlines in 1989, is acquired in 1989 by Checchi group, Los Angeles, with KLM Royal Dutch Airlines and Australian conglomerate Elders IXL for $3.65 billion)... New York-based Celanese Corp. is acquired by West Germany's chemical giant Hoeschst for $2.8 billion... May Department Stores acquires Associated Dry Goods for $2.3 billion... Time: "Sorry, Your Policy is Canceled" (cites crises in product liability insurance)... In $606 million deal, approved by 4 unions, Frank Lorenzo's Texas Air takes over troubled Eastern Airlines, bankruptcy in 1989, to become U.S.'

largest carrier with 422 planes serving 226 cities worldwide... USAir, direct offspring of Pittsburgh's Allegheny Airlines, expands to West Coast with purchase of PSA for $400 million (adds Piedmont Airlines, deregulation success in expanding from regional to national system in 10 years, in 1989)... Ottawa-based real estate tycoon Robert Campeau acquires Allied Stores, 690-store chain, including Jordan Marsh, Brooks Bros. and Ann Taylor, and 5 major shopping centers for $3.6 billion...

Newsweek: "Peddling A Social Cause" (shows rewards realized by ad agencies in doing public-service ads)... With losses in petroleum and steel, 1961 conglomerate LTV, parent of U.S.' 2nd-largest steel maker and operator of 65 subsidiaries, declares bankruptcy despite profits in aerospace and defense business... Pepsico fails to buy 7-Up from Philip Morris for $380 million (buys Kentucky Fried Chicken, 6,500 outlets worldwide, from RJR Nabisco for $850 million to join its Taco Bell, 2,300 units, and Pizza Hut, 5,200 outlets, chains)... Coca-Cola buys Dr Pepper for $470 million...

Delta Airlines of Atlanta, founded 1929, buys Los Angeles-based Western Airlines for some $860 million... Business Week: "'Rocket Scientists' are Revolutionizing Wall Street" (shows trend since early 1970s of academics with computer expertise, quantitative techniques on Wall Street to make more money with less risks)... Following lead of Citicorp and Ford Motor Co., WSGP International, founded by Preston Martin and William Simon, acquires Honolulu Federal Savings & Loan, Hawaii's largest, as base to acquire 5 troubled thrifts, i.e., Western Federal, California's 5th largest, for $157 million, in 10 months for $225 million...

Sumitono Bank pays $500 million for 12.5% of Goldman, Sachs investment firm, followed by Nippon Life Insurance paying $538 million for 13% of Shearson Lehman Bros. brokerage... After incurring debt of $540 million and filing for bankruptcy, Miami financier, Victor Posner, CEO of DWG Corp. holding company of $4.1 billion, is tops in executive compensation with $12.7 million for 1985 (ends 8-year-battle, avoids disclosures with intricate financial network, with U.S. by pleading no contest to income tax evasion in 1987)...

When unable to get his money out from leveraged deal in 1985, corporate raider Carl Icahn takes over operating control of TWA (acquires Ozark Airlines for some $224 million, bids for bankrupted Eastern in 1989)... Time: "An Electronic Assault On Privacy" (covers rise of computer black lists so subscribers can avoid risky customers, clients, patients)...

Business Week: "Those Big Swings On Wall Street" (cites new role of 'program trading' in fluctuations of stocks when shares are bought, sold as commodities instead of investments)... 38 billion-dollar deals, mergers, acquisitions, and/or buyouts, are made during year... To compete in global market BBDO International, U.S.' No. 6, Doyle Dane Bernback Group, U.S.' No. 12, and Needham Harper Worldwide, U.S.' No. 16, merge to form world's largest advertising business with combined billings of nearly $5 billion, loses billings of $100 million in 6 months (is topped by London's Saatchi & Saatchi's 1986 acquisition of U.S.' Ted Bates Worldwide for billings of $7.5 billion, loses accounts over $300 million in several months)...

Newsweek: "The Dramatic Art of Dining" (shows trend of designer restaurants as theaters)... Time: "How Do You Say Beef?" (covers new light varieties of Chianina, Zebu, Beefalo, Brae for consumers wanting lean meats)... Fortune: "The Revolt Against 'Working Smarter'" (details resistance of executives to participative management, some 75% of all programs in early 1980s fail)... Business Week: "How Adversity Is Reshaping Madison Avenue" (shows ad agencies surviving by merging, diversifying, cutting costs)...

After purchasing Denver-based Frontier Airlines in 1985 after bidding war with Texas Air only to lose $10 million/month, Donald C. Burr, CEO of financially-troubled Newark-based People Express after growing from 3 planes in 1981 to 117 in 1986 by serving 107 North American cities plus Brussels and London with fare wars, fails to sell Frontier to United Airlines, blocked by pilots' union (is forced to sell People Express to Texas Air)... Business Week: "The Rewiring of America" (shows use phone lines as transportation system for information age)... Business Week: "The Job Nobody Wants" (covers risks, hassles being on a board of directors)...

In latest of international advertising combinations ad agency D'Arcy MacManus Masius, U.S.' 12th largest, merges with Benton & Bowles, 14th largest (shows billings growth of some 22% each year to 1989 to evolve as U.S.' 11th-largest, wins $50 million Maxwell House account of Kraft/General Foods Group and 50% of $215 million Burger King account in 1989)... After its parent company Ralston Purina was bought by British Petroleum, Foodmaker, runs Jack in the Box and Chi-Chi fast-food chains, goes private in $175 million leveraged buyout (highlights trend in farming out computing instead of operating a data center, cuts data processing costs by 17%)...

General Development Corp., Florida's largest developer of planned residential communities, buys plush Orlando resort, Vistana, to enter condo time-sharing market, imported from Europe in mid-1970s and sold to some 1.3 million U.S. vacationeers by 1989 (by 1989 operates 11 resorts from Texas to Hawaii with network of 200 sales agents, joined in 1989 market by Marriott, 6 developments in 5 years, and Disney with plans for time-share development at Orlando parks)...

General Electric Capital Corp. forms unit to seek borrowers in media and communications, by 1989 U.S.' 2nd biggest lender in cable systems after Canada's Toronto Dominion Bank... Newsweek: "Coping with the Ad Crunch" (covers overall decline in revenues of television networks, major national magazines)... Louisville Cardinals, first minor baseball team to draw one million fans in one season in 1983, is sold for $5 million, most ever paid for minor league team... Saul Steinberg's Reliance Capital forms Telemundo television network with handful of local Spanish stations for Hispanic market of 21 million... New York shuts down First Meridian financial planning business in alleging it took $55 million from investors paying inflated prices for art work, coins, and Florida real estate...

After building Kinder-Care as empire of 1,235 learning centers, founder Perry Mendel diversifies by 1989 with two Florida thrifts, specialty retail chain, and deer-hunter's magazine (is forced to restructure in 1989 by dissatisfied stockholders, rumors of takeover)... Marisol Malaret, Miss Universe in 1970, and San Juan publisher Manuel A. Casiano,

Jr., started <u>Caribbean</u> <u>Business</u> weekly in 1973, launch <u>Imagen</u> magazine for upscale, fashion-conscious Hispanic women... Shedding decades of adversarial union relations, National Steel's Japanese-style labor pact with workers is hailed as milestone in U.S. labor management, subject of union dispute in 1989... From 1975 two-thirds of FORTUNE 500 firms were convicted of serious crimes from price fixing to illegal dumping of hazardous wastes... Larry Leight, partners open upscale optical shop, Oliver Peoples with treasure trove of 1,500 antique frames, in Los Angeles, sales average $200/frame... Working mom Carol Smith-Carter, idea in 1982, opens successful cushy summer camp for mothers...

Hybritech, biotech firm started 1978, is sold to Eli Lilly pharmaceuticals for $400 million, 800 employees divide $80 million of sales price (inspires rise of 70 commercial biotech firms in San Diego area)... To escape corporate raider Fruehauf, 1918 maker of truck-trailers, spends $1.5 billion, $120 million in greenmail, to repurchase stock (after selling divisions to ease debt, exists only in name in 1989)... Reebok sells some $900 million of athletic-leisure footwear, $4 million in 1982... Thomas Stemberg launches Staples, 27 stores in Northeast by 1989, to pioneer rise of retail chains in office supplies, followed by Office Depot with 39 stores in South and Office Club with 21 stores on West Coast...

IBM invites key customers to participate in its strategic planning... Brunswick Corp. buys two major boat builders for $773 million to enter industry's 5-year boom, 4 more by 1989 for $78 million (puts up Industrial Products division for sale in 1989 to ride out sinking boat market... When other steel mills are closing Thomas Tyrrell, partners buy 3 steel mills from USX to form American Steel & Wire (transforms business, employees with same perks as executives, by creating learning organization to think, anticipate, develop)...

Founder of ProServe, sports marketing firm, Raymond Benton leaves to start bicycle tour companies in U.S. and Europe, biggest U.S. operator with sales of $4 million in 1988... L.A. Gear, founded 1982 by hairdresser Robert Greenberg to sell teenage girls Los Angeles lifestyle (imports canvas sneakers from South Korea in 1984), goes public, sales of $9 million in 1984 to $223.7 million by 1989 (diversifies with shoes for men, infants and children in 1986, sweatshirts, T shirts and shorts in 1987, jeans in 1988, and quartz watches in 1989).

1987

General Events

U.S. shows record deficit of $36.84 billion for last quarter of 1986... Dow Jones Industrial Average hits (January 8) 2000 mark for first time, first 1000 in 1972 (tops 2100 on January 22, 2200 on February 17, and 2300 points on February 20)... After rising record 51.60 points on Thursday and 64 points on Friday to high of 2210, Dow Jones Industrial Average drops (January 23) 115 points in 71 minutes... Dollar falls, January, sharply against major currencies... Paul Kennedy: <u>The</u> <u>Rise</u> <u>and</u> <u>Fall</u> <u>of</u> <u>the</u> <u>Great</u> <u>Powers</u> (relates economic change and military strength of countries from 1500 to 2000)... Scientists Paul C.W. Chu, University of Houston, and Mau-Kuen Wu, University of Alabama, report new breakthough in superconductivity, touted as introducing new industrial

revolution... Clean Air Bill passes (February 4) Presidential veto...
Newsweek: "Back to the Basics" (reports U.S. firms providing employees
with basic education in primary skills)... U.S. rescinds plan to impose
200% duties on agricultural products of European Community after winning
trade concessions... U.S. reports record trade deficit of $169.78 billion
for 1986... Four top Wall Street traders are named in insider-trading
probe... AFL-CIO building and construction trade department signs
agreement with National Construction Assn. (grants flexible work rules,
no-strike policy to stimulate industry)... Time: "I'll Take Manhattan-
Waikiki" (reports increasing investments of Japanese investors in U.S.
as dollar declines in value against Japanese yen)...

Conrail's 85% share owned by government, 15% by employees, is sold to
U.S. public for $1.65 billion, Wall Street's largest stock offering of 18
million shares... After dumping charges President Reagan plans (February
27) 100% retalitory tariffs on Japanese consumer products, leads to
lowest drop of U.S. dollar, 147.70, against yen since W.W. II... Bill to
raise national minimum wage to $4.65 by 1990 is introduced (March 25) to
Congress, vetoed by President Bush in 1989... Outgoing SEC chairman,
J.S.R. Shad, gives $30 million, largest received by school, to Harvard to
establish ethics program for MBA students...

San Francisco agrees to raise wages of women, minorities to level of men
on jobs of comparable worth... Time: "Show Me the Way to Go Home" (cites
trend of young adults living with parents)... U.S. Patent and Trademark
Office accepts applications for new forms of animal life... U.S. Supreme
Court backs Federal Reserve Board's approval for New York bank to open
subsidiary in Palm Beach, FL... U.S. Supreme Court upholds use of
arbitration over litigation to resolve securities-fraud claims of
investors against brokers... U.S. Supreme Court rules employers may favor
women and minorities over white men in hiring and promoting to achieve
balanced work force (rules in 1989 that such hiring practices result in
reverse discrimination unless employer has past history of discrimination
against women and minorities)...

U.S. awards printing contract for passports to Japan's Uno Seisakusho...
Foreign investors spend $40.3 billion for U.S. assets, $65 billion in
1988 with Britain paying $21.5 billion, Japan $14.2 billion, and Canada
$10.4 billion - U.S. ahead with total of $330 billion to $304 billion...
Federal Reserve, Germany's Bundesbank and Bank of Japan act (April)
simultaneously to rescue dollar... Massachusetts General Hospital
develops DXplain, world's first computerized diagnostic system... Austin,
TX, employer pleads no contest to criminally negligent homicide in death
of two employees... AFL-CIO provides cheap legal services to union
members, part of drive to boost dwindling membership, 14 million in 1983
to 13 million, in its 92 unions...

President Reagan proposes stiff tariffs on $300 million worth of Japanese
electrical imports... Time: "How Ripe for a Crash?" (cites possibility
of another Great Depression)... Florida passes sales tax on personal
services, covers State's share of national advertiser's share of audience
(after furor is rescinded)... U.S. Supreme Court upholds Indiana's
antitakeover law to restrict hostile bids... U.S. Air Force Major Stephen
R. Le Clair designs pioneering multiexpert computer program... Japan's
Sumitomo Corp. of America settles U.S. sex-discrimination suit of former
women workers... Alfred L. Malabre, Jr.: Beyond Our Means (shows U.S.'

long years of debt, deficits and reckless borrowing now threaten to overwhelm country)... Coined in 1970s by computer scientist Myron Krueger, Defense Advanced Research Projects Agency develops SIMNET, Simulation Network to provide 'Artificial Reality,' so tank crews in Kentucky can battle opponents in Germany with tank simulators... Time: "Rock Power for Health & Wealth" (covers New Age trend in use of crystals in personal therapy, Star Magic space-age gift shop, NYC, triples sales in 4 years)... Florida authorities close 8 travel agencies offering bogus bargains and sue 35 others, actions by IL, CA, and MO...

After 42.7% hike in malpractice insurance by State's largest carrier, South Florida doctors resign from emergency-room duties... Three U.S. government agencies start paying bills with computer transfers of money... Nebraska's Agricultural Department devises underground plow that doesn't wreck topsoil, increases soil's ability to hold water by up to 50%... Ravi Batra: The Great Depression of 1990 (warns of impending economic disaster as worst in history)... Six states pass parental-leave laws for employees, bring total coverage to 15... U.S. Supreme Court restricts use of 115-year-old mail-fraud law for protection of property rights... U.S. Supreme Court upholds exemption for religious groups from Federal law barring discrimination in employment based on religion... Dow Jones hits (June 16) a record 2400...

Minnesota bill blocks (June 25) takeover bid of Dart Group, discount retailer of Haft family, for Dayton Hudson Department Stores... U.S. Senate votes (June 30) to ban sales of Toshiba products in U.S. to protest illegal sale of militarily useful technology to U.S.S.R... Avco Corp., unit of Textron, pleads guilty to overcharging Defense Department, pays $4.6 million in plea-bargain... Cleveland ends bankruptcy by paying debt of 1978 financial crisis... Kidder, Peabody & Co. agrees to pay $13.7 million in profits from insider-trading and penalty of $11.6 million... National Endowment for the Humanities reports U.S. educational system puts too much emphasis on skill training instead of traditional knowledge...

U.S. law calls for international cooperation in monitoring catches on open seas, enforcing fishing constraints (tries to curb Japan's, Taiwan's use of killer nets, 40 miles wide and 40 feet deep, in 1989)... Garbage barge travels some 6,000 miles in 3 months before returning to Brooklyn, waste spurned by at least 5 states and 3 countries... After strike of 15 minutes, Director's Guild signs contract with Alliance of Motion Picture and Television Producers to avoid crippling walkout... To avoid decertification vote union ends 7-month-old strike with Iowa Beef Processors (wins rehiring of union members and higher wages and benefits, accepts two-tier wage system)... Lions service club abolishes 70-year-old ban on female members, Kiwanis follows suit...

Dow Jones hits (July 12) a record 2500... U.S. Treasury cancels 32-year-old treaty with Netherlands Antilles, one of world's most lucrative tax havens with 24,000 corporations registered in land of 200,000 people, to exempt investments from almost all taxes... Congress holds hearing on animal patents... President Reagan unveils (July 28) plan to develop commercial potential of superconductivity... Senate passes (August 4) bill to allow insolvent Federal Savings & Loan Insurance to raise $10.8 billion by issuing long-term bonds, bail-out bill of $100 billion plus in 1989... FDIC agrees to bail out First City Bancorp of Houston, last of sickest of Texas banks, for $970 million, 2nd largest rescue after 1984 Continental Illinois... Medium income is $29,460, 4.2% higher than in 1985... AFL-CIO ends 1977 dispute with Coors Brewery... Labor Department requires workers be given toxic warnings... FTC blocks corporate raiders with new reporting requirements... Twenty people, 12 union officials and 8 contractors, are indicted in Brooklyn on charges of labor racketeering in construction by rigging bids, manipulating awards of contracts, bribery, extortion, collusion, and fraud...

Casino dealers in Claridge Casino Hotel, Atlantic City, reject unionization... Association of Professional Flight Attendants, 12,000 members, plans merger with Association of Flight Attendants, 23,000 members... After topping (August 25) 2700 mark, Dow Jones drops (October 1) to 2639, 2549 (October 6), 2471 (October 12) and 2508 (October 13) before slumping (October 14) record 95.46 points to 2412.7 (hits 2355 on October 15, and to 2246, October 16, after record trading of 388.5 million shares in record drop of 108.36 points, drops, October 19, 508 points to 1738 and wipe out $500 billion in assets, struggles, October 20, to climb 360 points after Federal Reserve eases credit and banks lower prime interest rates to stabilize the economy and avoid financial catastrophe, reaches, October 21, 2027 before falling, October 22, to 1950.43 as stocks lose $107.79 billion to wipe out recovery, reaches 1793 on October 26, 1846 on October 27, 1993 on October 30, 1833 on November 30 and 1938, near beginning of January level, on December 31)...

U.S. trade deficit in July soars to record $16.5 billion... NFL players strike (September 22) over free agency, first walkout since 1982 of 57 days (is called off after 24 days with no agreement as union files antitrust suit)... President Reagan signs (September 29) bill to impose automatic reductions in Federal spending if Congress, President fail to reach annual targets... EPA sets (October 5) new water pollution controls for industries, largely unregulated, of plastics, synthetic fibers and organic chemicals... U.S. trade deficit rises to record $17.63 billion in October, up 25% from September...

Dollar falls (November 5) to new lows against major currencies... U.S. and Mexico, 3rd-largest trading partner after Canada and Japan, sign (November 6) bilateral pact to improve trade, $30 billion in 1986...Justice Department settles (November 10) its 10-year-old lawsuit against Teamsters Union Pension Fund, under Federal Court supervision in 1982 to eliminate influence of organized crime (recovers $21.5 million on misuse of funds)... President Reagan imposes (November 13) punitive tariffs on Brazilian imports in retaliation for Brazil's import restrictions on U.S. computer software... Federal Savings & Loan Insurance Corp. pledges record $1.3 billion to bail out Vernon Savings & Loan Assn., TX, bought 1982 by Dallas real estate investor Don R. Dickson to finance lavish lifestyle...

Federal Savings & Loan Ins. Corp. rescues or liquidates 48 thrifts during year... Federal Reserve Bank of NY names Nikko Securities of Japan, Lloyd's Government Securities of Britain as primary dealers of U.S. Government Securities... Federal Reserve reports (December 3) failure of 9 banks, most in one day since its creation... U.S., China agree (December 19) to limit growth of Chinese textile imports to U.S... United Auto Workers win union representation at Mazda plant in Flat Rock, MI... Teamsters union, expelled 1957 in dispute over ethics, rejoins AFL-CIO (seeks support on troubles with Justice Department's trial of President Jackie Presser on charges of racketeering and embezzling, on expected attempt to Justice to remove leadership for ties with organized crime)... Justice Department launches investigation of Chicago Board of Trade, Chicago Mercantile Exchange (in 1989 accuses 46 commodities brokers, traders in acting to defraud customers)... Dennis Walker, former church bishop in Southern Oregon, persuades church members to invest in offshore bank, over 150 investors lose over $8 million in fraudulent scheme (is followed by 1989 state report that false prophets, con artists bilk 15,000 believers out of $450 million in 1985-89).

Business Events

Carl Icahn drops $7.19 billion bid for USX (after selling Texaco shares for over $2 billion in cash in 1989, is rumored in new raid on USX)... To block takeover bid of Donald Trump, Bally Mfg., owns Atlantic City casino, Six Flags amusement parks, and several hundred health clubs and makes gambling machines, buys Atlantic City's Golden Nugget Casino/ Hotel for $439 million... After canceling Leisure and Picture Week earlier, Time Inc. scraps its 3-year-old unit to develop new magazine (after two years of study plans Entertainment Weekly to cover new movies, TV shows, videocassettes, recorded music and books in 1990) ... Newsweek prints its first ad for condoms, copied by other publications...

Eastern, Pan Am seek wage cuts from unions... Chrysler acquires Renault's share, bought 46% in 1979, of American Motors for $1.1 billion... National Amusements, 400 movie screens, acquires Viacom International, 1971 spinoff of CBS with radio and TV stations plus cable services, for $3.4 billion after bidding war (sues Time Inc. in 1989 for using its cable franchises to promote its Home Box Office channel, acquired 1973, at expense of Viacom's Showtime)... Three major banks reclassify Brazil debt as nonaccural... IBM launches its 2nd generation PCs... Chicago-based Amoco buys Dome Petroleum for $3.86 billion, forms Canada's largest oil and gas firm... New York Stock Exchange seat sells for record $1.1 million, bought 1964 for $200,000...

Surprising financial markets Citicorp reserves $3 billion to cover losses in Third World loans, copied by 9 other major banks... Primerica buys Smith Barney brokerage for $750 million to complement interests in insurance, mutual funds and asset management (caps efforts of Gerald Tsai to transform American Can into financial-services conglomerate by shedding over 25 firms and adding 15 others)... Salomon Bros. reports silver, gold and oil offering best returns on investment for 1987... CEO Richard J. Ferris, goal to build full-service travel company, is forced out by Allegis board (drops name for United Airlines to focus on air travel business, is takeover target in 1989)...

Ford recalls some 4.3 million cars, trucks to correct fuel systems... Thompson brothers of Dallas, hold 10.3% of Southland started by father, buy entire company, 8,207, 7-Eleven stores and 50% of Citgo Petroleum, for some $5.1 billion... Computer Associates buys archrival Uccel, two of biggest makers of software for mainframe computers, for $780 million... R.R. Donnelly & Sons, U.S.' largest printer with sales of $2.2 billion in 1986, acquires Metromail, services in direct-mail industry, for $282.6 million as match for its catalog-printing and distribution business... 1982 USA Today of Gannett Co. shows first profits... First Fidelity

Bancorp, 2nd-largest bank holding company, NJ, joins with Philadelphia's Fidelcor, most depositors in City, in largest interstate-bank merger to form U.S.' 18th-largest bank... BankAmerica, once world's largest to trail Citicorp's assets of $194.42 billion and Chase's $98.86 billion in U.S. with $96.9 billion, posts (July 23) net loss of $1.14 billion from loans to Third World, mismanagement... GM is sued on closing 64-year-old assembly plant in Norwood, OH... Vlasic Foods, 20 growers and Farm Labor Organizing Committee sign pact to cover cucumber harvest, 4th contract since 1986...

Corning Glassworks wins patent infringement against Japan's Sumitomo Electric Industries over design of optical fibers, forces Sumitomo to close its fiber optical plant... Body Glove Swimwear introduces neoprene suits... Time: "Massage Comes out of the Parlor" (cites increasing use of U.S.' 50,000 massage therapists at airports, clubs, offices, and shopping centers)... Chicago's Board of Trade, Mercantile Exchange begin 3-hour Sunday-night session to coincide with business hours in Tokyo (plan global automation for trading by computers in 1988-89)... NYC's 21 Club opens private breakfast club for over 300 business executives...

Coca-Cola spins off entertainment division, includes Columbia Pictures, Merv Griffin Enterprises and Embassy Communications, to join Tri-Star Pictures, joint venture with Time Inc. and CBS, in forming Columbia Pictures Entertainment, retains 49% stake in new company... Reichhold Chemicals accepts $540 million hostile bid of Japan's Dainippon Ink & Chemicals... Eli Lilly sells Elizabeth Arden cosmetic business to Faberge, controlled by Meshulam Riklis, for some $700 million... RJR Nabisco devises 'smokeless' cigarettes...

To reverse slide in profits and fight takeover of raider and largest stockholder Ronald O. Perelman, Salomon Bros. announces major retrenchment by abandoning municipal bond underwriting business, largest market share of any Wall Street house, dismissing 12% of staff, and dropping out of underwriting $1 billion office and residential complex...

Bank of Boston writes off $200 million of its $1 billion in loans to Third World countries... Goodrich sells 50% of UniRoyal Goodrich Tire for $225 million to leave traditional tire business... Home Shopping Network buys NYSE seat to provide financial services... Time: "Restructuring American Business" (cites efforts of firms for more organizational efficiency with staff reductions, etc.)...

Chicago investment firm, Knightsbridge Partners, buys Supercuts hair-care salon chain, founded 1975 (operates 500 units by 1989 to trim 1.5 million heads/month for sales of $139 million, plans to double its size in 5 years)... Home Shopping Network files $1.5 billion fraud, misrepresentation lawsuit against GTE, challenges traditional limited liability of telecommunications suppliers, phone companies, equipment suppliers and data communications firms in handling information...

After founding Waste Management in 1972, H. Wayne Huizenga, partners buy Blockbuster chain of 100 video rental "superstores," FL (expands to 700 outlets by 1989, plans 300 more by 1990, faces charges of overly aggressive accounting by Bear Sterns & Co.)...

Newsweek: "Silicon Valley's Newest Wizard" (covers evolution of high-tech-design operations to develop innovative consumer products)... After opening Foot Locker, 1,000 stores in 1989, in 1974 to sell running shoes and sporting togs and Lady Foot Locker, 486 outlets in 1989, in 1982, F.W. Woolworth's Kinney Shoe launches Kids Locker... After 15 years of research Procter & Gamble submits Olestra, new cholestrol-and calorie-free fat substitute, to FDA for approval... After dropping black powder in 1973, dynamite in 1978 and propellants in 1986, DuPont sells last of its exposive business, started 1802 with black powder, to Canadian firm... NFL owners approve new TV contract and cable viewing, $1.428 billion over 3 years (plan international spring league for 1990 or 1991)...

Peryl Gottesman starts Who's Minding the Store business in Portland, OR, to run small firms for owners on vacation, buying trips or emergency absences... Using technology of Gummi-Mayer, West Germany's largest tire retreader with innovative 1973 tire-burning plant, Oxford Action builds $41 million plant south of San Francisco to burn unusable whole tires, generates electricity for 14,000 homes... Chicago's USG adopts employee policy for acoustical plants in 8 states of no smoking on-and-off-the-job... CSX acquires Sea-Land Corp. for $803 million (if approved by ICC allows formation of largest rail system in East, leading barge line, natural-gas pipeline and truck line with largest U.S. ocean container shipper)...

General Motors replaces automated equipment at its car assembly plant in Lansing, MI, with traditional conveyor-belt system... Nuveen Municipal Value Fund raises record $1.5 billion in public offering for participation in closed-end fund... Newsweek: "The Chaotic World of Bonds" (covers tricky hedges and huge losses, $275 million by Merrill Lynch, Salomon Bros. and First Boston)... Glenn Friedt launches Books by Wire, modeled on Florists' Transworld Delivery... After first buying land in Australia in 1950s, turning North Queensland properties of tropical rain forests into pasturage, Texas-based King Ranch puts up rural properties and nearly 50,000 head of cattle for sale for $45 million (sells all interests in Spain, Venezuela and Argentina and reduces holdings in Brazil)...

Eastman Kodak, Fuji Photo introduce disposable cameras... Dinosaur toys are popular at NYC show... Boardwalk and Baseball, an old-fashioned amusement park featuring rides and midway games, opens in Baseball City, FL... Newsweek: "The Age of McFashion" (notes surge of specialty stores selling pre-packaged style, ebb of department stores)... Wendy's International uses automated teller machines in Dayton restaurants to attract cashless customers to its fast-food outlets... Australian-born Rupert Murdoch adds 170-year-old Harper & Row Publishing to media empire... Arena Football League, each of 14 teams a subsidiary, begins play during summer in air-conditioned stadiums, televised by ESPN cable for $1 million (averages attendance of 10,700/game, break-even is 8,000)...

Chrysler buys Italian luxury sports-car maker Lamborghini, employs 300 to make 450 cars/year for up to $127,000, for some $20 million... Protectel business opens in Berkeley, CA, to deliver condoms or sponges to door in 15 minutes... Avis rental car business plans chain of 1,700 quick-lube stops, pioneered by Jiffy Lube International in late 1970s with plans for 1,200 by 1990... Business Week: "ESOPs: Are They Good for You?" (shows new trend in employee stock-ownership plans to deter takeovers, save taxes and boost productivity)... Kroger grocery chain tests CheckRobot at several Georgia markets to let customers scan own purchases, pay receipt to cashier... Harcourt Brace Jovanovich, U.S.' largest textbook publisher, takes on $2.5 billion debt to block takeover of British press baron Robert Maxwell (is forced to sell Sea World marine parks, FL, TX, OH and CA, and Boardwalk & Baseball park and Cypress Gardens, FL, in 1989 to ease debt)... GM replaces 1918 executive cash-bonus plan with stock options... Campbell Soup offers up to 3 months of unpaid leave to all workers with newborn, adopted child, or sick family member, American Express adopts similar plan...

Fred G. Currey, partners buy Greyhound lines, 2,800 buses, from Greyhound Corp. for some $375 million (purchase industry's No. 2 Trailways, 1,200 buses, for some $80 million to control 80% of market, after approval by ICC shows 20% traffic increase in 1989 with rising air fares while original Greyhound struggles)... Promoters form pro volleyball league for women with 6 teams... Newsweek: "Fast-Cash Express" (cites entrepreneurs score big by taking firms public to become millionaires, i.e., Barry Minkow of ZZZZ Best rug cleaning, Ron Unkefer of Good Guys consumer-electronics, Bill Gates of Microsoft software, Bob McKnight of Quiksilver software and Paul Maestri of P.A.M. Transport)...

Chicago Board of Trade holds first night session in history of U.S. exchanges, plans global trading by computers in 1988-89... Combustion Engineering forms first U.S.-Soviet venture to make, sell refinery equipment in U.S.S.R., followed in 1989 by McDonald's with plans for two Moscow outlets and consortium of U.S. health care companies with Soviet Health Ministry, 34 health care organizations... Executives of CBS buy its magazine unit, 21 publications, for $650 million... Group of sport promoters form International Basketball Assn., 6 franchises, to play June-September in 1988 (sets maximum height of players at 6'4" and team salary cap of $600,000)...

Newsweek: "A Small World Grows Tinier" (notes micro machines may be next industrial wave)... San Francisco's KRON-TV is first station in major TV market to air condom ads... Marriott, 899 limited-menu eateries with chains of Big Boy and Roy Rogers, seeks $900 million acquisition of Denny's 1,185 family-style restaurants for No. 1 place in market... GM's South African subsidiary pledges financial support to any black employee using beaches reserved for whites (forces Port Elizabeth to desegregate its beaches)... Wall Street Journal carries 9-page advertising supplement by Soviet Union to promote investments in U.S.S.R...

Mayway Corp. of Lau family, North America's biggest wholesaler of Chinese herbs, opens Emperor Herbal Restaurant in San Francisco, every dish on menu formulated to be good for what ails you... Fuller Brush Co. publishes its first national mail-order catalog, plans two retail outlets later in year for Dallas area... "The Electronic Supervisor: New Technology, New Tensions" report shows worker morale drops as computers monitor output, rest breaks...

Business Week: "Videos Are Starring in More and More Training Programs" (shows use of interactive video to teach job skills)... Catalog Retail of Connecticut distributes mail-order catalogs of some 200 businesses to local news outlets for sale... Citibank, Coca-Cola adopt programs in

South Africa to support black economic development, education... Quality Inns starts economy hotel chain to operate up to 300 inns by 1989... American Airlines introduces Capture, electronic service allows firms to monitor travel and expense reports... Ford buys Britain's 69-year-old Aston Martin Lagonda to enter luxury-sports-car market... After 4 different owners in 4 years, Avis car-rental firm sets up employee stock-ownership plan for 12,700 workers to buy business from Wesray Capital for $1.75 billion... Loral Corp. of NY acquires Goodyear Aerospace...

Al Dziuk, brother start Texas Microwave Popcorn-on-the-Cob on whim, sell 19,000 packages of novelty food in 1988 and 20,000 in 6 months of 1989... First Clean and Lean Laundromat with fitness center opens in Vista, CA (with success sells franchises in 1988)... Moscow's Viyacheslav Zaitsev, favorite Soviet fashion designer of First Lady Raisa Gorbachev, makes U.S. debut in NYC... Former travel agent Donna Walker starts business to make authentic passports issued by nonexistant nations for travelers worried about terrorists...

Apple Computer markets HyperCard, guide to new software generation... Coleco introduces $35 Couch-Potato doll for new market trend... Young Americans Bank opens in Denver for kids doing grown-up business... U.S. is world's top international contractor with 25% of market, 45% in 1980... Humana hospital chain, founded 1962 as nursing home business (builds first hospital in 1968, sells 41 nursing homes in 1972, acquires American Medicorp to double size in 1978, starts Health Services Division in 1981 to administer MedFirst emergency clinics - closes 102 facilities in 1987), buys troubled Florida HMO, International Medical Centers, to start Humana Medical Plan (operates in 1989 market, 1960 Hospital Corp. of America as largest, 1968 National Medical Enterprises as 3rd and Community Psychiatric Centers as 4th and 1956 American and Medical Insurance as 5th, as 2nd largest with 83 hospitals, 49,400 employees and 17,323 beds)...

Westinghouse-Airship Industries, joint venture of Westinghouse Defense Electronics and Britain's Airship Industries, beats out Goodyear Aerospace to win U.S. Navy's $170-million contract for some 50 blimps... Sematech is $250-million consortium created by semiconductor industry, 14 firms such as AT&T, Texas Instruments, Intel, IBM and Motorola, to restore U.S. competitiveness in making chips, joins consortiums of Japan, 6 firms join in 1976 to produce world's highest capacity memory chip and 9 firms form Fifth Generation to develop advanced technologies, such as artificial intelligence and parallel processing, in 1981, and U.S., MCC in 1983 with 19 firms, such as Boeing, Control Data, DEC and 3M, to work on advanced technologies and artificial intelligence and U.S. Memories, 7 firms including IBM and Digital Equipment, in 1989 to make dynamic random-access memory chips)...

London's Airship Industries flies first U.S. commercial blimp service in 50 years from Oakland, CA, over San Francisco... Leading Wall Street firms announce, (December 6,7, and 14) major layoffs... Ford guarantees employment, except for industry-wide sales slump, for 140,000 workers, down from 190,000 over past 10 years, in new 3-year contract with UAW, followed by GM with similar pact... With success of France's state-owned Videotex services, seven Baby Bells are allowed to expand into transmission of electronic services (eases concerns of electronic publishers), denied permission to provide long-distance service and manufacture phone equipment....

Baseball owners lose 1985 free agency case... After acquiring Knickerbocker plush toys in 1983, Milton Bradley games and its Playskool unit for $360 million in 1984, and Scruples board games in 1985, Hasbro, founded 1923, acquires Pogo Ball and Schaper games (adds Coleco, Cabbage Patch dolls with games of Scrabble, Trivial Pursuits and Parcheesi, in 1989 for $111 million to become U.S.' largest toy business with product line for all ages)... American Express introduces Optima credit card, first with installemnt payment at lower variable interest rate (follows appearance of dog-tag-like plate by Farrington Mfg. in 1927 for use by Filene's of Boston after use of cards after W.W. I by oil companies for motorists and modern charge card of Diner's Club in 1950 designed by Frank McNamara, Ralph Schneider in 1949)...

Amoco is first oil company to phase out leaded gasoline for high-octane grades (starts marketing frenzy with gas stations peddling whatever)... Michael Milken, head of Drexel Burnham Lambert's junk-bond business, earns $550 million in 1987 (after Drexel's deal with SEC for his dismissal, resigns in 1989, faces 98 counts of racketeering and fraud charges, to start International Capital Access Group to create "ownership opportunities" for employees, minorities and unions)... Retailers spend some $250 million, up nearly 10% from 1986, to stop shoplifters (spawns use of high-tech firms in war on theft)... From 1977 executive pay, bonuses jump 120% over factory workers' wages...

U.S. producers hold 1% of U.S. market in phonographs vs. 90% in 1970, 10% of color TVS vs. 90% in 1970, 0% of audiotape recorders vs. 40% in 1970, 1% of videotape recorders vs. 10% in 1970, 35% of machine tool centers vs. 99% in 1970, 25% of telephones vs. 99% in 1970, 65% of semiconductors vs. 89% in 1970, and 74% of computers vs. 97% in 1975... McDonald's tries to sell single-serving pizza (dumps idea after ad attack by Pizza Hut with 6,000 stores, tests regular pizza menu in 1989 for 10,500 outlets)... Unilever buys Chesebrough-Ponds, Prince Matchabelli perfume and cold cream products (considers buying Faberge and Elizabeth Arden in 1989 to take on Japan's Shiseido Cosmetics, No. 2, and France's L'Oreal, No. 1, in world market and Estee Lauder, 38%, and L'Oreal's Cosmair, 13.4%, in U.S. field)...

Ferruzzi Finanziaria, Italy's 2nd largest private firm, buys Indiana's Central Soya to become 3rd largest U.S. soybean processor after Archer Daniels Midland and Cargill, suspected of market manipulation on Chicago's Board of Trade in 1989... After bid by Dart group, Revco, largest U.S. drugstore chain in 1986, evades takeover with $1.3 billion LBO as advised by Salomon Bros. (is largest LBO to seek bankruptcy protection from creditors in 1988)...

Ted Turner is rescued from debt load of $1.2 billion after financial misadventures with MGM/UA and CBS by $550 million firm cable industry, Ted Malone's Telecommunications, 31 cable operators and Time Inc. (revives business by 1989 with 3 of U.S.' 6 highest-rated basic-cable stations to oversee $5 billion empire: $165 million in real estate, $150 million in sports franchises, $1.5 billion in Cable News Network and Headline News, $1.5 billion in superstation TBS, $1 billion in library of 3,700 movies, 1,700 hours of TV shows and hundreds of cartoons, and $615 million in new cable Turner Network Television to reach 29.2 million homes)... GE swaps its consumer electronic business, maker of RCA TV sets for 40 years, to French state-owned Thomson S.A. for its diagnostic imaging business and cash (starts GE Medical Systems Asia in Tokyo, anchored by GE-owned Yokogawa Medical Systems, to become world leader in field)...

Holiday Inn incurs debt over $2 billion to block takeover by Donald Trump (sells North American chain of over 1,400 inns to Britain's pub-and-brewery giant Bass PLC for $2.23 billion in 1989 to focus on its chains of Embassy Suites, Hampton Inns, Homewood Suites and Harrah's casinos)... Health-care expenditures equal some 46% of corporate operating profits, 9% in 1965...

Pear Brewing Co., entered market in 1961, and Pabst brewery sells 2 million cases of non-alcoholic beer, 1.6 million in 1983... NYC's Sullivan & Cromwell law firm is finally allowed to open Tokyo office for local clients eager to invest in U.S., joined by 20 others (are blocked from most international work by Japanese rules).

1988

General Events

President's Task Force on Market Mechanisms reports (January 8) "Financial System Approached Breakdown" on Tuesday, October 20, 1987... Amoco Corp. is fined $85.2 million for 1978 oil spill of Amoco Cadiz supertanker off Britany Coast; Exxon castigated for Alaskan oil spill in 1989 costing over $100 million... U.S. reports exports of November, 1987 climbed 9.4% to record $23.8 billion... Los Angeles federal grand jury charges 9 members of Caro Quintero's Mexican drug ring with 1987 slaying of U.S. Drug Enforcement Administration agent... U.S. indicts Panamanian General Manuel Noriega, de facto ruler, for international drug trafficking... Delaware, home base for 180,000 corporations, 45% of those listed on NYSE and 56% of Fortune 500, passes antitakeover law to protect firms from hostile raids...

U.S., Mexico sign pact to widen access of Mexican textiles to U.S. markets... President Reagan proposes in 1989 budget to eliminate ICC, Economic Development Administration, Appalachian Regional Commission, Urban Development Action Grants, and Small Business Administration and loans and subsidies for Amtrak (proposes pilot programs for private operation of Federal prison industries, minimum security prisons, cargo inspection, military commissaries, Coast Guard buoy maintenance and management of undeveloped federal lands)... Federal Home Loan Bank plans to rescue 143 ailing Texas thrifts at initial cost of $6-7 billion...

Federal Reserve Board liberalizes (February 18) restrictions on U.S. banks swapping Third World debt for equity... Federal Reserve Board chairman Alan Greenspan warns (March 15) stronger economic growth in 1988 could lead to renewed inflation... U.S. Supreme Court upholds 1981 Federal law barring striking workers from receiving food stamps... Senate votes (March 30) to grant banks wider underwriting powers... U.S. Senate imposes economic sanctions on Mexico for failing to do enough in blocking narcotics trade... Dow Jones Industrial Average slides (April 14) 101 points, 5th worst in history, after release of February U.S. merchandise trade figures... Federal appeals court strikes down law as unconstitutional for barring publisher Rupert Murdoch from owning both newspapers, TV stations in NYC, Boston... U.S. bans Japanese fishing in U.S. waters to protest its continued slaughter of whales...   Commerce Department reports sizable narrowing of U.S. trade imbalance in March with "4 Tigers" of Hong Kong, Taiwan, South Korea and Singapore (cancels special trading privileges in 1989)... SEC reports (April 18) stock-index arbitrage may have accelerated market decline on January 8 when Dow Jones dropped 140 points... Occupational Safety and Health Administration fines Iowa Beef Processors, U.S.' largest, $3.1 million for "willfully ignoring" a health hazard... Dow Jones index surges (May 31) 74.68 points to 2031.12, most since January 4 and 6th largest in history... Federal Home Loan Bank Board liquidates two insolvent Southern California thrifts at record cost of $1.35 billion...

Federal Jury finds Liggett Group partly to blame for death of a cigarette smoker, first such ruling in over 300 tobacco liability lawsuits from 1954 (is ordered to pay $400,000)... New York's Suffolk County regulates use of video-display terminals in workplace... Drought hits 50% of U.S. farm counties, grain stocks plunge... Federal Home Loan Bank posts (June 21) losses of $3.78 billion for troubled thrifts in first quarter, $7.6 billion for 1987... Dow Jones reaches (June 22) new post-October 1987 crash high of 2152.20... U.S. files (June 28) suit to oust leaders of Teamsters and to have a trustee run union until free elections are held... TVA reduces work force by 20%, 7,500 employees, to cope with financial problems...

Federal Court rules First City Financial Corp., Vice President Marc Belzberg deliberately "parked" Ashland oil stocks with Bear, Sterns & Co. to avoid disclosure... After death of Jackie Presser, William J. McCarthy of New England union is (July 15) new President of International Teamsters... SEC rules "one share, one vote"... Reagan accepts (August 2) plant-closure bill, requires 60 days' notice for layoffs, closures...

After 4 years and Presidential veto, Senate passes (August 3) comprehensive trade bill, most extensive in 25 years, to open foreign markets, to retaliate against unfair trade practices (triggers action against Brazil, Japan, India in 1989)... FDIC sells insolvent First RepublicBank Corp. of Dallas, Texas' largest with 40 banking subsidiaries and bad loans from 1987 takeover of ailing Dallas Interfirst, to NCNB of North Carolina for some $4 billion... U.S. warns (August 4) European Community against protectionism... Some 9,000 movie and television scriptwriters end strike of 22 weeks, longest ever for Writers Guild...

U.S. trade deficit widens, $12.54 billion, in June with record imports of $39.35 billion, reaches record $125 billion by 1989 with $155 billion budget deficit... Federal Reserve Board reports (August 16) factories operating in July at 83.5% of capacity, 8-year high... Federal Home Loan Board merges (August 26) 10 insolvent thrifts with 5 healthy ones at cost of $948.5 million... Federal Home Loan Board plans (August 31) takeover of 14 insolvent Oklahoma thrifts for reorganization as 6 larger regional institutions... Chicago federal grand jury indicts, convicts two sports agents for fraud, racketeering, extortion... Baseball arbitrator rules major league baseball team owners had violated collective bargaining agreement with baseball players by colluding against free agent players... FCC sets (September 1) high-definition guidelines for TV... U.S. passes (September 19) U.S.-Canada trade accord to open market for free trade, approved by Canada by 1989... President Reagan vetoes (September 28) bill to restrict textile imports...Space-shuttle <u>Discovery</u> ends (October 3) successful mission, first since 1986 loss of <u>Challenger</u>... U.S. federal grand jury charges (October 11) Luxembourg-based Bank of Credit & Commerce in laundering over $32 million in profits from alleged cocaine sales by Columbia's Medellin Cartel, responsible for 80% of cocaine imports to U.S... Federal Home Loan Board (is saved by 1989 S&L federal bailout of $150-$200 billion) rescues (October 14) 11 Texas thrifts with $1.3 billion...

U.S. grants (October 17) short-term loan of up to $3.5 billion to Mexico, largest U.S. loan to debtor nation since Latin American debt crisis in 1982... Dow Jones hits (October 18) post-crash high of 2159.85... Over 6,000 computers across U.S. are shut down (November 2-3) after being sabotaged by computer virus, planted by Cornell University graduate student to explore security of computer system... U.S. mergers reach record $129.4 billion in first 6 months... Labor Department lifts (November 10) 45-year-old Federal ban on 5 different kinds of work at home, denounced by organized labor...

U.S. and 10 central banks support (November 17) tumbling dollar... 80,000 farms face foreclosure in November... Arbitrators order Fujitsu of Japan to pay IBM $833.2 million to settle 6-year software copyright dispute (is followed by 1989 settlement of 5-year suit between NEC, Intel that a microcode for industry microprocessors can be copyrighted)... Federal Government indicts Ruben Sturman, world's leading pornographer using over 200 shell corporations to control over 50% of U.S.' $8 billion industry, in Las Vegas and Cleveland for racketeering, income tax evasion and tax fraud... In penny-stock probe, New Jersey federal grand jury indicts Erick M. Wynn, others for defrauding investors of $640,000 in defunct jewelry firm, Renaissance Enterprises...

Illinois puts sales tax on marijuana, cocaine and other illegal drugs... Massachusetts is first state with comprehensive health-insurance plan... Overseas investors put $65 billion into U.S. enterprises, $31.6 billion in manufacturing, $8 billion in retailing and $5.8 billion in insurance... U.S. agrees (December 14) to open dialogue with PLO...

General Services Administration awards 10-year contract, largest ever for $3-$10 billion by Government outside military and space programs, to AT&T, US Sprint... Dow Jones ends year at 2168.57, climbs to record 2734.64 (August 24, 1989)... From mere $1.2 billion in 1979 U.S. trade with China jumps to $13.4 billion, almost $5 billion in U.S. exports of farm goods, aircraft and oil-drilling equipment and $8.5 billion in Chinese imports of clothing, toys, and sporting goods (results in over 600 joint ventures or wholly owned U.S. subsidiaries, only allowed by China, Viet Nam, Poland and Hungary, is halted with government suppression of student protests in 1989)... Clyde V. Prestowitz: <u>Trading Places</u> (recognizes Japan has invented new type of capitalism more efficient than U.S., follows Chalmers Johnson's <u>MITI</u> <u>and</u> <u>the</u> <u>Japanese Miracle</u>, pioneers revisionist views, in 1982)... Families spend 5.4 nights on "getaway" vacations, 6.3 nights in 1983... FDA investigates generic-drug firms, a 1988 scandal.

Business Events

Kodak saves Sterling Drug from Hoffman-LaRoche takeover in $5.1 billion deal, faces overcapacity from competition by Fuji Photo and Polaroid in 1989... After rejecting $3 billion offer of Paris-based Sanofi, drug maker 60% controlled by French state-owned Societe Nationale Elf Aquitaine oil firm, A.H. Robins accepts $3.2 billion bid from American Home Products... After bid of E-II Holdings for American Brands, American Brands makes hostile offer for E-II to block takeover in "Pac Man" defense (acquires E-II for $1.1 billion)... For first time NYSE curbs electronic program trading to reduce volatility in stock market...

Monsanto's NutraSweet unveils "Simplesse" low-calorie, cholestrol-free fat substitute... New York Post, founded 1801, avoids closure as publisher Rupert Murdoch, unions agree to cut costs by $22 million (sells paper to real estate developer Peter Kalikow for $37.6 million)... Stop and Shop, based in Braintree, MA, with 114 supermarkets and 171 Bradlees discount department stores in New England and Mid-Atlantic states, rejects hostile takeover of Dart group in accepting bid of takeover specialists Kohlberg Kravis Roberts for $1.23 billion...

Dun & Bradstreet, publishing and business information concern owning Nielsen Marketing Research, buys IMS International, NYC-based market research and data base publishing service, for $1.77 billion... Exxon, Occidental Petroleum get permission to drill for oil off California coast... Honda of America settles Federal job-bias charges against blacks, women for $6 million... Thrifts report (March 24) record $6.8 billion loss in 1987... Northwest Airlines bans smoking on all domestic routes and nearby international routes... DuPont phases out production of chlorofluorocarbons... United Artists Communications with 800,000 cable subscribers and 2,050 movie screens, United Cable Television with 1.48 million subscribers merge to form 3rd largest system in U.S...

Westinghouse, Asea Brown Boveri AG of Switzerland form two joint ventures for steam turbines and energy transmission... Developer Donald Trump buys NYC's fancy Plaza Hotel, opened 1907 as "world's most luxurious hotel," for $410 million, highest price paid for a hotel... Apple sues Microsoft, Hewlett-Packard for copyright infringements, casts pall over computer industry on software rights... For first time, IBM allows U.K.'s Ferranti PLC to sell its PCs under Ferranti name... After 3-month battle, West Point-Pepperell buys 1817 J.P. Stevens for $1.2 billion in cash, makes West Point-Pepperell U.S.' largest producer of bed linen and 2nd-largest producer of bath towels...

Kodak, entered copier market in 1975, buys IBM copier business to take on Xerox... Five leading Wall Street securities firms temporarily suspend index arbitrage for program training... After pressure by pilot's union to restructure with sale of Hilton International for $1.07 billion, Westin Hotels & Resorts for $1.35 billion and Hertz for $1.3 billion, Allegis, owner of United Airlines sells 50% of its Apollo computer reservation service to USAir and 4 European airlines for $499 million... LTV, U.S.' 2nd-largest steel maker, unveils reorganization plan to end 1986 bankruptcy... Japan's Daiwa Securities launches $2.5 billion mutual fund in U.S.... International Lease Finance Co. of Beverly Hills orders 100 Boeing planes and 30 Airbus craft for $5.04 billion, largest single purchase of commercial aircraft... In heated takeover battle Koppers Co.

agrees to $1.71 billion buyout by Britain's Beazer PLC... American Stores, 339 in 14 states, buys Lucky Stores, some 580 supermarkets in California, Midwest, Florida and Southwest, for $2.51 billion to operate 2,000 stores nationwide as U.S.' largest supermarket chain over Kroger, Safeway... Campbell Soup acquires frozen-food producer Freshbake Foods of Britain for some $202 million, 4th European acquisition since 1985...

Chicago law firm of Baker & McKenzie merges with Los Angeles-based MacDonald, Halsted & Laybourne, world's largest with 1,154 lawyers in over 40 cities... McGraw-Hill sells 49% of Japanese joint publishing venture to Nihon Kezai Shimbun for $283 million as it did not suit its global strategy of providing products, services worldwide... NYSE, Chicago Mercantile Exchange announces (July 7) trading limits to deter sharp drops in stock and stock-index futures market... Hunt brothers settle 2-year battle with group of 13 banks by ceding 50% stake in Penrod drilling, $50 million in cash, $500 million note and real estate holdings to emerge from Chapter 11 of U.S. Bankruptcy Code (agree to drop $14 billion 1986 conspiracy suit against banks)...

Robert M. Bass Group agrees to acquire American Savings & Loan of Stockton, CA, U.S.' largest insolvent thrift, with $550 million and $2 billion in Federal assistance plus $500 million note... Sanford Weill's Commercial Credit acquires Gerald Tsai, Jr.'s Primerica, struggling with Smith Barney brokerage with post-Crash problems, for $1.7 billion... After losing $130 million suit to Minpeco S.A. of Peru for attempt to corner silver market in 1979-80, Hunt brothers file for personal bankruptcy to stay execution of judgment...

Nine large personal-computer makers, Compaq, Epson, Hewlett-Packard, Tandy, Zenith, NEC, Olivetti, Wyse and International Data, join forces to challenge IBM with new computer electronic conduit so computers can communicate with each other... Bank of New York wins $1.45 billion bitter year-long hostile takeover battle for Irving Bank, creates U.S.' 12th largest with over $43 billion in assets... Pritzker family, Chicago, buys 50% of Norwegian Miami-based Royal Admiral Cruises for $567 million...

Republic New York buys 40% of Geneva-based Safra Republic for some $900 million... U.S.' Whirlpool forms $470 million household appliance joint venture with Holland's N.V. Philips... Rockefeller & Co., investment firm managing $4 billion in assets for 85 Rockefeller heirs, invests $85 million in French holding company of Marine-Wendel, France's oldest industrial dynasty left after nationalization of 1978... Hershey sells Friendly Ice Cream chain for $375 million in cash, ends 9-year involvement in restaurant business (buys London-based Cadbury Schweppes for some $300 million)... Westinghouse, 3rd-largest in U.S. elevator market after Otis and Dover, sells interests to Swiss-based Schindler, world's 2nd largest after Otis...

Kraft, U.S.' largest independent food company with sales of $9.9 billion, accepts $13.1 billion bid from Philip Morris, nation's largest tobacco firm and U.S.' largest food processor with General Foods and Miller Brewing, in 2nd largest merger ever after Chevron buy of Gulf for $13.4 billion in 1984 (replaces British-Dutch Unilever as world's largest-food company, world's largest advertiser)... Maytag acquires Chicago Pacific, Hoover appliances and vacuum cleaners with plants in 8 countries, for $1 billion to expand in overseas markets... Commodity Exchange, New York

Mercantile Exchange agree for first time to coordinate futures market in gold, platinum... DuPont sells genetically 'engineered' mice... To end bitter dispute with UAW, Chrysler pays $250 million to close Kenosha, WI, American Motors plant... GE acquires chemical business of Borg-Warner for $2.3 billion... Hospital Corp., founded 1968 to become U.S.' largest hospital chain, accepts $3.61 billion leveraged buyout from management plagued by declining occupancy rates and falling profits after 1983 cuts in costs of Medicare...

Armco sells 40% of its Eastern Steel to Kawasaki Steel of Japan for some $350 million, largest joint venture of Japanese steel firm in U.S. in topping $310 million for 50% purchase of National Steel in 1984 by NKK... Ames Department Stores buys Zayre discount stores for $800 million, U.S.' 3rd-largest discount retailer with 736 stores after K mart and Wal-Mart... 3M expands into Europe with purchase of Spotex unit of Paris-based cleaning-products concern Chargeurs S.A. for $182 million... Major airlines discontinue discount fares as of November 23...

Fighting off rivals Kohlberg Kravis Roberts engineers record $25.07 billion takeover of RJR Nabisco... American Express, Dow Chemical, Pfizer, Sara Lee apply to SEC for approval to retire large portions of their common stock and issue new financial instruments, called Unbundled Stock Units... Donald Trump sells NYC's fancy 700-room St. Moritz Hotel, purchased 1984 for $31 million, to Australian Alan Bond for $180 million... Tootsie Roll, 2nd-largest lollypop maker, buys Charms, largest lollypop maker, for $65 million... First Henrys Supper Shop opens in Portland, OR, to provide full-course take-home meals...

KPMG-Peat Marwick, world's largest accounting firm, shows revenues of $3.9 billion, is topped in 1989 by merger of NYC's Arthur Young, world's 4th largest, and Cleveland's Ernst & Whinney, world's 5th largest, for combined sales of $4.2 billion with 6,100 partners and some 70,000 employees, 2,105 partners and 25,391 employees in U.S., worldwide (talks in 1989 by Arthur Andersen & Co. with Price Waterhouse for a $5.1 billion merger)... The Atlanta Journal and Constitution accuses city banks in discriminating against blacks, similar iniquities in Chicago, Washington, DC, Baltimore and Denver...

Once variety chain pioneer F.W. Woolworth Co., operator of different specialty chains such as Champs for sporting goods, Kids Mart, Harold's Square for party goods, Woolworth Express as specialty variety, Kinney Shoe, Afterthoughts boutiques, and Face Fantasies for discount cosmetics, opens 1,100 new stores in year to sell 40-plus store brands in U.S., Canada, West Germany and Australia, shows sales of $8.1 billion in 1988, 13% over 1987... Black Enterprise reports sales of 100 largest black-owned firms up 10.2%, 7.6% for Fortune 500 firms... Los Angeles-based Thrifty, 640 drug stores and discount stores in 9 western states and 3 sporting goods chains with 194 stores in midwest and west, acquires 110 Pay 'n Save drug stores and its Bi-Mart discount merchandise chain with 37 stores, for $232 million to enter Northwest market...

Kellogg Associates is formed (monitors 150 stocks to spot issues in trouble before they drop for clients such as institutional investors, short-sellers and other speculators)... Some 5 Chicago banks lose nearly $70,000 on checks that disintegrate shortly after deposit... Everybody's Delivery is started in Portland, OR, to deliver full-course meals from any of 11 City's restaurants to diner's homes, echoed by Feed Me Now in Salem with home delivery of movie videos and meals from 15 restaurants...

AT&T buys 20% of 1982 Sun Microsystems, needs capital and protection from hostile takeovers, to revive its computer business... Black & Decker, power-tool and household appliance business, launches $1.8 billion takeover of American Standard, New York-based maker of plumbing, air conditioning, automotive brakes and mass-transit controls... Struggling to shake 3 years of slow growth, IBM, CEO John Akers, reorganizes to further decentralize into seven autonomers units, speed product development and improve service as market moves from mainframe machines to smaller, more powerful desktop computers...

Reliable Waters, MA, installs desalination plant, computer-operated to achieve its mission without any outside advice, in Canary Islands (simulates judgment of skilled operator to make and control decisions)... Jan Bell Marketing, supplying jewelry to 75% of U.S.' 327 price clubs with growth of 30%/year by selling merchandise at cut-rate prices, shows profit of $9.3 million, 86% surge over past 3 years, on sales of $120 million... Pillsbury accepts $5.7 billion offer of Grand Metropolitan, largest non-oil takeover by British company, to become world leader in foods, retailing...

After previously buying two insolvent Michigan thrifts Ford Motors First Nationwide Financial acquires 4 troubled thrifts, assets of $7.7 billion, for $170 million and $1.6 billion from Federal Home Loan Bank Board, becomes U.S.' 2nd-largest-thrift, $34 billion, behind Home Savings of America with $38 billion in assets... Wear and Share, Austin, TX, introduces condom earrings, sells 1,200 pairs, $4.50 each, in 3 months...

B.A.S.S., Inc., Montgomery firm founded 1967 to hold fishing contests (promotes activities with weekly cable-TV, magazines and network of 2,000 amateur fishing clubs), shows revenues of $30 million, twice level of 5 years earlier... Indianapolis suburban art dealer Peg Goldberg is steered to four Byzantine mosaics by Amsterdam dealer (buys art in Geneva for $1.2 million, after 1989 suit is required to return smuggled goods to Orthodox Church of Cypress and Cypress, outcome sets precedent for world antiquities market)... U.S. firms move over 500,000 workers, up some 6% since 1986...

First U.S.-made Hondas are unloaded in Japan... Coalition of 7 U.S. firms, Archer Daniels Midland, Chevron, Eastman Kodak, Ford, Johnson & Johnson, Mercator and RJR Nabisco, as American Trade Consortium signs agreement with Soviet Foreign Economic Consortium to pursue joint ventures... GM spends $4.754 billion on research and development, U.S.' No. 1, followed by IBM, $4.419, Ford, $2.930, AT&T, $2.572, DuPont, $1.319, Digital Equipment, $1.307, GE $1.155, Eastman Kodak, $1.147, Hewlett-Packard, $1.019, and United Technologies with $932 million on R&D...

With 1,234 outlets Kinder-Care Learning Center is U.S.' largest child-care chain, followed by La Petite Academy with 700 centers, Children's World Learning Centers with 470 units, Gerber Children's Centers with 118 units and Children's Discovery Centers with 81 units... Conde Nast Publications sacks Grace Mirabella, editor of Vogue since replacing legendary Diana Vreeland in 1972, for British-born Anna Wintour to take on 1985 U.S. version of <u>Elle</u>, French fashion magazine started 1945 (revives <u>Vogue</u> with trendy look while Mirabella launches <u>Mirabella</u> in 1989)... Minor league baseball attendance, 196 clubs in 19 minor leagues in 1989 is most since 1957, is 21.6 million, highest since 1952 and near big league mark of 28.5 million... After making millions in corporate takeover bids in part by illegally "parking" stocks for resale later and failing to takeover 4 different firms in 1985-86, Paul A. Bilzerian manages to acquire defense contractor Singer when no one else wanted it after 1987 stock-market crash (is convicted, first in Government's 3-year crackdown on insider trading, in 1989 on 9 counts of securities fraud, conspiracy, and tax violations)...

Robert E. Allen is new CEO of AT&T (launches revolution to change entrenched corporate culture, writes off $6.7 billion in equipment to show $1.67 billion loss, first ever since 1885 incorporation, spends $250 million to buy rival Paradyne, manufacturer of data communications equipment, to reduce dependency on home-grown products, decentralizes by products to bring AT&T closer to customers and to operate profit centers, and forms joint ventures and consortiums in U.S., overseas)... Tidewater Mets is one of top moneymakers in minor league baseball with profit of some $250,000...

Sears is top in U.S. retailing (spawns field of firms checking customer service, i.e., PROVE, NC, in 1978) with market share of 29%, No. 1 in 1971 with 44%, followed by K mart with 26%, 3rd in 1971 with 13% as Kresge, Wal-Mart with 20%, not in 1971 top 5, J.C. Penney with 14%, 2nd in 1971 with 21%, and Dayton-Hudson with 18%, not in 1971 top 5 (omits Woolworth, 4th in 1971 with 12%, and Montgomery Ward with 10%)... After focusing on service to children, stately Four Seasons Clift Hotel, San Francisco, hands out some 1,200 comic books in pampering little guests, joining trend in 1989 is Hyatt Hotel's Camp Hyatt facility for kids at 97 hotels, resorts...

After dropping its credit card in 1982 to become cheapest gas supplier in the West, Atlantic Richfield, Arco, is No. 1 in California market while competitors battle each other with array of goods, services... After Baltimore Orioles suffer record 21-game losing streak in opening baseball season, New York businessman, Eli J. Jacobs buys, hapless franchise for record $70 million (sees team reach top of American League East by June 28, 1989 with 6-1/2 game lead)...

After debut in 1939 comic book, movie serial in 1940s, and in 1966-68 campy TV series, production of "Batman" movie is started, rights secured in 1979 (premiers in 1989 to rake in some $44 million on 1st weekend while over 100 licensees with some 300 products, T-shirts biggest seller, and national tie-in with Taco Bell add extra income, "Ghostbuster II" in 1989 with some 60 licensees and 150 products)... After founding Dallas-based Southwest Airlines in 1966 with $20,000 stake in investment fund of $560,000 and adding Muse Air in 1986 for $68 million, closed 1987 after losing $2 million/month, Herbert D. Kelleher's no-frills operation posts revenues of $860 million, U.S.' 9th-largest carrier (opens new routes in California, Midwest in 1989 to aim for $1 billion in revenues and $2 billion by 1995)...

Meshulam Riklis, as former stockbroker started career of wheeling and dealing in 1957 in using Rapid-American Corp., office machine, printing and Christmas-card business, to expand with mechandising, tire, apparel and packaging firms via high-yield debt and stock swaps (adds McCrory variety stores in 1960, with disasterous earnings liquidates all holdings except 51% of McCrory in 1963, sells International Playtex and BVD units in 1974 to avoid financial ruin, signs consent decree in 1979 in SEC complaint of illegal discounts, is involved in Britain's 1986 Guinness financial scandal in takeover of Distillers Co., sells Schenley Industries in 1986 to Guinness for $419 million), buys E-II Holdings from American Brands for $1.2 billion (faces suits by E-II bondholders after removing $925 million in cash from E-II in exchange for Rapid's Faberge and its Elizabeth Arden unit)...

New products for supermarkets grows by 3.7%, 26% in 1987 (leads to chains demanding fees to carry new items)... IBM forms group to develop applications software, i.e., word processing programs, for market... Christiansen/Cummings Associates report Americans spend some $208 billion on legalized gambling: $2 billion on bookmaking, $4 billion on bingo, $4 billion in cardrooms, $17 billion on lotteries, $18 billion on pari-mutuals, $37 billion on slot machines and $126 billion on casino table games... Japanese exports of dry beer invade U.S...

Pepsi-Cola splits U.S. into four regional companies for more focused advertising, Campbell operates in 22 advertising zones in 1989... Theme and amusement parks cite record 249 million visitors and revenues over $4 billion... John Sullivan, believing kids like disgusting things to upset parents, introduces Boogers candy, grosses $2 million by 1989... Former real estate lawyer William Parish starts first commercial plant, CA, to produce electricity by burning cattle dung from nearby feedlots, produces power for 15,000 homes (plans 2nd alternative-energy plant in 1989 to burn crop wastes)...

Lands' End, started 1963 by Gary Comer, former ad copywriter for Young & Rubicam, as catalog supplier of sailboat hardware before switching to moderately priced, well-made leisure clothing in 1977, racks up sales of $456 million, L.L. Bean No. 1 in sportswear mail-order industry with $580 million... After leaving First Boston's mergers-and-acquisition group, Bruce Wasserstein and Joseph Perella open own shop, 65 deals worth over $150 billion by 1989 as Wall Street's most active investment firm, worldwide staff of 100, (joins Nomura Securities in 1989 to open merger boutique in Tokyo) after Morgan Stanley as First Boston slips from No. 1 to No. 8...

Warner Communications acquires Lorimar Telepictures for $1.2 billion, makes Warner U.S.' largest producer of TV shows (plans $10 billion merger with Time Inc. in 1989, attracts $10.7 billion hostile takeover of Time by Marvin Davis' Paramount, leads to Time offer of some $14 billion for Warner, counter offer of $12.2 billion by Paramount for Time, court challenges, retreat by Paramount as Delaware judge favors Time in backing directors over stockholders in determining fate of firms, and creation of Time Warner as world's largest media concern, $4.4 billion in TV and films, $2.8 billion in publishing and $2.0 billion in music, in 1989, soon followed by $11.2 billion merger, Bristol-Myers and Squibb, to form world's 2nd largest drug firm, merger of Smithkline Beckman with London's Beecham Group and Dow Chemical's pharmaceutical subsidiary with Marion Laboratories)... U.S.' Sandy Reitan wins biggest purse ever awarded, $33,000, in professional women's darts at Tokyo's Japan Grand Prix, 125

U.S. tournaments/year for some $1.5 million in total prizes... Dexter Corp., founded 1767, CT, with purchase of sawmill, is oldest member of NYSE (chooses first non-family member in 1989 to head $827 million manufacturer of plastics, sealants and coatings, sales of $9.5 million in 1958)... Tokyo meat importer Zenchiku Ltd. pays $13 million for Selkirk ranch, MT, of 77,000 acres, trend of $50-$100 million invested in U.S. beef industry by 1989...

Portland Trailblazers, paid $3.7 million for NBA franchise in 1970, goes for some $72 million... Sinjin Smith, beach-volleyball's top professional, earns nearly $135,000 on circuit, 6 others win over $100,000... With new ad image and targeted promotions, Folgers coffee gets 32% of total U.S. market, 24% in 1982... Golfers pay $5.7 billion in fees to 13,626 courses... U.S. ships $841 million worth of beef to Japan, $26 million, up 1,400%, to Korea...

Orange's TRW, leading credit bureau in 1989 with Atlanta's Equifax (buys National Decision Systems, sells computerized breakdowns of neighborhoods, towns with profiles of spending habits, for $21 million) and Chicago's Trans Union, buys Chilton, 140 million files (gives 3 total of 400 million records on 160 million individuals, 90% of U.S. adult population), for $330 million (designs Financial Lifestyle Database in 1988 for any customer, i.e., mail-order house, phone solicitor, or political party)...

Gross revenues for major leagues total some $2.7 billion, $1 billion to major league baseball, $935 million to NFL, $450 million to NBA, and $350 million to NHL... Bowlers spend some $4 billion at 7,000 centers.

Selected Bibliography

Boorstin, Daniel J. The Americans (Vols. I, II, III), New York: Vintage Books, 1958.

Brooks, John (ed.). The Autobiography of American Business, New York: Doubleday & Co., 1974.

Bursk, Edward C. Clark, Donald T. and Hidy, Ralph W. (eds.). The World of Business (Vols. I, II, III, IV), New York: Simon and Schuster, 1962.

Cable, Mary. American Manners & Morals, New York: American Heritage Publishing, 1969.

Chamberlain, John. The Enterprising Americans: A Business History of the United States, New York: Harper & Row, 1963.

Chandler, Alfred D., Jr. and Salsbury, Steven. Pierre S. du Pont and the Making of the Modern Corporation, New York: Harper and Row, 1971.

Chandler, Alfred D., Jr. The Visible Hand: The Managerial Revolution in American Business, Cambridge, MA: Belknap Press of Harvard University Press, 1977.

Chandler, Alfred D., Jr. Strategy of Structure, Boston: The M.I.T. Press, 1962.

Cochran, Thomas C. 200 Years of American Business, New York: Basic Books, 1977.

Daniel, Clifton (ed.). Chronicle of the 20th Century, New York: Chronicle Publications, 1987.

d'Estaing, Valerie-Anne Giscard. The World Almanac Book of Inventions, New York: World Almanac Publications, 1985.

Douglas, Elisha P. The Coming of Age of American Business, Chapel Hill: University of North Carolina Press, 1971.

Gannet, Lewis (ed.). The Age of the Moguls, New York: Doubleday & Co., 1953.

George, Claude, S., Jr. The History of Management Thought (2nd ed.), New York: Prentice-Hall, 1972.

Graff, Henry F. (ed.). The Life History of the United States, (12 vols.), New York: Time-Life Books, 1963.

Great American Stories of American Businessmen, New York: American Heritage Publishing, 1972.

Groner, Alex. American Business & Industry, New York: American Heritage Publishing, 1972.

Grun, Bernard. The Timetables of History, New York: Simon Schuster, 1975.

French, Wendell, L. The Personnel Management Process (5th ed.), New York: Houghton Mifflin, 1982.

Furnas, J.C. The Americans: A Social History of the United States 1587-1914, New York: G.P. Putnam's Sons, 1969.

Hendrickson, Robert. The Grand Emporiums, New York: Stein and Day, 1979.

Holbert, Hayward Janes. A History of Professional Management in American Industry, New York: Arno Press, 1976.

Houndshell, David A. From the American System to Mass Production 1800-1932: The Development of Manufacturing Technology in the United States, Baltimore: The Johns Hopkins University Press, 1984.

Ingham, John N. Biographical Dictionary of American Business Leaders (Vols, I, II, III, IV), Westport, CT: Greenwood Press, 1983.

Jensen, Oliver. Railroads in America, New York: American Heritage Publishing, 1975.

Josephson, Matthew. The Robber Barons, New York: Harcourt, Brace & World, 1962.

Kennedy, Paul. The Rise and Fall of the Great Powers, New York: Random House, 1987.

Laing, Alexander. Seafaring America, New York: American Heritage Publishing, 1974.

Morgan, Hal. Symbols of America, New York: Viking Press, 1986.

Morris, Richard B. (ed.). Encyclopedia of American History, (6th ed.), New York: Harper & Row, 1982.

Morris, Richard B. Government and Labor in Early America, New York: Harper & Row, 1946.

Porter, Glenn (ed.). Encyclopedia of American Economic History, (Vols. I, II, III), New York: Charles Scribner's Sons, 1980.

Room, Adrian. Dictionary of Trade Name Origins, London: Routledge & Kegan Parl, 1982.

Schlesinger, Arthur M., Jr. (ed.). The Almanac of American History, New York: G.P. Putnam's Sons, 1983.

Seavoy, Ronald E. The Origin of the American Business Corporation, 1784-1855, Westport, CT: Greenwood Press, 1982.

Steinberg, S.H. Historical Tables, 58 B.C. - A.D. 1978, New York: St. Martin's Press, 1964.

Thernstrom, Stephan (ed.). Harvard Encyclopedia of American Ethnic Groups, Cambridge, MA: The Belknap Press, 1980.

Walton, Gary M. and Shepherd, James F. The Economic Rise of Early America, New York: Cambridge University Press, 1979.

Williams, Trevor, I. The History of Invention: From Stone Axes to Silicon Chips, New York: Facts on File Publications, 1987.

Wren, Daniel A. The Evolution of Management Thought, New York: Ronald Press, 1972.

Index

About the Compiler

RICHARD ROBINSON has survived a career of teaching, with tours of duty at Indiana University, Evansville College, University of Washington, and Portland State University and visits to Copenhagen's Institute of Industrial Organization, Rotterdam's Institute of Economics, and Thessaloniki's Graduate Industrial School. He is currently working on a book entitled *World Business History: A Chronology,* and in addition to continuing as a management consultant he plans to design games for pleasure and profit.